# Political Parties in America SECOND EDITION

# Political Parties in America SECOND EDITION

**Robert J. Huckshorn**
Florida Atlantic University

Brooks/Cole Publishing Company
Monterey, California

Brooks/Cole Publishing Company
A Division of Wadsworth, Inc.

Collage on p. 299 courtesy of the *American Journal of Nursing, Common Cause Magazine,* the
National Education Association and the *NEA Advocate,* the National Organization for Women
and the *National NOW Times,* the *American Rifleman,* and *Public Affairs Newsletter.*

Printed in the United States of America
10  9  8  7  6  5  4  3  2  1

**Library of Congress Cataloging in Publication Data**

Huckshorn, Robert Jack, [date]
    Political parties in America.

    Bibliography: p.
    Includes index.
    1. Political parties—United States.    2. Elections—
United States.    3. United States—Politics and
government.    I. Title.
JK2265.H8     1984          324.273          83–14299
ISBN 0-534-02885-3

Sponsoring Editor: *Marquita Flemming*
Production Editors: *Gay L. Orr and Richard Mason*
Manuscript Editor: *Steve Bodian*
Permissions Editor: *Carline Haga*
Interior and Cover Design: *Katherine Minerva*
Cover Photo: © *Ken Kobre/PictureGroup*
Art Coordinator: *Rebecca A. Tait*
Interior Illustration: *John Foster*
Typesetting: *Graphic Typesetting Service*
Cover Printing: *Phoenix Color Corporation*
Printing and Binding: *Halliday Lithograph*

*To Rosamond Huckshorn and Josephine Stefanides*
*and in memory of*
*Jack Huckshorn and Victor Stefanides*

# PREFACE

When I first began teaching courses on political parties and interest groups twenty-seven years ago, the world of American politics was very different. The two great American parties, although not as influential as they once had been, still commanded public respect and voter allegiance. President Dwight D. Eisenhower was destined to be overwhelmingly reelected to office in that fall of 1956, but even after four years in office, and in spite of recent evidence to the contrary, he still considered himself to be a "bipartisan" or "apolitical" national leader. On the day Ike was reelected, the Republicans failed to win control of either house of Congress. That division in voter attitudes was symbolic of the problems that were to face the parties and the political system in the next quarter century. The trend toward weakened parties—indeed, some describe the period as an "antiparty" age—has covered a period in which an entire generation of Americans has grown to maturity. Those young men and women do not remember when parties were influential and occupied an important place in American society. They cannot relate to parties in the same way their parents and grandparents did. Many are unsure of what role political parties should play in their lives. The drama, the pathos, the excitement, the tragedies and the triumphs of political campaigns and party work escape them.

Just about everyone writing about parties today must necessarily do so from the perspective of change. The changes in the party system and in the way the American voter responds to the party system have been pervasive. Yet most college students today do not have a frame of reference with which to evaluate parties and politics. The thread that runs through this book is that of change. As in the first edition, I have sought in the chapters that follow to present a reasonably comprehensive framework that will permit students to view today's political system with a bit of yesterday's perspective. It is not an entirely neutral presentation. I confess, here at the beginning, that I like political parties. I think they are important. I believe that in one way or another they must be revived. At the same time I understand that the end result of that revival can never lead us back to the good old days of party power; democratization of the political process has gone too far for that to occur. However, the parties must be given, or must assume, a more meaningful role in the political process than they now possess. The people must be provided with reasons for identifying with and working for a political party. Because the antiparty web has filaments that radiate in many directions and intersect with many other political, social, and economic conditions, the decline of parties will not be easy to reverse; some knowledgeable people will not even agree that this reversal is an important goal. They may be right, but I do not think so. At the very least, the people should be afforded an opportunity to opt for stronger parties and for a more meaningful relationship to politics.

This book differs in several respects from most other books on political parties. First, it is written in such a way as to stimulate student interest in politics and parties. Second, it presents a short history of American political parties as a means of providing today's student with some historical perspective. I hope that the contemporary political system can be made more meaningful by providing a milestone map of the political past. It goes without saying that this brief history is necessary to an understanding of the changes that have occurred and the transformations that are widely predicted. Third, the recent rise in importance of political interest groups has had a profound effect on political parties. Since I do not believe that today's politics can be completely understood without addressing the impact of interest groups on the political process, I have provided two chapters to that end. Finally, I offer an assessment of the transformations currently taking place in the political system.

A number of changes and improvements have been incorporated into this edition. Most importantly, this edition includes much new and much updated material. For instance, the 1980 and 1982 elections are now included, along with complete coverage of the Carter administration and the first two years of the Reagan administration. Sections on campaign finance and public funding of elections have been updated and expanded. The first edition provided detailed coverage of the revitalization of the Republican National Committee, and this one also includes the post-1980 efforts to reinvigorate the Democratic National Committee. *Political Parties in America* now includes an additional chapter on the important issue of interest groups and lobbying. Another of the book's major expansions is material that describes and analyzes state and local politics and parties. Finally, the new edition contains a report on recent conferences and research on the future of American parties and transformations that are taking place in the party system.

Many of those writing about political parties today are understandably pessimistic about the future of parties. It is difficult not to share that view after reviewing the decline in party fortunes over the past quarter century. Nevertheless, I hold to the more optimistic conviction that the current transformation can also lead to party renewal. If the American people will engage themselves in the political process under the aegis of the political parties and if the parties themselves can offer them reasons for doing so, we might, in fact, contribute to an age of national renewal that far transcends politics and parties. Since publication of the first edition, I have been encouraged by the number of scholars, political leaders, party conferences, and symposia that have unequivocally endorsed the goal of strengthening the party system. Increasingly greater attention is being focused on the problems that weakened parties present to a democratic society, and it is important that new generations of college students be prepared to take part in this continuing debate.

I owe the customary debts of gratitude to assistants, colleagues, friends, and family. I especially wish to thank my colleagues around the nation who gave so generously of their time to read parts of the manuscript for the first and second editions. For the first edition they included Robert Agranoff, Indiana University; Douglas S. Gatlin, Florida Atlantic University; Bernard C. Henessy, California State University at Hayward; David J. Vogler, Wheaton College; and Robert Craig, University of New Hampshire. The second edition was read by Cornelius P. Cotter, University of Wisconsin, Milwaukee; Robert Adams, Wright State University; William J. Crotty, Northwestern University; and both editions were read by John F. Bibby, University of Wisconsin, Milwaukee. Their helpful suggestions and intelligent criticism helped immeasurably to strengthen the final versions. Obviously, none of them can be responsible for any errors of fact or interpretation that remain. Parts of the manuscript for the second edition were typed by Christine Mikulski and Cathy Goetzl and the whole by Ann Bendall. Finally, it has been a real pleasure to work with the people at Brooks/Cole Publishing Company, particularly Marquita Flemming, Richard Mason, Gay Orr, Katherine Minerva, and Carline Haga. My wife, Carolyn, and my children, Kevin Ann, Kristin, and Dana, have all offered their encouragement and understanding.

*Robert J. Huckshorn*

# CONTENTS

# The Changing American Political System

It is ironic that the American people are credited not only with inventing political parties but also with undermining their effectiveness by adopting reforms to make them more democratic. Having created parties as a method through which voters' preferences could be transmitted into political reality, we then adopted the direct primary, nonpartisan elections, and presidential preference primaries—each a reform that made parties less effective. Perhaps even more ironic is the fact that we have erected barriers that make it difficult for parties to operate and proceed to blame them for not doing their job. We are indisputably in an antiparty age. We may be in an antigovernment age.

Parties are not the only institution to suffer a decline in public esteem. Congress, the presidency, the media (both electronic and print), and the educational, legal, and medical professions have all experienced severe losses in public support. Cynicism is widespread in the United States; it began long ago and was accelerated by the Vietnam War and Watergate. Only two presidents since the Second World War have escaped it (Eisenhower and Kennedy), and the rest have suffered public disapprobation, as witnessed by such phrases as: "To Err Is Truman," "wheeler-dealer" Lyndon Johnson, "Tricky Dick" Nixon, "stumbling" Jerry Ford, and, more recently, a "cold and ineffective" Jimmy Carter. Ronald Reagan has been called a former B-movie actor who is not quite in charge of his own administration. Congress, too, is at an unprecedented low in public esteem. Some of the disenchantment with parties may be a reflection of the fact that the president and members of Congress are also representatives of the two political parties.

The American people expect a great deal from political parties. They count on them to select good candidates who will campaign fairly, discuss the issues, and, if elected, carry out their pledges. They assume that party leadership will be at once enlightened and pragmatic. The voters have removed much of the party's control over selecting their own candidates, but they want the party held responsible for the actions of their own officeholders. Public expectations regarding political parties reflect a certain nostalgia for the past. It is almost as though the public holds parties to frontier agrarian standards of nomination, organization, and campaigning but expects them to operate in a space-satellite age. When parties cannot measure up to this contradiction between expectation and actuality, they inadvertently add to the antipartyism that prevails.

Party systems change because sociopolitical systems change. During the past quarter century the American party system has undergone vast change. The old system appeared to be outmoded and unresponsive to modern political needs. Population growth and the communication/transportation revolution forced new demands on the parties. The old New Deal coalition that undergirded the Democratic party for so long is in an advanced stage of disintegration. The Republican coalition of the early part of this century was undercut by the New Deal and has been unable to reform and regroup in such a way as to attain majority status. Voters have established a pattern of electoral independence that is often situated outside the familiar two-party structure. People have turned to special-interest groups as a source of voting cues in preference to the more exclusive allegiance demanded by party loyalty. The growth of groups has accelerated to such an extent that some political observers fear that these groups have taken over some important party functions. Greater educational attainments combined with the spectacular growth of the national and international media network have shifted emphasis away from parties and diminished their value in the eyes of many citizens. Party rules, once the preserve of party organizations, have become increasingly imbedded in statutory law. The changes that have taken place have been profound, and the transformation is clearly not complete.

One can vividly demonstrate the changes that have occurred by perusing a typical 1940s textbook on political parties. Almost any of them will do. One book tells us that the "chairman of the national committee is a potent figure" who "manages the national campaign." The "county chairman . . . is in general command of local strategy and possesses considerable power." Forty pages are spent describing political bosses and big-city machines. An entire section is devoted to whispering campaigns, slogans, and symbols, campaign songs and parades, and sobriquets such as "Honest Abe" and "Old Hickory." There are sections on the white primary, the distrust of female candidates, and a new innovation, the voting machine. The chapter on interest groups includes descriptions of the National Civil Service Reform League, the American Liberty League, the Anti-Saloon League, the National Security League, and the Navy League of the United States. Leagues seemed to be in vogue in those days. The giant late-twentieth-century economic groups—the American Federation of Labor, the Congress of Industrial Organizations (at that time not joined together), the Chamber of Commerce, and others of familiar ring—are treated almost as afterthoughts. The change has been profound in the intervening years. That author was no doubt correct in describing politics as they existed at that time, but any student can see the differences between the descriptions in that book and the politics of today.

We now speak of the "Old Politics" and the "New Politics." We draw distinctions between traditional campaigns and technological campaigns. Speculation is rife about the transformations that are taking place and about the future of American parties. Books are published and scholarly papers are read that debate questions of party dissolution or party realignment. The dangers of single-interest politics as opposed to multi-interest parties are raised. The changes that have taken place offer an obvious framework on which to build a discussion of present-day parties and politics. Change, therefore, is a thread that can be used to tie this narrative together.

None of the events discussed in these pages suggests that the party system is dead, although many observers believe that it is seriously ill. Certainly the traditional roles played by the political parties have changed dramatically. Citizens and voters have sought new means of political expression and influence as a way of meeting new social and economic goals. Undoubtedly, then, we are in the midst of a transformation in party politics, but its direction is in dispute. From the opening fragment of a 1952 lecture to the closing assessment of where we are and where we appear to be going, we shall attempt to describe the system from the point of view of the changing perspectives of political parties and party politics. The chapters will describe past developments in the party system and will seek to outline the structure of the continuing conflicts in the political firmament.

We shall begin by considering some of the basic assumptions that underlie the American political party system. Chapter 1 deals with four questions: What is a political party? What constitutes political party leadership? What characteristics distinguish the American party system? What functions are performed by the political parties? Chapter 2 presents a brief history of the American parties at different stages of their development and considers various types of party systems.

Chapter 3 discusses party organization and functions at the national, state, and local levels. The nominating process, both for the presidency and for lesser offices, is discussed in chapter 4. Chapter 5 deals with the electoral process itself, including techniques of campaigning. Campaign finance and its regulation, as well as the costs of American politics, are covered in chapter 6. American electoral behavior is discussed in chapter 7: turnout, administrative obstacles to voting, and voter participation.

Chapter 8 considers the political role of the executive in policymaking, and chapter 9 discusses the political role of legislative bodies, national and state. A brief case study is used to illustrate the many points of impact of politics on governmental decision making. Interest groups are the focus of chapter 10. The growth in the influence of groups vis-a-vis parties makes it imperative for us to briefly discuss groups and their organization, membership, and manner of operation. The techniques of groups, both lobbying and grass-roots pressure, are discussed in chapter 11. The final chapter, 12, assesses the role of parties in American politics in the latter part of the twentieth century and suggests some of the prevailing theories of party transformation.

On concluding this book, the student will, it is hoped, have gained a better understanding of where we have been in the political past, where we are in the current process of party transformation, and where we might be going in the future. Possibly, this discussion of party politics today will provide a greater understanding of the changes in political society that will take place tomorrow.

# CHAPTER ONE

# American Political Parties: Dynamics and Change

A fragment of a lecture that might have been delivered in late 1952 by a political science professor who described the political scene as he saw it:

And so, students, as we wind up this unit on American politics, there are some obvious characteristics of our party system that you should remember. What we have learned this semester is based on experience, and experience is the handmaiden of history. It is clear, it seems to me, that the two major parties control presidential nominations so tightly that we will continue to face choices between moderates like General Eisenhower and Governor Stevenson. It would simply not be possible, as I see it, for a candidate for president to emerge from the ideological left or right. The nature of our party system ensures that fringe candidates cannot gain enough delegates to be nominated. The pressure groups that form such an important part of the support base of our parties would not take such a risk. It is inconceivable, for instance, that the Democrats would nominate a candidate who was not acceptable to the AFL and the CIO.

It should be clear by now that presidents will always be renominated if they want to be. Presidential power and political party loyalty are so strong that a sitting president need only make known his desire to run again and the nomination will be his. National conventions are closely controlled by party leaders, and they will see that the delegates do not change leaders in midstream. Only one incumbent president who wanted his party's nomination for another term has been denied it, and that was many years ago. By the same token, the successive defeats of Governor Dewey and Governor Stevenson would suggest that the office of governor will no longer be a stepping-stone to a presidential nomination.

The presidential preference primary is on the wane. From a high of twenty-six primaries in 1920, at the height of the Progressive era, the number of states using the primary as a means of registering preferences for president has declined to fourteen in 1952. There is little reason to believe that this decline will not continue and that the preference primary will not die out. The party organizations are clearly reasserting themselves against the reformers. Delegate selection, it can safely be said, will be returned to party-dominated caucuses and conventions.

Those who believe in strong party organization have little to hope for in future years. Party organizations show little more life now than they have in the past. State parties are in such sad shape that few even maintain operating headquarters. The national committees continue to be dominated by unknown state party functionaries who, for the most part, have demonstrated little capacity for or interest in party leadership. They remain loose, episodic, and unstructured organizations with few functions to perform. State party organizations are not even represented at the national organizational level.

Finally, big money continues to dominate politics. Every attempt to raise large sums of money in small contributions has failed. One need only be reminded of the recent failure of Beardsley Ruml's plan to raise large sums in $5 contributions to see that. That effort resulted in a total collection of only about $285,000 in 1952. Obviously, politics today is big business, and the costs are great. Small contributor programs do not work, and it does not seem likely that legislators can be persuaded to adopt enforceable restraints on campaign contributions and spending. So, unfortunate though it may be, we have a system through which unrestricted amounts of money, mostly in large contributions, are derived from the rich and the powerful as well as from pressure groups. The prospects for tighter controls over campaign finances do not appear to be very bright.

There you have my assessment of American politics today as we are about to begin 1953 under a new Republican president. Change does not appear to be inevitable. Indeed, one would be hard-pressed to provide evidence that the party system will change at all anytime in the third quarter of this century. But I hope that you have paid enough attention, read enough assignments, and learned enough to better prepare you to watch the political drama with a more discerning eye.

---

**M**ore than thirty years have passed since that mythical professor's peroration to his class. If he has kept abreast of his field, he has had to rewrite his lecture many times. Seldom in American political history have so many changes occurred in so short a time. Each statement made by our imaginary professor was an accurate representation of reality in late 1952. Now, however, in the last quarter of this century, few of his assertions still hold true.

Each party has held a convention that nominated a candidate from an ideological fringe. Both Barry Goldwater in 1964 and George McGovern in 1972 proved that an established party organization is strikingly vulnerable to carefully engineered challenges by narrow bands of inspired supporters. In 1968 Eugene McCarthy, building on a small base on the Democratic left, helped to dissuade an incumbent president, Lyndon B. Johnson, from seeking nomination for another term. The AFL-CIO, after merging in 1955, became one of the most important supportive groups in the Democratic coalition. But when Senator McGovern sought his party's nomination in 1972, the leaders of organized labor bitterly opposed him. Having failed, and having been humiliated in the process, big labor sat out the election rather than support the nominee. In 1980 Ronald Reagan cut deeply into the labor vote, making major inroads in blue-collar areas despite the endorsement of President Jimmy Carter by most labor unions.

Although it was certainly true in 1952 that only one incumbent president, Chester A. Arthur in 1884, had been denied nomination to a second term, it was apparent in 1976 that President Gerald R. Ford might well have lost the nomination of his party at any one of several points during the preconvention period. Furthermore, Lyndon B. Johnson was forced to withdraw in 1968 under the pressure of an unpopular war in Vietnam. The advent of additional primaries, widespread media influence, and more open procedures had changed the complexion of national conventions and of the nominating process itself.

Far from disappearing, presidential preference primaries gained new strength in the 1970s. Almost three-fourths of the delegates to the national conventions in 1976 were chosen in primaries held in thirty states. In 1980 the number of states selecting delegates through presidential primaries had risen to thirty-seven. Furthermore, in 1972, 1976, and 1980 the delegates were a new and different breed. Greater numbers of young people, females, and blacks were elected—a far cry from the stereotypical cigar-chomping delegate of earlier years.

Party organizations also showed signs of growth and change. By 1976 almost every state party—over ninety of them—had permanently staffed headquarters, and one-fourth were led by full-time paid state chairpersons. Each state chairperson also held a second party post as a voting member of his or her respective national committee; collectively, these officials wielded considerable influence in both parties. The Democratic National Committee, freshly restructured in 1972, was called upon to select a vice-presidential candidate to replace one who resigned from the ticket. The Democrats also adopted an unprecedented national party charter and held off-year miniconventions in 1974, 1978, and 1982.

In recent years the office of governor has reasserted itself as a spawning ground for presidential candidacies. In 1980 alone, candidates Jimmy Carter, Ronald Reagan, Edmund G. Brown, Jr., and John Connally had served their respective states in the office of governor.

Big money was still required for party politics, but beginning in 1962 the Republican National Committee and several presidential candidates—Barry Goldwater, George Wallace, George McGovern, and Eugene McCarthy—all succeeded in collecting large sums through mass-mailed solicitations for small contributions. Personal contributions from the wealthy and from private interest groups were still important, but reform efforts in the 1970s made it more difficult to raise and spend money from most of these traditional sources. New state and national laws limited the size of contributions, required that contributors be named publicly, and limited how the money could be spent. The excesses of the 1972 campaign, Watergate, court convictions of political contributors, and the attendant adverse publicity initially served to dampen the enthusiasm of many who might ordinarily have sought to buy a piece of influence with the government. By 1980, however, changes in the Federal Election Campaign Act of 1971, while eliminating large contributions to the publicly funded presidential contests, had brought a surge of political action committee (PAC) money into congressional and other campaigns. The advent of public funding of presidential elections and PAC contributions to lesser contests dramatically affected the 1976 and 1980 presidential and congressional elections and will continue to help reshape the politics of the future.

All of these changes of the last quarter century have profoundly influenced the political system in the United States. Although we lack perspective on these events, they do offer a framework for discussion of parties and politics. We are not just interested in changes. In order to grasp the dynamics of politics in our own time, we need to review traditional aspects of politics as well. This introductory chapter attempts to set the stage for the more detailed discussion that follows by suggesting answers to several questions important to an understanding of American political parties and politics. What is a political party? What constitutes political leadership? What are the characteristics that distinguish the American from other party systems? And, finally, what functions are performed by the political parties?

## What Is a Political Party?

Most people acknowledge that political parties are vitally important to American democracy. They represent the principal means through which we select the leaders of our nation. But they do a good deal more than that. They help to run the election machinery. They serve as vehicles for political campaigns. They serve as checks on the activities of extremists from both sides of the political spectrum. They stimulate public discussion of important issues. And, possibly most important of all, they serve as a bridge between the people and their governments. Neither of our two parties may perform all of these functions well all of the time. But each of them has performed them well enough to escape serious challenge to its supremacy for over one hundred years. However ineffective they may at times seem to be, they have been responsible for providing the channel through which our elected leaders have been chosen almost from the beginning of the constitutional era.

When Lord James Bryce wrote *The American Commonwealth* almost a hundred years ago, he said that "perhaps no form of government needs great leaders so much as democracy."[1] The political environment demands leadership because the people who elect are dependent on cues being furnished to guide them in their electoral choices. This is especially true in a geographically large and demographically diverse country like the United States. Yet one of the most common complaints heard today is that American political leadership is uncreative, self-serving, and directionless. Furthermore, where political cues for public guidance should be the stock-in-trade of political parties, it is said, the American versions have been allowed to atrophy and have ceased to perform that important function. Citizens, who in another country might be active party workers, are often disenchanted with poor leadership, frustrated, and helplessly uninspired. Some of our most productive minds and industrious hands have been channeled into nonparty citizens' efforts such as Common Cause, Nader's Raiders, and a variety of conservative activist groups, including many recently organized by fundamentalist religious groups led by television evangelists.

The American people, who invented the modern political party, have shown a remarkable lack of interest in its continued good health. The various institutional diseases from which the parties are supposed to suffer have been diagnosed time and again. Through this process the diagnosticians—journalists, politicians, and political scientists—have come to a number of conclusions as to what political parties are, what they perhaps ought to be, and the characteristics that differentiate them from each other and from other kinds of organizations. Let us begin, then, by attempting to answer this question: What is a political party?

Most political scientists no longer question the importance of political parties to modern government. One influential political scientist has stated flatly

> that the political parties created democracy and that modern democracy is unthinkable save in terms of the parties. As a matter of fact, the condition of the parties is the best possible evidence of the nature of any regime. The most important distinction in modern political philosophy, the distinction between democracy and dictatorship, can be made best in terms of party politics. The parties are not therefore merely appendages of modern government; they are in the center of it and play a determinative and creative role in it.[2]

This statement, published in 1942, not only provides a reference point for those who believe political parties are essential to democratic government, but also includes an implicit warning that is particularly applicable to the conditions of the parties in the 1980s. Parties are simply vehicles through which we channel the efforts of people and groups who seek influence over the policies of government. Definitions of the political party are as numerous as the authors who have formulated them. They range from simple statements incorporating some basic concepts to more complex, multifaceted efforts designed to cover all aspects by incorporating within a single definition most of the functions that parties perform.

### Burke's Normative Definition

One of the earliest and most widely quoted definitions was by Edmund Burke, British political theorist and politician, who wrote in 1771 that "Party is a body of men united, for promoting by their joint endeavors the national interest, upon some particular principle in which they are all agreed."[3] Burke's definition is not acceptable today because, in important respects, some parties do not fit within it; it also states what parties ought to be rather than what they actually are. Furthermore, Burke attributes characteristics to all parties that are only appropriate to some of them.

### Downs's Rational Voter Definition

Some authors, like Anthony Downs, have attempted to define party in terms of the people included within it. Most scholars have considered that voters are important participants in party affairs. Downs, however, disagrees, insisting instead that parties consist of "teams" of "office seekers." He therefore defines party as "a coalition of men seeking to control the governing apparatus by legal means." He believes that parties are motivated only by the desire to seek and control office. He goes on further to amplify his definition.

> By *coalition,* we mean a group of individuals who have certain ends in common and cooperate with each other to achieve them. By *governing apparatus,* we mean the physical, legal, and institutional equipment which the government uses to carry out its specialized role in the division of labor. By *legal means,* we mean either duly constituted elections or legitimate influence.[4]

According to Downs's definition, then, the party is basically an elite group of people who are seeking office. The voters can be compared to consumers who respond to public policy initiatives offered them by competing sets of office seekers. Voters are rational individuals who evaluate alternatives in terms of a cost-benefit ratio. Obviously, Downs sees voters and parties (as exemplified by office seekers) as two clearly separate groups of people. The distinction is explicitly made when he says, "Therefore we can treat citizens and political parties as two mutually exclusive groups without unduly distorting reality."[5] Critics of Downs argue that voters are not necessarily rational all the time; they also point out that the party's motivation is not purely one of winning offices. Downs offers a thought-provoking model of party government, but many political scientists are unable to accept some of its underlying assumptions.

## Sorauf's Tripartite Party Definition

Frank Sorauf describes the party organizations as "three-headed political giants." He maintains that this tripartite structure includes a party organization, a party in office, and a party in the electorate. The party organization is composed of the party leaders, activists, and members. These party organizers make and carry out decisions in behalf of the party; they work through committees, caucuses, conferences, and conventions, and they are controlled by the state laws and party bylaws. The party in government is made up of those who have run for and won public office—presidents and governors, members of Congress and legislators, commissioners and council members. These officeholders make pronouncements in behalf of the party because the enunciation of policy is a part of their job. They are semiautonomous and are frequently at odds with the people who work in the party organization itself. The party in the electorate, the most difficult to describe, is made up of all of those who have some degree of loyalty to the party, vote for it most of the time, but do not take an active part beyond that civic duty. These people are the clientele group for the party, and they are responsible for providing the votes that elect men and women to office.[6]

## Schlesinger's Nuclear Party Definition

Another theory that deserves notice is Joseph Schlesinger's concept of the "nuclear party." Schlesinger suggests that the basic unit of party organization is the small nuclear group where collective effort helps elect a single candidate to office. These nuclei may work for a presidential candidate or be nothing more than a few supporters for an obscure local candidate. The nuclear party is based on contributors rather than members. In fact, the nucleus eliminates the necessity to come to grips with the question of what constitutes membership. It is simply the cooperative efforts of a group of supporters in behalf of a candidate.[7]

## Statutory Definitions of Party

Many state legislatures have attempted to write a legal definition of political party; these are usually descriptive of organization and duties. As is typical of many states, Florida statutes include this section on party committees:

**Powers and duties of the executive committees**

1. Each state and county executive committee of a political party shall have the power and duty:

    a. To adopt a constitution by two-thirds vote of the full committee.

    b. To adopt such bylaws as it may deem necessary by majority vote of the full committee.

    c. To conduct its meetings according to generally accepted parliamentary rules.

    d. To make party nominations when required by law.

    e. To conduct campaigns for party nominees.

    f. To raise and expend party funds.

    g. To make any assessment it requires of candidates, for the purpose of meeting its expenses or maintaining its party organization.

2. The state executive committee shall by resolution recommend candidates for presidential electors and deliver a certified copy thereof to the Governor prior to September 1 of each presidential election year.

3. The chairman and treasurer of an executive committee of any political party shall be accountable for the funds of such committee and jointly liable for their proper expenditure for authorized purposes only.[8]

A more straightforward definition is exemplified by the Missouri statutes, which define an established political party as one that, "at either of the last two general elections, polled for its candidate for any statewide office more than two percent of the entire vote cast for the office. . . ."[9]

## Epstein's All-Inclusive Definition

This review should also contain an all-inclusive definition that can be extended beyond the American experience. Political scientist Leon Epstein offers one that he claims will fit almost everything that is called a party in any Western democracy and that he describes as "any group, however loosely organized, seeking to elect governmental officeholders under a given label."[10] He believes that having a label rather than an organization is the crucial defining element, since this permits a group of aspiring officeholders, even though they have no organized following, to seek votes under a collective name. Epstein clearly does not believe that parties or party organizations are crucial to democracy.

## A Pragmatic Definition of Party

Clearly, there is little agreement as to those qualities that go to make up a political party. Different cooks toss different ingredients into their particular political stew. It is time, therefore, to offer our own definition of political party. For our purposes, *the American political party is an autonomous group of citizens having the purpose of making nominations and contesting elections in hope of gaining control over governmental power through the capture of public offices and the organization of the gov-*

*ernment.* An inclusive definition of this type always opens one to attack. Almost every element in the definition can stir debate between scholars and political observers. But it is important to keep in mind that the overall goal, regardless of party definition, is to select governmental leadership.

## What Characteristics Distinguish the American Party System?

Explaining the American party system to a foreign visitor is like explaining Christianity to an Amazon tribesman. Each explanation is a revelation, and each revelation deepens the mystery. Two thousand years from now an anthropologist attempting to explain the American political system might be hard-pressed to describe how it worked or even how it survived for so long. Many of its antecedents lie buried in history, and many of its characteristics arise from the peculiar qualities of the people themselves. Every political system in the world is unique in some fashion. Parties in a democracy are the products of a functional response to voting by the electorate, but they are also tools through which governmental actions are justified and channeled. Totalitarian systems, on the other hand, often use parties—usually a single one—as a facade behind which the government can exercise its will while maintaining the fiction of popular support. Our future anthropologist would quickly discover that he or she could not describe superficially the characteristics of the American party system in the twentieth century. The system is too complex for simple explanations to serve. The system does, however, have certain distinguishing characteristics; we are now prepared to review some of the chief of these.

### A Two-Party System

The *first* and most notable characteristic, one that sets off the American from virtually every other party system in the world, is that there are only two major parties. As we have already noted, most of the dictators of the world maintain a single official party to cater to the purposes of the government. Many political scientists argue that these organizations are mere devices, not parties in the true sense of the word. Most of the other democracies are served by systems embracing several parties. Some democracies, such as that of Great Britain, have two major parties, although third parties have sometimes garnered enough votes to be important in the formation of a parliamentary majority. The Liberal party was displaced as a major force after World War I and was replaced by the Labour party, which has been the major competitor of the Conservative party since that time. Although the Liberal party today has little influence, with less than a dozen seats in the 635-member House of Commons, in 1981 a new split in the ranks of Labour brought about the creation of a new Social Democratic party that some observers of British politics believe represents an important and potentially influential third-party force. Other Western European countries have six, nine, or thirteen parties. But, from the inception of parties, the United States has had only two. One major reason for this has been the multiclass and heterogeneous base of support of each of the two parties. The American people, regardless of political beliefs, have been able to fit themselves under the two-party umbrella. This characteristic has not only distinguished the American system from multiparty systems, but has also been an important factor in the failure of third-party movements. Hundreds of efforts have been made to organize and nurture third-party movements, but none, save the Republican party that emerged just before the Civil War, has had any lasting effect. In chapter 2 we shall discuss the two-party system in detail.

## Decentralization

Americans are accustomed to centralized organizations with clear lines of authority and responsibility extending vertically through the levels of the hierarchy. Most American organizations fit that pattern. The people at the apex of the organizational pyramid exercise authority over the people in the lower levels; this authority includes the power to discipline. Most of the political parties in the democratic systems of the world conform to this centralized structure. Parties in the United States, however, do not.

Therefore, the *second* distinguishing characteristic of American political parties is that they are decentralized, with elements of power distributed throughout the system, although concentrated toward the state and local levels. It is ironic that this is the case. For almost half a century the flow of power has been toward the federal government in Washington. Concern has long been voiced over the growth of federal programs and the national bureaucracy. Politicians have declared the need to return power to the people. But only recently has there been perceptible growth in national party power. The principal national organizations of the parties consist of the national committees and the national nominating conventions. These bodies have traditionally had little power to force action by state and local parties, for they have had no sanctions to apply and few rewards to give. Each state and local committee was (and still is, for the most part) self-governing and self-perpetuating. National party leaders normally could not attempt to force a state party to act, because each separate unit had its own sources of support and influence and could easily exist without the national party organization.

Essentially, the same problem existed with the national conventions, which have the added burden of meeting only quadrennially. Even though the conventions are the lawmaking bodies of the parties, their primary purpose is to nominate candidates for president and vice-president. Nevertheless, their powers to perform these functions have been so circumscribed that decentralization has actually been furthered. With the advent of large numbers of presidential preference primaries in the 1970s, three-fourths of the delegates to the 1980 conventions were chosen outside of party channels, and many hundreds of them who were in attendance owed allegiance to a particular candidate—and only secondarily to the party. Insofar as nominations are concerned, the primaries have undercut the deliberative functions of the conventions. Furthermore, even those delegates who are still selected by methods other than primaries represent the state and local parties rather than the national parties.

The success of the national committees, particularly that of the Democrats, in enforcing delegate "quotas" in 1972 suggests that sanctions can be applied to state and local parties. At the present time, however, the national committees are formless coalitions that publicize the national parties, organize the national conventions, and ratify decisions made elsewhere. An increase in their responsibilities might provide for a more centralized party system. Several events of the past few years suggest that the national party committees are in fact striving to increase their power and authority over the state committees. As discussed in chapter 3, such a trend might ultimately bring about increased centralization.

## Diffused Leadership

Americans have frequently referred to "the great game of politics" as though it were a form of competition on a playing field. If that were actually the case, considerable conjecture would certainly arise as to the identity of the coach. The *third* characteristic of the party system, therefore, is our perpetual difficulty in determining who party leaders are. The decentralization of the system, lack of party responsibility, and separation of powers have often combined to thwart any effort by party faithfuls to point a finger and say, "That is our leader."

Those who wish to strengthen party organization see the results of that revitalization as a means of bringing forth new leaders. Those who seek to build responsible parties in the British mold hope that greater responsibiliity will help to entice new leaders into the arena of political and governmental battle. Those who wish to concentrate on improving the electoral process believe that such effort will result in greater choice among leadership cadres.

Leadership, however, is a difficult, elusive issue with which to deal. Henri Peyre has described leadership as one of three topics "on which no wise man should ever attempt to write."[11] The problem, of course, is that no fixed set of qualities is common to all leaders. Characteristics that may be relevant to one leader may not be to another. The result is that different political cultures define their own criteria for leadership. Austin Ranney and Willmoore Kendall have assigned three different meanings to the word *leader*. According to them, it connotes either: (1) one whose attainments, in terms of a particular set of standards and values, rank high when compared to the attainments of his or her contemporaries; (2) one to whom persons engaged in a particular activity defer because of the status he or she enjoys; or (3) one who emits stimuli to which members of the group may respond in order to advance the activities and performance of the group.[12] Obviously, if no agreement exists concerning the general concept of leadership, neither is there a consensus concerning the more specific question of the development of political leaders, although the latter is a role clearly expected of the political parties.

Let us emphasize that there are really two categories of party leaders. Some persons are party leaders, although they never run for public office. These persons are *organizational* leaders, and they devote themselves to party affairs—the well-being of the party and its candidates for office. This group includes national and state party chairpersons; county, city, and borough leaders; members of the national committees; and others who perform political functions but whose names never grace a ballot and who have never occupied a public office.

*Public* party leaders, on the other hand, run for nominations, campaign for office, and, if elected, serve as officers of the government. They, of course, include governors, legislators, commissioners, and council members. Furthermore, considerable movement may take place from one group to the other. Between 1964 and 1980, for instance, 45 percent of all those who served as heads of state parties subsequently ran for *public* political office.[13] The path also runs the other way. Numerous examples exist of *public* officeholders who, upon the expiration of their terms, were elected to serve in party *organizational* offices.

Leadership is an elusive concept, as we have noted before. More often than not, power is shared among many. Sometimes it resides in unlikely places. For two decades the late Mayor Richard J. Daley of Chicago was the Democratic leader of Illinois, regardless of who occupied the governor's chair or who served as state party chairperson. Because of his control over the Cook County organization, Daley, in effect, controlled the Illinois Democratic party, although a variety of other people held the offices we normally think of as leadership positions.

One would assume that, for the party controlling the presidency, it would be an easy task to identify the president as the leader. Even that is not the case, however, for some presidents have shown little interest in their party leadership role. One of the criticisms leveled at Jimmy Carter during his term as president was that he ignored the Democratic party organization and treated its leaders with disdain. Furthermore, even highly politicized presidents have directed their energies towards personal campaign organizations, at times leaving their party splintered and quarreling.

For the party out of power, identification of leadership is even more difficult. Many may claim to be the party leader, but their claims are sometimes not supported by any sizable following. Contenders for the honor of leading the party may include a former president, recent presidential candidates, congressional leaders, national chairpersons, or even some party functionary who does not hold party or public office.

Opinions often differ concerning the identity of the real leader in state and local politics. In some states even the governor is not always the leader of his or her party. Some governors have isolated themselves from party politics, leaving the political machinery in other hands. State party chairpersons are sometimes recognized leaders, at other times they are not.[14] In short, there is no clear-cut, easily identifiable leadership in many cells of the hierarchical structure. Politics is a game with many coaches. Party leadership is often shared, which by itself sets the American system uniquely apart from the systems of other democratic countries, particularly those with parliamentary forms of government.

## Lack of Ideological Commitment

A *fourth* characteristic distinguishing the American from other party systems is the failure, indeed the inability, of our two major parties to adopt ideological or programmatic statements of belief. Most of the world's democratic parties appeal to voters by adopting platforms that set forth their views on major issues or make an ideological commitment. These parties are able to do so because in multiparty systems the voters can be reached with a narrow appeal based on a limited program. Platform statements serve to impart to the voters the views of the party leadership on issues of the day. Sometimes, in particular countries, the commitment is strongly ideological, representing deeply held beliefs in communism, socialism, fascism, or laissez faire capitalism. Although some parties try to blur the edges of their programmatic commitments in order to alienate as few voters as possible, they are able to maintain a semblance of ideological purity.

In the United States, with its two-party system, it is much more difficult for the parties to adopt strong statements of belief. Both the Republicans and the Democrats draw support from a wide range of groups and voters. Some of these adherents are conservative, others are liberal, and still others are in-between moderates. Furthermore, little relationship exists between the foreign policy and domestic policy views of the various groups. A conservative Democrat may also be an outspoken internationalist; an isolationist may be a domestic liberal.

Weak party organizations and loose ideological and programmatic commitments lead to widespread ticket splitting in the United States. American voters are increasingly making voting choices that disregard party affiliation, relying instead on personal appeals, candidate programs, and responses to campaign tactics. At times these appeals are little more than veiled exploitations of charismatic qualities carefully crafted for television by advertising specialists. The increase in ticket splitting may merely reflect what some believe to be a traditional streak of antipartyism in the American people. Even though many citizens express a preference for one or the other of the parties, their actual behavior in the polling booth suggests a degree of fickleness unmatched in most other life experiences.

Naturally, if the voters do not vote according to party affiliation, the ideological range of officeholders is bound to be great. Each of the Democratic congresses of the post–World War II era, for instance, has included members in the majority who range over the entire spectrum of political beliefs from right to left. Conservative southern Democrats vie for power with northern and western liberals. Internationalists and isolationists sit side by side in the chambers. As Clinton Rossiter noted in 1960: "The parties, moderate and tolerant and self-contradictory to a fault, are interested in the votes of men, not in their principles, and they care not at all whether the votes they gather are bestowed with passion or with indifference—so long as they are bestowed and counted."[15]

Americans are not the only people who are dissatisfied with the ideological or programmatic commitment of their political parties. Members of a variety of European parties long identified as ideological have expressed dismay as their leadership has "forsaken" ideological purity for broader electoral support. For several years the British Labour party has been torn with dissension over the commitment of the leadership to established party doctrines. Dogmatism in support of principles sometimes gives way to pragmatism in the quest for votes.

Anthony Downs maintains that the chief goal of the party is to win elections and that, to do so, the parties must run candidates who appeal to the voters' self-interest. The population diversity in this country makes it very difficult to determine what is the collective self-interest of the voters. Consequently, most candidates attempt to direct their appeals to the center by adopting positions that straddle the issues and that thus might appeal to voters who perceive themselves as centrists—between liberal and conservative.

This became harder to do after the presidential campaign of 1964, which turned, to a large extent, on an ideological disagreement over the role of government. By 1972 the conflict had become much more complicated. Traditional ideological divisions broke down as political debate expanded to encompass new realities—disagreements over the Vietnam War, unfulfilled racial and minority aspirations, federal poverty programs versus individual self-help, efforts by the New Left to increase personal freedoms as it saw them, and proposals to reform and restructure governmental institutions. Many candidates, to avoid becoming impaled on the sharp edges of these controversies, sought to rely on personality, while others concentrated on selling themselves through media campaigns—a technique that guarantees that the voters cannot talk back.

The campaign of 1980 was another in which issues seemed to dominate the presidential contest. Each of the major candidates discussed differences over the role of the United States in world affairs, the troubled economy, the tragedy unfolding in Iran, the Panama Canal Treaty, the Equal Rights Amendment, and a host of newly minted moral questions. Some observers believed that we might be moving toward a period of more issue-oriented electoral outcomes. It is more likely, however, as we shall see in chapter 7, that voter decisions will continue to be made on the basis of candidate personalities and that issues will continue to be of lesser importance. It is true that some political scientists believe we may be undergoing an evolutionary change that will eventually thrust issues and ideology more to the fore, but there is little evidence of that having happened to date. American campaigns still normally reflect the desire of parties and candidates to occupy the middle ground, a characteristic more or less unique to the American political party system.

## Lack of Responsible Parties

If decentralization is the most descriptive word applied to American parties, then lack of responsibility is the most discussed. This *fifth* characteristic of our parties simply means that candidates elected to office under party labels and on party platforms are free to ignore those platforms without having to account for their actions. In simple fact, once elected, candidates are not required to honor their pledges, and their party is not able to enforce discipline against them.

Advocates of responsible parties contend that legislators elected under the party name are obligated to act in unison to carry out the policies identified with the party. In their view, legislators should adhere to party positions, that is, maintain a high degree of cohesiveness, so that the voters can successfully distinguish one party's program from the other. Yet three of the four characteristics thus far discussed work to undercut responsible party behavior. Decentralization of power, lack of coherent leadership, and the failure to adopt ideological positions are all factors in the disinclination of the American parties to behave in a "responsible" manner.

The key to responsible parties is internal cohesion. Cohesion usually means the degree to which the members of the party in the legislature are able to join together in support of party positions. Although there is sometimes more party unity in Congress than is credited, on the whole the American parties have been unable to achieve any consistent and effective degree of cohesion at the national level. Legislatures in some states have shown a much greater degree of partisan unity. Party responsibility based on a strong organization and supported by powerful leaders has been a hallmark of the New York legislature, regardless of which party controlled the state. Many legislatures, however, particularly those in one-party and modified one-party states, have suffered from the same organizational looseness and lack of responsibility that has suffused Congress for so long.

The fact that the legislative parties do not vote cohesively means that the party organization that elected them cannot hold them responsible for their failure to support party positions. Even though the party has enjoyed unity during the course of a campaign, once the successful candidates become incumbent officeholders, party support scores decline, and dedication to partisan principle and campaign rhetoric evaporates. Sometimes this occurs because the demands of citizens, interest groups, and party leaders are contradictory and ill-defined, but it can also be a by-product of the governmental structure.

Congressional candidates, serving in national office, are nominated by local party systems. Once in office, however, congressional representatives often cease to view the local party as their patron and strike an independent stance aimed at reelection under the auspices of their own personal organization. Because of that, neither the national party nor the state or local parties can exercise control over the congressional representative's actions or votes. Indeed, the original purpose in organizing the congressional campaign committees in Washington was to provide the members with their own channel to the voters, thus, in effect, removing them from the established presidentially oriented party hierarchy.[16]

Another factor is that congressional district lines cut across political jurisdictions with little regard to other electoral boundaries. Counties are separated from their neighbors and precincts from their cities. Seemingly haphazard congressional district lines slice through states without apparent reason. As a result, few state and local parties have an abiding interest in or loyalty to a candidate seeking election to the House. Legislators, for their part, see little to be gained from tying their futures to a party organization that may take an ideological line or adopt a policy position that directly threatens their political careers.

The question of whether more responsible parties are desirable has plagued political scientists for years. At one time it was believed by some that adjustments might be made in the American system that would have the effect of making the parties more responsible. Most of the recommended reforms, however, involved serious tampering with the constitutional mechanism and appeared to some to be designed to bring the system into closer alignment with that of the British.

In the United Kingdom, both parties impose much greater conformity on members of the House of Commons than do their counterparts in the United States. Republican members of Congress can repeatedly vote in opposition to their own party, defy their own president, oppose policies enunciated by Republican leaders, and still return home to be reelected by their constituents. Members of the House of Commons acting in comparable fashion, however, would have less hope of reelection, since the party leadership has a variety of sanctions that can be levied to bring them into line. The ultimate penalty would be for the party to run officially "endorsed" candidates against the renegades in the next election, thus either winning the seats with new members of greater loyalty or splitting the vote so that the opposition party wins. Members of Commons are elected because they are expected to support the party's programs and its leaders. Deviation from that support is considered to be a defiance of their mandate. It is unlikely that such a system could be imposed on the American electorate, and many question whether it would be desirable even if it were possible.

In 1950 the American Political Science Association (APSA) sponsored a wide-ranging study of party responsibility. The results were published as a monograph entitled *Toward a More Responsible Two-Party System.*[17] The report, written by a group of distinguished political scientists, concluded that "Party responsibility means the responsibility of both parties to the general public, as enforced in elections," and argued that "An effective party system requires, first, that the parties are able to bring forth programs to which they commit themselves and, second, that the parties possess sufficient internal cohesion to carry out these programs."[18]

The report recommended a series of reforms that would, in the view of the committee that wrote the report, strengthen and make more responsible the entire political system in the United States. Publication of the report triggered a controversy that simmers to this day in political science circles.

Those supporting the committee's judgment contended that the parties could be made more responsible, could bring forth programs to which they committed themselves, and could carry out the programs, provided reforms were instituted that would guarantee the necessary party cohesion. Many political scientists today disagree with the APSA study and even denounce the goal of "more responsible parties." Critics argue that the committee ignored the political realities of American life and did not take into account the price that would have to be paid in order to gain more disciplined and responsive parties. Some believe that this price would include a deterioration of the federal system, greater difficulty in achieving compromise between opposing groups, and the almost certain development of a multiparty system. The critics also point to sharp and irreconcilable differences between the British system and the American, as well as between the people of the two countries.

Opponents of the "responsible party" theorists note that the United States is populated by a vast, heterogeneous, and diversified people, who need parties to nurture compromise and moderation. The United Kingdom, on the other hand, is populated by a more homogeneous people, for whom a more responsible party system is appropriate. Austin Ranney has noted that greater unity in the American parties would destroy the two-party system, that "the congeries of bipartisan and intraparty 'blocs' in Congress is, in effect, a multiple-party system, masquerading under the labels and formalities of a two-party system."[19] He goes on to observe that, as long as our basic population and interests remain the same, "centralizing and disciplining our national parties would very likely result in a multiple-party rather than a two-party system."[20]

Thus the lack of cohesion and the lack of party responsibility really stem, according to these critics, from the diversity of American interests and the divisions engendered by the Constitution, which often combine to force legislators to engage in bipartisan negotiation and voting behavior in order to survive. The parties themselves, under such a system, have no choice but to remain permissive and to refrain from attempting to enforce greater regularity among their officeholding members.

## Lack of Commitment to Politics

A *sixth* and final characteristic is a characteristic more of our political culture than it is of our party system, yet it deserves mention just the same. Clinton Rossiter has pointed out the absence in our national behavior of a commitment to politics as a way of life. As Rossiter explained:

> Americans give less scope to politics, are less stirred by the rhetoric of politicians, and expect less from the political process than do Frenchmen or Belgians or Italians or even Canadians. Even at the height of a presidential campaign, when the air is purple with the promises and threats of a legion of orators, the political temperature of most Americans remains low and steady.[21]

The evident coolness of the American people toward politics is illustrated in a number of ways: (1) the shifting of allegiance of citizens between the two parties or into independent status; (2) the failure of the parties to require anything in exchange for membership—attendance at meetings, payment of dues, or performance of specific duties; and (3) the failure of the party organizations to enlist masses of people in their cause.

The rapid growth in the number of citizens claiming independent status may attest to a general negative attitude toward politics and politicians. When opinion analyst George Gallup first asked a national sample of voters in 1944, "If you have a son would you like to see him go into politics as a life work when he gets out of school?"

only 21 percent answered affirmatively. Most of those who furnished negative answers described politics and politicians as "crooked," "rotten," "corrupt," or "unethical." In subsequent years the percentage responding favorably has remained about the same. In 1981 Gallup asked a sample of over 1,500 people to rate the honesty and ethical standards of workers in different occupations and only salespeople, car salespeople, and advertising practitioners ranked lower than public officeholders. Only 20 percent of the people in the sample gave a "very high" or "high" rating to U.S. senators, while congressmen and local and state officeholders ranked lower still, with 15, 14, and 12 percent, respectively.[22] A 1979 Louis Harris poll revealed that, of fifteen listed occupational choices judged by prestige, the politician ranked near the bottom, with only 17 percent of the people assigning that occupation "great prestige."[23]

A separate body of data, based on survey research, has shown a precipitate decline in public identification with the political parties. The University of Michigan's Center for Political Studies has been surveying a weighted sample of eligible voters every election year since 1952. The respondents have been asked the same two questions in every survey. The first question requires interviewees to identify themselves as Democrats, Republicans, or Independents. The second question seeks to measure partisanship by requiring the self-described Democrats and Republicans to categorize themselves as strong or weak identifiers. Independents are asked to designate whether they lean more toward the Republicans or the Democrats. According to the Michigan survey, both parties have lost supporters in recent years as more and more people have declared themselves Independents.

The number of people describing themselves as Democrats has declined from 47 percent in 1952 to 41 percent in 1980, and those self-identified as Republicans have declined from 27 to 23 percent. While the number of people identifying with the two parties has fallen, the percentage describing themselves as Independents rose from 22 percent in 1952 to 37 percent in 1974 and back to 34 percent in 1980. In that span of twenty-eight years, therefore, the number of Independents surpassed the number of Republicans and came within seven percentage points of matching the Democrats (see table1-1).[24] Nevertheless, if strong and weak Republicans and Democrats are combined, 63 percent still claim party affiliation.

It should also be noted, however, that party-leaning Independents have a stronger record of party voting than do weak party identifiers. Arthur H. Miller and Warren E. Miller, two of the political scientists responsible for the University of Michigan data gathering and analysis, have found that Independents who lean toward either party have, on the average, followed their party preferences more closely in presidential voting than have weak Democrats and Republicans.[25]

Viewed over time, these shifting allegiances confirm Rossiter's assessment that the American people do not have a lasting commitment to politics and political affairs. But, obviously, many of them do. Every candidate and each of the parties can always count on some volunteers who will spend the long hours necessary to keep the intermittent political machine chugging along without stalling. Politics in the United States tends to be highly personal rather than an institutional affair. What is it that does cause some people to lend themselves to political campaigns? Why do they get involved?

Most people become active in politics, whether on a sustained, long-term basis or as a part of a particular campaign, because the incentive system makes it worth their while. Party members and volunteer workers participate because they want to get

TABLE 1-1  Party identification of the electorate, 1952–1980

| | 1952 | 1954 | 1956 | 1958 | 1960 | 1962 | 1964 | 1966 | 1968 | 1970 | 1972 | 1974 | 1976 | 1978 | 1980 |
|---|---|---|---|---|---|---|---|---|---|---|---|---|---|---|---|
| Democratic | | | | | | | | | | | | | | | |
| Strong | 22% | 22% | 21% | 23% | 21% | 23% | 26% | 18% | 20% | 20% | 15% | 18% | 15% | 15% | 18% |
| Weak | 25 | 25 | 23 | 24 | 25 | 23 | 25 | 27 | 25 | 23 | 25 | 21 | 25 | 24 | 23 |
| Subtotal | 47 | 47 | 44 | 47 | 46 | 46 | 51 | 45 | 45 | 43 | 40 | 39 | 40 | 39 | 41 |
| Independent | | | | | | | | | | | | | | | |
| Lean Democratic | 10 | 9 | 7 | 7 | 8 | 8 | 9 | 9 | 10 | 10 | 11 | 13 | 12 | 14 | 11 |
| Independent | 5 | 7 | 9 | 8 | 8 | 8 | 8 | 12 | 11 | 13 | 13 | 16 | 14 | 14 | 13 |
| Lean Republican | 7 | 6 | 8 | 4 | 7 | 6 | 6 | 7 | 9 | 8 | 11 | 8 | 10 | 10 | 10 |
| Subtotal | 22 | 22 | 24 | 19 | 23 | 22 | 23 | 28 | 30 | 31 | 35 | 37 | 36 | 38 | 34 |
| Republican | | | | | | | | | | | | | | | |
| Weak | 14 | 14 | 14 | 16 | 13 | 16 | 13 | 15 | 14 | 15 | 13 | 14 | 14 | 13 | 14 |
| Strong | 13 | 13 | 15 | 13 | 14 | 12 | 11 | 10 | 10 | 10 | 10 | 8 | 9 | 8 | 9 |
| Subtotal | 27 | 27 | 29 | 29 | 27 | 28 | 24 | 25 | 24 | 25 | 23 | 22 | 23 | 21 | 23 |
| Apolitical, don't know | 4 | 4 | 3 | 5 | 4 | 4 | 2 | 2 | 1 | 1 | 2 | 2 | 1 | 2 | 2 |

Source: "Party Identification 1952–1974: Michigan Survey," in *Politics and Parties Between Elections*, National Journal Reprint (Washington, D.C.: Government Research Corporation, 1977), p. 8. Data for 1976, 1978, and 1980 are from *American National Election Studies*, Center for Political Studies, University of Michigan. Reprinted by permission.

something out of the experience. Some rewards are intangible, reflecting the personal satisfaction derived from taking part. Others are tangible, arising from the individual's desire to earn an opportunity for appointment to a government job or some form of personal recognition. In general, the incentive system embraces three categories of rewards: (1) economic or material incentives, such as jobs, contracts, favors, and, in some places, even bribes or graft; (2) personal or social incentives, founded on the wish for social contacts and friendship and perhaps greater prestige; and (3) ideological incentives, based on the desire to influence public policy or to implement or defeat a particular philosophy.

Undoubtedly, other characteristics exist that distinguish the American parties from parties in different parts of the world. Each of the qualities we have discussed—the two-party pattern, decentralization, dispersed leadership, lack of ideological and issue commitments, nonresponsibility, and citizen disinterest—can be and has been treated as a criticism of the system itself. Regardless of the tone of resignation that often seems to permeate discussions of the American parties, until recent years relatively little reform has been attempted. Furthermore, most of the changes that have taken place have been evolutionary in nature, designed to meet the needs of a particular moment.

## What Are the Functions of Political Parties?

Political parties in a democracy have important responsibilities and must perform certain functions necessary to carry them out. In a broad sense, the party in power has the responsibility to govern: that is, to assume command of the machinery of government and use it to see that the party's policies are adopted and carried into effect. The party out of power, of course, plays a different role. It has the duty to oppose, and it can do this by proposing alternative courses of action and by focusing public attention on the shortcomings of the incumbents. Ideally, opposition by the party out of power takes constructive forms. Occasionally, however, the minority party may fall into a pattern of opposition for opposition's sake, merely publicizing the failures of the party in power without offering any constructive alternatives.

Earlier, in defining the "American political party," we listed as its purposes *making nominations, contesting elections, gaining control by capturing public offices,* and *organizing the government* once the offices have been won and the candidates have been seated. Here, then, are the functions performed by the American parties.

### Nominating Candidates

Political scientists generally agree that the nomination of candidates is the most important function performed by political parties. E. E. Schattschneider maintains that "Whatever else they may or may not do, *the parties must make nominations.*"[26] This role distinguishes parties from other types of political organizations, such as interest groups. Obviously, if the party leadership is unable to field candidates who can be elected, or at least make an honorable attempt, the leadership cannot exploit its chances to capture control of offices and to run the government. Without political parties to screen and select candidates, the voters would find it most difficult to make rational choices from the array of candidates who would present themselves. The nominating process, therefore, is not just a system for candidate selection; it is also a system for cue giving to the party's voters.

During the period after the American Revolution, candidates were chosen in party caucuses composed of party leaders, legislators, officeholders, and others who simply met together for the purpose of maintaining party control over those men running under the party label. This system, however undemocratic by today's standards, had the advantage of allowing the custodians of the party to select those who were to represent it. The caucus as a system of candidate selection fell into disrepute, first during the Jacksonian era, and then later during the Progressive period, as party members rebelled against the system of candidate selection by those already in office.

Gradually a system of party conventions emerged as a more democratic method of nomination. Delegates selected in the lower echelons of the party hierarchy met together in convention to nominate candidates and to write statements of party principles. Abuses of the system by party "bosses" eventually brought the convention system into disrepute, and reformers began casting about for a more democratic way of making nominations.

The direct primary system of nomination first gained popularity in Wisconsin in 1904 as a tenet of LaFollette progressivism. Even though the direct primary had been used in isolated governmental units at the local level for several decades, Wisconsin was the first state to adopt it as a statewide nominating method. The primary movement spread across the nation and by 1915 had been adopted in some form or another in every state. Use of the party primary permits each party member to vote on candidates to represent the party on the general election ballot. Although the primary appears to be a more democratic system of nomination, it has been attacked in recent years because of the usually low turnout of voters and the removal of the party organization from candidate selection.

## Providing a Channel for Political Struggle

The second function of the party is to afford a channel for the struggle for political power. The arena for political conflicts is large, and the dimensions of the political struggle woud be unmanageable were it not for the parties. With large numbers of elective offices to fill at all levels of government, it is essential that the voters be given some form of guidance in their choice of candidates. The political parties provide the mechanism for that guidance.

Parties also offer a vehicle through which complex issues and policy proposals can be simplified so that voters may better understand them. This sometimes results in campaign themes being reduced to simple slogans or catchwords, but for many voters this decrease in complexity permits them to cast their votes with at least some sophistication.

An important part of the representative system is voter expectation that a winner will emerge to provide the continuity necessary to maintain stable government. The parties furnish an umbrella under which various people with somewhat similar beliefs can come together with a reasonable expectation of winning some of the time. Political parties also have a fair chance of regrouping their forces when they fail to win. Thus parties constitute a channel for political action that is most important to the success of a representative democracy. The winners govern, but the losers do not have to mount the barricades to have a chance to govern in the future.

## Organizing the Machinery of Government

The third function of political parties is to organize the machinery of government so that its business can be transacted properly. This is often not so simple as it might seem. When the same party controls both the presidency and Congress (or the governorship and the legislature), theoretically, it can put its programs, presumably as outlined in its platform, into effect. If control of the two branches is split between parties, as has been the case for most of the past quarter century, reaching agreement on policy outputs and fixing responsibility for policy outcomes become more difficult. The executive branch must then propose policy alternatives and do what it can to get them accepted by an opposition Congress. Those who advocate greater party responsibility believe that changes should be considered that would reduce the chances for divided control of the executive and legislative branches. Only with such change, they maintain, can the parties responsibly perform their governing function.

## Political Socialization

Political parties share with the family, church, and school responsibility for socializing the individual. Political socialization is the process through which citizens acquire the values and attitudes that influence their political decisions. For many dedicated members the party serves as a key to personal decision making on partisan issues and selection of candidates. Political socialization is essentially a matter of political education. The party performs this function whenever it tries to influence voters through press releases, pamphlets, campaign literature, and press conferences. The American parties have never approached their socialization function very systematically. Unlike some European and Latin American parties, they do not make much of an effort to influence young people, and they have little or nothing to do with the public or private education systems on an organized basis. They have approached the problem, if at all, in a more haphazard manner. Nevertheless, they do have responsibility for establishing political values and for making information available to the citizenry.

## Providing a Focus for Policy Concerns

When the citizen tells the pollster that he or she is not going to vote because the parties both stand for the same things or do not stand for anything, that citizen is, in effect, opting for a system of policy advocacy for the parties. When a newspaper editorial fusses because a candidate does not come to grips with the "real" issues facing the voters, that editorial board is calling for a greater policy emphasis. When a candidate claims to be the only one in the race who is talking about the issues, he or she is assuming the self-awarded mantle of policy advocate.

The American political system has been moving toward an emphasis on policy advocacy for some time now. But in order to achieve this, the parties must be able to demonstrate that the election of their candidates is an endorsement of their platform and policy pronouncements. That, however, cannot be accomplished in the American system for four reasons. (1) The parties and candidates often are not in major disagreement on important policy issues. (2) Our elections do not always represent mandates, because those who vote do not necessarily transmit the wishes of all people. (3) We are unable to define what a mandate is because we do not know why people voted as they did, nor do we always elect all of the candidates for a variety of offices from the same party. (4) Individual officeholders elected in the same election from the same party often disagree on major policy positions.

Elections, in short, cannot serve as referenda on the issues of the day. Voters still cast their ballots because of ingrained habit, not because the party candidate that they support is an advocate of some particular collection of policy initiatives. A Republican voter may vote for the Republican candidates on the ballot because he or she always has. The voter may vote the straight ticket because of a liking for the candidate who heads that ticket, even though some of those lower down the ballot are less compatible. Some cast their ballots because they like a candidate's personality or the way he or she appears on television. Others may vote for a particular ticket because they were taken to the polls and given a "palm card" with that party's candidates listed on it. Meanwhile, the policy or issue voter may spend considerable time analyzing the positions taken by the candidates, assessing their abilities to carry them out, and trying to make a personal determination of the kind of leadership they will give. Yet, when all the votes are cast and all the ballots are counted, we do not know which citizens voted for what reasons. We only know that one candidate for one office received more than 50 percent of the vote and the other received less.

Those who win an election may believe that they have a mandate, but in reality they would be hard-pressed to prove what their mandate means. Even so, most candidates attempt to work toward the adoption of the policies they advocated during the campaign. In most cases those policy preferences will not differ much from the positions taken by the defeated candidate. Political intuition, public opinion polls, letters to the editor, newspaper editorials, mail from the general public, and representations from interest groups all offer some degree of insight into what the collective public thinks. The candidates and the leadership of both parties read the same tea leaves. They may take diametrically opposing sides on some particular issue, but on most of them, collectively, they will ordinarily not be far apart.

Some people may think that they perceive a difference between Republicans and Democrats. Seventy-seven years ago Senator George F. Hoar, a Republican from Massachusetts, declared:

> The men who do the work of piety and charity in our churches, the men who administer our school system, the men who own and till their own farms, the men who perform skilled labor in the shops, the soldiers, the men who went to war and stayed all through, the men who paid the debt and kept the currency sound and saved the nation's honor, the men who saved the country in war and have made it worth living in peace, commonly and as a rule, by the natural law of their being, find their places in the Republican party. While the old slave-owner and slave-driver, the saloon keeper, the ballot box stuffer, the Ku Klux Klan, the criminal class of the great cities, the men who cannot read or write, commonly and as a rule, by the natural law of their being, find their congenial place in the Democratic party.[27]*

Senator Hoar saw a dichotomy between Democrats and Republicans that most of us would reject and few of us would endorse. But most observers who have tried to describe the policy differences between the parties have found this a difficult task, not because no policy differences exist, but rather because the differences are often philosophical rather than issue oriented. The key to this difference is the citizen's attitude toward the use of government as an instrument to accomplish public goals. Democrats usually view government as an instrument of action for solving social and economic

*This and all other excerpts from *The Making of the President—1972* by Theodore H. White are reprinted with the permission of Atheneum Publishers. Copyright © 1973 by Theodore H. White

problems. They see government as a tool by which they can help people who cannot help themselves and protect these people from other people who would do them social or economic harm.

The Republican philosophy, although less clearly defined, holds that the citizen bears a private and community responsibility that transcends that of the government. Many Republicans believe that the government, particularly since 1932, has trespassed on private rights and has blunted personal initiative. This too, of course, is related to the source of Republican popular support. Neither of these philosophies is universally held by all members of the respective parties. It is doubtful that either position is held even by a majority of those who call themselves Democrats and Republicans. Most persons who claim party membership do so, as we have noted, for other reasons. But these two views of the function of government do serve as a theoretical underpinning for the parties—a framework on which party platforms and candidate positions can be stretched. Whether there is significant difference between the two frameworks is of little importance in this context. The people still believe that the parties should adopt programmatic goals that will benefit those who make up party memberships. Realizing the impossibility of pleasing all of the people, party leaders attempt to please as many as possible by carefully distributing policy rewards among them. Thus the political parties provide a focus for policy concerns.

Neither of our two major parties performs all of the actual or theoretical functions described here in a creditable manner all of the time. Nevertheless, as Lord Bryce observed in the early part of this century, "the spirit and force of party has in America been as essential to the action of the machinery of government as steam is to a loco-motive engine. . . ."[28]

## Political Parties in the 1980s

American political institutions have fallen on hard times during the past half century. Public support for parties and political leaders has eroded. As we have seen, former Democrats and Republicans now call themselves Independents and vote accordingly. Campaigns are run by private businesses, with candidates being hawked on television like detergent. A few elected leaders are sent to jail or removed from office and in the process cast all politicians in a bad light in the eyes of undiscriminating voters. Private interest groups grow in membership, whereas those who consider themselves political party members decline in number. For those who support strong parties, lists such as this are read as a litany of despair. Even though we are more sure of the diagnosis, we are less sure of the cure.

The blame for this state of affairs is not easy to assign. Some of the fault lies in the nature of the political system itself. Those very characteristics that have enabled the party system to survive for two hundred years are also blamed for some of the problems that beset it. Party characteristics are converted into criticisms. Thus, the critics say, a two-party system may well serve a heterogeneous and diverse population, but it also limits the degree of ideological choice between candidates and issues. Heterogeneous parties, their dual nature locked in by law, necessarily strive for moderation and compromise. Many people, however, believe that it is a party's responsibility to take clear-cut ideological or programmatic positions regardless of how far to the left or right they may be. Whether called "Goldwaterites," "McGovernites," "Wallaceites," or "Reaganites," their goals are to force the parties to select candidates and leaders who will grapple with complex issues without treating moderation as a virtue.

When thwarted in their ambitions, some seek out and become members of interest groups or even form third parties through which they hope to gain a fairer hearing and make a wider impact. Others neither work within the established parties nor join interest groups. Instead, these individuals become free-lance amateur partisans, supporting first this candidate and then that with little regard for party affiliation. Such defections, and it should be recognized that they occur all the time, contribute to the diffusion of public support for the parties and further erode voter commitment to the two-party choices that they are offered.

Criticism has also been directed at the inability of the system to produce a well-defined leadership cadre with real power. The multiplicity of leaders is one result of decentralization, with its many hundreds of separate party units. Each of these units—city, ward, county, congressional, or state—is essentially autonomous, and their very independence militates against greater party responsibility and cohesion. Thus we return full circle to the weaknesses of the two-party system, with its consequent limits on programmatic and ideological choices and ticket splitting and divided government that result.

It is small wonder that so many of the American people show little disposition to give politics a more central place in their lives. The wonder may well be that the Democratic and Republican parties are, in fact, the two oldest democratic parties in the world. Admittedly, two hundred years may not seem a very long time in the great skein of history, but it is a substantial portion of the period during which democracy has existed. The perseverance of the two parties and their ability to overcome adversity suggest that they will probably survive and endure. The two-party system is an American invention, and its continued good health may well be an American obligation.

To prepare us for that obligation, if indeed it is one, it might be helpful to review briefly the history and development of the American parties and to consider some of the alternatives that are used elsewhere in the world. Such a review should help bring into focus our more detailed discussion of the functions of parties.

---

## Notes

1. James Bryce, *The American Commonwealth* (New York: Putnam's, 1959), vol. 2, p. 432.
2. Elmer E. Schattschneider, *Party Government* (New York: Holt, Rinehart and Winston, 1942), p. 1.
3. Edmund Burke, "Thoughts on the Cause of Present Discontents," in *Works* (Boston: Little, Brown, 1971), vol. 1, p. 151.
4. Anthony Downs, *An Economic Theory of Democracy* (New York: Harper and Row, 1957), pp. 24–25. See also Norman Frohlich, Joe A. Oppenheimer, Jeffrey Smith, and Oran R. Young, "A Test of Downsian Voter Rationality: 1964 Presidential Voting," *American Political Science Review* 72, no. 1 (March 1978): 178–197.
5. Ibid., p. 26.
6. Frank J. Sorauf, *Party Politics in America*, 4th ed. (Boston: Little, Brown, 1980), pp. 8–10.
7. Joseph A. Schlesinger, "Political Party Organi-
zation," in *Handbook of Organizations,* ed. James G. March (Chicago: Rand McNally, 1965), pp. 764–801.
8. State of Florida, *Election Laws* (Tallahassee, Fla.: Secretary of State, 1978), ch. 103, sec. 121, p. 80.
9. State of Missouri, *Comprehensive Election Act of 1977* (Jefferson City, Mo.: Secretary of State, 1977), Sec. 1.025, para. 10, p. 9.
10. Leon Epstein, *Political Parties in Western Democracies* (New York: Praeger, 1967), p. 9.
11. Henri Peyre, "Excellence and Leadership: Has Western Europe Any Lessons for Us?" in *Excellence and Leadership in a Democracy,* eds. Stephen R. Graubard and Gerald Holton (New York: Columbia University Press, 1962), p. 1.
12. Austin Ranney and Willmoore Kendall, *Democracy and the American Party System* (New York: Harcourt Brace Jovanovich, 1956), p. 244.
13. There is a discussion of the exchange of roles by

public and organization party leaders in Robert J. Huckshorn, *Party Leadership in the States* (Amherst: University of Massachusetts Press, 1976), chapter 2. Data on subsequent office-holding by former party leaders who served between 1962 and 1972 is contained in Huckshorn and was updated in 1982 to include the years 1973 through 1980 as a part of a research project conducted by Cornelius P. Cotter, John F. Bibby, James Gibson, and the author.

14. Ibid.

15. Clinton Rossiter, *Parties and Politics in America* (Ithaca, N. Y.: Cornell University Press, 1960), p. 11.

16. Congressional attitudes toward campaigning and the regular party hierarchy are discussed in depth in Robert J. Huckshorn and Robert C. Spencer, *The Politics of Defeat: Campaigning for Congress* (Amherst: University of Massachusetts Press, 1971); and Jeff Fishel, *Party and Opposition: Congressional Challengers in American Politics* (New York: McKay, 1973).

17. "Toward a More Responsible Two-Party System," *American Political Science Review* 44 (September 1950): Supplement, pp. 1–2.

18. Ibid., pp. 17–22.

19. Ranney and Kendall, *Democracy and the American Party System,* p. 531.

20. Ibid.

21. Rossiter, *Parties and Politics,* pp. 24–25.

22. *The Gallup Report,* no. 192, September 1981.

23. *Louis Harris and Associates Survey,* October 8–16, 1977. Reprinted in *Public Opinion* 4, no. 4 (August–September 1981), p. 33.

24. "Party Identification 1952–1974: Michigan Survey," in *Politics, Parties, and 1976,* National Journal Reprints (Washington, D. C.: Governmental Research Corporation, 1975), p. 800. 1976, 1978, and 1980 data were added from the Center for Political Studies, University of Michigan.

25. Arthur H. Miller and Warren E. Miller, "Partisanship and Performance: 'Rational' Choice in the 1976 Presidential Election," paper presented at the annual meeting of the American Political Science Association, 1977, Washington, D. C., pp. 6, 10–13.

26. Schattschneider, *Party Government,* p. 101.

27. Quoted in Theodore H. White, *The Making of the President—1972* (New York: Atheneum, 1972), p. 363.

28. Bryce, *The American Commonwealth,* p. 134.

# Two-Party Politics
# in America

*We will never have a time again, in my opinion, in this country when you are going to
have a polarization of only Democrats versus Republicans. I think you are going to
have the Independents controlling basically the balance of power.*

President Richard M. Nixon
Television/Radio Interview,
ABC Network, March 22, 1971

**R**ichard Nixon was not the only president to recognize that a political transformation of some kind was under way in the United States. Indeed, virtually every president of recent times has had something to say about the status of the two-party system and the future of electoral politics. The 1980 Virginia ballot (figure 2-1) demonstrates one effort by third-party organizations and ideological groups to keep themselves before the voting public as alternatives to the established order. In this chapter we shall review the idea of party, the nature of party politics, and some of the alternatives to the two-party system.

In a democracy, politics should be the preoccupation of free men and women, for its very existence is the principal test of freedom. Politics provides a method by which

| PRESIDENT AND VICE PRESIDENT (Vote for not more than one) |
|---|
| **DEMOCRATIC PARTY** PRESIDENTIAL ELECTORS FOR<br>**JIMMY CARTER,** PRESIDENT<br>**WALTER MONDALE,** VICE PRESIDENT |
| **REPUBLICAN PARTY** PRESIDENTIAL ELECTORS FOR<br>**RONALD REAGAN,** PRESIDENT<br>**GEORGE BUSH,** VICE PRESIDENT |
| **INDEPENDENT** PRESIDENTIAL ELECTORS FOR<br>**BARRY COMMONER,** PRESIDENT<br>**LaDONNA HARRIS,** VICE PRESIDENT |
| **INDEPENDENT** PRESIDENTIAL ELECTORS FOR<br>**JOHN B. ANDERSON,** PRESIDENT<br>**PATRICK J. LUCEY,** VICE PRESIDENT |
| **INDEPENDENT** PRESIDENTIAL ELECTORS FOR<br>**CLIFTON DeBERRY,** PRESIDENT<br>**MATILDE ZIMMERMANN,** VICE PRESIDENT |
| **LIBERTARIAN PARTY** PRESIDENTIAL ELECTORS FOR<br>**ED CLARK,** PRESIDENT<br>**DAVID KOCH,** VICE PRESIDENT |

**FIGURE 2–1**   An example of one effort to maintain alternatives to the two-party system. *(Source: Segment of 1980 General Election Ballot in Virginia.)*

to rule society without resorting to bullets. Indeed, in America, we rely on ballots to choose our governors, because politics has proceeded through a system of political parties and elections. We have already noted that parties are "organized groups," but just how did they become organized? We have experienced a domination of two-party politics for so long that we take it for granted. Yet parties are not even mentioned in the Constitution, and those august men who took part in the creation of the new government were not favorably disposed to them as an institution. Even so, the new American baby had hardly become a toddler when the first seeds of faction sprouted. Organized factions, or parties, had been widely predicted but had not been sought. The purpose of the framers was not so much to eliminate factional politics as to minimize it. They soon learned that the influence of party politics could not even be minimized. Parties, in fact, became widespread and pervasive. The evolution of the American party system, in most respects, was not unlike that in other parts of the world.

## The Idea of Party

Throughout modern history, political parties have more often than not been developed by private groups of citizens banding together to support or oppose some proposed governmental policy. Long before the invention of modern democratic government, organized groups were seeking to be heard. These groups usually did not possess any of the characteristics normally associated with political parties, but they were certainly the harbingers of those parties. Political historians generally agree that the first of these factions to bear a real resemblance to modern parties arose in the mid-1600s in England. The most dramatic escalation in the development of party systems, however, took place during the period of the democratic revolutions that swept through many countries in the eighteenth and nineteenth centuries. Those revolutions, including the one in America, generated demands for a popular role in government. Parties, therefore, arose as the vehicle through which the people's will could be properly registered.

Party politics is far from universal. In many developing nations, for example, parties still do not exist. Furthermore, the form in which they do exist in some more mature states runs counter to most of our own concepts of democracy; this fact marks a major difference between the political processes of free and authoritarian societies. Most authoritarian governments, if they permit parties to exist at all, authorize only one. In the Soviet Union, for instance, only the Communist party is legally permitted to exist. Competition based on voter choice is not allowed, because government leaders expect the single party to perform functions that are not compatible with free choice. That this is true in the Soviet Union, however, does not mean that all Communist parties everywhere operate within a noncompetitive system.

The Communist parties of Western Europe, and even the Communist party in the United States, do work competitively within an environment of organized elections. In some of those countries the Communists are truly in competition and regularly win enough seats in parliament to gain at least some voice. In the 1976 parliamentary elections in Italy, for instance, the Communist party made dramatic gains and became a force with which the ruling Christian Democrats had to contend. These Communist gains were the result of free elections in a multiparty state. In other countries, however, the Communists represent little more than a small group of dissidents using the party vehicle as a means to disseminate propaganda. Authoritarian governments, though, view parties as instruments of the government. Consequently, they permit only one party to exist, to be used as a tool for the rulers, who can thus wield power behind a democratic facade.

Among the democratic nations, two or more parties is the norm because democratic government requires competition in order to give citizens a choice between candidates and issues. Democracy (*demos,* "the people"; *kratos,* "authority") demands a decision-making system based on majority rule, but with minority rights protected. That definition in itself suggests more than one party. Consequently, party systems are often classified by the number of individual parties competing in them. Focusing attention on the number of parties underlines the uniqueness of the American two-party system.

The very nature of a society will often determine the type of party system that emerges. Most of us are aware of the great differences in the political process between free and authoritarian societies. The nightly television news regularly brings home that distinction. A free society requires that three political conditions be met: (1) general acceptance of and shared belief in the political, social, and economic institutions of the nation; (2) open competition of political ideas embracing both the policy ends sought and the means for attaining them; and (3) the existence of basic freedoms, including the freedoms of speech, press, and association, that enable the people to fully express their views.

Authoritarian societies by definition cannot meet these three criteria. Although it is less troublesome, in our view, to have general sharing of beliefs in national institutions, it is not at all necessary. In authoritarian societies dissenters are simply not tolerated or, if tolerated, are not given opportunities to translate into action their disagreement with the government. Political leadership emanates from the government and imposes its will from above. Ordinarily, a controlled press makes this reasonably easy to accomplish; at the same time, of course, the basic freedom of expression enjoyed in more open societies is abrogated.

Not all one-party systems are found in totalitarian dictatorships, however. Mexico's Institutional Revolutionary Party (PRI) has ruled that country since 1929. The president has great power but cannot run for reelection after serving his six-year term. He can, however, select his successor, and in late 1981 President José López Portillo announced that his planning and budget minister, Miguél de la Madrid Hurtado, would be the party's candidate in the 1982 election. President López Portillo ran unopposed in 1976, as had been customary. But in 1978 a reform law was passed opening the ballot to five minor parties. A vigorous campaign was waged by de la Madrid and the other candidates and on July 4, 1982, the PRI again won the presidency by an overwhelming margin. Mexico has served as an example of a democratic one-party system for over half a century, but many observers of Mexican politics believe that its dominance may be coming to an end.

Although it is common to discuss the notion of one-party systems, it is not universally agreed that they even exist. For instance, Sigmund Neumann, a respected political scientist, has questioned whether it is ever possible to call the one-party apparatus used by totalitarian governments a political party system. Neumann points out that a single party is used to retain a semblance of popular rule but in reality is little more than a device for manipulating mass consent rather than converting popular belief into governmental policy. The whole concept of single-party systems is paradoxical to him, because the term *party* implies a plurality of units.[1] Nevertheless, it has become common to discuss political systems in terms of the number of parties that they contain. Thus the uniqueness of the two-party system in the United States is worth exploring. That this system has persisted for so long and has not been copied by other nations lends importance to the way in which it developed. Let us look briefly, then, at the origins and history of the American parties.

## A Brief History of the American Political Parties

American political parties trace their lineage back to Great Britain, where the first party-like political groups were organized. Popular division occurred in England over the policies of Charles II, and parliamentary factions composed of supporters and opponents began to meet to plan strategy. The two groups eventually found themselves engaged in partisan conflict as "Whigs" and "Tories," terms which later became common in pre–Revolutionary America. By 1800 the philosophical dichotomy was more formalized and showed more and more aspects of party faction. Each colony had divisions in the colonial assemblies representing various member attitudes toward the British-appointed governors. Thus there arose a "court" party and a "country"

party, with supporters of the governors called "Tories" or "Loyalists" and their opponents labeled "Whigs" or "Patriots."

The American people emerged from the Revolutionary War believing that they had
thrown off the yoke of a domineering kingdom and prepared to embark on an experiment in reconciling the conflicting and competing forces of authority and republicanism. Their optimism was short-lived, however, because they were to face two decades
of factionalism, attempted foreign intervention, and changing constitutional mechanisms before settling on a form of government that would prove to be lasting. Their
high hopes for some form of "pure" representative democracy soon ran aground on
the shoals of controversy. Politics, indeed, had preceded party.

In *Federalist Paper* no. 10, James Madison wrote of his fear of faction, but partisan
division was already an accomplished fact in many of the colonial assemblies. One
example, the so-called Boston Junto, led by Samuel Adams, was organized in the
Massachusetts Assembly to fight against outside interference in colonial affairs. For
the most part, such groups bore little resemblance to political parties, being more
accurately described as patriotic societies. Although they disappeared during the Revolutionary period, they served as models for the advent of full-fledged parties.[2]

## The First American Party System

Once the Constitution was approved and the first president was elected, real party
development got under way. The factional divisions that ultimately led to the organized parties began in the early 1790s. They came about as the result of continuing
controversies over the policies and programs of Alexander Hamilton, the secretary of
the treasury. Hamilton soon became the recognized leader of the faction calling itself
"Federalist." This group advocated a government based on strong executive leadership, centralization of power, and economic programs that would benefit business and
commercial interests. They chose the name *Federalist* to signify to the people that
Hamilton and his followers wanted to maintain a strong central or national government. The designation also permitted them to claim to be the true supporters of the
federal system so recently unveiled as a part of the Constitution. As described by
William Nisbet Chambers:

> Hamilton sought a happy and fruitful marriage between the special interests of "moneyed
> men" and the larger interests of orderly national government, from which the one might
> derive strength and authority, and the other gain. An Anglophile, he admired the hierarchical
> political order he saw in Great Britain and its elitist, ministerial style of government; to foster
> the marriage of wealth and government in America, he would copy the English model as far
> as he could.[3]

Growing in opposition was a coalition of small farmers, small property owners,
and local political leaders, principally from the southern and Middle Atlantic states,
who were loyal to the secretary of state, Thomas Jefferson. Fearing Hamilton's monarchical tendencies, the members of the Jefferson faction came to call themselves
"Republicans" in order to make clear their stand on the issue of government by the
people.

Ironically, President Washington, who disdained party faction, was forced to sit
idly by while his two favorite cabinet officers assumed leading roles in the formation
of the first parties. Partly as a result of the internal fighting, Jefferson left the cabinet
in 1793 to work with the developing state and local organizations to build a party

substructure. By 1794 three dozen such grass-roots groups, in various stages of development, were operating in the states. They were predominantly anti-Federalist, but they were also performing some of the more positive chores associated with party building. They issued statements, held protest meetings, sent resolutions to Congress, and endorsed candidates. Nevertheless, formal party-like organizations were still not widespread.

The growth of Republicanism was not solely the work of Jefferson, although he was the faction's recognized leader. Many of the first signs of organized opposition to Hamilton's policies originated in Congress. James Madison, James Monroe, and Aaron Burr in the Senate and William Giles and Nathaniel Macon in the House drew nearer to Jefferson as President Washington drew closer to Alexander Hamilton. The internal congressional organizations that they built were designed to complement and strengthen those being constructed at the state and local level. By the end of the eighteenth century these leaders had invented the congressional caucus (which was also used to nominate candidates for president and vice-president), the offices of Speaker of the House and floor leader, and the congressional committee system. Albert Gallatin, a leading congressional Republican, joined with Madison to create the House Ways and Means Committee as an instrument through which Hamilton's financial undertaking might be examined.

Jefferson was a candidate for president in 1796 but was narrowly defeated in the Electoral College by Vice-President John Adams. During the next four years Jefferson continued to work to organize the Republicans at the state and local levels, and he came back in 1800 to be elected as the third president. By then the Federalists, although they had made belated efforts to stem the erosion of their support, were clearly destined for oblivion. A few state organizations worthy of the name remained, but the Federalist period had run its course. By 1816 the Federalists had ceased to exist. The Jefferson presidency ushered in a new era and inaugurated the first American political party system.

Historians do not agree on the details surrounding the origin of parties. Some believe that Jefferson forged the Republican party from a coalition of existing state and local factions. Claude Bowers, for instance, described Jefferson as pondering the question, "Why not consolidate these local parties into one great national organization and broaden the issue to include the problems of both State and Nation."[4] Wilfred Binkley concurs, noting that, "Like all our major political parties, this earlier one to organize constituted a loose federation of local parties. . . . Jefferson set out to negotiate the necessary connections and understanding among them."[5]

Other historians, however, suggest the need to reappraise the common thinking about the origins of the party system. They note that the mass of evidence does not support the earlier theories of local origin. They consider it much more likely that parties developed at the national level out of the continuing division between the Congress and the administration. According to this theory, party growth was clearly a product of national, not local, political forces. Issues such as the Jay Treaty served as catalysts for political divisions and for the development of party organization. Most of the early groups that organized in the states were little more than committees of correspondence. Although they had frequent meetings, listened to speeches, elected officers, and sent memorials to Congress and the state legislatures, they did not perform any of those functions normally associated with parties, namely, to nominate, campaign, and elect.[6]

The first party system was destined to fail. By 1815 the Federalists had dropped by the wayside and the Republicans had succumbed to factionalism. The Republican victories had been based on the availability of members of the "Virginia Dynasty"—Jefferson, Madison, and Monroe—to serve as presidents and party leaders, but these successes also arose from fortuitous Federalist weakness and disintegration. By 1824, when John Quincy Adams won the presidency in a bitter and divisive struggle, the Republicans had split into two factions—the Democratic-Republicans and the National-Republicans. That election served as a last rally for the Republicans. Divided and quarreling, they were no match for the dedicated followers of General Andrew Jackson. Jackson, after losing the presidency in 1824, was elected in 1828, an event that inaugurated the second American party system.[7]

## The Second American Party System

Historian Richard McCormick has described the advent of the Jackson Democrats in 1828 as the beginning of the second American party system.[8] This system emerged from the chaos of the election of 1824 and the divisions that continued to beset the Jeffersonian Republicans. The election of Adams had been a bitter disappointment to Jackson and his followers. It took place during a period of great political turmoil and change. The Republican congressional caucus had become weak and discredited. The seemingly endless supply of Virginians ready to run for the presidency had come to an end. Sectionalism had appeared: Jackson's support came from the South and West and Adams's from New England. A new political era had clearly dawned as Andrew Jackson assumed the office of president of the United States.

Lasting two-party politics came to the United States between 1824 and 1840. During that period parties were formed in every state, based largely on the reaction of the people to the personalities and the issues of the day. In all but a few states the parties were balanced and competitive. The glue that held them together was the public's attitude toward Andrew Jackson. Party organizations might properly have been termed Jacksonian and anti-Jacksonian, but in reality they were called Democrats and Whigs. Both of them possessed the economic and geographic characteristics of national parties. Jacksonian popular democracy created more public offices and, as people sought to fill them, ballots grew longer. Early party committees appeared, and in some cities bosses emerged. Platforms developed as a means of communicating ideas to the voters, and the mass-membership, two-party system became an entrenched idea.

Between 1840 and 1856 the Whigs and the Democrats alternated in winning the presidency. The emergence of slavery as an issue of national importance eventually doomed the Whig party. Again factionalism developed within the parties, and in 1848 the antislavery Whigs joined with the antislavery Democrats to form a new party pledged to prevent the further extension of slavery. They were joined by the old Liberty party and became known as the Free Soil party, for they were dedicated to the principle established in the Wilmot Proviso that excluded slavery from the territories of the United States. Whig candidate Zachary Taylor won the office of president, the last candidate of his party to become president. In 1852 Franklin Pierce, the Democratic candidate, was elected; this was the last election in which the Whigs competed with a candidate of their own. It was also the last election to feature any of the other leaders who had dominated politics since the 1820s. Jackson, Adams, Calhoun, Clay, and Webster were all dead. Van Buren was in retirement, and others had dropped from active participation. Their places were filled by newer and younger men who were soon to take part in the evolution of the third party system and the destruction of the Union.

## The Third American Party System

The election of 1856 was the turning point in the development of the new party system, although it did not assume national dimensions until the 1870s. Democrat James Buchanan won the presidency against John C. Fremont, the candidate of a coalition of antislavery parties. The Whigs denounced both the Democrats and the new Republicans and endorsed a third-party candidate. The next years were to witness some of the great dramatic events in American history—the Dred Scott case, the Lincoln-Douglas debates, and the founding of the present-day Republican party. With the election of Abraham Lincoln as the first Republican president, the outbreak of war subordinated everything to preserving the Union. The Civil War and the Reconstruction period profoundly affected American political history. The Republicans began a domination of the presidency that was to last for nearly seventy-five years. The Democratic "Solid South" evolved as a major regional influence on party politics that was to last for almost one hundred years. The domination of the presidency by the Republicans forced the Democrats to nurture the concept of "the loyal opposition."

During this long period of Republican dominance, the party broadened its constituency to include a wide spectrum of social, economic, and geographic support. Its tariff policies attracted new voters on the northeastern seaboard; its land policies solidified the support of farmers in the Midwest; its financial policies, including sound money and government support for railroads, won the votes of merchants and industrialists; and its antislavery policies won it the allegiance of the newly freed black Americans. In short, the Republicans during this era were truly the party of the Union, transcending sectional and class divisions.

Although it won every presidential election during this period except those that brought Grover Cleveland and Woodrow Wilson to office, the Republican party was not without problems. Internal disagreements and dissension between eastern and western supporters often clashed with the more liberal views of the Republican farmers and workers of the Midwest. Scandals of major proportions erupted during the Grant and Harding administrations, and the era of Republican dominance came to a close with the economic collapse of the late 1920s.

## The Fourth American Party System

With the landslide election of Franklin D. Roosevelt in 1932, the period of Republican domination ended. This election, like those of 1824 and 1860, was a landmark in the history of American politics. The overwhelming economic impact of the Great Depression and the failure of President Hoover to take decisive action to offset its effects brought massive switches in party allegiance in almost all classes of voters. Unskilled workers, union members, Catholics, Jews, black Americans, and urban dwellers joined with the traditional Solid South to create a new electoral majority that lasted into the 1960s. This new alignment of voters heralded the fourth American party system. Even though the Republicans won the presidency five times, with Dwight D. Eisenhower in 1952 and 1956, with Richard M. Nixon in 1968 and 1972, and with Ronald Reagan in 1980, these victories tended to be personal rather than party. During the entire

*"Has the possibility occurred to you, Senator,*
*that you're a Democrat and don't know it?"*
(Drawing by Dedini; ©1955 The New Yorker
Magazine, Inc.)

period from 1932 to 1984, the Republicans gained control of both houses of Congress only twice, although they won control of the Senate a third time in 1980. Furthermore, the number of voters willing to identify themselves as members of the Republican party declined to 23 percent in 1982. The Republican party remained in a decidedly minority position for most of this fifty-year period, even though they continued to win the presidency periodically. In chapter 7 we will consider some commentary on the current state of the party system.

Politics in the United States has always been more personal than ideological or institutional. Party growth was out of phase from state to state, and different plateaus were reached at different times, but the parties eventually became national organizations. Federalism virtually guaranteed that the party system would be decentralized, and the separation of powers made it likely that the executive and legislative branches would be at loggerheads from time to time. But the party system has survived and appears likely to continue into the future.

## The Two-Party System in the United States

Foremost among the characteristics of the American political system is its federal and two-party nature. From the time the political structure first took shape, two parties have existed, and for most of that time they have been organized both at the national level and in the individual states. Since 1860 every presidential election has been won by either a Republican or a Democratic candidate nominated by representatives of the state parties through caucuses, conventions, or primaries. Since 1862 virtually all of the members of the House and the Senate have been elected under one of the two major party banners, and each has been chosen through one of the state party systems. Furthermore, with few exceptions, state and local officers have also been chosen as representatives of the two major parties. In short, our politics has followed a two-party format almost from the beginning, and our candidates have been selected through an integrated national and state system of parties. There have been a number of theories as to the causes for the development of the two-party system in America.

## Historical Theories

Historically, the two-party system may have resulted from a basic duality of interests within the structure of American society. Political, economic, and social conflicts helped shape the nation and its institutions from the beginning, and each conflict has almost always had two sides. The Revolution itself divided the people, as did the ratification of the Constitution. The issues that emerged from the constitutional period caused division between the eastern commercial interests and the western agrarian frontier interests. The parties to this division soon had national leaders in the persons of Thomas Jefferson and Alexander Hamilton. Andrew Jackson, while rightly honored for his political contributions to the nation, also exacerbated the basic conflicts between the sections. These economic controversies eventually gave way to the North–South split over slavery and plantation economics, and this, in turn, divided the people into two groups as they prepared for war.

The Civil War and the Reconstruction period that followed have been cited as the catalysts for the urban–rural split of the twentieth century. Moreover, some believe that differences between urban and rural interests are crucial to an understanding of attitudinal conflicts between liberals and conservatives. The theme of duality runs throughout this recitation. Proponents of theories of historical dualism maintain that most issues throughout American history have been debated by two opposing groups and that these evolved quite naturally into two political parties. The theory does not explore the root cause of the two-party system, but it offers that system a readily understood rationale.

## Institutional Theories

Maurice Duverger suggests that the explanation for two-partyism is simple and uncomplicated. He notes that the two-party idea "seems to correspond to the nature of things," since "political choice usually takes the form of a choice between two alternatives."[9] Thus the two voting groups in the electoral system express themselves through institutional arrangements such as the single-member district system with plurality election. Under this plan, only one representative, rather than several, is elected to serve in a given office from a single district. Election by plurality means simply that only one candidate is elected on a winner-take-all basis, and the winner is the candidate who receives the most votes, regardless of whether his votes constitute a majority. Under this system, minor parties are encouraged to join forces with one of the major parties in the hope of being associated with a winner. The alternative to single-member plurality election is multimember proportional representation.

Institutional theorists argue that the two-party system emerges from the plurality electoral system, which almost always produces a single winning candidate in a single-member district. Thus there are no rewards for also-rans. The winner takes the office, and the loser retires from the fray. This stands in stark contrast to systems that use multimember districts, elect by proportional representation—and usually emerge with multiple parties. Proportional representation is a system devised to guarantee that minorities will have representation fairly equal to the strength they can muster at the polls. Thus a party gaining 25 percent of the votes may win approximately 25 percent of the seats. The prospect of winning a share in the government, even a small one, is encouraging to minority parties and helps sustain multipartyism. In America, if a candidate does not win a plurality, he or she does not win anything. This, so the theory goes, discourages the establishment and survival of third parties.

Another aspect of the institutional theories is the "natural" dualism associated with the election of the president. Electing presidents through the Electoral College is an all-or-nothing system. In each state the entire slate of electors receiving the most votes is elected. Again, no reward is given for coming in second. If one candidate receives 51 percent of the popular votes of the citizens of New York State, he or she will receive 100 percent of the electoral votes of that state. These provisions in and of themselves do not require a dual party system, but the way in which they have come to be used certainly encourages such a system.

The election of state governors by plurality also tends to perpetuate two-partyism. Here, too, the winner takes the prize, and the loser goes home empty-handed. The office itself is indivisible and, in order to have any chance at all of winning it, the two parties must do all in their power to emphasize their strengths. This means that they must create a system in which the rise of an effective third party is made most difficult. Since nearly all state legislatures are controlled by Democrats and Republicans, the election laws that they pass are geared to protect the two-party system. The monopoly of power in the two parties is real, and they must use their resources to protect their cartel. They usually are successful in guaranteeing that a gubernatorial contest, as well as most others, will be between representatives of the two major parties.

The evidence suggests that the American people and their leaders have subscribed to a value judgment in favor of a two-party system. They have built an electoral institution that supports bipartisanship and that, in turn, is supported by it.

## Cultural Theories

Some authorities believe that the two parties resulted from a high degree of cultural heterogeneity; that is, the American people are inclined ordinarily to compromise in order to reach consensus. They do not yield to the divisiveness of dogmatism. Americans would, on the whole, rather come to an agreement that is less than satisfactory to all in order to avoid actions that would ideologically undermine the whole. Advocates of this theory point to the usually tepid feeling with which Americans express ideological views. Political pragmatism is the keystone for retaining a two-party system. Those peoples who have opted for two parties have reached a national realization that they must make accommodations with each other in order to avoid the weaknesses that they envision resulting from third-party development.

This accommodation has been made easier because most Americans accept the prevailing social, economic, and political institutions. They have been willing to bring about change within the basic governmental structure and the framework of the Constitution. They have not experienced a class society in the same sense that other countries have. In short, they have collectively avoided matters that would divide them and have sought solutions in compromise within the existing two parties rather than through the vehicle of ideologically narrow third-party movements.

These are all high-sounding theories that may in fact have some truth. We actually do not know why the United States has two parties and has resisted every temptation to expand that number. Nor do we know whether these theories represent causes or effects. Each of them incorporates elements that might have caused the development and maintenance of the two-party system. But, at the same time, these views may merely have arisen because of a system that hinders the development of third parties and forces electoral choices to be made only through two-party channels. Whatever the cause, and regardless of the effects, the American people developed deep-seated loyalties to the two parties and the two-party system. This loyalty has been so strong that the parties have overcome every prediction of their demise. Their longevity is indisputable: they are now the two oldest democratic parties in the world.

## Two-Party Competitiveness

If one were to sit down over coffee with a Republican leader from Louisiana and another from Ohio, one would soon realize that each saw Republican politics from a different perspective. Louisiana Republicans, until recently, have had little luck in making a mark on either their state or the nation. They elected their first Republican congressman since 1888 in 1972 and presently have 2 out of 8. In 1982 no members of the Louisiana Senate and only 9 of 105 members of the Louisiana House of Representatives were Republicans. The party's biggest victory came in 1979 when it elected its first governor since Reconstruction. Although a Republican organization exists in Louisiana, it seldom runs candidates and has virtually no grass-roots organization. A Louisiana Republican leader would have to admit that his or her party does not perform many of the functions normally expected of more mature party organizations.

An Ohio Republican, in contrast, would describe real two-party competitive campaigning based on a solidly established organization. He or she would be able to claim substantial victories and the thrill of winning after the election-night cliffhanger. Such a politician might be able to discuss the spoils of victory—public service, jobs, contracts, favors for friends—and the immense satisfaction that comes from political power. This midwestern Republican could talk about old victories and compare them to modern successes, because Ohio Republicans have been a force for many years. He or she could refer to policy initiatives brought about under top leadership. Truly, the witness to this discussion might not recognize that these two Republicans, one from Louisiana and the other from Ohio, were members of the same political party.

The contrasts between the separate state versions of the same party arise from differing degrees of competitiveness. Some parties are clearly competitive most of the time, with both parties performing essential roles. Others, however, operate with little or no opposition, the same party always winning and never being threatened. Discussion of degress of competitiveness, to be meaningful, demands some means of measurement. What constitutes a competitive party? How does a scholar or a politician decide to what extent some particular party in some particular state at some particular time meets the test of competitiveness?

Many efforts have been made to develop schemes to classify the American states according to the degree of competitiveness between the parties. These are not merely exercises in political research engaged in by ivory-tower academicians. They offer evidence that has a decided influence on our understanding of political inputs and policy outputs, and they suggest styles of campaigning to be followed by political candidates. Furthermore, different degrees of party competitiveness are related to other important aspects of party government—cohesion in legislative bodies, control over nominations, and organizational proficiency.

Austin Ranney analyzed the percentages of the two-party popular vote for governor for each party in each state between the years 1962 and 1973, along with the percentages of seats won by each party in both houses of the state legislature in each election. From these data Ranney computed four basic figures: (1) the average percentage of popular vote won by Democratic candidates for governor; (2) the average percentage of seats in the state senates won by Democrats; (3) the average percentage of seats in the state houses of representatives won by Democrats; and (4) the percentages of all terms for governor, senate, and house in which the Democrats had control.[10] Ranney then averaged together the four percentages for each state to produce an "index of competitiveness," ranging from 0—representing total Republican success—to 1—representing total Democratic success. On this scale, 0.5 represents absolute two-party competition. Bibby, Cotter, Gibson, and Huckshorn have since updated Ranney's analysis to include data through 1980. Their results, using classifications based on the Ranney Index, are shown in table 2-1.[11] The classification produced five categories of interparty competition in the states: one-party Democratic, modified one-party Democratic, two-party, modified one-party Republican, and one-party Republican. No states were classified as one-party Republican throughout the period covered by both studies.

In his original study Ranney cautioned that this party competitiveness measure should be treated like a snapshot that catches a degree of interparty competitiveness at a given moment in a moving continuum. The extent of change can be seen by comparing a state's score for the 1974–1980 period with its score for 1962–1973. For example, six states that were modified one-party Republican in 1962–1973 (Colorado, Idaho, Kansas, South Dakota, Vermont, and Wyoming) became two-party states in the 1974–1980 period. At the same time another group of southern and border states (Alabama, Louisiana, South Carolina, Tennessee, Texas, and Virginia) moved in the opposite direction and became more Republican in the latter period. Even so, during the 1974–1980 period a majority of the states became more Democratic. This can be noted by looking at the overall mean index score for all fifty states. This mean moved from 0.5435 in 1946–1962 to 0.5845 in 1962–1973 to 0.6430 in 1974–1980. These data would suggest that a significant number of state political systems have been only marginally competitive between 1974 and 1980.[12]

This analysis is based solely on state elections and does not take into account how the state voted in presidential elections. Some states are highly competitive in national elections but much less competitive at the state level. For example, Ronald Reagan, running as the Republican candidate for president in 1980, carried six of the eight one-party Democratic states and sixteen of the nineteen modified one-party Democratic states. Similarly, as Bibby and his colleagues point out, six of the one-party Democratic states have Republican U.S. senators.

Finally, it should be noted that the interparty competition scores give more weight to partisan control of a state legislature than they do to winning the governorship. One result of this is that recent Republican capture of gubernatorial offices in traditionally Democratic states (Arkansas, Louisiana, North Carolina, and South Carolina) make a smaller contribution to determining an index score than does the heavy Democratic dominance of the state legislatures in those states.[13]

It should be reemphasized that techniques such as those used by Ranney and by Bibby and associates are but tools that permit analysts to better understand party politics. Each of these studies, as well as several others, has helped us to comprehend

**TABLE 2–1    The fifty states classified according to degree of interparty competition, 1974–1980**

| One-party Democratic | Modified one-party Democratic | Two-party | | | Modified one-party Republican |
|---|---|---|---|---|---|
| Alabama (0.9438) | South Carolina (0.8034) | New Jersey (0.7330) | Montana (0.6259) | Kansas (0.4671) | North Dakota (0.3374) |
| Georgia (0.8849) | West Virginia (0.8032) | Virginia (0.7162) | Michigan (0.6125) | Utah (0.4653) | |
| Louisiana (0.8762) | Texas (0.7993) | New Mexico (0.7113) | Ohio (0.5916) | Iowa (0.4539) | |
| Mississippi (0.8673) | Massachusetts (0.7916) | California (0.7081) | Washington (0.5806) | Arizona (0.4482) | |
| Arkansas (0.8630) | Kentucky (0.7907) | Oregon (0.6954) | Alaska (0.5771) | Colorado (0.4429) | |
| North Carolina (0.8555) | Oklahoma (0.7841) | Missouri (0.6932) | Pennsylvania (0.5574) | Indiana (0.4145) | |
| Maryland (0.8509) | Nevada (0.7593) | Minnesota (0.6680) | Delaware (0.5490) | New Hampshire (0.3916) | |
| Rhode Island (0.8506) | Hawaii (0.7547) | Tennessee (0.6648) | New York (0.5390) | Idaho (0.3898) | |
| | Florida (0.7524) | Wisconsin (0.6634) | Illinois (0.5384) | Wyoming (0.3879) | |
| | Connecticut (0.7336) | | Nebraska (0.5166) | Vermont (0.3612) | |
| | | | Maine (0.5164) | South Dakota (0.3512) | |

The index has a possible range of 0 (total Republican success) to 1 (total Democratic success), with 0.5 representing absolutely even two-party competition. When the states are listed in descending order of index numbers, the resulting clusters suggest the following categories and definitions:

0.8500 or higher: one-party Democratic
0.6500 to 0.8499: modified one-party Democratic
0.3500 to 0.6499: two-party
0.1500 to 0.3499: modified one-party Republican
0.0000 to 0.1499: one-party Republican

**Source:** The original classification study was done by Austin Ranney, and an earlier version was published in "Parties in State Politics," in *Politics in the American States: A Comparative Analysis,* 3rd ed., eds. Herbert Jacob and Kenneth Vines (Boston: Little, Brown, 1976). This version was compiled by John F. Bibby, Cornelius P. Cotter, James L. Gibson, and Robert J. Huckshorn and is published as "Parties in State Politics," in *Politics in the American States: A Comparative Analysis,* 4th ed., Copyright ©1983 by John F. Bibby, Cornelius P. Cotter, James L. Gibson, and Robert J. Huckshorn. Reprinted by permission.

the degree of competitiveness between the parties and to classify the states according to party competition, instead of having to rely on conventional wisdom. The studies do make it clear that to speak casually of the "two-party system" is misleading. Organizationally, we do have a two-party system throughout the United States, but some of the state parties are far more competitive than others, and degrees of competition are quite fluid.

Computations and indices can never tell us everything we want to know about our complex political system. It is divided by federalism into national and state parties. It is also divided by constituencies and differing terms of office, so that some officials are elected in different years in response to different issues and events. The voters can choose a candidate for president and then split their tickets to vote for candidates of the opposite party for lesser offices.

In 1980 a dramatic illustration of ticket splitting occurred in Utah: 73 percent of the voters supported Ronald Reagan, the Republican candidate for president, 74 percent voted for the Republican candidate for the U.S. Senate, but 55 percent split their tickets to vote for the Democratic candidate for governor. Reagan also carried Ohio with an 11 percent margin over President Carter, but at the same time 71 percent of the vote for the U.S. Senate was going to the Democratic candidate. Substantial ticket splitting occurred in three eastern states (Connecticut, New Hampshire, and Vermont), six southern states (Arkansas, Georgia, Louisiana, Maryland, North Carolina, and South Carolina), four midwestern states (Illinois, Kentucky, Missouri, and Ohio), and four western states (California, Colorado, Montana, and Utah) (see table 2-2). These results were not unusual. Different branches and levels of government are often under the control of different parties. Cooperation is necessary between the Democratic and Republican officeholders representing these different branches and levels if the government is to work—which is why many observers feel that the loose, decentralized, and generally non–issue-oriented American party system fits the country well. A programmatic and doctrinaire party system would create many difficult problems, given the various possibilities for divided control.

## Governing by Coalition

As we have seen, American politics can be baffling to the uninitiated observer. We elect a president every four years at the same time that we are electing all members of the House of Representatives and one-third of the Senate. Usually, but not always, the party with an elected president has also elected majorities in both houses of Congress. But, at the midterm or off-year elections, the opposition party may come back to capture control of one or both houses. One might assume that, in those years when the presidency and the Congress are controlled by the same party, a unified and cohesive program would emerge bearing that party's imprint. This, however, is not

TABLE 2–2    Split-ticket outcomes in statewide voting, 1980

| State | President | Senator | Governor |
|---|---|---|---|
| Arkansas | R | D | R |
| California | R | D | |
| Colorado | R | D | |
| Connecticut | R | D | |
| Georgia | D | R | |
| Illinois | R | D | |
| Kentucky | R | D | |
| Louisiana | R | D | |
| Maryland | D | R | |
| Missouri | R | D | R |
| Montana | R | | D |
| New Hampshire | R | R | D |
| North Carolina | R | R | D |
| Ohio | R | D | |
| South Carolina | R | D | |
| Utah | R | R | D |
| Vermont | R | D | R |

often the case. Presidents Roosevelt, Truman, Kennedy, Johnson, and Carter all had, for all or most of their terms, Democratic congressional majorities (sometimes ranging up to two-thirds of all the members), but they were often unable to get significant segments of their individual programs adopted. A coalition of Republicans and southern Democrats was frequently able to block action on the presidential programs.

Such presidential difficulties with Congress are bipartisan in nature. President Eisenhower, whose Republican administration was in office through most of the 1950s, had more difficulty getting his programs through the Republican Congress elected in 1952 than through the Democratic congresses that succeeded it. More recently, Ronald Reagan had some remarkable legislative successes during his first two years in office in spite of the fact that the Democrats held a substantial majority in the House of Representatives. Obviously, control of the government by representatives of a single political party does not necessarily guarantee that that party's programs will be put into effect.

Most voters live in the urban areas of the nation—the big cities and suburbs. For many years, until the 1962 Supreme Court case of *Baker* v. *Carr,* they were underrepresented in the House of Representatives because gerrymandering tended to preserve the rural influence. Equal representation by states in the Senate, regardless of population, also assured the less urban states stronger representation than they deserved in terms of the proportion of their population.

By the same token, voters in large urban states gain influence in presidential contests because the popular vote is a statewide vote, thus permitting political control to reside where the people live. Therefore the system tends to favor more moderate to liberal candidates for presidential office and more conservative to moderate candidates for congressional office. Evidence for this view is the influence of the "conservative coalition" in Congress, a development with antecedents in the later Roosevelt years.

*Congressional Quarterly Weekly Report* (CQ) has analyzed conservative coalition vote scores for both houses of Congress since 1957. CQ considers a conservative coalition vote to be one in which a majority of Republicans and a majority of southern Democrats oppose a stand taken on an issue by the northern Democrats. For definitional purposes CQ considers the South to consist of Alabama, Arkansas, Florida, Georgia, Kentucky, Louisiana, Mississippi, North Carolina, Oklahoma, South Carolina, Tennessee, Texas, and Virginia. Every other state is classified as the North in this analysis. Until 1982 the most successful year for the coalition was 1971, when it appeared on 30 percent of the votes and won 83 percent of the time. Its worst year was 1965, when it appeared on 24 percent of the votes and won only 33 percent of the time. The 1981 session of Congress, however, set a new record for coalition success. The alliance appeared on 21 percent of the votes in both houses, with a success rate of 92 percent.[14] Although a gradual upward trend had been taking place since 1978, 1981 clearly represented the success of the Reagan presidency in translating its economic program into law. This was something of a departure from patterns of the past when the coalition normally manifested itself in contests between liberal presidents and conservative congresses. Reagan was able to mobilize members of the coalition in behalf of his program with considerable success. As noted earlier, the conservative alliance, cutting across parties in both houses of Congress, is dependent on political coalition. We will return to our discussion of the conservative coalition in chapter 11 when we consider the role of political parties in the legislative process.

## One-Party Domination in a Two-Party System

Even though we have a two-party system in the United States, some of the state parties are more two-party in character than others. A sizable number of states can be categorized as one-party or modified one-party. Yet they operate within the confines of a two-party framework, and we do not think of them in the same sense that we think of one-party arrangements in totalitarian systems.

A great difference exists between the one-party system of the Soviet Union and that operating in Louisiana or Alabama. The monopoly party of the Soviet Union is designed specifically to thwart public dissent and to obstruct competition. One-party dominance within a two-party setting, on the other hand, simply means that a large majority of the people in that area, for one reason or another, have established a sustained pattern of support for a single party. Normally, that party has controlled the government offices for a long period of time. This differs from a one-party system *imposed* by government, because the channels of competition remain open and parties are free to compete for votes. The fact that some parties do not win many offices or attract many votes is an accident of history rather than an imposition of governmental control. Even so, the "single-party" rubric includes a range of American phenomena, from big-city machine monopolies to dominant nonpartisan citizens groups and large personal followings not based on party. Without attempting to cover all of these bases, we should understand the one-party dominant system that has prevailed in some areas of the nation for so long. Indeed, the modern analysis of American parties began with V. O. Key's *Southern Politics,* not with studies of the more competitive systems found in most parts of the nation.[15]

Two-party competitiveness has grown remarkably in some of the southern states in the past two decades. Although the states in the Old Confederacy began to divide their electoral vote for president and vice-president between Democrats and Republicans in 1952, the origin of the fissures in the Solid South lies in the election of 1948. In that year southern resentment of northern control over the Democratic party and its national conventions, which had been quietly seething for years, boiled over. Ever since 1933, southern Democratic influence in the selection of presidential nominees and platform writing had been on the wane. As early as 1944 southern Democrats, including most of the power structure of Congress, had been discontented and had increasingly posed a threat to party unity. In 1948 the eruption finally came, precipitated by the demands of President Harry S. Truman that Congress adopt laws guaranteeing the right to vote to all citizens, providing fair employment practices, and agreeing to antilynch laws. Southern leaders, including most of the Democrats in Congress, lost no time in making known their displeasure at what they considered to be another in a long line of attacks on southern customs and laws.

At the Democratic National Convention in June, the northern liberals threw down the gauntlet to the southerners by adopting a strong civil rights plank. When the vote on the plank was announced to the convention, all of the Mississippi delegation and half of the Alabama delegation walked out of the hall in a dramatic display of disaffection. Those southern delegates who remained cast their votes for one of their own— Sen. Richard B. Russell of Georgia. The convention adjourned in turmoil and bitterness.

A few weeks later a conference of southern leaders met in Birmingham and "nominated" Gov. J. Strom Thurmond of South Carolina for president and Gov. Fielding

Wright of Mississippi for vice-president. The strategy of the southerners was designed not to elect the Thurmond-Wright ticket, since they knew that they could not succeed, but rather to demonstrate enough support to strengthen their hand in the Electoral College when it met to choose the winner of the election. A united South would have substantial bargaining power in the ultimate choice of a president.

On election day the "Dixiecrats," as they had been labeled, won four states—Alabama, South Carolina, Mississippi, and Louisiana. They polled a total of 1,154,000 votes in the four states where they were declared the official Democratic nominees. It is always difficult to measure the lasting effects of such movements as that of the Dixiecrats. Possibly the national (northern) Democrats treated their southern brethren with more deference in succeeding years; and perhaps the 1948 revolt had some intangible effect on the growth of the Republican party in the South. One should note, however, that the Democratic presidential candidate did win in 1948 in spite of the defection of the Dixiecrats, and, with the exception of South Carolina, the remaining three states that supported Thurmond in 1948 have been far less responsive to Republican party incursions. By the same token, Republican candidates fared better in the South as a whole after 1948 than they had at any period since 1928. Governor Thurmond, of course, was later elected to the U.S. Senate as a Democrat but switched parties in 1964 to become a Republican. Senator Thurmond might be termed a personal symbol of the changes taking place in mid-century southern politics.

Since 1948 the southern states have divided their vote for president between the Democrats and Republicans. Four states cast their votes for Dwight D. Eisenhower, the Republican candidate, in 1952; and in every election since, except for 1960 and 1976, at least five southern states have gone Republican. In 1960 Richard M. Nixon carried only three southern states; in 1972 he carried all eleven. In 1976 Georgia's Jimmy Carter carried all of the southern states except one, but in 1980 all except Georgia voted for Ronald Reagan.

Below the presidential level, southern two-party growth has been notable. The most striking successes have been the Republican gains in governors, U.S. senators, and members of Congress. In 1966 both Florida and Arkansas elected their first GOP governors since the post–Civil War period. They were joined in later years by Republican chief executives in Tennessee, Virginia, North Carolina, Texas, and Louisiana. Also during this period the Republicans of Florida, Mississippi, North and South Carolina, Texas, Tennessee, Virginia, Georgia, and Alabama elected United States senators. Furthermore, every one of the southern states had elected at least 1 Republican member of Congress by 1980, with 39 elected in that year alone. By 1980 a total of 304 Republicans had been elected to southern state legislatures (see table 2-3).

A shift to two-party competition has also been apparent in a number of formerly one-party Republican states. For more than a century, several states in New England (Maine, Vermont, and New Hampshire) and others in the Midwest (Kansas and Nebraska) were dominated by the Republican party. In recent years, however, each of them has elected one or more Democrats to high office. Edmund Muskie's election as governor in 1954, followed by his election to the U.S. Senate in 1958, represented the first time a Democrat had been elected to either of those two offices in Maine. During the 1950s and 1960s Vermont elected a succession of Democratic governors and is presently represented by its first Democratic U.S. senator. The same pattern of Democratic encroachment has developed in most of the other states that were formerly Republican preserves. Organizationally, however, even though the old one-party states

**TABLE 2-3    Republican office holders, 1948-1980**

| Year | Governors | Senators | Members of congress | State legislators |
|------|-----------|----------|---------------------|-------------------|
| 1948 | 39.6% | 43.8% | 39.3% | 45.0% |
| 1950 | 52.1 | 49.0 | 45.7 | 44.3 |
| 1952 | 62.5 | 50.0 | 50.8 | 51.0 |
| 1954 | 43.7 | 49.0 | 46.7 | 44.0 |
| 1956 | 39.6 | 49.0 | 46.2 | 44.0 |
| 1958 | 28.6 | 34.0 | 35.2 | 34.0 |
| 1960 | 32.0 | 35.0 | 39.8 | 38.0 |
| 1962 | 32.0 | 33.0 | 40.5 | 40.0 |
| 1964 | 34.0 | 32.0 | 32.1 | 34.0 |
| 1966 | 50.0 | 36.0 | 43.0 | 42.0 |
| 1968 | 62.0 | 43.0 | 44.1 | 42.9 |
| 1970 | 42.0 | 44.0 | 41.3 | 39.4 |
| 1972 | 19.0 | 42.0 | 44.1 | 40.0 |
| 1974 | 24.0 | 39.0 | 33.1 | 31.4 |
| 1976 | 24.0 | 38.0 | 33.3 | 30.0 |
| 1978 | 36.0 | 41.0 | 36.6 | 35.8 |
| 1980 | 46.0 | 53.0 | 44.1 | 40.0 |

All of the percentages shown exclude third-party and nonpartisan officers.

**Source:** Robert J. Huckshorn and John F. Bibby, "The Republican Party in American Politics," in *Parties and Elections in an Anti-Party Age,* ed. Jeff Fishel (Bloomington: Indiana University Press, 1978), p. 56. 1980 data added. Reprinted by permission.

have become more competitive and have elected major officers representing the former minority parties, many of them remain beset by intraparty factionalism.

Factionalism in any organization is debilitating. In the one-party systems of the South, though, factionalism was sometimes a substitute for the interparty competition that was missing from the state political system. The competition that did exist was between factions within the single party—which, in the South, was the Democratic party. As early as the 1940s V. O. Key, Jr., suggested that political parties could be categorized according to the degree of factionalism found within them. For many years state parties were categorized as cohesive (unified), bifactional, or multifactional.[16] If a party appears to be reasonably unified, willing to follow elected leadership, and in agreement on some shared goals, it can be described as cohesive. Obviously, cohesive parties can be found in either two-party or one-party systems. They represent the ideal, since internal cohesion is often used as a principal criterion in measuring party effectiveness. In this discussion, however, most of our attention will focus on the long-standing concepts of bifactionalism and multifactionalism in one-party systems.

## Bifactional Politics in the South

For many years another kind of politics was to be found in some of the southern states. In those states, factions within a single party competed with each other in an approximation of two-party politics. Key labeled such systems "bifactional." At the time of Key's study several southern states could be described as bifactional, the best known being Louisiana, which represented an almost classic case of two factions within the same party contending for power over a period of many years. The two factions of the Louisiana Democratic party reflected a long-standing rivalry between the Long family and the anti-Long faction. Allan Sindler's 1955 study of Louisiana politics describes the conflict and attributes it to the commanding figures of Huey and

Earl Long. From 1918, when Huey Long was elected to the state railroad commission at the age of twenty-five, until his death by assassination in 1935, "Longism" dominated the politics of the state. The voting strength of the two principal factions came from two distinct groups.

Each of the groups displayed a "continuity of political attitudes going back to the muted class conflicts of the previous century."[17] The bifactional cleavage grew out of antagonisms between city and rural dwellers and between wealthy planters and small dirt farmers. It offered meaningful choices with worthwhile political rewards for the winning faction. The two organizations employed the "ticket system," a version of traditional slate making in which candidates for office had to compete for the endorsement of the local machine and, if they won it, were well on their way to election. By 1932 Long had expanded the slating system to the point that all major candidates for state office ran on a slate. For twenty-eight years, incorporating eight consecutive elections, the runoff primary in Louisiana was between Long and anti-Long candidates. The conflict between the two factions ended in 1960 when the Long group failed to place a candidate in the runoff primary. It has now deteriorated to the point where recent elections suggest that Louisiana is no longer bifactional but is now multifactional, centered around ad hoc coalitions and personalities that shift from election to election.

Although Louisiana was the best known of the bifactional systems in the south, V. O. Key, Jr., found that a bifactional system was also dominant in the Georgia Democratic party. From 1926 to 1948 the stronger faction was led by Eugene Talmadge and later by his son, Sen. Herman Talmadge. The Talmadge faction was entrenched in the "black belt" of the central part of the state, where most of the rural whites lent their support. Much of the strength of the Talmadge faction was built on the old (now unconstitutional) county-unit system, in which votes were cast as "county units" (much like the National Electoral College), and rural Georgia counties controlled about 60 percent of the votes. The election of Herman Talmadge to the U.S. Senate in 1956 brought the pro- and anti-Talmadge factions to an end, but Georgia's primary voting patterns still reflect an ingrained rural–urban split.[18] Just as clearly, the 1980 election of a Republican governor of Louisiana and the defeat of Talmadge by a Republican for the U.S. Senate signaled a new era in the politics of those formerly bifactional states.

As early as the 1940s Key found that politics in most of the southern states were "multifactional." Typically, a Democratic primary for statewide office might find as many as six or eight candidates running for each office. Each candidate would have the support of significant numbers of voters and his or her own coterie of party and elected leaders. Each would run a separate, distinctly personal campaign. The results, of course, were so splintering that most of the states in the South invented the runoff primary just to ensure that the eventual winner would be elected by a majority vote.

## The Multifactional Politics of Florida Democrats

At the time Key was studying southern politics, the premier multifactional party was in Florida. Like other southern states, Florida had no Republican party except at the presidential level. The kaleidoscopic politics of the Sunshine State was described by Key as "every man for himself." In 1936 fourteen men ran for governor in the Democratic party primary, and the one who outdistanced the rest received only 15.7 percent of the votes. Forty years later, in the 1974 senatorial primary, there were eleven candidates, and the front-runner garnered only 29.1 percent of the vote and went on to lose the runoff to the primary runner-up.

In 1978 the Democratic primary race for governor presented the voters with a list of seven candidates, almost all of them major names in state politics. Few of the candidates in these or other intervening elections were able to build and sustain state-wide campaign organizations. Many of them found it difficult to raise money, and the large number of candidates simply exacerbated this problem. Campaign organizations were built around local constituencies whose support was assumed, and organizational efforts were devoted to selected areas in other parts of the state. Key noted thirty years ago that Florida Democratic politics was little more than an electoral lottery. One needed only to pay the filing fee, work to get a spot in the runoff, and hope that Lady Luck was on one's side when that warm September day rolled around. A tropical rainstorm on election day could result in the voters choosing a totally unexpected candidate. As one 1974 candidate for the Senate wryly noted, "You pays your money and you takes your chances!"

Florida is not the only multifaceted and factionalized state. Key found that most of the states in the South had elements of multifactionalism. Although the political systems in some of the southern states have matured somewhat, others remain multifactional. In those states electoral outcomes are often determined by a fluid and ever-changing field of candidates representing different locales and ideologies, with little carry-over from one election to the next. The electorate is up for grabs after every election contest. Clearly, this is a highly fragmented and personal kind of politics.

Americans tend to think of one-party politics in terms of Hitler's National Socialists (Nazis) or Andropov's Communists, each a totalitarian government with authorized and controlled single parties designed to provide the trappings of democracy. But there are different degrees of dictatorship, just as there are significant differences between democracies. Every state in the Union has a two-party organization and in every state each party runs some candidates for office. Few Republicans actually get elected in Mississippi and few Democrats in Vermont, but some are elected. Therefore some state party systems can be described as dual in nature but dominated by one party. The minority party is legal, operates in the open, and may win elections on occasion. These features help distinguish such state systems from the one-party politics of the Soviet Union. Recognition of that distinction has led to greater speculation regarding multiparty systems as an alternative for the political structure of the United States.

## Third-Party Politics in the United States

Almost everyone has listened to an address on the virtues of the two-party system at one time or another. The speaker normally reviews those aspects of the one-party system that make it unpalatable to Americans but also explains the coalition problems that beset multiparty systems, such as those in the Western European parliamentary democracies. A parliamentary system is one in which the authority of government is vested in the legislative body from which the parliamentary majority leader chooses his cabinet to carry on the day-to-day operations of administration. The prime minister and cabinet remain in power only so long as they command majority support in the parliamentary body. In most of the parliamentary nations of Europe and Scandinavia the multiparty system prevails. It is usually based on a system of proportional representation requiring that a coalition of several parties holding seats in parliament be brought together to form a government. Such governments, normally negotiated through compromise, are notoriously unstable, and the defection of one key element in the coalition can bring down the government. The Italian parliamentary democracy, for example, has had forty-two different governments since 1943.

European and Scandinavian parties differ in many respects from those in the United States. They are highly centralized, have a mass membership, and are much more ideological than ours. One study of the ideological and socioeconomic group support of the leading parties in seventeen Western nations listed seven major ideological groups around which parties had been built: communists, democratic socialists, Christian democrats, liberals, democratic conservatives, antidemocratic conservatives, and antidemocratic radicals. These party groups, ranging from the left to the right, splinter the electorate and make it difficult for any one party to gain a parliamentary majority.[19] That fact necessitates coalition building if a viable government is to emerge. Thus one of the major parties will bargain for support from one or more of the lesser parties, seeking to persuade their leaders to join in a coalition government. In recent years the Scandinavian countries have been more politically stable than the Western European nations because a single party has been so dominant that coalition building was less demanding. Even so, defenders of the two-party arrangement can point to their system as being considerably more stable.

Both the two-party and multiparty systems are based on coalitions of support groups. The difference is that in the United States the coalition building takes place *within* the parties, while in the European democracies coalitions form *between* the parties. The American coalitions of voters group themselves before and during elections, whereas the European parties group themselves after the election has taken place and the results are known. As American citizens, we are used to two political parties, each sheltering people of different ideological beliefs. We do not consider it particularly startling that the Republican party can include both Sen. Lowell Weicker, a liberal from Connecticut, and Sen. J. Strom Thurmond, a conservative from South Carolina. This phenomenon merely points up the fact that people of radically different views can live together, albeit sometimes uncomfortably, in the same party.

In Western Europe and the Scandinavian countries people with strongly held beliefs are more likely to join a party that most nearly represents their views—not so difficult to do, given the number of parties. After the voting is over, the parties get together to form coalition governments; the choice of partners in the coalition lies with the party leadership in the parliament. Therefore, although the individual citizen makes the initial choice of party, he or she eventually leaves it to that party's leaders to determine what role they will play in the government. In contrast, the fact that American voters can subordinate their own personal beliefs to party loyalty has helped to preserve the two-party system. What fragmentation has occurred historically has resulted from efforts by dissatisfied groups of citizens who have sought to break out of the two-party mold by establishing rival third parties. Most of them did not have a permanent multiparty system in mind but were attempting to displace one of the two major parties.

Although American third parties have never been able to capture control of the national government, they have achieved considerable success in influencing public policy. Periodically, they have captured some state and local offices, and, on occasion, even a congressional seat. Nevertheless, even though they perform many of the electoral functions of major parties, they can seldom accomplish the essential feat of mobilizing a majority of the voters in behalf of their candidates. Their lack of electoral success, however, has not prevented groups of like-minded citizens from struggling to establish third parties. The Center for Political Studies at the University of Michigan has compiled a list of all of the third-party movements in American history. Most of the eleven hundred parties were short-lived, with limited support. The nature of their narrow appeal is suggested by the following selections from the list:

> High Tariff Whigs Party
> Liberation Whigs Party
> Tariff for Revenue Democrat Party
> Unconditional Union Party
> Protectionists Party
> Greenback Labor Reform Party
> National Anti-Monopoly Party
> Felician Republicans Party
> Middle of the Road Populists Party
> High Life Party
> Light Wines and Beer Party
> Blacksmith Party
> The Third Party
> Pathfinders Party
> Nebraska Democrat Party
> Four Freedoms Party
> Cincinnatus Nonpartisan Movement Party
> Poor Man's Party[20]

As odd as some of these third parties may sound to us today, we should recognize that some of them have had a most decisive impact on American politics and on the two major parties. Their failure to win office cannot detract from their effect on government policy. The presence of third parties has often stimulated interest in emerging issues and has even, on rare occasions, divided the vote in such a way as to influence election outcomes. Walter Burnham has noted that there are two basic kinds of large-scale, third-party activity. One is the *majority party bolt* type, which detaches the most acutely disaffected voters from a major party's coalition. We can see an excellent example of such a development in the double split from the Democratic party in 1948: the Progressives on the left (under Henry Wallace) and the Dixiecrats on the right (under Strom Thurmond, then a Democrat) both bolted at the same time. Neither defection, however, kept the Democrats from retaining the presidency—Harry S. Truman was reelected.

The second type of third-party movement described by Burnham is the *protest movement,* which draws support from across party lines and may have broad appeal for a limited period of time. Examples may be found in the Anti-Masonic party in 1832, the Free Soil party in 1848, the Greenback party in 1878, the Populist party in 1892, the LaFollette Progressives in 1924, George Wallace's American Independent party in 1968, and John Anderson's independent candidacy in 1980.[21]

One of the third parties in the second group, the Populists in 1892, serves as a good example of the positive effects such groups can have in stimulating the discussion of new issues and in invigorating the leadership of the established parties. Although it never experienced much success at the polls, the Populist (People's) party of the 1890s eventually saw virtually its entire platform taken over, debated, and partially adopted by the two major parties. At one time or another the Populists advocated: (1) a graduated income tax; (2) women's suffrage; (3) postal savings banks; (4) direct democracy through initiative and referendum; (5) increased antimonopoly actions by the government; (6) tighter immigration laws; (7) abolition of national banks; (8) free silver; and (9) government ownership of the railroads. By the end of the next quarter century all but the last three of these propositions had become law, even though many of them were considered radical at the time. Not all the credit for these actions could be claimed by the Populists; indeed, the party only lasted a few years, but its platforms forced the Republicans and Democrats to wrestle with important issues and to broaden their appeal to the voters.

The Populists also had an important impact on the electorate. The party was composed of remnants of the old Greenback Labor, Farmers' Alliance, and Knights of Labor parties and polled over one million votes for its presidential candidate in 1892. Although the Populists gained only twenty-two electoral votes, theirs was the best performance to date for a third party. In 1894 Populist candidates for Congress received over half a million votes and by that time had elected two U.S. senators and fourteen members of the House. By 1895 they had gained five senators, but the number of their congressmen had declined to seven. The beginning of the end occurred in 1896 when the Populists were faced with the Democrats behind William Jennings Bryan. The fusionists won the day, and they joined in support of the Bryan nomination. Republican William McKinley won the presidency, however, and the Populist party finally disbanded in 1912.

## Modern Third Parties

The appeal of third parties has not declined in modern America. In every presidential election numerous vegetarians, prohibitionists, progressives, socialists, communists, states' rights advocates, and other party candidates are listed on the ballots of some states. Some of them, such as the Minnesota Farmer-Labor party, survive to become a lasting influence in politics. At one point in the 1930s the Farmer-Labor party was the dominant force in Minnesota and actually won the governorship in 1930, 1932, and 1936, beating both the Republicans and the Democrats. The emergence of liberal Republican Harold Stassen on the scene brought the Republicans into dominance, and in the 1940s the Farmer-Laborites joined forces with the Democrats to become the Democratic Farmer-Labor Party. The DFL subsequently assumed an important place in Minnesota political history and dominated the major offices in the state until 1978, when the Republicans won both U.S. Senate seats and the governorship.

One of the best known of the modern third- (and even fourth-) party movements arose in New York State in the 1970s. The state of New York has a history of third-party movements going back to the early nineteenth century. The real impetus to third-party development came in the early twentieth century when the law was changed to permit a candidate to run on more than one party ticket. This opened the way to highly ideological parties, which have the option of running their own candidates or endorsing the candidates of one of the major parties. The latter arrangement permits the candidate receiving the endorsement to have his name on two lines of the ballot, that is, to be cross-listed. The result is that some third parties have succeeded in achieving influence in the party system far in excess of their numerical strength.

Since 1962 there have been two significant minor parties in New York. The Liberal party was organized in the mid-1940s by David Dubinsky of the International Ladies Garment Workers Union. The Liberal party quickly became a favorite of reform Democrats (i.e., anti–Tammany Hall) and the large New York City Jewish population who worked in the clothing industry. The significance of the Liberal party's influence cannot be overemphasized. It provided the margin of victory for Herbert Lehman when he ran for the Senate in 1950; for Averill Harriman in his race for governor in 1954; for John F. Kennedy in the presidential contest of 1960; and for John Lindsay in his campaign for mayor of New York City in 1965. When Lindsay ran for reelection in 1966, he did not receive the Republican nomination but ran on the Liberal line alone and again won. Under the tutelage of the late Alex Rose, the Liberals have seldom run their own candidates, following the alternative strategy of endorsing a candidate of another party. In addition to the 1966 Lindsay victory, the only successes registered by the party on its own were in a 1949 congressional election and a 1951 victory in a contest for presidency of city council. Yet, because the Liberals have occasionally provided the margin of victory, candidates have not been disposed to ignore them.

The New York Conservative party was organized in 1962 as a means of shifting New York to the right by applying pressure on the Republican party. Using essentially the same tactics as the Liberals, the Conservatives first attracted serious attention in 1966 by winning over half a million votes for their gubernatorial candidate, a college professor who was not widely known. They made believers of many skeptics when they outpolled the Liberal party in supposedly liberal New York City. That accomplishment entitled them to the coveted third line on the ballot, and in 1970 Conservative party senatorial nominee James L. Buckley was elected over incumbent Republican Senator Charles Goodell and Democratic nominee Richard Ottinger. Goodell ran with the endorsement of the Liberal party.

The impact of third-party politics in New York can be seen by reviewing the results of that election. Buckley (C) received 2,288,190 (37.2 percent) of the votes to Ottinger's (D) 2,171,232 (35.3 percent) and Goodell's (R-L) 1,434,472 (23.3 percent). In order to avoid the pitfalls of maintaining an effective independent status in the Senate, Buckley assumed his seat as a Conservative-Republican and voted with the Republican minority on organizational matters. Neal R. Peirce, an astute political observer, claims that the "fundamental reason for success [of the Conservative party] was that a political vacuum existed in New York." He notes that:

> Both Republicans and Democrats were for big government, civil rights, and, by their deeds if not their words, high taxes. Practically, there was no difference between the major parties. The Conservatives provided an alternative on spending issues, opposed school busing, took the side of the police in the civilian review board controversy in New York City, and provided the only political voice continuing to call for victory in Vietnam.[22]

The Conservative and Liberal movements in New York offer good examples of issue-oriented parties that have been able to bargain endorsements into real power. They were able to do so because of a New York law permitting dual endorsements. In recent years, however, both groups have declined in influence. The death of Alex Rose in 1976 and the failure of the Liberals to broaden their appeal has seriously eroded their strength. In 1966 they lost their third line on the ballot to the Conservatives when Liberal candidates received fewer votes than Conservatives, and in 1978 they finished fifth behind the fledgling Right to Life party. The Conservatives, too, appear to have peaked, and party leaders have increasingly been content with endorsing the nominees of the Republican party. It is clear that both the Conservatives and the Liberals in New York have suffered from some of the ills that traditionally beset third-party movements in general.

A cursory review of the historical literature will bring home the fact that all third-party movements have failed except one, the Republicans, who survived to become a major party. The failures have resulted from several factors. In some cases, such as the Populist and the Socialist parties, the Republicans and Democrats merely coopted their platforms and eventually translated their more popular planks into law. Being issue oriented, the third parties themselves could not survive the loss of their issue base. Other third parties have been little more than the personal coteries of a particular candidate whose eventual removal from the scene caused the organization itself to slide into oblivion. Some minor parties have been so ideologically extreme that they were unable to accommodate themselves to the mold that is considered acceptable or appropriate by the American voter. They often collapsed from the inside as factional disputes over party dogma undermined their foundations.

The two major parties have controlled the state legislatures and Congress for so long that some of their actions have helped perpetuate their control. They have, for instance, carefully constructed a framework of election laws that makes it most difficult for a third party to operate over a period of time on a continuing basis. In 1968 George Wallace, running for president as the candidate of the American Independent party, was able to meet the legal requirements to get on the ballot in every one of the fifty states.

That achievement cannot be overestimated. At one point Governor Wallace had a staff of twenty-five lawyers traveling from state to state researching election laws, filing suits, and getting petition signatures to meet local requirements. In all, he and his supporters collected 2.7 million petition signatures to guarantee his position in those states requiring them. Even then, Wallace ran under nine different ballot designations and party labels. On election day he received 13.5 percent of the popular vote, the most impressive showing of any national third-party candidate to date. Nevertheless, much of the groundwork was undercut by state laws requiring third parties to maintain a minimum percentage of the vote in order to remain on the ballot in the future. Had Wallace run again as a third-party candidate, much of his effort would have had to be repeated in order to place his name on the ballot again. It is no accident that the election laws passed by Republican and Democratic state legislators raise road blocks to the candidacies of third-party candidates. The demands of democracy and the Constitution make it essential that minor parties be permitted to run, but state legislators do not hesitate to set up hurdles that minor parties must overcome in order to get on the ballot.

In 1980 third-party candidate John Anderson faced the same hurdles that Wallace had faced in 1968. He too was able to get listed on the ballot in all fifty states, but his support declined from the 20 percent shown by the polls in mid-summer to the 7 percent he actually received on election day. His best showing was in Vermont and Massachusetts, where he received 15 percent of the vote. He did not win any electoral votes, but his 7 percent did qualify him for federal matching funds, which enabled him to pay off his campaign debts.

A final aspect of the electoral system that works to the disadvantage of third parties is the single-member district plan. This plan, widely used in the United States, is almost perfectly attuned to the two-party system, as has been noted earlier. Under the single-member district system, only one representative is elected to office from each constituent district. Obviously, only one victor is possible in each district, since the winner of a plurality is the winner of the election. Since political parties, by definition, always seek to win elections, the single-member district plan enhances the chances of the two major contenders and undercuts the chances of third parties. Given all of these factors, plus the enduring loyalty of the American voters to their party, it is not surprising that the two-party system has overcome all threats from third-party challengers.

## Nonpartisan Elections

American society has always had a strain of antipartyism. In his Farewell Address in 1797 George Washington called on the nation to be wary of the "baneful effects of the spirit of party." This warning was a natural result of events that took place in his own administration and that signaled the development of party factions. But antipartyism has never been far beneath the surface of American consciousness, and it emerged in full flower in the latter part of the nineteenth century in the midwestern states. There are many varieties of nonpartisanship. Some supporters of the nonpartisan concept are opposed to majority rule itself. Others are simply against political parties and party organizations; they view politics as dirty, divisive, and conducive to the compromise of principles.

The nonpartisan concept became an article of faith of the LaFollette Progressives in the early part of this century. The theory of nonpartisan elections holds that, by eliminating the party designation of candidates and allowing all voters to take part in elections, partisan politics will be reduced and officeholders will owe allegiance to all of the electorate, not just the party that elected them. It has become apparent over the years that nonpartisan elections do not really place a moratorium on politics. They simply substitute a different kind of politics for the old partisan type.

Nonpartisanship has the effect of removing the party as a cue giver to the voter. If voters cannot rely on their political parties for advice and leadership in casting their votes, how then do they decide which candidate to vote for? Let us review some valuable research that has been done in an attempt to answer that question.

1. Nonpartisanship does weaken the political parties. That was its intent, and it succeeded in those places where it was tried. The parties are weakened because the number of people interested in becoming involved in party activities usually diminishes. Most nonpartisan activity is at the municipal level and has often been accompanied by implementation of the city manager plan, with its concomitant increase in appointive rather than elective officers. With fewer offices to fill, fewer candidates run, and often fewer campaign workers become active. Less incentive exists for people to become involved, since fewer rewards are provided for political activity. Furthermore, nonpartisan systems remove the principal function of the party: the recruitment and election of candidates. Even if the parties find a way to become involved behind the scenes, they cannot claim credit for electoral successes.

2. Nonpartisanship results in a shift in influence to nonparty groups. Eugene Lee found that in California the electorate relied heavily on newspapers (mostly Repub-

lican), business people, service clubs, and women's organizations, in that order. Labor unions had less influence than they normally do in a partisan system, partly because members' working hours do not readily lend themselves to campaigning.[23] Other studies have shown that nonpartisanship tends to reduce the turnout of Democrats; as a result many cities, which vote heavily Democratic in state and national elections, elect local candidates who are quite conservative.[24] Organizations are sometimes formed to choose candidates and fight election campaigns outside the partisan arena. Groups such as "citizens associations," "charter committees," and "good government committees" become substitutes for local parties by helping in the selection of candidates and assisting with their campaigns. They are, in effect, slate-making organizations established to perform a neoparty function.

In Los Angeles, selection of candidates is made by a group representing the downtown business and commercial interests, who agree to contribute corporate funds toward the requisite professional public relations campaign.[25] Where parties are excluded, it has become commonplace for nonpartisan groups to move in to fill the vacuum. Many of those who believe strongly in political parties are convinced that nonpartisanship undermines the electoral process. If the parties were doing their job efficiently and effectively, that might well be true. However, especially in local government, political parties have permitted themselves to be taken over by local bosses, a development that also thwarts the electoral process. Furthermore, the decline in the number of incentives that could be offered by party officials has made it difficult for many of them to operate in the usual partisan sense.

3. Campaigns and elections in nonpartisan systems are more likely to be decided on the basis of the personal qualities of the candidates than on the issues that were the basis for adopting the system in the first place. A nonpartisan system tends to cast the voters adrift in the sense that they are left without the crutch of party label on which to base a voting decision. Even candidates chosen by slate-making groups are often selected because of qualities that have little to do with the issues. Voters are asked to decide between candidates according to television presence, impersonal public relations campaigns, or characteristics of race or ethnic background. Obviously, candidates of this kind are chosen in partisan systems too. Nevertheless, the choice of candidates on the basis of personal characteristics appears to be more common in nonpartisan systems. Charles Adrian, in what was probably the earliest academic study of the effects of nonpartisanship, describes a Detroit council candidate who campaigned on the "implicit platform that he had been an able shortstop on the Detroit Tigers' baseball club."[26]

The concept of nonpartisanship has enjoyed widespread adoption. Nonpartisan elections are used in most cities in the United States, including some large cities, such as Los Angeles. Partisan politics still reigns in most of the very large cities, such as New York, Chicago, and Philadelphia. At the state level most offices are elected on a partisan ballot, although Nebraska elects state legislators on nonpartisan ballots. In some jurisdictions, even though nonpartisan elections are held, parties and individual partisans operate informally to influence the outcome of elections. A summary of the literature concerning nonpartisan elections leads to the following inescapable conclusions: incumbents are usually reelected; the influence of the middle class is increased because their turnout is greater; nonparty groups often assume the burdens normally associated with partisanship; and candidates are more likely to be elected because of some particular personal characteristic or identification with some specific popular issue.

## Two-Party Politics and 1984

For almost a century and a quarter, the president, the members of Congress, most state constitutional officers, and many local officials have been elected under the auspices of one of the world's two oldest democratic parties. Despite repeated warnings that one or the other of them was doomed, each has always bounced back to win and to rule. The American parties have never been ideologically grounded. Parties based on ideology normally develop in societies with deep social and institutional conflicts. The American people have certainly been divided by conflict at times, but the electorate has developed a high degree of consensus and political integration on important matters, such as support for constitutional government and the free use of private capital. Minor third parties have, on occasion, attempted to carve out a place for themselves in the system, but they have seldom survived for very long. The two major parties have outlasted the assaults of the antiparty and nonpartisan forces and have even transcended the reforms designed to do them in.

America's two hundredth birthday provided us with an opportunity to look back to see where we have been. The arrival of 1984, the year selected by George Orwell to represent his depiction of the future, forces us to look forward as well. From this point in time it would be possible to describe our political parties as both sturdy and fragile. They have endured, and they seem to be firmly established in the public mind and consciousness. But they also show signs of stress and of public alienation. Their efforts to cope with organizational problems and to regain public acceptance are among the topics discussed in chapter 3.

## Notes

1. Sigmund Neumann, "Toward a Cooperative Study of Political Parties," in *Modern Political Parties: Approaches to Comparative Politics,* ed. Sigmund Neumann (Chicago: University of Chicago Press, 1956), pp. 395–421.
2. Austin Ranney and Willmoore Kendall, *Democracy and the American Party System* (New York: Harcourt Brace Jovanovich, 1956), pp. 95–96.
3. William Nisbet Chambers, *Political Parties in a New Nation—The American Experience 1776–1809* (New York: Oxford University Press, 1963), p. 37.
4. Claude C. Bowers, *Jefferson and Hamilton* (Boston: Houghton Mifflin, 1925), p. 143.
5. Wilfred E. Binkley, *American Political Parties: Their Natural History,* 4th ed. (New York: Knopf, 1963), p. 78.
6. Noble E. Cunningham, Jr., *The Jeffersonian Republicans* (Chapel Hill: University of North Carolina Press, 1957), p. 65.
7. Richard P. McCormick, *The Second American Party System: Party Formation in the Jacksonian Era* (Chapel Hill: University of North Carolina Press, 1966).
8. Ibid.
9. Maurice Duverger, *Political Parties* (New York: Wiley, 1954), p. 217.
10. Austin Ranney, "Parties in State Politics," in *Politics in the American States: A Comparative Analysis,* 3rd ed., eds. Herbert Jacob and Kenneth Vines (Boston: Little, Brown, 1976), pp. 51–92. Most of the interparty competition classifications, including Ranney's, involve three basic dimensions originally proposed by Richard Dawson and James A. Robinson: (1) the degree of success, as measured by the percentage of votes won by each of the two parties in statewide races and the percentage of legislative seats won; (2) the time factor, as measured by the length of time each of the parties has controlled statewide offices and/or the state legislature; and (3) the divided control factor, as measured by the percentage of time the parties have divided control over the governorship and the legislature.
11. John F. Bibby, Cornelius P. Cotter, James L. Gibson, and Robert J. Huckshorn, "Parties in State Politics," in *Politics in the American States: A Comparative Analysis,* 4th ed., eds. Virginia Gray, Herbert Jacob, and Kenneth Vines (Boston: Little, Brown, 1983), pp. 59–96.
12. Ibid.
13. Ranney, "Parties in State Politics," pp. 60–61; and ibid., pp. 65–67. For a different method of measuring interparty competition, see David G.

Pfeiffer, "The Measurement of Inter-Party Competition and Systemic Stability," *American Political Science Review* 61, no. 2 (June 1967): 457–467.

14. *1981 Congressional Quarterly Almanac* (Washington, D.C.: Congressional Quarterly, 1982), pp. 35-C–36-C.

15. V. O. Key, Jr., *Southern Politics in State and Nation* (New York: Knopf, 1949).

16. Ibid., ch. 14. Also see Malcolm E. Jewell and David M. Olson, *American State Political Parties and Elections*, rev. ed. (Homewood, Ill.: Dorsey Press, 1982), pp. 56–67.

17. Allan P. Sindler, "Bifactional Rivalry as an Alternative to Two-Party Competition in Louisiana," *American Political Science Review* 49 (September 1955): 641–642.

18. Key, *Southern Politics*, pp. 106–129.

19. Austin Ranney, *The Governing of Men*, 3rd ed. (New York: Holt, Rinehart and Winston, 1971), pp. 337–339.

20. Center for Political Studies, "Party Code List" (mimeographed) (Ann Arbor: University of Michigan, undated).

21. Walter Dean Burnham, *Critical Elections and the Mainsprings of American Politics* (New York: Norton, 1970), pp. 27–28.

22. Neal R. Peirce, *The Mega States of America* (New York: Norton, 19792), p. 63.

23. Eugene C. Lee, *The Politics of Nonpartisanship* (Berkeley: University of California Press, 1960), pp. 76–96.

24. Edward C. Banfield and James Q. Wilson, *City Politics* (Cambridge, Mass.: Harvard University Press and M.I.T. Press, 1963), p. 159.

25. Ibid., p. 162.

26. Charles R. Adrian, "Some General Characteristics of Non-Partisan Elections," *American Political Science Review* 46 (September 1952): 773n.

# CHAPTER THREE

# Party Organizations: National, State, and Local

---

*Five men, one of whom said he is a former employee of the Central Intelligence Agency, were arrested at 2:30 a.m. yesterday in what authorities described as an elaborate plot to bug the offices of the Democratic National Committee....*

*Washington Post,* June 18, 1972, p. 1.

---

That front-page story in the *Washington Post* on June 18, 1972, opened one of the great political dramas in American history—Watergate. The story also, no doubt, brought to the attention of many Americans for the first time the existence of the national party committees. Although many people believe that parties exist as an essential conduit for democratic government, few ordinarily know much about them, and fewer still understand the organizational interrelationships of the various units.

We tend, in fact, to think of all organizations as pyramidal in structure. The U.S. Army, for instance, is headed by generals who preside over an expanding hierarchy of colonels, majors, captains, lieutenants, noncommissioned officers, and privates. Authority and responsibility flow up and down the official hierarchical levels. An order from the top is supposed to sift down through the layers until it reaches a level where it can be carried out. The person in authority who executed the order expects it to be obeyed, and his enforcement powers will usually work to see that it results in some appropriate action. More or less the same pattern exists in corporations, universities, and other social institutions, although the response to an order may not be so clean. Thus, because we are familiar with institutions that are organized as vertical pyramids, we assume that all organizations follow this structure. Political parties may appear to fit the pyramidal pattern, but in reality they do not. Parties do not exhibit the clean-flowing lines of authority and responsibility that seem to exist in other pyramidal organizations.

It is reasonably easy to depict a political party graphically as a pyramid (see figure 3–1). One might well assume that the national chairperson, occupying the apex as he or she does, would also exercise control over those units lower down the pyramid. In fact, looking at the organization from its base, one might expect the larger units at the bottom to be responsible to those above. In reality, although the pyramid pictured in figure 3–1 is a reasonably accurate picture of the *organizational* structure of American parties, it does not realistically portray their *power* structure. A true picture of the party's power structure would show a series of stratified layers of committees with overlapping boundaries and interlocking memberships. Instead of a central national office with power radiating downward through the layers to the bottom of the hier-

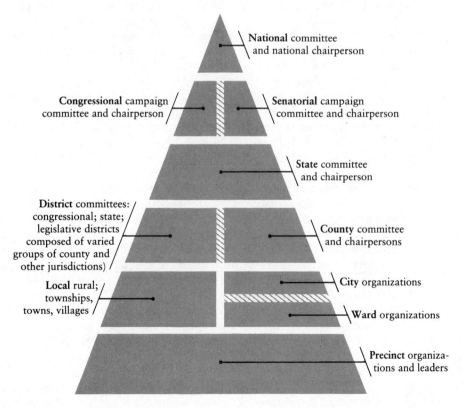

**FIGURE 3–1**  Organizational units and party officers at various levels of hierarchy.

archy, our organizational pyramids are topped by national committees that have little power and few responsibilities. National committee members are really delegates from "sovereign" state parties, and national committee chairpersons are often little more than agents representing the party's presidential nominees or incumbent presidents. State and local parties operate more or less independently, and the party committees devoted to the election of congressional representatives and senators operate even more separately. In this chapter we will attempt to describe the various levels of the party organization and to explain the relationships of each to the other. Like the Watergate burglars, let us begin by looking at the national party committees from the inside.

## National Party Committees

Both of the major parties maintain a full-time, staffed national headquarters in Washington. The Democratic National Committee (DNC) was created by the National Convention of 1848; the Republicans followed suit with their own organization in 1856. Before 1952 the methods of selecting members for the two national committees were similar. Each of the states, territories, and possessions of the United States was entitled to one national committeeman and one national committeewoman, the latter being added after the adoption of the Nineteenth Amendment. In 1952, however, the Republican National Convention voted to add the state party chairperson from each state that either elected a Republican governor, cast its electoral vote for the Republican presidential candidate in the last election, or elected a congressional delegation composed of a majority of Republicans.

The result of this change was that those states with viable and active Republican organizations had more power in the national party councils. The shift in power within the national committee was illustrated by the floor fight that erupted over the change proposed at the 1952 convention. The two groups who actively opposed the additional members were the women delegates and those state chairpersons who represented southern states. Since virtually all state chairpersons were male, the addition of most of them to the national committee effectively diluted the role of women members from one-half to approximately one-third. Furthermore, the standards by which the new members could be added excluded many of the southern chairpersons, who, at the time, could not even visualize the election of a governor or a majority of the congressional delegation. By 1948 several southern states had cast their votes for Republican presidential candidates, but that was an uncertain means of gaining added members. Once these changes were made, the membership of the Republican National Committee (RNC) remained unaltered until 1968, when the rules were again revised to include *all* Republican state chairpersons.

The Democratic National Committee did not change its membership until the 1972 national convention, when, spurred by the newly established Association of State Democratic Chairmen, the rules were changed to restructure the national committee and to include, among others, the state party chairpersons and vice-chairpersons— representing an equal number of men and women. This was not entirely satisfactory to the state party leaders, since they were furnished with only one-half of a vote each. However, this particular structure lasted only a short time, and in 1974, after a two-year study by the Democratic Charter Commission, the national committee was again

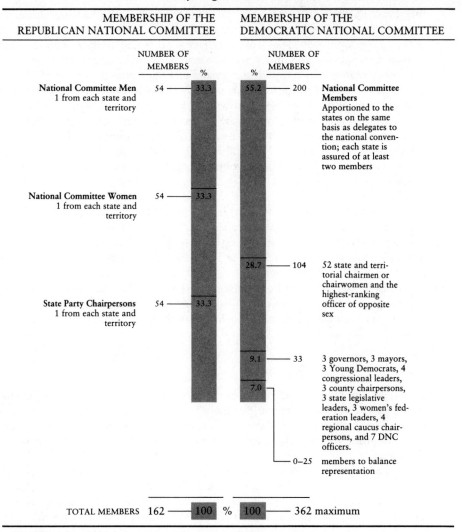

FIGURE 3–2 Comparison of Democratic and Republican National Committee membership, 1982.

redesigned. The new structure included the highest ranking officer of each sex in each state (with a full vote), elected national committee members, governors, the congressional leadership, officers of the national committee, mayors, Young Democrats, and additional members selected to bring racial and ethnic balance to the body. In 1981 the charter was amended to add representatives from the National Federation of Democratic Women and the chairpersons of the four regional caucuses (see figure 3-2). The total number of members on the newly constituted committee could range up to 362.[1]

As shown in figure 3–2, both committees are composed of about two-thirds national committeemen and committeewomen and one-third state chairpersons and ex officio members. The real difference is in the manner in which they are apportioned. The Republicans furnish each state and territory with three members per state, regardless of the size or population. The Democrats have apportioned the bulk of the membership of their new national committee according to the formula used to allot national convention delegates, thus giving the larger and more populous states considerably more power than the smaller ones. The Democratic National Committee is also more representative of minority groups, and women have greater representation, since both the chairman (or chairwoman) and the officer of the next highest rank (always of the opposite sex) from each state are members. Thus approximately one-third of the members of the Republican National Committee are women, in comparison to just under one-half of their Democratic counterparts. Most of the members are well known inside the party organization and hold important offices in their parties, but they are usually not widely recognized outside the hierarchy. In 1981 newly elected Democratic National Chairman Charles Manatt, Jr., persuaded the national committee members to approve the appointment of fifteen leaders of organized labor as part of the twenty-five members reserved for guaranteeing racial and ethnic balance. This restored labor's influence after an eight-year absence from the party hierarchy following the 1972 campaign of George McGovern.

The leader of the national committee is the national chairman or chairwoman. The names of these party leaders do not roll lightly off the tongue, but inside the parties they are important, and they normally have established reputations in national or state politics.

## National Party Chairperson

No job description can be applied universally to a national chairperson; the job changes as the party's fortunes change. But the key to understanding the role of the party chairperson is whether or not the party controls the presidency or the governorship. The role of the in-party chairperson differs substantially from that of the out-party chairperson.

The national chairperson of the party controlling the presidency is almost always the personal choice of the president. He or she serves, in effect, as the agent representing the president to the party organization. Sometimes he or she is given responsibility for carrying out the duties that belong to the president in his role as party leader. At other times the chairperson may serve only as party administrator while taking orders from the political advisors in the White House. From 1961 to 1968 John Bailey was Democratic national chairman under John F. Kennedy and Lyndon B. Johnson. Yet he was not on the inside of either president's personal political circle. In contrast, Dwight D. Eisenhower relied for political advice and strategy on both Leonard Hall and Senator Thurston Morton during their terms as Republican national chairman. Jimmy Carter used his national chairman, John White of Texas, as a principal liaison between the White House, the campaign staff, and the Democratic National Committee, and during the 1980 campaign period considerable interplay occurred between the three groups, including several exchanges of personnel.

Chairpersons of the party out of power have more often been party leaders in the real sense of the word. The power of titular party leaders, such as former presidential candidates, evaporates quickly once they have been defeated. The same is true of former presidents, who are usually willing to assume the role of elder statesman and leave party building to others. Thus the mantle of leadership often falls squarely on the shoulders of the national party chairperson. This situation brings both advantages and disadvantages. Without the presidency, for example, the chairperson has little patronage to dispense and few favors to distribute. But, on the other hand, he or she is more likely to be viewed as the real party leader without the added problem of being subservient to the president. He or she is able to concentrate on the daily activities and routines of staff conferences, research, public relations, personnel matters, and diplomatic relations with the congressional party leaders.

In 1965, after suffering one of the worst defeats in history, the tattered leadership of the Republican party met to select someone who could put the party organization back together. The choice was the Ohio state chairman, Ray C. Bliss, who described himself as a political "nuts and bolts" man. By that he meant that he viewed party work as primarily organizational. Throughout his five years as national chairman, he placed special emphasis on and invested substantial funding in organizational and rebuilding efforts. He was particularly concerned about the low status of GOP organizational activities in the big cities. He worked to overcome the traditional hostility between the Republican leaders from the congressional and the presidential wings of the party. And, unlike many chairpersons, he maintained a low personal profile, speaking as little as possible and leaving public relations to others.[2]

After the 1976 election the Republican National Committee chairwoman, Mary Louise Smith, resigned, and a search began for a new leader to take over the party machinery. None of the elected leaders, including outgoing President Gerald R. Ford, could muster enough influence to force the election of a personal choice for the post. At the national committee meeting in January 1977, five candidates contended for the office in the first actual contested election since 1949, and ultimately, on the third ballot, former U.S. senator William Brock of Tennessee was elected.[3]

Some chairpersons are selected specifically to serve as spokespersons for the party. This is particularly true when the presidency has been lost and the party's leadership is fragmented. It can also be the case when a president wishes to rise above the political battle and have a party spokesperson who is not connected to the White House. Sen. Robert Dole, Republican of Kansas, was chosen to be national chairman by President Richard M. Nixon specifically because of his articulate vocal support for the administration's programs during the Nixon first term. Dole, during his tenure in office, left much of the day-to-day administration of the national party to subordinates while he traveled the land speaking in favor of the Nixon administration. He also continued to serve his Kansas constituents in the Senate. Senator Dole's dual role brought to the fore an old and divisive question that has plagued the Republican party for years. That is the practice of selecting a sitting member of Congress to serve as chairperson of the national party.

The Republicans have chosen members of the Congress on several occasions in recent years, including, in addition to Dole, Senators Hugh Scott and Thruston Morton and Representatives William E. Miller and Rogers C. B. Morton. This practice has been favored by some Republicans because they believed that GOP power was centered on Capitol Hill and that congressional forces should therefore be strong inside the party councils. Many observers, however, do not believe this practice should be followed, since it forces a single individual to assume two posts, with the result that one or both will usually be neglected. The job of a member of Congress now takes considerable time, with greatly extended work days being common. It is simply not pos-

sible, it is argued, for a member to find the time necessary to devote to both positions.*
It is said that Massachusetts congressman Joseph Martin visited the national committee headquarters only twice in the twenty-eight months he served as its chairman
in the early 1940s.[4] Many staff members of both national committees consider a visit
by their head who is also a member of Congress to be an event worthy of special note,
so rarely do such visits occur.

Admittedly, however, the practice does have some advantages that should not be
overlooked. For the party out of power, Congress offers the principal source of policy
initiative and input, and members of the body are often better able to enunciate those
policies because of their daily familiarity with them. One may also argue that a national
chairperson who serves simultaneously in Congress may bring greater insights into
the politics of midterm congressional campaigns. On balance, though, these would
appear to be rather small rewards for the sacrifice of full-time party leadership and
the chairperson's undivided attention to party affairs. It has been said that a national
chairperson must be a "thousand-fingered Dutch boy" plugging the holes in the political dikes. National committee heads are responsible for too many day-to-day activities
for the parties to allow them to spend the lion's share of their time in other professional
pursuits.

Even under the best of circumstances, few national committee heads have been
capable of performing all aspects of the job equally well. Some have been good party
spokespersons, others have been campaign strategists, and still others have concentrated on party building and organization. Occasionally a presidential candidate selects
a national chairperson to serve during the interim between the convention and the
election or inauguration. Thus, immediately after his nomination in 1960, John F.
Kennedy asked the national committee to elect Senator Henry "Scoop" Jackson to
serve until after the election. Most of the people who have held the position as party
leader have not served out the full four-year term. During the five-year presidency of
Richard M. Nixon, for instance, four different men served as national chairman. John
Bailey, Democratic national chairman from 1960 to 1968, served two full terms, but
others in both parties have served but a few months. All of those who have been
elected to the top party post have been males except for Jean Westwood, who was
presidential candidate George McGovern's choice in 1972, and Mary Louise Smith,
who was recommended by Gerald R. Ford shortly after he became president.

Since World War II several national party chairmen have emerged with reputations
for leadership that place them well above the average. Democrats Paul M. Butler
(1955–1960) and Robert S. Strauss (1972–1977) served at two different periods during which their party was at a low ebb. Both were innovative, and both involved
themselves in party pursuits that had not been explored before. In the Republican
party the programs implemented by Ray C. Bliss (1965–1969) not only revived the
party after its disastrous loss in 1964 but provided new dimensions to the office of
national party chairperson. All three were leaders of parties that did not control the
presidency. More recently, William Brock, who served as Republican national chairman from 1977 to 1981, has received widespread attention for the many innovations
and reforms that he inaugurated during his term. Brock concentrated on a party-
building program based on shoring up the Republican state and local organizational

*The bylaws of the Republican National Committee were amended in 1976 to require that the national
chairperson serve full-time. This created a problem in 1982 when President Reagan indicated his desire to ask
the RNC to elect his close friend, Sen. Paul Laxalt of Nevada, to the post. The problem was solved by naming
Laxalt "general chairman" of the party and electing Frank Fahrenkopf, state chairperson of Nevada, as the
national chairperson in charge of day-to-day operations.

(From Herblock on all Fronts, New
American Library, 1980)

base. He appointed regional political directors and finance directors to assist state chairpersons with organizational development and fund raising. He set up a sophisticated data-processing network to provide computer services to state parties at minimal cost and created a local elections division to provide technical, staff, and financial assistance to state legislative campaigns. The national committee under Brock's leadership developed an impressive organization to assist in state legislative and congressional redistricting after the 1980 census. But probably the most controversial and one of the most successful efforts undertaken by Brock was to involve the national committee directly in state and local elections, both in recruiting and training candidates and in providing them with campaign funds and services to help get them elected. These efforts clearly expanded the role of the national committee and provided impetus to the nationalizing trends within both the parties.[5]

## National Party Committee Functions

Once one has established a responsible party model, one may quite easily demonstrate that the party organizations in the United States do not conform to it. As discussed in chapter 1, any responsible party model demands that the people hold the party in power responsible for the actions of its officials in the government. It also requires that all the governmental machinery, both the legislative and executive, be controlled by the same party. Divided government does not permit the voter to place the blame clearly or give credit for actions taken. Responsible government requires that the political party, its officers, candidates, and public officials be held accountable. If they are allowed to deny responsibility for official actions, the principal criterion for responsible parties is removed.

One problem, of course, is the division of powers in the national government. By requiring the president and members of the House and Senate to be elected for terms of differing lengths and by different constituencies, we almost guarantee periodic divided government, in which it is not only difficult to determine responsibility but almost impossible to make changes that will immediately result in greater attention to public demands.

Another problem lies in the federal system, which has power divided between the national government and the states. The parties, having evolved over a period of years in a seemingly unplanned fashion, were simply superimposed on the federal governmental structure. At no time were party leaders furnished with the kind of power that would permit them to command support from their elected officeholders. Party leaders, therefore, have had to accomplish their goals by persuasion and compromise. In some important ways the parties are much like the federal system of government. Each is composed of a large number of independent units ranging from local to national, and each of those units represents one foundation stone in the national political structure. Yet, unlike the national and state governments, there is no constitution to provide a division of powers and no Supreme Court to decide which party can do what to whom, or how. Most national party leaders are temporary creatures of incumbent presidents or of transient presidential candidates. State parties are often mere collection points for a profusion of precinct, ward, city, and county groups, each representing a distinct and separate part of a giant political jigsaw puzzle.

Partly because of the division of powers and responsibilities between branches of the national government, and partly because of the constitutional divisions of powers between the national and state governments, party organizations have never been able to develop a role that would permit them to claim to be "responsible." Even so, the national party organizations exist in full panoply. What, then, do they do? Do they perform services for other party units further down the hierarchy? Do they serve party officeholders? Do they participate in policy formation? Do they engage in campaigning? Are they involved in the recruitment of candidates for various offices? Do they take an active part in the nominating process?

The answer to each of these questions is a modified yes—modified, because the national party committees are seldom in a position to impose themselves on party units lower down the hierarchy or even laterally at the congressional level. They make political merchandise available, but their customers—the state and local parties—do not have to buy. The merchandise they have in stock takes the form of service activities performed by the national commitee staff persons. These activities can be categorized as research, public relations, campaign management, auxiliary group activities, fund raising, and management of the national conventions, miniconventions, and other party conferences. For a variety of reasons, neither of the national committees performs these functions equally well all of the time, but, as indicated earlier, in recent years the Republican National Committee has taken the lead in servicing state and local parties in ways that have never been tried before. The Democratic National Committee has been unable to emulate its Republican counterpart for a number of reasons, one of which has been a multimillion dollar debt that until recently has effectively hindered an expansion of its services. Nevertheless, both national committees furnish certain services, although in almost every category the Republicans have far outdistanced the Democrats. Let us turn now to the specific functions of the national party committees.

**Research.**   Political party organizations conduct research in order to provide information and analysis required by candidates and campaign managers in their efforts to influence voters. Party-generated research may be candidate/campaign directed, or it may be organization directed. Research designed specifically for use in campaigns by candidates consists of fact books, position papers, speech materials, and compilations of voting records of incumbent officeholders. These are materials intended to help candidates and campaign managers compete in election contests.

Organization-directed research is geared to the party apparatus and to officers and candidates. It consists of "how-to" manuals (e.g., "How to get out the vote," "How to purchase television time"); handbooks for campaign managers, precinct workers, and telephone canvassers; and statistical analysis of voter registration, electoral participation, and voting patterns of specific groups. These materials are for internal use in the strategic decision making of the campaign.

Both national committees have moved into data processing and computer services during the past several years. The Republicans, however, have developed a sophisticated system that not only serves the campaign and election efforts of the party but was heavily involved in the 1981 legislative redistricting efforts throughout the country. The Republican National Committee also developed REPNET, a nationwide network of computer services specifically designed to aid state party organizations that wish to tie into the system. Both committees use computers for fund raising and campaign finance accounting. The Republicans also maintain a legal services division that offers counsel to RNC staff regarding campaign finance laws, election laws, and ballot security. These services, too, are available to state Republican parties.

**Public relations.** The techniques of establishing and maintaining contacts with the voting public are the realm of public relations specialists. These activities serve as vital tools of interpretation and integration between the party organizations and the voters. Public relations experts should be both informative and persuasive—a combination of talents that explains why so many of them came originally from the field of commercial advertising. Although much of the public relations function in American politics is now performed on a contract basis by private firms, the party organizations usually have regular staff people working in a public relations capacity.

The national committees have always maintained a close alliance between public relations and research. Speeches, press releases, policy statements, and other such pronouncements are research based, but their effective use demands public relations skills. Consequently, both national committees have ordinarily maintained a small staff for this purpose. Also, from time to time the national committees have contracted with private public relations firms to carry the party's message to the public in the most effective manner. Some of the largest firms in the nation have undertaken such assignments.[6]

Another public relations function performed by national committee staff persons in the past has been the maintenance of speakers' bureaus. At some time during the campaign, many local candidates request the assignment of a "name" speaker to campaign personally for them. The Republican National Committee, for instance, maintains a list of 500 prominent speakers composed of party and administration officials. Both the DNC and the RNC have been involved in scheduling presidential appearances when their party controls the White House.

The public relations function of the national committees has only been sporadically successful, depending on the support funds available. At the present time, because of their superior funding and organization, the Republican National Committee has the most successful public relations program. Since 1980 the staff has shifted from being the primary voice of the party to being a support organization for the president. The communications division performs issue research, monitors the activities of the Democrats, and contracts with private firms for surveys of public opinion. It also operates an information retrieval system, publishes several magazines, newsletters, and other periodicals, and handles press relations. On a smaller scale the Democratic National Committee performs some of these functions, but since it represents the party out of power, it is more of a recognized party voice.

**Candidate and campaign staff training programs.**    There is no universally accepted method of training candidates to run for public office. Districts and constituents differ, and training for candidacy usually takes place during the campaign. In recent years, however, political strategists have realized that some matters can be imparted to candidates to enable them to make the best use of their resources and to assist them in avoiding the political pitfalls of increasingly complex laws. This has become particularly important in light of the post-Watergate efforts to provide legislative direction on financial disclosure, campaign contributions, and other aspects of political ethics.

Both national committees organize training programs specifically designed to assist candidates, managers, and other staff persons to understand the intricacies of election and campaign finance laws, suggest effective campaign techniques, provide issue briefings, and furnish instruction in the technicalities of campaign management. The committees have run campaign schools for congressional candidates for a number of years, but in recent years the Republican National Committee has carried political education and training to its highest form in history. In preparation for the 1980 campaign the RNC sponsored 16 regional campaign workshops for a total of 800 students recruited by regional political directors, field personnel, and staff members of state and local campaigns. For campaign managers and senior field representatives in congressional races, a Campaign Management College six-day course was provided to give participants an opportunity to study actual campaigns, learn to develop strategy, conduct survey research, raise money, and effectively use the media. Nearly 85,000 volunteers participated in 486 leadership meetings designed to identify voters and get out the vote. The Concord Group, established in 1978 by the RNC, was designed to attract young business and professional people and to train them in local campaign planning and operations. In 1980 the Concord Group trained more than 600 people through five regional workshops held in Rhode Island, Tennessee, Washington, Illinois, and Arizona.

For the 1982 off-year elections the Republicans planned 26 seminars and workshops for nearly 2,000 operatives nationwide. Forty-eight workshops and seminars were scheduled to train up to 4,000 candidates, campaign staff aides, and state and local party leaders. These included workshops in campaign management and workshops for incumbent members of Congress, finance personnel, communications and press specialists, and black and Hispanic Republicans. Obviously, all of these training programs are dependent on the successful fund-raising programs developed by the Republican National Committee since the early 1960s.[7]

**Auxiliary group activities.**    Voter groups are composed of people with similar backgrounds based on ethnicity, religion, or other common sociological or psychological determinants. Considerable data has been gathered correlating the voting behavior of groups with party support. Traditionally, at least since the 1930s, the Democratic party has had the support of most Catholics, Jews, blacks, and labor union members. Republican votes were more likely to be gathered among Protestants, farmers, business people, and the better educated. In recent years Hispanics have emerged as the fastest-growing ethnic group in America, and both political parties have sought to capitalize on the potential voting strength of these Spanish-speaking people. Furthermore, as women have taken a more active and vocal role in politics, and as specific women's issues have emerged, they too have been targeted for special consideration.

All of these groups represent voting blocs worth cultivating. Consequently, both national committees have included a variety of special-group divisions designed to develop appeals to particular group needs. These divisions have changed over the years as different groups have emerged as keys in the political process. Both committees have periodically maintained minorities divisions aimed at improving their party's percentage of the black and Hispanic vote, and both have created divisions designed to appeal to senior citizens, youth, farmers, and labor union members. During the early 1960s the Republican National Committee spent vast sums on its southern division ("Operation Dixie"), which was charged with building a Republican party in the South.[8] Both committees have supported activist women's divisions and youth divisions. Each special-group activity publishes materials designed to interest voters who are members of the group, and efforts are made to register and get out to vote those who belong to these special groups. Neither national committee has ever furnished consistent support to the activities of these special voter group divisions; however, they often show more interest during periods when they do not control the presidency.

In 1981 and 1982, for example, at meetings of the Democratic National Committee, a number of groups were scheduled to meet in one or a series of caucuses to discuss problems applicable to the groups or to their constituent voters. Thus, during the three-day semiannual national committee meetings, meetings were scheduled for the black caucus, the women's caucus, the Hispanic caucus, and the ethnic caucus. The Republicans, for their part, have developed a successful advertising campaign in ethnic and religious newspapers across the country.

**Fund raising.**   When dealing with political money, one must distinguish between political party finance and campaign finance. Party finance includes all the money necessary to keep local, state, and national party organizations and machinery operating between elections. Millions of dollars are required to keep various party headquarters open, pay permanent staff persons, and conduct the various political enterprises carried out by a modern political organization. Campaign finance, naturally, is concerned with the collection of money for campaign purposes, and is directed both to the organization and to the candidate. Candidates need money to pay for their own personal campaigns. They must be able to tap resources, both party and personal, to support the cash drain of public relations, media costs, research, travel, and communications associated with any campaign. Most of these monies come from candidate resources; some come from party-collected funds that are ordinarily distributed according to some criterion, such as the estimated chances for election.

At this point let us look briefly at the role of the national committees in raising political money. Until the 1960s the Republican National Committee was quite successful in raising operating money through what came to be known as the quota system. Each state party was assigned a quota based on a complicated formula devised to include such factors as state population, percentage of Republican votes, and personal income. Individual contributions from a particular state were credited to its quota. The system worked in approximately two-thirds of the states until a number of events transpired to undermine it, including the development of the Congressional Boosters Club to raise money for GOP congressional candidates, the impact of the Goldwater nomination's alienation of moderate Republicans, and the development of a continuing, sustaining program based on small contributions.

The Democratic National Committee was never so well organized in its fund-raising efforts. Until the early 1960s fund raising was largely a product of the individual effort of whoever was currently serving as the national finance chairperson or treasurer of the national committee. Since 1968 the DNC has been saddled with a multimillion dollar debt that it has only recently been able to pay off.

In the late 1970s and early 1980s, financial strength of the Republican party organizations has been widely noted by journalists, politicians, and political scientists. The fund-raising activities of the Republicans at the national level are carried out by three separate organizations: the national, congressional, and senatorial campaign committees. These three groups combined in 1980 to raise over $100 million, an amount partially made possible by the high degree of cooperation between them. Since the early 1960s the Republicans have pioneered a small-contributors sustaining program that raised nearly $70 million in 1980, in two million individual contributions averaging slightly less than $30 each. This direct-mail effort provides a steady flow of cash in both election and nonelection years and permits the Republicans to engage in longer-range planning and more carefully thought-out campaign strategy. The Democrats, too, have a small-contributors program, but it has not been nearly so successful.

In addition to the small-contributors sustaining program, the Republicans have also developed a number of large-contributors efforts that accounted for nearly one-third of all receipts in 1980. The success of these two efforts has made it possible for the GOP to develop their organizational strength on a secure financial base.[9] We will discuss most of the problems associated with campaign finance in more detail in chapter 6.

The advent of public funding has made it unnecessary for the national parties to raise and set aside enough money to put on their national conventions. Even so, each of them must raise money to run day-to-day political operations. Furthermore, under the 1974 campaign finance act, each national committee may raise and spend up to $3.2 million in behalf of its presidential nominee.[10]

**National convention management.**    The national nominating conventions occupy the center of power in the American parties. They represent the most visible of the party units and are responsible for nominating candidates for president and vice-president, adopting the platform, and passing party laws in the form of rules changes and resolutions. They also serve as a means of attracting national media attention and as a kickoff rally for the campaign. The Democratic National Committee has usually been more casual about convention management than the Republican. The Democrats have treated each convention as a separate entity and until recently have not attempted to maintain an ongoing staff responsible for carrying out convention responsibilities. The Republican National Committee maintains a full-time convention office presided over by a director with responsibilities that cover many aspects of management. The Republicans had the same convention director for many years, and until her recent retirement she had organized and managed every national convention, national com-

## The Republican National Committee and the 1980 Elections

The performance of the Republican National Committee in the 1980 election has attracted widespread notice and praise from political scientists and the media. Far from the traditional service and clearinghouse role usually associated with the national committees, the RNC, under the leadership of Chairman William Brock, was fully engaged in the 1980 campaign at virtually every level of the party structure. As reported by the RNC in the *1981 Chairman's Report,* these activities were impressive to those accustomed to the secondary role traditionally assigned to the national committees—a role usually restricted to support efforts for the independently run presidential campaign committee.

Finance

Raised $30,000,000 through a variety of fund-raising programs.

Provided $4,600,000 direct cash support to the Reagan–Bush campaign. Carried out a $9,400,000 national advertising campaign for Republican candidates, including a concentration of television advertising during the last 16 days of the presidential campaign.

Provided $6,200,000 direct cash support and in-kind contributions to candidates for the U.S. Senate, U.S. House of Representatives, governorships, and state legislatures.

Increased the Sustaining, Campaigner, and Life Member programs for small contributors by disseminating information, fund-raising letters, and so on to 1,200,000 contributors.

Conducted eight fund-raising seminars for state parties and candidates; split over $4,000,000 with state and local party organizations; conducted direct-mail campaigns for state and local candidates.

Increased participation in the Eagle Program of $10,000-per-year contributors to 865, the most since it was established in 1975.

Raised $4,000,000 through "Prelude-to-Victory Dinners" held on September 30, 1980, sponsored by RNC and state party organizations and addressed by Ronald Reagan, George Bush, and Gerald Ford on closed-circuit television.

Formed the PAC 40 Club, composed of representatives of the first 40 political action committees (PACs) to make an annual contribution of $5,000 or more. Members provided issue and politics briefings at monthly breakfasts.

Spent over $5.5 million to attract new contributors to the GOP through the Contributor Recruitment program. The program brought in over 400,000 new Sustaining, Campaigner, and Life Members and $7,200,200.

Computer Services

Wrote 700 computer programs, processed 130 surveys for candidates plus five national surveys, and processed over 20,000,000 names and addresses for voter registration and get-out-the-vote drives through its computer services staff.

Surveyed electoral data from 175,000 precincts and, after combining this with demographic data, provided Republican candidates with targeting information to assist them in determining the best allocation of campaign resources.

Established the computer assistance redistricting system (CARS) to analyze census data and political history and provide Republican state legislators with assistance in drawing new legislative and congressional districts following the 1980 census.    *(Continued)*

| | The Republican National Committee and the 1980 Elections, *continued* |
|---|---|
| Legal Services | Provided assistance by inside and outside counsel in furnishing RNC staff with legal opinions and other services required by federal, state, and local election laws. Made legal services available to state parties and state fund-raising efforts. Prepared a program for the state and local parties on the legal ramifications of ballot security problems. |
| Election Services | Coordinated the campaign efforts of the Reagan–Bush Campaign Committee, the National Republican Senatorial Campaign Committee, the National Republican Congressional Campaign Committee, the Republican Governor's Association, and the RNC local elections division. Worked directly with over 4,000 Republican candidates for state and local offices, including financial assistance, survey research support, and campaign staff training. |
| Publications | Published dozens of daily, weekly, monthly, and special newsletters, magazines, and reports, including: *First Monday*—a monthly that deals with issues and party personalities and is distributed to over half a million supporters, media representatives, and opinion leaders. *Commonsense—A Republican Journal of Thought and Opinion*—published quarterly as a semiprofessional journal of opinion containing articles and essays on politics, public issues, and ongoing research projects. *Promises, Promises*—a compilation of Carter Administration actions compared to Carter campaign promises. Published three times during the campaign at six-month intervals. *Democrat Watch '80*—a weekly digest of statements by Democratic candidates and party leaders. *Public Opinion Report*—published the results of major national polling organizations for weekly distribution to party and campaign leaders across the country. *County Line*—a monthly report to local party chairmen and chairwomen to keep them informed of party activities, polls, and news of interest. |

mittee meeting, and other party meeting since 1956. The convention director is also responsible for assisting the site selection committee in its quadrennial search for a city in which to hold the national nominating convention.

## Congressional and Senatorial Campaign Organizations

Although they are often overlooked, four major party committees are based on Capitol Hill: the senatorial campaign committees and the national congressional campaign committees for each party. These committees are, in every sense of the word, party organizations devoted to the "external politics" of the Congress. They are responsible for providing aid to members of Congress seeking reelection and for attempting to elect new members. They are a part of the official national party apparatus and should not be confused with the "internal" party units, which help to organize and run the House and Senate once their members have been elected (see chapter 11).

The four committees are composed entirely of members of the respective houses of Congress. The National Republican Congressional Committee, for instance, is made up of one Republican from each state that elects a member of that party. Three of the committees are housed in government buildings, and the House Republicans have space in the party's Eisenhower building adjacent to the House office buildings. The congressional campaign committees developed historically from the differences between the president and Congress during and following the midterm elections of 1866. Policy divisions between the post–Civil War Congress and President Andrew Johnson led to a four-way split in the congressional parties. All four groups held midterm congressional conventions, and after its conclave in Philadelphia the Union party mounted a nationwide campaign to strengthen its control of Congress. It was the Union party's congressional campaign committee that later became the National Republican Congressional Committee (NRCC). The Democratic Congressional Campaign Committee (DCCC) developed out of the same campaign after the incumbent Democrats organized in an effort to increase their numbers in that congressional election.

Today, the National Republican Congressional Committee has far outstripped its Democratic counterpart in the scale of its operations, its services to candidates, and its influence within the party. Several factors account for this superior position, the most important of which is that Congress was the principal center of power for the national Republicans between 1932 and 1968. The Democrats have controlled the White House for thirty-four of the last fifty years and have held a majority in both houses of Congress for all but four years during the same period. During those years of Democratic hegemony, the burden of providing opposition voices and issues fell to the Republicans in Congress, since they represented the only elected representatives of their party in Washington. A second reason for the growth in influence of the Republican House campaign committee was an outgrowth of the first. After the 1964 election debacle the National Republican Congressional Committee established a fund-raising group called the Republican Congressional Boosters Club. The boosters were organized specifically to raise money for congressional campaigns in districts where Republicans were attempting to unseat Democratic incumbents. In recent years the boosters have given way to other fund-raising techniques and programs.

The National Republican Congressional Committee also raises substantial amounts of money through direct-mail solicitation and receives large sums from political action committees (PACs). The amount of money raised by the NRCC has grown considerably in the past few years. For instance, the NRCC spent just over $1 million in the 1974 off-year election, in comparison to nearly $50 million budgeted for 1982.[11] Much of the money is used to support campaign staff and services to Republican congressional candidates. The Federal Election Commission reported that in 1980 the NRCC contributed almost $35 million to GOP candidates for the House, whereas the Democratic Congressional Committee furnished only $2 million to its candidates.[12]

The NRCC maintains a staff of forty full-time professional experts in research, public relations, campaign tactics, field services, fund raising, and all of the other areas of expertise needed by the modern political organization. Old rivalries between the Republican Congressional Committee and the Republican National Committee have been muted in recent years as the two have held weekly joint strategy meetings and have shared fund-raising and candidate support activities.

The Democratic Congressional Campaign Committee is anemic by comparison with the House Republican group. It has restricted itself, for the most part, to fund-raising ventures geared to contests within individual congressional districts. However, in 1982 the committee mailed "care packages" to its congressional candidates containing political issue papers, suggested speeches attacking the Republicans, and current economic statistics to illustrate "the Reagan recession."[13] The DCCC is short staffed and under-funded and, because Democratic majorities have remained high over the past quarter century, direct political involvement in campaigns has not seemed necessary. Recent Republican successes, however, have stimulated some action on the part of House Democrats to increase the funding and services of the DCCC to make it more competitive with its Republican counterpart.

Both of the party committees in the Senate are chiefly fund-raising organizations, usually built around dinner speeches and direct mail and not furnishing any significant level of campaign services. Most of the money raised by the Democratic Senatorial Campaign Committee (DSCC) is distributed to incumbent senators, whereas just the reverse is true of the Republican committee. The Republican Senatorial Campaign Committee spent $21 million in 1980, in comparison to $2 million for the DSCC.[14]

The congressional party organizations still remain somewhat separate from the "regular" party organization. Representatives and senators tend to run their own campaigns and raise their own money, and many of them make minimal use of the party organization. Congressional districts are unlike any others in the nation. Composed of groups of counties and pieces of counties in rural areas and wards and pieces of wards in urban areas, the congressional district seldom ever fits the established party organizational structure. Normally, no other officeholder is elected from the district except the member of Congress. Consequently, most members build their own districtwide personal organization and rely on it for their reelection effort. Clearly, this undercuts any role the regular party organizations might want to play in developing a responsible following in the Congress. It is only natural that the party leaders at the local level are more interested in races for sheriff or tax collector and that the leadership at the state level is more interested in the party's candidate for governor, attorney general, or any one of several other state constitutional officers. The congressional candidate and his or her district, therefore, do not have a natural place in the party organizational hierarchy.[15] But the same cannot be said of the state organizations; many observers and students of politics believe that the real power in American parties is at the state and local levels.

## State Party Organizations

Even though many observers consider that political party organizations are essential to the conduct of government, few ordinary citizens know much about them. This is especially true of the party organizations in the fifty states. The state parties have always been overshadowed by their national counterparts. National party leaders make national news and even occasionally appear on evening network news programs. But few people know who occupies the position of state chairperson, and state party leaders are seldom considered newsworthy. The lack of visibility associated with state party organizations arises from several factors. National events in Washington politics cast celebrities in major roles that make it more difficult for state leaders to compete for public attention. State officials in Bismarck, Boise, or Baton Rouge cannot normally gain recognition outside the boundaries of their own states for any of their accomplishments, partly because news coverage of state capital events is limited. And, in view of the fact that many of the more important political activities are hidden from public view, it is not surprising that few people understand the importance of state party organizations.

Nevertheless, in the past decade state party organizations have grown considerably, and many show signs of maturity unknown in the past. In 1956 V. O. Key, Jr., stated:

> The most apparent, and perhaps the fundamental, incapacity of state parties lies in the frequency with which the leadership corps is fractionalized and lacking in both capacity and organization for action. Some state party organizations, to be sure, have an evident vitality as well as a fairly high degree of coherence. Yet a more common situation is the almost complete absence of a functioning statewide organization.[16]

Now, a generation later, state parties are emerging from their lethargy. Certainly, some of them continue to suffer from organizational weaknesses associated with the proliferation of candidates (engendered by the long ballot), a lack of volunteer workers, financial anemia, widespread member apathy, and occasional local bossism. The greater number, however, show more vital signs than they have in their long history. More of them have full-time paid chairpersons, often assisted by professional executive directors. Most of them have permanently staffed state headquarters, usually located in the vicinity of the capitol building. Significant numbers of them have developed ongoing fund-raising programs that have permitted them to move into new and innovative technocratic methods of campaigning. The record of progress has been uneven in accomplishment and pace, but the new signs of life have encouraged those who believe in a strong party system.[17]

## Organizational Development

State political parties, as we know them today, emerged from the trauma of the Civil War period. For the most part they remained relatively stable until after World War II, when a number of hitherto one-party or modified one-party states nurtured competitive second parties. The earliest evidence of this growth and change emerged from the southern states, where Republican presidential candidates received increasingly impressive voter support during the 1940s and 1950s. Later these successes were translated into Republican gains in senators, members of Congress, and governors. In 1966 Florida and Arkansas elected their first GOP governors since Reconstruction. By 1974 every one of the southern states had elected at least one Republican member of Congress, and their successes in electing state legislators were impressive.[18] Only slightly less striking, as noted earlier, were the successes scored by Democrats in formerly solid Republican states. Traditional Republican strongholds, such as Iowa, Nebraska, Kansas, Maine, Vermont, and New Hampshire, all elected Democratic governors, and several sent Democratic senators to Washington. Obviously, where such breaches of customary voting habits occur, the result is usually greater party competition.

One effect of the growth in competitive states has been a general strengthening of organizational capabilities at the level of the party structure. Organization is most important to party building. Many practitioners of politics believe that it is the most important single undertaking for state parties. Strong organization provides the capability for fund raising, service, research, public relations, recruitment, and special projects, such as get-out-the-vote drives. Clearly, a strong, well-organized state party does not guarantee that all of these things will be done, but it offers a better chance that they will be.

A party leader, such as a state chairperson, has four intraparty responsibilities, all more or less dependent on the existence of an effective organizational structure. *First,* the state party leader must maintain a working relationship with the local or grass-roots units of the organization. Many authorities think that the real strength of American parties lies at the county level. Usually the state organization is the only viable vehicle through which county organizations can be fashioned into an effective political unit. By its very nature, American politics generates natural tensions between elected officials and party leaders at various levels. Each group represents different constituencies, and both compete for money and workers, but neither can command loyalty or cooperation from the other. One of the many phenomena of the past two decades has been the intensified efforts of state party leaders to bring the local party leadership into a closer relationship with the state organization. These efforts have required the skills of a political impresario because much rivalry and jealousy exists within the levels of the party cadre.

A *second* intraparty responsibility of the state party leaders is to maintain an effective working relationship with their central committee, the elected governing body of the state party. These governing bodies are elected in a variety of ways. They are either chosen within the party under party rules, or they are selected under whatever statutory law the legislature has seen fit to pass (see "A Sampling of Legal Definitions of State Central Committees," page 77). These central committees may be made up of ex officio members serving by virtue of their election to some lower party post, or they may be elected by party primary, caucus, or convention. They range in size from small bodies representing congressional or other electoral districts to groups with several hundred members selected to represent a wide variety of party units. The state chairpersons must decide just how they will use the central committee or, depending on their own particular role in the party, whether they are to be used by the committee.[19] That, in turn, depends to a great extent on the quality of their leadership and on whether the party controls the governorship.

*Third,* a relatively new undertaking for most of the parties has been to serve as a source of substantive and political aid to elected officeholders, particularly those in the state legislature. To some extent this represents a lobbying role for the party leadership. These party leaders often are responsible for selling the programmatic or policy goals of the party. If the party holds the governorship, these policies may simply represent the governor's program. If not, the party may be pushing its own platform in an effort to get it adopted as law.

A *fourth* responsibility of the state leadership is to maintain the state headquarters. Parties, like any large organization, require an administrative structure to accomplish the goals that are set out for them. People must be hired, funds raised, candidates recruited, policies developed, and services performed. Each of these responsibilities requires space and staff resources. In recent years the rapid growth of competitive politics in more and more states and the simultaneous growth of technocratic innovations in management and campaigning have brought the various functions of the state headquarters to the fore.

Obviously, not all political parties perform all political functions equally well. Indeed, on account of the great variety of party systems in the states, some do not perform any of them at all. Nevertheless, the rapid growth in party headquarters and the development of additional service functions have signaled the willingness of many party leaders to invest the resources necessary to enhance the value of the political party operations in the states.

---

## A Sampling of Legal Definitions of State Central Committees

**16–233.**

The state committee of each party shall consist, in addition to the chairman of the several county committees, of one member of the county committee for each four hundred votes or major fraction thereof cast for the party's nominee for governor or for presidential electors for the nominee of the party for president at the last preceding general election. The state committeemen shall be chosen at the first meeting of the county committee from the committee's elected membership.

**Arizona Revised Statutes, 1977**

**1–14–108 (2)(a)**

The state central committee shall be constituted of the chairman and vice-chairman of the several county committees, together with the elected United States senators, representatives in congress, governor, lieutenant governor, secretary of state, state treasurer, attorney general, members of the board of regents, members of the state board of education, state senators, state representatives, and such additional members as provided for by the state central committee bylaws. Two additional members shall be allowed the political party from each county that polled ten thousand votes at the last preceding general election for its candidate for governor or president of the United States. Two additional members shall be allowed for each additional ten thousand votes or major portion thereof so polled in such county. The additional members shall be elected by the county central committee of the political party.

**The Election Laws of the State of Colorado, 1978**

**8660.**

The Democratic state central committee shall consist of:
a. All delegates to the state convention.
b. The chairman of each county central committee of the party.
c. Members appointed pursuant to this part.
d. The national committeeman and national committeewoman of the party.
e. Any person elected to fill a vacancy in the State Legislature in a special election.
f. The immediate past chairman and the immediate past northern and southern section chairmen.

**Deering's California Code, 1977**

**2–102**

The members of the state committee of each party shall be elected from units of representation as the state committee shall by rule provide. The number of members representing each unit may vary, but each member shall be entitled to an equal vote within his unit. Each member of the state committee shall be entitled to cast one vote unless the rules of the party shall provide otherwise.

**State of New York, 1977–1978**
**Election Law**

## State Party Leadership

The two major parties each have a state central committee and a state chairperson in all of the fifty states. The central committees are elected in a variety of ways, and their composition differs from state to state (see "A Sampling of Legal Definitions of State Central Committees," page 77). Some have hundreds of members; others are composed of a small group of men and women who may or may not be powerful figures in inner party circles. Each of them elects or ratifies a person to serve as chairperson of the party.

Political party chairpersons are normally discussed in the context of whether their political party is in or out of power. At the national level that is probably an accurate method of considering the roles of the office, in view of the fact that it is so closely tied to the presidency. As noted by Cotter and Hennessy, "How the national chairmen play their roles will be determined, in large part, by the presence or absence of a political superior in the White House."[20] For the in-party there is no ambiguity of leadership, and the chairperson does as he or she is told. The out-party leader, in contrast, gains recognition by virtue of his or her position but may not exercise control simply by possessing the office of chairperson. Even a national chairperson must compete with other party leaders in Congress, among former presidential candidates, and within the ranks of his or her party's governors. At the state party level, however, the definition of the chairperson's role is more complex.

State party chairpersons play three distinct roles. First, some are *political agents* who serve as a partisan arm of an incumbent governor. Political agents bear organizational responsibilities and serve as managers of the party, but their power derives from the governor who selected them. These chairpersons seldom exercise real control over the party, deferring instead to the governor. Often they have attained their position in spite of the fact that they do not have a large personal following in the party. Many of them served as campaign managers to the governor and have undertaken to supervise his or her political operations from their position as chairperson. Many of them do not rate the party leadership role very high on their list of party responsibilities.

One chairman who serves as an agent of the governor described his role in this way:

> I was his [the governor's] campaign manager and have been a lifelong friend. When we won, he asked me to be state chairman in order to have a trusted colleague in the office to keep control over the party. I am really the governor's agent to the party, and whatever power I have comes from our control of the governor's office. He really acts as party leader, and I am his liaison with the county chairmen and the city leaders. I take the flak when the party people don't like what he is doing.[21]

Political agents occupy a peculiar and often self-effacing role. At times they are totally overshadowed by the governor and operate in obscurity behind the scenes. Other political agents, however, are in the forefront of the political battles, leading the fight for the governor and deflecting some of the partisan sniping.

The second type of chairperson might be called the *in-party independent*. Such an individual serves the party that controls the governor's office but does so as a legitimately elected leader who achieved office without the assistance of the incumbent governor. At times this type of chairperson was the choice of a defeated candidate for governor and merely retained his or her position after the election. Others occupy places of party power in their own right and campaigned for and won the office of chairperson on their own. Sometimes the chairperson has a fixed term that antedates that of the governor. States with long traditions of party independence often have chairpersons who operate independently of a governor in their own party. Connecticut's Democratic chairman John Bailey was first elected to the post in 1946 and served until his death in 1975. He took a leading part in the election of four Democratic governors, each of whom supported his reelection as chairman. He also retained the office during periods of Republican control. In view of the fact that the average tenure of state chairpersons is a remarkably short two and one-half to three years, Bailey was obviously an exception. But, even so, he represented perfectly the type of chairperson who serves as in-party independent.

One midwestern chairman of this kind has described his role as follows:

> In ——— we think it is a mistake to tie the chairmanship and the governor's office too closely together. The party will never be able to function in the way it was meant to unless it is independent. We maintain our independence by electing the governor in different years from the chairman. So the chairman is always already in office when a governor takes office. I guess a governor could pressure a chairman to resign, but it would be a heck of a fight and probably not worth the effort. Most of our governors in both parties consider the party organization to be a tool, and they leave us alone.

Finally, the third type of party chairperson is the *out-party independent*. These chairpersons preside over party organizations that do not control the governor's office. They are normally elected from a personal power base or are the personal choice of a defeated candidate for governor and have continued in office as the out-party leader. Obviously, most of the southern Republican parties are led by out-party independents. But such chairpersons do not exist only in one-party and modified one-party states. They are also in office in strong two-party competitive systems. They, in effect, serve as the real party leader when the party has failed to win the governorship or, at times, any other office. Some parties have difficulty finding men and women to become chairpersons when the party is out of power. In other parties members engage in strategic infighting to gain election to the office of chairperson. One of the out-party independents described his relationship to the party in this way:

> I seem to have emerged as the key man in the party. We lost the governorship two years ago and we only have one other statewide office under our control, and the man who holds it is not really interested in the party. We do have a United States Senator, but he has his own separate campaign organization and leaves us alone. So I am the spokesman for the party, negotiate with the legislature, try to build up local organizations, and recruit candidates. The worst part is fund raising, but if we can lick that we should be able to recapture the governorship two years from now.

Each chairperson approaches his or her office within the boundaries laid down by party law, party tradition, and party history. Control of the governorship, however, is the key to the style in which chairpersons carry out their duties and to the degree of power they exercise. Political agents wield power on behalf of an incumbent governor, consequently building power for themselves. In-party independents are often viewed as the "organizational" leader, while the governor is looked on as the "political" leader. And, finally, the out-party independent is usually recognized as the real party leader and is usually powerful in his or her own right.

## Legal Structure of State Parties

Political parties in the United States developed without the aid of the state, but they are governed and even defined by laws adopted by the state (see "A Sampling of Legal Definitions of State Political Parties," page 80). Most states provide by law for a formal

## A Sampling of Legal Definitions of State Political Parties

7–2.

A political party, which at the general election for State and County officers then next preceding a primary, polled more than 5 per cent of the entire vote cast in the State, is hereby declared to be a political party within the State, and shall nominate all candidates provided for in this Article ... under the provisions hereof, and shall elect precinct, township, ward and State central committeemen as herein provided.

**Illinois Election Laws, 1978**

441

A political party shall be recognized in this state if one of its candidates for presidential elector received at least five percent of the votes cast in this state for presidential electors in the last presidential election, or if at least five percent of the registered voters in the state are registered as being affiliated with the political party. A party which receives more than five percent but less than ten percent of the votes cast in the last presidential election shall not be entitled to representation on a parish board of election supervisors.

**Louisiana Election Code, 1977**

120.140.

Definitions.

1. The term "political party" shall mean any "established political party" and shall also mean any group which shall hereafter undertake to form an established political party, provided that no political organization or group shall be qualified as a political party, or given a place on a ballot, which organization or group advocates the overthrow by violence of the established constitutional form of government of the United States or the state of Missouri.

2. An "established political party" is hereby declared to be a political party which, as to the state, at the last general election for state and county officers, polled for its candidate for governor more than two percent of the entire vote cast for governor in the state; and, as to any district or political subdivision of the state, a political party which polled more than two percent of the entire vote cast in such district or political subdivision at such election.

**Election Laws of the State of Missouri,**
**1973–1974**

structural framework for the political parties and describe, sometimes in great detail, the powers that can be exercised by party officials. These laws vary widely. Some are so minimal as to be almost nonexistent; others are hundreds of pages long. The election laws of the state of California, for instance, are bound in two volumes containing almost fourteen hundred pages, over half of which deal with parties and campaigns. Other states have only a few election law provisions that apply directly to parties.

We have noted before that the American party system is not truly pyramidal. It could more accurately be described as resembling a layer cake, with each layer exercising considerable autonomy over its own affairs. The state party layer is always positioned midway between the national and local party layers, but that strategic location does not carry with it the power necessary to capitalize on the position.

The problem, of course, lies in our federal system with its divided powers and responsibilities. The political parties, having evolved in an unplanned fashion over a period of years, were simply superimposed on the existing federal structure. At no time were party leaders furnished with the basic power that would permit them to command support from subordinates or allegiance from party members. The party leaders have always had to accomplish their goals by persuasion and compromise. Like the government itself, the parties are federal, each representing only one foundation stone in the national political structure. Yet, unlike the national and state governments, parties have no constitution to provide a division of powers and responsibilities; nor do they have a supreme court to decide which party can do what to whom, or how.

Some political organizations operate outside the normal party channels and are dominated by an individual leader who maintains personal control over the apparatus. For years the late Mayor Richard J. Daley controlled the Illinois Democratic party through his domination over the city of Chicago and Cook County. Other parties in other states are also sometimes dominated by a single politician, and the organization works within the shadow of the man. The New York Republicans under the late Nelson Rockefeller and the Massachusetts Democrats under Edward Kennedy are examples of this phenomenon. In Arkansas the revived Republican party of the 1960s was unable to survive the defeat of its creator and benefactor, the late Gov. Winthrop Rockefeller.

In some other states, weakened party structures have permitted extralegal party groups to play an expanding role in politics. The historical weaknesses of political parties in California paved the way for the emergence of three important extraparty groups—the California Republican Assembly, the United Republicans of California, and the California Democratic clubs. In the same vein, the New York Democratic reform movement has occupied an important place in the recent history of that party, although its influence has diminished in the last few years. Although strong personalities and extraparty political groups occasionally have an important impact on state politics, it is more important, for our purposes, to describe the normal state political party organizations as they exist today.

## Strengthening State Party Organizations

Each of the two parties has a state party organization in each of the fifty states, complete with officers, bylaws, and, in most cases, headquarters. Each organization is headed by a state chairperson and one or more vice-chairpersons. These top officers are chosen in a variety of ways but are generally elected by the state central committee or some auxiliary thereof. Most of the state committee members have few responsibilities in their parties, meeting periodically to ratify those actions that have been taken by the state chairperson or the governor. In some states, though, the state party organizations have traditionally relied on the support of committee members and have assigned them regular responsibilities.

Political scientists have found it difficult in the past to study state parties on a comparative basis because of their widespread geographical distribution, their failure to maintain and retain usable records, and the rapid changes in fortune that beset them as they go through the repetitive electoral process. In the past few years, however, a number of studies have been conducted that have begun to build a substantial comparative literature on state party organizations and operations.[22] Many political scientists and practitioners believe that a strong state party organization is dependent on a strong party headquarters operation. Strong organizations offer the capability for systematic fund raising, professional research, day-to-day public relations, candidate recruitment programs, and increased modern campaign services. These capabilities are important in other ways. They offer the party organization an opportunity to compete with the outside consulting firms that have been increasing their role in political campaigns in recent years, and they establish a presence for the party. Obviously, no amount of organizational capability can guarantee victory on election day, but a strong state party organization with effective leaders can offer a better chance for success.

Scholars have disagreed on which organizational attributes constitute the formula for political success. It has been suggested, however, that three attributes are important to party strength and may contribute to electoral success: maintenance of a permanent headquarters; a regular fund-raising program that provides a steady source of funds for operations and campaigns; and the services of a professional staff.

- In 1960 only half of the state party organizations had a permanent headquarters. Today, only five do not maintain a headquarters on a regular basis. Most headquarters are located in the state capital, with easy access to the centers of state government. Some are not very well funded and are understaffed, but their mere existence demonstrates a recognition of the importance of having a permanent, staffed headquarters operation if the party is to maintain its rightful place in the political arena.

- A large majority of the state party headquarters are staffed by a full-time paid executive director, and over 90 percent of them are run on a day-to-day basis by either an executive director or a full-time paid chairperson. Again, this represents a major improvement over the 1960s, when only 63 percent of the state organizations had a full-time officer in charge. The principal problem of staffing is the difficulty posed by the relatively short tenure of state chairpersons. The state chairpersons who have served during the past thirty years have averaged a little over two years in the job, and each change of party leader brings with it some change in staff. Obviously, this poses a problem of continuity and probably has a deleterious effect on the organizational programs. At the present time state headquarters staffs average about seven persons, but 25 percent have ten or more. Not much staff specialization exists, but many parties do have a research director and a full-time staff person in charge of ongoing fund-raising activities.

- A regular source of operating funds is probably the most important ingredient in the maintenance of a state headquarters. In addition to the traditional sources of such money, such as fund-raising dinners, many state parties, following the lead established by the Republican National Committee in the early 1960s, have moved into computer-based small-contributors programs, large-contributors clubs, and telethons. In a few states the political parties still get money from patronage programs, although the rise of civil service and merit systems has cut deeply into that source of revenue. A few states, notably Indiana, give a portion of the revenue from each car license sold to the political parties. However, the newest source of party funds is the growth of state public funding programs. In 1982 seventeen states had some kind of public funding for political campaigns, half channeled through the party organization and half provided directly to the candidates. Most of the money was raised through some version of an income tax checkoff (see chapter 6). One study found that the fifty-three state party organizations sampled had an average annual budget of $340,000, with budgets ranging from $14,000 to $2,500,000. This figure represents a dramatic increase since 1960, when the average state party budget was less than $190,000.

The purpose of the state headquarters, the staff, and the regularized fund raising is to allow the party organization in the states to offer services to their candidates. The activities carried out by the state party headquarters are of two types: organization building and assistance to candidates. Organization building includes services provided by the party for the general good of the party, such as fund raising, development of issues, public relations, opinion polling, and electoral mobilization. Campaign services to candidates include media assistance and advertising, advice on compliance with election and campaign finance laws, training seminars, voter registration and get-out-the-vote drives, and distribution of literature. About 50 percent of the state parties offer some combination of these services.

Having reviewed this organizational progress, what has been the effect on the strength of the state party system? Bibby, Cotter, Gibson, and Huckshorn have developed an index of party organizational strength for the state parties using organizational and programmatic characteristics to assign each state party a score. This measure of party institutionalization demonstrates important differences in the strength of the two parties at the state level. The Republicans have a decided organizational advantage (see table 3-1), with thirty-five of the forty-five (78 percent) falling into the moderately strong or strong classifications, whereas thirty-two of forty-five Democratic parties (71 percent) fall into the moderately weak or weak categories.[23] Both parties were strongest at the state level in the Midwest. The next-strongest Republican parties were in the South, the third-strongest in the West, and the weakest in the East. The Democrats, in contrast, had their second-strongest parties in the West, the third strongest in the East and the weakest in the South. The mean index of institutionalization suggested to the researchers that the state party organizations have become more institutionalized since 1960—not less institutionalized, as some of those who foresee the demise of parties have argued.[24]

TABLE 3–1   Organizational strength of state parties, 1975–1980

| Organizational strength | Number of state parties Republican | Democratic | Total |
|---|---|---|---|
| Strong | 8 | 2 | 10 |
| Moderately strong | 27 | 11 | 38 |
| Moderately weak | 9 | 26 | 35 |
| Weak | 1 | 6 | 7 |
| Total | 45 | 45 | 90[a] |

[a]Data were available for 90 of the 100 state parties.

Source: From John F. Bibby, Cornelius P. Cotter, James L. Gibson, and Robert J. Huckshorn, "Parties in State Politics," in Virginia Gray, Herbert Jacob, and Kenneth N. Vines, eds., *Politics in the American States: A Comparative Analysis,* 4th ed., p. 83. Copyright ©1983 by John F. Bibby, Cornelius P. Cotter, James L. Gibson, and Robert Huckshorn. Reprinted by permission.

## Local Party Organizations

The folklore of politics has commonly ascribed certain roles to local party leaders that, in fact, are not often performed. Local party systems are spiderwebs of interlocking districts and committees ranging from precincts to counties and usually meshing with constituent districts from which candidates are elected. Throughout most of the country, the lowest-ranking (but by no means the least-important) party officer is the precinct leader. In many of the large cities the chief party officer is the ward committeeman or committeewoman, who usually appoints the precinct leaders—often called captains to distinguish them from precinct committee members. The highest level of local party organizations is the county committee, composed of committee members and a county chairperson. Some of them are powerful and effective—they truly make the party machine move. Many, however, do little in behalf of their party, and their inactivity is a testament to the problems of local party organizations.

## Precinct Organizations

In *The Great Game of Politics,* a classic early work on political parties written by newspaperman Frank R. Kent in 1923, the precinct committeeman (and they were all men in those days) was described in this way:

> While he is the smallest, he is also, by long odds, the most vital. . . . He is the bone and sinew of the machine. He is its foundation and the real source of its strength. If he does not function, the machine decays. If he quits, the machine dies. He is the actual connecting link between the people and the organizations, and he is the only connecting link—the only man in the machine who has any point of direct contact with the voters, who knows anything about them, who has any real influence with them. All that the boss has in the way of power comes from the precinct executives. All that the machine has in the way of substance and solidity, he gives it. Without him there is no machine. He is the indispensable cog in the wheel.[25]

Although writing in an era of big-city machine politics, Kent clearly recognized that votes are the principal commodity in which the political parties deal. Even today, in an ideal, strong local party apparatus, the precinct leader is responsible for making sure the voters are registered, that they get to the polls, and that they vote for the party's candidates. He or she distributes literature, organizes telephone banks, sees that mailings go out, and attempts to woo independents and members of the opposition party. Each of these responsibilities is an *external* function—external in the sense that the goal is to reach out to people who are important to the party's success on election day but are not a part of the cadre who run the party day to day. The precinct leader also has *internal* roles, which include the raising of campaign funds, the recruiting of candidates, the care and maintenance of the organization, and, sometimes even the clearing of patronage appointments. Obviously, these roles are important only if the precinct is a part of an effective operating party organization.

Kent would be astounded at how few of the precincts live up to the model in today's political parties. The men and women who hold these positions no longer can gain support in votes in exchange for coal to warm the voters and food to feed them. Few precinct leaders, outside of a small number of highly structured machines in a few big cities, fit that romantic nineteenth-century image. Today's precinct leaders are more likely to have little organization, no patronage, and few favors. They do well just to keep their voter lists up to date and to maintain a minimum degree of contact with the people in the precinct. Nevertheless, strong and effective local organizations remain the goal for many state and local party officials.

Precinct leaders are elected in one of two ways: by vote of the party members in locally held caucuses or by vote of the party members in primary elections. The vast majority are chosen by the latter method. On occasion, contests between party factions produce campaigns that attract considerable attention and create a great deal of excitement within the party. More often, however, the election of precinct leaders is a pro forma exercise that attracts little attention and produces few fireworks. In many cases the leaders are elected without opposition. In others no one is elected at all.

Many positions in local party organizations remain vacant year after year. In the early 1960s, for instance, one study by William Crotty found that only one-third of the North Carolina counties had full complements of precinct officers in the minority Republican party, whereas three-quarters of the Democratic positions were filled.[26] Another study by Paul A. Beck, using data collected by the Survey Research Center at the University of Michigan, found that one-half of the county chairpersons sampled reported that 90 percent or more of the precincts in their counties had leaders.[27] Gibson and associates, using a larger sample, found a comparable figure of 90 percent with leaders in the late 1970s.[28] Both studies also found that about one-half of the precinct leaders were rated as "effective" by the county chairpersons surveyed.

The minority party in any given area finds it particularly difficult to recruit qualified and energetic people to run for precinct office. There are few rewards for much hard work, and every election constitutes a new disappointment. Yet, without an active and competing local party organization, the minority has little chance of becoming a majority.

## Intermediate-Level Party Organizations

In most big cities an intermediate level of party organization operates midway between the precincts and the counties. Although these intermediate bodies vary from city to city (and even from one area to an adjacent area), they usually follow a pattern of combining numerous precincts into a ward organization. Sometimes the wards are the principal unit of organization in a borough or county. The duties of a ward leader are about the same as those of a precinct leader, only on a grander scale. Some, like the leaders of the county (borough) party organizations in New York City, are people of eminent power. They still perform old-fashioned constituent services, for which they hope to collect payment in the currency of voter support.

In 1970 the *New York Times* described the voter-related activities of James V. Mangano, one of the forty-six Brooklyn Democratic leaders. In one week, Mangano arranged for an Army private to be brought home from Vietnam to visit his ailing mother, secured school crossing guards for a parochial school, managed an interdepartmental transfer of an employee in a private business, and arranged for a retarded child to be admitted to a specialized school. He acknowledged his hope that constituent satisfaction would be translated into votes for Democrats on election day.[29]

Each ward or borough organization even within the same city may differ in structure and political activities. In the Bronx, next door to Mangano's Brooklyn, over thirty-seven hundred local committee members are elected. They, in turn, elect district leaders for each assembly (legislative) district, and the district leaders in their turn elect the county leaders. In recent years several Democratic borough leaders have been defeated for reelection in the party conventions because they backed the wrong candidate for higher office, because the level of services within the district had declined, or because the performance at the polls had not measured up. Each party organization in each of the five boroughs is different. Furthermore, what is true of New York City may be completely at variance with systems in other large cities.

## County Party Organizations

Many political scientists believe that the county party organization is the most important in our political system. Yet not much comparative research has been done on county party systems. Scholars have concentrated instead on studies of individual county leaders or of county systems in small regions or areas that do not constitute a good sample. The disparity of these studies makes it difficult to generalize from them. At the county level, however, it is clear that the key individual is the county chairperson. As we have seen, in the big cities the county leader may be a person of substantial political power operating a voter service center. In other cities the key to political influence may rest in the city organization controlled by the mayor or some other influential officeholder.

In rural counties, particularly in the Midwest and the South, the party chairperson is usually intimately tied to courthouse politics. Party efforts are often directed to county offices, such as sheriff, property appraiser, tax collector, or superintendent of schools. Rural party leaders are in a position to personalize politics to a considerable extent, and rewards and punishments have a greater and more obvious impact on party affairs. An active party leader keeps in close touch with the officeholders, who represent visible evidence of success. Many party leaders work diligently to build precinct organizations and to see that the leadership positions at that level are filled. Nevertheless, as we have seen, many precinct positions are vacant, and in many areas of the country the county and the precinct organizations are virtually moribund.

In many states the county party leader is the representative of the local party to district and state committees. In some states he or she serves as an automatic delegate to state conventions. In many states the county organizations are so closely intertwined with those at the state level that one cannot be discussed separately from the other. Strong state parties are built on a base of strong county and precinct organizations.

Recent research has demonstrated that county committees engage in two general types of activities. As one might expect, the first focuses on campaign assistance, including working with candidate organizations. One recent study found that over three-fourths of the county committees are involved with the distribution of campaign literature, and about two-thirds are active in fund raising and the distribution of campaign money. About the same number are engaged in using advertising, running telephone banks, organizing meetings and rallies, and dealing with the media. With a few exceptions both parties at the county level perform approximately the same kinds of services. The second type of activity engaged in by the county committees is organizational, such as scheduling regular meetings, budgeting, and building a strong organization between elections.

Both parties are almost equal in strength at the county level, and both share the same levels of strength by region: strongest in the East, second-strongest in the West, next-strongest in the Midwest, and weakest in the South. They also share another characteristic: their strongest county organizations are in the more populous areas.

Recent evidence does not indicate that the county committees are declining in strength. In fact, 58 percent of the Republican and 50 percent of the Democratic chairpersons said that their county organizations were stronger now than they were a decade ago.[30]

Many county parties are quite active in election campaigns. One study of a national sample of county parties found that they could be divided, according to their campaign activities, into two types. First were what might be termed *persuasion* parties: their goal was to persuade voters who normally would not be considered party loyalists or who remained unconvinced. The second type might be called *mobilization* parties, which concentrated on mobilizing voters already known to support the party. Those that emphasized persuasion were more apt to use television to build voter support, whereas those that sought to mobilize party adherents used traditional methods to get them to register and to get them to the polls. Republican county parties in both the North and the South tended to stress mobilization of known supporters in competitive counties; even when Republicans were in a minority in the North, they also emphasized mobilization. Mobilization of supporters in the Democratic party did not vary between the North and the South or according to the competition level. Persuasion in both parties increased in rural and predominantly Republican areas in the North but in the South was not related to either competition or population characteristics.[31]

It is very difficult to generalize about local party organizations in the United States. Few of them meet the demands imposed on them by textbook definitions. Local party groups not only differ from place to place, but the same organization may also vary from time to time. In some areas the precincts and counties may be quite close to the ideal as reflected in definitions of party activities. The local leaders may recruit candidates, groom them for office, help them get nominated, aid them in campaigning, raise money for them, and do all the other things that we normally think of as meeting the demands of the ideal political organizations. Most local party units, however, cannot meet all of those responsibilities.

Often the local party organization is merely a collection of elected officers (who may or may not have followers) and allied interest groups or a floating collection of individuals who coalesce during every election season around the candidacy of a particular individual. In the next election these same people will regroup around another candidate. These candidate-oriented groups may be made up of individual activists, or they may represent organized satellite groups outside the party structure. They may be ideologically based (liberal or conservative), lifestyle based (e.g., residents of condominiums), issue based (e.g., environmentalists), or candidate based. In some areas they may constitute the only political organization.

## Shifting Power Relationships Among Party Levels

We have previously noted that decentralization has been one of the most consistent and pervasive characteristics of American political parties. Historically, the national party organizations have not been able to exercise control over those party units located at subnational levels. Since responsibility and authority were not readily placed, the state and local party units have often gone their own way, paying little heed to the wishes of national party leaders or groups. In America the need for organizational unity and the desire for political purity have always run aground on the shoals of the competing need for winning office. Party organization has been viewed quite simply as an adjunct to vote seeking and electoral success. Admittedly, this has not been the case only in the United States. Almost all parties in the Western democracies have tied their *organizational* structure to their national election structure. For each level of offices in the governmental pyramid there has been a corresponding level of party agencies in the political pyramid. The result, of course, has been that the political parties maintain both national and subnational organizations, and the different levels are often in conflict over nominating procedures, party rules, the allocation of funds, and the formulation of policies.

Traditionally, national party officers have had no way of imposing their will (assuming that to be desirable) on those occupying positions in the subnational party offices. They have been required to resort to pleading, cajoling, and threats in order to encourage cooperation on party matters they considered to be important. The leadership of both parties has often expressed frustration at the immovability of their brethren at the state and local levels.

In recent years there has been increasing indication, particularly in the Democratic party, that the national party committees may be establishing more substantial control over the state and local parties. As is often the case with organizational change, the evidence has mounted slowly, and the apparent shift has been evolutionary in nature. After the 1952 election the Democratic National Committee declared a member's seat vacant after he elected to support the Republican candidate for president. In 1958 a move to force the resignation of a member of the national committee because he was "soft" on questions of racial segregation failed when the committee refused to accept the removal and to approve the member elected in his place. In both instances the states involved were southern, and the national committee's actions represented the first time in many years that any national party agency had successfully imposed its will on state party units.[32]

At the 1968 Democratic National Convention the "regular" Mississippi delegation was denied seats, and a substitute delegation composed of "loyal" Democrats was seated. This represented a natural follow-up to the party's efforts to prevent southern delegations from bolting the convention as they had in 1948. That same convention was responsible for the resolutions that led to the establishment of the McGovern-Fraser Commission on Party Structure and Delegate Selection as well as the O'Hara Commission on Convention Rules. These commissions were mandated by the 1968 national convention, appointed by the national chairperson, and supported by the national committee. The recommendations of the two commissions were, for the most part, accepted and became a part of party law. The guidelines recommended by the McGovern-Fraser commission were approved by the national committee and forced most of the state parties to make radical changes in their rules and operating procedures. The result was a reaffirmation of the power of the national committee to exercise control over the procedures used in the states to select national convention delegates. The O'Hara commission was successful in effecting changes in convention procedures and operations and had the support of appropriate national party agencies in seeing that they were carried out. Together, the work of the two commissions represented a significant shift in power to the national party organization.

After the 1972 convention, the Democrats undertook a new series of reforms that further enhanced the power of the national party. A Conference on Party Organization and Policy, euphemistically called a miniconvention, was held in 1974 and adopted a new charter for the Democratic party. The charter, another first in American politics, further strengthened the position of the national committee and the national chair-person. The new constitution created a "new" national committee composed of members distributed in such a way that the most solidly Democratic states hold the balance of power (see figure 3–2). Such redistribution, in effect, gives control of the committee to the more reform-minded elements in the party.[33]

In order to prepare for the 1980 national convention, the Democratic National Committee created a new Commission on Presidential Nomination and Party Structure headed by Michigan state party chairman Morley A. Winograd. The Winograd commission report and recommendations, with a few exceptions, were adopted by the national committee in June 1978.

The latest of the Democratic reform groups, the Commission on Presidential Nominations chaired by Gov. James B. Hunt, Jr., of North Carolina, reported its recommendations in mid-1982 and successfully steered them through the Democratic National Committee later that year. The recommendations were designed to bring more politicians back into the national convention selection process and to impose a few additional restrictions on the activities of the state parties in delegate selection. These various Democratic party reform efforts are reviewed in chapter 4, since they have had a decisive impact on presidential politics.

Republicans have not been idle during this reform period. They too reformed convention delegate selection after the Committee on Delegates and Organization (the DO committee) made recommendations in 1970–1971. The 1972 convention adopted almost all of the recommendations and implemented them as part of the delegate selection process for 1976. The recommendations were directed toward the same goals as the McGovern-Fraser guidelines but did not carry the same level of implementing sanctions to be applied by the national committee.

All of these changes have brought more power to the national party levels. Furthermore, in the case of the Democrats, the reforms have been imbedded in party law so that they would appear to be lasting. The Republicans have not gone so far, but it is much more difficult for the party controlling the presidency to accomplish change, and the Republicans occupied the White House all during this reform, through 1976. One of the first acts of the newly elected Republican national chairman, former U.S. senator William Brock, after taking office in January 1977, was to announce his intention to work toward training a corps of one hundred professional political organizers who could help to "whip state party operations" into shape. He conceded that some state party leaders would consider the proposal an intrusion into their affairs but expressed confidence that they could be persuaded to take part.[34]

The Watergate burglars focused public attention on the national party organizations. Other events, however, have usually been responsible for leading the parties to actually reform themselves. It is doubtful that the Democrats would have undertaken such reforms had it not been for the events at the Chicago convention in 1968. The trauma of that violent week left indelible marks on the party and caused some leaders to view the organization with an eye for change. The massive election loss of 1972 forced the Democratic National Committee to recognize the need for new directions and gave impetus to those who wanted change. Republicans, too, have undergone other periods of political trauma besides Watergate. The 1964 presidential loss was so sweeping that party leaders were forced to lay aside party-splitting ideological battles in order to rebuild—and, indeed, possibly to survive. The 1960s and 1970s have constituted a truly remarkable period in American political history. More structural reform has occurred than at any other time since the early part of this century. Many of the reforms of both periods have been directed at the nomination process—the subject of chapter 4.

## Notes

1. *Democratic Party Charter,* art. 3, sec. 2, adopted in Kansas City, Mo., December 8, 1974.
2. John F. Bibby and Robert J. Huckshorn, "Out-Party Strategy: Republican National Committee Rebuilding Politics, 1964–1966," in *Republican Politics: The 1964 Campaign and Its Aftermath,* eds. Bernard C. Cosman and Robert J. Huckshorn (New York: Praeger, 1968), pp. 117–123.
3. *Congressional Quarterly Weekly Report,* "Brock chosen to lead rebuilding of GOP" (January 22, 1977): 142–144.
4. Cornelius P. Cotter and Bernard C. Hennessy, *Politics Without Power: The National Party Committees* (New York: Atherton Press, 1964), p. 63.
5. For a more complete description of Republican National Committee activities under Chairman Brock, see John F. Bibby, "Political Parties and Federalism: The Republican National Committee Involvement in Gubernatorial and Legislative Elections," *Publius* (Fall–Winter 1979): 229–236; and Robert J. Huckshorn and John F. Bibby, "State Parties in an Era of Political Change," in *The Future of American Political Parties,* ed. Joel L. Fleishman (New York: American Assembly, 1982), pp. 70–100.
6. See John S. Saloma III and Frederick H. Sontag, *Parties: The Real Opportunity for Effective Citizen Politics* (New York: Knopf, 1972), ch. 9; Larry J. Sabato, *The Rise of Political Consultants* (New York: Basic Books, 1982); "Professional Managers, Consultants Play Major Role in 1970 Political Races," *National Journal* (September 26, 1970): 2077–2087.
7. Republican National Committee, *1981 Chairman's Report* (Washington, D.C.: Republican National Committee, 1981).
8. Cotter and Hennessy, *Politics Without Power,* pp. 162–164; also see Robert J. Huckshorn and Robert C. Spencer, *The Politics of Defeat: Campaigning for Congress* (Amherst: University of Massachusetts Press, 1971), p. 175.
9. See F. Christopher Arterton, "Political Money and Party Strength," in *The Future of American Political Parties,* ed. Joel L. Fleishman.
10. Federal Election Campaign Act Amendments of 1974 (88 stat. 1263).
11. *New York Times,* "Parties stayed with national roles" (May 4, 1982): 14.
12. Federal Election Commission press release, February 21, 1982.
13. *New York Times* (May 4, 1982): 14.
14. Ibid.
15. Huckshorn and Spencer, *Politics of Defeat,* pp. 15–17.
16. V. O. Key, Jr., *American State Politics: An Introduction* (New York: Knopf, 1956), p. 271.
17. See Robert J. Huckshorn, *Party Leadership in the States* (Amherst: University of Massachusetts Press, 1976), for a thorough discussion of the changes in state parties.
18. Ibid., pp. 227–228.
19. Ibid., pp. 12–19.
20. Cotter and Hennessy, *Politics Without Power,* p. 81.
21. The three quotations used to illustrate this section on types of state party leaders were taken from interviews conducted in preparation of the author's *Party Leadership in the States,* ch. 4.
22. The material in this section on state party organizations has been derived from the following sources: Huckshorn, *Party Leadership in the States;* Huckshorn and Bibby, "State Parties in an Era of Political Change"; Cornelius P. Cotter, James Gibson, John F. Bibby, and Robert J. Huckshorn, "State Party Organizations and the Thesis of Party Decline," unpublished paper delivered at the annual meeting of the American Political Science Association, Washington, D.C., 1980; Gibson, Cotter, Bibby, and Huckshorn, "Assessing Party Organizational Strength," *American Journal of Political Science* (May 1983); Bibby, Huckshorn, Gibson, and Cotter, "State Party Chairmen Role Orientations and Institutional Party Strength," paper delivered at the annual meeting of the Western Political Science Association, Denver, Colo., 1981; and Bibby, Cotter, Gibson, and Huckshorn, "Parties in State Politics," in *Politics in the American States: A Comparative Analysis,* 4th ed., eds Virginia Gray, Herbert Jacob, and Kenneth Vines (Boston: Little, Brown, 1983).
23. See Gibson, Cotter, Bibby, and Huckshorn, "Assessing Party Organizational Strength," for a complete description of the institutional index.
24. John F. Bibby, James L. Gibson, Cornelius P. Cotter, and Robert J. Huckshorn, "Trends in Party Organizational Strength, 1960–1980: Institutionalization in an Era of Electoral Dealignment," *International Political Science Review* (4[1], 1983), pp. 21–27.
25. Frank R. Kent, *The Great Game of Politics,* rev. ed. (Garden City, N.Y.: Doubleday, 1930), pp. 1–2.
26. William J. Crotty, "The Party Organization and Its Activities," in *Approaches to the Study of*

*Party Organization*, ed. William J. Crotty (Boston: Allyn & Bacon, 1968), p. 298.

27. Paul A. Beck, "Environment and Party: The Impact of Political and Demographic County Characteristics on Party Behavior," *American Political Science Review* 68 (September 1974): 1240.

28. Gibson, Cotter, Bibby, and Huckshorn, "Trends in Party Organizational Strength," pp. 21–27.

29. *New York Times* (June 1, 1970): 1.

30. Gibson, Cotter, Bibby, and Huckshorn, "Trends in Party Organizational Strength," pp. 21–27.

31. Beck, "Environment and Party," pp. 1238–1241.

32. Austin Ranney, *Curing the Mischiefs of Faction: Party Reform in America* (Berkeley: University of California Press, 1975), pp. 180–181.

33. Frank J. Sorauf, *Party Politics in America,* 3rd ed. (Boston: Little, Brown, 1976), pp. 118–119.

34. *New York Times,* "Brock plans corps for training G.O.P." (January 22, 1977): 9.

# CHAPTER FOUR

# The Nominating Process

*Under the new leadership of Bill Brock, the Republican National Committee is venturing cautiously into a politically perilous area: backing one Republican among two or more competitors in a party primary.*

*Under the unwritten code long observed by both parties, national intervention in a primary for a Senate or House nomination, much less state legislative office, has been virtually unthinkable. The ironclad rule has been to let candidates fight it out among themselves, then after the primary support the winner.*

*But Mr. Brock, the new national chairman, who is charged with reviving Republican fortunes in the face of adversity, had decided that hard times demand hard solutions. In the interest of nominating candidates with the best chance of winning the election, he is prepared to ignore selectively the old requirement for Washington impartiality.*

Warren Weaver, Jr., *New York Times*, May 30, 1977.

Old-time politicians were surprised in 1977 when the new Republican national chairman, William Brock, began to involve the national committee directly in party primaries at the local level. Party leaders have almost always operated according to an unwritten code that discourages intervention in a party nominating contest between two or more candidates of the same party. It has always been assumed that, should the leadership give its support to a primary candidate who then lost the nomination, the winning candidate would owe even less to the party than usual. Yet the headlines were indisputable: Brock had not only intervened once but several times and not only in races for the U.S. Congress but in selected state legislative contests. Furthermore, he had also set up an entire division within the Republic National Committee (RNC) to provide direct assistance to state and local party campaigns.[1] Both actions were unprecedented on the part of a national party chairman, but, when elected to the chairmanship, Brock believed he had an unspoken obligation to rebuild the Republican organization and revive party fortunes. To do that, he concluded, he must be prepared to intercede selectively in party nominating contests in order to provide assistance to those who would better serve the party as candidates in the general election. If successful, of course, the candidates benefiting from such help would presumably owe greater loyalty to the party leaders who helped put them in office. That, Brock reasoned, was what party responsibility was all about.

The Republican chairman's first intervention was in behalf of a black candidate for the California State Assembly who was in a nominating race with four white Republican opponents. This particular effort was successful. His second intercession was on the side of a Republican in a special election for the House of Representatives in Louisiana, and again his candidate won handily over another Republican and was later elected to Congress—the first Republican from that district in over one hundred years. In two other congressional district special elections the Republican candidate was successful; in a third he was not. As Brock's term progressed he intervened in dozens of such races.

Although often successful, Brock's initiative was somewhat restricted by a rules change at the national convention in 1980. Some state party leaders—chagrined that Brock channeled RNC resources to at least one U.S. Senate candidate who went on to lose the Republican primary—led a successful effort to amend the rules to prohibit contributions in a contested primary until the state chairman and both national committee members from the state agreed.[2] It is too soon to determine the effect that this rules change will have on future efforts by Republican national party leaders to intercede in local campaigns.

William Brock's successors after 1981, Richard Richards and Frank Fahrenkopf, continued the selective intervention in primaries and extended the local campaign efforts of the national committee to the county level. For instance, in 1981 a large number of indictments for graft against Oklahoma county commissioners opened a number of commission seats to new elections. Richards put over $100,000 of national committee money into these county races in an effort to build the Republican party in that state at the grass-roots level.[3]

The efforts of Chairmen Brock, Richards, and Fahrenkopf were but the latest of many devised by party leaders over the years to try to undercut the effects of the direct-primary system of nomination. Complaints about the direct primary are an old refrain among political party leaders. A self-starter candidate running in opposition to a carefully recruited and nurtured candidate can spell havoc for party cohesion and for strong control by the leadership of the party. Nevertheless, the party primary provides encouragement for candidates to run, regardless of whether they have any backing within the party. One party leader has described the problem he and his party faced in one such contest:

> My recruitment committee and I worked for weeks to talk a particular individual into running for the state senate. We visited his place of business, invited him to party strategy discussions, asked his friends to work on him. He was very reluctant to undergo a campaign that was, at best, a 50–50 chance. Now, he was quite frank in saying he would like to be in the senate. He just needed to be persuaded to make the run. We finally made him some promises of campaign help that he couldn't resist. He agreed to run. And damned if a guy none of us even knew didn't announce three weeks later. We had practically promised ———— that he would go through to the nomination without opposition. Well, I had to do something I do not normally like to do—that is, intervene in a primary. The chairman and I both put our necks on the line by personally endorsing our man. Fortunately, he won, but we were a little worried.[4]

## Nomination of Candidates

In chapter 1 we discussed the functions of political parties, the first being the nomination of candidates. In the United States, nominating methods can be distinguished according to the method used and the level of the office sought. All nominations, even those for president and vice-president, are accomplished either by the primary system or by the convention system, except in a few rural areas that continue to make local nominations by means of a caucus (meeting) of party leaders. Every state now requires that candidates for some or all public offices be nominated by the direct-primary method. Primary elections are used to nominate local candidates, party choices for county and state offices, and candidates for the U.S. House of Representatives and the U.S. Senate. All direct primaries are provided for by state law, and most are administered by state officials. Conventions, in contrast, are usually operated under party rules, are administered by party officers, and nominate indirectly through delegated authority.

Of course, presidential candidates and their vice-presidential running mates are nominated in national conventions. But, even there, the primary system has become the chief means of selecting the delegates who will attend the convention. In 1980 nearly three-fourths of the convention delegates from thirty-seven states and territories were chosen by the voters in party presidential primaries. As recently as 1968 only one-third of the states held presidential primaries, and less than half the delegates were chosen through them. The trend has been away from party choices and toward voter choices. Both the direct-primary system of nomination of candidates for lesser offices and the presidential preference primaries have undercut the influence of party leaders in candidate selection.

## The Direct Primary

Definitions of the term *political party* generally list the purposes of the party organization, and these lists always include making nominations as a party function. Indeed, the job of nomination separates the political party from all other types of political organizations. Citizen groups do not make nominations, nor do political interest groups.

Only political parties have this responsibility. The nomination of candidates is possibly the most important function of the political party. The belief is widely held that a party that cannot effectively recruit and nominate candidates for office is unlikely to remain viable and competitive for long. Such a party may not be able to exploit its opportunities to capture offices and, if successful, to provide direction to government.

The following are the principal conditions of office seeking, for which the American parties are the vehicle: (1) a large number of offices must be filled at every level of the governmental hierarchy; (2) selection of most of the candidates for these offices is made through the direct primary system; (3) no formal prerequisites exist for holding office, other than age or residential requirements; and, (4) in order to win, candidates must usually run as either Democrats or Republicans. This combination of almost unlimited political opportunity and a restrictive two-party structure places the prospective office seeker as well as his or her party in an almost untenable position.

From the point of view of the candidate, the direct-primary campaign may be a nightmare round of poorly attended rallies, embarrassing pleas for money, fruitless efforts to enlist illicit support from party leaders, and fratricidal campaign attacks on fellow party candidates. These events may be especially disappointing to a candidate who has been groomed by party leaders and has been led to expect more. The primary campaign often appears to party leaders to be a counterproductive use of energy and funds, both of which could be better employed in the general election.

From the point of view of the party leaders, the primary election experience is not much rosier. A carefully recruited candidate may find his or her resources being squandered on an unanticipated party primary with the potential for intraparty polarization that sometimes occurs. Furthermore, the party may be saddled with a candidate who has little potential in a competitive general election campaign.

From the vantage point of the self-starter candidate, however, the primary presents an open door to political involvement. Perfectly respectable candidates (and some not very respectable ones) may have been locked out by the party apparatus. Efforts to secure party backing may have been unavailing. Endorsed candidates may appear to be inferior and to have less potential for success. The person who feels qualified to run may have found the paths to office seeking closed by the very party organization under whose aegis his or her candidacy was to blossom. The role of self-starter is all that remains to such a hopeful individual.

The voter, on the other hand, takes a different view of the candidate selection process. Most voters are interested in and participate in two-party competitive politics of the variety that takes place in the general election campaign. Republicans want to contest with Democrats. Internecine warfare holds little appeal for them. Many voters still respond to the party label in spite of the recent upsurge in ticket-splitting and self-proclaimed independence. In the primary election, though, without the party label as a guide, many voters are unable to distinguish between the dozens, even hundreds, of candidates who present themselves for election to various offices.

The nominating system presents a problem that does not lend itself to easy solution. In earlier years candidates were chosen by the party leaders in controlled and generally inaccessible caucuses. Party bosses, legislative leaders, officeholders, and others simply met together for the purpose of deciding who would occupy which slot on the ticket. Obviously, this was not a particularly democratic system, but the party caucus did give the leadership control over who used its name and who campaigned under its banner. If an officeholder stole the public funds or offended public morality, it was at least theoretically possible to hold the party responsible for presenting that person to the voters as a candidate. Nevertheless, in those jurisdictions controlled by political machines, the party members had little or no influence in choosing candidates to run for office. As a result, callous party bosses could, and did, fill the offices with their cronies and their henchmen, and the public found that it had little to say about the candidates selected to run for public office. The caucus system gradually fell into disrepute as scandal became more prevalent, and party members eventually rebelled against the system of candidate selection controlled by those who already held public office.

Gradually, during the Progressive era following 1900, a system of party conventions emerged as a more democratic method of selecting nominees for the general election. Typically, the lower echelons of the party hierarchy met to elect delegates to the next higher level. These conventions, usually at the state level, nominated candidates and wrote the party's platform. Conventions offered a means of promoting unity and reducing factionalism, and they provided a mechanism through which balanced tickets could be worked out within the trappings of a democratically selected delegate system. They operated under the dual advantages, it was thought, of permitting ordinary party activists to take part as delegates while considerable control remained in the hands of party leaders.

The convention system of nominations lasted for many years, until abuses by party bosses brought it into disrepute and reform-minded citizens began casting about for an alternative system that would be even more democratic and outside the control of the bosses. The degeneration of the convention system stemmed from gross abuses. In some places unscrupulous politicians brought in criminal elements to "enforce" the preferred decisions. The lowest elements in political life often dominated conventions. Although possibly atypical, one Cook County (Chicago) convention in 1896 was composed of 723 delegates; of these, 265 were saloonkeepers; 148 were political employees; 130 were pickpockets, ex-burglars, and other minor criminals; 17 had been tried for murder; 2 were keepers of houses of ill repute; 71 had no discernible occupation; and 92 were lawyers, farmers, and business and professional people.[5] Publication of such rosters caused growing public concern, and again calls for nomination reform were heard.

The first statewide mandatory direct primary was enacted by the Wisconsin voters in 1903 at the urging of Gov. Robert M. LaFollette, Sr. Although the primary had been used in some localities for many years, this represented the first time that it had been adopted as a statewide system of nomination. The next fifteen years saw the system spread across the nation until it had been adopted in one form or another in all but four states (Connecticut, New Mexico, Rhode Island, and Utah). In 1955 Connecticut became the fiftieth state to adopt the primary as a system of nomination.

In some contests, however, conventions are still used to select candidates. In Delaware and Michigan, for instance, nominations for some statewide offices (e.g., lieutenant governor and secretary of state) are still made in party convention. In Connecticut and New York a "challenge" primary combines the convention and primary systems—ostensibly to bring the best features of both to the nominating process. Each party in Connecticut holds a convention to nominate candidates, who then automatically go onto the general election ballot if not challenged by another candidate. To make such a challenge, a candidate must have actively sought the nomination during the convention, must have received at least 20 percent of the delegate votes, and must have filed nominating petitions. No statewide primary was held in Connecticut until 1970, fifteen years after adoption of the system.

In most states all nominees of both parties for all major offices are direct-primary choices. Until recently several southern state Republican parties retained the convention system as a nominating method, and Virginia still does. In ten states "sore loser" statutes forbid a candidate who loses the primary from seeking to run in the general election as an independent or the candidate of another party.

Many of the states that have retained some form of convention control have strongly competitive and centralized two-party systems. The convention system permits the party leadership to maintain control over candidate selection while avoiding the potential bloodshed of a divisive primary. In short, those who control the party organization in these states are able to maintain their strength by determining the selection of nominees.

In most states the system of direct primaries allows every party member to vote for candidates. The extent to which that right is exercised is largely determined by the type of primary used in the state.

## The Closed Primary

Thirty-nine states use the *closed* primary system, which requires the voter to affirm a party preference or affiliation before being allowed to take part in an election. The proof required usually consists of a sworn statement at the time of registration that he or she (1) has voted in the party's primary in immediate past elections; (2) presently considers himself or herself to be a member of the party; or (3) intends to support the party's candidates in the coming general election. Obviously, since the ballot is secret, it is not possible in those states to prove the accuracy of the statements of party affiliation.

Having proclaimed party membership, the voter appears at the polls on primary election day and is given the ballot of the party shown in the official records maintained by polling officials. Should the voter refuse to declare a party affiliation at the time of registration, he or she cannot vote in the primary election. The theory behind the closed primary system is that voters are willing to identify themselves as party members in order to take part in that party's candidate selection. In most states there is nothing to keep the voter from switching from one party to another between elections so long as the procedures for changing registration are followed. Those who register as Independents are not permitted to take part in closed primaries. They have, in effect, disenfranchised themselves by not choosing to register as members of a legally recognized party. Party leaders usually prefer the closed primary, as opposed to other types of primaries, because it provides them with a list of party members to whom campaign strategies can be directed. Other primary systems that do not require registration by party deny the party leadership an identifiable constituency.

## The Open Primary

Throughout American history political reformers have often been antiparty, an attitude arising from what they considered to be abuses of the democratic system by party leaders. One result was the invention of the *open* primary, in which no party membership tests for voter participation are allowed. In open primary states the primary voters who appear at the polling place are furnished with the primary ballot of all parties running candidates in that particular election. They are not required to identify their party choice or their party affiliation at any time.

A variety of systems exist for protecting the open primary's secrecy of the vote. In some states each voter is given the party ballots of all the parties and chooses one in the privacy of the polling booth. The marked ballot is placed in the ballot box, and the remaining unmarked ones are placed in a separate receptacle. In other states the voter is given all of the party ballots on a single perforated sheet, uses one, tears off the rest, and deposits the marked and the unmarked ballots in separate boxes. Whatever the system, the voter may participate in only one party's primary, but the choice of primary is his or hers and is completely secret.

Just as its major advantage is the total secrecy surrounding the voter's party identification, the major disadvantage of the open primary is the practice of "raiding," which is occasionally suspected in certain states. The theory behind the open primary is that a voter who does not wish to identify his or her party affiliation can take part without having to do so. In most cases that is the undoubted result; however, situations sometimes develop in open primary states that lend themselves to a more sinister political purpose. In a highly disciplined party system the leaders of one party may instruct the voters in that party to choose the ballot of the opposition in order to "help" nominate one of the weaker candidates in their primary. If successful, a raid can nominate a potential loser to oppose the raiding party's stronger candidate (see "The Democrats Organize a Raid on a Republican Primary"). Raids are not always easy to detect. Some unexpected primary nominations may appear to have resulted from a raid by the opposition when, in reality, the surprise nominee was the result of decisions independently arrived at by the voters.

Another, more innocent kind of raid can also take place. If one party has an uninteresting primary with few real contests, the voters associated with the party may choose to cast their votes in the other party's primary simply because more meaningful contests are involved. Thus a larger number of Republicans may vote in the Democratic primary, assist the Democrats with nominating their slate of candidates for various offices, and then vote Republican against those very nominees in the general election. This may represent a simple, straightforward effort on the part of some voters to play a significant role in the nominating process. Just as obviously, it undercuts any attempt to maintain a responsible party system in which the party leaders can be held responsible for their nominees. It should be noted that some authorities are not convinced that organized raiding is very widespread.

## The Blanket Primary: Washington and Alaska

First in Washington and later in Alaska an even more open form of primary was adopted. In the *blanket* primary not only are voters not required to identify their party affiliation, but they can vote in the primary of more than one party. One vote can be cast for a Democratic candidate for U.S. senator, another for a Republican candidate for sheriff, and yet a third for a Democratic choice for the state legislature. Obviously, a vote cannot be cast for both the Republican and Democratic candidates for the same office, but the parties can be mixed from office to office. The ballot is arranged so that the candidates' names are listed according to office sought rather than according to party. Thus all candidates for all parties for the office of governor are given separately in an "office block." The party affiliation of each candidate is shown after the can-

## The Democrats Organize a Raid
## on a Republican Primary

Raiding is often difficult to detect, and one can never be absolutely sure that a raid has taken place in an open primary state. A hypothetical example in a mythical state follows.

The Democrats control the office of governor. The incumbent governor is very popular. He is running for nomination and reelection but is possibly vulnerable to a challenge by a strong Republican gubernatorial candidate. The Democratic governor is guaranteed renomination because he has no serious opposition.

Four Republicans announce their candidacies for governor. They are:

Mr. *Stronge,* a popular state senator with a large following who has never lost an election and is considered by knowledgeable observers to be a potential threat to the Democratic governor;

Mr. *Politicus,* the Republican state chairman, who is popular within the party organization but virtually unknown to the voters and is given only an outside chance for success;

Ms. *Radfem,* a noisy leader of the radical feminist movement in the state, who is widely regarded as being a far-left Democrat and is running as a Republican only because she has no chance against the Democratic governor;

Mr. *Feeble,* an unknown local party politician, who has tied his entire campaign to a personal crusade to abolish taxes and substitute legalized casino gambling as a source of revenue for the state.

Democratic leaders, including the governor's campaign aides, quickly realize that Mr. Stronge is their greatest threat. Unfortunately, he is also most likely to be nominated. His would be a serious challenge and would endanger the Democrats' chances for remaining in power for four more years. Although not as serious a threat, Mr. Politicus might prove troublesome as a nominee and, because of his popularity in the organization, could get the nomination. Ms. Radfem, everyone agrees, would stand no chance of being nominated with or without Democratic help. The choice, then, devolves on Mr. Feeble, whose support of gambling as a revenue-generating device would not be popular in this conservative and religious state.

The Democratic leaders, quietly and without fanfare, pass the word through party channels that Democratic voters on primary election day should cast their votes in the Republican party for Mr. Feeble. On election night it becomes obvious, with the surprise nomination of Mr. Feeble, that thousands of Democrats have crossed over to raid the Republican primary in order to "help" that party nominate its weakest candidate. Returns clearly show that in many heavily Democratic areas more Republicans voted than there were Republicans living there.

Having helped with the Republican nomination, the raiders cross back over to their own party in the general election, vote for their own gubernatorial nominee, and send him back to Capitol City for another term. The Republicans have been ambushed by a Democratic raid that brought about the nomination of a Republican candidate who was sure to make a poor general election showing, thus guaranteeing the governor's reelection.

didate's name. Only one candidate in each office block can receive a vote. Voters can vote for a single party's candidates for each office or can mix up their votes between the parties as long as they cast only one vote in each block. (Louisiana recently adopted a *nonpartisan* primary for statewide and congressional races that is similar to the blanket primary except that all the candidates for each office are listed on the ballot without regard to party identification.) These systems give the voter maximum flexibility, but, as one might expect, they are not usually popular with party leaders, who consider them to be free-for-alls that discourage effective participation by strong partisan supporters.

## Cross-Filing

Until 1959 California permitted the practice of cross-filing, another device intended to give voters the widest possible choice of candidates in a primary. Candidates were allowed to file nominating petitions in both the Republican and the Democratic primaries, although members of each party were only permitted to vote in the primary of their own party. The classic success story under cross-filing was Earl Warren's; he won both the Republican and the Democratic primary nominations for governor in 1946 and went on to win the general election without opposition. Supporters of party discipline and party responsibility finally convinced the legislature to abolish the system as a needless roadblock to stronger parties.

The only other practice similar to cross-filing is used in New York, where minor parties have been cross-listed on the ballot. New York does not allow cross-filing unless the parties approve, and both major parties in that state have refused to allow the practice. Consequently, it is used primarily by the Conservative, Liberal, and Right to Life parties, all of which have had a greater impact than most other minor parties. Even so, the influence of these three parties appears to have waned in recent years.

## The Runoff Primary

In chapter 2 we reviewed the multifactional and bifactional one-party politics that exists in some southern states. As we have noted before, even though the Republicans in the South have had considerable success in electing candidates to high state and national office, party organizations there are weak and undernourished. The primary nominating system in that region is beset by twin problems, the *first* being the large number of self-starter candidates who emerge to run for each office. Neither the Democratic nor the Republican organization is strong in most of the southern states. The Republicans are newly emerging as a challenger party, and the Democrats, never having had to compete with another party before, have never needed to maintain a party organization. The resultant lack of strong leaders and party discipline encourages many hopeful self-starter candidates to try for nomination.

The *second* problem is related to the first. With several candidates contending for each office, often none of them is able to emerge from the first primary with a majority vote. Most states have shown little concern with this problem of democracy. But in the South, ten states (plus Oklahoma) have adopted a *runoff* primary to ensure that party nominees carry a mandate from a majority of the voters. The runoff is held some weeks after the initial primary and is usually a contest between the two highest vote getters. Having only two candidates ensures that one of them will receive a majority of the votes cast and can validly claim to represent the party's voters in the upcoming general election. Opponents of the runoff system contend that voter turnout in primary elections is usually so low that the winning candidate, whether of the first or the runoff primary, cannot claim to represent more than a minority of the party members anyway.

## Preprimary Conventions

Since 1912 Colorado has had a system in which a candidate receiving 20 percent or more of the delegate votes in a state party convention is then placed on the ballot for a primary election. Other candidates are permitted to run in the primary as "challenge" candidates, and they have occasionally won nomination. The state of Utah has used preprimary conventions since 1947 to designate two candidates for each office in the primaries, although, should one candidate receive 70 percent of the convention vote, nomination is automatic. In Rhode Island a state party convention is permitted to endorse or identify on the ballot the choices of the state party committees. The endorsed candidates are either designated on the ballot or listed first. Colorado lists the endorsed candidates in order of the number of convention votes received. The party-endorsed candidates usually win the nomination. Other states that have tried some form of preprimary selection or endorsement include Idaho, Massachusetts, and New Mexico.[6] Some observers believe that the preprimary convention system is one answer to the problem posed by the popularity of the direct primary and the need to bring party leaders back into the nominating system. Nevertheless, it has never achieved widespread success.

## Indirect Party Intervention in the Primary Process

Party leaders discover rather quickly that the easiest way for the party to determine the outcome of a primary is to become involved early enough to control prospective competition to a favored candidate. If self-starters without party support are to be discouraged, it is the party leader's role to provide the discouragement. This can be done through arbitration between candidates who have indicated an interest or by coaxing an attractive potential candidate to become a full-fledged contender. Those who can be discouraged may be offered an alternative patronage position or simply dropped from contention. Most, if they have been involved in politics at all, may recognize the disadvantages of attempting to run against the party organization's choice. Occasionally, such a candidate beats the endorsed contender, but, in reality, that does not happen very often.

What kinds of assistance can a party leader promise to an unofficial choice? In most states party involvement in primary elections is extralegal. Committee members may be urged to help the candidate circulate nominating petitions. In some states the party issues small "palm cards" with the names and offices of the preferred candidates printed on them. These cards can be taken into the polling booth by the voter to minimize reliance on personal memory. In other areas, when the party sends drivers to take voters to the polls, the driver uses the trip to pass the word about the leadership's choices. Sometimes experienced party workers are encouraged to work in a favored candidate's behalf. In other places candidates are included in the official party advertising or are offered a part of the money derived from fund-raising events. All of these methods, and many more, have been used as unofficial means of letting the party faithful know which candidates bear the party's stamp of approval. Where the organization is well structured and influential, these assists can go a long way toward providing a slate of candidates the leadership can support.

Sometimes a tightly structured organization, such as that presided over for many years by the late mayor of Chicago Richard J. Daley, can combine the recruitment and nomination processes in such a way that a winning slate is virtually guaranteed. Potential candidates in Daley's bailiwick were usually expected to demonstrate loyalty through long years of diligent effort and party support. When these individuals were deemed ready, the leaders would encourage them to present themselves before the Democratic "slating committees" that were assigned the responsibility for interviewing the various candidates and for debating their merits.

Meeting first in Springfield and then in Chicago, the slating committees would hear the contenders for various offices present their cases in tightly guarded and closed sessions. The mayor himself presided over the Chicago committee meetings, acting in his capacity as Cook County party chairman. After hearing all the potential candidates, the slating committee would emerge to announce its choices for each office in the upcoming primary. Generally, the organization's endorsement was all that was necessary to win nomination on election day, but occasionally a challenger would refuse to abide by the slate and would run in opposition to the "hand-picked" choices of the organization. In 1972 Daniel Walker filed against the slated choice in the gubernatorial primary and defeated him. He then went on to win the office of governor of Illinois in the general election. In 1976 the slating of a Daley colleague as a candidate for governor was so unpopular that a strong Republican contender won the office.

Other state party organizations have attempted to use formal and informal endorsement proceedings to indicate to party members the leadership's choice among primary candidates. In 1981, for example, the Florida Republican executive committee adopted guidelines for endorsement of primary candidates that permit such designations. Under the rule it would take a unanimous vote of the full state and county executive committees to endorse a state or county candidate in a primary in which two or more Republicans are seeking nomination.

All of these approaches represent different methods of involving the party in the candidate selection process. Naturally, those parties with strong bases of support and established leadership cadres are more likely to prevail in the prenominating battles. Such intervention, according to one study, is more common in two-party competitive systems where strong candidates are more likely to face strong opposition.[7] In one-party areas the organization may be dominated by incumbent officeholders, and competitive primary contests may be rare.

## Primary Elections: Competition and Participation

The reform groups that advocated the direct nomination of candidates through party primaries believed that people were interested in having a major participatory role in the selection of candidates to run in the general election. Studies that have been made since the direct primary was inaugurated in the first two decades of this century suggest the following generalizations:

1. Excluding the southern states, voting participation in primaries is much lower than in general elections. Austin Ranney, using his own index of competitiveness

discussed in chapter 2, analyzed the mean percentage of voting turnout in both primary and general elections for governor and U.S. senator between 1962 and 1972 for four of the categories of states. As noted in table 4-1, participation in southern (one-party Democratic) gubernatorial primary contests has been almost as high as that in general elections. In the other three categories, however, turnout has averaged 27.5 percent in primaries and from 22 to 39 percent higher in general elections. Lower primary turnout is not evenly distributed across all the states. Participation varies from state to state according to the kind of party system in the state, as can be seen in the Ranney table; thus participation in primaries for governor was 36.7 percent in one-party Democratic states (the South), 29.9 percent in modified one-party Democratic states, 25.8 percent in two-party competitive states, and 27.0 percent in modified one-party Republican states.

These figures suggest that low turnout outside the South sometimes stems from the small number of candidates competing for a single nomination and/or the lack of important issues in the party primary.[8] Obviously, a rather small minority of party voters can have considerably greater impact on the primary outcome than their number would warrant. Furthermore, the minority may not be representative of the whole of the party's voters. Should this be the case, and it often appears to be, the party may go into the general election with a candidate who has little appeal to the general membership of the party or to independent voters, who must be attracted in order to win a majority.

One recent analysis of gubernatorial primary turnout in forty-seven states over a quarter century suggests the following conclusions: (a) among the states there are large variations in turnout for contested races; (b) higher turnout is more likely in states that share certain characteristics, such as high general election turnout, numerous

TABLE 4–1   Mean percentage voting turnout in primary and general elections for governor and U.S. senator, 1962–1972

| Type of state | For Governor | | |
| | Primary elections[a] | General elections | Difference |
|---|---|---|---|
| One-party Democratic | 36.7 | 37.7 | −1.0 |
| Modified one-party Democratic | 29.9 | 52.0 | −22.1 |
| Two-party | 25.8 | 57.1 | −31.3 |
| Modified one-party Republican | 27.0 | 63.4 | −36.4 |
| | For U.S. Senator | | |
| One-party Democratic | 27.5 | 34.9 | −7.4 |
| Modified one-party Democratic | 23.3 | 48.9 | −25.6 |
| Two-party | 25.1 | 58.8 | −33.7 |
| Modified one-party Republican | 22.3 | 61.6 | −39.3 |

[a]Includes all primary–general election pairs in which at least one party's primary was contested and the general election was contested by both parties.

*Source:* From Austin Ranney, "Parties in State Politics," in Herbert Jacob and Kenneth N. Vines, eds., *Politics in the American State: A Comparative Analysis,* 3d ed. (Boston: Little, Brown and Co., 1976), p. 71. Data from Richard Scammon, ed., *America Votes* (Washington, D.C.: Governmental Affairs Institute and Congressional Quarterly, Inc., 1962–1972). Copyright © 1976 by Little, Brown and Company (Inc.). Reprinted by permission.

contested primaries, open primaries, and relatively weak party organizations; (c) higher turnout is generally found in parties that have been dominant over a long period of time; (d) variations over time in the relative turnout rates of the two parties result from changes in two-party competition or from the existence of an open primary system; and (e) large differences in turnout levels exist in southern Democratic primaries, with the highest found in states that have the least two-party competition as well as the highest levels of competition within the primary.[9]

2. Contests in which an incumbent officeholder is running draw fewer challenger candidates in the primary than do those in which no incumbent is running. Incumbents are usually hard to beat. Not only are their names better known to the voters, but they have been in office and have been able to do things for their constituents. Generally speaking, incumbents also find it far easier to raise money for their campaigns, and they are more likely to have ongoing campaign organizations.

Malcolm Jewell and David Olson found that incumbency had a major effect on contests for governor. In thirty-six northern states incumbents were running in nearly one-third of the primaries, and 54.0 percent of those races where incumbents were running were contested, as compared to 78.7 percent of those without incumbents. In the southern states almost all of the elections with or without incumbents were contested, in contrast to only half the Republican primaries (almost always without incumbents). They also found that the average vote for the winner in all races with incumbents in the forty-seven states included in their survey was 64.6 percent, in contrast to 55.9 percent for races without incumbents.[10]

Jewell and Olson also studied the proportion of contested primaries in various categories of states, broken down by incumbency. As shown in table 4-2, regional differences are pronounced. The levels of competition in the southern and border states are much higher than anywhere else, particularly in the Democratic party. Until recently Republican opposition in those states was very weak, and elections were usually decided in the Democratic primary. Even though the Republican party in the South has grown, GOP leaders have had difficulty finding candidates in many areas, and only about half of the primaries with a Republican candidate have actually been competitive. Primary competition has been lowest in the Midwest and the Northeast. Jewell and Olson attribute this to the existence of stronger political party organizations that, in a number

TABLE 4-2 Percentage of primaries contested, by party and incumbency and by region, 1946–1950 to 1980

| Categories of states (N) | Total | Democratic | | Republican | |
|---|---|---|---|---|---|
| | | Incumbent Runs | No Incumbent | Incumbent Runs | No Incumbent |
| All states (47) | 72.8 | 64.2 | 82.1 | 54.0 | 74.8 |
| South (11) | 82.4 | 97.1 | 94.9 | (100.0) | 54.5 |
| North (36) | 70.7 | 55.2 | 78.2 | 52.8 | 79.2 |
| Border (4) | 95.8 | (100.0) | 100.0 | (33.3) | 97.0 |
| West (13) | 76.0 | 68.1 | 87.0 | 54.8 | 81.0 |
| Midwest (10) | 64.5 | 40.5 | 69.6 | 50.0 | 81.3 |
| Northeast (9) | 63.0 | 48.5 | 69.0 | 56.3 | 66.7 |

*Source:* A portion of a table in Malcolm E. Jewell and David M. Olson, *American State Political Parties and Elections,* rev. ed. (Homewood, Ill.: The Dorsey Press, 1982), p. 123. Percentages in parentheses are based on very small numbers of cases. In some states the first election included was 1950; in states where four-year terms were used consistently, the 1946 or 1948 election was included to ensure coverage of a larger number of elections.

of cases, use some form of endorsement procedure, thus discouraging others from running.[11]

From a different perspective it is clear that, when a party has a good chance of winning an election—for instance, with an incumbent officeholder running—it is more likely to have contested primaries. For a long time the proportion of contested primaries in both parties has been higher in two-party states and in one-party Democratic states. In a competitive two-party state the chances of winning are relatively even, and in a one-party Democratic state the chances of winning the general election are excellent for the winner of the Democratic primary.[12]

## The Direct Primary: Hope versus Reality

The decline of party organization and influence in America since the turn of the century has been largely due to the reforms that grew out of the Progressive movement. The Progressives' advocacy of institutional innovation may have strengthened democracy, at least by their definition, but it also had a number of unhappy effects on party organization and party leaders. The deleterious effects of the primary are sometimes overdrawn, but it does constitute a threat to the well-being of the party and often causes damaging inconveniences and disruptions, which can be summarized as follows:

• The loss of organizational control over nominations is costly to the party in a number of ways. It encourages people to self-declare and, having done so, to go their own way. In effect the self-starter candidate has borrowed the party's name and reputation and has run under the party's banner, but has done so often without the party's permission and occasionally with the party's outright opposition. By denying the party control over nominations, the primary has diminished the leadership's ability to demand any degree of loyalty from its elected officeholders. Since many of those who have won office did so without benefit of party assistance in gaining their nomination, they feel no obligation to the party on matters of policy or substance.

The primary can easily permit the nomination of a candidate who is hostile to the party's positions, opposed to the party's platform, and embarrassing to the party's image. A candidate nominated in a divisive primary may well represent only 10 or 12 percent of the voters and be generally out of sync with the large majority of those who consider themselves loyal partisans. At worst the primary may produce a loser or an embarrassment.

• Contrary to the hopes of the Progressives, the direct participation of the people in the nominating process did not stimulate any massive increases in popular concern for nominating good candidates. Low voter turnout persists, and it is not uncommon for the ultimate victor in a primary to win the support of only 10 to 15 percent of the eligible electorate in the party. In a multicandidate primary a simple plurality of a 30 percent turnout does not constitute much of a mandate for the winner to represent his or her party in the general election. Furthermore, the primary can easily saddle the party with an unbalanced ticket for the general election. In a voting district represented by diverse regional, religious, racial, and ethnic groups, it is quite possible, with the right combination of bloc voting, that the party will end up with an unbalanced ticket composed of a large number of representatives of one such group but none of the others. Most party officials would prefer to enter a general election contest with a more balanced attempt to appeal to various voter groups—an approach that is possible under the convention system. The question remains whether those who take part in primaries reflect the broad spectrum of those who identify themselves as party members. One study of the primary electorate in Wisconsin found that those who vote in primaries differ from those who claim a party membership but do not take part. Wisconsin primary participants tended to be older and better educated, to have higher incomes, to be longer-term residents, and to be predominantly male.[13]

• The costs of politics escalated dramatically with the use of the direct-primary system of nomination. If the party has an endorsement procedure, the cost of candidate support in the primary is an added financial burden to the party, and the money spent on primary campaigns often depletes the amount available for the general election campaign.

The principal cost, however, is to party unity. In a strenuous party primary between two or more candidates seeking the party's nomination, the scars that result can be lasting and devastating. A primary is, after all, a family fight and can leave wounds that are difficult to heal and bitterness that is impossible to assuage.[14]

Thus far we have considered nominations at all levels below the presidency and vice-presidency. The presidential nomination is brought about through a unique system that has changed rapidly in recent years. Although the nomination takes place in a national convention setting, the power of the people to determine the ultimate success of one candidate through their preconvention activities has taken a decided upswing since 1972.

## Nominating the President: The Democrats

In the small hours of the second night of the Democratic National Convention in 1968 the delegates loyal to Eugene McCarthy and Robert F. Kennedy won the only victory they were to have in Chicago. The convention leadership, caught by surprise, was unable to defeat a resolution introduced by the Ad Hoc Commission on the Democratic Selection of Presidential Nominees, and that late-night vote set in motion the most thoroughgoing review of national convention nominating practices ever witnessed in American history. California, New York, and other presidential primary states voted overwhelmingly for the resolution. Connecticut, Illinois, Ohio, and Pennsylvania—all strong party organization states—voted in opposition. If the representatives of those parties feared that party influence in delegate selection would be undercut by proposed reforms, they were right. By 1976 citizen input into the delegate selection process, particularly in the Democratic party, had literally changed the nature of the presidential nominating system.

To implement the resolution passed that night, Democratic National Chairman Fred Harris in early 1969 appointed two commissions, each with twenty-eight members. One was a commission on party structure and delegate selection headed by Sen. George McGovern (who was later succeeded by Rep. Donald Fraser). The other was a commission on rules chaired by Rep. James O'Hara. In the ensuing months a wide-ranging set of reforms was agreed to by the two commissions, most of which were adopted by the Democratic National Committee and put into effect before the 1972 election.

### The McGovern-Fraser Commission

The McGovern-Fraser commissions recommended eighteen guidelines requiring radical revisions in state party rules and state laws governing delegate selection. Once these guidelines were adopted, the national committee made compliance with them a precondition for the seating of state delegations in the 1972 convention (see "McGovern-Fraser Commission Guidelines," below).

The changes in party rules and practices generally fell into three categories:

1. The commission found that a broad range of procedures were followed by the states in delegate selection. Some states had no written party rules at all, leaving the selection of delegates to elected and appointed state officials. Proxy voting was widely used, as was the "unit rule," an old practice employed since 1936 by which the majority on a delegation could bind the minority to vote for the majority's choice. In the words of the commission report, the selection of the 1968 delegates was made without "meaningful participation of Democratic voters."[15] The recommendations set about to change that.

2. A second area examined by the commission was the level of participation by black, female, and young delegates. Only 5.5 percent of the 1968 delegates were black, although that group constituted 11 percent of the nation's population; 13 percent of the delegates were women, although over half the population was female; and only 4 percent of the delegates were under the age of thirty, although 27 percent of the

---

## The McGovern-Fraser Commission Guidelines

The McGovern-Fraser Commission proposed a series of guidelines for the state party organizations, and these were imposed by the Democratic National Committee. The guidelines urged the committee to:

1. Adopt explicit written party rules governing delegate selection
2. Adopt procedural rules and safeguards for the delegate selection process in order to
   —forbid proxy voting
   —ban the use of the unit rule
   —require a quorum of not less than 40 percent at all party committee meetings
   —limit mandatory fees to no more than $10
   —ensure, except in rural areas, that party meetings are held on uniform dates in public places
   —ensure adequate public notice of all party meetings involved in the delegate selection process
3. Seek a broader base for the party by
   —adding antiracial discrimination standards to state party rules
   —encouraging representation on the state's convention delegation to minority groups, young people, and women, in a reasonable relationship to their presence in the state's population
   —allowing all persons eighteen years of age or older to participate in all party affairs
4. Make the following changes in the delegate selection process:
   —select alternatives in the same manner as delegates
   —ban designation of ex officio delegates
   —conduct the entire process of delegate selection within the calendar year of the election
   —select at least 75 percent of the total delegation at conventions at a level no higher than congressional districts, and follow apportionment formulas
   —designate procedures by which delegate slates are prepared and may be challenged
   —select no more than 10 percent of the delegates by state committee

population was between the ages of eighteen and thirty. Commission recommendations were aimed at correcting those deficiencies.

3. Finally, the commission noted a third set of structural inadequacies. It found that 38 percent of the 1968 delegates were selected in the states before Sen. Eugene McCarthy even announced his candidacy and that the choice was usually made by party committees that merely ratified slates previously prepared by elected or appointed party officials. In some cases fees were assessed against delegates by state party organizations, thus effectively blocking those with smaller incomes from participating. Many other practices had been used in 1968 and in earlier preconvention periods that excluded many people from meaningful participation.

Change did not come easily. Eventually, all Democratic state parties carried out the mandate of the national committee, at least at a minimal level. The performance of the state parties was mixed, but the new guidelines did significantly increase the number of 1972 delegates who were black (15.5 percent), female (40.0 percent), and under the age of thirty (21.4 percent). All delegates were chosen during the 1972 calendar year, with much more local participation in the process. Except for California, where party leaders flatly refused to comply, the unit rule was abolished, and no delegates were assessed fees.

Two events led to further changes in the law and the practices of the states in presidential nominating politics. One was the Watergate break-in, which resulted in the resignation of a president and the emergence of an unelected president. The second was the devastating defeat of Sen. George McGovern as the Democratic presidential candidate in 1972. The McGovern defeat convinced many Democrats that the post-1968 reforms had gone too far and that, although it was too late to turn back, the rules could be recast in order to avoid some of the more dangerous pitfalls encountered in the 1972 campaign and election. Changes resulting from Watergate included the new election finance law that was passed in 1974, modified and partially overturned by the Supreme Court in 1976, and readopted by Congress two months later. The Watergate scandals also contributed to the second major change—the adoption of new delegate selection rules and the spread of presidential primaries.

Reform had swept the Democratic party before 1972, and those reforms were blamed by some for the defeat that engulfed its presidential candidate in November. The implementation of the quota system to ensure the election of certain minimum numbers of blacks, women, Chicanos, and young people divided the party. Although party leaders carefully refrained from calling the effort a quota system, the press and the public did not; thus after 1972 many party faithfuls believed that the rules should be modified to remove the more absolute and stringent requirements that had resulted from the McGovern-Fraser reforms.

## The O'Hara Commission

While most of the attention of the press was directed to the work of the McGovern-Fraser commission, the O'Hara Commission on Rules was preparing proposals for procedural reforms. The new procedures, ultimately endorsed by the Democratic National Committee and implemented in time for the 1972 convention, provided for fewer and shorter speeches, abolished floor demonstrations, detailed the means through which credentials challenges were to be decided, and ordered that seating on the convention floor, the housing of delegates in particular hotels, and the order of the roll call by states be determined by lot.

## The Mikulski Commission

At the midterm party conference in Kansas City in December 1974, the Democrats adopted the first national charter of any American party. It also banned quotas, prohibited discrimination, and provided for an affirmative action program to encourage the election of black, female, and young delegates. These modifications emerged from the new Commission on Delegate Selection headed by Baltimore city councilwoman Barbara Mikulski. The Mikulski commission adopted twenty rules, many of them identical to the McGovern-Fraser guidelines but some significantly different. The principal changes were the following:

> States were required to establish affirmative action plans to encourage full participation by all Democrats, with special provisions to include minority groups, Native Americans, women, and youth, "as indicated by their presence in the Democratic electorate." There would be no quotas.
> There must be a fair reflection of voters' presidential preferences at all levels of the delegate selection process. At least 75 percent of the state's delegation, in both primary and convention states, had to be selected in units no larger than a congressional district. Winner-take-all primaries were abolished.
> The new rules required that all feasible steps be taken to restrict the delegate selection process to Democratic voters only, thus outlawing crossover primaries such as the one in Wisconsin.
> Candidates for delegate who desired to run associated with a particular presidential candidate were subject to approval by that candidate.
> A compliance review commission was created, composed of twenty-five members charged with reviewing and monitoring the implementation of state affirmative action and delegate selection programs.

These new rules caused many state parties and state legislatures to change the system under which delegates were selected. Thirty states provided for some form of presidential primary in 1976, and only seventeen states held no primaries at all, instead selecting their delegates in state conventions. Most states used a tiered system of caucuses and conventions starting at the local level, with delegates to each higher level reflecting the presidential preferences of those who had elected them. Thirteen states were permitted to use "loophole" primaries, allowing the election of delegates in congressional districts without proportional representation—in effect permitting winner-take-all at the congressional district level. This loophole was approved by the Mikulski commission and the national chairman, who ruled that the credentials committee would not hear any challenges based on the nonproportionality of representation.[16]

## The Sanford Commission

In the initial thrust of reform, the 1968 Democratic National Convention authorized investigations and recommendations for change in party organizational structures. Both of the early reform commissions, McGovern-Fraser and O'Hara, claimed jurisdiction in this area but eventually became stalemated. Both commissions then jointly proposed a new party charter, but it did not survive the conflict generated by the 1972 divisions within the party. The 1972 convention, as one of its last acts, authorized a new charter commission, and former North Carolina governor Terry Sanford was selected as chairman. The Sanford commission, with 164 members, worked for two years to draft a new charter for the party and eventually arrived at a consensus that was presented to the 1974 midterm (mini) convention in Kansas City and passed without much formal opposition.

The most important result of the Sanford commission's deliberations was the newly structured 350-member national committee described in chapter 3. In addition to specifying the makeup and powers of the new DNC, the charter also:

> Required state parties to adapt their rules and practices to the national party's standards
>
> Allocated national convention delegates through a choice of different formulas giving equal weight to either population or electoral vote and to the Democratic vote for president
>
> Established a judicial council to review and approve state plans for the election of delegates to the national conventions and to adjudicate challenges and credentials disputes
>
> Provided that all meetings of the national committee, the executive committee, and official party commissions operate in the "sunshine" (i.e., in the open)
>
> Required all state parties to adopt and provide to the national committee written rules for the conduct of party business[17]

The adoption of the Democratic charter was an effort to inject new spirit into the party and to provide mechanisms through which internal squabbles could be resolved without the rending and tearing that had taken place in the years immediately preceding its adoption.

## The Winograd Commission

In order to prepare for the 1980 Democratic National Convention a third commission was established—the Commission on Presidential Nomination and Party Structure headed by Michigan state party chairman Morley A. Winograd. Although the work of the commission reopened old controversies concerning delegate selection left over from the McGovern-Fraser and Mikulski commissions, the final report was adopted in early June 1978. The new rules for the 1980 convention were considered a victory for President Jimmy Carter because they made it more difficult for a "fringe" candidate to win delegates to the convention. They shortened the period during which delegate selection can take place from six to three months, required primary states to set candidate-filing deadlines from thirty to ninety days before the election, increased the size of delegations by 10 percent to accommodate state party and elected officials, and limited participation in the delegate selection process to Democrats only. This last rule, in effect, banned crossover primaries, such as the one in Wisconsin, where voters may participate in the Democratic election without designating their party affiliation.[18] Critics contended that the crossover primary permitted Republicans and Independents to have too much influence in the selection of a Democratic candidate. The Wisconsin Supreme Court had ordered the DNC to seat the Wisconsin delegation to the 1980 national convention even though they were selected through the open primary in violation of the party's rules. In early 1981 the U.S. Supreme Court reversed the Wisconsin ruling and upheld the Democratic National Committee's right to determine the rules by which states can choose delegates. The ruling was a victory not only for the national party but also for those attempting to bring greater centralization and nationalization to the political party structure.

## The Hunt Commission

In the aftermath of the 1980 loss of the White House, the Democratic National Committee turned once again to a new commission to revise the delegate selection rules for the 1984 convention, the fourth such effort since 1972. Chaired by Gov. James B. Hunt, Jr., of North Carolina, the Commission on Presidential Nominations worked for a year and was successful in getting approval of new rules in mid-1982. A number of rules changes were approved, including the following:

> Provided that 14 percent of the delegates to the nominating convention be chosen on the basis of their office or party status and without commitment to a candidate. This change would act to restore to participation a greater number of practicing politicians, officeholders, and others with political experience, some of whom would become delegates semiautomatically and others of whom would be chosen by the state parties.
>
> Reinstated the "loophole primary," which had been banned by the 1976 national convention. Under the new rule a candidate winning a clear plurality of the district vote can win all of the delegates and not have to divide them proportionally with other candidates who did not fare as well.
>
> Tightened the "window" of three months during which national convention delegates must be chosen in presidential election years. The new rule shortens the thirty-six days that elapsed between the 1980 Iowa caucuses and the New Hampshire primary to eight days, thus reducing the campaign period by five weeks.[19]

These Democratic party reform commissions were a response to the disastrous 1968 Chicago national convention and to the general reform efforts that later gained momentum after the Watergate affair. Once started, the reform movement maintained its own momentum. The earliest of the reform efforts were partially responsible for the nomination of Sen. George McGovern as the 1972 presidential candidate. His landslide defeat by Richard M. Nixon triggered new demands for revocation of some of the reforms and inaugurated a long quadrennial battle within the Democratic party for control of the nominating process. The activist-reformers wanted to open the party to greater participation by amateurs, whereas the traditionalists wished to maintain the role of professional politicians in the nominating process. The subsequent series of reform commissions and rules changes have largely been an effort to resolve that problem and to arrive at a system that was more open and democratic but at the same time was willing to listen to and use the practical experience and wisdom of old-time party leaders.

American parties have traditionally been little more than collections of state associations. But the new Democratic charter and the new delegate selection rules to be enforced by the national party served to concentrate power at the top. The Democrats were not alone in the party reform movement of the 1970s. The Republican party, too, was active in undertaking change.

## Nominating the President: The Republicans

Because the Republicans controlled the White House during the decade of reform, there was less demand for internal change in the party organization or in the way presidential nominees were selected. Furthermore, many Republican leaders believe that their party is less in need of reform because it has never engaged in some of the practices, such as the unit rule, that led to demands for change in the Democratic party. Nor do the Republicans have the same fratricidal factional pressures from within, since the conservative wing has dominated party councils since the early 1960s, leaving the moderates and liberals divided and weakened. In spite of this, the Republicans established two separate reform committees after the 1968 and 1972 elections. They were active during the same time period as the Democratic reform groups but worked with less fanfare and produced more modest changes.

## The Delegates and Organizations Committee

The first reform committee was an outgrowth of the 1968 national convention, which adopted a rule empowering the Republican National Committee to establish a delegates and organizations committee (the DO committee). Composed entirely of party officials, the DO committee was headed by the national committeewoman from Missouri, Rosemary Ginn. In 1971 the DO committee issued two reports calling for many of the same kinds of reforms recommended to the Democrats by the McGovern-Fraser commission. The DO committee's recommendations included the following:

> Open meetings should be held throughout the delegate selection system as one way to guarantee that all qualified citizens are encouraged to take part.
> No fees should be assessed against delegates as a requirement for taking part in a national convention.
> No proxy voting should be allowed at a convention.
> No automatic delegates should be allowed, i.e., those who become delegates by virtue of some party or elected office held.
> The membership of each convention committee, in addition to the traditional one man and one woman from each delegation, should be increased to include one delegate under the age of twenty-five and one delegate who is a member of a minority ethnic group.
> Each state should be required to seek equal representation between men and women in each delegation.
> Each state should be required to seek delegate representation by persons under the age of twenty-five in proportion to their voting strength within the state's general population.
> The Republican National Committee should assist the states in their efforts to inform citizens on delegate selection processes.[20]

Unlike the Democratic party, which only requires approval of rules changes by the national committee, the Republican rules require approval by a variety of party agencies and ultimately by the next national convention. Thus the DO committee recommendations could not become operative until approved by the 1972 Republican National Convention. Eventually, all were approved except for the one calling for proportional representation for young people. The key difference between the two parties in their new delegate selection processes was that the Democrats, through the McGovern-Fraser commission guidelines, initially attempted to make the quota system mandatory, whereas the Republicans only recommended the election of greater numbers of delegates from the affected minorities.

## The Rule 29 Committee

At the 1972 national convention the Republican delegates passed Rule 29(b), calling for the creation of a new committee to study the party rules with the goal of further opening the selection process to greater participation by women, youth, racial and ethnic minorities, and the elderly. The response to that change was a series of recommendations that would require each state to create a broadly representative Rule 29 committee and to publicize the details of the state's delegate selection process. The state parties would be required to file reports on their positive action programs with the national committee, and that body would be empowered to review and comment on them. The new committee's proposals were considered by a national committee meeting in 1975, and this provision on report filing and reviewing became the principal bone of contention. Opponents, mostly from the conservative wing of the party, contended that it was an emulation of Democratic efforts, which had, they said, resulted in the 1972 defeat of that party. By a vote of seventy-five to seventy-four the provision was deleted. A revised rule was adopted that allows the national committee to review and comment on a state's positive action program only on the request of the state. Quotas were specifically disallowed, but efforts to increase delegate representation from among women, minorities, youth, and the poor were approved.

---

# Critiquing Convention Reforms

A general thrust of these convention reforms, particularly in the Democratic party, has been to enhance democracy by involving more and more people. Some informed critics of the delegate selection reforms have noted that they have not only involved more people but may have simply transferred power to a different set of elites within the party. These new insiders may, in many cases, not be party oriented at all but may owe their allegiance to a particular ideology or an ideologically inclined candidate. The result may be that the reform movement has created a new set of rules that makes it possible to more easily nominate a fringe candidate or one who does not have a national following and is not in the mainstream of opinion within his or her party. The constantly changing delegate selection rules have also caused concern among some that the proliferation of primaries, the deliberate exclusion of many professional and experienced politicians, the rapid increase in campaign costs, and the exceedingly long time period needed for delegate selection have made the presidential nominating system so cumbersome as to demand change. The reforms since 1968 have indisputably brought some improvements to the nominating system. Undemocratic practices in delegate selection have been reduced. Formerly underrepresented groups, particularly women and blacks, have been included in ever-increasing numbers. People who had never before been involved have become active political participants. But the fact remains that no two national Democratic conventions or presidential campaigns since 1968 have been conducted under the same set of rules. To many the nominating system appears to be somewhat haphazard and unstable.

One result has been that a number of conferences, usually sponsored by academic institutions, have been convened in recent years to study the question of presidential nominations.* One of the best known of these was the Commission on the Presidential Nominating Process sponsored by the University of Virginia in 1982. Chaired by former secretary of defense Melvin Laird and former senator Adlai E. Stevenson, the commission issued a report recommending:

1. That the number of presidential primaries be reduced to no more than sixteen. If implemented, this recommendation would automatically bring about a better mix of primaries and caucuses, with a relaxation of state laws or rules (particularly in the Democratic party) to permit greater discretion on the part of delegates.

2. That more than 20 percent of the delegate slots at the conventions be granted to elected officials. This would permit the inclusion of greater numbers of representatives, senators, governors, and party officials who would not be bound by the results of state delegate selection contests. It would help to guarantee a more independent judgment on the part of the convention and would return to the political arena the invaluable experience of the elected officeholder in electoral politics and public office.

3. That all primaries and caucuses be held between the first week in March and the first week in June in primary election years, thus shortening the campaign and the election season. Implementation of this recommendation would reduce costs as well as candidate and voter fatigue.

4. That those states continuing to hold primaries be required to schedule them in blocs defined by time zones, with the order of the primary blocs to be determined by lottery. The commission noted that in 1980 the nomination decision had been made before nearly one-fifth of the population went to the polls to choose their delegates in the June 3 primaries. Another effect of this recommendation would be to undercut the importance of the early Iowa caucuses and the New Hampshire primary, both of which have an unjustifiably large influence because of the media impact of their decisions on the voters in other areas.

5. That changes in campaign finance laws be made to increase the limits on individual campaign contributions from $1,000 to $5,000, thus relieving the candidates of the burden of time-consuming fund raising directed to small contributors.

The commission also recommended that Congress should abolish state-by-state limitations on campaign expenditures. The commission emphasized that "no change is more important than to return to the delegates and the conventions the practical possibility of making an independent judgment. Once delegates and conventions possess this authority, it is essential that the delegates themselves have the qualities and qualifications to exercise their authority with wisdom and discretion."[21]

The presidential nominating process is a consummate political event. It involves a contesting of vital interests over important issues, and it culminates in the selection of

*Three other conferences on political parties and the nominating process were held at approximately the same time, in 1981 and 1982. The Duke University Institute of Policy Sciences and Public Affairs, in conjunction with the Woodrow Wilson International Center for Scholars, sponsored a Forum on Presidential Nominations chaired by former governor Terry Sanford. The main proposals of this group included: the removal of barriers to convenient delegate participation; revitalization of the local party caucus; the concentration of presidential primaries within a four-month period, with one day set aside in each month for the holding of the primaries; designation of major party and public officials as designated delegates; and the freeing of delegates to vote as they wish at the time of the conventions. A Conference on the Parties and the Nominating Process was held at Harvard University in late 1981, sponsored by the Institute of Politics. This conference did not attempt to arrive at a set of proposals but did consider most of the issues raised by the other groups. In April 1982 a conference sponsored by the American Assembly at Columbia University was held at Arden House in Harriman, New York. This Conference on the Future of the American Political Parties addressed a wide range of issues concerning the party organizations themselves and the nominating system. The recommendations of the participants at the American Assembly will be discussed later in the book.

candidates, one of whom will go on to be the leader of the most powerful nation in the free world. As the various reform commissions have found, the repeated revision of the rules and the changing of the standards of selection do not necessarily guarantee better candidates or more democratic participation. Nowhere was that demonstrated more vividly than in both the 1976 and 1980 presidential contests, each of which produced candidates who divided their party faithful and neither of which produced candidates who had a base of support broad enough to reverse the long, steady decline in voter participation.

# The Presidential Nominations in 1976 and 1980: The Battle for Delegates

The reform efforts in both parties were designed to democratize the delegate selection process. There is little question that they did broaden the base from which delegates are chosen and that they provided more representation for certain constituency groups. But the principal result of the new 1972, 1976, and 1980 guidelines was substantial proliferation of presidential preference primaries. The primaries provided the means by which Jimmy Carter captured the Democratic nomination in 1976 and at the same time served as the vehicle used by Ronald Reagan in his nearly successful effort to wrest the Republican nomination from President Gerald R. Ford. In 1980 a hard-fought series of primary and caucus battles between President Carter and Sen. Edward Kennedy badly split the Democratic party. In contrast, Ronald Reagan, after a rocky start, went on to dominate the Republican delegate selection process.

## Jimmy Carter Takes on the Democrats: 1976

With the nomination of Jimmy Carter, the Democratic party endorsed a man about whom it knew little, an outsider to the national political arena. Carter had never been a national candidate before and had no significant experience in or ties to Washington. Furthermore, as a candidate from the Deep South, Carter was distrusted by many in the old New Deal coalition as well as by many who had served in the upper echelons of the Democratic party. Carter and his aides, realizing that they would need to prove themselves as vote getters, entered most of the thirty presidential primaries. Two successes early in the election year gained him national attention and brought an end to much of the skepticism concerning his candidacy.

His first success came in the early Iowa local caucuses, the initial step in the selection of Iowa convention delegates. He followed that by gaining more votes in the New Hampshire primary than any other Democratic candidate. Although he received only 23,373 votes in New Hampshire, that 28 percent share in a nine-candidate field established his legitimacy. He suffered a setback a week later when he ran fourth in the Massachusetts primary but recovered a week after that by winning in Florida. Even when he lost elections, he won additional delegate strength because of the rule dividing delegates proportionally between the contenders. On May 25 he lost three of the six primaries held that day but gained 107 of the 179 delegates chosen in those states. He lost five of the last twelve primaries held during the final three weeks of the election season but in each case added to his delegate count. His successes brought an increase in his public opinion poll ratings and in his campaign contributions, and his major

*"After they've chewed up a few, you get
your pick of what's left"* (From *Herblock on
All Fronts,* New American Library, 1980)

opponents gradually dropped by the wayside. The steady cumulative increase in Jimmy
Carter's delegate strength eventually reached almost 40 percent—none of his opponents had even half that number. By the time the convention opened in New York,
the Georgian was the certain nominee.

As mentioned earlier, Carter, like John F. Kennedy sixteen years before, was something of an outsider to party politics of the kind practiced in the nation's capital. He
had served one term as governor of Georgia and had received national exposure as
chairman of the Democratic campaign committee for the 1974 off-year elections.
Kennedy, although not obscure, was not widely recognized as a national leader until
he decided to seek the presidency shortly after the 1956 election. He too bore some
handicaps that had to be overcome—his youth, his Catholicism, and his rather undis-
tinguished record in Congress.

Both Carter and Kennedy needed the presidential primaries. Both needed a vehicle
to permit them to demonstrate to the power brokers within the Democratic party that
personal popularity and charisma could outweigh political liabilities. Both were able
to use the presidential primaries to accomplish that purpose, and both were successful—Kennedy in proving that he could get large voter support and Carter in establishing that he could build great delegate strength.

## Ronald Reagan Takes on Gerald Ford: 1976

Incumbent presidents normally do not have serious challenges for renomination from
within their party. But President Gerald R. Ford was different from most incumbent
presidents. He was not elected to the office, having succeeded Richard M. Nixon at
the time of the latter's resignation. He had not even been elected to the vice-presidency,
for he was appointed to that post after the resignation of Spiro T. Agnew. In fact, he

had never run for public office in an area larger than his own former congressional district in Michigan. But, in spite of the fact that Republican leaders, on the whole, do not like intraparty political fights, former governor Ronald Reagan of California decided to challenge Ford and almost succeeded in wresting the nomination from him in 1976.

Reagan had a number of factors working in his behalf. Watergate had damaged the authority and the prestige of the presidency, and Ford's pardon of Richard Nixon brought a diminution of his own personal popularity. The new campaign finance laws provided the means for a challenger like Reagan to approach a national campaign on a more equal footing than had ever been the case before. Furthermore, a shift in the delegate apportionment formula, engineered by the conservatives at the 1972 convention (with a view to helping Vice-President Spiro T. Agnew, then still in good graces, win the 1976 nomination) worked to Reagan's advantage by giving a larger share of delegates to states in the West and the South. Finally, the proliferation of presidential primaries helped Reagan, since they made the nomination less susceptible to the influence of party leaders, most of whom favored Ford.

Nevertheless, President Ford won the first four primaries, in New Hampshire, Massachusetts, Florida, and Illinois. Reagan won in North Carolina in late March, and then the order of the primary calendar gave added impetus to the challenger's campaign. The battle for primary delegates shifted to the South and the West, areas of Reagan popularity where, in some cases, crossover voting permitted conservative Democrats to vote in the Republican primaries. All of the Texas delegates went to Reagan, as did most of those in Indiana. By the time the primaries and state conventions were over, Ford led in the delegate count by a slight margin, with enough delegates still uncommitted to decide the nomination. At the Kansas City convention Ford eventually won with a 117 vote margin out of 2,259 votes cast. Reagan had capitalized on his personal popularity in the generally conservative Republican party. He had captured many delegates in state caucuses and conventions and had won enough key primaries to demonstrate his appeal to voters. In the contested primaries Reagan actually emerged with a slight advantage, but it was not great enough to overcome Ford's strength in uncontested primaries and state conventions.

The race again brought home the deep ideological fissures in the Republican party. This debilitating split began in the early 1960s as the conservatives successfully wrested control of the party machinery from the eastern establishment that had controlled it for many years. The moderates had captured every presidential nomination between 1936 and 1960 and had elected governors and senators from virtually all of the largest states. Their mixed success in winning the presidency and their outright failure to gain control of Congress opened the moderate leaders to charges of "me-tooism" and "neo-liberalism," which had little appeal to the conservatives of the South and West. Sen. Barry Goldwater's capture of the 1964 nomination for president was the most visible sign of the conservative surge inside the Republican party, but it had started before that and continued apace thereafter.

In 1976 Ronald Reagan, although he ultimately lost the nomination, had again demonstrated the attraction of conservatives for the Republican rank and file. He had proved once again that presidential primaries tend to shift power from party leaders to party voters. In so doing, he also demonstrated that the power residing in an incumbent president was not invincible.

## Jimmy Carter Seeks Renomination: "The Best Place to Campaign for President"

Gerald Pomper, a political scientist, has noted that the 1980 campaign of President Jimmy Carter demonstrated the truth of the cliché "The presidency is the best place to campaign for President." The president, as have many of his predecessors, based his campaign for renomination and reelection on his incumbency. As Pomper has noted:

> He emphasized the experience he had gained as the nation's chief executive, an asset unavailable to any Democratic contender. Without any special effort, he could be assured of daily news coverage and could request network time for "non-political" events at any time. Every visit of a foreign dignitary, every signing of legislation, and every speech to Congress or news conference was a reminder that Jimmy Carter was the president, while others only hoped for the job.[22]

The renomination strategy was constructed around the advantages of already being in the White House. This "Rose Garden" strategy required that the President remain in Washington, thus removing himself as a target of criticism. By controlling responses to events in foreign policy, he limited the attention of the media to his rivals. By exercising the powers of the office, he effectively made use of the political calendar. As Pomper notes, the Olympic boycott was formally proposed the Sunday before the Iowa caucuses, and a United Nations commission was sent to Teheran the weekend before the New Hampshire primary. On the day before the Wisconsin primary he set a deadline for the transfer of the Iranian hostages.[23]

Carter also used the traditional benefits of the incumbency to his advantage. Funds were released from federal agencies for state and local projects, and federal appointments were made to best capitalize on their electoral impact. Under normal circumstances this would have been enough to guarantee success. But 1980 was not normal in that the incumbent president had major opposition within his own party from Sen. Edward Kennedy of Massachusetts. Furthermore, it appeared, in the summer of 1980, that Jimmy Carter was vulnerable. His approval rating in the Gallup Poll was 21 percent, the lowest of any president in the nearly forty years of polling, including the rating for Richard Nixon just before he resigned.

Senator Kennedy began the campaign with what appeared to be strong support and apparent popularity. His strategy was to capitalize on what was perceived to be President Carter's unpopularity and on the Kennedy organization's efforts to revive the old Democratic coalition of urban residents, union members, Catholics, Jews, and blacks. His apparent support began to dissipate quickly as he was transformed from popular liberal leader to potential president. The issues of personal character, including the decade-old events at Chappaquiddick bridge, gained new emphasis, and his campaign was never able to generate momentum.

After Kennedy's loss to Carter in the Iowa caucuses, the campaign moved on to the New Hampshire primary, a neighbor to Kennedy's Massachusetts, where he not only lost the primary but lost the support of working-class areas on which he had hoped to build his coalition. In Florida Kennedy was badly beaten by Carter, receiving only 23 percent of the popular vote, and his showing in the Illinois primary a week later was a disaster. Not only did the popular vote go to Carter by a margin of two to one, but the effect was exaggerated because Illinois was one of the "loophole primary" states in which delegates were not divided proportionately but were selected in each congressional district. This turned a two-to-one popular margin for the President into a twelve-to-one delegate advantage and gave Carter 10 percent of all the delegates he needed to gain the nomination.

Kennedy's victory in the New York primary revived his campaign for a time, while world and national events conspired against the image of presidential leadership so carefully nurtured by the Carter campaign advisors. Even so, Carter swept the southern primaries and held a decisive delegate advantage over Kennedy. A free-swinging Pennsylvania campaign tipped that state to Kennedy by a narrow popular margin but contributed another 92 delegates to the Carter total—just one less than the number won by Kennedy.

As the final phase leading to the eight primaries on June 3 unfolded, almost nothing went right for the Carter campaign. The attempt to rescue the Iranian hostages failed with loss of life; the Council of Economic Advisors predicted the worst economic downturn in years; Miami was being flooded with Cuban refugees, including a large contingent of criminals pulled from Cuban jails and pushed onto the boatlift; a ten-cents-per-gallon increase in gasoline taxes demanded by the White House was refused by the Democratic Congress; and America's Common Market allies gave legal recognition to the Palestine Liberation Organization. Events seemed out of control, and the president appeared to many to be an ineffectual leader.

Of the final eight primaries, Kennedy won five, including California and New Jersey, and Carter won three, including Ohio. But, at the bottom line, the delegate count showed President Jimmy Carter with 1,971 delegates to Kennedy's 1,221. The Carter margin guaranteed his renomination. Yet the cost of the victory in prestige and public confidence was enormous. Widespread discontent in the nation had come to focus on the president, and Republican Ronald Reagan was to be the benefactor.

## Ronald Reagan Finally Wins the Republican Nomination: 1980

Ronald Reagan, former movie actor, former Democrat, and former governor of California, had run for the presidency in 1976 but finally lost the nomination to President Gerald R. Ford. After a brief respite from his quest, he again undertook a campaign to win the nomination and the office in 1980. Rivals for the nomination of the Republican party were numerous: George Bush, John Anderson, John Connally, Philip Crane, Robert Dole, Howard Baker, and a collection of others, most of whom did not last long into the campaign season. For one brief two-week period former President Ford made it clear that even he would accept the nomination, but his effort, too late to have an impact on the remaining primaries, was quickly abandoned. There were two reasons for the great interest in the Republican nomination: Ronald Reagan, the acknowledged front-runner, was perceived to be too old (he was, in fact, the oldest person ever to be elected and the oldest ever to serve as president); and the unpopularity of Jimmy Carter appeared to be an opportunity that few Republican politicians wished to pass up.

Even though George Bush won the Iowa caucuses, he failed to gain momentum and lost the New Hampshire primary to Reagan. Lack of electoral enthusiasm soon forced all of the candidates from the race except Reagan, Bush, and Anderson. The Illinois primary was crucial to the Anderson campaign because it was the congressman's home state. He worked hard to win, and, although he defeated Bush, he lost to Reagan. He then ran poorly in both Connecticut and Wisconsin, centers of Republican liberalism that should have been drawn to his campaign. At that point Anderson withdrew as a Republican candidate and announced his candidacy as an Independent.

Finally, the race for the nomination came down to Reagan and Bush. Although Bush won primaries in Connecticut, Michigan, and Pennsylvania, Ronald Reagan continued to pile up large numbers of delegates in the South and the West and eventually won a majority of the popular vote. By the end of May Reagan had the necessary majority of delegates to win the nomination. He had shown a broad base of support in the center of new Republican strength in the Sunbelt and the western states. He had established considerable appeal to people of traditional Democratic persuasion, such as labor unions, Catholics, and conservative Democrats. When the Republican Convention took its presidential roll call, Reagan won 1,939 of the 1,994 votes.

Reagan did not make the mistakes that had been made by Sen. Barry Goldwater in 1964. He reached out to his vanquished foes, offered modifications of platform positions to appeal to moderates, and kept the moderate and highly regarded national party chairman, William Brock, in office. His most obvious effort to mend the rifts in party unity came in his selection of a vice-presidential candidate. After a curious and abortive attempt to persuade former President Ford to become his running mate, Reagan chose George Bush, his most persistent opponent in the nominating campaign. The Republicans left Detroit convinced that their unity, their superior campaign resources, their overwhelming financial backing, and the divided and quarreling Democratic party led by an unpopular candidate augured well for success in the November elections.[24]

## Choosing the Vice-Presidential Nominees

Since 1945 the United States has had eight presidents, three of whom succeeded to the office from the vice-presidency. Harry S Truman took over after the death of Franklin D. Roosevelt in the midst of the greatest war the country has ever fought. Lyndon B. Johnson succeeded John F. Kennedy as the unpopular and divisive war in Vietnam was getting under way. And Gerald R. Ford succeeded to the office on the resignation of Richard M. Nixon in the aftermath of the deepest political scandals ever to beset the nation. Each was elected or appointed to the office of vice-president at the behest of a single man—Roosevelt, Kennedy, and Nixon, respectively.

Vice-presidential nominations are made quickly and almost always on command of the newly nominated presidential candidate. Sometimes history suggests that little thought has gone into the choice. The tone of consultations over potential nominees is usually in terms of the potential benefits to the ticket, not in terms of the candidate's qualifications as a possible presidential successor. One recent vice-president (Spiro T. Agnew) was forced to resign after it was revealed that he had evaded income taxes, and in 1972 the Democratic nominee (Thomas Eagleton) resigned from the ticket in mid-campaign after it became known that he had been treated for mental illness. In short, most presidential candidates, in the afterglow of their own nomination, are forced to make late-night, often hasty and ill-considered decisions that can, and often do, vitally affect the nation's future. Critics generally agree that the system should be changed, but few agree on how best to change it. Most people agree that the presidential candidate should not be laden with a running mate with whom he has no rapport and with whom he may not share a mutual respect. Most presidential candidates have approached the choice of a running mate in personal political terms rather than in terms of the nation's best interest. Most proposals for change have centered around extending the period of time between the presidential selection and the necessity for final vice-presidential choice. Nevertheless, little has been done to revise the system effectively, and important institutional changes do not appear imminent.

## The National Conventions

The national nominating conventions have been a fixture of American government since the mid-1800s. They have often been rowdy, gaudy, flamboyant, ridiculous, and noisy, but they have also, at their best, produced nominations for Abraham Lincoln, Theodore Roosevelt, Charles Evans Hughes, Woodrow Wilson, Franklin D. Roosevelt, Adlai Stevenson, Dwight D. Eisenhower, and John F. Kennedy. In most cases even those candidates who fell short of greatness were respectable leaders and acceptable choices. At their worst the national conventions have earned the ridicule heaped on them by H. L. Mencken in 1932:

> It is instructive to observe these great men at the solemn business of selecting a First Chief for the greatest free Republic ever seen on earth. . . . One sees them at close range, sweating, belching, munching peanuts, chasing fleas. They parade idiotically, carrying dingy flags and macerating one another's corns. They crowd the aisles, swapping gossip, most of it untrue. They devour hot dogs. They rush out to the speakeasies. They rush back to yell, fume, and vote.
>
> The average delegate never knows what is going on. The hall is in dreadful confusion, and the speeches from the platform are mainly irrelevant and unintelligible. The real business of a national convention is done down under the stage, in dark and smelly rooms, or in hotel suites miles away. Presently a State boss fights his way out to his delegation on the floor and tells his slaves what is to be voted on, and how they are to vote.[25]

Nowadays, it is rare that a "boss" tells his "slaves" how to vote, because most of them were elected in a presidential primary and their votes are committed. But, as any convention watcher can testify, this colorful description by Mencken is still in many respects not too far from the mark. The color and excitement of the convention would be lost if the nominating system were changed; and that, in the opinion of many observers, would be an unfortunate loss for American politics.

Formal authority in national politics flows from the quadrennial conventions. As we have seen, each convention is composed of delegates selected from the states and territories who meet together once every four years to perform four major functions: (1) to nominate candidates for president and vice-president; (2) to write a platform or to ratify one written elsewhere; (3) to adopt formal party rules and changes in procedures; and (4) to serve as a kickoff for the fall campaign and/or as a healer of wounds that have been caused by conflict over the nomination.

Few changes in the roles of the national conventions have occurred since they were first used as a nominating vehicle. As we have seen, though, there have been important developments in the presidential primary system of selecting delegates: the growth of influence of radio, television, and public opinion polls; the decline in power of the political boss; and the increase in preconvention campaigning. Some changes have been made in recent years in the way in which both the Republican and Democratic national conventions function.

The basic work of each convention is carried out by four major committees. Their duties have remained the same for many years, although the Democrats have changed the political calendar so that, in some cases, the more important committee sessions for that party take place before the opening of the convention itself. The Republican committees meet either during the convention week or, in the case of the platform committee, the week before the opening of the convention.

## Permanent Organization Committee

This committee selects the permanent officers who will direct the proceedings of the convention. In the past these designees were chosen by the national chairperson and ratified by the committee. The new Democratic rules, however, call for each of the four committees to choose its own chairperson, and some of the early preliminary skirmishes in the 1976 and 1980 presidential conventions took place at these committee meetings. The Republican committees are all composed of one male and one female delegate from each state, and the membership of each committee selects its own chairperson. The convention officers are chosen by the permanent organization committee and include the permanent chairperson, secretary, and sergeant at arms. These officers are important since they, to a large extent, control the direction and the timing of the convention.

## Credentials Committee

In terms of the outcome of the presidential nomination battle the credentials committee may well be the most crucial of the convention units. That is because, in a close contest, the credentials committee's decisions can be important in deciding who ultimately can vote on convention decisions. One of the most memorable credentials fights took place at the 1952 Republican convention when the committee supported the pro-Taft delegation from Texas, only to have the decision overturned on the floor with the seating of the pro-Eisenhower delegation. If the Taft delegates had been seated, the Ohio senator would have led General Eisenhower on the first ballot, a psychological and political boost that might have resulted in Taft's nomination.

A more recent credentials conflict took place at the 1972 Democratic convention in Miami Beach when the credentials committee, after a heated conflict between the McGovern and anti-McGovern forces, chose to split the California delegation between them. Although later overturned on the convention floor, this challenge was representative of more than a dozen that were fought in an effort to decide which delegates could vote. Ultimately, the power of the McGovern forces won most of the crucial battles, once again bearing out the old adage that determinations of this kind in national conventions are made on the basis of who has the most votes—not of what is "fair" or "right." Undoubtedly, credentials fights are the most crucial to the candidates and to the orderliness of a convention. The outcome of these conflicts can actually determine whether one or another candidate receives the required votes to win.

## Rules Committee

As the name implies, the rules committees determine the rules under which conventions proceed. These matters are usually of little public interest, but each convention requires the settlement of disputes over the length of nominating and seconding speeches, access to the floor, demonstrations, and the order in which delegations will be polled. In short, the rules committees deal with matters that affect the progress of the convention.

They can be important in the nominating battle, but their work is not widely noted unless an issue arises that has a direct effect on the nomination. One such incident was the repeal of the two-thirds rule of the Democratic convention in 1936. The effect of this change was to erode seriously the power of the southern delegation in the nominating contest. The rule, requiring that two-thirds of the votes in a convention were necessary to nominate, meant that the southerners were often able to thwart the nomination of candidates they considered unacceptable. At the 1976 Republican convention the Reagan forces sought to change the rules to require presidential candidates to designate who their running mates would be.

In 1980 the Republican rules committee changed the time of election for the national chairman and, as mentioned earlier, made it more difficult for the national committee to make contributions to primary candidates. The Democratic convention became involved with a major rules fight over an effort of the Kennedy forces to defeat a Carter-backed "open convention" rule to bind all delegates to vote on the first ballot for the presidential candidate under whose banner they were selected. The Kennedy people lost in the rules committee but filed a minority report that placed the matter on the agenda of the convention itself. A Carter victory in getting the new rule adopted would guarantee against last-minute defections from the president; a Kennedy victory would open the possibility that enough Carter delegates would have second thoughts about the electability of their candidate and would switch sides at the time of the roll call. After a vigorous and contentious debate the rule was adopted, thus guaranteeing President Carter the nomination.

## Platform (Resolutions) Committee

The citizens who make up the American parties are never completely united on every issue. The ideological factions within the party make total agreement impossible. Liberal and conservative factions wrestle each other for control of the party machinery, and the very ideological terms used to describe them indicate their disagreements over policy. Such basic disagreement makes platform writing difficult but often interesting as well. The platform (resolutions) committee is composed of delegates who are expected to resolve party differences as far as possible in order to present the voters with a statement of beliefs on current policy questions. The need to "paper over" factional dissension turns most platforms into documents of compromise.

Gerald Pomper has noted that, according to conventional political wisdom, platforms are largely irrelevant to subsequent governmental policymaking. He summarizes the charges against platforms this way: (1) platform statements are usually not very important, are ambiguous, and are often contradictory; (2) since few differences exist between the platforms of the two parties, platforms hold little value for the voters; and (3) the statements of party principle agreed upon do not bind the candidates who are eventually chosen as standard bearers for that year. In short, the principal function of the party platform is as a campaign device that has little relevance to governing or government.

As Pomper points out, though, these criticisms are not entirely valid. Many party platforms have indeed taken unequivocal stands on important issues. The Republicans, from their earliest conventions, clearly opposed the extension of slavery to the territories and favored the protective tariff. The 1948 Democratic platform, as well as those that have followed, called flatly for the repeal of the Taft-Hartley Act (the Labor-Management Act of 1946), and that party's platform has often called for extensions of the Social Security program. Thus, although platforms are often ambiguous, they are not universally so.

Finally, Pomper notes that the most accurate criticism of platforms is that candidates are not bound by party promises. In a number of cases the candidate has actually repudiated the planks with which he disagreed. Presidential failures to carry out platform pledges are common. Pledges are often more precise when they touch on the special interests of party support groups, since party leaders and candidates want to forge an effective coalition of group support. On many occasions language suggested by certain groups has been incorporated into platform statements. The platform is a road map of the interest-group constituents to whom the party plans to appeal. It is both a campaign document and a policy statement. The party platform represents the confluence of many streams: ideas, phrases, and paragraphs may be originated by the president's office, the departments of the government, congressional offices, interest-group headquarters, or ordinary citizens. But, once adopted by the platform committee and the convention, these provisions constitute the pledges of the party.[26]

In recent national conventions some of the sharpest debate and most interesting candidate strategies have emerged during conflicts in the platform committees and during convention consideration of controversial planks. In 1980 Sen. Edward Kennedy's supporters were able to modify the platform proposals to make some of them distasteful to President Carter. The Kennedy forces were also successful in getting a new rule adopted requiring presidential candidates to state in writing their differences with the platform and to pledge to carry out its provisions. At the time the rule was adopted the Kennedy people hoped that the obligation to endorse the platform would prove embarrassing to Carter and might be used to win additional delegates for the senator. This effort was doomed, however, with the adoption of the "open convention" rule. Furthermore, President Carter responded to the platform proposals with a written statement that neither rejected nor accepted them. The 1980 Republican platform, in contrast, reflected the convention control wielded by Ronald Reagan, and the conservatives and moderates worked out their differences in order to present a united front.

## Healing the Wounds of the Nominating Battle

Finally, the national convention allows the presidential candidate to repair fractured egos, heal political wounds, and forge new alliances with his former enemies. The long season of presidential primaries, caucuses, and, occasionally, bruising convention fights often leaves party solidarity in a shambles. Comments have been made during the heat of the delegate battle that need to be retracted. Promises have been given that cannot be kept. Disagreements have arisen over position statements. The final day of the convention offers the successful candidate and his vice-presidential choice a final chance to weld together party factions in order to prepare for the fall campaign.

Sometimes the choice of a running mate is in itself an attempt to mend fences. The selection of Lyndon B. Johnson by presidential nominee John F. Kennedy not only strengthened the Democratic ticket in the South but also assuaged the anger of the Johnson partisans, who deeply resented their candidate's failure to win first place on the ticket. Because of his commitment to a campaign of total conservatism, 1964 Republican candidate Barry Goldwater chose another conservative, Congressman William E. Miller of New York, in a move widely believed to have been a tactical mistake.

This act did not extend an olive branch to the moderate and liberal segments of the party, and it was interpreted by many as a deliberate insult.

On the final night of the 1976 Democratic convention in New York, the national television audience witnessed a parade of hundreds of party leaders and followers as they crossed the platform to display their solidarity to the nation. Friends and enemies alike embraced Jimmy Carter and Walter Mondale in a mass exorcism of factional demons. This scene was repeated in 1980 with added drama as President Carter anxiously waited to see if Senator Kennedy would make an appearance on the podium— an appearance that was eventually made but that caused comment due to its brevity. These rites of reconciliation demonstrate the importance of the hours after the nominating battle as a time, when the party leadership is assembled, to bring together a coalition of partisan factions and to begin the process of healing self-inflicted wounds.

## The Proposed National Presidential Primary

The reform movements of the past decade have been designed to democratize the delegate selection process. They have carried the parties a long way toward broader participation by citizens and toward more open conventions. Some advocates of reform, however, believe that nothing can ever overcome what they consider the intrinsically undemocratic nature of the convention system itself. These critics note that few people actually participate in the election of delegates and that those who do are one or two steps removed from the actual nomination process at the conventions. One proposal that has been considered for many years in one form or another is to create a national presidential primary.

The idea for a primary to be held throughout the nation on the same day, with the voters choosing between the announced candidates, has sometimes had a large following. Former Senate majority leader Mike Mansfield and various cosponsors introduced bills calling for a national primary in successive sessions of the Senate over a thirty-year period. The idea has always generated strong support in public opinion polls, although some believe that support to be built on rather shaky foundations of public understanding. Advocates of the idea argue that the national primary could shorten campaigns by virtue of its scheduling, would cost less in campaign expenditures for the candidates, would eliminate the hoopla and circus atmosphere of the national conventions, and would ultimately result in a true reflection of the wishes of the voters in each party as to who should be their candidate for president. All of these arguments sound persuasive to many people and become more so as the frustration level rises during the quadrennial spring primary marathon.

Although it is acknowledged that the sponsors are well intentioned, the national primary concept has found few friends among serious students of the nomination process. Most who have studied the idea have concluded that the disadvantages of the system far outweigh any gains that might be won. The arguments against the national primary can be summarized as follows:

1. The proposed system would go far toward destroying what remains of the party system. For those who believe that political parties are an important bridge between the people and the government, the further erosion of the system would be intolerable. The national convention system would no longer be necessary, unless some form of

convention was held to draft a platform, and the parties would lose what little control over candidate selection they still retain.

2. Most of the proposals that have surfaced over the years have contained a provision that, should no candidate receive some designated percentage of the votes (usually 35 or 40 percent), a runoff election would be necessary. Given the number of times the average American voter goes to the polls today, the addition of these two national elections could adversely affect turnout because of voter fatigue. Furthermore, most proposals have called for these national primaries to be held early in the fall, a time when interest might be low due to the end of the vacation season, the opening of school, and the celebration of Labor Day.

3. The national primary would necessarily be closely tied to television as a vehicle through which to carry the campaign to the people. Not only would that be enormously expensive, possibly doubling the cost of electing the president, but it would put a premium on the candidate who projected well over the tube. Critics of the national primary note that the handsome, articulate, and well-groomed candidate might well win votes in spite of being empty-headed. Yet, because of the limited time available for the campaign, particularly the runoff primary, candidates would be forced to use television to reach the maximum number of people in the shortest period of time.

4. Finally, the probability is high that the majority of candidates in both parties would be representative of the center, making it more likely that the moderate vote would be split. This could conceivably make it possible for a candidate representing a large left or right ideological fringe, a particular geographic region, or a single issue to perform well enough to be nominated. Under such circumstances a small turnout of centrists divided among several candidates might be overwhelmed by a large outpouring of support from a dedicated, even fanatical, ideological fringe. The choices of the primary might thus represent the extremes of the party coalition.[27]

Critics of the national primary proposals do not argue that the present system is perfect or that it has always produced first-rate nominees. It does, however, require that successful candidates perform well in a variety of political environments and successfully negotiate a series of political shoals. The system is an exhausting one for both the candidates and the voters, but it is spread over a period of time long enough to permit people to make judgments about the various candidates. It does allow candidates who are less well heeled and those who have more difficulty raising campaign funds an opportunity to remain in contention by permitting them to choose those primaries that will be the best showcases for their candidacies. For all its faults, most observers and students of the nominating process believe that what we have is better than what we would get under the proposed national primary. They maintain that the national convention system has served us well and has produced some truly great statesmen.

## Nomination: A Public Enterprise

The attempts by former Republican national chairman Brock to reassert the influence of party in the nominating process may prove transient. Most party leaders are reluctant to involve themselves in nominating contests because the political dangers are too great. However, regardless of the duration of the experiment, Brock has helped to focus attention on the enormous impact on nominations brought about by greater public involvement. Primaries, whether to select a county commission candidate or to vote on a presidential nominee, are no longer party enterprises. The nominating system, under the impetus of reform, has become a public enterprise. Every major change in the nominating system in the past fifty years has further eroded the control of the party over the process of selecting candidates. This fact may well constitute the principal reason for the decline in party influence.

No convention of either party since 1952 has taken more than the first ballot to nominate its presidential candidate. In fact, with the exception of Gerald R. Ford, every nomination during that period has been determined before the convention even met. The ability of candidates to win first-ballot victories is impressive evidence of the decline of the national convention as an arena in which nominations are arrived at through the brokers of party power. This has come about because of important changes that have occurred in the nominating process. Pomper notes that the candidates are now judged and evaluated by representatives of the mass media. Reporters, editors, and commentators have displaced delegates as the certifying agents.[28] Collectively, they are what *New York Times* columnist Russell Baker has labeled "the Great Mentioner," the source of self-fulfilling stories that a person has been "mentioned" as a possible presidential nominee. They label candidates as "front-runners" or note that they are "moving up fast." They exaggerate the importance of particular events, such as the New Hampshire primary, which sometimes raises an obscure candidate to the level of a contender in spite of the fact that it brings about the election of a mere handful of delegates by one of the smallest states in the Union. A tearful public defense by a candidate (Edmund Muskie) of his wife against political attack can convince millions, through the medium of television, that he is not as stable as one might hope. An offhand remark about being "brainwashed" can suggest to the nation that a candidate (George Romney) is unsuited to the high office.

New federal laws to reform political finance by providing public funding for campaigns permit candidates to wage campaigns without party support or assistance. New state laws creating presidential preference primaries take away from the party organization the right to select its own convention delegates. Population growth and social change give impetus to the use of the electronic media, thus furnishing a vehicle through which the people can be reached. All of these changes have undercut the traditional role of the national convention. Each of them has transferred key elements of political power to the voters at large. But, in the process, the changes have further eroded party power and altered the face of American politics.

All of these changes have had an enormous effect on the content of campaigns and the style of campaigning. Since World War II the changes in campaigns and the impact they have on candidate selection, elections, and voter choice have been nothing short of phenomenal. In chapter 5 we will further consider campaigns and other factors that affect electoral outcomes.

# Notes

1. Republican National Committee, *1981 Chairman's Report* (Washington, D.C.: Republican National Committee, 1981), pp. 23–24.

2. *Congressional Quarterly Weekly Report* 38, no. 29 (July 19, 1980): 2012.

3. "Republicans flex party muscle in push to win fall elections," *New York Times* (October 25, 1981): 33.

4. Robert J. Huckshorn, *Party Leadership in the States* (Amherst: University of Massachusetts Press, 1976), p. 103.

5. William Anderson and Edward W. Weidner,

*American Government,* 4th ed. (New York: Holt, 1953), p. 436.

6. Richard S. Childs, "Inside 100 State Parties," *National Civic Review* 56, no. 10 (November 1967): 568–571.

7. Samuel C. Patterson, "Characteristics of Party Leaders," *Western Political Quarterly* 16, June 1963: 348.

8. Austin Ranney, "Parties in State Politics," in *Politics in the American States: A Comparative Analysis,* 3rd ed., eds. Herbert Jacob and Kenneth Vines (Boston: Little, Brown, 1976), pp. 70–72.

9. Malcolm E. Jewell, "Voting Turnout in State Gubernatorial Primaries," *Western Political Quarterly* 30, no. 2 (June 1977): 236–254.

10. Malcolm E. Jewell and David M. Olson, *American State Political Parties and Elections* (Homewood, Ill.: Dorsey Press, 1982), p. 122.

11. Ibid., pp. 122–123.

12. Ranney, "Parties in State Politics," pp. 70–72.

13. Austin Ranney, "The Representativeness of Primary Electorates," *Midwest Journal of Political Science* 12 (May 1968): 224–238. See also Austin Ranney and Leon D. Epstein, "The Two Electorates: Voters and Non-Voters in Wisconsin Primary," *Journal of Politics* 28 (August 1966): 598–616.

14. For the effects of contested primaries, see Donald B. Johnson and James R. Gibson, "The Divisive Primary Revisited: Party Activists in Iowa," *American Political Science Review* 68 (1974): 67–77; Robert A. Bernstein, "Divisive Primaries Do Hurt: U.S. Senate Races, 1956–1972," *American Political Science Review* 71 (1977): 540–545; and John Comer, "Another Look at the Effects of the Divisive Primary," *American Politics Quarterly* 4 (1976): 121–128.

15. Commission on Party Structure and Delegate Selection, *Mandate for Reform* (Washington, D.C.: Democratic National Committee, 1970), p. 10.

16. Louis Maisel and Joseph Cooper, eds., *The Impact of the Electoral Process,* Sage Electoral Studies Yearbook, vol. 3 (Beverly Hills, Calif.: Sage, 1977), p. 42. See also *Congressional Quarterly Weekly Report* (August 16, 1975): 1812.

17. Democratic Charter Commission, *Charter of the Democratic Party of the United States* (Washington, D.C.: Democratic National Committee, 1974). Adopted in Kansas City, Mo., December 7, 1974.

18. *Congressional Quarterly Weekly Report* (June 17, 1978): 1571–1572.

19. *New York Times* (January 15, 1982: 6; January 17, 1982: 13; and March 27, 1982: 1 and 8.)

20. Delegate and Organizations Committee, *Programming for the Party Future, Part I* (Washington, D.C.: Republican National Committee, January 15–16, 1971); and Delegates and Organizations Committee, *The Delegate Selection Procedures for the Republican Party, Part II* (Washington, D.C.: Republican National Committee, July 23, 1971).

21. *Report of the Commission on the Presidential Nominating Process,* White Burkett Miller Center of Public Affairs, University of Virginia, 1982.

22. Gerald M. Pomper et al., eds. *The Election of 1980: Reports and Interpretations* (Chatham, N.J.: Chatham House, 1980), pp. 20–32.

23. Pomper, *Election of 1980,* p. 21.

24. Two other reviews of the 1980 nominating campaign worth noting are Ellis Sandoz and Cecil V. Crabb, Jr., eds., *A Tide of Discontent: The 1980 Elections and Their Meaning* (Washington, D.C.: Congressional Quarterly Press, 1981); and Theodore H. White, *America In Search of Itself* (New York: Harper & Row, 1982), chs. 8, 9, 10, and 11.

25. H. L. Mencken, *Making a President* (New York: Knopf, 1932), pp. 28–29.

26. Gerald Pomper, *Nominating the President: The Politics of Convention Choice* (Evanston, Ill.: Northwestern University Press, 1963), pp. 68–82. See also Pomper, *Elections in America* (New York: Dodd, Mead, 1968), ch. 7.

27. For a good discussion of the national primary, see William J. Crotty, *Political Reform and the American Experiment* (New York: Crowell, 1977), pp. 229–230.

28. Gerald Pomper, "Nominating Contests and Conventions," in Pomper et al., *The Election of 1976* (New York: McKay, 1977), pp. 33–34; and William R. Keech and Donald R. Matthews, *The Party's Choice* (Washington, D.C.: Brookings Institution, 1976), p. 13.

# CHAPTER FIVE

# Campaigns and the Electoral Process

As the candidate drove home from his last campaign appearance, he hoped to get some sleep before the dawn of election day. He recalled the night the delegation of party leaders called upon him to ask if he would consider being the party's candidate for Congress. They assured him that, in their collective opinion, he would make an excellent candidate and, with their money and support, he might defeat the entrenched incumbent congressman. They outlined for him the ways in which they could help. They would see to it that other candidates did not file for the nomination. They could arrange with national and state leaders to furnish a big-name speaker during the campaign. Money could be raised, and volunteers could be enlisted. Everyone knew, they said, that the incumbent could be beaten with the right opponent. He was little more than an errand-boy who had never in six terms made an important contribution. All of that had been months ago. But, as he pulled into his driveway, he sighed over lost opportunities, failed promises, and faded hopes. He knew in his heart that tomorrow night the congressman would be reelected—thereby adding one more opponent's pelt to his office wall.

Nothing much had worked during the campaign. He had learned that few local party organizations are so well organized and cohesive that promises could always be kept. In spite of the leader's assurances, a self-starter candidate had filed, siphoning off precious resources for a primary when they could have been better saved for his general election campaign. No nationally recognized speaker was assigned, because national party leaders considered the incumbent to be "safe" and unchallengeable.

Campaign money was spent on candidates who had a better chance. Small contributions were hard to come by. The promised legions of workers did not volunteer, and the campaign fell to the candidate's personal organization, his family, and his friends. The congressman's reputation as an errand-boy paid off handsomely. He had performed hundreds of favors for constituents and interest groups. Money flowed to his campaign uninterrupted, paying for television ads, radio spots, and hired professionals to run the campaign. The emoluments of the office— staff, paid travel, the franking privilege—all contributed to an aura of invincibility. The congressman's hold on his office seemed to be invulnerable.

Armchair political experts and campaign devotees like to think of politics in competitive terms—as a horse race or a prize fight from which the "best" candidate will emerge victorious. This stereotype is based in about equal parts on a nostalgia for earlier days of party rallies, stump speeches, and brass bands and on a misunderstanding of modern campaign techniques and costs. In the Alice-in-Wonderland world of current politics, "things are seldom what they seem." Our mythical candidate had learned a hard lesson. He now understood what his college political science teacher meant when he talked about decentralization, lack of party responsibility, the nonideological nature of parties, and the absence of public commitment to politics. In the process he also discovered that campaigning was quite different from what he had conceived. The old style of campaigning, popular when he was younger, had given way to a new technocratic style that demanded greater sophistication and understanding of public relations and the media.

In this chapter we will review the art of campaigning and consider the impact of campaigns on electoral outcomes. We will see that, since World War II, scientific developments such as television, computers, opinion polls, and other social and technological inventions have revolutionized midcentury office seeking. Except in some rural areas or in some local campaigns, one can no longer rely exclusively on speeches, rallies, and door-to-door campaigning, nor can one depend on party organizations for needed resources. The changes in campaign methods can be considered from the point of view of the "old" versus the "new."

## The Old Politics: Meeting the Voters

Campaigning is hard work. It does not matter whether one refers to the old style of campaigning, built on shoe leather and handshakes and managed by the party, or the new style, composed of candidate-oriented media appeals: television debates, telephone banks, and mass mailings. The goals are the same; only the methods differ.

Most campaigns, at whatever level, have traditionally not been very well planned. They have combined the problems of organizational management with the nebulous practices associated with old-fashioned circuses and carnivals. Many resemblances, in fact, exist between the sawdust trail and the campaign trail. A political campaign is a seasonal pilgrimage of a candidate's nomadic entourage, moving from place to place for limited appearances and always looking for a crowd before which to perform.

Most candidates would agree with former California governor Edmund "Pat" Brown who, after unexpectedly defeating former vice-president Richard M. Nixon in the 1962 gubernatorial election, responded with the victory statement: "What a Hell of a way to make a living."[1] Campaigning has changed considerably over the years. Politics, too, has altered. Most of the changes have come about since World War II, which ushered in the great technological revolution of television.

Robert Agranoff, a political scientist who has studied campaign styles, points out four important distinctions between the old style and the new. *First,* the candidate, rather than the party, tends to be the major focus of modern campaigns. Candidates sometimes delete references to their party affiliation from their campaign literature, seeking to link the issues of the day with their own name, rather than with their party. Furthermore, generally the most impressive campaign organizations are those run by candidates, not by parties. A well-financed candidate can build an organization devoted exclusively to his own election. The party organization must support many candidates for different offices. At the same time, it should be noted that not all campaigns have become candidate oriented. In some areas unified party-run campaigns are still undertaken, and successfully so.

*Second,* in the new modes of campaigning that have emerged since World War II, the use of party professionals to run campaigns has given way to the technical professional—the management specialist, the pollster, the advertising person, the public relations consultant. When it became evident that the political parties did not have available people with the skills to organize and run a modern campaign, candidates turned to those who already had the necessary skills in the world of business—planners, market researchers, public relations and advertising professionals. New complex campaign finance laws forced candidates and parties alike to look to the public accountant for help.

The *third* distinction between the old and the new style of campaign management stems from improved technology itself. Political professionals from earlier times were forced to rely on reports from precinct captains and seat-of-the-pants judgments. The new campaign manager uses systematic research gathered through polls and surveys and processed through a computer. These technological modes of campaigning have replaced the precinct or party worker in many places.

Finally, a *fourth* change has come about because of the communications revolution. In earlier times the party organization had control of campaign communications. Information was distributed to the voters through speeches, handouts, and party rallies. Services and favors were the staples of the precinct captain and the ward boss. They extended from ordinary taxpayer supported services, such as garbage collection (which might be better because the captain was overseeing it), to the help provided for immigrant families looking for a link to a new and strange government. The party man was there to help fill out government papers, explain the tax system, help find jobs, and take care of bureaucratic tangles. The payoff came on election day, when the votes were counted. The precinct captain was expected to deliver or, if he did not, to step aside for someone who could.[2]

Today, control over the distribution of campaign information has been transferred to the candidate and his staff. It includes computer-printed personalized letters, professional telephone banks, television and radio advertising, and mass door-to-door distribution of materials. As Agranoff notes, "Television has become the surrogate party worker, the vehicle for conveying candidate style, image, and issues." The key to all of these changes has been the transfer of campaign emphasis from the political party organization to the candidate organization. The tools of the transfer have been modern communications, expert research, and computer analysis.[3]

The old politics still has an important place in many campaigns. Candidates and party officers in many areas of the country still canvass votes, distribute literature outside shopping centers, and take people to the polls on election day. Many candidates who are underfinanced are forced to rely on these traditional methods of campaigning. Party organizations use newspaper advertisements to urge the election of all the candidates on the ticket. Volunteers keep open the doors of storefront headquarters. The old techniques still serve the parties and their candidates well in some places for some campaigns.

Nevertheless, we have embarked on a political road that is marked by both voter and candidate independence from the party. The new styles and the new tools of campaigning blend well with the new independence. The change has not been universal. Pockets of party-run campaigns still remain, and some of the surviving political machines still rely on the power generated for the precinct captains by patronage appointments, but even the machines have adopted many of the new techniques of campaigning.

Even those political leaders who have embraced the new technology still long for an earlier era when political campaigns were a form of entertainment. Political rallies were held in public parks, and large audiences were perfectly content to listen for hours to political speeches interspersed with music, dancing, games, and repasts. These events were usually run by the party organization for the entire ticket. Professor M. Ostrogorski describes one such event from an earlier time:

> The whole neighborhood is invited to a "rally," a big meeting; the farmers generally come in large numbers, on horseback, in breaks, or on foot, often with their families. Political speakers sent down by committees hold forth in a covered enclosure to audiences which, especially in the West, are composed of both men and women. In the daytime a "procession" takes place: the faithful followers of the party, adorned with emblems, scour the country, headed by a band; the negro village barber, wearing a costume trimmed with gold, beats time with indescribable dignity. In the evening the houses of all the party faithful are illuminated, and a torch-light procession concludes the "Chinese business." The fete, however, still goes on; the speakers reappear, and, in the open air, on the green, by the flickering glare of the torches, they harangue the assembled crowd. But the attention of the wearied public is distracted, there are only a few groups listening here and there, the rest are talking, the young people are flirting in the dim light.[4]

Clearly, Ostrogorski was describing a social and recreational event as well as a political one. Politics in the old days was more of a social function. It was a means for getting people together as well as an exercise in democracy. But politics as a form of social intercourse and as a form of entertainment has suffered in competition with new diversions. It was always an art, with few prescribed rules. There was a considerable store of conventional wisdom, and most campaigns were organized to take advantage of that wisdom. But the basic overriding goal was to meet as many people and gain as much recognition as possible. In an era of small populations, closer community ties, and stronger parties, that goal was relatively easy to achieve. The old style of politics gradually gave way to the new because of: (1) the decline of political parties; (2) the decline of party voting; (3) the growth of the mass media; and (4) the advent of professional campaign management.

*"Frankly, Al, we feel it wasn't your style, your platform, or the people around you the voters wouldn't buy. What they wouldn't buy was you."*
(Drawing by Lorenz; © 1974 The New Yorker Magazine, Inc.)

## The New Politics: Reaching the Voters

New techniques in political campaigning have arisen because of profound changes in American politics; these changes have centered around weakened party structures and greater personalism. Traditional party organizations that were able (at least in some places) to mobilize voters and get them to the polls to "vote the ticket" have given way to a new form of politics based on the use of mass communications that reach the voters through electronic means.

### Decline of Party Organizations

Students of politics almost all agree that the principal causes for the shift to technocratic campaigning have been the steady decline of party organizations and the rise in available technology. As we have noted before, party strength has gradually eroded throughout this century on account of the loss of control by party leaders over such things as candidate selection, campaign management, issue positions, and the distribution of political rewards. The rise of the mass media has hastened this decline and permitted professional campaign managers to move in to do what parties had traditionally done in an earlier age.

We have noted the loss of organizational control over candidate selection through the spread of the direct-primary system of nomination. With the loss of control the parties also lost their influence over candidates' issue positions. Candidates running for office today frequently stake out their positions very early—often at the time they announce for the nomination. They become locked into positions that may not fit within the party's programmatic scheme. Republican candidates may well find themselves supporting issues in direct opposition to party platform pronouncements. And, as we have pointed out before, once a candidate has been without party support, he or she is quite able to operate outside the influence of party leaders.

Coupled with the decline in party influence over candidates has been a parallel decline in party influence over voters. Until recently, party loyalty, as measured by the self-identification of party members, was a reliable indicator of support. During the 1950s and 1960s the figures remained relatively stable, but in the 1970s considerable shifting of voter allegiance occurred. According to the Gallup Opinion Survey, between 1940 and 1972 the number of Democrats averaged about 44 percent of all voters, with the Republicans and Independents dividing up the remaining 56 percent. In 1971, however, the number of self-identified Independents began to increase, until, by 1977, 31 percent of the people described themselves as Independents. The Republicans, during the same period, began to lose adherents, until by 1977 only 20 percent of the electorate termed themselves members of the GOP. By mid-1982 the number of Republican identifiers had edged up to 26 percent, with the same number claiming to be Independents, according to the Gallup organization.

At the same time the Democrats registered modest gains, at least partly due to their presidential victory in 1976, so that, by 1977, 49 percent of the people called themselves Democrats. Only once since 1940 has an American party claimed more than 50 percent of the voters: the Democratic party in 1964, when the Republican nominee was Sen. Barry Goldwater. The important factor in these figures is the rise of the Independent voter. Not only are Americans less likely to identify with an established party, but they are more inclined toward ticket splitting and party switching. In 1964, 66 percent of those calling themselves Independents voted Democratic in the presidential contest, but in 1972, with the nomination of Democratic senator George McGovern, 66 percent voted Republican.[5] In both 1976 and 1980 Independents voted for the Republican candidates by sizable margins—57 percent in 1976, in comparison to 38 percent for the Democrats, and 55 percent in 1980, in comparison to 29 percent for the Democrats and 14 percent for John Anderson.[6] We will return to the subject of electoral behavior in chapter 7.

These shifts in voter allegiance present serious problems for campaign strategists. They have helped to siphon resources away from regular party channels and toward media campaigns, which can more readily reach the increasing numbers of Independents. These shifts have also helped to direct voter attention to personality and specific issue appeals. This, in turn, has helped to weaken traditional party loyalties even more.

## Growth of the Mass Media

The decline of party organizations and changing patterns of voter identification have been paralleled by growth in the use of the mass media to mobilize voters. As noted by James M. Perry: "There are two essential ingredients of the new politics. One is that appeals should be made directly to the voters through mass media. The other is that the techniques used to make these appeals—polling, computers, television, direct mail—should be sophisticated and scientific."[7]

The advent of the new politics had its antecedents in the development of market research: from selling products to selling candidates and issues was not a very long step. Most early political public relations experts came from the field of advertising. Not uncommonly, one group of employees in an agency was preparing advertisements for soap or corn flakes, while another group in the same agency was busy drawing up plans for a gubernatorial campaign.

The world of mass-media politics is a world of research, press releases, radio and videotapes, time buyers, and image promotion. Millions are spent on television alone, and many candidates, virtually unknown before their campaign, have effectively employed the media to capture the nomination and the election. Politics has been brought into the living rooms of the people (see "Bob Graham: Working for Florida," below).

---

## Bob Graham: Working for Florida

When D. Robert Graham decided to run for the office of governor of Florida, he had many natural advantages. A multimillionaire lawyer/businessman/dairy operator, Graham represented a Miami district in the state senate and had constructed a progressive record extending over many policy areas of importance to the state. He had served in both houses of the Florida legislature for a total of twelve years but had not been a part of the leadership. He was a leader of the south Florida urban coalition and had earned the enmity of many north Florida conservative leaders.

When he first announced for governor in 1977, less than 1 percent of the people recognized his name in a respected statewide poll. At the beginning of the Democratic primary, facing six other candidates, he showed the support of only 5 percent of the Democratic voters in the state. His Democratic primary opponents represented a formidable group: a popular and effective attorney general from Miami who was widely regarded as the front-runner; the popular mayor of Jacksonville; the secretary of state, who was young and personable and the son of one of the most popular political figures in the history of the state; the only former Republican governor of the state (who had changed parties to run as a Democrat); the popular and widely respected lieutenant-governor, who had the tacit support of the incumbent governor; and a successful businessman who was not considered to be a serious candidate. The Republican candidates were the founder of a successful drugstore chain, who had previously run for statewide office twice and who was willing to spend whatever portion of his $57 million fortune was necessary to get elected, and a popular and effective Republican congressman from the central part of the state.

Graham had a formidable problem in overcoming his lack of statewide recognition and in neutralizing the vaunted organization of his principal opponent, the attorney general. He hired Robert Squier, a nationally known political consultant, and Patrick Caddell, the polling expert who had worked on presidential candidate Jimmy Carter's campaign. The strategy worked out was to have Graham spend one hundred workdays over a period of one year at various blue-collar jobs. The workday strategy was a natural for television and press attention and enabled Graham to overcome criticism of his wealth, his Harvard education, and his urban background. No candidate from south Florida had ever before been elected.

Graham worked as a citrus picker, a stable boy, a bellhop, a teacher, and an actor. His expensive television ads, some of the most effective ever seen in Florida, were built around the workdays. His name recognition grew, and just before the first primary a statewide poll showed him running second, with 18 percent of the vote. In fact, in the first primary he received 25 percent; the attorney general led the race with 35 percent. In the three weeks before the runoff primary, Graham closed the gap and won the nomination with 54 percent of the vote, overcoming a 103,000 vote deficit in the first primary. He went on to win the general election against the drugstore executive, with 56 percent of the vote.

Graham was not the first candidate in the nation to use the workday concept, but he had become the best known. In the age of the media campaign it proved to be the decisive factor.

Theodore H. White recently noted the influence of television in this way:

> Politicans have always spread their messages wherever people crowded—at county and state fairs, at factory gates, grange halls, and union halls, outside the churches and in the lunch-hour crush of big-city streets. But Americans have been gathering for the past twenty years at their television sets. In 1950 only 4.4 million American homes boasted television sets. The next ten years saw an explosion: during some weeks in that decade, no less than ten thousand people every day were buying their first television sets. By 1960, 45 million homes in America had television, and television was ready to set the stage of modern politics. By 1980, 80 million homes owned television sets—as close to saturation as was statistically possible. And the traditional transcontinental stage of American politics had shrunk to a thirteen-inch or nineteen-inch tube at which, sometimes, as many as 100 million citizens gathered for a single episode.[8]

Television did not adapt to politics—politics adapted to television. The presidential nominating contests in the states are tailored to a series of television events. The national conventions have been redesigned and scheduled to fit times of maximum viewing. The predictions of network computers on election nights are sometimes believed to influence the voters in those areas of the country that have not yet voted. Campaigning has been structured to create an event worthy of inclusion in the nightly news. The age of political technology is here, and the media, particularly television, are the catalysts.

## The Advent of Professional Campaign Management

In the mid-1930s a California newspaperman and lobbyist named Clem Whitaker became the first person to see political campaigning as a lucrative business venture. During one of his first campaigns he met Leone Baxter, married her, and inaugurated a new era in American politics. The firm of Whitaker and Baxter was greatly aided by the proclivity of Californians for direct legislation—the old Progressive institutions of the initiative and the referendum. Hardly an election has been held in that state in the past thirty years that has not presented the voters with one or several issues for decision. Whitaker and Baxter specialized in putting these sometimes complex issues before the voters through media campaigns carefully planned and executed to sell the point of view of their clients. The firm has also been involved in the campaigns of some of California's leading political figures.[9] The success of this venture spawned other competing firms in California (sometimes headed by former employees), and the concept of campaign consulting spread nationwide.

A recent study by the *National Journal* showed that of sixty-seven contested elections for the U.S. Senate in 1970 only five did not employ professional consultants. Thirty hired media consultants, twenty-four contracted for the services of national opinion-polling firms, and sixty used commercial advertising companies.[10] Obviously, an important by-product of such political entrepreneurism is a diminution of loyalty by the candidate to the party. These services have generally been contracted for important offices—president, U.S. senator, congressional representative, governor. But, more and more, candidates for lesser offices are also contracting for consultant services.

The development of these new campaign strategies has been gradual. It had to await the invention of the electronic media that project the candidate's image to the voters. The result has not been good for the political parties, but it has nurtured an entire new political industry, which performs some of the same functions as the parties.

Larry Sabato, in his book on political consultants, sums up the impact in this way:

Political professionals and their techniques have helped to homogenize American politics, added significantly to campaign costs, lengthened campaigns, and narrowed the focus of elections. Consultants have emphasized personality and gimmickry over issues, often exploiting emotional and negative themes rather than encouraging rational discussion. They have sought candidates who fit their technologies more than the requirements of office and have given an extra boost to candidates who are more skilled at electioneering than governing.[11]

## New Campaigning Techniques

Campaigns for local office have changed little over the years. Candidates for city, county, and lesser state offices have relatively little money to spend on campaigns and, as a result, work to reach the people in more traditional ways. Since the advent of campaign technocracy, however, candidates for important offices or in highly populated districts have resorted to media campaigns insofar as their budgets will permit. These campaigns are usually run by professional consultants. In some races there almost appears to be no limit to how much money can be spent. Recent examples include the following:

Richard L. Ottinger, Democratic candidate for the U.S. Senate in New York in 1970, spent $2 million in his successful quest for the nomination and another $2 million in a three-way general election campaign, which he lost. Almost all of it went to television in an effort to saturate the airwaves with the name of Ottinger.[12]

In 1974 New York gubernatorial candidate Hugh Carey spent $2.5 million to get the Democratic nomination and another $2.5 million to win the election. In the general election campaign alone he spent $750,000 on the media.[13]

The 1978 Florida gubernatorial campaign began with nine candidates: seven Democrats and two Republicans. Republican Jack Eckerd, a drugstore magnate, won his nomination in the first primary, but two Democrats engaged in a hard-fought and expensive media campaign to determine the winner of the runoff primary. By the time Robert Graham was elected in November the nine campaigns had cost the candidates a total of $10 million. Graham himself spent $2.4 million; Republican Eckerd spent almost $3 million.[14]

In 1980 Gov. John D. Rockefeller IV of West Virginia spent nearly $12 million in his successful bid for reelection, much of it going for television advertising. Some of the advertisements were broadcast over stations in Washington, D.C., and Pittsburgh because those stations reached voters in northern and eastern sections of the state. All but $245,000 was contributed by Rockefeller to his own campaign.[15]

The 1982 campaign for the U.S. Senate in Minnesota between incumbent Republican Dave Durenberger and wealthy department store heir Mark Dayton was one of the most expensive on record. By the time of the election Dayton had spent nearly $8 million on campaign consultants and media advertising in order to "offset the advantages of an incumbent."[16]

These five campaigns illustrate the high cost of running media campaigns by candidates who are not well known to the general public. They are not unusual. Similarly expensive media campaigns have taken place in virtually every state, most often in those that are populous or have weak party organizations. Obviously, professionalization of campaigns has occurred in races for offices other than governor or senator. Quite frequently now, many state legislator or big-city commissioner campaigns are being managed by campaign professionals.

Candidates must use the electronic media to reach the masses of people who will be casting their votes. This is an expensive business, requiring serious candidates to confront the question of money before they approach other important campaign problems. Ironically, mass appeals for campaign funds, even for the personally wealthy, are themselves based on expensive computerized mailing operations. Campaign technocracy is involved from the moment a candidate decides to run.

## Campaign Management Services

Experienced campaign managers generally agree that, to achieve victory on election day, three ingredients are necessary: (1) careful and rational planning; (2) realistic budgeting; and (3) the gathering of information about the mood of the electorate. Most campaign efforts are somewhat disorganized and haphazard. Campaigns for more important offices, however, can be made less haphazard and can be more cleanly organized with the help of professional campaign managers or consultants. Although the development of professional campaign management is not new, the general availability of firms in this field is a relatively recent phenomenon.

Many firms today will not undertake the management of an entire campaign. They are more likely to sign on as consultants for some particular services, such as polling, counseling on media relations, campaign organization, or direct-mail solicitation. Most firms prefer to work for candidates of either one party or the other—not both. Larry Sabato has listed thirty major political consulting firms according to party preference and ideology. Of that group he found that fourteen work for Democrats, twelve for Republicans, and four for candidates of either party. Of those who concentrate on campaigns for Democrats, eleven preferred to work for liberals or moderate liberals and three for moderates. Of the Republican consultants eight worked for moderates or moderate conservatives, two for conservatives, and one for liberals.[17]

In addition, many firms will not undertake the role of campaign consultant unless convinced that the candidate has sufficient money and backup resources to make the effort worthwhile. The candidate must consider the quality of the work and the win–loss record of the firms; the executives in the firm must determine whether a candidate has a reasonable chance of winning. They are in business, and their business acumen is judged by the number of successful campaigns with which they are associated. They cannot afford to damage their reputation by managing a succession of losing efforts.

Campaign services offered by these firms include public relations counseling, advertising, advancing campaign tours, fund raising, and special telephone programs. Information services include market research, public opinion polling, various kinds of computer analyses, demographic analysis, and other statistical components. The largest group, reflecting the mass voter base, is composed of the media experts who offer a wide variety of specialties, such as speech writing and coaching, radio and television production, time purchases, graphic design, and direct-mail advertising. A campaign may contract with one firm to undertake an entire campaign or select certain specialists from one or a variety of firms to carry out selected missions.

The media campaigns constructed by these experts today are based on a careful analysis of the voter group and are designed to exploit a variety of slogans, symbols, and themes. They are, in effect, attempting to achieve scientifically what old-time party strategists sought to do by common sense and conventional wisdom. The new technicians are engaged in media campaigning as a vehicle for selling a candidate to the public. Some have noted that the media experts are often trying to shape the views of the public to fit the client-candidate, whereas the traditional campaign managers were trying to use their resources to mobilize preexisting sentiments and to capitalize on identified party memberships.

The relationship between the new and the old experts is not always an easy one. The new specialists are apt to believe that the politicians are misdirecting their energies and wasting their time. The political managers are likely to view the campaign "scientists" with distrust and condescension. There is, in fact, a place for both in most important campaigns. A media expert with little experience or understanding of politics can destroy a campaign as easily as a seasoned political operative with no insight into the nature of the electorate. In most campaigns, though, each has a distinct role to play. The 1974 *Campaign Manual* prepared by the Democratic National Committee distinguishes between the kinds of activities that the established party organization might perform and those that the management professionals might carry out (see "Sources of Campaign Management," below).

But this partnership is not always entirely successful. Campaign crises often develop as the campaign consultants and the political organizers disagree over strategy. In fact, many of the activities listed under campaign organization in "Sources of Campaign Management" are also performed by professional managers. Most modern campaigns for major office are a blend of both methods. Furthermore, even a perfect blend does not always produce a winning candidate. As the *National Journal* noted, "In the 1970 campaigns for governor and senator, nine national media consultants worked in thirty-eight campaigns; the score was ten winners for the Democratic consultants and five for the Republicans, suggesting that professional imagemakers do not always have the formula for victory and that other factors are at work."[18]

---

## Sources of Campaign Management

**The Campaign Organization**
1. Day-to-day campaign management
2. Researching and statements for press and candidate on campaign issues
3. Preparation of the candidate's campaign speeches
4. Recruiting and organizing volunteer workers
5. Organizing and conducting telephone campaigns
6. Fund raising
   a. Door-to-door canvass
   b. Telephone
   c. Fund-raising dinner
7. Voter registration
8. Get-out-the-vote drives
9. Scheduling
10. Analysis of past voter information
11. Election-day activities

**Professional Management**
1. Counseling on media relations
2. Counseling on overall strategy
3. Advertising
   a. Time and space buying
   b. Graphic design
   c. Film production
   d. TV advertising
   e. Radio production
   f. Printing
4. Direct-mail programs
5. Fund raising: direct mail
6. Budgeting
7. Public opinion polling

*Source:* Democratic National Committee, *Campaign Manual* (Washington, D.C.: Democratic National Committee, 1974), p. 33.

## Public Opinion Polling

Public opinion measurement by scientific instruments began in the mid-1930s, came into its own in the 1940s, was accepted by the public and politicians in the 1950s, and has been a key part of political campaign planning ever since. Modern polling had its origins in newspaper straw votes and market research. In 1824 the presidential preferences of the electorate of Wilmington, Delaware, were surveyed by the *Harrisburg Pennsylvanian.* Andrew Jackson won the straw ballot by a vote of two to one over the eventual winner of the electoral vote, John Quincy Adams.[19] Newspaper straw votes became fashionable in the 1880s and were popular until 1936, when the most famous straw poll in history, conducted by *Literary Digest,* a widely read weekly magazine, predicted the defeat of President Franklin D. Roosevelt by Republican Alf Landon. Roosevelt's landslide victory not only undermined straw polling but also caused the collapse of the *Literary Digest.* Scientific polling, however, was already being perfected as George H. Gallup adapted the application of the mathematical laws of probability to the sampling of human behavior and beliefs.[20] Since their historic setback in 1948, when the major polls erroneously predicted the election of Thomas E. Dewey to the presidency, the professional polling organizations have made steady gains toward proving their value as campaign instruments.[21]

Politicians have always harbored a certain amount of suspicion toward polling. In many instances, polls have been misused during campaigns through loaded questions, leaked results, and faked findings. Nevertheless, most political users no longer need to be persuaded that a properly structured, carefully conducted, and accurately analyzed poll can be a valuable asset to a campaign.

First used widely in presidential campaigns, polls became increasingly popular in state elections during the 1960s. Nationally known leaders, such as the late Gov. Nelson Rockefeller, made widely publicized use of polls as tools of campaign management, and campaign planners throughout the nation began to clamor for reliable information on public opinion. Polling organizations developed well beyond the original restricted group of national concerns until eventually most states and regions were served by companies offering opinion analyses.

Polls are essential tools in the determination of campaign strategy. Candidates and managers (including professional consultants) can learn the strengths and weaknesses of their own campaign as well as that of their opponent. They can pinpoint salient issues to be used with specified voter groups. A more careful analysis and determination of how best to spend the campaign dollar can be made. Furthermore, scheduling, timing, canvassing, and the tone of the campaign can be affected by the results of survey research. Other uses of polling include estimating voter turnout, voter predispositions, determining extent of candidate-name recognition, and attitudes of independent voters.

According to long-time pollster Louis Harris, most of the polling done for campaigns is directed to gathering information in three specific areas. First, as Harris's clients have informed him, his most valuable assistance has been the key-group breakdowns that dissect the anatomy of the constituency, such as area differences, racial and religious patterns, nationality group differences, and occupational patterns. This information enables the candidate and his or her managers to determine where best to try to put together a majority. Second, the candidate can find out what the electorate thinks of him or her as a public figure—his or her name familiarity, idiosyncrasies, and public record. Harris notes that the pollster is put in the position of having to tell the candidate that he or she is perceived by the electorate as being spineless, arrogant, loud-mouthed, cold, poor at public speaking, or just plain unknown. He also notes that, in his experience, candidates are seldom able to change in order to gain a more favorable image.

Third, candidates have found information useful that helps define issues. This information is gathered in two principal ways: (1) the voters are allowed to express their own views toward problems that they believe should be of interest to the government; and (2) voters select from prescribed lists and reply to structured questions regarding issues. The collection of these data permits the opinion analyst to compare responses between particular voter groups and certain issues and, if carried out over a period of time, to isolate any vote switching that is taking place. It is then up to the candidate to make the best use of the data provided.[22] In recent years, scientific polling has been used to determine the media habits of voters, thus permitting shifts in advertising emphasis both to improve timing and to determine specific audiences.

Nowhere has this third use of polling been more evident than in the White House itself. Franklin D. Roosevelt recognized the usefulness of polling by hiring a Princeton psychologist, Hadley Cantril, to assist in the interpretation of public opinion in the prewar era. John F. Kennedy was also intrigued by polls but did not maintain his own polling apparatus. The honor of bringing professional polling to the White House belongs to Lyndon B. Johnson, a renowned addict of opinion polls, who made them an institution during his presidency. Albert H. "Tad" Cantril, Hadley Cantril's son, was put on Johnson's staff to analyze public opinion and interpret published polls. Most of President Johnson's biographers have noted that he kept favorable polls in his pocket to use when he needed to impress visiting politicians or journalists of the rightness of his actions.[23]

Jimmy Carter was even more fascinated by public opinion polling than Johnson. Through a contract with the Democratic National Committee, Carter secured the services of Patrick H. Caddell, who had come to public attention as candidate George McGovern's pollster in 1972, and Caddell quickly emerged as an important member of the White House inner circle of advisors. Caddell monitored opinion not only during the 1976 campaign but also during the administration itself. At the end of the 1980 campaign it fell to him, early on the morning before the election, to break the news to Carter's staff, and hence to the president, that they were going to lose the election and that Ronald Reagan would be the next president. President Reagan contracts with Richard B. Wirthlin of Decision Making Information, a California firm, for his polling services. Wirthlin was very influential in the Reagan campaign and has continued to conduct regular polls for the White House during the Reagan presidency.

As might be expected, public opinion polling is an expensive enterprise. Polling costs have more than doubled in the last ten years and are now one of the most expensive aspects of a sophisticated campaign. A forty-five-minute "benchmark" interview can easily run to six figures, although most are scaled down to $50,000 or so (see "Types of Opinion Polls," page 142). Most firms using telephone polls charge from $12 to $23 per call, with polls often totaling up to $20,000.[24] Even though telephone polls cost less than those that rely on home interviews, they are often less useful because they do not produce the depth and variety of information that campaign strategists need. Usually, a professional pollster targets the types of voters to be called, and the actual calls are made by employees of the polling firm. Opinion polling has

## Types of Opinion Polls

In a major campaign four types of public opinion polls may be employed.

1. *Benchmark poll:* starting as early as a year or more before an election, a benchmark survey may be taken to assess the way in which the public perceives a candidate. Usually armed with lengthy interview forms, polltakers visit homes seeking to determine the mood of the public and the strengths or weaknesses of candidates. The benchmark poll will normally range from 2,500 to 4,000 interviews and will cost from $25 to $35 each. These polls may be followed up by a survey of 500 to 1,000 people to identify more precisely voter concerns and candidate assessments. A specific element of the population may even be singled out for a follow-up survey.

2. *Panel survey:* pollsters may, after the passage of several months, conduct a panel survey of up to half the respondents previously polled. The panel is used to gauge shifts in voter attitudes and is usually conducted by telephone with 300 to 400 people. To account for the fact that these subjects are more likely to be politically aware and therefore more likely to vote, separate panels composed of new respondents are sometimes asked the same questions as a base for comparison.

3. *Focus group polls:* the focus group is not a survey at all, but is rather a discussion group of 10 to 15 people brought together with a leader who will focus attention on the way in which voters think about candidates and issues.

4. *Tracking polls:* many pollsters "track" the voters right up to election day. Many professional public opinion experts believe that tracking is the most important phase of polling. The process involves calling 50 to 100 respondents each night to ask five or six specific questions. This tracking process is especially useful in keeping tabs on undecided voters and last-minute voting shifts. The cost of tracking calls is about $12 per call. Thus, pollsters must constantly attempt to balance costs and reliability.

*Source:* Interview with pollster Lance Tarrance, Houston, Texas, April 2, 1980, "When a Presidential Candidate Moves, A Pollster May Be Pulling the Strings," *National Journal,* December 15, 1979, pp. 2092–2095; "Houston's Tarrance Builds Reputation for Accuracy," *The Houston Post,* November 26, 1978, p. 14.

assumed an important place in the strategic arsenal of political candidates and campaign managers. The successful use of polls in campaign planning and execution has also gone hand in hand with the spread to the political arena of automatic data processing.

## Automatic Data Processing: The Computer Age

For more important offices, the ability to make effective operational decisions is one of the major keys to successful campaigning, but such decision making has become more difficult with the increasing mobility, complexity, and sophistication of the electorate. Just as good intelligence is crucial to military success, good information is necessary to political success. The decision makers in a political campaign need to know the economic, social, and political composition of the electorate to whom the appeal is being directed. They must pinpoint which issues are the most important and to which group of constituents these are most likely to appeal. And, above all, the campaign strategist is dependent on up-to-date precinct lists that can be used during the campaign and on election day. Most campaign strategists understand that there is no effective way to reach all of the voters; therefore, it is important to reach selected voters who might feel a sympathetic kinship with the candidate. This kind of information can be provided by a voter profile of the district or the state. None of these kinds of information lend themselves to compilation and analysis by hand. They all, however, are suitable for computerization.

Not long after the development and spread of the computer, political leaders recognized the value of automatic data processing in election campaigns and party organizational activities. In fact, some academic observers have noted a considerable shift of political power from party leaders to communications experts.[25] As has often been the case, the "amateur" political strategists were forced to turn to the "expert" computer analyst in order to derive the most benefit from the information sources that were made available.

The national party leadership recognized the value of computers in the mid-1960s. In 1966 the Republican National Committee authorized a study of centralized data processing and produced a handbook to explain computer technology in lay terms. It also undertook a pilot program based on test precincts and sponsored training conferences designed to provide updated information to Republican state party leaders. The Republican headquarters in Washington issued a total of sixteen manuals and eleven computer programs, which were made available to the states; and by 1969 twenty state GOP organizations were using data processing in one form or another.[26]

In 1981 the Republican National Committee transferred the computer services department from the administration services division to the political affairs division, a signal that computers are now recognized as a major tool in political decision making, not just as instruments for accounting. In the 1981 legislative and congressional redistricting effort the computer assisted redistricting system (CARS) was established at the RNC to assist state legislators in their efforts and to protect Republicans by providing computer-generated maps, incorporating census bureau and political history information into the districting equation and permitting quick response to Democratic counterproposals.[27]

The RNC had plans to provide regional political and finance directors with briefcase-size computers. This would enable field personnel to have instant access to a variety of statistical data, including precinct voting history, last election data, talent bank information, and accounting. In addition the RNC maintains REPNET, a national network of computer services available to state parties.[28]

As shown in figure 5-1, the uses of computer technology in campaign management are almost limitless. As Robert L. Chartrand has noted:

> It has been shown that an increasing number of candidates are finding that they must delve more deeply into the myriad files of campaign-related information, which will allow them to understand their environment, reach out to their constituents, and address the issues of the times. While the role of the new technology has yet to be fully defined, thoughtful persons in high places are showing a willingness to learn about, and evaluate, the innovations.[29]

Campaigns by smaller party organizations and for lesser offices usually cannot afford the cost of automatic data processing. For a major campaign the cost can be many thousands of dollars per month, and the candidate and his or her managers must determine to their own satisfaction that the benefits are worth the costs. Even if the candidate cannot afford to pay for computer technology, other sources of computers are available. Industry and labor are sometimes willing to allow campaign access to their computers if, of course, they are supporting the candidate or the party requesting the use. The Democrats, both at the national and state levels, have been given access to computer equipment by the AFL-CIO, and Republican party organizations have been given "free" time on the computers owned by businesses and corporations. Some candidates are personally wealthy and can absorb the costs without undue hardship, but in a few instances state parties maintain computers that can be used by candidates.

Most party officials do not believe that the use of electronic data processing will displace older, more established forms of political analysis. Even though vast amounts of data can be assimilated and manipulated, the results must still be put to good use by men and women who have the political maturity and judgment to interpret them.

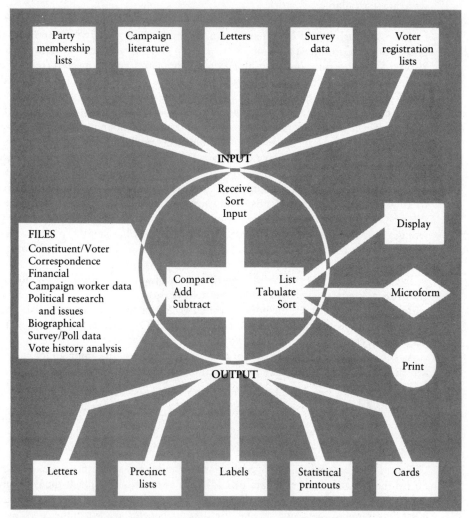

**FIGURE 5-1**  Typical campaign headquarters information handling system.
(*Source:* Robert L. Chartrand, *"Information Technology and the Political Campaigner,"* in Robert Agranoff, *The New Style in Election Campaigns,* 2nd ed. (Boston: Holbrook Press, 1976), p. 157. Reprinted by permission.)

## Radio and Television in the Campaign

In 1924 Calvin Coolidge decided that it was unbecoming for a president to go barn-storming around the country campaigning for an office he already held. Therefore, he stayed in Washington and conducted much of his campaign through radio speeches. He outspent his Democratic opponent three to one ($120,000 to $40,000) and out-polled him in the election three to one. Four years later, the 1928 Democratic candi-date, Alfred E. Smith, warned his radio studio audiences to hold their applause until the end of his speech because "it doesn't cost anything then." With eight million radios reaching forty million people, the cost of media campaigning had already begun an upward spiral that has not really stopped to this day.[30] It is ironic that Calvin Coolidge, one of the most colorless and uninteresting men ever to hold the presidential office, originated mass-media campaigning.

Although mass-media campaigning began with radio, it now encompasses a wide variety of vehicles through which the candidates' messages are communicated: tele-vision, direct mail, billboards, newspapers, and even skywriting. Most of these use a mechanical means of transmission. They are all expensive, but they have not always had the impact on voter attitudes that many expected, for their effect on voting behav-ior depends on certain conditions. First, how one votes and whether one votes at all are closely related to party affiliation, one's perception of group interests, one's opin-ions about long-standing issues, and one's view of party performance in managing governmental affairs. Campaign communications do not easily alter these attitudes, which are generally stable and are more likely to be reinforced than changed.

Second, campaign communications always find the voter in a particular context. Voters are affected by their acquaintances, and set behavior patterns prevent them from veering far from expected convictions. Each of us is tied to other people, and these established relationships serve to anchor our opinions and to deflect the impact of communications on them. Our opinions have been shaped by our primary associ-ations, group memberships, and other relationships that develop out of the context of our lives. Because of these attitudes, it is difficult, but not impossible, for media cam-paigns to induce opinion changes in the short-run world of a campaign for office.

Finally, it can be argued that the media can create new opinions more easily than they can change existing ones because new issues are less likely to run afoul of unsym-pathetic predispositions, established group norms, or the views of opinion leaders. Robert Agranoff notes that, although the effects of the electronic mass media on voter behavior are somewhat muted, they are still significant in a number of ways.

1. The size of media audience is important in itself, since no other means of com-munication can offer the same potential for reaching large numbers of voters in a relatively short period of time, and the larger the audience, the more likely it is to include segments of the electorate who are persuadable.

2. Regardless of the impact on the great majority of the audience, the electronic media can influence and convert some voters during the campaign. This small but growing margin of opinion conversion is attractive to candidates and media experts, especially in an election perceived to be close.

3. Some evidence suggests that the media exert a considerable influence on the voters' perceptions of the personal qualities of the candidates. These candidate-ori-ented stimuli are, for the most part, new to most voters, and thus are less likely to be subject to the forces that make change of opinion difficult. This phenomenon is respon-

sible for the emphasis placed on candidate image in American elections, and the mass media offer an ideal vehicle for projecting the desired image.

4. Finally, the media serve as important agencies of campaign reinforcement, since advertisements, televised rallies or speeches, and campaign hoopla can help to inspire the faithful and reinforce the resolve of the workers. In this sense the media have taken the place of the old-fashioned parade or political rally.[31]

Because of their crucial importance to modern campaigns the electronic media demand a large share of the campaign budget; consequently, the people who are put in charge of the media campaign must know how to derive the most benefit from it. Since professional campaign consultants should be responsible for all phases of the media campaign, they are at the very center of campaign planning. Candidates must be coached on improving their formal television performances as well as their informal appearances, such as press conferences, talk show interviews, and news events. Planning the media campaign demands the early purchase of television and radio time, with a thorough understanding of the market and the impact on the campaign budget. Attention should be paid to getting as much free exposure as possible. Campaign staff members must be trained in the care and feeding of the press as well as in how best to create and use news in behalf of the candidate. Contracts must be signed with agencies to produce spot announcements or longer in-depth productions—a procedure requiring an intimate knowledge of which agencies do the best job with certain kinds of presentations. No set formulas are applicable to all candidates and all campaigns. A review of the literature on campaign consulting reveals that few of the experts agree on the best ways to approach a campaign. They usually tailor the campaign to the existing situation as it is affected by the client-candidate.

Through extensive studies of media use in the 1972 and 1976 presidential campaigns, Thomas E. Patterson and Robert D. McClure found that, in 1972, political commercials had no effect on the voters' perception of the candidates but had a substantial effect on their perception of the candidates' positions on issues and platform promises. Furthermore, they found that commercials had considerably more influence than did the nightly television news presentations. Even if one grants that the same findings might not hold true below the presidential level, they are somewhat startling. For instance, Patterson and McClure discovered that, between September 18 and November 6, 1972, the bulk of the campaign period, more than one hour of television commercials was used to tell of President Nixon's policies on China, Russia, Vietnam, and the American allies. In contrast, the average network devoted only fifteen minutes to those stories. Furthermore, many viewers remembered more of the content of the commercials than of the newscasts.[32]

As the same two authors' analysis of the 1976 presidential campaign concluded:

> One dimension of the election fits perfectly the networks' demand for good pictures. It is the "horse race" aspect of the run for the White House. For a presidential election is surely a super contest with all the elements that are associated with spectacular sports events: huge crowds, rabid followers, dramatic do-or-die battles, winners and losers. It is this part of the election that the networks emphasize.[33]

In support of that conclusion the authors report that the "horse race" aspects of the campaigns in both 1972 and 1976 dominated political television. Sixty percent of the coverage was given to "horse race" topics, 28 percent to substantive issues, and 12 percent to miscellaneous matters.[34]

Patterson recently published a book on the role of the mass media in the 1976 election in which he compares the results of his study with those of an early classic study of the 1940 election conducted by Paul Lazarsfeld, Bernard Berelson, and Hazel Gaudet. The comparison of these two studies of the television and newspaper media in two presidential elections thirty-six years apart is informative. First, the press in 1940 emphasized issue positions, leadership qualities, and group commitments, whereas in 1976 the emphasis was on the competitive struggle ("horse race") between the candidates. Second, there is a consistent journalistic model of campaign coverage that places considerably greater emphasis on the struggle for power than on the winner's impact on national policy. Finally, based on a panel survey of voters, Patterson concluded that the electorate's response to the media coverage took two forms: (1) in 1976 they were less concerned about candidate policy stands or personal qualifications than they had been in 1940; and (2) their level of knowledge of the candidates' positions on issues was considerably lower in 1976 than it had been in 1940. In support of the first of these findings, Patterson notes that, in 1940, 67 percent of the voters talked about policy, compared with only 34 percent in 1976. In support of the second conclusion, he reports that only 25 percent of the voters knew the issue positions of the candidates in 1976, compared with 37 percent in 1940.[35]

Some had hoped that the coverage of recent presidential debates would improve by placing more emphasis on positions and issues. However, recent studies have shown that, although the debates themselves have been issue oriented, news coverage has paid more attention to candidate appearance, performance, and personality. The media have been more concerned with who won than with what was said.[36]

The candidate who chooses to campaign by television and radio—and almost all of them do—faces a formidable financial burden. The costs of media campaigns are high, whether at the national, state, or local level. Under federal law each presidential campaign was given $29.4 million in public funds after the 1980 national conventions. Of this sum, both campaigns spent approximately $19 million on television and radio commercials. Another $10 million was spent on travel and political organizations, much of it devoted to arranging travel to make the most of local news and photo opportunities for television and the press. Much of the spending for commercials was devoted to spot announcements on prime-time, top-rated television shows—which can run as high as $60,000 to $80,000 per thirty seconds.[37] Local spots are also very costly to local candidates, and the price has been rapidly escalating. A thirty-second prime-time spot in Portland, Oregon, in 1974 cost only $35; by 1980 that same spot had gone up to $3,000, according to the *Washington Post*. In San Diego the 1974 cost for thirty seconds was $509; this had also escalated to $3,000 by 1980.[38]

State and local campaign costs also depend on the size and configuration of the district and the availability of television and media coverage. In Louisiana in 1979, according to Herbert E. Alexander, six candidates for governor spent a total of $20.7 million, almost half of which ($9.8 million) went to mass-media advertising.[39] One of the classic television campaigns was that of the late Nelson Rockefeller, running for his third term as a governor of New York in 1966. (See "Nelson Rockefeller's 1966 Campaign for Governor of New York," p. 149.)

For lesser offices, less is spent for television and radio, but the necessary funds are just as difficult to raise. A series of late-afternoon radio spots of ten, fifteen, thirty, or sixty seconds, designed to catch the commuter as a captive audience, can cost many hundreds of dollars. Fifteen-second television spots are expensive even for a local market, and the candidate may find that his spot has been lumped with three or four others, thereby blurring any distinction he hoped to gain. Nevertheless, in this age of media campaigns, most candidates are afraid not to use television and radio appeals to the extent that their budgets will allow.

The availability of tangible campaign resources such as money, professional staff, and experienced management is obviously very important to a campaign. In any election year, however, there are other resources that will naturally benefit one candidate or party over the other. One of the most important of these advantages is incumbency. Existing possession of office, at almost any governmental level, is an advantage to the candidate and his or her party, and for many reasons: the incumbent is more likely to be known to the voting public; will usually receive the lion's share of campaign contributions (particularly from political action committees); will likely receive more extensive press and media coverage than his or her opponents; and will gather more volunteer workers. Furthermore, the incumbent will have the resources of office to use in subtle ways on behalf of the reelection campaign. In fact, for the party holding office the entire campaign can be built around the incumbency and the benefits of continuing it.

Other advantages that might benefit one candidate over another are personal wealth, public-speaking expertise, experience with the electronic and print media, or personal stamina. Each of these qualities may not only provide a natural advantage for a candidate but may also lend itself to exploitation in the campaign.

When all is said and done, even the best-managed campaign can produce a loser. Sometimes both opposing candidates are about equal in strength and have about equal public support, but one must lose. On other occasions one candidate is clearly superior to the other, and one of them, not always the superior one, wins. And others, who may have done everything right during the campaign, wind up losing the election because of conditions beyond their control. Let us consider the impact of campaigns on electoral outcomes.

## Do Campaigns Make a Difference?

We are now spending close to half a billion dollars to elect candidates to public office at all levels in a presidential election year. The late Nelson Rockefeller spent an estimated $6.5 million to get reelected governor of New York in 1966 and another $8 million in his quest for the Republican presidential nomination in 1968. Nine candidates for governor of Florida spent a grand total of $10 million before a winner finally emerged in November 1978. In 1980 candidates for the U.S. Senate and House spent $250 million in their bids for election.

When the campaign is over, whether it has been an "old" style campaign or a "new," the loser often claims that just a little more money would have turned the trick. Candidates and managers always want just a few more ads, a few more billboards, a few more paid staff members, or a few more door-to-door canvassers. We spend a full year of campaigning to elect a president, and some campaigns extend over two-, three-, or four-year periods. The barrage of campaign literature, television ads, telephone calls, and public meetings is mind-boggling to candidates and voters alike. Yet we do not really know much about the impact of campaigning on election outcomes.

Most politicians and campaign specialists take for granted the efficacy of campaigns. Almost every one of them can cite examples of an obscure candidate who, through a

## Nelson Rockefeller's 1966 Campaign for Governor of New York

The 1966 campaign of Nelson Rockefeller for reelection to a third term as governor of New York was a classic contest—classic in the sophisticated use of the media as a campaign tool and classic in its cost. Governor Rockefeller had already served two four-year terms by 1966. He was regularly being written off as politically dead, weighted down by the attrition of those eight years in office, the dislike of disappointed office seekers, the fallout from two major tax increases, and a series of scandals in the state liquor authority.

Rockefeller's standing in the public opinion polls was so low that one pollster told the governor, "You couldn't be elected dogcatcher." But Rockefeller and his political advisors undertook a massive campaign to reverse public opinion and to keep the governor in Albany for another term. They unfolded the most expensive campaign ever waged for a governor's office at that time.

The campaign was pure media, and it cost pure money. Waves of the slickest television commercials ever seen up to that time were released, starting as early as the Fourth of July. It has been estimated that between three and four thousand commercials were used before election day. Different commercials were directed to specific audiences. One extolled the Rockefeller record in highway construction, another his role in building a system of higher education for New York State, and still another was directed toward the senior citizen. Each, however, was designed to praise the Rockefeller record and to imply that more good things would come were the governor reelected. The state was inundated by 25 million pieces of printed literature, four items for every New Yorker who turned out to vote. Dozens of different kinds of brochures were directed at the interests of each group of voters. A staff person was assigned to see that each different audience was reached by the appropriate brochure. If, for example, a meeting on higher education was held in any part of the state, a staff person would be in attendance to see that the governor's views on the subject and his accomplishments in the field were made known.

A paid staff of more than three hundred people worked full-time on the campaign. Almost two hundred of them were garrisoned at the New York Hilton for the duration of the campaign.

The estimated total cost ranged from the officially reported figures of $4.8 million to a more realistic cost of around $6.5 million.

*Source:* Adapted from Herbert M. Baus and William B. Ross, *Politics Battle Plan* (New York: Macmillan, 1968), pp. 298–299.

masterful campaign, rose in popular esteem and visibility to capture the ultimate prize. Jimmy Carter is one obvious example, but almost any state has some officeholder who climbed from obscurity by virtue of a highly effective campaign. Often one can offer little tangible evidence to support these claims, but logical deduction, as well as the lack of any other explanation, leads one to conclude that the campaign was indeed the determining factor in the victory of one candidate over another.

It is difficult to make generalizations about campaigns, for they range from campaigns for president to campaigns for city council member. Obviously, a campaign for president differs substantially from one for congressional, state, county, or city government office. Campaigns vary according to the kind of office being sought: executive, legislative, or judicial. They differ in degree of competitiveness and, in judicial and local races, they may even be nonpartisan. Some candidates may have no intention of winning but may be running for name identification in anticipation of a future race. Some altruistic candidates may be running in a hopeless contest just to help the party fill its ticket. Some candidates, who are virtually assured of election, may gear their campaign to obtaining a necessary bare majority (or plurality). Others may be trying to put together a big margin in order to demonstrate their vote-getting capabilities for some future election for a higher office. The campaign for nomination may be fought in the public arena to convince a primary electorate, or it may be fought in a party arena to influence a majority of convention delegates. Whatever the type of election—except those of token opposition—candidates will attempt to develop support of four kinds: financial, party, group, and electoral.[40]

In today's world of media concentration, campaign finances assume considerably more importance than they did in earlier eras. The campaign may rise or fall on the availability of money to reach the voter through media exposure. Thus the chief fund raiser may be the most important campaign aide, and his or her success will ordinarily determine the limits to which the campaign can be extended.

Loyal party members seldom have much difficulty in deciding how to vote. Even so, the campaign may have an impact in the sense that their support is reinforced. They may be stimulated to take a more active and participatory role. A Republican candidate, for instance, may represent the minority party. His or her campaign strategy must be concentrated on holding the Republican vote while winning a majority of the Independents and some of the Democrats. The Democratic candidate in a Democratic district, however, may need only hold the support of his or her party adherents to win. The campaign strategies of the opposing candidates will be directed to those separate goals.

The rise in importance of interest groups has focused more and more attention on winning group endorsements. Labor unions, for example, will normally support an incumbent Democrat even though he or she may not be as prolabor as the opponent. From the union leaders' point of view the very fact of incumbency may be important, for it probably has permitted the Democrat to build seniority in a legislative body. Labor strategists may decide that it is preferable to reelect a generally prolabor officeholder with a proven record than to take a chance on supporting the opponent on the basis of promises. Furthermore, the incumbent is already accessible, and access is a key to interest-group success.

Candidates seek group support because it is assumed that group leaders have influence on the voting behavior of group members. Although this assumption is often not true, it underlies the relationship between the group and the candidate. The candidate will probably have preconceived notions as to which interest groups will most probably lend support. Most candidates, however, will not take that support for granted and will actively woo the group leaders for positive endorsement as well as campaign support and financial assistance. They will also work for the endorsement of those groups that are not as likely to lend support automatically.

Finally, as we have seen, campaigns are usually directed toward convincing a majority of the electorate. The ultimate goal of the campaign is to get as many votes on election day as possible. Most people maintain an identification with one of the two parties, and most of those committed voters will vote for the candidates of their party. This fact is crucial to campaign planning. A Democratic candidate in a solidly Democratic district can win election (all other things being equal) by virtue of being on the ballot—he or she can gain a majority simply because the Democrats are a majority. The Republican in that district, however, is the candidate of a minority party. Republicans alone cannot elect this hopeful to office. His or her campaign must be directed toward holding all of the Republican vote, getting a substantial portion of the Independent vote, and even cutting into the Democratic vote. If such a candidate is successful, he or she may put together a winning coalition on election day. The committed party voter is usually easiest to convince. The uncommitted voter, or one who normally supports the opposition party, is the most difficult to persuade. The success of the candidate during the campaign in convincing such a voter may be the key to election.[41]

## Maxims for Developing a Campaign Strategy

Louis Froman, Jr., has synthesized social science research on campaigns and voting behavior to arrive at a set of maxims for developing a candidate strategy. He notes that tactics vary, depending on the electoral situation and the available resources, but he believes that the following are useful in most situations:

1. *Get others involved.* It is important to elicit support and participation from groups, since the most effective pressure on people is group pressure. The candidate should get as many people as possible to work in the campaign by urging others to vote for him.

2. *Use as much personal contact as possible.* Social scientists have verified the intuitive beliefs of politicians that personal communication is most important. Candidates should meet as many people as possible and should take part in as many group meetings as can be fitted into their schedule. As we have noted, the age of media campaigns has put more emphasis on the electronic connection. If there is limited time for personal participation in meetings, television and radio campaigns are the next best thing.

3. *Be brief.* Spot announcements scattered throughout the day are more likely to be effective than a single extended speech. Short announcements are more apt to reach captive audiences, and their spread throughout the day will reach a wider variety of audiences.

4. *Do not publicize the opponent.* A campaign is a method of candidate exposure and a mechanism through which voters can be persuaded. Arguments with the opponent should be avoided because they give the opposition free advertising and because the adversary might win the argument. Carried to its logical extreme, this would preclude live or television debates. Many campaign strategists believe that the front-runner errs in engaging in such debates because they favor the lesser-known challenger, who gets wider exposure and who might appear to win the debate.

5. *Have a simple campaign theme.* A candidate benefits from having a few general themes around which to build a campaign. This can involve concentration on favorable issues to the exclusion of others, and it can also be little more than the widespread use of an effective slogan.[42]

As we noted earlier, it is difficult to generalize about campaigns. No list of maxims can fit every campaign situation or all candidates. Nevertheless, these general rules are useful even in the age of the new politics.

## When Do Voters Decide?

One way to look at the question of the influence of campaigns on voter decisions is to determine at what point voters make up their minds during presidential election years. As shown in table 5-1, voters made their presidential choices in each election year between 1952 and 1980 at about the same time. With the exception of the 1956 rematch between President Dwight D. Eisenhower and Adlai Stevenson, about one-third of the electorate decided on a candidate before the national conventions even met, another third reached a decision during the conventions, and the final third decided during the campaign. Slight deviations occurred in 1964, when the Republicans nominated Barry Goldwater, and in 1972, when the Democrats nominated George McGovern, but the fact that both were running against incumbents was probably more important than the fact that they were both ideological choices for their respective parties. In 1968, 1976, and 1980 exceptionally large numbers of voters reported making their choices during the postconvention campaign period. Fully 10 percent of the voters decided on election day in 1948—a figure that probably helps to explain President Harry S. Truman's surprise victory in the face of contrary polls.

TABLE 5-1    Time of decision on voter choices for president, 1952-1980

| Time of Decision | 1952 | 1956 | 1960 | 1964 | 1968 | 1972 | 1976 | 1980 |
|---|---|---|---|---|---|---|---|---|
| Before conventions | 34% | 57% | 30% | 40% | 33% | 43% | 33% | 31% |
| During conventions | 31 | 18 | 30 | 25 | 22 | 17 | 20 | 18 |
| During campaign | 31 | 21 | 36 | 33 | 38 | 35 | 45 | 50 |
| Don't remember, NA | 4 | 4 | 4 | 3 | 7 | 4 | 2 | 1 |
| TOTAL | 100 | 100 | 100 | 100 | 100 | 99 | 100 | 100 |
| Number = | 1251 | 1285 | 1445 | 1126 | 1039 | 1119 | 1667 | 1614 |

*Source:* Preelection and postelection surveys at the Survey Research Center, University of Michigan, 1952–1980.

Table 5-2 shows in greater detail the breakdown of voters according to the time of their decision in the 1980 election. Aside from 1956, the largest number of voters to reach a decision before the conventions was in 1972, when 43 percent did so. Although in 1980 the largest percentage made their decisions before the primaries even got under way, most of the remaining voters were scattered throughout the primary, convention, and campaign periods. We do not have comparable data for congressional, senatorial, gubernatorial, or local elections, except in isolated cases. These data on presidential choices, plus observation of other elections at other levels, suggest that to a considerable degree most people have made up their minds before the opening of the postnomination campaign period. If so, the benefits of the campaign may come down to the success with which the candidates can make their views known to the largest number of people. Most elections appear to be run under conditions that enhance the chances of one candidate over the other. Incumbency, resources, advantageous issues, and national trends may be the keys to victory. Even so, most candidates attempt to exploit whatever advantages they perceive and, in most cases, are never really sure what factors actually determined the outcome.

## The Art and Science of Getting Elected

Getting elected to office is both an art and a science. It also requires a little bit of luck. Campaign craftsmanship is based on a knowledge of the district, composition of the constituency, and the ability to exploit personal qualities that may generate support. It also often rests on the construction of a campaign apparatus designed to use a

**TABLE 5–2    Time of decision on voter choices for president, 1980**

*How long before the election did you decide that you were going to vote the way you did?*

| Time | Percent |
|---|---|
| Knew all along; always vote for the same party; before the convention; before the primaries | 20 |
| During the primaries; several months | 9 |
| Before the convention, because of Carter's or Reagan's candidacy; as soon as Carter or Reagan said they would run | 11 |
| At the time of the Democratic convention, when Carter was nominated | 6 |
| At the time of the Republican convention, when Reagan was nominated | 12 |
| After the conventions; during the campaign before the debates | 8 |
| Five to seven weeks | 2 |
| One month, three weeks | 6 |
| Within two weeks of the election; after the third debate | 10 |
| In the last few days of the campaign | 7 |
| On election day | 9 |
| Other | 0 |
| Don't know | 0 |
| No answer | 0 |
| N = 1614 | 100 |

*Source:* Center for Political Studies, University of Michigan, *The CPS 1980 American National Election Study: Codebook,* vol. 1 (Ann Arbor, CPS, 1981), pp. 596–597.

candidate's natural advantages, advantages that might include party support, public recognition, family connections, readily available campaign funds, and personality. None of these will automatically guarantee victory on election night, and none necessarily requires the services of professional campaign strategists. Nevertheless, candidates for higher offices in larger constituencies often bring in professional assistants who can make the most of natural advantages and can get the most for the campaign dollar.

And the campaign dollar cannot be underestimated. With the rapid escalation in the number of political action committees (PACs) in recent years, as well as their already established favoritism for incumbents, it is becoming increasingly clear that large amounts of campaign funds are required for consultants and the media. Funding specialists have emerged in important roles to support the hiring of professional campaign specialists and consultants. These professionals should be well versed in up-to-date campaign mechanics, while at the same time being aware of some of the traditional strategies for winning votes. This is not an easy blend to achieve. Professional politicians and the technicians of the new campaign styles often clash over planning and execution. Much depends on the candidate's personal reputation and style. Modern campaigning, especially for higher office, extends from the first decision of the candidate to run all the way through the closing of the polls on election night. The careful candidate who is serious about getting elected cannot afford to let down his or her guard at any point along the way.

## Notes

1. Herbert M. Baus and William B. Ross, *Politics Battle Plan* (New York: Macmillan, 1968), p. 7.
2. For a fuller description, see Mike Royko, *Boss—Richard J. Daley of Chicago* (New York: Dutton, 1971), pp. 62–64.
3. Robert Agranoff, *The New Style in Election Campaigns* (Boston: Holbrook Press, 1972), pp. 4–10.
4. Quoted by Stanley Kelley, Jr., "Elections and the Mass Media," in *Law and Contemporary Problems, The Electoral Process, Part I* (Durham, N.C.: Duke University Press, 1962), vol. 27, no. 2 (Spring 1962), p. 314. Taken from M. Ostrogorski, *Democracy and the Party System in the United States* (New York: Macmillan, 1926), p. 200.
5. *Gallup Opinion Index, Monthly Reports* (1970–1978 and June 25–28, 1982). In mid-1982 other national polls showed the Republicans with a higher percentage of the identified voters: Louis Harris, 29 percent; *Time*/Yankelovich, Skelly, and White, 30 percent; NBC News/Associated Press, 30 percent; CBS News, 29 percent; ABC News reported the same 26 percent as Gallup, *Public Opinion*, American Enterprise Institute, August–September, 1982, p. 29.
6. James L. Sundquist and Richard M. Scammon, "The 1980 Election: Profile and Historical Perspective," in *A Tide of Discontent: The 1980 Elections and Their Meaning*, eds. Ellis Sandoz and Cecil V. Crabb, Jr. (Washington, D.C.: Congressional Quarterly Press, 1981), p. 22. See also Paul R. Abramson, John H. Aldrich, and David W. Rohde, *Change and Continuity in the 1980 Elections* (Washington, D.C.: Congressional Quarterly Press, 1982).
7. James M. Perry, *The New Politics: The Expanding Technology of Political Manipulation* (New York: Potter, 1968).
8. Theodore H. White, *America in Search of Itself* (New York: Harper & Row, 1982), p. 165. (Italics are the author's.)
9. The activities of Whitaker and Baxter were first publicized in Carey McWilliams, "Government by Whitaker and Baxter," *Nation*, Stanley Kelley, Jr., described the firm in detail in *Professional Public Relations and Political Power* (Baltimore, Md.: Johns Hopkins University Press, 1956).
10. "Professional Managers, Consultants Play Major Roles in 1970 Political Races," *National Journal* 2 (September 26, 1970):2084–2085. These totals are not contained in the article but are a count of each category from the information furnished about each campaign.
11. Larry J. Sabato, *The Rise of Political Consultants: New Ways of Winning Elections* (New York: Basic Books, 1981), p. 7.
12. Herbert E. Alexander, *Financing Politics: Money, Elections and Political Reform* (Washington, D.C.: Congressional Quarterly Press, 1976), pp. 52–53.
13. Ibid., pp. 234–235.
14. Division of Elections, State of Florida, Tallahassee, Fla.
15. *New York Times* (December 6, 1980):12.
16. Associated Press report of October 1982 carried in the *Fort Lauderdale* (Fla.) *Sun-Sentinel* (October 18, 1982): 3.
17. Sabato, *Rise of Political Consultants*, Appendix C, pp. 247–255.
18. "Washington Tensions Increase as Both Parties Claim Election Gains," *National Journal* 2 (November 7, 1970):2432.
19. Described in Sabato, *Rise of Political Consultants*, p. 69.
20. Ibid.
21. Various analysts have attributed the 1948 miscue to faulty sampling, failure to reach voters in lower-income groups, and especially to errors in assigning the undecided vote.
22. Louis Harris, "Polls and Politics in the United States," *Public Opinion Quarterly* 27 (Spring 1963):3–8.
23. Sabato, *Rise of Political Consultants*, p. 70. Also see White, *America in Search of Itself*, pp. 377–383.
24. Sabato, *Rise of Political Consultants*, p. 79.
25. Walter DeVries, "Information Systems and Political Consulting," paper presented at the Seminar on Information Systems, Computers, and Campaigns, American Association of Political Consultants, New York, March 20–21, 1970, p. 3.
26. Robert J. Huckshorn, *Party Leadership in the States* (Amherst: University of Massachusetts Press, 1977), pp. 136–137.
27. Republican National Committee, *1982 Chairman's Report*, p. 24.
28. Ibid., p. 22.
29. Robert L. Chartrand, *Computers and Political Campaigning* (New York: Spartan Books, 1972), p. 122.
30. Robert MacNeil, *The People Machine: The Influence of Television on American Politics* (New York: Harper & Row, 1968), pp. 126–127.
31. Robert Agranoff, *The New Style in Election Campaigns* (Boston: Holbrook Press, 1972), p. 260. This and a later edition are excellent books on modern campaign techniques.
32. Thomas E. Patterson and Robert D. McClure, *The Unseeing Eye* (New York: Putnam's, 1976), p. 104.
33. Ibid., pp. 40–41.
34. Ibid., p. 184.
35. Summarized from Thomas E. Patterson, *The Mass*

*Media Election: How Americans Choose Their President* (New York: Praeger, 1980); and Patterson, "The Role of the Mass Media in Presidential Campaigns: The Lessons of the 1976 Election," *ITEMS,* newsletter of The Social Science Research Council 34, no. 2 (1980):25–30. Compared with Paul F. Lazarsfeld, Bernard Berelson, and Hazel Gaudet, *The People's Choice: How the Voter Makes Up His Mind in a Presidential Campaign,* 3rd ed. (New York: Columbia University Press, 1968). (First published in 1944.)

36. David O. Sears and Steven Chaffee, "Uses and Effects of the 1976 Debates: An Overview of Empirical Studies," chapter prepared for inclusion in *The Great Debates, 1976: Ford vs. Carter,* ed. Sidney Kraus (Bloomington: Indiana Univer-

sity Press, 1979); cited in John Kessel, *Presidential Campaign Politics* (Homewood, Ill.: Dorsey Press, 1980), p. 190.

37. Sabato, *Rise of Political Consultants,* p. 181.

38. *Washington Post* (April 1, 1980): 1.

39. Herbert E. Alexander, "Financing Gubernatorial Election Campaigns," *State Government* (Summer, 1980):141–142.

40. Stanley Kelley, Jr., *Political Campaigning* (Washington, D.C.: Brookings Institution, 1960), p. 5.

41. See Lewis A. Froman, Jr., "A Realistic Approach to Campaign Strategies and Tactics," in *The Electoral Process,* eds. M. Kent Jennings and L. Harmon Zeigler (Englewood Cliffs, N.J.: Prentice-Hall, 1966), pp. 1–20.

42. Ibid., pp. 15–17.

# CHAPTER SIX

# Campaign Finance: The Costs of American Politics

Public interest in campaign finance is a phenomenon of recent origin. *The Readers' Guide to Periodical Literature,* a cumulative author/subject index of American journals of general interest, listed only eight references under the category of "campaign funds" between December 1944 and November 1948. Between 1948 and 1952 the number of entries rose to forty-two. In 1955, fifty-six articles were listed, and by 1982 the number of entries was averaging about forty per year.

The outpouring of scholarly books and monographs in the area of political finance was no less impressive. National conferences on campaign funding had become commonplace by 1982, and independently funded foundations had emerged to further the research output of interested scholars. Legislative bodies, from Capitol Hill to the statehouses, were debating and adopting far-reaching campaign finance laws, and government agencies at all levels had been established to supervise or enforce the new laws. Seldom in American history had so much activity been generated around a relatively narrow area of political interest.

**B**ecause General George Washington did not have to campaign for president, his selection for that office by the Electoral College cost him nothing. Both Thomas Jefferson and Alexander Hamilton hired the services of political writers and editors to serve their respective party newspapers and paid them either with a patronage job or with money collected from friends and supporters. It is supposed to have cost Abraham Lincoln only 75 cents to get elected to the House of Representatives, and he was elected president in 1860 for only about $100,000. In 1904 Theodore Roosevelt spent $2,096,000 in the general election; in 1924 Calvin Coolidge spent $4,020,478.

After World War II campaign costs for the presidency began a steady climb that has not stopped. In 1972 President Richard M. Nixon spent a record $61.4 million and Democrat George McGovern spent $30 million.[1] In 1976 $72 million was disbursed in public funds alone: $24.3 million to presidential candidates in the primaries; $4.1 million to the major parties for their national conventions; and $43.6 million to presidential candidates Ford and Carter. In addition, about $50 million was raised through private contributions.[2]

The 1980 presidential campaign is estimated to have cost more than any other in history—one-quarter of a billion dollars, a 56 percent increase over the 1976 contest.[3] Candidates Reagan and Carter spent $20.7 and $18.5 million, respectively, just in their quest for the nomination. All candidates for president spent $186.9 million in the preconvention period and $74.8 million in the general election period. In addition, however, the party committees spent a total of $28.8 million and individuals and groups an additional $31.7 million throughout the campaign. When all expenditures are totaled for 1980, it is estimated that the Democratic candidates spent $96.0 million, the Republicans $136.1 million, and others, including Independent John Anderson, $15.8 million.[4]

One should not look just at the presidential election costs. Campaigns have become very expensive at all levels of government. In 1978 Republican senator Jesse Helms of North Carolina spent $7.5 million in his bid for reelection, a record for a statewide race that held until 1982. In that year two Republican gubernatorial candidates spent about $12.5 million in their quest for office. Both Gov. William Clements of Texas and Republican candidate Lewis Lehrman of New York, however, lost their elections. Democratic candidate Mark Dayton of Minnesota spent nearly $7 million in 1982 in an unsuccessful attempt to become a senator. The year 1982 was also one in which a half-dozen candidates for the House of Representatives exceeded expenditures of $1 million, and Democrat Tom Hayden spent $1.3 million to get elected to the California General Assembly.[5]

Much of the money goes to pay the high costs of technocratic politics, as noted in the last chapter. Politics has changed in virtually every regard in the past two hundred years. We have clearly come a long way from that time in 1828 when John Quincy Adams asserted in his private journal that "the presidency of the United States was an office neither to be sought nor declined. To pay money for securing it, directly or indirectly, was in my opinion incorrect in principle."[6]

# The High Cost of Politics

When dealing with the costs of politics, one must distinguish between party finance and campaign finance. Party finance includes all the money necessary to maintain the operating machinery of the national, state, and local party organizations between elections. Millions of dollars are required to keep the various party headquarters open, pay permanent staff members, carry out the party's public relations functions, and do the dozens of other things that are important to the viability of a party. Levels of expenditures vary greatly from state to state and region to region, with some party organizations responsible for spending hundreds of thousands of dollars each year, while others are barely able to maintain a downtown storefront office with a part-time secretary.

Campaign finance, in contrast, is the collection and expenditure of money for campaign purposes to assist a candidate in his or her effort to get elected. This operation may or may not be centralized in a particular unit of the party structure, and it is most frequently shared among volunteer citizen groups, interest-group organizations, individual donors, and, above all, the resources of the candidate and his immediate family and associates. Both organizational and campaign costs have escalated in recent years at an alarming rate. Party officers and candidates are spending considerable amounts of time, effort, and money just to provide themselves with the resources necessary to perform their primary electoral function.

As we noted in the last chapter, the growth in technocratic politics, especially the high cost of media campaigns, has provided the major impetus to the increased costs of running for office. We often think of these costs in the restricted terms of campaigns for the presidency, but much of the demand for money comes from congressional campaigns, gubernatorial and other statewide campaigns, and thousands of local efforts scattered across the nation. Most of us recognize the fact that it is difficult to raise $50 million to nominate and elect a presidential candidate, but it is often no less difficult to raise $10,000 to elect a rural county sheriff.

Herbert E. Alexander, an authority on campaign finance, has estimated that the costs of campaigns at all levels in presidential years more than tripled between 1952 and 1976 and nearly doubled again by 1980 (see table 6-1). Much of the money has been funneled into presidential campaigns, and much of the growth in expenditures

*"Time to hit the campaign trail"*
(© 1982 Engelhardt in the *St. Louis Post-Dispatch*.
Reprinted by permission.)

can be attributed to changes in campaign styles associated with the mass media. The growth in total campaign spending from $140 million in 1952 to over $900 million in 1980 can be partially attributed to inflationary factors, but most of the increased expenditures have resulted from the explosion of media campaigning. The relatively small incremental growth in campaign spending between 1972 and 1976 was probably due to contribution limits that prevailed under the federal law and in approximately half the states. Other factors that might have slowed spending during that period included the advent of public funding and the residue of resistance to contributing that followed the Watergate scandals. The massive escalation in expenditures between 1976 and 1980 was a result of the 1979 amendments to the Federal Election Campaign Act, which reduced the paperwork associated with campaign reporting and expanded the financial support that state and local parties could provide to federal candidates. The escalation was also a result of the substantial expansion of the role of political action committees (PACs) that was permitted by the 1974 amendments. These changes formalized the role of PACs but expanded their level of expenditures, particularly in congressional elections.

As might be expected, the largest portion of total expenditures goes to presidential campaigns. In 1968, 33.3 percent of the total ($100 million of $300 million) was devoted to presidential politics; in 1972, 32.5 percent ($138 million of $425 million) was spent for that purpose.[7] Although the costs of presidential campaigns were rising faster than those of other campaign efforts until 1976, spending by congressional candidates also escalated dramatically. In 1976 candidates for the House of Representatives spent about one-third more than they had two years earlier. In that year 860 House candidates spent a record $60.9 million, $16.2 million more than they had spent in 1974 and $20.9 million more than in 1972. The average expenditure by Democratic candidates for the House in 1976 was $80,965, and the average for the Republican candidates was $77,440, with incumbents outspending challengers by $2.3 million.[8]

TABLE 6–1 Campaign expenditures for all offices in presidential years, 1952–1980, in millions

| Year | Total expenditures |
|------|--------------------|
| 1952 | $140 |
| 1956 | 155 |
| 1960 | 175 |
| 1964 | 200 |
| 1968 | 300 |
| 1972 | 425 |
| 1976 | 500 |
| 1980 | 900 |

*Source:* The 1952 and 1956 data are from Alexander Heard, *The Costs of Democracy* (Chapel Hill: University of North Carolina Press, 1960). The data for 1960, 1964, 1968, and 1972 are from Herbert E. Alexander's succession of studies: *Financing the 1960 Election* (Princeton, N.J.: Citizens' Research Foundation, 1962); *Financing the 1964 Election* (Princeton, N.J.: Citizens' Research Foundation, 1966); *Financing the 1968 Election* (Boston: Heath, 1971); and *Financing the 1972 Election* (Boston: Heath, 1976). The 1980 data are from *Dollar Politics,* 3rd ed. (Washington, D.C.: Congressional Quarterly, 1982), p. 9, and are based on data from Alexander.

In 1976 sixty-four candidates for the U.S. Senate spent over $38 million, with Democrats outspending Republicans by a slight margin.[9] In 1978 candidates for the Senate in thirty-three states spent close to $45 million in the general election, a figure that does not include all of the candidates who lost in the primaries. By 1980 the costs of all Senate campaigns had risen to $105.2 million, with the Democrats again spending 51 percent of the total. House candidates in 1980 greatly exceeded earlier levels, with total expenditures of $137.3 million. Expenditures to elect the Congress in 1980 totaled $242.5 million.[10] In 1974 both candidates in one campaign each spent more than $500,000; in 1978 nine House candidates spent that much, and in 1980 twenty did, including one, Congressman Robert Dornan of California, who spent $1.8 million. The average campaign expenditures for a freshman member of the House were $106,000 in 1974; $141,000 in 1976; $229,000 in 1978; and $275,000 in 1980.[11]

In 1978 the amount of money contributed by national party organizations to congressional campaigns began to escalate. In one typically competitive district without an incumbent, the Republican candidate received almost $30,000 from nine different GOP committees.[12] In 1980 the two parties used their resources to aid both incumbents facing opposition and open-seat contestants. Democratic incumbents received an average of $1,476; Democratic candidates for open seats received nearly $3,500. Republican incumbents in that year were given an average of $7,986, whereas open-seat contestants received $6,977. Democratic challengers of incumbent Republicans were given $935; Republican challengers were furnished with $2,712.[13]

Expenditures of this size by party organizations in congressional races are unusual. In the past the Democratic Congressional Campaign Committee has seldom extended much financial help to candidates for Congress, and the Republicans have provided assistance only in races considered to be close. The expenditure of sums such as those in 1978 and 1980 are a new departure for the national and state political party organizations.

A final comment needs to be added regarding the impact of campaign funds on races by challengers as opposed to incumbents. Much has been written in recent years concerning the advantages the incumbent has over the challenger in a campaign. This is particularly true at the congressional level, where incumbent congressional representatives and senators have important and costly perquisites of staff, the franking privilege, government-sponsored campaign assistance (in the form of facilities for radio and television reports to the people back home), paid trips to the district, and newsletters. All of these factors contribute to the invulnerability of most incumbents. Furthermore, the officeholder is in a position to perform services for constituents and to gain advantages for the district. These assets are difficult to overcome for a less well known challenger. Consequently, most observers have doubted that House elections will become any more competitive in the foreseeable future than they are now. They believe that what turnover does occur will come about through retirement rather than defeat.

Political scientist Thomas E. Mann disagrees. He believes that House elections may very well become more like Senate elections, where the advantages of incumbency are often neutralized by highly visible and well-financed challengers and where the challenger is much more apt to be successful. Mann notes that such an increase in competition would require stronger effort on the part of challengers. At the present time, he contends, many House seats are not seriously contested. He notes that, in the 1976 elections for the House, challengers spent an average of $49,000, compared to $80,000 for incumbents, and that over 40 percent of the challengers spent less than $20,000. Mann argues that the lack of competition in many districts reflects the decision of local elites not to mount a serious effort.[14] It might also reflect, however, the inability of nonincumbents to raise money from interest-group sources, which have become much more important in campaign finance since the adoption of the 1974 Federal Election Campaign Act Amendments. Groups usually put their money on incumbents because the odds are so great that they will be reelected. In the face of that fact, the challenger often has difficulty raising funds, regardless of how hard he or she tries.

Just the same, when challengers do mount an effort to raise and spend money, it does make a difference. Gary C. Jacobson, in a recent study of the effects of campaign spending on congressional elections, found

> that spending by *challengers* has a substantial impact on election outcomes, whereas spending by *incumbents* has relatively little effect; the evidence is particularly strong for House elections. . . . The more incumbents spend, the worse they do; the reason is that they raise and spend money in direct proportion to the magnitude of the electoral threat posed by the challenger, but this reactive spending fails to offset the progress made by the challenger that inspires it in the first place.[15]

In other words, incumbents spend more when challengers spend more, and the former are able to adjust their level of spending to the gravity of the threat from the latter. Even so, Jacobson found that the more challengers spend, the better they do.

Jacobson contends that the implications of this finding for public policy are clear: in order to increase competition in House races, the challengers' access to campaign funds must be increased, either through public subsidies or with measures that make it easier for them to raise money. Limiting contributions and putting ceilings on spending only serve to dampen competition further. That fact has not been lost on incumbent members of Congress, who, after all, are the only ones who can vote on bills proposing such limitations.[16] Should public funding of congressional elections be approved sometime in the future, it is quite possible that competition levels between incumbents and challengers in congressional races will escalate significantly. If the efforts to secure public funding fail, competition may increase anyway because of the significant growth in contributions to challengers by the parties and by interest groups.

## How Is the Money Spent?

Campaign contributions are collected for the express purpose of helping candidates to make themselves known to the voters. The recent growth of technocratic campaigning has channeled much of the available money into radio and television, professional campaign management, and other technical areas of political marketing.

### Radio and Television Costs

Whether or not a candidate for office is able to profitably use radio and television as campaign media depends in large part on the office being sought and the needs of particular types of campaigns. A candidate for a congressional seat that covers a few acres in a teeming big city will probably find that radio and television are an unduly expensive way of reaching voters in a restricted area. A television spot announcement can cost thousands of dollars in a large city and will reach everyone in the city and the suburbs. But if only one voter in ten can vote in that particular congressional race, such a tactic is not only inefficient but probably foolhardy. In contrast, a rural district may cover an entire viewing area for a centralized television station; in this situation, television might well afford a candidate the most efficient and least costly means available for reaching most of the voters. Decisions such as these must be made by the candidate and his or her advisors early in the game in order for the candidate to develop the best campaign strategy possible for that particular race.

Radio and television offer obvious advantages to candidates for the presidency or those running in statewide contests. The area that can be covered is wide, and the cost per voter is relatively inexpensive. As shown in table 6-2, the expenditures for radio and television in 1968 and 1972 were very high. In 1972 all candidates in all elections spent $59.6 million on the electronic media, with approximately one-fourth of this total being spent by presidential candidates. The only reason that more money was not spent on media campaigns was that new federal campaign spending laws (later repealed) placed a legal limit of $8.5 million on broadcasting.

The magnitude of general election spending for media can be seen by reviewing the percentage of federal funds spent by each presidential candidate from 1968 to 1980 for television, production costs of commercials, newspaper and radio advertisements, and so forth (see table 6-3).

We have noted that the cost of media advertising, both electronic and print, is already very high and is rising. Yet, when 95 percent of the homes in America have at least one television set, it is no wonder that candidates and managers are willing to budget the money necessary for maximum coverage. That coverage is usually defined in terms of available dollars and the locale where the campaign is being waged. A recent edition of the *Spot Television Rates and Data Report,* a monthly service for the television industry, reported the cost of a thirty-second prime-time spot announcement for NBC affiliates in selected cities (see table 6-4).[17]

Obviously, it costs less to campaign by television and radio in some markets than in others. The candidate in Laredo, Texas, can buy eighty thirty-second spots to the New York candidate's one. Not only does the candidate in a less populated but geographically larger district get cheaper time, but he or she probably also gets better and broader coverage, since the range of the station's signal may better match the lines of the congressional district. A congressional candidate running in a district composed of a few acres of New York City may be foreclosed from using television at all because coverage is so much wider than the district boundaries.

Finally, some candidates, particularly those for president, senator, congressional representative, or governor may have access to "free" time in the form of invited appearances on panel shows or better coverage on the local or national news. Some public television stations offer time for candidates for all offices to present their views. Proposals have even been made to require private broadcasting stations to make available some of their public air time as a part of their public service commitment. Media executives, for the most part, oppose the "donation" of time on the grounds that other industries are not forced to make political contributions and that broadcasters should not be singled out in this way.

Intuitively, candidates believe that television and radio offer the best channel for reaching large numbers of voters. Not only do they offer sight and sound, but they reach audiences accustomed to watching and hearing. The use of color and music adds dimensions that are not available in the print media. The size of the audience

**TABLE 6–2    Expenditures for radio and television in the 1968 and 1972 elections, in millions**

|  | 1968 | 1972 |
|---|---|---|
| Nomination and election of all presidential candidates | $28.5 | $14.3 |
| Republican presidential ticket | 12.6 | 4.3 |
| Democratic presidential ticket | 6.1 | 6.2 |
| U.S. Senate candidates | 10.4 | 6.4 |
| U.S. House candidates | 6.1[a] | 7.4 |
| All candidates in all elections | 58.9 | 59.6 |

[a]Off-year congressional election in 1970.
*Source: Congressional Quarterly Weekly Report* (May 12, 1973): 1134–1135. The CQ report was derived from the Federal Communications Commission's Report to Congress on broadcast spending in the 1972 election. No report has been published for the 1976 or 1980 elections.

**TABLE 6–3    General election campaign spending for media, 1968–1980**

| Year | Candidate | Percentage for Media |
|---|---|---|
| 1968 | Humphrey (D) | 61% |
|  | Nixon    (R) | 44 |
| 1972 | McGovern (D) | 37 |
|  | Nixon    (R) | 11 |
| 1976 | Carter   (D) | 44 |
|  | Ford     (R) | 57 |
| 1980 | Carter   (D) | 67 |
|  | Reagan   (R) | 66 |

*Source:* F. Christopher Arterton, "Dollars for Presidents: Spending Money Under the FECA," in *Financing Presidential Campaigns: An Examination of the Ongoing Effects of the Federal Election Campaign Laws Upon the Conduct of Presidential Campaigns,* Institute of Politics, John F. Kennedy School of Government, Harvard University, Cambridge, Mass., January 1982, pp. 3–41. Reprinted by permission.

**TABLE 6–4    Cost of a 30-second prime-time spot announcement for NBC affiliates in selected cities**

| City | Cost per spot | Households served |
|---|---|---|
| New York City | $10,000 | 6,288,500 |
| Chicago | 5,400 | 2,679,400 |
| Kansas City | 1,500 | 617,300 |
| Phoenix | 775 | 534,000 |
| Little Rock | 550 | 360,800 |
| Laredo | 125 | 21,800 |

*Note:* Highest prime-time rates are shown; actual time may vary from station to station.
*Source: Spot Television Rates and Data,* vol. 59, no. 12, December 15, 1977 (Skokie, Ill.: Standard Rate and Data Services, Inc.). Reprinted by permission.

reaches levels that are not possible through any other kind of campaign effort. Candidates use television because they believe it works. And they believe it works because they have heard some of the more spectacular successes of media campaigns that have resulted in the election of virtual unknown candidates to high offices. The list of such candidates lengthens with each election, and the successes spawn more such campaigns as well as rapidly increasing campaign costs. Nevertheless, expensive media campaigns do not always guarantee election. Both in 1980 and 1982 a considerable number of high-spending media candidates lost to opponents who often spent less and won the election anyway. In fact, a growing number of knowledgeable observers believe that there may be a limit to what a media campaign can achieve.

## Costs of Professional Campaign Management

The growth of modern campaign technology has automatically carried with it the need for expert consultants who know how to put it to work. That, in turn, has brought new and heavy demands for more and more campaign money. Professional consulting firms offer a wide variety of services, and a candidate can usually contract for particular services or for an entire campaign. One firm, Matt Reese and Associates, has advertised the availability of the following services:

> Advance and Candidate Scheduling
> Bond Issue and Referenda Campaigns
> Campaign Counseling
> Campaign Management
> Demographic and Audience Research
> Election-Day Activities
> Issue Research
> Media Planning, Coaching, and Buying
> Opinion Polls/Survey Research
> Political Party Management and Organization
> Press Relations
> Public Relations
> Speech and Script Writing
> Staff Recruitment and Organization
> Volunteer Recruitment and Organization
> Voter Registration Drives
> Computer Letters and Direct Mail
> Computer Software Services and Data Processing
> Telephone Communication Consultants[18]

The candidate who contracts for some of these services will find that the cost is high. A public opinion poll in a statewide campaign can cost from $3,000 to $50,000. A mass mailing will involve paper, printing, and postage, all rapidly escalating in price. The rental fee for a hall can be contracted by the hour or charged according to the number of people who show up. Full-scale campaign management might run into hundreds of thousands of dollars in some states, but by negotiating for specific services the cost can be greatly reduced.

Most campaign management firms do not publicize their fee schedules, and no two of them use precisely the same system of charges. Larry Sabato reports that campaign consultant Stuart Spencer charges $1,000 per day, from $20,000 to $50,000 for a statewide campaign contract for consulting, and up to $100,000 for a total management package. Bob Goodman, another major consultant, charges from $50,000 to $100,000 to manage both the primary and general election campaigns and adds a 15 percent commission on the production and placement of his own media advertisements. Others charge by the month ($10,000 or more) or by the day ($750, for example). Such charges are estimated to account for about 20 percent of the average campaign budget.[19] Obviously, these fees reflect the costs of professional management; they also represent one of the reasons for the dramatic escalation in campaign costs and the need for funds.

Even election reform has proven to be a costly campaign expense. Most consultants are now advising clients to reserve from 5 to 10 percent of their total campaign budget for accounting, computer time, and the legal costs associated with increased campaign finance disclosure requirements. Campaign consultants are expensive, but they are increasingly believed to be a necessity rather than a luxury. Because of that attitude, political consulting has become a major growth industry, and campaign funding has become an important part of the candidate's strategy.

Clearly, major responsibility for the rise in campaign costs lies in the expense of media advertising, particularly television, and the employment of professional management consultants. Other components of the increased cost of campaigning have included those expenses associated with a candidate's headquarters (rent, salaries, mailing, telephone service, and supplies) and technical needs, such as computerized mailing, travel, and organized telephone banks. All of these have risen in cost in recent years because of changes in campaign styles and inflationary growth. As the demand for campaign money grows, pressure to expand the traditional sources of campaign money have increased. Let us turn now to the problem of raising the money to pay for the campaigns.

## Where Does the Money Come From?

No area of American politics generates a greater disparity of viewpoints than the question of money to finance campaigns. Many people express extreme cynicism; they consider campaign funds to be the foundation on which a corrupt system is based. Others, however, expressing a more idealistic view, believe that campaign contributions are one of the truest forms of democratic expression and participation. It is not likely that the people holding these opposing views will ever find a common ground, but recent reform efforts requiring financial disclosure, regular reports of campaign contributions and expenditures, funding limitations, public finance of elections, and stronger enforcement agencies may eventually prove to be the catalyst that triumphs over the extremes of viewpoint.

Campaign funds generally derive from two sources: private contributions and the public treasury. As we have seen, political campaigns have become increasingly expensive at all levels. Candidates have been forced to seek funds from a wide variety of sources. Almost everyone would agree that a campaign supported entirely by small contributions from individual citizens would be ideal. But the escalation in campaign costs and the reluctance of people to contribute have made that ideal difficult to achieve in most races. Consequently, candidates often accept contributions from organized interest groups and PACs, and these raise significant questions of ethics and representational roles. Groups usually provide campaign funds to candidates whose support they hope to have after the election—a perfectly legitimate expectation. However, for the newly elected official, the expectation sometimes provides the ingredients for important moral and political dilemmas. If the official casts a vote for the position represented by the group that provided campaign funds, he or she may face accusations of "selling out." But, should that vote be cast against the position of the group, the public official may lose future campaign contributions and suffer a decline in voter support from constituent members of the group. This dilemma has plagued office-holders since the beginning of representative democracy. The problem has been exacerbated in recent decades as the influence of political parties has waned. The impact of large group contributions to candidates has, in fact, served as a spur to people who advocate the public funding of elections.

## Traditional Funding from Private Sources

Traditional sources of campaign funds continue to be important in most races below the level of the presidency. This private funding has traditionally derived from small-contributor programs, large private contributors, dinners and other special events, government employees in political patronage positions, telethons, and political action committees (PACs).

**Small contributors.** In the early days of the Republic, campaign money was usually limited to contributions from the candidates, party organizations, and assessments against officeholders. By the mid-1880s wealthier businessmen and corporations had begun to invest heavily in politics, giving candidates who seemed to best represent their interests an important assist while providing a safe investment. Big contributors continued to play a major role in campaign finance into the 1960s, although the powerful interest groups—labor, business, medicine, and the law—had all emerged as major contributors. The same patterns of giving were apparent throughout state governments.

Through the years many people persisted in believing that politics should and could be financed by large numbers of small contributions. The theory held that if the citizenry in general would only give small amounts (usually from $1 to $10), the accumulated total would pay for campaigns while not shackling candidates to any one special-interest segment of the population. Thus freed of political obligations, it was argued, officeholders would be able to act in the best interests of all of the people while not becoming beholden to major campaign investors.

In fact, however, as the studies of the Survey Research Center at the University of Michigan have repeatedly shown, only about 10 percent of the people have ever contributed during the presidential year.[20] Furthermore, most of the money came in sums of $100 or more, and before 1956 two-thirds of the contributions were in amounts exceeding $500. Since 1960, however, several events have occurred that shifted patterns of political giving. Furthermore, because of changes in the laws, we now know more about the sources of campaign funds than ever before.

Before the 1960s there had been a number of small-contributors programs in both parties, but few of them had been successful. In 1962, however, the Republican National Committee inaugurated a $10 sustaining program based on the use of private nonparty mailing lists borrowed from friendly interest groups or subscription rosters borrowed from friendly publishers. Letters signed by prominent party leaders were mass-mailed to the names on these lists, and a citizen who returned a check was sent a membership card and a subscription to a party publication. By 1963 the gross receipts of the sustaining program were $1.1 million, collected from over 100,000 contributors. In 1964 almost $2.4 million was raised in small sums, and the program has continued to produce significant amounts of money to this day. In the months before the 1972 national convention the Republican sustaining program generated $5.3 million, and each contribution averaged $20.[21] By 1980 the RNC and its congressional counterpart committees had increased the number of regular direct-mail contributors to over two million, with an average individual contribution of under $30. The three committees combined raised approximately $70 million for the 1980 election.[22] The Democratic National Committee has not been able to successfully launch a direct-mail fund-raising effort, but in 1981 it contracted with a private firm to undertake such a program. By 1982 the DNC reported that the firm had mailed two million pieces, but did not indicate the amount of money raised.

Other successful mail solicitation drives have been organized by individual presidential candidates who offered a more clear-cut ideological choice than is usual in American politics. Sen. Barry Goldwater raised some $5.8 million from about 651,000 contributors in 1964. Gov. George C. Wallace, running the costliest third-party campaign in history, raised about $5 million from 750,000 people in 1968. Before the Democratic National Convention in 1972, Sen. George McGovern raised $3 million in small contributions and added another $12 million after receiving the nomination. In both the Wallace and McGovern campaigns individual contributions averaged under $100.[23]

In 1976 and 1980 a number of candidates for president in both parties raised most of their campaign money in small contributions through direct-mail appeals. In 1976 George Wallace, Fred Harris, Morris Udall, Frank Church, and Ronald Reagan all received more than 80 percent of their individual contributions in amounts under $500—in fact, mostly under $100. Lesser-known, ideologically-oriented candidates such as Philip Crane raised almost all of their money through direct mail, but even better-known candidates placed heavy emphasis on mailed appeals. The Kennedy, Bush, and Baker campaigns raised approximately 40 to 50 percent of their campaign funds in this way.[24]

Several factors account for the recent successes of direct-mail solicitation drives. The use of general mailing lists (as contrasted with lists of known supporters) has broadened the base of contributors to include millions of people who would not normally receive a political appeal. Companies now sell such lists for solicitation purposes. Furthermore, the most successful candidates each had large personal followings that constituted a broad base to receive the mailed appeals. Finally, the advent of computerized mailing and handling brought the administrative costs of such appeals down to a level permitting a greater net gain. Nevertheless, direct-mail fund raising can be very expensive (see table 6-5).

**Large contributors.**   "Fat cats" have been a traditional source of campaign money in America. In 1908 and 1912 Charles P. Taft gave $250,000 to his brother's campaign for president, and in 1928 Alfred E. Smith, the Democratic presidential candidate, received individual donations from four supporters of $360,000, $275,000, $260,000, and $150,000, respectively. Big contributors continued to play an important role from the 1940s through the 1960s.

Personal contributions to the 1972 Nixon campaign included two for $300,000, another for $250,000 and four for $100,000. Each of the contributors was appointed to an ambassadorship. W. Clement Stone, an insurance executive from Chicago, reportedly contributed $7 million to President Nixon and other favored candidates during the late 1960s and early 1970s. Also in 1972 Stewart R. Mott, heir to a General

TABLE 6–5    How to raise $2 million by direct mail

*Persistence and a large mailing list are needed to raise $2 million through direct-mail appeals. According to the National Federation of Republican Women, it takes 11,878,458 letters, at a cost of $2,161,644, to raise $4,196,586. Using a federation example, here is how it is done:*

|  | Bank Balance |
|---|---|
| 1. Raise $200,000 to pay for first mailing. | $ 200,000 |
| 2. Use the $200,000 to pay for 1,142,857 letters. | 0 |
| 3. With a response rate of 2.6% and each donor giving an average of $9.18, the mailing returns $272,777. | 272,777 |
| 4. Use the $272,777 and mail letters to 1,558,726 new names. | 0 |
| 5. The rate of response will be slightly lower (2.45%). With the same average gift ($9.18), the mailing will bring in $350,573. | 350,573 |
| 6. At about the same time, mail again to previous donors. It will cost only $23,087 and should produce a response of 15%, with an average of $13 per donor. The profit will be $109,324. | 459,897 |
| 7. Take the $459,897 and send out 2,627,982 letters to a new list of individuals (called "prospects"). With a response of 2.3% and an average gift of $9.18 each, the mailing will return $554,872. | 554,872 |
| 8. Take the $554,872 and send out another "prospect" mailing of 3,179,697 letters. With a 2.1% response at $9.18 each, there is a return of $611,247. | 611,247 |
| 9. Assuming six to eight weeks have passed since last mailing to the donor list, mail to it again. The mailing will cost $66,277 and, with a 15% response and an average donation of $13, it will yield $380,117. | 925,087 |
| 10. Take $500,000 and do a final "prospect" mailing to 2,857,143 new names. With a 1.9% response and $9.18 per gift, it will yield $498,343 (a slight loss) and new names for the donor list. | 923,430 |
| 11. With primaries under way, mail to donor list every five weeks, getting a 20% response (up to 24%) and a higher per-gift average (about $20). The first mailing, at an average of $20 and a 24% response, will bring in $1,196,246 at a cost of $84,734. | 2,034,942 |

*Source:* National Federation of Republican Women, Republican National Committee, Washington, D.C.

Motors fortune, gave a total of $830,339 to Democratic candidates, with $400,000 going to presidential contender George McGovern.[25]

Prior to 1972 a small number of wealthy contributors often provided a substantial proportion of the funds raised by presidential candidates. Federal Election Campaign Act limitations and court decisions limiting contributions have effectively excluded those donors. Even so, there has been some mobilization of networks of $1,000 contributors who together have furnished large sums to particular candidates. Furthermore, independent expenditures, both in the nominating and election campaigns, have become important conduits for large donations to campaigns. Such independent expenditures are permitted under the law so long as the candidate or his organization have not been consulted. They became popular after the Supreme Court's ruling in *Buckley* v. *Valeo* removed the limitations on independent spending. A large contributor can also aid a presidential candidate by contributing funds to state and local parties (within the limitations of state law), and that money can be used to help the national ticket.

**Dinners, receptions, and other special events.**    One of the most popular and traditional methods of raising campaign money, one that is universally used, is the dinner or reception. Many such events center around Lincoln Day and Jefferson-Jackson Day celebrations. The cost may be anywhere from $5 to $1,000 per person, but most dinners at the state or local level fall into the $25 to $100 range. Well-known entertainers are sometimes used as an enticement. Blocks of tickets are sold to interest groups and lobbyists. Some state party organizations finance their entire annual budget from the proceeds of one annual dinner. A statewide dinner for a U.S. Senate candidate (particularly an incumbent) might gross as much as $200,000 to $300,000. Net proceeds of $50,000 or more are not unusual.

It is not uncommon for testimonial dinners in honor of a president to bring in huge amounts of money. In 1968 a twenty-two-city hookup by closed-circuit television on behalf of the Nixon campaign grossed $6 million and produced a profit of $4.6 million.[26] On January 20, 1978, an Atlanta Salute to Carter dinner raised $950,000 for congressional campaigns. About two thousand people attended, at $1000 per couple.[27]

In January 1982 the Republican Eagles Club, composed of contributors of $10,000 annually, met for a dinner honoring the first anniversary of the Reagan inauguration. Held at the Washington Hilton, the 200 tables were each worth $10,000, and the event was attended by the president, the vice-president, the cabinet, and other GOP notables and show-business personalities. The money raised from the event was used to pay the cost of campaign trips by President Reagan and Vice-President Bush in behalf of Republican congressional candidates in 1982.[28]

On occasion, dinners are tied to patronage, with profitable results. One Democratic state chairman has reported that he raised nearly $1 million for his party with a $100-per-plate dinner; all thirteen thousand state patronage appointees were invited to this occasion and were urged to attend. In effect, those who attended contributed $100 apiece to the party that helped them get their jobs.[29] A Democratic state chairman in New York scheduled a fund-raising dinner at Toots Shor's Restaurant and bought the closed-circuit television rights to the Ali-Frazier fight for $16,000. Tickets sold for $250, and the net proved to be a substantial windfall for the party.[30] At the opposite extreme some more egalitarian candidates have sponsored $5 box lunches in an effort to raise large amounts of money from small individual contributions while still maintaining their self-described status as a "people's" candidate. The variety of fund-raising events is endless. Political money has been raised at cocktail parties, wine-and-cheese parties, theatre parties, and other such events. These events have proved to be an important source of political funds for candidates, from the mightiest to the smallest.

**Government employees in patronage positions.**   Every student of government knows that not much political patronage is left to enable political parties to reward their faithful workers with jobs after an election victory. Merit and civil service systems have taken their toll of patronage and spoils. However, in some states and big cities, many government jobs are still filled by the party in power and with the acquiescence of the local party officials. Four state political parties developed a system through which they "taxed" those who received government jobs under party auspices. Probably the best known of these was the system used in Indiana for many years, called the Two Percent Club. Under this system, state employees were requested to contribute 2 percent of their net wages to the party in power each year. They were not generally coerced into compliance, but many feared for their jobs or for promotion opportunities should they not comply. In 1973 these "contributions" amounted to about $400,000 for the Republican State Committee, while between $50,000 and $60,000 went to the Democrats from employees loyal to the party that had originally appointed them in earlier years. Party officials in both parties hailed the system for making it possible to budget with some accuracy and at the same time reduce the influence of wealthy contributors.[31]

Herbert E. Alexander has noted that in 1974 Pennsylvania governor Milton Shapp's reelection campaign was bolstered by $300,000 raised from state employees. The fund raiser for the Democratic State Committee levied assessments according to job category. In the state highway department, for instance, a laborer was expected to contribute $60; a foreman, $120; and contractors, $100 per snow removal machine used.[32]

Generally speaking, federal employees are not as subject as state employees to such efforts to elicit political contributions. In one study only 3 percent reported that they were encouraged by their superiors to vote for a particular candidate or party, and only 2 percent were urged to contribute money.[33] There have been occasional reports that presidential appointees at the cabinet and subcabinet levels have pressured top-level employees to attend fund-raising dinners or cocktail parties, but this is not a common occurrence.

**Telethons.**   The changes wrought by technology are evident even in the efforts of the parties and candidates to raise money. Small-contributors programs are dependent on the lower costs associated with mass mailings, commercial mailing lists, and computer-printed letters. Television has provided the vehicle for telethons and televised appeals by charismatic leaders. Telephone banks have permitted massive calling drives on a national basis. Each of these has proved to be an important means of raising campaign money. At the same time, however, the old tried-and-true methods have continued to produce significant amounts of political cash. Government jobholders are sometimes expected to contribute as a function of their appreciation for their jobs. Large contributors continue to furnish sizable contributions either for selfish, civic, or ideological reasons. And dinners continue to be an important source of political funds (while also contributing to creamed-pea-and-chicken–induced national dyspepsia).

One of the most productive new sources of political money for a number of years was the nationally televised "telethon." Beginning in 1972, the Democratic National Committee inaugurated the first of these events in an effort to pay part of the party's $9.3 million debt left over from the 1968 elections. About 300,000 people pledged almost $4.5 million, and, after production costs were paid, the party netted about $2 million. Telethons were also held in 1973 and 1974, but the proceeds declined and the costs rose until they were no longer so profitable. Furthermore, new federal election laws complicated the financial arrangements through which the time could be bought from a network, and internal party strife arose over how the proceeds should be divided among candidates and the national and state parties.[34] Nevertheless, in 1983 the Democrats were again planning to hold a telethon.

National television has also been used successfully by individual candidates as a means of raising large sums of money. In 1976 Republican presidential candidate Ronald Reagan bought a half hour of prime network time for $80,000 and raised over $1 million as a result of his televised appeal.[35]

## Political Action Committees

The political action committee (PAC) represents one of the newest, and unquestionably one of the most interesting, changes in campaign finance. To some, PACs represent an insidious means for business, labor, professional, and other groups to exercise more control over the political process. To others, they represent an expanded means through which individuals and groups can participate in the political process by contributing funds to campaigns. Everyone agrees that they have emerged within the last few years as an important influence in congressional elections. Yet they have had little impact on presidential races because those campaigns have been funded since 1976 by public money collected through the income-tax checkoff. PACs have had some limited impact on prenomination presidential contests, but only individual contributions are matched by public funds, and in 1980 only $2 million in PAC money was given to presidential candidates.

Many believe that the political action committee is a new innovation. That is not the case, however. Organized labor began forming political action committees over half a century ago, and the AFL-CIO's Committee on Political Education (COPE) has had an influential role in American politics since the mid-1940s. Indeed, since the Civil War big labor and big business have been important forces in American politics, not only because they represent millions of voters who are tied to them through employment or membership, but also because they have vast financial resources that can be channeled into political campaigns. Because of their power, both groups have long been singled out by Congress and some states for regulation of their role in politics. As early as 1907 Congress made it illegal for corporations to contribute money to federal election campaigns, and in 1947 the Taft-Hartley Act contained a provision forbidding contributions and expenditures by both labor and business in federal elections. Both retained the right to make contributions in state and local campaigns unless prohibited by law.

Although direct corporate giving was prohibited, the officers of companies were often encouraged to contribute as a civic responsibility. In 1968 *Congressional Quarterly* surveyed one thousand top executives of large corporations and found that 219 contributed a total of $783,000 to the Republican party, and 26 gave $132,000 to the Democratic party.[36]

Organized labor became a significant force in campaign finance in 1936 and has maintained its role ever since. Labor has traditionally used four methods to raise money for politics. The *first* and best known of these is COPE, an early form of political action committee originally formed to collect voluntary contributions from union members for use in political campaigns. These funds could be used directly to assist candidates in their campaigns, and COPE represented a way in which labor could get around the legal limitations on direct union contributions. A *second* method involves funds taken directly from union treasuries to be used for "educational" purposes, such as get-out-the-vote drives, voter registration drives, and the distribution of such educational materials as congressional voting records and issue analyses. Most of these efforts were directed toward aiding the Democrats and were focused in districts where the benefits would accrue largely to candidates of that party.

A *third* means of influencing elections is through public service activities, such as the distribution of union newspapers and magazines, and through radio programs and other such media events. Finally, a *fourth* category includes those sums spent in state and local elections where state laws did not restrict union political efforts. Studies have shown that labor has contributed as much as 20 percent of the funds for major Democratic candidates in some states and often represented the largest single organizational contributor.[37] Clearly, in spite of federal legal restrictions of many years standing, both business and labor have found ways to be involved in helping to finance the campaigns of favored parties and candidates. The real impetus for extended political action came in the mid-1970s, however, and the face of American politics has changed dramatically since that time.

The 1971 Federal Election Campaign Act (FECA) was amended in 1974 to limit the amount that an individual citizen could contribute to a federal candidate to $1,000 for each primary, runoff or general election, and an aggregate total contribution of $25,000 to all federal candidates in any one year. Organizations, political committees, or national or state party organizations were permitted to contribute $5,000 for each election with no aggregate limit imposed. This provision has itself stimulated the rapid growth of political action committees since 1974.[38]

The FECA modified the ban on corporate and labor contributions by permitting the use of money "for the establishment, administration, and solicitation of contributions to a separate, segregated fund to be utilized for a political purpose."[39] The Supreme Court later upheld the constitutionality of separate segregated funds supported by voluntary contributions.[40] A major breakthrough for PACs came in 1975 when the Federal Election Commission (FEC), created by the 1971 law, issued a far-reaching ruling in a case involving the Sun Oil Company's request for permission to use general treasury funds of the company to establish SUNPAC, its own political action committee. This ruling clarified for business firms what actions they could legally take in permissible fund raising and spending.[41] Organized labor was not happy with the decision, since labor leaders believed that it opened the way to a massive infusion of corporate money into the political process. Labor was successful in getting the FECA amended in 1976 to expand the range of options open to labor and to put some restrictions on how PAC money could be raised and spent. Nevertheless, labor's concerns proved to be well founded as the number of corporate PACs proliferated, and by mid-1982 they outnumbered labor PACs approximately 1,500 to 400. Nearly 3,500 PACs of all types were registered with the FEC at that time (see table 6–6). In spite of the discrepancy in the number of PACs, labor contributions to campaigns exceeded those of business throughout the 1970s.[42]

At the end of 1982 the Federal Election Commission released a preliminary report showing that PACs contributed $38 million during the first eighteen months of the 1981–1982 election cycle, almost all of it to congressional candidates. This represented a considerable growth in contributions over the 1979–1980 election cycle, when only

TABLE 6–6   **The increasing number of political action committees, 1974–1982**

| Committee type | 12/31/74 | 11/24/75[a] | 5/10/76[b] | 12/31/76 | 12/31/77 | 12/31/78 | 8/79 | 12/31/79 | 7/1/80 | 12/31/80 | 7/1/81 | 12/31/81 | 7/1/82 |
|---|---|---|---|---|---|---|---|---|---|---|---|---|---|
| Corporate | 89 | 139 | 294 | 433 | 550 | 784 | 884 | 949 | 1,106 | 1,204 | 1,251 | 1,327 | 1,496 |
| Labor | 201 | 226 | 246 | 224 | 234 | 217 | 226 | 240 | 255 | 297 | 303 | 318 | 389 |
| Trade/Membership Health | 318 | 357 | 452 | 489 | 438 | 451 | 481 | 512 | 542 | 574 | 577 | 608 | 655 |
| Non-Connected | | | | | 110 | 165 | 209 | 250 | 312 | 378 | 445 | 539 | 794 |
| Cooperative | | | | | 8 | 12 | 13 | 17 | 23 | 42 | 38 | 41 | 49 |
| Corporation without stock | | | | | 20 | 24 | 27 | 32 | 41 | 56 | 64 | 68 | 96 |
| TOTAL | 608 | 722 | 992 | 1,146 | 1,360 | 1,653 | 1,840 | 2,000 | 2,279 | 2,551 | 2,678 | 2,901 | 3,479 |

[a]On November 24, 1975, the commission issued Advisory Opinion 1975–23, "SUNPAC."
[b]On May 11, 1976, the president signed the Federal Election Campaign Act Amendments of 1976, P.L. 94–283.
*Source:* Federal Election Commission press release, January 1982. 1982 data added from *Federal Election Commission Record* 8, no. 11 (November 1982): 5.

$25 million was contributed. Table 6–7 shows those PACs that raised the most money for federal candidates during 1981–1982, and table 6–8 shows those that made the most contributions.

Those who manage corporate and interest-group PACs use a variety of ways to determine how the money is to be spent. Some support only incumbent officeholders, whereas others contribute equally to both the incumbent and the challenger. Some make judgments based on candidate interviews and analyses of voting records and platforms, whereas others engage in complex decision-making processes. The 20 trustees of the Realtors PAC held a dozen strategy sessions in Chicago in 1982 to decide which of the congressional candidates would receive support from their group. Each member had a report on voting records, issue briefs, and intelligence materials prepared with the aid of eight full-time staff field specialists. Candidates seeking money from the realtors were required to submit answers to a six-page questionnaire.[43]

TABLE 6–7 Top ten PAC fund raisers

| Political Action Committee | Amount Raised 1/81–6/82 |
|---|---|
| National Congressional Club | $7,695,037 |
| National Conservative Political Action Committee | 7,223,209 |
| Realtors Political Action Committee (National Association of Realtors)[a] | 2,225,645 |
| American Medical Political Action Committee (American Medical Association) | 2,172,477 |
| Citizens for the Republic | 1,945,809 |
| Fund for a Conservative Majority | 1,915,763 |
| Committee for the Survival of a Free Congress | 1,786,675 |
| National Committee for an Effective Congress | 1,623,820 |
| Committee for the Future of America, Inc. | 1,457,835 |
| Committee for Thorough Agricultural Political Education (Associated Milk Producers, Inc.) | 1,378,406 |

[a]The connected organizations (i.e., sponsors) of separate segregated funds are indicated in parentheses.
*Source: Federal Election Commission Record* 8, no. 4 (November 1982): 4.

TABLE 6–8 Top ten PAC contributors to candidates

| Political Action Committee | Amount Contributed 1/81–10/82 |
|---|---|
| Realtors Political Action Committee (National Association of Realtors)[a] | $2,045,092 |
| American Medical Political Action Committee (American Medical Association) | 1,638,795 |
| United Automobile Workers Political Action Committee | 1,470,354 |
| Machinists Non-Partisan Political League (International Association of Machinists & Aerospace Workers) | 1,252,209 |
| National Education Association Political Action Committee (National Education Association) | 1,073,896 |
| American Bankers Association Political Action Committee (American Bankers Association) | 870,110 |
| National Association of Home Builders PAC | 852,745 |
| Associated Milk Producers Political Action Committee | 842,450 |
| Automobile & Truck Dealers Election Action Committee | 829,945 |
| AFL-CIO COPE Political Contributions Committee | 823,125 |

[a]The connected organizations (i.e., sponsors) of separate segregated funds are indicated in parentheses.
*Source: Federal Election Commission Record* 9, no. 2 (February 1983): 6.

Smaller PACs often look to larger, more sophisticated ones for assistance and guidance. The U.S. Chamber of Commerce and the AFL-CIO both publish "opportunity lists" to provide leads as to where PAC money will do the most good. The Chamber of Commerce in 1982 produced a videotape of its "opportunity list" for broadcast in a four-hour closed-circuit television show called "See How They Run." The broadcast was directed to 150 PAC managers in seven cities and provided an analysis of 50 key congressional races.[44]

As one would expect, the proliferation of PACs has not been without controversy. Those who favor the PAC system argue that, regardless of the method used, special-interest money will continue to flow into election campaign coffers and that it is better to have a system that is regulated and open to the public. Furthermore, they maintain that PACs represent a way in which small donors can pool their money to have a greater impact on the political process. Finally, the ultimate argument has always been that people have a constitutional right to involve themselves in the electoral system and that PACs are a legitimate means of exercising that right.

Those who are opposed to the rapid acceleration in PAC activities maintain that they undermine the effectiveness and integrity of Congress. These opponents argue that, unlike independent contributions, PAC money represents organized interests that will follow up their contributions with lobbying and grass-roots pressures on congressional representatives. Some members of Congress have suggested that PACs tend to pull members away from broad consensus building toward more narrowly defined and selfish goals. Opponents also maintain that most PAC money goes to incumbents representing an unfair advantage that the challenger is hard-pressed to overcome. Finally, many criticize PACs for undermining political parties by usurping the traditional party role in campaigns. By providing large infusions of campaign funds, PACs aid candidates in buying professional campaign consulting services, thus reducing their reliance on party organizations. Furthermore, PACs that represent large membership groups can mobilize group members into voting blocs, which further reduces the candidates' need for the voter mobilization services available through the party.

Other observers believe that the negative impact of PACs on parties is exaggerated. They point out that the decline in the parties' role began long before the advent of PACs and that in many cases PAC money is making available to candidates campaign technology that is no longer available from the party organization in many areas.

Several solutions to the PAC problem have been suggested. Some have argued that public financing of congressional campaigns (following the pattern established for presidential campaigns) would eliminate the problem. Others wish to raise the $1,000 limit that an individual can contribute to a campaign, thus helping to dilute the influence of PACs. Still another option would be to limit the amount an individual candidate can accept from PACs. Whatever proposals are considered, however, it will be most difficult to persuade incumbent members of the House and Senate to cut off this source of funds or to limit its application. Incumbents receive the bulk of PAC money, and it is the incumbents who will have to vote on any reforms that are made.

## Public Funding of Election Campaigns

The rise in campaign costs, the influence of family wealth and large contributors, the impact of illegal contributions brought into focus by Watergate, and the advantages enjoyed by incumbents have all joined in recent years to raise public awareness of the

THE NEW YORK TIMES, SUNDAY, FEBRUARY 6, 1983

# A DECLARATION OF WAR

The time has come to draw the line. Political Action Committees (PACs) have put Congress on the take. And *you're* being taken for a ride. Consider your health: PAC money from doctors helped convince Congress *not* to pass a bill that would help keep your hospital costs from skyrocketing. Consider your protection from fraud: PAC money from auto dealers helped convince Congress *not* to pass a bill that would require used car dealers to tell you what's wrong with the second-hand car you're buying. Consider your savings: PAC money from the dairy industry has helped to convince Congress, year after year, *not* to make needed cuts in dairy subsidies, which artificially inflate the price of the milk, butter and cheese you buy. Consider yourself *mute.* Your voice is being *drowned out* by the ringing of PAC cash registers in Congress.

Senator Robert Dole, Chairman of the Senate tax writing committee, says, "When these PACs give money, they expect something in return other than good government." These are contributions with a purpose—a legislative purpose. And the PAC system works according to the golden rule, says former Congressman Henry Reuss: "Those who have the gold make the rules."

We're not talking about illegal campaign contributions of the sort that ten years ago created a national scandal called Watergate. We're talking about $80 million in campaign contributions that are *perfectly legal,* creating a new national scandal corrupting our democracy. And *that* is a crime.

Unless we change our system for financing Congressional campaigns and change it soon, our representative system of government will be gone. We will be left with a government of, by and for the PACs.

We can't let that happen. We *won't* let that happen. Common Cause has declared war — a war on PACs. Ours has always been a government of, by and for the *people.* We must keep it that way.    Common Cause.

Common Cause advertisement opposing political action committees.

need for reform. One aspect of that reform effort was the advent of public funding of presidential election campaigns, which went into effect in the 1976 campaign. The money for federal funding is derived from a tax checkoff through which every individual whose federal tax liability for one taxable year is $1 or more can designate on his or her federal income-tax form that $1 be placed in the Presidential Election Campaign Fund. Those filing joint returns can earmark $2. Any candidate nominated by a major party—defined as a party receiving at least 25 percent of the vote in the previous presidential election—is entitled to participate. Minor party candidates are eligible to take part if they meet certain requirements. The amount of money that a third-party candidate may receive is determined by a formula that incorporates his or her share of the popular vote in comparison to the average popular vote of the major-party candidates. Since no third-party candidate qualified, all public funds in 1976 went to Democratic and Republican candidates. In 1980 Independent candidate John Anderson was certified to receive matching funds.

The federal checkoff system provides for the accumulation of money during each tax year, with all payments made in the presidential election year. The number of taxpayers taking part has increased steadily, from 4 percent in 1972 to 27.4 percent by 1980. By 1982 the fund contained a balance of $114 million and had, with the exception of 1979, showed steady growth from year to year.[45] Public funds in the amount of $31.3 million were distributed to ten candidates in 1980 during the pre-convention period and $29.4 million to each of the major party candidates during the general election campaign (see table 6-9). For the first time in the brief history of the FECA, the Federal Election Commission certified payment of $4.2 million to a third-party candidate, John Anderson. Furthermore, each of the national party committees received the maximum entitlement of $4.4 million for their national nominating conventions.[46]

The commission certifies matching funds to eligible presidential primary candidates who have qualified by raising more than $100,000 in amounts exceeding $5,000 from each of twenty states. This provision is an attempt to guarantee that candidates have broad national support. Up to $250 of an individual contribution may be matched by federal funds, and candidates must agree in advance to limit expenditures to $10 million plus a cost-of-living adjustment. In 1980 the total limit, including the adjustment, was set at $14,720,000.

The experiment in public funding of presidential elections, which seemed to work well in 1976 and 1980, provided a fundamental change in campaign finance. Consid-

TABLE 6-9    FEC-certified matching funds for 1980 presidential primaries

| Reagan | (R) | $7.3 million |
|---|---|---|
| Bush | (R) | 5.7 |
| Carter | (D) | 5.2 |
| Kennedy | (D) | 4.2 |
| Anderson | (I) | 2.7 |
| Baker | (R) | 2.6 |
| Crane | (R) | 1.9 |
| Brown | (D) | .9 |
| LaRouche | (D) | .5 |
| Dole | (R) | .4 |

*Source:* Federal Election Commission press release, February 1982.

ering the fact that President Nixon spent more than $60 million in 1972 and Senator McGovern over $30 million, the new limits were clearly more restrictive. Some thought that it would not be possible to run a presidential campaign for the amounts allowed, but neither candidate nor party appeared to be seriously inconvenienced. Given the rate of inflation and the spiraling costs of campaigning, however, it appears doubtful that future campaigns can be carried out without expanding the amount of money available.

The federal government is not alone in experimenting with public funding of elections. Between 1974 and 1980 seventeen states enacted legislation to provide public funding of some state-level campaigns. Led by New Jersey, the states of Hawaii, Idaho, Iowa, Kentucky, Maryland, Maine, Massachusetts, Michigan, Minnesota, Montana, North Carolina, Oklahoma, Oregon, Rhode Island, Utah, and Wisconsin have enacted legislation setting up some form of public financing. Ruth S. Jones has noted that each of these states has unique features in their individual plans and that they vary in four categories of policy choice: (1) fund collection, (2) fund allocation, (3) types of elections to be subsidized, and (4) the means of administration and enforcement.[47] Let us briefly review the way in which each of the states has approached each of these policy choices.

1. *Campaign fund collection.* The first of the four choices legislators have had to make concerns the overt role of political partisanship in the collection of public funds. In five states (Iowa, Kentucky, Maine, Oregon, and Utah) the political parties are specified as the direct recipients of public funds; in eight states the funds are collected in a general fund; and in four states the contributor can designate either a partisan or general fund allocation.

Fourteen states provide for a $1 contribution per taxpayer, and three permit the individual taxpayer to contribute $2. Thirteen states use a checkoff system, similar to the one used at the federal level, through which the taxpayer earmarks a portion of his or her tax to be used for public funding by checking a box on the tax form. Under this system the tax liability of the individual is not increased, but some funds that would normally go to the state's general fund are set aside for public funding of campaigns. Four states rely on the "add-on" system, in which the taxpayer increases the amount of the check written to the state by the amount of the political contribution. Generally, the "add-on" system produces less money than the checkoff system, and the states permitting a $2 checkoff produce considerably more than those allowing only $1. Participation levels have been similar across the states, with about one-fifth of the taxpayers taking part.[48]

2. *Campaign fund allocation.* The second policy decision concerns the method through which money is to be allocated, either directly to individual candidates or to the political party organizations. The states divide almost equally on this issue: eight allocate money to parties, eight allocate directly to candidates, and Oklahoma provides a small amount for parties, with the remainder going to candidates.

3. *Election to be subsidized.* The states have varied considerably in their determination of which elections to subsidize. Most of the states have limited public funding to the general gubernatorial election, but Massachusetts, Michigan, and New Jersey also provide funds in gubernatorial primaries. A second question has had to do with the number of campaigns to be subsidized. In Michigan and New Jersey, only gubernatorial campaigns are subsidized, but in Wisconsin and Minnesota public funds

are provided for all state constitutional offices and legislative races. In Hawaii and Maryland the coverage extends from state constitutional offices to selected local campaigns.

4. *Program administration and enforcement.* The fourth policy decision to be made involves the way in which public funding is to be administered and enforced. One determination is whether to rely on an established state agency or to create a new one for the particular purpose. If the latter choice is made, decisions must be made as to the powers to be given the new agency. By 1980 seven states had chosen to place these responsibilities with an existing agency, and ten had created new agencies for the purpose. The states vary considerably in the authority they grant to these agencies: some agencies have only advisory powers and rely on traditional law enforcement offices for enforcement, whereas others have the power to investigate, subpoena, and prosecute.

Ruth Jones has found that five of the seventeen states did not use public funds in 1980 but that the remaining twelve used $2,875,000 in that year. Although levels of participation have varied somewhat, the number of participants has remained generally constant year after year. Taxpayer participation rates for the tax year of 1979, which provided money for the 1980 elections, ranged from 7.5 percent to 41.0 percent in tax checkoff states and from 0.5 percent to almost 3.0 percent in the "add-on" states. Among the states in which taxpayers can designate a partisan preference, the balance shifted slightly toward the Republicans, but only in Utah did the Republican party receive more than the Democratic party. Allocations remained about equal in Iowa and Idaho, and the Democratic party maintained an advantage in the remaining states.[49]

Jones concludes that a general evaluation of state public funding of elections demonstrates that public campaign finance brings a significant amount of new money into state campaigns; one-fifth to one-fourth of the taxpayers voluntarily take part in the tax checkoff system; the Democrats usually get more than the Republicans in absolute dollar amounts, due largely to the fact that they outnumber the Republicans in the active electorate; and taxpayer participation has remained rather constant. Other findings are as yet not confirmed or are contradictory.[50]

Public funding, both at the national and state levels, is too new for an accurate assessment of its effects to be made with any certainty. It is not known whether there will be a long-range benefit for one party over the other or for challengers over incumbents. Based on the 1976 and 1980 experiences, we cannot accurately assess the prospect that more candidates will run because of the financial guarantees provided by public funding. In those states that allow more discretion in the expenditure of funds the party organizations might well be strengthened. The party leadership will have funds with which to campaign, and that, in turn, might ultimately increase party responsibility. By the same token, in those states that bypass the party organizations by furnishing funds directly to candidates, one may reasonably expect a diminution in party influence.

## Regulating Campaign Finance

In 1867 a federal law was passed designed to protect government employees from having to kickback a percentage of their salary to the officeholder who hired them. The Civil Service Reform Act of 1883 broadened the prohibition against soliciting government workers and expanded it to prevent federal employees from collecting political money from each other. Congress adopted laws in 1907 to forbid banks and corporations from making direct contributions to federal candidates and in 1910 enacted the first disclosure law, which, when amended in 1911, applied its provisions to primaries as well as general elections. The new law also limited the expenditures of congressional candidates. In 1921 the Supreme Court (*U.S.* v. *Newberry*) limited the law's coverage and removed federal jurisdiction over nominations.

The Federal Corrupt Practices Act of 1925 codified existing law and required candidates for the Senate and the House to disclose contributions and expenditures. It also established spending ceilings for House and Senate races but excluded presidential contests. Although the spending limits were unrealistic ($2,500 to $5,000 in the House and $10,000 to $25,000 in the Senate, depending on the size of the constituency), this law remained one of the principal federal election laws until the 1970s.

The Hatch Act, adopted in 1939 (with amendments in 1940), put a $5,000 limit on individual contributions to federal campaigns and a $3 million maximum on the expenditures of political committees, including the national committees. Other restrictions were placed on participation by federal workers, who were forbidden to act as campaign managers or poll workers or to take part in election-day activities. Penalties were provided for in the Hatch Act, including both fines and prison terms. For three-quarters of the twentieth century, therefore, the Federal Corrupt Practices Act and the Hatch Act constituted federal law governing election financing. Prohibitions on corporate giving, first enacted in 1907, were extended to include labor unions by the Smith-Connally Act of 1944 and later by the Taft-Hartley Act of 1947. None of these laws was ever vigorously enforced, and few people, including members of Congress, paid them much attention. After World War II several state legislatures adopted campaign finance laws, the best known of which was Florida's "Who Gave It, Who Got It" law, but few of them, including Florida, provided enforcement machinery to implement their provisions.

## Campaign Finance Reform in the 1970s

One of the first of the new wave of reform efforts was the Long Act, passed in 1966. Sponsored by Sen. Russell Long of Louisiana, the bill provided a federal subsidy for presidential elections to be paid for by a tax checkoff by taxpayers who filed federal returns. The checkoff permitted the taxpayer to designate $1 to be paid into a Presidential Election Campaign Fund beginning in 1968. Under the distribution formula each of the two major parties would have received about $30 million in 1968. This law was repealed, however, a year later. Nevertheless, the Long Act was a first step in the direction eventually taken by the lawmakers.

**Federal Election Campaign Act of 1971.**  The turning point came with the passage of the Federal Election Campaign Act (FECA) of 1971. In addition to repealing the Federal Corrupt Practices Act of 1925, FECA set limits on candidate expenditures for communications media in federal elections; placed a ceiling on contributions by candidates or their immediate families; stipulated that the appropriate federal officers to supervise election campaign practices were the clerk of the House, the secretary of the Senate, and the comptroller general; required congressional candidates and their campaign committees to file duplicate reports with the secretary of state or a comparable officer in their home state; required each political committee and candidate to report, on specified dates, total expenditures, including names, addresses, occupations, and places of business for [each contributor,] as well as the amount of the contribution; and required a complete financial statement of the costs of the presidential nominating conventions within sixty days after each affair.

**Federal Election Campaign Act amendments of 1974.**    Public pressure generated by the Watergate scandals spurred Congress to additional reform efforts in 1974. The resulting law was signed by President Ford and went into effect on January 1, 1975. Its major provisions can be summarized as follows:

1. *Contribution limits.* Individuals may contribute no more than $1,000 to any candidate for president or Congress in any one election and no more than $25,000 in all federal elections. Political committees may not contribute in excess of $5,000 per candidate per election, and candidates and their immediate families may not contribute more than $50,000 for an entire presidential campaign, $35,000 for a Senate race, or $25,000 for a House contest. Contributions were also defined in greater detail than had been the case in the past.

2. *Spending limits.* No more than $10 million may be spent to obtain a presidential nomination, and no more than $20 million in the presidential election. Limits of $100,000 for a Senate nominating contest and $70,000 for a House primary race were set; in the general election a House candidate was allowed an additional $70,000 and a Senate candidate was permitted $150,000. A separate formula for House and Senate races was established for populous states where the limits might not be high enough. A ceiling of $2 million was placed on national nominating conventions costs; nonpartisan registration and voting drives were exempt from the spending limitations; and the media spending limits in the 1971 law were repealed. Political parties and political committees were permitted to contribute up to $5,000 per federal candidate per election. Finally, national party committees were allowed approximately $2.8 million (figured at 2 cents for each potential voter) without this figure's counting against the nominee's spending limits.

3. *Presidential financing.* Money collected from the $1 checkoff on the federal income-tax form was to be disbursed according to the distribution previously discussed: $2 million for the national conventions; $20 million for each major party presidential candidate; and matching money for each contribution of $250 or less, after a candidate qualified by raising $5,000 in each of twenty states in contributions of $250 or less.

4. *Disclosure provisions.* All candidates were required to form one central campaign committee and to report all contributions, loans, and expenditures that exceeded $100.

5. *Enforcement.* This provision created an eight-member Federal Election Commission, with two members to be nominated by the president pro tempore of the Senate, two by the Speaker of the House, and two by the president, to be confirmed by a majority vote of both the Senate and House. The secretary of the Senate and the clerk of the House were made nonvoting ex officio members. The commission was empowered to give advisory opinions, to promulgate rules and regulations, and to seek injunctions and other civil remedies in court, in addition to sending criminal findings to the Department of Justice for prosecution.

**Buckley v. Valeo: The Supreme Court intervenes.** Whenever government undertakes to regulate the amounts of money that can be collected and spent in election campaigns or to use tax money for the support of political campaigns, important questions of representative democracy and constitutional government are raised. One of the most crucial of these questions is how the law will be interpreted and enforced. Who will fill in the blanks in the general legislation? How can we guarantee that the public funds will be disbursed fairly and conscientiously? In short, how can fairness be maintained so that some candidates or parties do not suffer undemocratic consequences?

In passing the Federal Election Campaign Act Amendments of 1974, Congress chose to spell out some of the administrative guidelines on contributions, expenditures, and disclosure, but most observers believed that the most important provision of the new law was the establishment of the strong enforcement agency—the Federal Election Commission. No complex law can be adequately and fairly enforced and administered without a reasonably clear legislative mandate to do so. Congress provided that mandate in the 1974 law by giving the FEC impressive powers and by requiring it to act expeditiously. Nevertheless, whenever a new law is passed and a new agency is created with general enforcement powers, some citizens, candidates, or parties feel threatened or intimidated. In this case those who belonged to third-party movements or ran as independents outside the mainstream of two-party politics were especially concerned.

A few days after the law became effective in January 1975, a case was brought against it in a federal action challenging many of its key provisions. The plaintiffs in the case included a wide-ranging assortment of liberals and conservatives, Republicans, Democrats, and Independents, incumbents and challengers, and wealthy citizens accustomed to making substantial political contributions to favored candidates.

A year later, in January 1976, the Supreme Court, in the case of *Buckley* v. *Valeo*, struck down the Federal Election Commission because its members were not all presidential appointees and a part of the executive branch of the government. But the Court upheld the *concept* of the enforcement commission and gave Congress three months to rewrite the law to comply with the decision. The 1976 amendments included a newly reconstituted Federal Election Commission composed of six members appointed by the president (plus the same two ex officio members) and more clearly defined its executive functions. The new commission had the power to promulgate rules and regulations, issue binding advisory opinions, take enforcement actions, and certify public funds to candidates. On May 11, 1976, a new commission was sworn in and began the difficult job of enforcing the revised law.

**1976 amendments to the Federal Election Campaign Act of 1974.** As a result of *Buckley* v. *Valeo* and the new 1976 amendments, the commission gained exclusive jurisdiction over civil enforcement of the law (in contrast to the 1974 provisions, which required that findings be referred to the Department of Justice for prosecution). The scope of commission advisory opinions was reduced in order to place more emphasis on the promulgation of rules and regulations. The Court struck down expenditure limitations as direct and substantial restraints on the quantity of political speech. This applied to limits on both individual citizens and on candidates using their own money, but an exception was made for those candidates who accepted public funds, in which case such limits could be imposed as a condition for accepting such funds.

The Court upheld limits on contributions both by individuals and by groups and sustained all the disclosure requirements of the law. Under these provisions all candidates were required to maintain a single campaign committee, and organizations collecting or spending $1,000 or more for a political purpose had to register with the Federal Election Commission. Furthermore, all individual contributions of $100 or more were to be reported. Additional restrictions were placed on labor and business.

**1979 amendments to the FECA of 1974.** By 1979 most of the provisions of the current election law were in place, but candidates and party officials continued to complain of excessive paperwork and red tape associated with the reporting requirements. The 1979 amendments to the FECA were designed to reduce or eliminate much of the paperwork, both for candidates and for the Federal Election Commission. Congressional approval was expedited when it was decided to avoid controversial issues, such as limitations on PACs and public financing of congressional campaigns, and President Carter signed the new legislation early in 1980. The changes were not very dramatic in themselves, but their overall effect was to significantly overhaul the law.

The 1979 amendments reduced the paperwork required in several ways: it decreased the number of reports federal candidates had to file with the FEC from twenty-four to nine; it eliminated the requirement that candidates who raised and spent less than $5,000 had to file reports; it allowed local political party organizations to avoid filing reports with the FEC if expenditures for certain activities were less than $5,000; it reduced from eleven to six the categories of information required on registration statements of political committees; it established new standards for seeking advisory opinions from the FEC and provided for a quicker response from that agency; and it increased from $2 million to $3 million the allotment to the political parties to finance their nominating conventions.

## FECA and the Political Parties

Any assessment of the national campaign finance laws and their effect on the political parties must conclude that the results have been mixed. In some respects the law facilitates party activity by permitting individual contributions of up to $20,000 directly to the party while only allowing $1,000 to individual candidates. Party organizations are also given some favored status in assisting candidates for federal office by allowing higher limits for contributions for party candidates as opposed to nonparty committees. For legislative candidates the law provides separately for support by the national and state parties. The Republicans, in fact, have set up a series of "agency agreements" in which both the RNC and the state parties designate the relevant national campaign committee as their agent, thus permitting a concerted fund-raising effort that may lead to a better use of campaign money. In addition, state and local parties are allowed to spend unlimited funds in behalf of their candidates for president for specifically exempted activities, such as support for volunteers and get-out-the-vote drives.

Those who believe that the federal campaign finance laws are detrimental to parties—and they have a strong case—point to the fact that public funding is provided directly to the candidates for president rather than being channeled through the parties. Furthermore, the law allows wealthy persons and political action committees to spend unlimited amounts of money independently while limiting the amount that can be spent by the parties. Finally, the act restricts campaign budgets by limiting spending on presidential campaigns and limiting contributions, thus possibly indirectly forcing candidates to rely more heavily on media campaigns rather than on traditional activities orchestrated by the parties. The complexities of the law can be seen by reading through Arterton's list of ten ways to spend money in a federal campaign (see box below).

---

## Ten Ways of Spending Money in Federal Elections

1. *Campaign treasuries of presidential candidates.* Public funding is provided directly to presidential candidates in both the prenomination and general election races. In return, the expenditures of the candidates are strictly limited.

2. *Compliance funds.* Presidential candidates can raise and spend additional funds for costs of complying with the laws. Although theoretically unlimited in amount, the expenditures from this account are subject to FEC audit to determine their appropriateness.

3. *National party conventions.* The national nominating conventions of major parties are financed out of the public treasury and strictly limited in the total that can be expended. Clearly, this category of spending benefits the party, the presidential candidates, and other party officeholders.

4. *National party spending directly associated with the presidential campaign.* A limited amount of funds can be raised from private sources by the national party committees. In both major parties these funds are entirely controlled by the candidate committee; they are treated as merely a separate bank account.

5. *Party money for congressional and senatorial candidates.* Party committees may expend money in behalf of their candidates for federal office. One of the national committees and the state party can each spend $10,000 for a congressional candidate and 2 cents per voting-age citizen or a total of $20,000 (whichever is larger) for a senatorial candidate. These amounts are increased by cost-of-living adjustments; thus the limitation for congressional candidates in 1980 was $14,700 (i.e., a total of $29,400), whereas spending for senators varied from a high of $485,024 (California) to a minimum of $29,400. These allotments can be doubled if both the state party and the national committee are spending in the candidate's behalf.

In addition, either the national party committee or the campaign committee may contribute $17,500 to senatorial candidates in either the primary or general election, and both committees may each contribute $5,000 to a congressional candidate in both the primary and general elections (i.e., $20,000 total). Finally, the state party committees may contribute $5,000 to Senate and House candidates in both types of elections, as can any local party committee that can prove it is independent of its state committee.

6. *National committee operating budgets.* The normal operation of the national parties can be funded quite separately and is essentially unlimited as long as it does not involve the express advocacy of the defeat or election of a specific candidate. Under this provision, the Republicans sponsored the "Vote Republican for a Change" ads.

*(continued)*

7. *Grass-roots activity of local party committees.* An exemption was included in the act in 1979 for certain classes of party spending for citizen-to-citizen contact and get-out-the-vote activities. In addition, local party committees that raise and spend under $5,000 can avoid the reporting requirements of the FECA.

8. *State party money.* State law may regulate the contributions and expenditures to state parties, but these are only affected by the federal law when these committees are involved in federal elections. During a presidential election, these funds, referred to as "soft money," can be mixed with the legally limited federal money in proportion to the number of candidates on the ballot in a given location, thereby allowing campaigners to spend more for ticketwide activities.

9. *Labor union, trade association, and corporation money.* These organizations can spend funds for get-out-the-vote efforts or "internal communications" to their membership without reporting these expenditures under the act.

10. *Independent expenditures.* Individuals and groups can spend unlimited amounts advocating the defeat or election of federal candidates as long as the expenditures are independent of the candidate, that is, not made in consultation or coordination with the candidate or his or her representatives.

*Source:* "Political Money and Party Strength," by F. Christopher Arterton. From the book *The Future of American Political Parties,* edited by Joel L. Fleishman. © 1982 by The American Assembly, Columbia University. Published by Prentice-Hall, Inc., Englewood Cliffs, NJ 07632. Reprinted by permission.

## FEC Enforcement of the FECA

Although the Federal Election Commission is involved in many different activities, one of the most public duties it performs is enforcement of the FECA. In 1980 the commission issued 134 advisory opinions on a wide variety of subjects. These opinions dealt with everything from the qualifications for being considered a national committee to whether a contribution of 100 silver dollars should be counted at face value (i.e., as a $100 contribution) or as an in-kind contribution that the candidate could barter for a greater amount. Disclosure reports were received from thousands of candidates and committees, and 194 compliance cases were closed during the year, leaving 214 pending future action. Thirty-three cases in litigation were pending as the year began, 31 new ones were filed, and 33 others were closed. The commission won 31 cases and lost 2.[51]

It is not possible to determine whether or not the 1976 and 1980 experiences were representative of future elections. Nevertheless, the years in which the commission has been active offer some evidence that it is settling into a routine. Unloved as it may be, it appears to be here to stay, and a number of observers believe that it is functioning about as well as can be expected, given the highly sensitive nature of its mission.

## Election Law Enforcement in the States

Between 1972 and 1980 virtually every one of the fifty states enacted new election laws, most of them including stringent campaign finance requirements. Most states had to rewrite their laws in the aftermath of *Buckley* v. *Valeo* in order to bring them into line with the Supreme Court's decision. One-half of the states created bipartisan independent commissions to oversee elections (see, for example, "Campaign Finance Laws, State of Florida," below). As Herbert E. Alexander has noted:

> The commissions represent an attempt to isolate as much as possible from political pressures the functions of receiving, auditing, tabulating, publicizing, and preserving the reports of political campaign receipts and expenditures required by law. The commissions generally

---

### Campaign Finance Laws, State of Florida

All candidates must:
— have a designated campaign treasurer.
— maintain a single campaign depository.
— follow designated rules on the use of bank checks.
— deposit campaign monies by legal deadlines.
Contribution limits for single contributor:
— $1,000 for all municipal, county, multicounty, or lower-level judicial races.
— $2,000 for judge of district court of appeals.
— $3,000 for all statewide offices, including justice of supreme court.
— all contribution limits treat primary, runoff, and general elections as distinct.
Expenditures:
— must be made through designated depository.
— permit petty cash funds at rate of $500 per week for statewide races and $100 per week for others.
Testimonials:
— defined as breakfast, dinner, luncheon, rally, party, reception, or other affair.
— notice of intent to hold required before money can be raised or spent.
Political advertisements:
— must be attributed to person or organization contracting for.
— must show party affiliation of general elections campaign.
— must be used with permission of candidate.
Enforcement:
— Florida Election Commission—six members and a chairman appointed by governor for four-year terms, approved by cabinet and confirmed by senate.
— investigates allegations of violations of above requirements.
— exempt from Sunshine Law; holds hearings in secret; results publicized after formal determination made.
Power of subpoena:
— may levy civil fines up to $1,000 per violation.
— may enforce orders of court.
— may refer criminal cases to state attorneys.

*Source:* Election laws of State of Florida, Division of Elections, Department of State, Tallahassee, Fla., June 1981.

**TABLE 6–10    Regulation of political finance by the states**

| State | Election Commission | Disclosure Before and After[a] | Individual Contribution Limits | Expenditure Limits[b] | Public Subsidy | Credit | Tax Provisions Deduction[e] | Checkoff |
|---|---|---|---|---|---|---|---|---|
| Ala. | | | | | | | | |
| Alaska | ✔ | ✔ | ✔ | | | ✔ | | |
| Ariz. | | ✔ | | | | | ✔ | |
| Ark. | | ✔ | ✔ | | | | ✔ | |
| Calif. | ✔ | ✔ | | | | | ✔ | |
| Colo. | | ✔ | | | | | | |
| Conn. | ✔ | ✔ | ✔ | | | | | |
| Del. | | ✔ | ✔ | ✔ | | | | |
| Fla. | ✔ | ✔ | ✔ | | | | | |
| Ga. | ✔ | ✔ | | | | | | |
| Hawaii | ✔ | ✔ | ✔ | ✔ | ✔ | | ✔ | ✔ |
| Idaho | | ✔ | | | ✔ | ✔ | | ✔ |
| Ill. | ✔ | ✔ | | | | | | |
| Ind. | ✔ | ✔ | | | | | | |
| Iowa | ✔ | ✔ | | | ✔ | | ✔ | ✔ |
| Kan. | ✔ | ✔ | ✔ | | | | | |
| Ky. | ✔ | ✔ | ✔ | | ✔ | | ✔ | ✔ |
| La. | ✔ | ✔ | | | | | | |
| Maine | ✔ | ✔ | ✔ | | ✔ | | | ✔c |
| Md. | ✔ | ✔ | ✔ | ✔ | ✔ | | | ✔c |
| Mass. | | ✔ | ✔ | | ✔ | | | ✔c |
| Mich. | | ✔ | ✔ | ✔ | ✔ | | ✔ | ✔ |
| Minn. | ✔ | ✔ | ✔ | ✔ | ✔ | ✔ | ✔ | ✔ |
| Miss. | | ✔ | | | | | | |
| Mo. | ✔ | ✔ | | | | | | |
| Mont. | | ✔ | ✔ | | ✔ | | | ✔c |
| Neb. | ✔ | ✔ | | | | | | |
| Nev. | | ✔ | | | | | | |
| N.H. | | ✔ | ✔ | | | | | |
| N.J. | ✔ | ✔ | ✔ | ✔ | ✔ | | | ✔d |

[a]Only one state, North Dakota, requires no disclosure. Two states, Alabama and Wyoming, require disclosure only after an election. In some states, disclosure requirements are not identical for primary and general elections.
[b]Expenditure limits were declared unconstitutional by the U.S. Supreme Court on January 30, 1976, in *Buckley* v. *Valeo* unless the candidate accepts public financing. Four states, Michigan, Minnesota, New Jersey, and Wisconsin, have expenditure limits that apply only to candidates who accept public financing. In another four states, Delaware, North Carolina, North Dakota, and Utah, expenditure limits have not yet been repealed by the state legislatures. In 1979 Hawaii enacted a public financing system that ties a contributor's income tax deduction to a candidate's acceptance of spending limits.
[c]Maine, Maryland, Massachusetts, and Montana have surcharge provisions.

have replaced partisan election officials, such as secretaries of state, who traditionally were repositories of campaign fund reports but whose partisanship as elected or appointed officials did not make them ideal administrators or enforcers of election law.[52]

The recent experiments in election and campaign finance reform have provided an excellent example of the theory of the Founding Fathers that states might serve as laboratories for experiments in law. Some have adopted strong laws requiring full disclosure, realistic contribution limits, restrictions on certain kinds of contributions, and even public funding of elections.[53] As suggested by table 6–10, the variety of law is infinite, and revisions are almost unending. All but one state, North Dakota, requires disclosure of political funds, and four-fifths of them demand disclosure both before and after the election. New restrictions have been placed on contributions by corporations and by labor unions. In some cases the states have gone beyond the federal government in attempting to stretch campaign reform to its limits.

**TABLE 6–10**    *continued*

| State | Election Commission | Disclosure Before and After[d] | Individual Contribution Limits | Expenditure Limits[b] | Public Subsidy | Credit | Tax Provisions Deduction[e] | Checkoff |
|---|---|---|---|---|---|---|---|---|
| N.M. | | ✔ | | | | | | |
| N.Y. | ✔ | ✔ | ✔ | | | | | |
| N.C. | ✔ | ✔ | ✔ | ✔ | ✔ | | | ✔ |
| N.D. | | | | ✔ | | | | |
| Ohio | ✔ | ✔ | | | | | | |
| Okla. | ✔ | ✔ | ✔ | | ✔ | | ✔ | ✔ |
| Ore. | | ✔ | | | ✔ | ✔ | | ✔ |
| Pa. | | ✔ | | | | | | |
| R.I. | ✔ | ✔ | | | ✔ | | | ✔ |
| S.C. | ✔ | ✔ | | | | | | |
| S.D. | | ✔ | ✔ | | | | | |
| Tenn. | | ✔ | | | | | | |
| Texas | | ✔ | | | | | | |
| Utah | | ✔ | | ✔ | ✔ | | ✔ | ✔ |
| Vt. | | ✔ | | | | ✔ | | |
| Va. | ✔ | ✔ | | | | | | |
| Wash. | ✔ | ✔ | | | | | | |
| W.Va. | ✔ | ✔ | ✔ | | | | | |
| Wis. | ✔ | ✔ | ✔ | ✔ | ✔ | | | ✔ |
| Wyo. | | | ✔ | | | | | |
| D.C. | ✔ | ✔ | ✔ | | | ✔ | | |

[d]New Jersey enacted a state income tax after the subsidy program, which was applicable to the 1977 gubernatorial elections, became law. The new income tax system included a checkoff, but the 1977 funding was appropriated by the legislature.

[e]Some additional states that used to allow indirect tax deductions tied to the federal tax deduction no longer can do so because the tax deduction under federal law was repealed as of January 1, 1979. The federal tax credit for political contributions remains in force, but there is no indirect benefit for a taxpayer paying state income tax based on the federal system.

*Sources:* Based on data as of July 1979, combined from: *Analysis of Federal and State Campaign Finance Law: Summaries and Quick Reference Charts,* prepared for the Federal Election Commission by the American Law Division of the Congressional Research Service, Library of Congress, Washington, D.C. (December 1977); *The Book of the States, 1976–1977,* XXI (Lexington, Ky.: The Council of State Governments, 1976), pp. 223–226; Karen Fling, ed. "A Summary of Campaign Practices Laws of the 50 States," *Campaign Practices Reports, Report 4* (Washington, D.C.: Plus Publications, Inc., October 1978); *Federal-State Election Law Updates: An Analysis of State and Federal Legislation,* prepared for the Federal Election Commission by the American Law Division of the Congressional Research Service, Library of Congress, Washington, D.C. (December 1978). Compiled by Herbert Alexander and published in *Financing Politics: Money, Elections and Political Reform,* 2nd ed. (Washington, D.C.: Congressional Quarterly Press, 1980), 130–132. Reprinted with permission.

# Do We Spend Too Much on Political Campaigns?

We spent $900 million at all levels to elect candidates to office in 1980—a quarter of a billion to elect the president alone and over 9 million dollars just to hold the national nominating conventions. Sums of this magnitude often make Americans blanch. Do they represent too large an investment in politics? Are the dollars well spent, and do we get our money's worth? How much is democracy worth?

Herbert E. Alexander, a leading authority on campaign finance, has answered these questions in an interesting manner. He points out that the $540 million spent for campaigns at all levels in 1976 was a fraction of 1 percent of the amounts spent for government at the federal, state, county, and municipal levels. The $160 million spent to elect a president in 1976, including prenomination campaigns and minor-party candidates, was just under half of what Americans spend in one year on clock and table radios. Furthermore, the total $540 million campaign expenditures were less than the total advertising budgets for that year of the two largest corporate advertisers, Procter and Gamble and General Motors. And, compared with what is spent in other nations on elections, the U.S. total is not excessive. The average cost per voter falls somewhere near the mean for world democracies, clustered with those in India and Japan and far lower than the cost per voter in Israel. Alexander notes that, all things being equal, two conditions enhance the power of money: (1) money is most important in the prenomination period, and (2) wealthy candidates seem to have a head start on those without wealth.[54]

Although campaigners often believe that a few more dollars might have made the difference between victory and defeat, this argument is usually hard to sustain. Nevertheless, the expenditure of additional money on politics would not seem to be so extravagant as some might have us believe. At the same time, there is no denying that much money is wasted in political campaigns, a problem that might well be ameliorated with additional emphasis on public funding and expenditure and on contribution limits.

## The Cost of Democracy

It has always been popular to describe political money as the "mother's milk of politics." Given the remarkable growth of campaign costs, the expensive new techniques of campaigning, and the proliferation of candidates and offices, that catch-phrase is more appropriate today than ever before. From the beginning of American history, a comfortable relationship has existed between big money and politics. From the selling of public lands to the railroad barons to routine construction contract graft, those with plenty of money have sought to buy influence with those possessing the power to make policy. Long-time efforts on the part of political reformers to reduce the influence of the wealthy were unrewarded until the 1960s; then politicians themselves proved that small-contributors programs could be successful under certain circumstances, making large contributions less necessary. Moreover, the advent of public funding of campaigns in the 1970s appeared to reduce the influence of big money even further. The recent growth of PACs and the escalation of independent expenditures, however, has again brought big money to the fore.

The significance of these developments should not be overlooked. For the first time, the American people have demonstrated a willingness to consider new and different ways to finance elections. The result has been a range of federal and state laws requiring controls on contributions and expenditures, financial disclosure, public funding of elections, tax incentives to contributors, and even the requirement that some of the public's business be transacted in the "sunshine." Each of these reforms could inhibit the practice of politics, but so far there is little evidence to indicate such inhibition.

There has always been some danger that reforms in political finance might undercut the relationship among private citizens, interest groups, and political parties. If the reform efforts should succeed in establishing a direct link between government money and small contributions, on the one hand, and the candidates, on the other, the role of political parties would be further diminished. Political parties have already been damaged by the advent of the direct-primary system of nomination, the removal of government jobs from party patronage, and the growth of nonpartisan elections. They might not survive the further erosion of influence that would probably come about as a result of diminishing their financial role in elections. In 1980, however, the national and state parties provided more campaign money through direct contributions to candidates than ever before. A continuation of this practice, allowed under the new federal campaign finance law, would significantly increase the power of these party organizations.

Many have voiced concern over restricting the relationship between candidates and interest-group leaders. Politics is an exercise composed of citizens—individual and organized. People who join groups such as labor, business, or professional associations do so because the group represents yet another channel through which the government can be approached. Reforms in campaign finance, desirable as they may be, should not be carried to such an extreme that both parties and groups are unduly impaired in their political operations. This is a difficult balance to gain and to maintain. Few would contend that it has been achieved at this time. Most would argue that important strides have been made in the reforms of the past decade but that, at the same time, additional efforts must attempt to reach a better balance among constitutional participation, political pragmatism, and institutional protection.

# Notes

1. From data collected by Herbert E. Alexander, *Financing Politics: Money, Elections, and Reform*, 1st ed. (Washington, D.C.: Congressional Quarterly Press, 1976), pp. 16–21.

2. Federal Election Commission, *Annual Report, 1976* (Washington, D.C.: Federal Election Commission, 1977), p. 14.

3. F. Christopher Arterton, "Dollars for Presidents: Spending Money Under the FECA," in *Financing Presidential Campaigns: An Examination of the On-going Effects of the Federal Election Campaign Laws Upon the Conduct of Presidential Campaigns*, a research report by the Campaign Finance Study Group to the Committee on Rules and Administration of the United States Senate, prepared by the Institute of Politics, John F. Kennedy School of Government, Harvard University, Cambridge, Mass., January 1982, pp. 3–9.

4. Ibid., p. 7.

5. "Slinging Mud and Money," *Time* (November 15, 1982): 43–44.

6. Quoted in Jasper B. Shannon, *Money and Politics* (New York: Random House, 1959), p. 15.

7. The 1968 figures come from Herbert E. Alexander, *Political Financing* (Minneapolis, Minn.: Burgess, 1972), p. 5; the 1972 figures are from Alexander, *Financing Politics*, p. 16.

8. "House Races: More Money to Incumbents," *Congressional Quarterly Weekly Report* (October 29, 1977): 2299.

9. "Money, Incumbency Failed to Guarantee Success in 1976 Senate Races," *Congressional Quarterly Weekly Report* (June 25, 1977): 1291–1294.

10. *Federal Election Commission Record 7*, no. 5 (May 1981): 11.

11. Mark Green, "Financing Campaigns," *New York Times* (December 14, 1980): 14.

12. Frederick Burgess, *Miami Herald* (November 5, 1978): sec. D, pp. 1 and 4.

13. F. Christopher Arterton, "Political Money and Party Strength," in *The Future of American Political Parties*, ed. Joel L. Fleishman (Englewood Cliffs, N.J.: Prentice-Hall, 1982), p. 113. (An American Assembly book.)

14. Thomas E. Mann, *Unsafe at Any Margin: Interpreting Congressional Elections* (Washington, D.C.: American Enterprise Institute for Public Policy Research, 1978), pp. 106–107.

15. Gary C. Jacobson, "The Effects of Campaign Spending in Congressional Elections," *American Political Science Review 72* (June 1978): 469.

16. Ibid.

17. Data taken from the December 15, 1977 issue of the *Spot Television Rates and Data Report*, a monthly publication of Standard Rate and Data Services, Skokie, Ill. The rates in this report are presented in a technical series of tables, and those used here are the highest prime-time rate shown, even though the actual time may vary from station to station.

18. David Nichols, *Financing Elections: The Politics of the American Ruling Class* (New York: New Viewpoints, 1974), p. 67.

19. Larry Sabato, *The Rise of Political Consultants* (New York: Basic Books, 1981), pp. 51–52.

20. Herbert E. Alexander, *Financing the 1964 Elections* (Princeton, N.J.: Princeton University Press, 1966), pp. 68–69.

21. Alexander, *Financing Politics,* p. 92.
22. Arterton, "Political Money and Party Strength," pp. 104–107.
23. Alexander, *Financing Politics,* pp. 92–93.
24. Gary Orren, "Fundraising in the Primaries: An Analysis of Contributions to Presidential Campaigns," in *Financing Presidential Campaigns,* pp. 2–17.
25. Alexander, *Financing Politics,* pp. 61–76.
26. Alexander, *Political Financing,* p. 26.
27. "Salute to Carter Dinner," *New York Times* (January 21, 1978): 5.
28. "Of Eagles and Sparrows," *New York Times* (January 20, 1982): 10.
29. Robert J. Huckshorn, *Party Leadership in the States* (Amherst: University of Massachusetts Press, 1976), p. 145.
30. Ibid.
31. Ibid., pp. 148–149.
32. Herbert E. Alexander, ed., *Campaign Money: Reform and Reality in the States* (New York: Free Press, 1976), p. 305.
33. Gary M. Halter, "The Effects of the Hatch Act on the Political Participation of Federal Employees," *Midwest Journal of Political Science* 16 (November 1972): 739.
34. Alexander, *Financing Politics,* pp. 94–95.
35. Ibid., p. 96.
36. Congressional Quarterly, *Dollar Politics: The Issue of Campaign Spending* (Washington, D.C.: Congressional Quarterly Press, 1971), p. 35. Reprinted by permission.
37. Alexander, *Financing Politics,* pp. 105–106.
38. For a discussion of the emerging role of PACs in congressional elections, see M. Margaret Conway, "PACs, the New Politics, and Congressional Campaign Finance," unpublished paper presented at the annual meeting of the Midwest Political Science Association, Milwaukee, Wis., April 29–May 1, 1982; and Joseph E. Cantor, *Political Action Committees: Their Evolution and Growth and Their Implication for the Political System* (Washington, D.C.: U.S. Library of Congress, Congressional Research Service, 1981).
39. Congressional Quarterly, *Dollar Politics: The Issue of Campaign Spending,* 3rd ed. (Washington, D.C.: Congressional Quarterly Press, 1982), p. 43.
40. Conway, "PACs, Politics, and Campaign Finance," p. 2.
41. Congressional Quarterly, *Dollar Politics,* pp. 42–43.
42. Conway, "PACs, Politics, and Campaign Finance," p. 6.
43. *Time* (October 25, 1982): 23.
44. Ibid.
45. Federal Election Commission press release, February 1982.
46. Federal Election Commission, *Annual Report, 1980,* pp. 16–17.
47. Ruth S. Jones, "State Public Campaign Finance: Implications for Partisan Politics," *American Journal of Political Science* 25, no. 2 (May 1981): 344–346. Much of the material in this section on state public funding is based on Jones's work. Also see Herbert E. Alexander, "Financing Gubernatorial Election Campaigns," *State Government* (Summer 1980): 140–143.
48. Ibid., p. 348.
49. Ruth S. Jones, "State Election Campaign Financing: 1980," in *Financing the 1980 and 1982 Elections,* ed. Michael Malbin (Washington, D.C.: American Enterprise Institute, forthcoming).
50. Jones, "State Public Campaign Finance," pp. 360–361.
51. Federal Election Commission, *Annual Report, 1980,* p. 57.
52. Alexander, *Financing Politics,* pp. 169–170.
53. Jane E. Miller, *Guide to Ethics Boards and Commissions* (Madison: State of Wisconsin Ethics Board, 1977).
54. Herbert E. Alexander, *Financing Politics,* 2nd ed. (Washington, D.C.: Congressional Quarterly Press, 1980), pp. 19–20.

# CHAPTER
# SEVEN

# The American Voter
# and Electoral Behavior

*There is no scarcity of popular wisdom devoted to explaining why the American people vote as they do. They vote their interests (Truman), their fears (Nixon), and their aspirations (Kennedy). They vote for candidates (Eisenhower) and against candidates (Goldwater). They learn quickly (LBJ); they forget slowly (FDR). They know what they want (the New Deal, peace, prosperity) but they do not want very much (a persistent 35 percent do not vote at all). Party allegiances are stable (Humphrey almost won) but not determinate (Nixon did win). In short, we know a great deal after each election, but, over the long run, all electoral explanations seem to cancel each other out.*

Peter Natchez, *"Images of Voting: The Social Psychologists,"* Public Policy [*18 (1970)*]: 553.

The emergence of modern representative government put a special emphasis on popular elections. Undoubtedly, elections perform important functions in a democracy, for they provide a vehicle through which the leaders of government can be chosen and public policy questions can be debated. They also offer a means whereby candidates and voters can interact with each other and, one hopes, sensitize those who are elected to popular will and public need. The outcome of an election often affords, at least in general outline, guidance as to the policy direction toward which the people wish government to move. Political parties have traditionally served as a mechanism for a somewhat systematic choice of alternatives of both candidates and issues. Furthermore, campaigns and elections perform important educational functions that encourage citizens to learn more about current issues and potential officeholders than they would otherwise have an opportunity to do. Although the opening quotation is quite apt—that explanations of the meaning of the electoral experience often cancel each other out over the long haul—it is also true that over the short haul elections furnish a worthwhile reading on public opinion and a road map for public policy development.

## The American Voter

The American people have always viewed elections as almost sacrosanct. We hold frequent elections and use them to elect long lists of public officers, from land surveyor to president. Any move to shorten the ballot by increasing the number of appointed officers almost always triggers a campaign by those who argue that it is un-American to "take away the people's right to vote." Efforts to adopt new constitutions or constitutional amendments or local charters reducing the number of elected officials are usually strongly opposed. Historically, these deep-seated feelings stem both from the early days of the Republic, when the reaction against monarchical rule was at its height, and from the early twentieth-century effort by the LaFollette Progressives to improve democracy by imposing more democracy.

Consequently, the United States is one of the most election-conscious countries in the world. The national affinity for elections not only extends to the selection of officeholders but includes referenda, bond issues, constitutional amendments, and even government-sponsored straw votes. We have even removed the power of the political parties to nominate candidates to run under their name and have given that power to the people through the system of direct primaries. And, as we have noted earlier, we have undercut the authority of the national nominating convention by electing more and more pledged delegates through the expanding presidential primary system. An observer might expect that our purported love of elections would carry with it a high rate of participation. That, however, would be an erroneous assumption. The American people have one of the lowest voter participation levels among all the world's democracies. On the one hand, we insist on voting on as many things as possible; on the other, only about half of us vote—or only vote in some races.

The large number of elections in the United States is partly a result of governmental structure and partly a reaction to the ingrained beliefs of the people in participatory democracy. The separation of powers guarantees that we elect executive officers as well as legislative officers. Many states even elect most of their judicial officers. The federal system assures that we elect parallel officeholders at three different levels—federal, state, and local. Presidents are matched by governors and mayors. Congressional representatives and senators are matched by state legislators and city and county commissioners. Thus these functional and geographic divisions that were written into the original constitutional plan by the Founding Fathers all contribute to the large number of positions that must be filled by direct elections.

*"And now I appeal to you non-voters. According to the latest polls, I have a substantial lead. Please do not spoil this by surprising us and coming out to vote."*
(© 1982 by Sidney Harris.)

The American people have believed in maximum participatory democracy from the earliest era of the first two-party system. Both Thomas Jefferson and Andrew Jackson were advocates of election by the people. As the system developed, however, the latter part of the nineteenth century brought the spoils system, big-city bosses, political corruption, and a loss of faith in democratic principles on the part of the people. Bribery, vote fraud, and voter intimidation were common in both city and rural life. Electoral reform seemed to be the answer to these problems, and the Progressive movement capitalized on the situation by proposing reforms guaranteed to return control to the hands of the people: the direct-primary system of nominations; the secret ballot; the initiative, referendum, and recall; and nonpartisan local elections. These reforms increased the number of offices to be filled, expanded the number of candidates seeking to fill them, and multiplied the number of issues that could be voted on directly by the people. The reforms did not, however, provide any means for ensuring that all eligible voters would actually vote.

In the past three decades, studies of American voting behavior have burgeoned. Studies abound of legal obstacles to voting, the socioeconomic aspects of electoral behavior, political socialization, party identification, and the apathetic and alienated nonvoter. The role of issues in electoral decision making has moved almost full circle. Methods of classifying elections have proliferated. In short, the literature on electoral behavior is large and growing. Some of the findings are contradictory, and many are fresh for a time but become outdated as the mood of the electorate changes. Volumes have been written about what is now known about voting behavior. Additional volumes are required just to keep the level of knowledge up to date.

In this chapter we will concentrate on three topics of more than passing concern. First, we will examine the institutional factors that affect voting decisions—that is, the legal qualifications for voting and their impact on the electorate. For years some have believed that residence requirements, restrictive voter registration laws, the poll tax, age restrictions, and other such technical requirements inhibited voters and kept the percentage of turnout low. Many of these inhibitions have now been removed. What has been the impact of their elimination on turnout and voter participation rates?

Second, since it is the people who vote, one must examine closely the influences that cause them to vote as they do. Why are some apathetic and others alienated from the political system? What aspects of personal life are a part of the overall voter equation? That is, how do educational level, income, sex, race, religion, and occupation affect voter decisions? Does it matter where one's ancestors emigrated from? In short, what aspects of socioeconomic life have an impact on how people vote?

Finally, we will consider the role of issues and how they affect voting preferences. A purist's definition of political party will include both the choice of candidates and positions on issues. Yet for many years voters showed little interest in issues as a reason for casting their votes. Issues are more important now, and they have the added dimension of serving as a principal factor in the coalescing of people into interest groups. We will therefore review how issues affect voter decisions and also examine the growth of popular democracy as seen in the use of the initiative and referendum.

A number of questions must be answered; not all of them have very clear answers. Needless to say, American politics has seldom been so fluid as it has been since World War II. Changing partisan alignments, the decline of old-style party organizations, ticket splitting, and the rise of media candidates and campaigns have all profoundly influenced American politics. Let us first address ourselves to the question of voter turnout and levels of participation.

## Turnout Factors in Electoral Participation

Many people have expressed concern over the declining levels of voter participation during the past three decades. A record 85.1 million people voted for the three major candidates for president in 1980, and another million cast their votes for eighteen lesser-known candidates. But, as shown in table 7–1, the percentage of voter turnout among the voting-age population was the smallest since the 1948 contest between President Harry S Truman and Gov. Thomas E. Dewey. There was a steady growth in turnout among voting age population in congressional elections between 1950 and 1966, but in 1968 and each succeeding year until 1982 the turnout declined. In 1982, as shown in table 7–1, there was a modest upturn to about the same level as 1950. Even so, the percentages of turnout ranged from 45.4 percent in both 1962 and 1966 to a low of 36.1 percent in 1974. Some analysts believe that concern over nonvoting and its effect on voter turnout is misplaced. These observers believe that it is a fairer measure of voter participation to consider the percentage of registered voters who vote rather than the percentage of eligibles. Thus they point out that in 1976, even though only 54.4 percent of the voting-age population actually went to the polls, 78.6 percent of those registered to vote did.

Even though voter participation increased slightly in the 1982 congressional elections, the trend has still been downward for the past twenty years. This is particularly troublesome since, during the same period, the size of the eligible electorate itself has

TABLE 7–1  Percentage of voting-age population voting in presidential and congressional off-year elections, 1948–1982

| Year | Presidential elections | Off-year elections House of Representatives |
|------|------------------------|---------------------------------------------|
| 1948 | 51.1% | |
| 1950 | | 41.1% |
| 1952 | 61.6 | |
| 1954 | | 41.7 |
| 1956 | 59.3 | |
| 1958 | | 43.0 |
| 1960 | 62.8 | |
| 1962 | | 45.4 |
| 1964 | 61.9 | |
| 1966 | | 45.4 |
| 1968 | 60.9 | |
| 1970 | | 43.5 |
| 1972 | 55.5 | |
| 1974 | | 36.1 |
| 1976 | 54.4 | |
| 1978 | | 39.3 |
| 1980 | 53.9 | |
| 1982 | | 41.0[a] |

[a]Figure for 1982 is an estimate.

*Source:* U.S. Department of Commerce, Bureau of the Census, *Statistical Abstract of the United States, 1977* (Washington, D.C.: Government Printing Office, 1977), p. 508; 1978 figures from *Pocket Data Book, USA 1979,* Bureau of the Census, p. 129; 1980 figures from *Congressional Quarterly Weekly Report* (Washington, D.C.: Department of Commerce, January 17, 1981): 138; and 1982 figures from *New York Times* (November 10, 1982): 1 and 10.

been expanding. On four separate occasions vast blocs of new voters have increased the eligible voter pool, opening voting to the following groups:

1. *Nonproperty owners and nontaxpayers.* Originally, only those citizens who owned property or paid taxes were considered to have enough of a stake in election outcomes to be permitted to vote. Gradually, in the early part of the nineteenth century the states began to rescind these restrictions, thus greatly expanding the number of white male voters. At the time of the Civil War no state required property ownership, and only a few still held taxpaying to be a prerequisite to voting. The last vestige of taxpaying requirements was the poll tax, which was finally abolished by a constitutional amendment in 1964 and a Supreme Court ruling in 1966.

2. *Women.* The fifty years between 1870 and 1920 saw ever-increasing pressure from women to be included as eligible voters. At first women sought remedial action at the state level, but after some years they concluded that a U.S. constitutional amendment was the only way to make sure that all women were granted the right to vote. In 1920 the suffragette movement finally accomplished its goal: approval of the Nineteenth Amendment forbidding states to deny the vote on grounds of sex.

3. *Blacks.* The expansion of black suffrage has been the most troublesome of all. After the Civil War a number of states began action to permit black people to vote as a direct result of the passage of the Fifteenth Amendment, which held that the right of citizens to vote "shall not be denied or abridged by the United States or by any State on account of race, color, or previous condition of servitude." Efforts by the judiciary and the Congress to enforce this amendment have continued to this day. Post–Civil War legal restrictions on black voters, including "grandfather clauses" and the "white primary," reduced black participation to a minuscule number. "Grand-

father clauses" provided that no person whose grandfather had not been a voter in 1867 could himself become a voter, and the "white primary" restricted voter participation in primary elections to white persons only. With the passage of the Civil Rights Act of 1965, blacks again began to register in large numbers, not only in the South but in other sections of the country, and participation of black voters and election of black candidates rose dramatically. Since 1940, when 250,000 black citizens were registered, the South alone has witnessed an increase in the number of registered black voters to 3,560,856—an increase from 5 to 59 percent.[1]

4. *Young people.* The final major expansion of the electorate has, for the most part, taken place in the 1970s. Until 1971 only four states permitted youths less than twenty-one years old to vote. Georgia and Kentucky allowed voting at eighteen, Alaska at nineteen, and Hawaii at twenty. In 1970, however, Congress passed a law establishing the right of all eighteen-year-olds to vote in both state and federal elections. A few months later the Supreme Court found that portion of the law devoted to federal elections to be constitutional but nullified the sections pertaining to state and local elections. Congress then passed and sent to the states an amendment to the Constitution lowering the voting age to eighteen for all elections. Rapid action by state legislatures led to the adoption of the Twenty-Sixth Amendment in 1971, and the new provisions took effect for the 1972 presidential elections.

Clearly, those who *take part* in the electoral process by voting differ in composition from those who are *legally enfranchised.* Each of the groups incorporated into the electorate has expanded the potential voting population by millions, yet three of them—women, blacks, and young people—have been slow to adopt the habit of regular voting.

Thomas Cavanaugh suggests that the decline in voter turnout is not due to a failure of any of these groups to vote but rather represents a large number of dropout voters. That is, significant numbers of voters simply decide to quit voting. Ten million voters dropped out in 1974 alone, and in 1976 over 27 million former voters did not bother to go to the polls.[2] Furthermore, even those groups that have traditionally constituted the active voting population have suffered a decline in participation rates. Clearly, the extent of voter participation depends on a number of factors. Among them are a series of administrative obstacles to voting that some authorities believe adversely affect voter turnout.

## Administrative Obstacles to Voting

In most of the Western democracies, levels of voter turnout are considerably higher than in the United States for a number of reasons. In part the problem grows out of the rules governing eligibility to vote. All fifty states require potential voters to register in advance of an election. The period between registration and actual voting may range from a few minutes to six months. In Minnesota a person can now register on election day by presenting proper personal identification and then can proceed immediately to vote.[3]

### Voter Registration

Beginning at the turn of the century, fear of widespread corruption and vote fraud brought about the enactment of laws designed to keep people from voting illegally. Literacy tests, residence requirements, strict registration, and complex procedures certainly provided more assurance of voter eligibility, but they also perpetuated a system that effectively excluded millions of people from voting at all. There was often good reason for concern in those days. Joseph Harris, author of a classic work on voter registration, cites an early *Chicago Tribune* of that era:

> In the Sixth Ward there were almost as many illegal votes as legal votes polled. Both parties canvassed the ward thoroughly before election and agreed that there were about seven hundred votes in the ward, and yet over twelve hundred were polled on election day. Can any sane man doubt that the most disgraceful frauds were perpetrated? ... A wagon load of voters openly attempted to vote in four wards and finally succeeded in voting by leaving their wagon at the corner and scattering themselves around.
>
> Early yesterday morning crowd after crowd of imported voters passed up Clark Street with their carpet bags in their hands, on their way to the depot, whence they took their departure for Joliet, Sycamore, and other places where they belong. They had accomplished their mission. They had received a dollar per head, voted, and were satisfied.[4]

Even though the *Chicago Tribune* was hardly an impartial observer in those days, the incident described did not differ materially from other abuses in other cities. Conditions such as these led to the establishment of voter registration systems, which were traditionally justified as a means to prevent fraud. The rationale was that prior registration assured that voters were legal residents of the state and the precinct and that they met age and length-of-residence requirements. Many of the conditions that gave rise to the restrictions ceased to exist many years ago. The system that was built to protect against abuse, however, has remained to this day—an administrative maze that often inhibits voting and perpetuates the status quo. Indeed, the system itself can be the deciding factor in some elections.

Many people do not know that in most states registration can be cancelled by election authorities for the simple act of moving, or failing to reregister at specified times, or even failing to vote in some consecutive number of elections. The burden of registering is placed on the voter. In most states government assumes no responsibility for attempting to register people to vote. This in itself distinguishes the American from the European method, where election authorities automatically update voter registration and, when a person moves, his or her registration is transferred automatically. In recent years a substantial movement to ease registration requirements has arisen in the United States. More states are experimenting with flexible, more decentralized, and more automatic systems, which should ease the burden on the voter.

These artificial requirements are so oppressive in some places that it is more prudent for candidates to spend their time working to register voters and to get them to the polls than actually campaigning. If candidates are running in districts in which registration levels in their party are low, one of their first priorities must be to get more people registered. Traditionally, the Democratic party has had a larger share of nonvoters than the Republican party because of the composition of their respective followings. Republicans tend to have higher incomes and more flexible work schedules and, as a consequence, more time to vote. Republican turnout is usually strong. Those voters who belong to the Democratic party tend to live in big cities, to have lower incomes, and to belong to various minority groups. They are less inclined to vote. These factors, along with the Democratic support by organized labor, have stimulated labor leaders to organize and pay for mass voter registration and get-out-the-vote drives in behalf of Democratic candidates. These drives sometimes appear to be more decisive factors in the election outcome than a candidate's qualities or the style of the campaign.

The first registration laws were adopted in the United States in the early 1800s, but the practice of registering voters did not come into common use until the post-Civil War period. Voter registration was not needed in early rural America. Settlements were small and closely knit. The people all knew each other, and a poll watcher from each party could easily identify each voter who came to the polls. Even in the cities the wards and precincts were small enough in population to allow party leaders to challenge any persons they suspected of not being a legitimate voter. But, with industrial expansion and urbanization, the nature of American life changed, and mass population migrations made it more and more difficult for poll workers to identify those who showed up to vote. These changes occurred at the same time that the big-city machines were being developed; thus machine politics was often based on systematic vote fraud. As we have seen, machine bosses sometimes arranged for people to vote, using the names on the tombstones of the cemetery, or they transported people in from out of town.

Some system needed to be developed to prevent unauthorized voters from taking part and to guarantee that those who did vote were breathing—or at least resided in the polling district. Registration of voters was the solution that emerged. Critics argue that the registration system is designed to discourage people from voting. They are especially critical of those systems that require each voter to appear in person at a central location and that demand periodic reregistration. Each such demand reduces the potential body of voters. One study found that, as jurisdictions adopt personal registration, participation drops between 8 and 12 percent from earlier levels. Even though considerable progress has been made in recent years toward reducing registration barriers, these requirements remain an impediment to voting in some areas.

The Voting Rights Act Amendments of 1970 imposed a maximum thirty-day residency requirement for presidential elections. New residents were also permitted to vote in their previous state either in person or by absentee ballot. A Supreme Court decision in 1972, *Dunn v. Blumstein,* declared Tennessee's one-year residency requirement unconstitutional; and that decision, in effect, restricted residency requirements in all other elections. Although the Court did not establish a new limit on residency, the decision was interpreted to mean that thirty days is the maximum that can be required before an election.

One major purpose of voter registration has been to enable the state to establish that the citizen is a resident and is eligible to vote in the coming election. The President's Commission on Registration and Voting Participation in 1963 estimated that 8 million people were unable to vote in the 1960 election because of residence requirements.[5] A 1978 study of the effects of registration laws on turnout found that if every state had had laws as permissive as the most permissive states in 1972, turnout would have been about 9 percent higher in the presidential election. Furthermore, it found that registration provisions have the most powerful effect on the least educated. Even so, as the authors point out, registration laws are not the only environmental variable that affects turnout. As we have noted before, the highest percentage of turnout recorded in modern times was in 1960, when residency requirements of one or two years, literacy tests, and poll taxes were quite common. Yet virtually all of these artificial barriers have been removed since 1960, and voter turnout has declined.[6]

In recent years reformers have made two major advances toward broader and more comprehensive registration laws. The first of these has been to permit voter registration by mail. Postcard registration proposals have had the strong support of organized labor and Democratic party officials, since it is assumed that many of the lower-income voters who would naturally be sympathetic to the Democratic cause would thus be added to the roster of eligible voters. Attempts to pass postcard registration have not been successful. The second has been an effort, both in the states (e.g., Minnesota) and in the nation, to permit registration by voters at the polls on election day. President Jimmy Carter included such a proposal in his election reform package that went to Congress in 1977, but neither house moved to pass the bills. In Ohio, the legislature did pass an election-day registration bill that was vetoed by the governor and then passed over his veto. Petitions were circulated, however, and the issue was put on the ballot in the form of a constitutional amendment that required voters to register at least thirty days before an election. The amendment was adopted with a 62 percent majority. Other states are also considering changes in registration as a means of increasing the number of voters who take part in elections. The problem of voter turnout is certainly affected by registration requirements, but other forces are obviously also at work.

## Ballots and Voting Machines

Another factor that can affect the outcome of an election campaign is the *system* used for voting (see figure 7–1). From the little research that has been done on the subject, it is apparent that the mechanical aspects of the voting system have an impact that, in some cases, can be decisive. Most studies have focused on the form of the ballot and on whether votes are cast by paper ballot or by voting machine. The most common form is the party-column ballot on which candidates are grouped in columns under the party name (see figure A–1 in the appendix). With this ballot, voters can more easily vote the "straight ticket." Party leaders often prefer this form because it lends itself to the election of those candidates for lesser offices whose names are located lower down the column, especially if the top of the ticket is strong.

The office-block ballot, sometimes called the Massachusetts ballot, groups the candidates according to the office for which they are contending (see figures A–2 and A–3). Thus all of the gubernatorial candidates of all parties are listed within one office block, and all of the candidates for sheriff are listed in another. Each candidate is identified within the block according to party affiliation. This style of ballot lends itself readily to "split-ticket" voting, since voters cannot cast all of their votes by merely making a mark but must consider each candidate for each office separately. If voters wish to vote for all of the candidates of one party, they must make a mark within each office block.

The voting behavior studies carried out by the University of Michigan's Survey Research Center for the 1952 and 1956 elections found that ballot form has less impact on straight-ticket voting among those who identify themselves as strong party supporters and has more impact among those who call themselves weak party identifiers.[7]

Another study has shown that ballot form has a considerable impact on voter participation in contests for lower offices because of a phenomenon called "roll-off" or "fall-off." "Roll-off" is the failure of voters to mark their ballots for offices of lesser importance. These voters make their choices for the important offices but either lose interest or suffer from voter fatigue and fail to complete the voting sequence for lesser offices. The result is that, whereas all voters who participate will cast their votes for

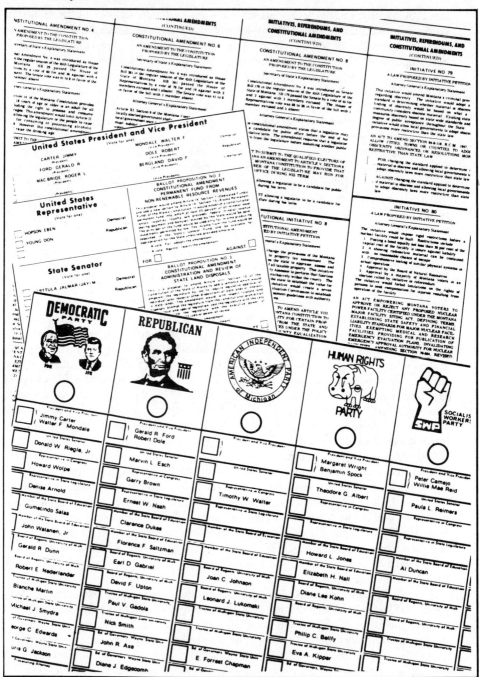

**FIGURE 7-1**  Examples of paper ballots used for candidate or issue elections.

governor or U.S. senator, the county offices or school board offices at the far end of the ballot may only have a fraction of the same participation rate. Jack L. Walker has found that states using the party-column ballot had consistently less roll-off than the states using the office-block type of ballot. Walker also showed that states switching from the party-column to the office-block type of ballot experienced greater ticket-splitting as well as substantial roll-off.[8]

When one considers that in some states ballots in major elections may have as many as one hundred or more names plus numerous referenda or initiative issues among which to choose, it is little wonder that many voters simply discontinue marking their ballots before the process is complete. This is one of the principal reasons why candidates seek name identification, since the average voter cannot be expected to follow every race or to enter the voting booth with a clear-cut choice in each contest.

Although paper ballots are still widely used in rural areas of the nation, most urban and suburban precincts use mechanical voting machines. In general, voting machines do speed up the process, but they also have disadvantages that are quite serious to those voters who are affected by them. The lever machine is quite formidable in appearance and literally frightens some voters. Older citizens may find the machine's candidate list difficult to see and understand. In some instances the spaces available on the machine have been inadequate to accommodate all the candidates running for office; the result has been confusing candidate listings that have caused difficulties for some voters. Machines have sometimes broken down, causing long lines to develop at the remaining machines. Even so, when the machines work well and are administered properly, they provide a rapid and effective way to permit large numbers of voters to cast their ballots in reasonably short periods of time. In the past decade there has been a movement, rapidly gaining acceleration, toward punch-card, computer-based voting machines (see figure 7–2). These systems are expensive to install and often require more time for the results to be reported on election night. However, they are thought to be more efficient and easier to use and are cheaper to buy than lever machines.

## Shortening the Ballot

Throughout much of American history there has been an inexorable movement toward electing more and more government officials. In spite of the fact that many studies have shown that the average voter knows little about most of the candidates, a mystique seems to exist in favor of electing officials instead of appointing them. Both political parties have usually supported election over appointment, since it offers the party a greater chance of putting some of its members in office and helps maintain the viability of the party system. The result has been an increasingly lengthy and complex ballot containing more choices than most voters could ever be expected to make reasonably or intelligently.

In most Western European countries, including the United Kingdom, voters are faced with far fewer choices, and their participation rate is much higher. Most of these countries operate under a parliamentary system that requires fewer electoral choices to be made by the individual voter. Additionally, because of the federal structure in the United States, the number of local, state, and national offices to be filled is more formidable.

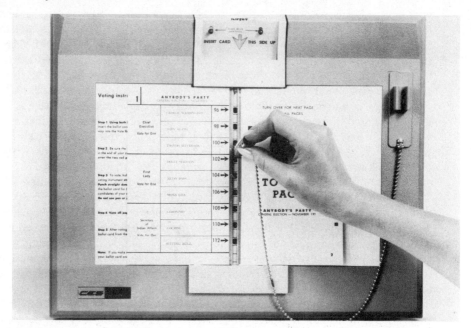

**FIGURE 7–2** Computer-based voting machine. *(Source:* Photo courtesy of Computer Election Systems, Inc.)

Those interested in reform have consistently fought for fewer elective offices because this shortens the ballot and allows the voter to concentrate his or her attention on fewer races and issues. Although a shorter ballot reduces voter fatigue and roll-off, it has been difficult to achieve in many locales because voters resist reducing the number of elective offices, often equating such a decrease with a loss of democracy. Furthermore, increased appointive powers for key elective officers or "bureaucrats" is believed by many people to build barriers between themselves and their government officials.

## Other Aspects of Ballot Form

As noted before, the way in which votes are cast can have a decided impact on electoral outcomes. Lengthy ballots, the roll-off effect, and paper versus machine voting all affect voting performance. Still other aspects of ballot form, however, deserve brief discussion.

First, the order in which candidates' names appear on the ballot in primary elections or on office-block ballots can affect outcomes. Clearly, many Americans do vote for the first name on the ballot for each office, regardless of who it is. Although the percentage of first-name choices varies from district to district, there is a perceptible advantage to being listed first. Some of the states have attempted to overcome the built-in advantage by requiring that the names for each office be rotated so that different candidates are placed at the top of a proportionate number of ballots. Others list candidates alphabetically or have them draw straws for the first spot.[9]

The second aspect of ballot form that can have an impact on election outcomes is the provision made for write-in votes. This is not of great importance in most elections, since few write-in candidates have ever been successful in their election bids. Some states require that the name written in must be correctly spelled and that no nicknames may be used—provisions that often invalidate many of the write-in votes cast. On the whole, this problem is not a serious one, but it does deserve mention.

Such technical rules concerning voting do affect voter turnout. They alone, however, do not explain the decline of voter participation. In fact, many of them have been abolished or changed to make them less restrictive. Some authorities believe that the question of voter turnout may be illusory; they suggest that nineteenth- and early twentieth-century participation figures are inaccurate, reflecting the widespread corruption and illegal voting that took place in that era. They hold that voting totals were consistently reported as being higher than they actually were, thus making meaningful comparisons with the more accurate figures of today almost impossible. Even if this thesis is true, we have no way of verifying it. It is worthwhile, therefore, to continue to view declining turnout as a significant political problem.

For whatever reasons, nonvoting is rapidly becoming epidemic in the United States. In 1980 only 53.9 percent of the voting-age population bothered to go to the polls to cast their votes, and in 1982 only 41 percent took part in the off-year elections for Congress and state offices. Yet it is widely believed that the survival of a democratic society is dependent on the active participation of citizens in choosing leaders. Curtis Gans of the Committee for the Study of the American Electorate, a nonprofit, bipartisan research group that studies voter turnout, has written:

> The central and perhaps the greatest single problem of the American polity today is . . . the degree to which the vital underpinnings of American democracy are being eroded. The legitimacy of a democratic leadership and the health of the democratic process depend squarely on the informed and active participation of the electorate. Yet the level of political participation is now sinking and the decline seems irreversible.[10]

When compared with other democratic nations, American voter turnout does not measure up well. When the British journal *The Economist* compiled voter turnout statistics for twenty-one democratic countries, it found that the United States ranked next to last in its level of voting for presidential candidates, surpassed only by Switzerland, a country that seriously challenges voter loyalty with repeated referenda on a great many subjects of public concern (see table 7–2). For those interested in voting

**TABLE 7–2**   Voter turnout in selected democratic nations

| Country | Turnout | Country | Turnout |
|---------|---------|---------|---------|
| Malta | 94.4% | Norway | 82.8% |
| Australia | 92.6 | New Zealand | 82.7 |
| Austria | 91.9 | Israel | 78.2 |
| Sweden | 91.4 | Ireland | 75.7 |
| Italy | 90.8 | Canada | 74.9 |
| Iceland | 90.3 | Great Britain | 72.8 |
| West Germany | 89.9 | Japan | 72.6 |
| Belgium | 88.3 | India | 60.5 |
| Denmark | 88.2 | United States | 54.4 |
| Holland | 87.5 | (presidential) | |
| France | 83.5 | Switzerland | 51.7 |
| | | United States (midterm) | 37.0 |

*Source:* From "Making More Americans Vote," *The Economist,* London, Vol. 269, November 11, 1978, p. 17. Reprinted by permission.

turnout as an important aspect of democratic choice, the continuing decline is of major concern. Clearly, more factors are at work than the prevalence of artificial administrative obstacles and technical rules. That being the case, we must look to other factors that affect the percentage of voter turnout. Let us next consider the matter from the perspective of the voter.

## Participating in Elections: The Voter's Perspective

Get-out-the-vote drives have always emphasized the importance of a single vote. In 1970, in the very first issue of the newsletter of Common Cause, the "citizen's interest group," founder John Gardner wrote:

> What difference does one vote make? It can make a lot. In most elections, those who fail to vote could have changed the result had they gone to the polls. For every vote in Richard Nixon's plurality over Hubert Humphrey in 1968, 150 people did not vote. The 1960 presidential election was decided by less than one vote per precinct. In 1962, the governorship of Minnesota was decided by just 91 votes out of more than one million cast. The outcome of the 1968 U.S. Senate election in Oregon turned on four-tenths of one percent of the 814,000 votes cast. Local races—for mayor, for city council, for school board—have sometimes been decided by a single vote.[11]

With only 53.9 percent of the eligible voters bothering to go to the polls in the 1980 presidential election and with the steady decline in the participation rate since 1960, nearly one voter is staying home for every one who casts a ballot. A 1976 survey of voters conducted by the U.S. Bureau of the Census found that nonvoting had many causes. As shown in table 7–3, 53.2 percent of the voters surveyed who were registered but did not vote said that they were unable to take part. Most attributed their nonparticipation to illness or some form of emergency; others claimed they could not take time off from work, had no way to get to the polls, were out of town, or found the lines at the polls too long. The 22.6 percent who deliberately chose not to vote claimed to be uninterested or alienated. Findings such as these are not unusual.

Peter Hart Research Associates, a respected polling firm, conducted a poll in July 1976 for Gans's Committee for the Study of the American Electorate and found that an estimated 10 million voting-age Americans had "dropped out" of the electoral system since 1968. The proportion of young nonvoters was far larger than the proportion of young people in the electorate as a whole. Forty-six percent of the nonvoters were under the age of thirty-five. Those surveyed were furnished a list of twenty-one reasons for nonvoting and were asked to rank the importance of each of the reasons. Sixty-eight percent said they believed that "candidates say one thing and then do another." Another 55 percent believed that "it doesn't make any difference who is elected, because things never seem to work out right." Fifty-two percent said that "Watergate proved that elected officials are only out for themselves."[12]

Political scientist and professional pollster Lance Tarrance has estimated the number of registered voters in each election since 1928 as well as how they divided between the parties. His findings are vividly illustrative of the problem of nonvoting. President Nixon, for instance, won a landslide victory in 1972 with the largest plurality ever received by a presidential candidate (47 million). But 62 million people chose not to vote at all. He also notes that Jimmy Carter won the presidency with 28 percent of

TABLE 7–3 Reported reasons for not voting and persons reported registered but not voting, November 1976

| | *Percent* |
|---|---|
| Unable to vote | |
| No way to get to the polls | 4.0 |
| Illness or emergency | 19.5 |
| Could not take time off work | 6.9 |
| Machines not working, lines too long | 2.2 |
| Out of town or away from home | 14.1 |
| Other | 6.5 |
| Total—unable to vote | 53.2 |
| | |
| Did not want to vote or not interested | |
| Did not prefer any candidate | 11.4 |
| Politicians not interested in my problems | 0.6 |
| Believed vote would make no difference | 1.2 |
| Didn't want to get involved | 1.1 |
| Not interested in election this year | 7.2 |
| Other | 1.1 |
| Total—did not want to vote | 22.6 |
| | |
| All other reasons | 16.7 |
| | |
| Don't know and not reported | 7.5 |
| Total | 100.0 |

*Source:* U.S. Department of Commerce, Bureau of the Census, Current Population Reports, series P-20, no. 322, "Voting and Registration in the Election of November, 1976."

the vote while 45 percent of the eligible electorate stayed at home.[13] Many of the reasons given by people for not taking part in elections can be viewed as measures of political efficacy.

## Political Efficacy

Political efficacy or effectiveness is the degree to which people believe that government can be understood and influenced by individual citizens. For voter participation to be maximized, citizens must believe that their vote counts for something—that it makes a difference in the outcome of the election and, ultimately, in how the government works. In a sense, political efficacy is a measure of people's faith in the system. It also encompasses the attitude of people that voting and taking part in politics constitute a civic obligation and are engaged in by "responsible citizens" as a matter of course.

The fact is, though, that those "responsible citizens" who do vote regularly and who do take part in the electoral process include only certain groups from within the general population. On the whole, the well-educated, higher-income, middle-aged, white Republicans have the best record and, therefore, the highest political efficacy. It should not be surprising that these particular groups are more likely to believe that their votes influence government decision making and help to decide elections. A wealthy person's vote does not count any more on election night than does the poor person's vote; but it does if the rich man votes and the poor man does not.

One would expect the better-educated to have higher incomes, just as one would expect that they would be white and that a greater proportion of them would vote

Republican. The less well educated are more likely to be poor and are less likely to believe that their votes will have impact. They are also less apt to go to the polls because of real or imagined job insecurities, baby-sitting problems, and other environmental factors. Furthermore, the less well educated, the poor, and the black, all heavily represented in the nonvoting population, tend to be Democrats. That is one reason the Democratic party has always shown more interest in organized get-out-the-vote drives than has the Republican party, whose members normally vote without having to be encouraged.

Political efficacy is not stable. It is a dynamic barometer of public attitudes toward government and politics. As table 7–4 indicates, efficacy has declined in recent years. The University of Michigan Center for Political Studies, which has conducted national surveys for many years, has asked a single series of questions about people's trust in government and political efficacy. Even if we assume that 1974 public views on the ongoing Watergate scandals affected the results, the end is the same. The growth of alienation and cynicism and the decline in trust and efficacy are plain to see, regardless of the cause. Clearly, Watergate was not the sole cause of shifting public attitudes;

TABLE 7–4   Trust, alienation, cynicism, and efficacy

|  | 1964 | 1968 | 1972 | 1974 | 1976 | 1980 |
|---|---|---|---|---|---|---|
| *Trust: How much of the time do you think you can trust the government in Washington to do what is right—just about always, most of the time, or only some of the time?* | | | | | | |
| Always | 14% | 8% | 7% | 3% | 3% | 2% |
| Most of the time | 62 | 53 | 45 | 33 | 29 | 23 |
| Only some of the time/ None of the time | 22 | 37 | 45 | 61 | 67 | 73 |
| Don't know/not ascertained | 2 | 2 | 3 | 3 | 1 | 2 |
|  | 100% | 100% | 100% | 100% | 100% | 100% |
| *Big interests: Would you say that the government is pretty much run by a few big interests looking out for themselves or that it is run for the benefit of all the people?* | | | | | | |
| For benefit of all | 64% | 52% | 43% | 24% | 24% | 21% |
| Few big interests | 29 | 39 | 48 | 65 | 66 | 70 |
| Other/depends/both | 4 | 5 | 3 | 3 | 2 | 0 |
| Don't know/not ascertained | 3 | 4 | 6 | 8 | 8 | 9 |
|  | 100% | 100% | 100% | 100% | 100% | 100% |
| *Honesty: Do you think that quite a few of the people running the government are a little crooked, not very many people are, or hardly any of them are crooked at all?* | | | | | | |
| Hardly any | 18% | 18% | 16% | 10% | 13% | 9% |
| Not many | 48 | 49 | 46 | 41 | 40 | 41 |
| Quite a few | 29 | 25 | 34 | 45 | 41 | 46 |
| Don't know/not ascertained | 5 | 8 | 4 | 4 | 6 | 4 |
|  | 100% | 100% | 100% | 100% | 100% | 100% |
| *Efficacy: People like me don't have any say about what government does.* | | | | | | |
| Agree | 29% | 41% | 36% | 40% | 41% | 34% |
| Disagree | 69 | 58 | 63 | 57 | 56 | 52 |
| Don't know/not ascertained | 2 | 1 | 1 | 3 | 3 | 14 |
|  | 100% | 100% | 100% | 100% | 100% | 100% |

*Source:* Survey Research Center, Center for Political Studies, University of Michigan.

the trends were already apparent before 1974. On the "trust" measure alone the number of people who believed that they could trust the government to do what is right all or most of the time declined from 76 percent in 1964 to 36 percent in 1974. In only one decade American people had reassessed their view of trustworthiness in federal government. At this point, future levels of political efficacy are difficult to determine. Unquestionably, however, public distrust of government and politicians will continue to have a wide impact on voting behavior.

## Party Competition and Turnout

Another factor that affects voter turnout is the degree of competition between the political parties and the candidates. As table 7–5 shows, the greater the degree of competition between the parties, the more people vote. We noted the differences in party competition between the states in chapter 2. At that time we were pointing out the differences that competition can make in the organizational activities of parties, but by using the same index of competitiveness, originally prepared by Austin Ranney, we can also see the contrast in voter turnout between competitive and noncompetitive

TABLE 7–5    1980 turnout of eligible voters compared to Ranney Index of state party competitiveness

| State | Competitiveness score | 1980 turnout of eligible voters |
|-------|----------------------|----------------------------------|
| States showing lowest degree of interparty competitiveness on Ranney Index, 1974–1980 | | |
| Rhode Island | 0.8506 | 60.6% |
| Maryland | 0.8509 | 50.7 |
| North Carolina | 0.8555 | 45.8 |
| Arkansas | 0.8630 | 53.6 |
| Mississippi | 0.8673 | 52.8 |
| Louisiana | 0.8762 | 47.1 |
| Georgia | 0.8849 | 44.0 |
| Alabama | 0.9438 | 49.4 |
| States showing highest degree of interparty competitiveness on Ranney Index, 1974–1980 | | |
| Delaware | 0.5490 | 56.1% |
| New York | 0.5390 | 48.1 |
| Illinois | 0.5384 | 59.0 |
| Nebraska | 0.5166 | 56.2 |
| Maine | 0.5164 | 66.2 |
| Kansas | 0.4671 | 55.8 |
| Utah | 0.4653 | 67.1 |
| Iowa | 0.4539 | 69.2 |

Average eligible voter turnout percentage:
Low party-competition states—50.5
High party-competition states—59.7

*Note:* The Ranney index has a possible range of 0 (total Republican success) to 1 (total Democratic success), with 0.5 representing absolutely even two-party competition. For this table all eight one-party Democratic states were used. There were no one-party Republican states. The middle eight two-party states were used. As revised by John F. Bibby, Cornelius P. Cotter, James L. Gibson, and Robert J. Huckshorn, "Parties in State Politics," in *Politics in the American States,* 4th ed., eds. Virginia Gray, Herbert Jacob, and Kenneth Vines (Boston: Little, Brown, 1983), p. 66.
*Source:* The turnout figures are from the *1981 Republican Almanac* (Washington, D.C.: Republican National Committee, 1981), p. 641. Based on total voting-age population as defined by the U.S. Bureau of the Census.

party states. In 1980 the average turnout of eligible voters in low party-competition states was 50.5 percent, whereas the average turnout in high party-competition states was 59.7 percent. Not all of that difference can be attributed to the competitiveness of the party system, but certainly a substantial amount of it can. Clearly, when party organizations are active and a high degree of competition for elective office exists, voter turnout swells. When a single party dominates the electoral system, as do some of the southern Democratic parties, voters may conclude that their votes are not important to the election outcome and accordingly may stay at home. When there is competition between the parties, candidates actively campaign, voter interest levels increase, and the participation rates escalate.

Gerald Pomper has noted that the parties have a basic electoral function to fulfill in a democracy. He suggests that most authorities consider the electoral function of the political party system to be one of its most important functions. Parties define alternatives, educate voters to the effects of choosing one alternative over another, and encourage citizens to use the franchise in order to have a role in choosing an alternative. Pomper suggests that the decline in partisan politics, which we observed earlier, may be a net result of the decline of the party's effectiveness in carrying out this role.[14]

## Socioeconomic Factors in Voting

It is no accident that some people become Democrats and others become Republicans. That choice is the result of political socialization. How people actually vote, though, is another matter. Some people are interested in and take part in political activities throughout their lifetimes. Others show some interest some of the time, and still others do not participate in any political activity during their whole lives. These patterns of political participation spring from differing social characteristics of the voters. As table 7–6 indicates, since 1952 the Gallup Public Opinion Poll has broken the presidential vote down into groups by sex, race, education, occupation, age, religion, politics, and region.

### Sex

When women won the right to vote in 1920, the percentage of women who actually availed themselves of the opportunity was quite small, and the percentage of turnout of the eligible voting population consequently suffered a substantial decline. Since that time the number of women casting votes has steadily increased until it is about the same as the number of men—only a 0.8 percent difference existed in the 1976 presidential election, according to the Bureau of the Census. Variations in participation levels do, however, occur within the group. Younger women tend to vote in greater numbers than older women. Furthermore, white women outside the South vote about as frequently as men, whereas those who live in the South vote less frequently than men. On the other hand, black women living outside the South participate at considerably lower levels than black men, but southern black women vote in greater numbers. These margins of difference have been narrowing since the passage of the voting rights acts of the 1950s and 1960s, and many authorities also credit the women's liberation movement with the improvement of their participation rates in politics.

## Race

Considering our legacy of slavery, discrimination, and lack of educational opportunities, it is not surprising that black voters have not turned out to vote in large numbers. The 1960s and 1970s, however, have brought new laws protecting and encouraging voting rights as well as a new higher level of black consciousness that has resulted in considerably more voter participation. After the Civil War those blacks who voted were solidly wedded to the Republican party—the party whose president proclaimed emancipation. But in 1932 black people were among the hardest hit by the depression, and, like many others, they blamed Republican president Herbert Hoover for their economic travail. The black vote switched almost en masse to the Democrats and has remained with that party ever since. The largest Republican percentage recorded since 1952, according to table 7–6, was the 39 percent black vote for President Eisenhower in 1956; the smallest was 6 percent for Republican candidate Barry Goldwater in 1964.

Prior to 1960, blacks in the South trailed far behind whites in their percentage of voter turnout. Since then, however, the South has been catching up among both blacks and whites. Most of the improvement in black participation has resulted from the civil rights acts of the 1950s and 1960s and the Voting Rights Act of 1965. Using a variety of legal procedures to eliminate discrimination and personal intimidation, these acts provided federal examiners for use in voter registration in certain areas, voided literacy tests and excessive residency requirements, and took other actions designed to increase voter participation. The result was a remarkable increase in registration for both whites and nonwhites. As shown in table 7–7, nonwhite registration increased from 29.7 percent in 1960 to 63.4 percent in 1970. Registration among southern whites increased by nearly 10 percent during the same period.

Black turnout nationwide has averaged ten to twelve percentage points less than white turnout during recent elections, but in 1980 in the South nonvoting among blacks and whites was approximately the same. In some local races in the big cities the turnout has occasionally reached 70 percent or more. Furthermore, another measure of black political maturity has been the rapidly increasing number of black officeholders in both the North and the South. These include black mayors elected in Los Angeles; Newark, New Jersey; New Orleans; Cleveland; Atlanta; Gary, Indiana; and Chicago.

## Education and Occupation

Many studies over long periods of time have demonstrated the positive relationship between economic status, as measured by occupation, and education. Voters with higher levels of education have occupations that provide higher levels of income. Furthermore, they are more likely to pay closer attention to campaigns, take part in election activities, and vote than are those with less education and smaller incomes. They are exposed to greater environmental pressures to take part and to vote; for example, they are more apt to be subjected to political influences at work from employers, union leaders, and coworkers. They are also subjected to more political discussion via television, newspapers, and magazines because they are more likely to be receptive to it.

Less-educated, unskilled, and lower-income individuals are less likely to be able to assimilate the masses of campaign information directed toward them and less likely

**TABLE 7–6  Presidential votes by groups, 1952–1980**

| | 1952 Stevenson | 1952 Ike | 1956 Stevenson | 1956 Ike | 1960 JFK | 1960 Nixon | 1964 LBJ | 1964 Goldwater | 1968 HHH | 1968 Nixon | 1968 Wallace |
|---|---|---|---|---|---|---|---|---|---|---|---|
| **National** | 44.6% | 55.4% | 42.2% | 57.8% | 50.1% | 49.9% | 61.3% | 38.7% | 43.0% | 43.4% | 13.6% |
| **Sex** | | | | | | | | | | | |
| Male | 47 | 53 | 45 | 55 | 52 | 48 | 60 | 40 | 41 | 43 | 16 |
| Female | 42 | 58 | 39 | 61 | 49 | 51 | 62 | 38 | 45 | 43 | 12 |
| **Race** | | | | | | | | | | | |
| White | 43 | 57 | 41 | 59 | 49 | 51 | 59 | 41 | 38 | 47 | 15 |
| Nonwhite | 79 | 21 | 61 | 39 | 68 | 32 | 94 | 6 | 85 | 12 | 3 |
| **Education** | | | | | | | | | | | |
| College | 34 | 66 | 31 | 69 | 39 | 61 | 52 | 48 | 37 | 54 | 9 |
| High school | 45 | 55 | 42 | 58 | 52 | 48 | 62 | 38 | 42 | 43 | 15 |
| Grade school | 52 | 48 | 50 | 50 | 55 | 45 | 66 | 34 | 52 | 33 | 15 |
| **Occupation** | | | | | | | | | | | |
| Prof. & business | 36 | 64 | 32 | 68 | 42 | 58 | 54 | 46 | 34 | 56 | 10 |
| White collar | 40 | 60 | 37 | 63 | 48 | 52 | 57 | 43 | 41 | 47 | 12 |
| Manual | 55 | 45 | 50 | 50 | 60 | 40 | 71 | 29 | 50 | 35 | 15 |
| **Age** | | | | | | | | | | | |
| Under 30 years | 51 | 49 | 43 | 57 | 54 | 46 | 64 | 36 | 47 | 38 | 15 |
| 30–49 years | 47 | 53 | 45 | 55 | 54 | 46 | 63 | 37 | 44 | 41 | 15 |
| 50 years and older | 39 | 61 | 39 | 61 | 46 | 54 | 59 | 41 | 41 | 47 | 12 |
| **Religion** | | | | | | | | | | | |
| Protestants | 37 | 63 | 37 | 63 | 38 | 62 | 55 | 45 | 35 | 49 | 16 |
| Catholics | 56 | 44 | 51 | 49 | 78 | 22 | 76 | 24 | 59 | 33 | 8 |
| **Politics** | | | | | | | | | | | |
| Republicans | 8 | 92 | 4 | 96 | 5 | 95 | 20 | 80 | 9 | 86 | 5 |
| Democrats | 77 | 23 | 85 | 15 | 84 | 16 | 87 | 13 | 74 | 12 | 14 |
| Independents | 35 | 65 | 30 | 70 | 43 | 57 | 56 | 44 | 31 | 44 | 25 |
| **Region** | | | | | | | | | | | |
| East | 45 | 55 | 40 | 60 | 53 | 47 | 68 | 32 | 50 | 43 | 7 |
| Midwest | 42 | 58 | 41 | 59 | 48 | 52 | 61 | 39 | 44 | 47 | 9 |
| South | 51 | 49 | 49 | 51 | 51 | 49 | 52 | 48 | 31 | 36 | 33 |
| West | 42 | 58 | 43 | 57 | 49 | 51 | 60 | 40 | 44 | 49 | 7 |
| **Members of labor union families** | 61 | 39 | 57 | 43 | 65 | 35 | 73 | 27 | 56 | 29 | 15 |

*Source:* "Presidential Votes by Groups, 1952–1976," *Gallup Opinion Index* (December 1976): 116–117; 1980 figures from Gallup Poll, "Dramatic Changes Seen in Vote Given Carter in '76 and '80," press release, December 21, 1980. Reprinted by permission.

**TABLE 7-6** continued

| | 1972 | | 1976 | | 1980 | | |
|---|---|---|---|---|---|---|---|
| | McGovern | Nixon | Carter | Ford | Carter | Reagan | Anderson |
| **National** | 38% | 62% | 50% | 48% | 41% | 51% | 7% |
| **Sex** | | | | | | | |
| Male | 37 | 63 | 53 | 45 | 38 | 53 | 7 |
| Female | 38 | 62 | 48 | 51 | 44 | 49 | 6 |
| **Race** | | | | | | | |
| White | 32 | 68 | 46 | 52 | 36 | 56 | 7 |
| Nonwhite | 87 | 13 | 85 | 15 | 86 | 10 | 2 |
| **Education** | | | | | | | |
| College | 37 | 63 | 42 | 55 | 35 | 53 | 10 |
| High school | 34 | 66 | 54 | 46 | 43 | 51 | 5 |
| Grade school | 49 | 51 | 58 | 41 | 54 | 42 | 3 |
| **Occupation** | | | | | | | |
| Prof. & business | 31 | 69 | 42 | 56 | 33 | 55 | 10 |
| White collar | 36 | 64 | 50 | 48 | 40 | 51 | 9 |
| Manual | 43 | 57 | 58 | 41 | 48 | 46 | 5 |
| **Age** | | | | | | | |
| Under 30 years | 48 | 52 | 53 | 45 | 47 | 41 | 11 |
| 30–49 years | 33 | 67 | 48 | 49 | 38 | 52 | 8 |
| 50 years and older | 36 | 64 | 52 | 48 | 41 | 54 | 4 |
| **Religion** | | | | | | | |
| Protestants | 30 | 70 | 46 | 53 | 39 | 54 | 6 |
| Catholics | 48 | 52 | 57 | 42 | 46 | 47 | 6 |
| **Politics** | | | | | | | |
| Republicans | 5 | 95 | 9 | 91 | 8 | 86 | 5 |
| Democrats | 67 | 33 | 82 | 18 | 69 | 26 | 4 |
| Independents | 31 | 69 | 38 | 57 | 29 | 55 | 14 |
| **Region** | | | | | | | |
| East | 42 | 58 | 51 | 47 | 43 | 47 | 8 |
| Midwest | 40 | 60 | 48 | 50 | 41 | 51 | 6 |
| South | 29 | 71 | 54 | 45 | 44 | 51 | 3 |
| West | 41 | 59 | 46 | 51 | 35 | 52 | 10 |
| **Members of labor union families** | 46 | 54 | 63 | 36 | 50 | 43 | 5 |

TABLE 7–7    Percentage of voting-age population registered to vote in eleven southern states, 1960 to 1970

| State | Nonwhite | | White | |
|---|---|---|---|---|
| | 1960 | 1970 | 1960 | 1970 |
| Mississippi | 5.2 | 71.0 | 63.9 | 82.1 |
| South Carolina | 13.7 | 56.1 | 57.1 | 62.3 |
| Alabama | 13.7 | 66.0 | 63.6 | 85.0 |
| Georgia | 29.3 | 57.2 | 56.8 | 71.7 |
| Virginia | 23.1 | 57.0 | 46.1 | 64.5 |
| Louisiana | 31.1 | 57.4 | 76.9 | 77.0 |
| Arkansas | 38.0 | 82.3 | 60.9 | 74.1 |
| North Carolina | 39.1 | 51.3 | 92.1 | 68.1 |
| Florida | 39.4 | 55.3 | 69.3 | 65.5 |
| Texas | 35.5 | 72.0 | 42.5 | 62.0 |
| Tennessee | 59.1 | 71.6 | 73.0 | 71.6 |
| Averages | 29.7 | 63.4 | 63.8 | 72.2 |

*Sources: Historical Abstract of the U.S., 1971* (Washington, D.C.: Government Printing Office, 1971); original report, *Voter Registration in the South*, prepared by the Southern Regional Council, Voter Education Project; see Frank Feigert and M. Margaret Conway, *Parties and Politics in America* (Boston: Allyn & Bacon, 1976), pp. 84–85.

to expose themselves voluntarily to the media through which it is transmitted. Such individuals are also less apt to take part in the election campaign and to vote. Sometimes this political apathy stems from a low level of interest resulting from poor education, and at other times it arises from lack of opportunity, attributable to lower income and less flexibility in lifestyle. Democracy is dependent on education. When combined with income, the two social measures of education and occupation emerge as key determinants of who votes and who does not.

## Age

For many years it was believed that one reason for lower voter turnout was the average four-year gap that young Americans experienced between graduating from high school at seventeen and gaining the right to vote at twenty-one. The reasoning was that most high school students were exposed to classroom propaganda about the importance of voting, but those who did not continue their education in college were forced to wait four years before they could cast their first vote and, in the meantime, lost interest. One of the arguments put forth by those advocating lowering the voting age to eighteen was that graduating high school seniors could move immediately into a regular voting status and would more likely develop the habit of regular voting. As table 7–8 suggests, the facts belie the conventional wisdom. The poorest voting performance of any age group is that between eighteen and twenty-four. In the 1980 presidential election only 35.7 percent of those between eighteen and twenty voted, and only 43.1 percent of those between twenty-one and twenty-four. All other age groups voted in significantly higher numbers. What, then, accounts for the relatively poor performance of the younger voting group?

A review of more recent research suggests that some of the factors may be unfamiliarity with registration procedures, a greater sense of alienation caused by the Vietnam War and the Watergate scandals, the greater mobility of young people as they seek careers, change jobs, and move from one locale to another more frequently,

**TABLE 7–8    Participation in 1980 presidential election, by age group**

| | Persons of voting age (Millions) | Persons reporting | | |
| --- | --- | --- | --- | --- |
| | | Voters | | Nonvoters |
| Age group | | Millions | Percent | Percent |
| 18–20 | 12.3 | 4.4 | 35.7 | 55.3 |
| 21–24 | 15.9 | 6.8 | 43.1 | 47.3 |
| 25–34 | 35.7 | 19.5 | 54.6 | 38.0 |
| 35–44 | 25.6 | 16.5 | 64.4 | 29.4 |
| 45–64 | 43.6 | 30.2 | 69.3 | 24.2 |
| 65 and older | 24.1 | 15.7 | 65.1 | 25.4 |

*Note:* Covers civilian noninstitutional population.
*Source:* U.S. Department of Commerce, Bureau of the Census, *Statistical Abstract of the United States,* 1981 (Washington, D.C.: Government Printing Office, 1981), p. 500.

the pressures of new marriages and new families, and the development of interests other than politics.

Those in the middle-aged group vote in heavier proportions than do those in the younger or the older groups. They are more likely to be settled, to have a stake in the community, and to be interested in taxes, education, and other issues that might stimulate them to vote. They are also more likely to be subjected to pressure in their work environment. Finally, they are more likely to be registered.

As table 7–6 indicates, all three age groups gave their support to Eisenhower in 1956, and all three supported Johnson in 1964 and Nixon in 1972. But in 1952 the younger group gave a bare majority of its votes to Stevenson, while the two older groups supported Eisenhower by wider margins. In 1960 the two younger groups (under forty-nine) voted for Kennedy, while the older group (fifty and older) supported Nixon. The same pattern held in 1968, with the two younger groups supporting Humphrey and the older one Nixon.

In 1976 the younger and older groups supported Carter, and the middle group (30 to 49 years old) gave a bare majority to Ford; in 1980 only the younger group voted for Carter, with the other two giving their votes to Reagan. Eleven percent supported John Anderson, the Independent candidate, in 1980, the largest percentage he received from any group other than political Independents (see table 7–6). In terms of presidential support none of the three age groups differs significantly in its voting choices over a long period of time, although patterns may differ within a given election year or series of elections.

## Religion

We have noted that income, occupation, and education are not easily separated in studies of voting behavior. A similar problem exists in trying to analyze the impact of religion on politics. Undoubtedly, differences appear in levels of political participation based on religion in the United States. Some religious groups, furthermore, are obviously more politically active than others, and some are more easily identified with one or the other of the political parties. Nevertheless, the relationship between religion and voting behavior is not clear-cut and can easily be overemphasized.

Ideologically, Jews, Catholics, and Baptists have ranked as the most liberal of the religious groups, while Congregationalists, Episcopalians, and Presbyterians have ranked as the most conservative. Yet, with the exception of the Jews, these differences appear to be based more on social class than on religion. The ranking of each of the other major denominational groups on political and economic issues is identical with the class-status rank of the group, whether measured as a condition of education, occupation, or income.[15]

Nevertheless, religious affiliation evidently does seem to bind certain denominations to particular ideologies and to one or the other of the political parties. The most easily recognizable of these is the Jewish attachment to liberalism and to the Democratic party. The altruistic liberalism of the Jews has led to strong and consistent support of candidates committed to the expenditure of public funds and the use of other resources for the amelioration of social problems. They have also been found to favor the distribution of economic power to lower-income groups through the extension of welfare programs, guaranteed employment, and distribution of federal tax money to poorer states. They are more internationalist than other religious groups, and they have been in the forefront of the civil rights conflict from the beginning.

These beliefs, which form the core of American liberalism, attracted Jewish voters to the Democratic party—and especially to Franklin D. Roosevelt's New Deal—where they have remained since.[16] Although data is scarce, the percentage of Jewish votes for Democratic presidential candidates is normally between 80 and 90 percent. Even in the 1972 election, when President Nixon received large majorities from most of the identifiable voting groups in the nation, Senator McGovern received 63 percent of the Jewish vote.[17] In 1976 Jimmy Carter's 68 percent Jewish vote was below normal Democratic expectations and possibly resulted from distrust of his evangelical Protestantism.[18] In 1980 Carter was supported by only 45 percent, with Ronald Reagan receiving 39 percent and John Anderson, 14 percent.[19] By the middle of Reagan's term, however, there were many indications that Jews were seriously dissatisfied with his administration due to disagreements over the president's policies toward Israel, social spending cuts, and the economic programs he supported.

Not only are Jews comfortable with the national Democratic party on domestic issues, but they have historically identified with it because of its early opposition to Nazism and its support for the state of Israel. Jewish voters may occasionally stray from the Democratic fold, but they have always returned.

Catholics also tend to vote more Democratic than the population at large. On economic issues Catholics have been in the forefront of the Democratic party, but on other noneconomic liberal policies of the party they have been in opposition. For instance, Catholics will vote on the basis of religious beliefs if the question involves an issue of church teaching, such as birth control or abortion, in spite of a contrary official position of the Democratic party on the issue.

Nevertheless, Catholic partisanship has impressed most analysts. For example, Catholics, unlike many other voting groups, have been found to retain their Democratic identification even when moving from the inner city to the suburbs. Most of the immigrant Catholics from Ireland, Poland, and Italy settled in the heavily populated cities of the Northeast. They came at a time when those cities were dominated and controlled by the old Democratic political machines and bosses, and they were openly courted by party leaders. In New York City, for instance, many of the men became policemen, since the New York Police Department was a ready source of jobs. The Irish influence remained dominant in the NYPD until the past decade, when black and

Puerto Rican policemen began to be hired in numbers more appropriate to their share of the population.

The typical Catholic voter was enough of a good Democrat to pass his party identity and loyalty on to his children, and this fidelity has remained essentially intact during subsequent generations, although there is some evidence that the number of Catholics who vote Republican is increasing. Most authorities feel certain that this Democratic party loyalty arises from social class and partisan belief rather than from Catholicism itself.[20]

As shown in table 7–6, Catholics have voted Democratic in all but two elections (1972 and 1980) since 1952. Even in the two Eisenhower–Stevenson contests, when other voting blocs were shifting to support the popular Republican candidate, the Catholic vote remained Democratic. From a Democratic margin of 56 to 44 percent in 1952, the Catholic vote narrowed to a Democratic margin of 51 to 49 in 1956. However, in 1960, with a popular Catholic Democratic candidate, John F. Kennedy, the shift back to the Democrats was massive, and the 78 to 22 margin was greater than in any other identifiable voting group. Two and one-half million Catholic voters who voted for Eisenhower in 1956 shifted to vote for Kennedy in 1960. Yet, in 1972, with a less popular midwestern Democratic candidate, Catholic voters joined many other groups in support of Richard Nixon, and in 1980 they narrowly supported Ronald Reagan.

The pattern of Protestant voting is less clear than the Catholic or Jewish patterns. Many early American colonies were settled by people of English heritage who came to this country because of religious dissent. Members of high-status churches—Congregationalists, Episcopalians, Presbyterians, Quakers, and Unitarians—dominated the political, economic, and social institutions of the eastern seaboard states. They tended to support political parties of the status quo, first the Federalists, then the Whigs, and later the Republicans. Lower-status Protestant denominations—Baptists, Methodists, and various fundamentalist groups—originally drew the preponderance of their members from lower socioeconomic areas of the population and were more disposed to support the Democratic party, which they viewed as the party of change. As these lower-status religious sects became upwardly mobile, they tended to shift party allegiance to the Republicans, but from socioeconomic motives rather than from factors associated with their religious preference. That remains the pattern today. The high-status Protestant denominations exhibit considerably greater allegiance to the Republican party than do lower-status denominations. Again, as table 7–6 shows, Protestants have voted Republican by fairly large margins in every presidential election since 1952, except for 1964.

## Regional Politics

Voting behavior by region is largely a product of history, culture, and level of party competition. The region traditionally singled out as most identifiable is the South. The cumulative results of the Civil War, the Great Depression, and subsequent events brought the Democrats to dominance in the South and kept that region Democratic until the middle part of the twentieth century. The "nationalization" of American politics is now a common phrase. This process means just one thing—the perceived convergence of the South with the political mainstream of the nation. Since 1948 various of the southern states have given their votes to Republican presidential candidates.

In chapter 2 we observed that competitive two-party systems have developed in some of the southern states and that Republican successes in electing officeholders in local, state, and national elections have been notable. The South is still a recognizable Democratic party entity, but it is much less so than it was twenty years ago, for several reasons. Civil rights has faded as an issue as the voting rights acts of the 1960s have increased black voter margins; the economy of the South is healthier than in many other areas of the nation; and a massive influx of northerners has eroded the old southern homogeneity. Although the process is not complete, the South will probably soon join the rest of the nation with more competitive two-party politics.

## The American Voter in Perspective

Having reviewed the growing body of information about voting behavior, we should caution that such data, though interesting, should nevertheless be treated warily. Groups are not homogeneous; Catholics do not all vote the same way, nor do women. Even Democrats do not always vote Democratic. We saw in an earlier chapter that split-ticket voting was developing rapidly into a common behavior pattern. Different candidates and changing issues can stir a political pot in such a way that a new voter mix pours forth. Businessmen, traditionally associated with Republicanism, switched in large numbers to vote for Democrat Lyndon B. Johnson in 1964. The Republican party, on the other hand, never considered a haven for labor union members, has always received significant labor support from some unions and in some areas. In recent elections, in fact, manual workers have cast over one-third of their votes for the Republican candidate. Furthermore, national and international events can bring both short-term and more far-reaching changes in the voting behavior of particular groups. Because of the fluidity of voting behavior, campaigns must be fashioned to appeal to as many members of the various social and economic groups as possible. The effect of such campaigns, however, is to blur the differences between the parties, with the result that media campaigning becomes even more significant. At the same time, though, the kind of campaign that is aimed at a variety of groups may lend stability to the political system as a whole.

Sen. Barry Goldwater lost the 1964 election by a whopping 16 million votes. Sen. George McGovern lost in 1972 by an even greater 17.5 million votes. Thus, within an eight-year period, two candidates, one from each of the two major parties, lost presidential elections to opponents who were not very popular and in circumstances that could not have been favorable to the winning candidate. Add to that the strong showing by third-party candidate George Wallace in 1968, the steady decline in levels of voter participation (in spite of rising numbers of eligible voters), the remarkable increase in split-ticket voting, and the weakening of party influence, and it becomes obvious that something of considerable importance is going on.

## Issues and the American Voter

Earlier, we noted that responsible party advocates believe that voter preferences should be tied to policy outcomes. They contend that, ideally, the voter should be able to distinguish between candidates according to their policy views and that, once the candidate is elected, mechanisms should come into play through which the officeholder could be forced to abide by his or her campaign promises. By now it should be clear that such a system does not exist in the United States. In order to have a responsible party system based on policy choices, three conditions would have to be met: (1) candidates would need to present policy alternatives during the course of their campaigns; (2) voters would necessarily be concerned with policy questions and issues and would register their preferences on election day; and (3) candidates elected to office would be committed to the positions they took during the campaign and could be held accountable for their public actions.

Unfortunately for responsible party advocates, none of these conditions is necessarily met in the American system. Candidates often do not discuss issues at all, and, even when they do, the "debate" is often ambiguous. Opposing candidates sometimes agree on major issues, and, even when they disagree, we have no way of knowing how voters respond to these conflicts in the privacy of the polling booth. Furthermore, the advent of the "New Politics" campaign techniques has had the effect of placing more emphasis on advertising candidate personalities at the expense of greater issue and policy discussion. The two-party system tends to muffle issue differences, with the result that both parties are in agreement on many issues, leaving the voter with restricted policy choices.

## The 1950s and 1960s

Beginning in the 1950s, a number of scholars began to undertake a series of studies of voter preferences, including how voters arrived at electoral decisions. The best known of these, and the one that probably had the greatest impact on political science, was *The American Voter* by a team of researchers at the Survey Research Center (SRC) at the University of Michigan.[21] This landmark study was based primarily on the 1956 presidential election, with additional material drawn from the 1952 presidential and the 1958 congressional elections. Subsequent SRC studies replicated the survey analysis every two years, thus providing the best long-term data base available at that time.

What did these studies, along with others, demonstrate about voting behavior? In summary, they found "an electorate that was only mildly involved in politics; that thought about politics in relatively simple and narrow terms; that was allied with one or the other of the major parties by ties that were more a matter of habit than of rational selection; and that was basically satisfied with the workings of the political system."[22]

The Survey Research Center group included a series of interview questions designed to ascertain public attitudes toward prominent public issues of the day. The response revealed a substantial lack of familiarity with issues and policy questions on the part of the voters. Some individuals showed considerably greater sensitivity to the full range of public political questions than did others. One factor in the degree of understanding of public issues was the level of education of the voter. To put it simply, those who were better informed were those with better educations (see table 7–9).

Philip Converse, one of the SRC team, has noted that, "for many people, politics does not compete in interest with sports, local gossip, and television dramas." Many people simply have no opinion about political issues. Only about one-third of the people, he commented, were able to identify legislative proposals that had been widely debated over a long period of time. Even those who could identify the proposals were unable to describe accurately the substance of the issue. Many people expressed contradictory and inconsistent positions. For instance, it was not unusual for a voter to

TABLE 7–9    Educational level and familiarity with policy issues

| Familiarity with issues | Less than 8 years of school | High school | College |
|---|---|---|---|
| High | 21% | 31% | 50% |
| Medium | 37 | 47 | 44 |
| Low | 42 | 22 | 6 |
| Total | 100 | 100 | 100 |

*Source:* A. Campbell, P. Converse, W. Miller, and D. Stokes, *The American Voter* (New York: John Wiley & Sons, 1960), p. 175. Reprinted by permission.

express support for tax cuts while at the same time favoring increased governmental services.[23]

Having arrived at this portrait of voter attitudes toward issues, the SRC group then proceeded to consider some of the ways in which people discuss politics. For instance, do they perceive politics in ideological or nonideological terms? These data were collected by asking respondents what they liked or disliked about each of the major parties and whether there was anything about each of the presidential candidates (Eisenhower or Stevenson) that would cause them to vote for or against him.

In analyzing the results, the researchers placed the responses into four "levels of conceptualization." First were those whose views were ideological in character. These particular responses were cast in terms of *liberalism or conservatism*. The researchers also sought out answers that were more abstract but were clearly formulated in ideological terms. Only 11.5 percent of the sample showed some form of ideological thinking (see figure 7–3).

A second group of 42 percent, representing the largest in the sample, conceptualized politics in terms of *benefits to the group* to which they belonged. Republicans, for example, were thought to aid the rich and business interests; Democrats were said to help working people or poor people. A third group associated the general *"goodness or badness"* of the times with a particular party or candidate. This group accounted for 24 percent of the sample. These respondents associated good or bad economic conditions with one or the other of the parties or suggested that one or the other was more likely to get us into war. The remaining 22.5 percent of the responses had *no issue or ideological* content at all. These respondents restricted their comments to platitudes about the candidates or parties or registered no views at all.

Obviously, the responses of this 1956 sample contain little ideological or issue content. These findings belied the generally held belief at the time that most people were interested in and somewhat informed about politics. Even among those with better educations only about one-third could be classed as ideologues. The result was the establishment of a new view that ideological thinking and issue orientation was quite rare among the voters.

The authors of *The American Voter* offered their own summary of their findings:

> When we examine the attitudes and beliefs of the electorate as a whole over a broad range of policy questions—welfare legislation, foreign policy, federal economic programs, minority rights, civil liberties—we do not find coherent patterns of belief. The common tendency to characterize large blocs of the electorate in such terms as "liberal" or "conservative" greatly exaggerates the actual amount of consistent patterning one finds. Our failure to locate more

## IDEOLOGICAL

| 11.5% |

Well, I think they're (Republicans) more middle-of-the-road—more conservative. They are not subject to radical change. . . .

I think they (Democrats) are supposed to be more interested in the small businessman and low tariff.

They're (Democrats) more inclined to help the working class of people, and that is the majority in our country. . . .

Well, they (Republicans) play up to individual rights, which is good. That's good—it makes a person feel more independent.

## GROUP BENEFITS

| 42% |

They (Republicans) are more for big business. . . . They cater to big men.

I think they (Democrats) have always helped the farmers. To tell you the truth, I don't see how any farmer could vote for Mr. Eisenhower.

I think they (Republicans) try to run the country without running into debt and keep us out of wars.

## GOODNESS OR BADNESS OF THE TIMES

| 24% |

My husband's job is better, . . . his investments in stocks are up. They go up when the Republicans are in.

My husband is a furrier, and when people get money they buy furs.

I like the good wages my husband makes. (*It is the Republicans who are in now*). I know, and it's sort of begun to tighten up since the Republicans got in.

## NO ISSUE OR IDEOLOGICAL CONTENT

| 22.5% |

I'm a Democrat, that's all I know. My husband's dead now—he was a Democrat.

I vote for who I think is the best man. The last two elections have been mudslinging, and the Democrats are responsible for this.

No, I don't know anything about political parties. I'm not interested in them at all.

**FIGURE 7–3** Voter responses to SRC interview questions in 1956, with percent of responses in each category. (*Source:* Adapted from A. Campbell, P. Converse, W. Miller, and D. Stokes, *The American Voter* (New York: John Wiley & Sons, Inc., 1960), pp. 216–265. Reprinted by permission.)

than a trace of "ideological" thinking in the protocols of our surveys emphasizes the general impoverishment of political thought in a large proportion of the electorate.

It is also apparent that there is a great deal of uncertainty and confusion in the public mind as to what specific policies the election of one party over the other would imply. Very few of our respondents have shown a sensitive understanding of the positions of the parties on current policy issues. Even among those people who are relatively familiar with the issues presented in our surveys—and our test of familiarity has been an easy one—there is little agreement as to where the two parties stand. This fact reflects the similarity of party positions on many issues, as well as the range of opinion within parties. But it also reflects how little attention even the relatively informed part of the electorate gives the specifics of public policy formation.

We have, then, the portrait of an electorate almost wholly without detailed information about decision making in government. A substantial portion of the public is able to respond in a discrete manner to issues that *might* be the subject of legislative or administrative action. Yet it knows little about what government has done on these issues or what the parties propose to do. It is almost completely unable to judge the rationality of government actions; knowing little of particular policies and what has led to them, the mass electorate is not able to appraise either its goals or the appropriateness of the means chosen to serve these goals.[24]

The excellence of the Survey Research Center studies tended to give them an aura of permanency—to freeze our understanding of voter behavior in the 1950s. But conditions have changed since that decade. We have moved from an age in which the popularity of President Eisenhower, concerns over the Cold War, bipartisan foreign policy, and other events pulled us together and tended to blur ideological differences and blend public attitudes. Since then, we have had one presidential candidate from the right and another from the left, a third-party candidate (Wallace) who deliberately and successfully brought ideology to the fore, and the emergence of such important issues as race, Vietnam, and Watergate, which led people to think in terms of issues again. As a result, researchers began to suggest that the level of issue consciousness and of ideological commitment had risen since the 1950s, and they started to undertake projects to test their hypotheses.

## The 1970s

The best known of the newer studies is *The Changing American Voter* by Norman H. Nie, Sidney Verba, and John R. Petrocik. These scholars note that the most dramatic political change in the American public over the past two decades has been the marked decline in partisanship. Party affiliation was a stabilizing influence in the post–World War II years, as the SRC team found, but the citizens were not issue oriented. Party identification and partisanship weakened in the 1960s, and in the 1970s issue differences emerged anew as important factors in the voter equation. In the past, citizens had coherent beliefs grounded in the political issues defined by Franklin D. Roosevelt and the New Deal. These issues tended to divide the parties, and people voted according to them. In the 1950s there was no such coherent set of issues, but the Goldwater candidacy in 1964 presented a clear choice and possibly stimulated new interest in issue positions.

Nie, Verba, and Petrocik found a high level of issue consistency in the presidential election years of 1964, 1968, and 1972 as well as in the intervening off-year elections. They conclude that "citizens have come to think about issues more consistently no matter what the specific electoral stimulus."[25] The old issues that had caused people to react in the 1950s also caused them to identify with the Democratic and Republican parties. But the Great Depression was over, and the social programs inaugurated by the New Deal had been accepted by the people and by both parties. Nothing arose in the 1950s to take their place, and the generation of voters emerging from that era, although they followed the partisan commitments of their parents, had no clear issue orientation. In short, they were available for new alignment.

V. O. Key, in a study published posthumously in 1966, argued that the mass electorate was a good deal less irrational, ill informed, and unconcerned about important policy questions than had been supposed. He urged that in a general way voters do behave rationally and responsibly.[26] Beginning in 1968, the Survey Research Center scholars found support for Key's thesis. Although they contended that in 1968 Wallace was an issue candidate, whereas Nixon and Humphrey were party candidates, by 1972 they found that issues had become very important. In that election they observed that the direct link between issues and the vote was stronger than the link between party identification and the vote. The results of these studies and others suggest that we can no longer accept the view that issues are of little importance in voter decisions, as was the case in the 1950s.[27]

The most potent issues in 1972 were the Vietnam War and amnesty, with legalization of marijuana and campus demonstrations also strongly related to the vote. Questions regarding desegregation and aid to minority groups were tied to the vote as well, but less strongly than the other four issues.[28]

## The 1980s

It is clear that, since 1964, issues have emerged once again to play a role in voter decision making. What is not clear is the nature of that role and the extent to which it has had an effect on elections. Some scholars believe that issue voting is replacing party voting and that the result is a decline in partisan affiliation and a rise in ticket splitting and political independence. They argue that the "departisanization" of the electorate has caused the voters to respond more directly to issues in recent years. Others believe that the issues of the 1960s—Vietnam, racial justice, the urban crisis, and environmental considerations—simply caught the attention of people and compelled them to make political decisions from the standpoint of issues. Finally, a more common argument holds that issue voting in the past has been overwhelmed by party voting based on habit and family tradition. In other words, voters were more attached to their political parties and tended to vote for the party's candidates regardless of their stand on the issues. These observers maintain that this state of affairs was overcome by the voters' realization that candidates were not responsive to the issue preferences being expressed at the polls. Clearly, if this argument is an accurate one, party loyalty and party voting will continue to erode in the face of increased issue voting.

So far, the 1980s have cast little light on the role of issues in the voter decision-making equation. The 1980 presidential election was one of the most issue oriented in many years. Just weeks before the election, polls showed that 85 percent of the electorate believed that Jimmy Carter was doing only a fair or poor job of handling the nation's economy, and 78 percent thought that his administration's foreign policy was only fair or poor.[29] The issues in 1980 were inflation, unemployment, the appearance of disorganization within the administration, and, above all, the hostages in Iran. A majority of citizens had clearly lost confidence in Carter, and they gave Ronald Reagan a 10 percent margin of victory on election day. But those voters who chose Reagan did not necessarily embrace his policies. Most pollsters found that, although two out of three people questioned believed that Reagan's economic program would lead to economic improvements, they disagreed on many of the specific parts of the whole. In other areas of national concern, opinion was sometimes in line with candidate Reagan's pronouncements and at other times widely at variance with them. In short, there were as many analyses and interpretations of the "meaning" of the Reagan election as there were writers and commentators discussing it. Just about everyone agreed that issues played a greater role than they had in any election since 1964—but that was about the extent of the agreement.

In the American democracy it is difficult to sort out why people vote as they do. Their voter decisions represent a potpourri that includes issues; party preference; and candidates' personality, talents, and personal attributes. The individual vote cast for a candidate may be stimulated by one or all of these factors. Often, even though we know who won and who lost, we find it difficult to ascertain why. One way to determine voter opinion on specific issues is through the instruments of direct democracy: the initiative and the referendum.

## Direct Democracy: The Voters Write the Law

Americans have long had the desire to maintain some degree of direct participation in government. This characteristic probably arises from a general belief that government officials cannot be fully trusted or relied upon to carry out the will of the people as registered in the election of candidates. The result has been the adoption in a number of states of measures through which citizens can take the "initiative" in placing policy matters on the ballot for a direct vote. Provisions also exist whereby legislative bodies can place matters on the ballot for a direct expression of support or disapproval. The first of these devices is the initiative, and the second is the referendum.

Fewer than half the states provide for some form of the initiative. The *direct initiative* permits voters to put a measure on the ballot by collecting a specified number of signatures of eligible voters (usually 5 to 15 percent); if the measure passes, it becomes law (see appendix for measures placed on ballot by initiative). Thirteen states provide for the direct initiative. The *indirect initiative* is used to petition the legislature to act on a measure before it is placed on the ballot. Five states provide for the indirect initiative, and three permit both forms. This device stemmed from the popular democracy of the Progressive era; only one state (Alaska) has adopted the initiative since 1918.

The *referendum,* used in over forty states, permits voters to review laws passed by the state legislature before they take effect. Once the legislature has passed a bill, those who are offended by it can seek the required number of signatures to place it on the ballot in an upcoming regular or general election. Until the election is held, the implementation of the bill is suspended, and, if the voters reject it, the bill is killed before it can become law. One widely used form of referendum requires a vote on bond issues or property tax increases. Another form is the *constitutional referendum,* frequently employed to amend state constitutions (see figure A–4, in appendix).

Supporters of the initiative and referendum view them as useful checks on elected representatives and as an expansion of democracy. Opponents argue that they undercut established government, which in turn undercuts representative democracy and legislative responsibility. The opponents believe that the mischief that can arise from using the two devices is too great a risk and overshadows any benefits to democracy.[30]

Until recently, the initiative and referendum were not used widely outside of California and a few other states that originally responded favorably to the Progressive movement. In more recent years, however, an upsurge of interest in and use of the initiative and referendum has caused some observers to express concern. In the 1978

**TABLE  7–10    Selected referendum propositions on the 1980 state ballots**

| State | Proposition | For | Against | Turnout |
|-------|-------------|-----|---------|---------|
| Arizona | Limit property taxes; tax increase possible only if approved by 2/3 vote of people or legislature | 30.1% | 69.9% | 46.0% |
| Massachusetts | Limit local taxes | 59.6% | 40.4% | 56.7% |
| Montana | Index state taxes to inflation rate | 69.4% | 30.6% | 60.0% |
| Missouri | Close down an operating nuclear plant | 39.1% | 60.9% | 55.3% |
| South Dakota | Prohibit disposal of nuclear wastes and construction of nuclear power plants except with voter approval | 48.4% | 51.6% | 62.4% |
| California | Extend requirement for designating smoking and nonsmoking areas in certain facilities | 46.5% | 53.5% | 48.1% |
| Iowa | Amend state constitution to guarantee rights of women | 44.2% | 55.8% | 50.7% |
| New Hampshire | Change all references in state bill of rights from "man," "men," and "men's" to "person," "people," and "person's" | 16.4% | 83.6% | 22.5% |
| Illinois | Reduce size of the state House of Representatives; replace multimember with single-member legislative districts; replace cumulative voting | 68.7% | 31.3% | 38.2% |
| Minnesota | Add popular initiative and referendum to lawmaking process | 53.2% | 46.8% | 61.7% |
| Nevada | Increase the types of crimes for which bail may be denied | 78.1% | 21.9% | 42.6% |

*Source:* Austin Ranney, "Referendums, 1980 Style," *Public Opinion* (February–March 1981): 40–41. © 1981 American Enterprise Institute. Reprinted by permission.

off-year elections, for instance, 350 different proposals appeared on the ballots of thirty-seven states, and uncounted numbers of issues were also presented to the voters in city and county elections. Of the statewide propositions, 40 were initiatives placed on the ballot by citizen petition, the highest number in an off-year election in over thirty years. The remainder were referenda proposed by legislatures and placed on the ballot for voter decision. The results were mixed. Thirteen states adopted restraints on taxes and spending, and several rejected proposals to expand legalized gambling. A few states or cities in recent years have voted on laws or ordinances extending homosexual rights, and a number have wrestled with a variety of environmental questions.[31]

In the presidential election year of 1980, the trend toward greater use of the instruments of direct democracy continued. Forty-two states and the District of Columbia had at least one referendum measure on the ballot. They ranged from tax cutting measures to political reform proposals and tended to reflect the conservative tenor of the election (see table 7–10). Austin Ranney has noted that the turnout for the referendum elections ranged from 22.5 percent in New Hampshire, on an amendment to remove sexist language from the state constitution, to a high of 64.4 percent in Utah, on a proposal to abolish the state sales tax—neither of which passed. The average turnout for all propositions was 52.1 percent, which was close to the national turnout for the presidential election.[32]

In 1982 the 237 measures on the ballot in forty-two states and the District of Columbia seemed to have a more liberal bent than those of the preceding election. By far the most common was the proposal for a bilateral nuclear arms freeze, which carried in most areas. Others dealt with the death penalty, can and bottle bills, and gun control.[33]

The rise of the initiative seems to be a part of a public quest for more responsive government. The increase in the number of referenda measures may well be a product of legislators' inability to read a volatile and changing electorate. Concern over abuses of the two direct-democracy devices recently led the National Municipal League to modify its long-standing support of the direct initiative in favor of an indirect initiative like that used in Massachusetts. In that state the legislature must first be petitioned for action before a proposition goes on the ballot.[34]

The recent increased popularity of the initiative and referendum has raised anew the old questions as to their impact on established governmental procedures. Undoubtedly, measures appearing on the ballot have strengthened voter interest and, in some cases, voter participation. But those same voters are not always in a position to know fully the ramifications of their votes. They can cut taxes, as they did in 1978 in California, Idaho, Nevada, and other states, but they do not bear the responsibility for deciding which governmental services are to be cut. Unpopular decisions sometimes must be made, and their very unpopularity will guarantee their defeat by the voters. That, however, may not be the central issue, and opponents of direct democracy argue that elected representatives are better able to make such judgments. Furthermore, public relations consultants have increasingly moved into the controversies generated by ballot propositions, with, frequently, a resultant blurring of public debate and obfuscation of public issues. A 1978 proposition to prevent smoking in public places in California was defeated—not necessarily because the voters made a rational decision to vote against it but more probably because the tobacco companies spent over $5 million in advertising against it.

Direct democracy has generated both support and opposition from knowledgeable observers. It does represent, however, one way in which citizens can register their views on particular issues in the privacy of the polling booth. To some extent it may be responsible for the increase in issue voting that has developed since the early 1960s.

## Voting Behavior of the American People

Within this context, analysts search for currents to describe the American political system of the future. Voter turnout is in decline, it is thought, because of administrative obstacles such as registration and residence requirements, but, as those restrictions ease, the number of voters does not increase. Some voters are alienated, and their personal disenchantment with the system causes them to drop out. Political efficacy is low among many people because they find it difficult to translate the importance of their vote into personal gain. They become nonvoters, thus guaranteeing that they will have no voice in running the government and no part in future political decisions. Voters turn more and more to pressure groups as vehicles for translating personal desires into policy reality. Yet the proliferation of groups and the wide variance in their aspirations mean that many people will have no greater voice through this vehicle than they believe that they had through party action (see chapters 10 and 11).

Admittedly, the study of voting behavior is fraught with difficulty. Most research has been based on presidential election data, ignoring voting behavior at the state and local levels that may be very different in outcome and in meaning. Furthermore, the development of the techniques necessary to study voting behavior has been concentrated in the period since World War II and is bracketed within a single party-alignment period. We have no way of knowing for sure whether our present experiences differ that much from those of earlier eras. Finally, the very fact that leading scholars and knowledgeable observers, using the same electoral data, come to very different conclusions gives one pause. Who is right? Which theory will prevail? What factors are really important, and which ones will ultimately decide the type of political system we will have? How long will we be in this tentative state of affairs? Conclusive answers do not exist.

The party organizations, the candidates, the officeholders, and the analysts agree that the political situation in the early 1980s is fluid. Some trends are apparent, but they are often contradictory. Politicians are, on the whole, running with the tide and constructing campaigns to fit their perception of the public mood. Many probably agree with the assessment of Richard Scammon and Ben Wattenberg in their widely read book, *The Real Majority,* published in 1970. They propose a blueprint for winning elections in this era of declining party influence and rising voter dissatisfaction. They suggest that the wise candidate will stay firmly in the middle of the road on key issues. He or she will not assume a stance that is either too conservative or too liberal, because most voters are in the center. The candidate, in general, should support social welfare legislation, increased minimum wage, social security, and aid to education but should take a hard line on drug abuse, crime in the streets, and permissiveness.[35] Some of the implications in their blueprint are disturbing, since they suggest that the candidate's goal is to win regardless of his or her true feelings about important issues. More than that, though, they raise questions regarding the effectiveness with which public desires are transferred through the political system to become public policy. They help to focus our attention on the role of the legislative and executive branches, both national and state, in the carrying out of political policymaking as reflected by electoral outcomes.

# Notes

1. David Campbell and Joe R. Feagin, "Black Politics in the South: A Descriptive Analysis," *Journal of Politics* 37, no. 1 (February 1975): 133.

2. Thomas E. Cavanaugh, "Changes in American Electoral Turnout, 1964–1976," a paper presented at the annual meeting of the Midwest Political Science Association, Chicago, April 1979, p. 23.

3. *Election Administration Reports* 8, no. 4 (February 15, 1978): 7.

4. Joseph P. Harris, *Registration of Voters in the United States* (Washington, D.C.: Brookings Institution, 1929), p. 82.

5. *Report of the President's Commission on Registration and Voting Participation,* November 1963, p. 13.

6. Steven J. Rosenstone and Raymond E. Wolfinger, "The Effect of Registration Laws on Voter Turnout," *American Political Science Review* 72 (March 1978): 41.

7. Angus Campbell and Warren E. Miller, "The Motivational Basis of Straight and Split Ticket Voting," *American Political Science Review* 51, no. 2 (June 1957): 293–312.

8. Jack L. Walker, "Ballot Forms and Voter Fatigue: An Analysis of the Office Block and Party Column Ballots," *Midwest Journal of Political Science* 10 (August 1966): 448–463.

9. Henry M. Bain and Donald S. Hecock, *Ballot Position and Voter's Choice* (Detroit: Wayne State University Press, 1957).

10. Curtis B. Gans, "The Empty Ballot Box: Reflec-

tions on Nonvoters in America," *Public Opinion* (September–October 1978): 54.

11. John Gardner, "Report from Washington," *Newsletter of Common Cause* 1, no. 1 (November 1970).

12. *Congressional Quarterly Weekly Report* (September 11, 1976): 2466. Also see Gans, "The Empty Ballot Box."

13. V. Lance Tarrance, "Suffrage and Voter Turnout in the United States: The Vanishing Voter," in *Parties and Elections in an Anti-Party Age,* ed. Jeff Fishel (Bloomington: Indiana University Press, 1978), pp. 77–85.

14. Gerald M. Pomper, "The Decline in Partisan Politics," in *The Impact of the Electoral Process,* eds. Louis Maisel and Joseph Cooper (Beverly Hills, Calif.: Sage, 1977): pp. 14–15.

15. Wesley Allinsmith and Beverly Allinsmith, "Religious Affiliation and Politico-Economic Attitudes: A Study of Eight Major U.S. Religious Groups," *Public Opinion Quarterly* 12 (Fall 1948): 377–389.

16. Edgar Litt, *Ethnic Politics in America* (Glenview, Ill.: Scott, Foresman, 1970), pp. 113–116.

17. *The American National Election Series: 1972,* Center for Political Studies, Institute for Social Research (Ann Arbor: University of Michigan, 1973).

18. Gerald Pomper et al., *The Election of 1976* (New York: McKay, 1977), p. 151.

19. Based on the *New York Times*/CBS News poll of exiting voters on election day and reported in the *New York Times* (November 9, 1980): 28.

20. David Knoke, *Change and Continuity in American Politics: The Social Bases of Political Parties* (Baltimore, Md.: Johns Hopkins University Press, 1976), pp. 19–37.

21. Angus Campbell, Philip E. Converse, Warren E. Miller, and Donald E. Stokes, *The American Voter* (New York: Wiley, 1960).

22. Norman H. Nie, Sidney Verba, and John R. Petrocik, *The Changing American Voter* (Cambridge, Mass.: Harvard University Press, 1976), p. 14.

23. Philip E. Converse, "The Nature of Belief Systems in Mass Publics," in *Ideology and Discontent,* ed. David E. Apter (New York: Free Press, 1964), pp. 213–230.

24. Campbell, Converse, Miller, and Stokes, *American Voter,* p. 543.

25. Nie, Verba, and Petrocik, *Changing American Voter,* pp. 348–349.

26. V. O. Key, Jr., *The Responsible Electorate: Rationality in Presidential Voting, 1936–1960* (Cambridge, Mass.: Belknap Press, 1966), pp. 7–8.

27. Philip E. Converse, Warren E. Miller, Jerrold G. Rusk, and Arthur C. Wolfe, "Continuity and Change in American Politics: Parties and Issues in the 1968 Election," *American Political Science Review* 63, no. 4 (December 1969): 1083–1105; Arthur H. Miller, Warren E. Miller, Alden S. Raine, and Thad A. Brown, "A Majority Party in Disarray: Policy Polarization in the 1972 Election," *American Political Science Review* 70, no. 3 (September 1976): 753–778.

28. Ibid., pp. 762–764.

29. NBC/Associated Press poll reported in *Public Opinion* (December–January 1981): 27.

30. Jack C. Plano and Milton Greenberg, *The American Political Dictionary,* 4th ed. (Hinsdale, Ill.: Dryden Press, 1976), pp. 172 and 182. The numbers of states cited come from Les Ledbetter, "More and More Voters Write the Law," *New York Times* (October 30, 1977): 1 and 22.

31. John Herbers, "Deciding by Referendum Is a Popular Proposition," *New York Times* (November 12, 1978): 4E.

32. Austin Ranney, "Referendums, 1980 Style," *Public Opinion* (February–March 1981): 40–41.

33. *Time* (November 15, 1982): 34.

34. Ledbetter, "More and More Voters," p. 22.

35. Richard M. Scammon and Ben J. Wattenberg, *The Real Majority* (New York: Coward-McCann, 1970).

# CHAPTER EIGHT

# The Chief Executive, Political Parties, and Policymaking

*This executive job of the Presidency is without parallel. Shortly after talking to President Nixon for the last time, I tried to find out just what the minimum legal burden of the executive was, in hard law. I learned the following: he is by statute responsible for choosing men and making the policy decisions for over fifty executive departments and agencies. He must appoint the policy makers who serve in 197 departments, agencies, commissions, and committees. He must direct the basic policy of all the statutory departments, some of which (such as HEW) have no less than 254 separate programs, on each of which he is supposed to give policy guidance. Plus Congress. In the year 1972, for example, 483 bills arrived at the White House from the Hill to be read and signed, which he did. Seventeen more arrived which he considered at length and then vetoed. In addition, he issued 55 Executive Orders to the government, and 77 Proclamations; moreover, he transmitted to Congress 110 reports from Presidential commissions and task forces, all of which, by law, were supposed to reflect his thinking. This was the statutory burden.*

Theodore H. White, *The Making of the President, 1972.*

*On the twenty-sixth of July, which out in Missouri we call "Turnip Day," I am going to call Congress back and ask them to pass laws to halt rising prices, to meet the housing crisis—which they are saying they are for in their platform. At the same time, I shall ask them to act upon other vitally needed measures, such as aid to education,*

*which they say they are for; a national health program; civil rights legislation, which
they say they are for; an increase in the minimum wage, which I doubt very much
they are for; extension of the social security coverage and increased benefits, which
they say they are for. . . . Now, my friends, if there is any reality behind that Republican platform, we ought to get some action from a short session of the Eightieth
Congress. They can do this job in fifteen days if they want to do it. They will still have
time to go and run for office.*

President Harry S Truman, acceptance speech at the 1948 Democratic National
Convention.

*[Part] of my heart will always be here on Capitol Hill. I know well the co-equal role
of the Congress in our constitutional process. I love the House of Representatives.
I revere the traditions of the Senate despite my too-short internship there. As
President, within the limits of basic principles, my motto towards the Congress
is communication, conciliation, compromise, and cooperation.*

*This Congress will, I am confident, be my working partner as well as my most
constructive critic. . . .*

*I do not want a honeymoon with you, . . . I want a marriage.*

President Gerald R. Ford, first address to a joint session of Congress, August 12,
1974.

T he first quotation from Theodore White captures the job of the president by describing the mechanics of the office.[1] Harry S Truman, opening what was supposed to be
a hopeless campaign for reelection, carefully plotted a strategy of attacks on the
Congress, which had been Republican-controlled since 1946. Gerald R. Ford was a
product of twenty-five years in the House and one year as Senate president. He was
the epitome of the congressional establishment, and his first appearance there as president reflected his deep affection for that body. Each of these quotations, then, represents a view of the presidential relationship with Congress; none of them truly
describes that relationship fully. No two presidents and no two congresses are alike.
The domestic and foreign issues change, and the political dynamics present a kalei-
doscope of ever-changing colorations between the two great policymaking branches.
But one common element holds them together and permits them to cooperate as much
as they do: both the president and the members of the House and Senate are affiliated
with one of the two political parties. That fact shapes many of their actions.

At the beginning of this book, it was noted that a political party makes nominations,
contests elections, and tries to capture offices in order to gain control of government.
Thus, until this point, emphasis has been placed on these three functions of political
parties. But, once a party has gained office, another element comes into play—the
policymaking power of those who control government. Most democratic systems are
built on the theory that a poor performance in the policy arena will result in the ouster
of those who control the government. As we have seen, this is often true in parlia-

mentary systems, where the executive and legislative branches are intermingled and inseparable. But in America we have a presidential system, with those two branches separated constitutionally and in fact.

The result of this separation of powers means that the links between party politics and government policy are not so easily defined. Our parties are not "responsible" in the sense that the party has power to demand support and allegiance from its officeholders. Thus, as we have seen in an earlier chapter, an American party has much less influence with its officeholding members than does its counterpart in a parliamentary system. Furthermore, the parties are presumed to be distinctive in ideology and in their promotion of alternative courses of action. The whole popular concept of blaming the party in power is based on the assumption that its officeholders have not lived up to their promises and that those of the other party could offer more popular alternatives. The electorate, however, is not often presented with such clear choices. The parties have long been accused of being Tweedledum and Tweedledee.

In addition, for a variety of reasons, the voters do not elect members of one party to all government positions; hence, it is often difficult to place blame or to give credit. Republican presidents in recent years have sometimes received more policy support from Democratic congresses than Democratic presidents have. Therefore, when voters go to the polls, they may very well reelect an incumbent Republican president while continuing to vote for those Democratic members of Congress who have been solid in their support of his programs. Furthermore, many believe that interest groups have supplanted parties as the more influential support system within the two houses of Congress. This fact, if true, lends support to the persistent complaint that the policymaking machinery of government is disorderly and incoherent. Those who make this argument say that the lack of orderliness in American policymaking results from the lack of ideology and the failure of the two parties to formulate coherent alternative programs. The complaint is directed at both the president and the Congress.

## The President and Policymaking

The government institution without a policy dimension would be little more than a referee between contending groups. A president without a program would preside over a government content to allow "natural" solutions to develop from conflicts between groups. Usually, the strongest groups would win, but that would not guarantee that the best policy outcome would emerge. In order to avoid this kind of political passivity, most Americans look to their president for program initiatives. In a general sort of way, they expect him to try to lead the nation in the direction of solving its problems. The solutions he proposes constitute his program. The policy process, however, is more complicated than that. One leading scholar has devised a list of "initial realities" to help define the scope of the policy process. These "realities" include the following:

Events in society are interpreted in different ways by different people at different times.
People have varying degrees of access to the policy process in government.
Most decision making is based on little information and poor communication.

Many programs are developed and implemented without the problem ever having been clearly defined.

Most people do not maintain interest in other people's problems.

No ideal policy system exists apart from the preferences of the architect of that system.[2]

The list contains other propositions, but this sampling is enough to suggest that, taken together, "these propositions suggest a highly relative and pluralistic decision-making system characterized by compromise, incrementalism, and continual adjustment."[3] With this list as a framework for analysis, let us turn to the politics of the executive and legislative branches. Presidents, senators, and members of Congress are elected under their party's banner. Some of them have adopted their party's platform as their own blueprint for solving the nation's problems. Others have run independently of the party, using its name and whatever influence it might have but keeping a distance between it and themselves. Some are more loyal to a particular interest group than they are to a party. And all are participants in a collective system of policy and decision making that makes it difficult for the average person to determine whether or not campaign promises have been fulfilled.

Without considering recent presidents, whose records history has not yet had time to evaluate, we may say that on almost every list of "great" presidents appear the names of George Washington, Thomas Jefferson, Andrew Jackson, Abraham Lincoln, Theodore Roosevelt, Woodrow Wilson, and Franklin D. Roosevelt. All these men understood the importance of presidential leadership, and each possessed some of the qualities necessary to exploit the potential of power that resides in the office. Each of the "great" presidents was a vital party leader, either establishing a new party or reviving an old one. Each had a hold on the imagination of the people and commanded loyalty and respect from wide segments of the population. Each was able to use presidential power and popular support in order to get most of his programs through Congress, at least during his first term.

The "weak" presidents, in contrast, generally viewed the office in narrower, more restrictive terms. They were either unable or unwilling to build strong public support for their programs. Most of them were reluctant to lead Congress or to impose their will in order to win congressional support. In short, they generally refused to exploit the political resources of the presidency. Some of them abdicated their role as party leader at a time when no one else was in a position to assume that role. With "strong" presidents, the political parties have ordinarily prospered. Traditionally, although it may not still be true today, party leaders have responded to dynamic presidential leadership. In its absence the multitudes of party followers have gone their own way and have suffered from indirection and indecision.

Most students of the presidency have concentrated on the way in which the men elected to that high office have used its powers in the governance of the nation. One reason for this emphasis is the vagueness with which the Constitution addresses the question of presidential power. Not only is the Constitution vague, but the section dealing with the presidency is quite brief. As Edward S. Corwin, one of the most respected of the scholars who have studied the presidency, has written: "Article II is the most loosely drawn chapter of the Constitution. To those who think that a constitution ought to settle everything beforehand, it should be a nightmare; by the same token, to those who think that constitution makers ought to leave considerable leeway for the future play of political forces, it should be a vision realized."[4]

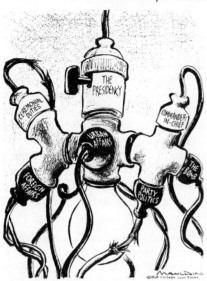

*Overload*
(By permission of Bill Mauldin and Wil-Jo
Associates, Inc. © 1969.)

The nonspecific nature of Article II did not reflect any lack of concern on the part of the men who wrote the Constitution. They argued at length over whether the president should be independent or a part of the legislative branch; over whether there should be a plural executive or one in which power was concentrated in the hands of one man; and over the way in which the office might be filled. Considerable attention was given, therefore, to the framework of the Electoral College that elects the president, but little detail as to the actual powers possessed by the man holding the office. Many writers have noted that Article II emerged from the Constitutional Convention reflecting greater concern for the mechanics of the office than for its powers.

The "executive power" was vested in the president, but no elaboration of the meaning of this power was included. The president was named as the "Commander in Chief," and he was authorized to "take care that the Laws be faithfully executed." He also received the power to reprieve and to grant pardons for offenses against the United States. He could require the opinion of his principal officers in writing, although those officers were not listed in the document. He was authorized to recommend to Congress such measures as he found necessary and expedient. This is the basis for his power to deal with the legislative branch and to implement his policy initiatives. The treaty-making power was his, but Senate ratification was required before a treaty could take effect. He was given the power to veto legislation passed by the Congress—an exercise that has emerged as an important tool of presidential leadership. He could appoint ambassadors and ministers (with the advice and consent of the Senate) and could receive ambassadors from other nations. Finally, he was required to provide Congress with a review of the state of the Union "from time to time." On this narrow base is constructed the office of the president, the most powerful elected officer in the world.

## The President as Party Leader

One leading scholar has noted that "the presidency is the work of presidents."[5] The presidential office and powers have developed out of constant redefinition and elaboration of the attributes of the position. That has been particularly true of the role of the presidents in leading their party in the development of policy initiatives. To be effective a president must impose his leadership on the party apparatus and come to terms with the competing party system that is represented in Congress. That is not always an easy task. It has served to define the nature of some of the presidencies in terms of their being "weak" or "strong." The president is aided in that effort by those people whom he has brought into his administration and those who work under them in the agencies. In general they are either members of the president's cabinet or of the White House staff in the executive office. Even with them, however, he sometimes does not find an easy relationship. As a one-time personal aide to President Truman once described it to Theodore H. White:

> The most startling thing a new President discovers is that his world is *not* monolithic. In the world of the Presidency, giving an order does *not* end the matter. You can pound your fist on the table or you can get mad or you can blow it all and go out to the golf course. But nothing gets done except by endless follow-up, endless kissing and coaxing, endless threatening and compelling. There are all those thousands of people in Washington working for you in the government—and every one is watching you, waiting, trying to guess what you mean, trying to get your number. Can they fool you? Can they outwait you? Will you be mad when you hear it isn't done yet? And Congress keeps shoving more and more power into the President's lap. . . . You can't do anything in defense unless you talk it over with your Secretary of State—and he'll have ideas, too. And then your Secretary of the Treasury will fight with you for days over a quarter-percent rise in the interest rate because it's important to him— but it's important to you, too. And those goddam bureaucrats—controlling *them!* Those regulatory agencies are so important now that they really control the whole economy. But who controls them unless you do? And a President gets out of those agencies only what he puts into them with his own energy.[6*]

Many of the problems described by President Truman's aide were political. They emphasize the importance of the role of the president as party leader, one of the most difficult of the presidential jobs to define. It is not spelled out in the Constitution, nor is it defined in law. It does not simply involve leadership of his party, for it is an interwoven complex of complementary and conflicting tasks. President Carter's 1978 attempts to achieve a peaceful solution to the Israeli–Arab conflict appear to be a major exercise of his foreign-policy role. But the initial success of these efforts led to a dramatic upturn in the president's support level in the public opinion polls and almost certainly provided him with new influence as leader of his party.

At almost the same time, however, his position as chief executive and chief administrator was beginning to generate political problems for him within the Democratic party. His vow to reduce the inflationary growth that continued to beset the nation's economy in 1979 brought him into conflict with the liberal wing of his party, which feared that his emphasis on cutting expenditures would reflect most adversely on government spending for social, welfare, and educational programs. Both his efforts

*Excerpts from *The Making of the President, 1960* by Theodore H. White are reprinted with the permission of Atheneum Publishers. Copyright © 1961 by Atheneum House, Inc.

at Camp David and his decision to cut government spending were manifestations of presidential powers given him by the Constitution. Nevertheless, each had a direct political impact on Carter as leader of the Democratic party, and both were generally well received by the press, which temporarily began treating him with greater deference and respect.

During his first year and one-half in office, President Ronald Reagan was notably successful in getting his program through a Congress in which the Republicans dominated the Senate and the Democrats the House. The skill of White House aides, plus carefully orchestrated interventions by the president, permitted domination of the Congress on many issues of importance to Reagan. Columnists and commentators wrote and spoke of a new Republican era led by a President who knew how to bend Congress to his will on policy matters by skillful use of presidential power, party influence, and congressional coalition building. By the end of the second year, however, the President's public opinion poll support had declined to 38 percent who thought he was doing a good job, and the 1982 elections cost his party twenty-six seats in the House of Representatives and seven governorships. The Republicans held on to the Senate, but a number of GOP members won election or reelection by very narrow margins. During the course of the first two years, Reagan also lost the support of many of the ideological conservatives who had been partly instrumental in getting him elected in 1980, and the worst recession since the Great Depression deprived him of the forward momentum that had dominated his first two years in office. Finally, because his program was so far-reaching and such a change in course for the nation, he was blamed by many for the failures as well as being credited for the successes. At the beginning of 1982 it appeared that many Republican members of Congress, as well as many of those conservative Democrats who had supported his policies during the first two years of his term, were prepared to follow a more independent course. Thus, both the strengths and the weaknesses of President Reagan's performance in office were greatly influential in determining how he measured up as a party leader and as a policymaker.

The president, it has been said, has two mandates: one from the party that nominated him and one from the electorate that elected him. The mandate from the party may well be the most important before an election. As the party's candidate, the president has to maintain a good relationship with party leaders and political stalwarts. In most cases, he has had to make promises and appeal to party members in such a way as to build enough of a consensus to obtain the nomination. Once nominated, however, he must seek to hold together the coalition of voters that makes up the party, at least until the election is over.

Once elected, though, many presidents have shifted their attention away from the party and have begun to address themselves directly to the general electorate. They see themselves as president of all the people, and they usually seek to create a national consensus that cuts across party and other lines. To be successful, most of them, and that includes all recent presidents, have found it necessary to exploit the uses of public communications and media. Franklin D. Roosevelt's imaginative employment of radio established an irreversible pattern that requires presidential mastery of media technology. Through the media a president can bring public pressure to bear on a recalcitrant Congress, even one controlled by his own party. He can use his personality, if it lends itself to such use, to build public support for his programs.

The result is that the president's capacity to appeal directly to the American public (as well as the world public) has tended to shift the thrust of his political leadership role from direct control of his party to indirect appeals to the public. Instead of calling on party leaders for support, presidents are more likely to "go public" through mass appeals. This may tangentially generate support for his party, but it often simply builds support for the president. It may, in fact, be an implicit call for new party activists loyal to him to work to overcome the traditional party leaders, who may be more loyal to the party than to their "temporary" party leader.

The presidency has, in a sense, become disengaged from party. The direct appeals to the public employed by every president since FDR have steadily exerted a weakening influence on the political parties.[7] Harry S Truman presided over one of the most serious splits in the Democratic party up to that time. Dwight D. Eisenhower is said to have showed little interest in Republican party affairs during his eight years in office, although recent research has suggested that Eisenhower in fact "exerted considerable influence over the Republican party and pursued a well-informed and sustained program to strengthen it."[8] John F. Kennedy, Lyndon B. Johnson, Richard M. Nixon, and Jimmy Carter presided over personal political organizations that were loyal to them, but they often ignored the established party leadership and organization. It was not the Republican National Committee that was involved in Watergate, but the Committee to Re-Elect the President (CREEP), Nixon's personal political organization in 1972. Gerald R. Ford made overtures to the Republican party leadership, but his time in office was so short that little came of them. Furthermore, the split between the Ford and Reagan camps increased throughout most of the Ford presidency as the two fought for delegates to the 1976 national convention. Jimmy Carter won the nomination for president in spite of the Democratic party; in fact, he ran as an outsider with few ties to either Washington or the party. Ronald Reagan, as noted earlier, has used his position as party leader to influence congressional Republicans to support his program and has exercised considerable control over the Republican National Committee throughout the first two years of his term. Obviously, each of these presidents, while occupying the White House, was the recognized leader of his party. Some, however, have performed their party leadership role at a distance or through the use of political agents operating out of the executive branch.

Ironically, this presidential leadership role has virtually guaranteed that the elected party leadership, as represented by the national party chairman or chairwoman, has had almost no power and very little influence. The focus of power for the party in power is the White House, not the political party organization. The late Democratic National Chairman John Bailey once said that, while serving as national chairman, he "found out what was going on in the White House by reading the *Washington Post*."[9] Seldom consulted by Kennedy or Johnson, Bailey presided over the Democratic party organization as an administrator, but the real political power rested with his mentors in the Oval Office. A later Democratic chairman, Robert Strauss, put it bluntly: "If you're Democratic party chairman when a Democrat is President, you're a . . . clerk."[10] As noted in chapter 3, however, the chairperson of the party out of power may play a considerably greater role as party leader than the chairperson of the party in power. The difference, of course, lies in the character of the presidency.

Even when the president wants to be an active leader of his political party, he is at the mercy of elements not entirely within his control. He may face difficult decisions with no politically satisfactory solution. He may simply be inept as a party leader. He may face a recalcitrant Congress whose very intransigence blocks him from successful party leadership. And to some extent he is a captive of those who surround him. The people who serve as his advisors and confidants in the cabinet, the executive office of the president, and other executive agencies may serve his party leadership aspirations well, or their actions may undercut his efforts. In most cases there will be both strengths and weaknesses in the cadre of advisors. Their activities, however, will have a direct and important impact on how the president does his job as party leader.

## The Cabinet

The president's cabinet is not specifically mentioned in the Constitution. As noted earlier, that document provides only that the president is entitled to "the opinion, in writing, of the principal officer of each of the executive departments." Acting on that vague reference, presidents, beginning with Washington, have appointed administrative department heads who have served collegially as the cabinet. As a useful presidential tool, the cabinet has been discussed from the beginning of the Republic. Presidents have often appeared to be uncertain as to how to use it. In 1983 there were thirteen cabinet members (see "The Cabinet and the Executive Office of the President," page 236). The individuals who are appointed to these posts must meet several criteria, mostly unwritten. They should normally be members of the president's party, although some have not been. They should have extensive administrative backgrounds in executive positions of importance, particularly within the field of interest of the department they head. They should be acceptable to most of the leadership of the major clientele groups with which the department works. The secretary of agriculture, for instance, will usually have a good working relationship with leaders of the various farm groups and should have some experience in agriculture. The secretary of labor should be acceptable to the leadership of important labor groups. Some presidents have expected cabinet appointees to have some experience in dealing with Congress, but that is not so important as other qualifications.

Other considerations are more political in nature. Cabinet officers should be loyal to the president and should be sympathetic to his programs. They should not be so controversial as to tarnish the president's personal image or jeopardize their confirmation by the Senate. Some presidents demand that they be "team players," sacrificing their own personal demands and those of their departments for the good of the team effort. The cabinet as a whole should be representative of the various voter groups that furnished support to the president's party. Some presidents have attempted to balance their cabinets by appointing representatives of particular religious or racial groups as well as women and members of the opposition party. Once the balance is gained and the members are confirmed and in office, the president must decide how best to use the cabinet—a matter that has proved thorny for some.

Presidents have differed over whether or not to hold regular meetings of their cabinet in order to seek its collective advice on pending policy or political matters. Most presidents have refrained from seeking such collegial judgments, however, because the parochial interests of each cabinet member have often worked against the general thrust of the president's total program. Cabinet officers usually believe that theirs is the most pressing program and that they need the most concentrated attention. Most presidents, therefore, have met with cabinet members individually or in small groups.

## The Cabinet and the Executive Office of the President

*Cabinet*
Department of Agriculture
Department of Commerce
Department of Defense
Department of Education
Department of Energy
Department of Health and Human Services
Department of Housing and Urban Development
Department of Interior
Department of Justice
Department of Labor
Department of State
Department of Transportation
Department of Treasury

*Executive Office*
Central Intelligence Agency
Council of Economic Advisors
Council on Environmental Quality
Council on Wage and Price Stability
Office of Drug Abuse Policy
Office of Management and Budget
Office of Science and Technology Policy
Office of the Special Representative for Trade Negotiations

*Other Officers with Cabinet Rank*
Vice-President
United Nations Representative
Counselor to the President

## The Executive Office of the President

As recently as the turn of the century, presidents performed their duties with the aid of a small staff consisting of a personal secretary, a messenger, and a few clerks, whose salaries they often paid out of their own pocket. The modern executive office dates only from the days of Franklin D. Roosevelt. Even then, the staff numbered only a few dozen, but the salaries were paid by the government. Since World War II the staff has increased immensely, paralleling the growth of government programs and services. Most of those who occupy key staff positions are people who have been close to the president during his quest for the nomination and for election. Their duties are highly political, and most presidents have tried to fill the various positions with political operatives. Each occupant of the White House must devise a staff plan and provide individuals who will implement it within the boundaries of his own personal definition and needs.

President Truman, succeeding to the presidency when Franklin D. Roosevelt died, needed immediate assistance from old Washington hands familiar with both domestic and foreign policy. President Eisenhower did not like politics much and chose a staff director who could protect him against the pressures of political influence. As a result, many believe that he passed up a rare opportunity to rebuild the Republican party in his own moderate image. President Kennedy put together one of the truly impressive collections of staff people in the White House and relied on them for direction and advice in trying to get his programs adopted. Although they were not very successful, they were widely respected.

President Johnson, taking over the presidency under difficult circumstances, used the Kennedy staff during the transition but gradually brought his own people into the White House. The Johnson staff that eventually emerged reflected the president's long-standing relationship with the Congress and his considerable political interests and talents. Richard M. Nixon constructed a highly politicized staff, the key members of which had little government experience but almost unprecedented power. Many decisions were made with a view toward the political implications for the president, regardless of their policy implications. The White House staff became deeply embroiled in the Watergate scandals and in the efforts to cover them up. Many of them were convicted and sentenced to prison for the illegal activities they engaged in during that corrosive period in American history.

President Ford retained many of the Nixon appointees remaining at the time of Nixon's resignation but gradually replaced them with his own supporters and confidants. President Carter was widely believed to suffer from a staff that was inexperienced in Washington; as a consequence, he was not able to develop a close working relationship with Democratic congressional leaders. Most of Carter's staff came to the White House from earlier experiences with the president when he was governor of Georgia, and most were with him at the time he began his campaign for the presidency. One factor in President Carter's swift decline in the public opinion polls during his term was a consistent public belief that the White House staff was not as strong as it might be. The president, however, was not willing to remove staff members whom he considered to be personally loyal.

The original Reagan cabinet was considered by many to be lackluster and to reflect many of the ideological support groups that made up his most identifiable constituency; it contained no women but did contain one black member. His executive office staff was relatively well balanced between political pragmatists and idea men and served well the president's need to delegate authority. Two key members of the Reagan staff triumvirate (Edwin Meese and Michael Deaver) were old associates from his days as governor of California; the third (James Baker) had been Vice-President George Bush's campaign manager. During the first two years of the Reagan term the three made much of the collegiality of their joint decision making, although there was considerable criticism over what some observers believed to be too much delegation of power. The Reagan cabinet and executive staff were remarkably stable during the first two years—only four cabinet officers left, and only lower-level resignations occurred in the White House. Two of the departing cabinet officers were replaced by women in early 1983.

The quality of presidential staff is important in understanding why some chief executives have been more successful than others in accomplishing their goals. Not only can strong staff people assist with the selling of presidential programs to the public, but they are also essential to the successful implementation of the policies in Congress, particularly when the president has a substantial majority of his own party in both houses of Congress, as have several recent Democratic chief executives.

The relationship between a president, the cabinet, and the White House staff is always somewhat difficult. Some presidents have not been able to come to terms with the problem throughout most of their term of office. On the one hand, the president expects loyalty and team effort on the part of his key advisors; on the other hand, he cannot afford to have only "yes" men who adopt as their own whatever attitude they perceive to be held by their leader. Presidents tend to want loyalists in key posts in their administration—men and women who will not sabotage the administration's programs and who will adapt themselves to adverse decisions once they have been made. But at the same time these same individuals are advisors and usually have high expectations that their advice will be sought and followed, especially if the problem involves their own area of expertise or their own clientele. These conflicting goals have not always been reconciled.

## Instruments of Presidential Leadership

In order to perform well as political leader of the nation the president must use a variety of tools. Some of these are mentioned in the Constitution, and others are not. Some of them offer extraordinary leverage with which the president can attempt to push his program through Congress and maintain his political leadership, whereas others are less well defined. Although there are a considerable number of these instruments of leadership, we will review but three of the principal ones here: federal job patronage, the presidential veto, and the press conference.

### Federal Patronage

Job patronage is the use of appointive governmental and political positions as a reward for past or future party work. Presidents and governors still trade in this important commodity, in spite of the inroads of civil service and merit systems throughout the federal government and the states. Federal patronage positions, particularly at high levels, are at the disposal of the president's party. State patronage is available, sometimes in large amounts, to the party of the governor. Patronage positions are usually of two types: (1) paid government positions involving the public's business and (2) unpaid honorary memberships in various party or government councils and committees. The former are the most important, since they bring the employee personal emolument as a reward for party service. Jobs, in short, sometimes represent the principal currency of politics. Honorary appointments are less important in terms of monetary rewards, but they do bring prestige to the recipients. In either case a president or a governor who is serious about using the party as a vehicle for political decision making can use patronage appointments as a means to maintain political control and to engender loyalty from those who are appointed.

For the party in power, patronage positions are a way of rewarding the party faithful. Control over them almost always rests with the White House or the governor's office, and the actual appointments are cleared through some type of political patronage network. The president, usually working through senators or members of Congress, consults with state party chairpersons or key party people within the state from which the prospective appointee comes. (For example, two years into his term, Ronald Reagan continued to experience difficulty in balancing the political needs of patronage against strong objections by leaders among his more conservative followers that some appointees were too moderate.) It is also important to clear away objections in the Senate if that body's approval is needed. Some administrations have treated the dispensation of federal jobs almost casually, playing down the "reward" aspects of the appointment. Others have demanded absolute loyalty from those receiving appointments.

In the past half century many states have adopted legislation placing most jobs under some type of merit system. Many local governments have also sought to reduce political influence in nonpartisan governments by instituting merit appointments. Even so, some states still maintain large numbers of patronage positions that are used in the brokerage of political power. One 1966 study of the Democratic party in St. Louis found that over 40 percent of the members of the party organization had been rewarded with patronage jobs of one kind or another.[11] Former mayor Michael Bilandic, who succeeded Chicago's late Richard Daley, retained control over the Chicago Democratic organization and an estimated 35,000 jobs with which to regularly oil the political machine. The governor of Pennsylvania has between 50,000 and 65,000 patronage positions to fill, and Indiana has about 8,000 patronage appointments out of 22,000 public employees.[12]

Patronage remains an important asset for political party leaders. It offers the president or the governor a political tool with which he can try to build support for his programs and loyalty within his administration.

## The Presidential Veto

The Constitution gives the president the power to veto an act passed by Congress. This power forces Congress to bear in mind presidential wishes in considering the passage of legislation, but it also forces the president to react to congressional initiatives. Presidents have great influence in helping to determine congressional agendas and legislative action. Even so, theirs is not the only influence, and bills often pass that are in some regard unacceptable. When that happens, presidents have the option of signing the bill into law (possibly attacking it as they sign), vetoing the bill to keep it from becoming law, or "pocket vetoing" the bill by failing to return it to Congress until after that body has adjourned. If a president does choose to use the veto, he must reject the entire law; he cannot veto one item and permit another to go into effect.

The veto does not have to be actually used in order to be effective. A president can simply threaten to use it and thereby force members of Congress interested in a bill either to remove the objectionable portion or to make a deal with the chief executive to include something in the bill in return for the presidential signature. Of course, if all else fails, and the bill is passed and sent to the president and he does cast his veto, it is up to supporters of the bill in Congress to muster the two-thirds of the House and Senate necessary to override the veto. This does not happen often.

Thomas Cronin, a leading presidential scholar, argues that the veto is a greatly overrated weapon in the president's arsenal.[13] He notes that those who cite it as such often justify their view by stressing the more than twelve hundred vetoes cast by Presidents Grover Cleveland and Franklin D. Roosevelt between them. They then emphasize that, of the more than three thousand vetoes cast since George Washington took office, less than ninety have been overridden. As Cronin notes, however, the vast majority of those vetoes were of bills of little significance or importance. Most of the bills vetoed were for the private relief of individual citizens, special immigration permissions, and individual pension claims. In most cases, questions of public policy were not even involved.

Presidents seldom veto major tax or appropriations bills, and, when they do, they may be attempting to make a point directed at some other matter—for example, vetoing an appropriations bill in order to strike an anti-inflationary posture.[14] President Carter used this approach when he vetoed a public works appropriations bill in 1978—a veto that was upheld by Congress in spite of opposition from the congressional leadership. He also vetoed the Defense Department weapons procurement bill because, he said, Congress had insisted on including money for an additional nuclear-powered aircraft carrier in spite of his belief that one was not needed. Many in Congress and in the press speculated, however, that an added motive might have been to use the veto to demonstrate to the Congress and the public that Carter was a strong chief executive despite his sagging public opinion poll standings.

President Reagan also attempted to make a point by use of the veto. In 1982 he vetoed a $14.2 million supplemental appropriations bill, calling it a "budget buster" and demanding more spending for defense and less for social programs. Congress, however, insisted on its right to help set budget priorities and overrode the veto.

In some instances, the threat is probably as important as the veto itself. Cronin notes: "It is said that Congress, especially members of the president's party, often act with White House reaction in mind. Warnings expressed by a president or conveyed through aides can prompt a measure to be modified or rewritten so as to avoid executive disapproval."[15] Cronin suggests, however, that the threat must be tempered with restraint. To threaten too often or not to carry through will devalue the president's hand. Furthermore, he must voice his objections in a manner that does not appear to be too combative or too truculent. Cronin proposes that the immediate override of Richard M. Nixon's veto of a $24.6 billion water pollution control bill in 1972 was a result of the president's efforts to assume for himself the role of fiscally responsible leadership.[16] Even so, Presidents Nixon and Ford exercised their veto power considerably more often than other recent presidents. Both had an overwhelming opposition in Congress to deal with. Both saw the veto as a means through which they could attempt to force congressional adherence to presidential policy initiatives and, at the same time, rally public support behind their presidencies. Congress, however, overrode a higher proportion of their vetoes than the vetoes of other presidents.

The veto is a seemingly important presidential power, but, like other constitutional powers, it is severely circumscribed in its uses by the realities of the political world as exercised in the federal government. The president cannot lead by using his veto power, and seldom can he even use it to shape national events. The veto is, on balance, an occasionally useful instrument that may be somewhat overrated as a vehicle of presidential power.

## The Presidential Press Conference

The presidential press conference is common to American politics, but few other world leaders have regular contacts with the press. Theodore Roosevelt is credited with the introduction of the press conference, the first of which took place in a barber shop while he was being shaved. Woodrow Wilson was the first to make the conference a regular weekly affair, receiving reporters in his office to expound on his views. Presidents Harding, Coolidge, and Hoover used the device but required reporters to submit written questions in advance.

The press conference came into its own as a political tool with the administration of Franklin D. Roosevelt, who enjoyed dealing with reporters and held a total of 998 conferences during his terms in office. Truman held 324, Eisenhower 192, and Kennedy 63.[17] Eisenhower permitted his press conferences to be televised for later showing, in whole or in part, and Kennedy allowed them to be televised and broadcast simultaneously, a practice that has been followed by all of his successors. All presidents in recent years have used the press conference as a principal means of communicating their ideas and their programs to the public at large; however, Reagan had met on numerous occasions with reporters in small group sessions. Some presidents have appealed directly to the public for support, and most have used the conference to focus attention on their legislative proposals as a means to pressure Congress into acting favorably on them.

Presidents in recent years have also sought to influence public opinion by addressing the nation on specific matters via television and radio. These addresses may concern a single piece of legislation, such as the various energy bills submitted by Ford and Carter, or they may deal with foreign affairs, such as the attempts by Presidents Johnson and Nixon to explain American policy in Vietnam, or in Central America by President Reagan. Merely addressing the nation, however, is not enough in many cases. The president must also be willing to use the other instruments at his command to further his efforts and to assist in focusing public attention in a way that will produce the most results for his program. This often proves to be the more difficult part of the enterprise.

The presidency is the most visible symbol of the party within the government. As chief executive and party leader, the president combines the functions that are most likely to provide the impetus for effective policy implementation. His is more than just a symbolic role. The powers of the presidency are often exercised through the constitutional and extraconstitutional grants that enable the incumbent to propose his own program and at the same time use his political persuasion to try to get it adopted. Whether or not the person holding the position is able to perform effectively depends on his own political skills and the political situation in which he finds himself. He can use patronage, the veto, the press conference, and any number of other instruments of power, but unless he is personally capable of making the most of them, he may discover his presidency bogged down and unable to function effectively as the focus of national leadership.

## Presidents and the News Media

Most of the news out of Washington is about the president. That is so because of the overwhelming importance of the various roles that he plays on the national and international stage. He occupies a position of great power, and, when he speaks or acts, others are forced to listen or react. He holds the initiative on many matters involving politics, legislation, public opinion, and world affairs. His decisions affect millions of people both positively and negatively; he also affects millions by indecision. The people, therefore, need to know what the president thinks and how he acts, and the chief links between the president and the people are the news media. Thus the media can be an extremely significant resource if the president knows how to use them effectively. But the media can also be an implacable enemy if the president is inept or out of step with media opinion leaders. Although it is important to democracy that the media be interested in the president, it is equally vital to the presidency that the incumbent be interesting in the media. The media, both print and electronic, use the president and his administration as sources of news. The president employs the media as a vehicle through which he can reach out to the people with his programs and performance.

Theodore Roosevelt, as noted earlier, originated the modern presidential press conference.[18] He is also credited with providing space in the White House for the press corps, thus stimulating the practice of assigning reporters specifically to cover the president. Franklin D. Roosevelt was the first to make extensive use of radio, speaking directly to the people to encourage their support of his programs and to inform them about his actions. He invented the "fireside chat," which helped to inspire confidence in his leadership and to calm the fears of the Depression generation. President Roosevelt was popular with reporters and knew how to make use of his office in order to cultivate a good press.

The age of television as a means of presidential communication began with the Korean War, which was announced via that medium to a nationwide audience by President Harry S Truman. However, it was President Eisenhower who became the first "television president." Eisenhower hired a TV consultant, former actor-producer Robert Montgomery, whose job it was to make the president appear to be informal, relaxed, and sincere. Given Eisenhower's nearly universal popularity and his winning personality, it is not easy to determine the effect of the professional efforts to enhance his image. Some experts think, however, that Montgomery was somewhat successful and that Eisenhower made increasingly good use of television as his two terms progressed.

The four televised debates between presidential candidates John F. Kennedy and Richard M. Nixon in 1960 were viewed by up to 75 million people. Many believe that Kennedy's performance during the first debate undercut Nixon's claim to greater experience and allayed some of the public's fears of the young, untried Massachusetts senator. As president, Kennedy's use of television was universally acclaimed. Televised press conferences, intimate meetings with a few reporter-questioners, and documentaries on Kennedy at work brought viewers close to the president and humanized the office as never before.

Lyndon B. Johnson and Richard M. Nixon increasingly employed the medium of television, but neither was as effective as their two predecessors. Johnson succeeded in reassuring the people of the continuity of government after the Kennedy assassination but, in the view of many, lost his command of the medium as he repeatedly attempted to explain to the people the United States's presence in Vietnam. Nixon, too, utilized television more effectively in his earlier years in office but came to be distrusted as the Vietnam War continued to escalate and the events of Watergate undercut popular faith in his esteem. As Nixon's fortunes plummeted, television displayed the presidential disaster for all to see. The effect not only was devastating for the president but was equally unhappy for the institution of the presidency.

Gerald R. Ford began his administration by promising an open government. After twenty-five years in the House of Representatives, during which he had a long-standing, open, and friendly relationship with the press, Ford was in many ways an ideal choice to restore public confidence in the office. During his time in office he held frequent press conferences, usually televised nationally, made special addresses to the Congress and the people, and met privately with selected reporters for wide-ranging discussions of important issues. The public opinion polls during the Ford era attest to the high points and the low in the president's popular appeal. After his televised pardon of former president Nixon, his public opinion poll ratings fell sharply; after his intervention in the Mayaguez incident, in which he ordered American forces to recapture a ship and crew taken by the Cambodians, his ratings rose by ten points.

Jimmy Carter, during his first two years as president, fared less well with the medium of television. As his public opinion support declined, many attributed the slide to a personality and speaking style that did not lend itself well to television. He attempted to revive the fireside chat, this time on television, and he held biweekly news conferences; but by 1980 the press openly questioned his ability to govern or to be reelected. His dramatic and effective use of television to announce the results of the Camp David summit talks with President Anwar Sadat of Egypt and Premier Menachem Begin of Israel, however, temporarily restored public confidence and revived his public image. On the night of September 17, 1978, in a prime-time unscheduled joint news event from the White House East Room, the president and his summit colleagues announced agreements that were designed to promote a Middle East settlement. The following night, Carter addressed a televised joint session of Congress, with Sadat and Begin watching from the gallery, to report on the summit and to announce the imminent departure of Secretary of State Vance to the Middle East to explain the agreements to other heads of state. Both events were dramatic and demonstrated once again that television is unsurpassed as a medium for presidential communications with the people—not just in the United States but throughout the world.

During his first two years in office, Ronald Reagan was labeled by the press as the "great communicator"—an appellation based more on his formal speeches and informal talks with small groups than on his press conferences. The president held fewer formal press conferences than others who had held the office, but most of them were televised in evening prime time. Critics claimed that he was often wrong in citing facts and figures extemporaneously and that he sometimes appeared to be ill at ease and uninformed. By the end of 1982, however, his performance at press conferences had improved somewhat.

Presidents now have the means to greatly influence public opinion and to bring its force to bear on national policymaking. Whether or not they are successful depends on many factors, including their own personalities, the sophistication of their uses of the media, and the events that shape their behavior. A president beset by unsettling economic or international woes may be unable to shape events, regardless of his own media abilities. Even so, some presidents have demonstrated a remarkable command of television technique, even in the face of adversity. (See "Building the President's Image," page 244.) Television is an instrument that can be used to impart wisdom and to build public support in every good sense of those words. It also represents a potential power of considerable danger, should the command of the medium fall into the wrong hands. Fred Friendly, respected former head of CBS News, has warned that

> no mighty king, no ambitious emperor, no pope or prophet, ever dreamt of such an awesome pulpit, so potent a magic wand. In the American experiment, with its delicate checks and balances, this device permits the First Amendment and the very heart of the Constitution to be breached, as it bestows on one politician a weapon denied to all others.[19]

Friendly's warning should be taken seriously. Nevertheless, the electronic and print media are essential to democracy as the means through which we educate and enlighten the citizen and voter. They also represent an important tool through which the president can exercise his power as political leader.

## Building the President's Image

Thomas E. Cronin, a leading expert on the presidency, has proposed a somewhat face-tious, but unnervingly accurate, list of precepts that a president might use to enhance his public image. Cynical? Yes! But, most of us can fit presidential names and events to each of the precepts:

I. Don't Just Stand There—Do Something!

II. Bend Over Backwards: Disprove Your Stereotypes!

III. Be Resolute and Firm: Appear Dominant—At All Costs Avoid Seeming "Soft"!

IV. Claim to Be a Consensus Leader When the Polls Are Favorable and a "Profile in Courage" Leader When They Are Not!

V. Travel Widely, Be a Statesman, Run for a Nobel Peace Prize—and Be Your Own Secretary of State!

VI. Do Not Let the Vice-President or Any Other Member of the Cabinet or White House Staff Upstage or Outshine You!

VII. Claim Credit When Things Go Right and Decentralize Blame; Be Very Selective in Choosing Problems for Their Potential Credit Value!

VIII. Proclaim an "Open Presidency" and an "Open Administration," but Practice Presidency-by-Secrecy, Manage the News, and Circumvent the White House Press Corps!

IX. History and Historians Reward Him Who Seems to Protect and Strengthen the Powers of the Presidency!

X. If All Else Fails, Wage War on the Press, Impugn Its Objectivity, Undermine Confidence in Its Fairness and Integrity; Denationalize Networks, Pacify Public Broadcasting, Investigate Reporters, and Intimidate Public Affairs Video Journalism!

Source: Thomas E. Cronin, "The Presidency Public Relations Script," in Richard G. Tugwell and Thomas E. Cronin, eds., *The Presidency Reappraised* (New York: Praeger Publishers, 1974), pp. 168–183.

# Shaping a Presidential Policy Proposal

President Carter's natural gas bill or his civil service reform bill, President Reagan's Caribbean Basin initiative or his "enterprise zones" proposal, were not found under cabbage leaves. They, and most other proposals that come out of the executive branch, arise from a variety of sources, and they represent another major role performed by the president, that of agenda-setter. The original idea for a new bill might come from a citizen or an interest group. It might stem from the president's party platform, or it might emanate from one of his cabinet officers or department heads. However con-ceived, a bill normally moves through a gestation period of a few days or a few years before being sprung upon the world as a new-born legislative proposal.

Regardless of the origin of the idea behind a bill, the initial assignment for shep-herding it through the executive labyrinth will usually be lodged with one of the departments or agencies under the president's purview. The agency will normally consult with the relevant congressional committee and/or subcommittee in order to keep the committee members apprised of the effort. Lateral discussions will be held with people in other executive agencies that might have an interest in the subject matter under consideration. Relevant interest-group leaders might be consulted, either to win early support or to blunt premature opposition. As a proposal takes shape, modifications are incorporated to accommodate the reactions that are received from these various interested parties.

Eventually, the proposed bill will be fully enough formed to send to the Office of Management and Budget (OMB), the chief clearinghouse within the White House for legislative proposals. The OMB is responsible for coordinating the dozens of programs emerging from agencies under the president's aegis and has considerable power over the shape of the bill or even over whether it will ever see the light of day. Most proposals cost money; some cost a great deal of money. The Office of Management and Budget is responsible for seeing that enough money is called for in the budget document to pay for the implementation of the proposed bill. If the money is insufficient, the director of OMB will propose to the president that the idea be dropped or modified to fit within available monies. The director may also recommend that the proposal be incorporated into some other piece of legislation or postponed until the next year. OMB is also responsible for keeping in touch with congressional committees in order to remain abreast of legislative developments in Congress—developments that might have an impact on the president's budget proposals.

---

A president attempting noble innovations thus stands in great need of public support and, especially, of strong partisan backing. A partyless government is almost invariably an arbitrary and reactionary regime. This country has an extraordinary need for revitalized parties: first, to serve as instruments of support for, and to discipline the whims of, elected leaders; and, second, to serve as vehicles for the two-way communication of voter preferences on policy. Too many presidents have looked upon their own party as an uninvited guest within the walls of their special brand of personalized or consensus government.

*Source:* Thomas E. Cronin, *The State of the Presidency* (Boston: Little, Brown, and Company, 1975), p. 318.

---

If the proposed bill survives OMB screening, the responsible agency may be given approval to seek congressional sponsorship, and a message may be written to accompany the bill when it is finally introduced. The general outlines of the proposal may be incorporated into the president's State of the Union Message and followed up with presidential initiatives to push for enactment. In order to provide for the survival of his bill as it negotiates the pitfalls of the legislative process, the president may use his personal prestige with members, or he may rely on his assistants for congressional relations; the latter are, in reality, lobbyists for the executive branch. He may find it necessary on particularly important pieces of legislation to go on television to enlist public support. The president and his administration have a variety of tools with which to mold congressional opinion. If these tools are successful, the president may ultimately find a revised version of the proposal on his desk for signature a few months or a few years later. He may also find that his work, and that of the Congress, must run the gauntlet of judicial review. The courts, too, are important actors in the policy arena.

## The President and the Judiciary

Back in the days when civics teachers told high school students that the judiciary was nonpolitical, the political impact of court actions was of little interest. But justice and courts have become controversial in the United States. Franklin D. Roosevelt tried to "pack" the Supreme Court in a blatant attempt to gain more favorable rulings on his New Deal measures. Richard M. Nixon was accused of trying to use the courts as a vehicle for persecuting anti-Vietnam War protesters, Black Panthers, and personal enemies. The trials of Benjamin Spock, the Chicago Seven, the Catonsville Nine, and other protesters convinced many Americans that the Court, dominated by Nixon-appointed justices, was an enemy of civil liberties. Civil libertarians, however, have usually viewed the judiciary as a bulwark against oppression and persecution.

In the 1960s southern conservatives tried to shield themselves from the liberal justices of the fourth circuit court by transferring South Carolina and Virginia to the fifth circuit, where they hoped they would get a friendlier hearing. Two of the most bruising fights between the Nixon administration and the Congress, in 1969 and 1970, resulted in the rejection by the Senate of two appointees to the Supreme Court, Clement Haynesworth and G. Harrold Carswell. Obviously, this sampling of events from a much longer list suggests that the judicial branch may well have political underpinnings.

At the same time, the careful student would do well to view such an assessment with considerable caution. The judicial branch is assumed to be above politics, and, except at the time of their appointment, judges are thought to be above partisan manipulation. Some truth, no doubt, resides in each of these views of the courts. Political scientists are just beginning to view the political role of courts more closely. The studies that have been done have concentrated on two concerns: the recruitment and selection of judges and the political implications of judicial decision making.

A major factor in the selection of Supreme Court and other federal judges, although by no means the only one, has been the partisan affiliation or the judicial philosophy of the prospective appointee. Theodore Roosevelt, on several occasions, sought to probe the "real politics" of prospective appointees. In a letter to his good friend Republican senator Henry Cabot Lodge, he wrote:

> The *nominal* politics of the man [Horace H. Lurton, a Democrat] has nothing to do with his actions on the bench. His *real* politics are all important. . . . He is right on the Negro question; he is right on the power of federal government; he is right on the Insular business; he is right about corporations; and he is right about labor. On every question that would come before the bench, he has so far shown himself to be in much closer touch with the policies in which you and I believe.[20]

In another letter to Lodge, Roosevelt wrote inquiring about a prospective appointee, Oliver Wendell Holmes, of the Massachusetts Supreme Court:

> In the ordinary and low sense which we attach to the words "partisan" and "politician," a judge of the Supreme Court should be neither. But in the higher sense, in the proper sense, he is not in my judgment fitted for the position unless he is a party man, a constructive statesman, constantly keeping in mind his adherence to the principles and policies under which this nation has been built up and in accordance with which it must go on. . . . The majority of the present Court, who have, although without satisfactory unanimity, upheld the policies of President McKinley and the Republican Party in Congress, have rendered a great service to mankind and to this nation. . . .
>
> Now I should like to know that Judge Holmes was in entire sympathy with our views, that is, with your views and mine and Judge Gray's [who was being replaced], just as we know

that ex-Attorney General Knowlton is, before I would feel justified in appointing him. . . . I should hold myself as guilty of an irreparable wrong to the nation if I should put in his [Gray's] place any man who was not absolutely sane and sound on the great national policies for which we stand in public life.[21]

This kind of examination was often being applied to prospective appointees both to the Supreme Court and to other federal courts. President Nixon's desire to appoint conservative, strict constructionists, for example, led him to Haynesworth and Carswell, and the senators' examination of their backgrounds and beliefs led to their rejection. Many presidents have appointed members of the opposition party to the Court, assuming that the minority party should have representation. But the overwhelming number of appointees have come from the president's party—in most cases over 90 percent (see table 8–1).

Jimmy Carter transformed the judicial appointment process during his term in office. Senators representing the individual states were asked to appoint committees in their respective states to screen candidates for the federal judiciary. The results of these screenings were then presented to the president for his consideration in making appointments. This process may be the reason for the decline in appointments from the president's party between the Nixon and Carter terms, as shown in table 8–1. Obviously, factors other than party are considered in these nominations—for example, geography, religion, and experience. The fact remains, however, that judgeships are an important source of patronage at the federal level in spite of presidential protestations that quality is the key factor. Even with his new system, President Carter appointed 86 percent of his nominees from his own party. To date, Ronald Reagan's most notable judicial appointment has been that of Sandra Day O'Connor to the Supreme Court, a Republican and the first woman ever appointed.

At the state level, there has been considerable movement in recent years toward some version of the "Missouri plan," devised as a means of removing judges from partisan campaign politics while maintaining their positions as elected officials. Under this plan, the governor appoints judges from a list of nominees submitted by a nonpartisan commission. Judges serve for one year before their names go before the voters for approval. There is no opposition candidate, each voter simply registering an affirmative or a negative vote on whether the judge should be retained for a full term. The

TABLE 8–1  Presidential appointments to the federal judiciary from his own political party

| President | Percentage |
|-----------|-----------|
| Roosevelt (T.) | 95.8 |
| Wilson | 98.6 |
| Coolidge | 94.1 |
| Roosevelt (F.D.) | 96.4 |
| Eisenhower | 94.1 |
| Kennedy | 90.1 |
| Johnson | 94.6 |
| Nixon | 93.2 |
| Carter | 86.0 |

*Sources:* Adapted by permission from table 15.4 in Frank Sorauf, *Party Politics in America,* 4th ed. (Boston: Little, Brown, and Co., 1980), p. 367; Nixon figure from George H. Sheldon, *The American Judicial Process* (New York: Harper & Row, Publishers, Inc., 1974), p. 121; Carter figure from *Congressional Quarterly Weekly Report* (February 14, 1981): 300.

principal problem with the "Missouri plan" and its imitators is that the voting public seldom has any clear notion of the judge's record or qualifications. Few have been rejected at the polls, although the selection process may work so well in most cases that the incumbent judge is clearly of superior quality. The various plans have had the effect of protecting judicial candidates from having to campaign on partisan issues or under political labels. The appointment-election system also permits them to avoid the indignity of having to accept campaign contributions, possibly from interests that might come before their courts.

The second area of concern to scholars has been the impact of politics on judicial decisions—a much thornier thicket to untangle. Some studies have shown a relationship between party affiliation of judges and decisions in certain kinds of cases. Men and women are not born judges; they become lawyers and then, in mid-career, are appointed or elected to judgeships. Because of the influence of law in American culture, the need for judges has become greater and greater. Political parties have usually looked with considerable favor on the creation of new judgeships. Parties are interested in new judgeships because these positions present additional offices to fill: courts and judges have their own patronage system of clerks, bailiffs, reporters, court-appointed guardians, attorneys, and executors. The prospect of filling these offices may entice many young lawyers into active party work. Finally, judges have been known to decide cases in line with their own personal philosophy, which sometimes corresponds with party positions.

This factor raises the question of whether or not political considerations come into play in the administration of justice. Do Democratic judges decide cases in one way and Republican judges decide them in another? Sidney Ulmer, in a study of Michigan judges, found that, even after moving to a nonpartisan election system, the public knew the party affiliation of the judicial candidates because the newspapers regularly reported it. Ulmer also noted considerable differences between Republican and Democratic justices, particularly with regard to unemployment and workmen's compensation cases. He noted that "Democratic justice is more sensitive to the claims of the unemployed and injured than Republican justice."[22]

Another study of the opinions of three hundred state and federal judges found similar characteristics, with Democrats taking a more liberal view than Republicans. The author concluded that judges do not vote according to their party convictions but rather reach decisions based on personal standards that are the same as those underlying their party affiliation.[23] In contrast, two other studies of judicial voting, in Wisconsin and in New York, found no party differences in the behavior of judges.[24]

And in a recent study, Thomas Walker reviewed 1,777 decisions made between 1963 and 1968 in civil liberties cases and compared them to the political affiliation of the federal district court judges involved, but he did not find that a relationship existed.[25]

Although we recommend caution in connecting political party influence with judicial decision making, there is a political component to the selection of many state judges, as table 8–2 makes clear. In fifteen states some combination of appellate and trial judges are elected as Democrats or Republicans on a partisan ballot. In sixteen states judges run on a nonpartisan ballot without reference to party affiliation. In ten states they are appointed by the governor with the approval of the legislature, and in four by the legislature itself. Finally, sixteen states use a combination of selection by a commission, appointment by the governor, and a later plebiscitary election (usually

**TABLE 8–2** Selection methods for state appellate and trial judges

| Partisan election | Nonpartisan election | Gubernatorial appointment | Legislative selection | Appointment and plebiscitary election |
|---|---|---|---|---|
| ALABAMA | [a] Arizona (Tr) | DELAWARE | CONNECTICUT | ALASKA |
| ARKANSAS | California (Tr) | Georgia (Tr) | Rhode Island (Ap) | Arizona (Ap, Tr) |
| Georgia (Ap, Tr) | Florida (Tr) | HAWAII | SOUTH CAROLINA | California (Ap) |
| ILLINOIS | Kansas (Tr) | MAINE | VIRGINIA | COLORADO |
| Indiana (Tr) | KENTUCKY | MARYLAND | | Florida (Ap) |
| LOUISIANA | [a] MICHIGAN | MASSACHUSETTS | | IDAHO |
| MISSISSIPPI | MINNESOTA | NEW HAMPSHIRE | | Indiana (Ap) |
| Missouri (Tr) | MONTANA | NEW JERSEY | | IOWA |
| NEW MEXICO | NEVADA | New York (Ap) | | Kansas (Ap) |
| New York (Ap, Tr) | NORTH DAKOTA | Rhode Island (Tr) | | Missouri (Ap, Tr) |
| NORTH CAROLINA | [a] OHIO | | | NEBRASKA |
| PENNSYLVANIA | Oklahoma (Ap, Tr) | | | Oklahoma (Ap) |
| Tennessee (Ap, Tr) | OREGON | | | Tennessee (Ap) |
| TEXAS | SOUTH DAKOTA | | | UTAH |
| WEST VIRGINIA | WASHINGTON | | | VERMONT |
| | WISCONSIN | | | WYOMING |
| Exclusive  10 | 11 | 7 | 3 | 8 |
| Combined  5 | 5 | 3 | 1 | 8 |
| *Total*  15 | 16 | 10 | 4 | 16 |

[a] State uses a nonpartisan ballot for electing judges after their nomination on a partisan ballot.

*Note:* States in CAPITAL LETTERS use only one selection system. All other states use two selection systems. The code in parentheses indicates that the system is used for trial (Tr) or appellate (Ap) courts.

*Source:* Compiled from Council of State Governments, *Book of the States: 1980–81* (Lexington, Ky.: Council of State Governments, 1980), 156–157. From Herbert Jacob, "Courts," in Virginia Gray, Herbert Jacob, and Kenneth N. Vines, eds., *Politics in the American States: A Comparative Analysis,* 4th ed., p. 238. Copyright © 1983 by Herbert Jacob. Reprinted by permission of the publisher, Little, Brown and Company.

in one year). Over the past few decades there has been a slow but steady trend toward the latter system—which is, of course, a variation of the "Missouri plan."

The office of judge is often attained without much public attention. Nevertheless, in spite of efforts to depoliticize judicial appointments, judges are not entirely immune to political considerations. They remain loosely linked to important political figures in the executive mansions and the legislatures; they must depend on partisan lawmakers for their budgets; and there is evidence that they are sometimes affected by the election returns. Even so, political distinctions in judicial decision making are more likely to arise from the personal background of a judge than from his or her party affiliation. Judicial behavior, like other kinds of behavior, is probably rooted in a magistrate's experience before he or she sits on the bench. The fact remains that politics and the political process pervade the search for new judges, the screening process for appointment, the electoral process for election, and, sometimes, the way in which decisions are made.

## The Governor and Policymaking

In the arena of subnational politics the state governor is without doubt the most important political figure. Since the 1950s state governors have moved from a position of relatively low visibility to one of increased attention and recognition. The governor has, in effect, become a federal systems officer for the state. The office of governor has been enhanced by the advent of revenue sharing, which combined with the established system of grants-in-aid to thrust the state governors into the forefront of policy implementation. At the same time the terms of office have been increased, and restrictions on succession have been lifted by many states. This has permitted some governors to extend their time in office and has provided them the means to become better-known political figures in the nation. As we have noted before, gubernatorial candidates were among the first at any level to take advantage of professional campaign managers, media experts, and computerized voter appeals; they are the new politicians of the new politics.

Paradoxically, enhancement of the office and greater recognition of gubernatorial roles have altered the structure of political opportunities for governors. Fewer have moved to the U.S. Senate, and fewer have received serious consideration for the presidency—Jimmy Carter and Ronald Reagan being conspicuous exceptions. The demands of the job have combined with its greater visibility to make governors more politically vulnerable and, consequently, more aware of the political implications of their administrations' proposals.

As the chief political officer in the state, governors serve as principal receptors for the demands made on the system. They must filter, interpret, and channel those demands into the political process through which they can be converted into public policy. Activist governors will accept responsibility for initiating those policies that undergird their own claims to be a popular candidate. The modern state governorship embodies an elaborate series of relationships with the legislature, the political parties, interest groups, staff persons, and administrators in the bureaucracy. The governor must keep one eye on past promises and the other on present performance. This political juggling act casts governors in a wide variety of political roles. Little is known about most of these roles; indeed, many of them may embrace little more than academic speculation.

We have discussed governors as political party leaders; let us consider them briefly as policy initiators.

The key factor that continues to dominate state governorships is the role originally assigned to them by constitution makers. In devising the presidency, the Founding Fathers were influenced largely by their experiences with colonial governorships, which were widely viewed as agents of the British monarchy. Thus, when the time came to create an executive office in the states, many of the men who took part reacted out of fear of strong executives and concentrated political power in the state legislatures. Both the presidency and the governorship have grown in power and influence since the eighteenth century, but the latter has always been the relatively weaker of the two. Even so, during the twentieth century the office of governor came into its own. New constitutions were adopted increasing the powers of the office in many states. The press of social and economic problems brought a realization of the weaknesses inherent in the strong legislative–weak executive framework. These problems needed quick solutions, and legislatures are notoriously slow to act. Governors assumed the responsibility for developing legislative programs and gained the power to call special legislative sessions.

At the same time, however, unlike the president, governors were often forced to share power with other elected statewide officers. The rise of the merit system concept removed a degree of the governors' political power by taking from them some of their ability to appoint and reward. The rise of state-level independent commissions covering a wide variety of responsibilities placed vast areas outside the governors' jurisdiction. Governors, in short, sometimes possess considerable power and at other times are circumscribed by constitutional restrictions.

In one area, though, governors have gained considerable influence. Like the president, most governors have assumed a major share of responsibility for providing leadership in legislative matters. Most of them periodically report to the legislature on the state of the state, and most are responsible for recommending a legislative program. Many have been furnished with budgetary powers that give them the leverage necessary to wrestle with legislative intransigence.

As political scientist Malcolm Jewell has pointed out:

> No factor is more important in determining a governor's legislative success than his relationship with the legislative leaders of his party. When that party is in the majority, these leaders— and particularly the House speakers—have broad powers to appoint committees, assign bills to committees, and guide deliberations on the floor. Moreover, these are the governor's spokesmen and representatives in the legislature. If they are ineffective or uncooperative, the governor is seriously handicapped. If he tries to bypass or undermine his leaders on one bill, he damages the effectiveness of the leadership on other legislation. The position of the governor is very much like that of the President: He must accept his legislative leaders for better or worse, once they have been chosen.[26]

Once the legislative leaders have been selected, however, governors will normally meet with them on a regular basis to plan strategy for getting their programs through the legislative maze. They may be required to use all of their powers of persuasion in this regard, since legislators' primary loyalty may well be to their own branch of government. Even so, such meetings will provide a governor with an estimate of the legislative temper and may warn him or her of potential obstacles. Obviously, in the larger states, the governor cannot personally conduct all of the administration's business with the legislature. During the hectic closing days of legislative sessions governors may be in the thick of the fight to keep their program alive or to undercut opposition to it. But during the bulk of the session much of the liaison with the legislature will be handled by legislative aides to the governor. These staff aides are responsible for keeping the governor informed of the progress of legislation and of transmitting messages from the governor to the legislative leadership. Sometimes, on particularly important bills, they may expand their level of contacts to include rank-and-file members of the legislature as they lobby for votes. If necessary, the governor may borrow staff members from government agencies when their expertise or their personal contacts are important to success.

Mention should be made here of the differences between one-party and two-party state governors and the ways in which they manage their relationships with the state legislature. The strength of the party organization, the breadth of the governor's constituency, the demands made on government by the people, and the resources that have been made available to the office of governor all have an effect on these relationships. A competitive two-party legislature requires a different plan of operations than does a one-party dominant legislature that is fragmented and incohesive. When most of the legislators are from one party, there is a tendency toward "every man for himself" politics. The governor is placed in the position of building a coalition of members to gain backing for his or her programs.

When the legislature is divided along party lines, however, even if the governor's party is in the majority, there is much greater likelihood that the legislative parties will be cohesive, especially in the larger industrial states. The governors of two-party states do have one variable with which their counterparts in one-party states need not contend: an organized opposition. If the opposition parties are reasonably cohesive, the governors must work to maintain cohesion within their own party. They cannot rely just on the fact of their own majority; they must work to hold that majority together. The great variety among the states in their political structures and relationships means that each governor has a different set of variables that affect his or her behavior. There are no set rules that influence more than a few governors at any particular time. The governance of a state today is a dynamic process and requires imagination and flexibility on the part of the chief executive and the legislature if the problems are to be confronted.

Sarah McCally Morehouse, a political scientist, has suggested that the governor's success in getting his or her program adopted depends on his or her ability as a party leader. She notes that all governors have resources available to this purpose but that their skill in using them makes the difference between success and failure. The resources that she believes to be important include:

1. *Patronage.* Jobs and contracts and other favors, where they still exist, can be used skillfully to dole out favors where they will do the most good for the governor's program.

2. *Publicity.* The guaranteed access governors have to the media means that they also have the ability to appeal to the public for support, thus putting constituency pressure on legislators where and when it will do the most good.

3. *Promise or threat of campaign support or opposition.* In some states the support of the governor in a primary or general election campaign can be a stimulus to a member of the legislature to lend his or her support to the administration, especially when the legislator is in a close race for nomination or election.

4. *Control over information.* This resource is related to governors' control over their own administration. If they have appointment powers sufficient to ensure loyalty from their administrators, they will automatically have control over access to information. If they do not have control over key appointments, this will not be a resource, since elected agency heads may be working in opposition to the governor.

5. *Influence over the scheduling of local legislation.* The governors can withhold their support from proposed local bills until the bill's sponsor in the legislature has agreed to conform to their wishes.

6. *Promise of advancement within the governor's party or faction within the legislature.* The selection of the legislative leadership, committee assignments, and other emoluments are important in state legislatures, and the governors in some states may be able to influence the choice of leaders in such a way that it builds support for their programs and administration.

As Morehouse says, most of these resources depend on the skill of incumbent governors and on the formal and informal relationships they have with their legislatures. These resources do not guarantee success, but in most states they are available if the governor wishes to use them.[27]

In another study, Thad Beyle, a student of the office of state governor, found that gubernatorial power varies considerably from state to state, and the degree of power that the governor has depends on many factors. Beyle believes that gubernatorial strength usually derives from a combination of personality, personal wealth, party influence, interest-group support, statutory authority, and the formal attributes of the office itself. Beyle surveyed thirty-nine incumbent governors in the mid-1960s and found that they believed the following factors to be most important in assessing their power:

1. *Tenure potential.* The ability of governors to succeed themselves, as well as the length of their term, significantly influences the extent of their power. Longer tenure can affect governors' intergovernmental relationships, the influence they have with the legislature, their ability to provide direction to their political party, and the extent to which they are able to attract quality appointees.

2. *Appointment power.* The power of appointment is fundamental to a governor's success. Not only will key appointments have a major part to play in the success (or lack of success) of his or her administration, but patronage opportunities provide a chief source of legislative influence and of control over the bureaucracy. Strong power over appointments represents one of the governor's most important strengths.

3. *Control over the budget.* An executive budget, centralized under the governor's control, is a major source of power for that individual. Being at the top of the budgetary process and in the position of chief lobbyist with the legislature is an important resource for getting his or her policies adopted. It not only gives the governor control over fiscal policy but also permits him or her to prioritize programs and provide emphasis to those he or she wishes to advance.

4. *Organizational power.* In recent years the governor's office in many states has expanded its role in the creation and abolition of offices, the assignment and reassignment of duties, and the organization of government. Many governors reported to Beyle that their powers were seriously constrained by their inability to control the executive branch. They strongly believed that the greater their organizational control, the better able they would be to control and manage government.

5. *The veto power.* The most direct power a governor can exercise in the legislative process is the veto power, particularly in the forty-three states that provide the governor with the ability to veto individual items in appropriations bills. The veto is a major tool in shaping legislation and controlling the budgetary process,* and the governor gains power both from using and from threatening to use it.

Obviously, as Beyle points out, this list outlines *formal* powers that provide the incumbent governor with the potential to be strong. But governors also have *informal* powers that, if properly used, can enhance their role in state government and their ability to perform duties at a higher level of effectiveness.[28]

In a follow-up study in 1978 and 1979, Lynn Muchmore and Thad Beyle interviewed fifteen former governors shortly after they left office. Among the questions asked of each governor were several dealing with partisan political matters, including his or her role in the political party. Findings revealed that the party is only marginally involved with personnel selection, is ideologically irrelevant, and has no influence on the course of policy development. In fact, none of the fifteen former governors viewed party leadership as an important duty. Furthermore, they did not perceive involvement in party affairs to be an obligatory role. In general they shaped their party leadership role as they wished and chose not to be enslaved to a partisan role structure that did not fit their concept of the governorship.[29]

It is interesting to compare these conclusions with those of the state party chairpersons interviewed by Huckshorn during the same period. Interviews with eighty state party chairpersons determined that, of twelve "responsibilities," service as "spokesman for the governor" ranked next to last, with only about 20 percent in each party listing it as "very important." Furthermore, the chairmen and chairwomen, many of whom were appointed by the incumbent governor, reported in 52.6 percent of the cases that the governor dispensed state patronage without their participation.[30] Thus they were in substantial agreement with the views of the governors on these two partisan roles.

Thomas Dye, in contrast, did not discover that the formal powers affected policy outcomes in any significant way. He observed that the economic development within the state was a more important influence than the governor's powers in determining policy outcomes, because the governors with strong formal powers come from the more wealthy urban and industrial states, whereas those with weak formal powers tend to come from states that are poor, rural, and agricultural.[31] In an earlier study, Joseph Schlesinger also found that the urban, more competitive states tended to give their governors more formal power. The formal strength of governors was positively associated with the size of the state, suggesting that complex state government enhances the governors' need for explicit means to control their administrations. Nevertheless, Schlesinger notes, a relationship does not necessarily exist between the formal devices for administrative control and the influence that the governor wields.[32]

Administering state government has become a difficult and risky political venture in recent years. Seemingly popular young governors with promising futures have been defeated for reelection; Christopher Bond of Missouri in 1976, Michael Dukakis of Massachusetts in 1978, and Bill Clinton of Arkansas in 1980 are cases in point. Interestingly enough, all three were later reelected to the office of governor one term

*Reprinted with permission from *Public Administration Review.* © 1968 by the American Society for Public Administration, Washington, D.C. All rights reserved.

later, suggesting just how volatile the politics of the office has become. The governorship of many states is a difficult position to fill. Legislatures become recalcitrant and reluctant to support the governor's program. Control over political parties sometimes eludes those governors who wish to exercise it and is not even sought by those who consider it to be unimportant. In some states the fragmentation of constituent groups within the legislature makes the construction of a cohesive majority almost impossible. In other states governors take charge, push their programs through the legislature, and accumulate bouquets and brickbats for their actions. The office is very different from the presidency. But both officers are responsible for the executive functions within their jurisdictions, both are recognized as the leaders of their party organization, and both have become legislative leaders to a greater and greater extent.

## The Chief Executive as Political Leader

This chapter has addressed the executive machinery for policymaking in the federal government and in the various states. The president and the governors of the states possess both formal and informal powers on which they rely to make themselves felt in the policy arena. Formal powers derive from constitutional and legislative grants, and informal powers arise from their positions as party and legislative leaders and the built-in advantages they enjoy as centers of public interest. The twentieth century has seen the rise of stronger executives in government. Both presidents and governors have gained increased powers with which to operate their offices. But this very change has created the unrealistic expectation that the chief executive should solve all problems, salve all wounds, and be all things to all people. Not only is this not possible, but most presidents and most governors of recent times would probably agree that the biggest restraint on their actions has been the combination of weak political parties, proliferating interest groups, and the necessary sharing of power with the Congress and the state legislatures. We cannot resolve this paradox. Nevertheless, in chapter 9 we will address the policy implications of legislative organization and behavior.

## Notes

1. Theodore H. White, *The Making of the President, 1972* (New York: Atheneum, 1973), pp. 363–364.
2. Charles O. Jones, *An Introduction to the Study of Public Policy* (North Scituate, Mass.: Duxbury Press, 1977), p. 8.
3. Ibid., p. 9.
4. Edward S. Corwin, *The President: Office and Powers, 1787–1948,* 3rd ed. (New York: New York University Press, 1948), p. 2.
5. Grant McConnell, *The Modern Presidency,* 2nd ed. (New York: St. Martin's Press, 1976), p. 9.
6. Theodore H. White, *The Making of the President, 1960* (New York: Atheneum, 1961), pp. 400–401.
7. See Lester G. Seligman, "The Presidential Office and the President as Party Leader, with a Postscript on the Kennedy-Nixon Era," in *Parties and Elections in an Anti-Party Age,* ed. Jeff Fishel (Bloomington: Indiana University Press, 1978), pp. 295–302. Originally published in *Law and Contemporary Problems* 21 (Autumn 1956): 724–734.
8. Cornelius P. Cotter, "Eisenhower as Party Leader," *Political Science Quarterly* (forthcoming). See also Fred I. Greenstein, "Eisenhower as an Activist President: A Look at New Evidence," *Political Science Quarterly* (Winter 1979–1980), pp. 575–599.
9. Interview with the author, July 21, 1971, Hartford, Conn.
10. Joseph A. Califano, Jr., *A Presidential Nation* (New York: Norton, 1975), p. 153.
11. Robert H. Salisbury, "The Urban Organization Member," *Public Opinion Quarterly* 29 (Winter 1965–1966): 558.

12. Robert J. Huckshorn, *Party Leadership in the States* (Amherst: University of Massachusetts Press, 1976), pp. 109–112.
13. Thomas E. Cronin, *The State of the Presidency* (Boston: Little, Brown, 1975), pp. 76–81.
14. Ibid., p. 79.
15. Ibid.
16. Ibid.
17. Hugh A. Bone, *American Politics and the Party System*, 3rd ed. (New York: McGraw-Hill, 1965), pp. 225–226.
18. Most of the following section is based on an excellent review of the presidential use of the news media written by William F. Mullen in his book *Presidential Power and Politics* (New York: St. Martin's Press, 1976), pp. 126–144.
19. Ibid., p. 143.
20. Henry Cabot Lodge, *Selections from the Correspondence of Theodore Roosevelt and Henry Cabot Lodge, 1884–1918*, vol. 2 (New York: Scribner's, 1925), pp. 228 and 230–231.
21. Lodge, *Correspondence of Roosevelt and Lodge*, vol. 1, pp. 517–519.
22. S. Sidney Ulmer, "The Political Party Variable in the Michigan Supreme Court," *Journal of Public Law* 11 (1962): 352–362.
23. Stuart S. Nagel, "Political Party Affiliation and Judges' Decisions," *American Political Science Review* 55 (December 1961): 845–847.
24. David W. Adamany, "The Political Party Variable in Judges' Voting: Conceptual Notes and a Case Study," *American Political Science Review* 63 (March 1969): 57–73; and Edward N. Beiser and Jonathan J. Silberman, "The Political Party Variable: Workmen's Compensation Cases in the New York Court of Appeals," *Polity* 3 (Summer 1971): 521–531.
25. Thomas G. Walker, "A Note Concerning Partisan Influences on Trial-Judge Decision Making," *Law and Society* 6, no. 4 (1972): 645–649.
26. Malcolm Jewell, "The Governor as a Legislative Leader," in *The American Governor in Behavioral Perspective*, ed. Thad Beyle and J. Oliver Williams (New York: Harper & Row, 1972), p. 133.
27. Sarah McCally Morehouse, "The Governor as Political Leader," in *Politics in the American States: A Comparative Analysis*, 3rd ed., eds. Herbert Jacob and Kenneth Vines (Boston: Little, Brown, 1976), pp. 196–241.
28. Thad Beyle, "The Governor's Formal Powers: A View from the Governor's Chair," *Public Administration Review* 28 (November–December 1968): 540–545.
29. Lynn Muchmore and Thad L. Beyle, "The Governor as Party Leader," *State Government* (Summer 1980): 121–124.
30. Huckshorn, *Party Leadership*, pp. 100 and 113.
31. Thomas Dye, "Executive Power and Public Policy in the States," *Western Political Quarterly* 27 (December 1969): 926–939.
32. Joseph A. Schlesinger, "Politics of the Executive," in *Politics in the American States: A Comparative Analysis*, 2nd ed., eds. Herbert Jacob and Kenneth Vines (Boston: Little, Brown, 1971), pp. 210–237.

# CHAPTER NINE

# Parties and the Legislative Process

*As you know, I'm one of the greatest critics of Congress. It's an outrageous and outmoded institution.*

*All Congress has ever done since I've been in Congress is pass the buck to the President and then blame him for what goes wrong.... Congress is gutless beyond my power to describe to you.*

Unidentified congressman quoted by Richard F. Fenno, Jr., "U.S. House Members in Their Constituencies," *American Political Science Review* (September 1977): 905.

*It is the strength of the House, and not its weakness, that it performs as a legislative chamber, skeptical, critical, independent, and not as a mere arm of the President and of some national partisan instrumentality called a party. For a political party is not what the reformists think it is. It is not a "conscience," but rather a form of pressure. It is not a "mind," but rather an expression of hope. It is neither "good" nor "bad"; it is only a hammer in the hands of men capable of governing; a device and not a principle.*

William S. White, *Home Place* (Boston: Houghton Mifflin, 1965), pp. 957–958.

*And right here is raised the dilemma of the Leadership. Yes, they lead, but they lead only because they win. If they cannot be certain of winning, they don't go.... Hence, the legislative timidity of the Congress, both House and Senate. Hence, the timidity is compounded in the face of a threatened veto, when one-third of either Chamber*

257

*becomes the majority in a very real sense. Hence, the great time lags for the consideration of legislation, stretching into years in many cases, while the Leadership waits for the pressures to build—pressures that will produce success. . . .*
*Righteousness with victory is a fine thing. Righteousness with defeat is nothing much at all.*

The late Congressman Clem Miller in his *Member of the House* (New York: Scribner's, 1962), pp. 91–92.

If the president looks on Congress with a wary eye, Congress has often looked on presidents with outright hostility. The president and the Congress are not equal when it comes to policymaking. This inequality arises from the general nature of the two branches as well as from the constitutional powers held by each. The president is the only national official (aside from the vice-president) who is elected from a national constituency. Power is concentrated in his office, and public attention is focused on his person. He is the symbolic head of government in both domestic and foreign affairs. He is the head of his political party. He is in the best position to articulate a program of national goals and in fact may have done so through his influence on the adoption of his party's platform. He has celebrity status, and, as the opinion polls have repeatedly shown, most of the American people want him to succeed.

Congress, on the other hand, is a multimember body in which the vast majority are unknown to the general public. Constituency pressures, whether from a relatively small congressional district or an entire state, tend to force members to pull in a variety of directions. Weak leadership, which has not been unknown in recent years, can leave the two bodies without rudder or direction. Many congressional representatives and senators have been elected without significant party support and do not owe any allegiance to the party under whose label they hold office. Furthermore, as a president's constitutionally limited two terms draw to a close, individual members of the legislative branch begin competing to replace him. Finally, members of Congress are subjected to intense personal lobbying by a multitude of special interests, some of which may have important ties to their constituencies.

An effective president can weave a tapestry of congressional support for his programs. In the parlance of bridge, most of the trumps are held by the president. If he and his aides do not know how to play them, however, the game can still go to his congressional opposition. In fact, some observers contend that Congress is more effective than the president on domestic matters. It is important to know that he and his staff, both at the cabinet level and in the White House, know the rules of the game and the way to play their cards effectively. And that requires a considerable knowledge of how the legislative branch responds to policy initiatives.

## Congressional Party Machinery

Party leaders in Congress strive mightily to unite their members into cohesive units that can be trusted to vote together on matters of policy and organization. They attempt to establish party discipline in what is basically an undisciplined body. Power is fragmented and is not concentrated in any one place. Rather, it is distributed among those holding formal leadership positions—the standing committee and subcommittee chairpersons (and ranking minority leaders)—and among certain leaders of ideological blocs and special caucus groups. These and other centers of power, always influenced by outside forces in the executive branch and among the various interest groups, all want to have a say in the making of policy. On different issues and at different times certain power centers emerge to exert influence, only to recede with the culmination of their particular interest.

Some issues are partisan in nature, and others are not. When confronted with an issue that contains the seeds of partisanship, party leaders sometimes have an easier time giving it the party imprimatur. On most issues, though, coalitions of individual members responding to stimuli of great variety eventually determine the outcome. Party discipline sometimes exists, but a leader finds it difficult to sustain discipline over a period of time extending across a variety of issues. Members of Congress and senators are elected from districts and states with differing degrees of heterogeneity. They are sometimes elected on the basis of local issues that have little to do with national problems. Until recently, few congressional candidates received significant party help in their campaigns, and, when help was forthcoming, the candidates seldom honored the party for providing it. Thus, when members of the House and Senate come together, their most partisan vote occurs when they elect the leadership. After that, the power is diffused and decentralized. Decisions to take a party vote on a given issue are rare and are agreed to only after much discussion and considerable leadership effort. As a result, although formal party machinery for partisan decision making exists, it is seldom used. Nevertheless, a brief review of the organizational edifice of parties is appropriate.

## Party Caucuses/Conferences and Policy Committees

The caucus, a meeting of party members, has been used since the first session of the first Congress but has occasionally fallen into disuse for long periods of time, allowing party leaders to assume more of the burden of leadership. Since the 1960s, however, caucuses have come into greater favor because of the initiative of the Democratic Study Group, an organization of liberal Democrats influential in the House since 1959. The revival of the House Democratic Caucus emerged from the adoption of a new rule in 1969 requiring a regular monthly meeting of the group. Those who sought this change believed that regular meetings would enable those interested in reform to gradually gain a greater influence in party policy. Although slow to develop, the caucus has been more effective in recent years, both in pushing for continuing internal reform and in making policy recommendations on substantive issues.

In 1973, the Democratic Steering and Policy Committee was established. Chaired by the Speaker of the House, it includes other party leaders, representatives of different geographic regions, and at-large members. In 1975 it was given its most important power—the right to recommend the selection of members and chairpersons to standing committees. It has also created substantive task forces to cooperate with Senate counterparts in the development of party policy on key issues. If this committee continues to develop as it has in the past few years, it could evolve into an important force in determining party policy positions. Nevertheless, as with other such groups in both houses of Congress, its ultimate role depends to a large extent on the willingness of the leadership to lend it encouragement.

The impact of the Democratic Steering and Policy Committee and the growth in influence of the Democratic Caucus have already created an important shift in power within the House. The influence of seniority has been weakened considerably, and the role and power of the committee chairpersons have declined. At the same time, partly as a result of these two shifts, the power of the revitalized subcommittee system has increased. That decentralization of committee power, plus the general inclination of members of Congress to vote according to the wishes of their constituencies, may mean that the caucus and the policy committee have gained about as much power as they are going to gain. The impact of party on congressional decision making is significant only when the individual member can fit it into his or her overall scheme for remaining in office, which necessarily focuses attention first on his or her constituents and only later on party allegiance.

The House Republicans, when they meet together as a party group, call themselves the "conference." The Republican Conference has met about twice a month in recent years to discuss issues and sometimes to take informal stands on policy matters. During the Nixon and Ford administrations the conference was sometimes briefed by White House aides seeking Republican votes on matters affecting the administration's programs. The conference seldom actually votes on substantive matters, and, when it does, the vote is usually not considered binding. Even so, the conference often meets just before an important vote, and the meeting is used to try to rally votes for the leadership's position. However, the most important function served by the group is to open up the process of internal House communications between the GOP leadership and the members.

The House Republican Policy Committee is a broad-based group composed of the leadership and representatives chosen from each of nine geographic regions in proportion to the number of Republicans in each. In addition, there are junior members representing those recently elected to the House and at-large members selected by the leadership. The policy committee meets weekly, and, if it reaches a general consensus, it may take a stand on a given issue. From 1959 to 1974 the policy committee issued about three hundred policy statements, an average of nineteen each year. One study of the Republican Policy Committee concluded that it was the most effective of the four committees dealing with party policy.[1] Another study, though, found that the policy statements issued by Republicans dealt with matters that already commanded broad agreement.[2]

In the Senate there are policy committees for both parties, but they have not developed into important leadership groups. The Senate Republican Policy Committee includes the minority leadership as ex officio members, and the rest of the membership rotates among other Republican senators, often including those running for reelection. The committee is not chaired by a party leader, as is the case among Democrats. The committee, which at any given time includes about half of all Republican senators, meets regularly for informal discussion and occasionally makes recommendations on pending legislation to the conference. The leadership has provided a staff for the policy committee, and it produces research reports on substantive issues for the use of Republican senators. On the whole, the Republican Policy Committee in the Senate has not proved to be a very effective instrument in policymaking, concentrating instead on providing a forum for internal party discussion.

On the Democratic side much the same was the case until recent years, when Majority Leader Mike Mansfield, before his retirement in 1976, worked to involve the Senate

Democratic Policy Committee more actively in party policymaking. The committee is composed of most of the leadership (Mansfield served as chairman), six members who serve on the committee as long as they serve in the Senate, and four other members who belong to the Legislative Review Committee, which screens less controversial legislation. The Policy Committee meets regularly and has been most effective in advising the leadership on legislative matters involving the scheduling of legislation, developing acceptable compromises, and, in a few cases, actually taking positions on some matters for consideration by the caucus. During the latter years of the Nixon administration, for instance, the Democratic Policy Committee adopted a number of resolutions urging the administration to speed American withdrawal from Vietnam.

## Party Leaders: Majority and Minority

Party leadership in the House and Senate is only as strong as the people who hold the leadership positions. The Speaker of the House is the most influential person in Congress. He controls an array of formal powers that permit him to manage the business of the House and to control the flow of legislation. The formal powers include recognition of members who wish to speak, voting to break tie votes, and referral of bills to the standing committees. However, often a Speaker's "informal" powers and reputation for leadership determine the record that emerges from the House. These informal powers are largely unwritten and depend to a great extent on the political skill and personality of the Speaker. A Speaker can frequently make things happen, for instance, by exerting pressure on key committee heads and members. He is largely responsible for scheduling the flow of legislation by controlling the calendar of floor consideration. Some Speakers, such as Sam Rayburn, who served in that office from 1940 to 1961 (with two breaks in service), have accumulated enormous power and have maintained it for many years. Others have been less successful in bringing the powers of the office to bear and have allowed the leadership to be shared and diffused. Without strong leadership, the House suffers from the centrifugal force generated by the individual goals and aspirations of its members.

There is little question that, as Congress has changed, the character of the Speakership has changed. The current Speaker, Thomas P. "Tip" O'Neill, has noted some of the contrasts between his role and that of Rayburn in the 1940s and 1950s:

> Old Sam Rayburn couldn't name twelve new members of Congress, and he was an institution that awed people. Only on the rarest of occasions could a Congressman get an appointment to see him. And when he called the Attorney General and said, "You be in my office at three in the afternoon," that Cabinet officer was there at three in the afternoon. Politics has changed. I have to deal in dialogue, in openness; if someone wants to see me, they see me. And of course they're highly independent now. You have to talk to people in the House, listen to them. The whole ethics question has changed. Years ago you'd think nothing of calling Internal Revenue and saying that this case has been kicking around for a couple of years, and it ought to be civil instead of criminal. You'd think nothing of calling a chairman of a committee and saying, "Put this project in, put this dam in." Well, you can't do that now.[3]*

Yet the Speaker remains the most influential member of Congress. The difference is that he now shares power with committee chairpersons, senior members, and spokespersons for various sections of the country.

*© 1977 by The New York Times Company. Reprinted by permission.

*"So far, my mail is running three to one in favor of my position."*
(Drawing by Robt. Day; © 1970 The New Yorker Magazine, Inc.)

The Speaker is aided by the majority leader, who serves as the chief floor manager and spokesperson for the party. Operating in concert, they schedule bills for consideration, serve as the nerve center of party strategy, and attempt to maximize the party's voting strength. The majority leader has usually been a confidant, indeed a protégé, of the Speaker and more often than not has succeeded to that office when a vacancy occurs. He is assisted by a majority whip, who is responsible for notifying members of pending debates and scheduled floor votes. The whip maintains a network of assistant whips who keep him informed of members' voting intentions and seek to guarantee their presence on the floor for key votes. The effectiveness of the whip organization is important to the party's policy success. The results of their repeated polls of members' intentions are important to the development of floor strategy and provide time for the Speaker and/or the majority leader to make personal contact with recalcitrant members.

The party officers of the minority parallel those of the majority. The minority leader and the minority whip carry out the same functions as their majority counterparts. The minority leader is the opposition party's candidate for Speaker—a contest decided by a straight party vote. The top leaders in each party confer regularly and cooperate in planning the schedule of the House.

Senate leaders have not been so strong as those in the House. This disparity has resulted from the earlier consolidation of power in the hands of the Speaker and the relatively later emergence of important Senate leaders. It has also stemmed from the smaller size of the Senate and the presence of more publicly recognizable members. Some Senate leaders—for example, Lyndon B. Johnson for the Democrats and Everett M. Dirksen and Howard Baker, Jr., for the Republicans—have impressed their personalities and political talents on the leadership posts of their respective parties and have provided a reservoir of strength that enhanced their power in the Senate. Normally, though, floor leaders and whips operate much as they do in the House, but with considerably less control over their members. Our emphasis here on the leaders is illustrative of their importance in orchestrating the influence of political parties in Congress.

Party leaders provide focus for party influence. Real power in the Senate and the House is diffused among the members, the committees, the informal groups, and other internal agencies and is strongly influenced by input from executive agencies. In view of the somewhat limited power of party leaders and in the face of the individual ambitions and objectives of the members, it may be that little more can be done to lead than is now done. The Senate and the House party leaders serve as strategists to schedule legislation, keep members informed, round up support for or against the president's program, and serve as party spokespersons when necessary. They arbitrate disputes between committees and subcommittees and various of the proliferating special caucuses. They serve as both legislative and political contacts with the White House, and they are often placed in the role of catalyst vis-à-vis the interest groups. Given the lack of responsible party government in the United States, political leadership in the Congress must act on the basis of both formal and informal powers as well as the personalities of the elected leaders. The job has always been difficult, but the recent rise of numerous informal groups, such as special caucuses, as well as the increasing power of the subcommittee network, has made it even more complex.

## Informal Groups in the House

Reform had not yet come to the House of Representatives in the 1950s. Even then, though, large numbers of newly elected, more liberal Democrats were entering the House only to find themselves frustrated and impotent when faced with the power structure that seniority had built. That power structure was represented by the slogan "To get along, go along." Committee chairpersons attained their powerful places in the hierarchy of the majority party by longer staying power based on the built-in advantages of their incumbency, the carefully drawn protective district boundaries that discouraged opposition, and their ability to deliver goods for their people back home. Most of them were southerners, representing one-party districts, where success in the primary guaranteed a free ride back to Washington in the next general election.

In 1959 about eighty liberal Democrats joined forces to establish the Democratic Study Group (DSG), a collection of issue-oriented, urban, and western Democrats. Dissatisfied with the party leadership and believing themselves isolated from the policy machinery of the majority of which they were a part, the group began to meet regularly and to study issues and tactics. They saw themselves, to some extent, as a counterweight to the dominant southern Democratic bloc that then held control. They used the discharge petition and other previously little-used parliamentary devices to demonstrate to their colleagues that they meant to have a voice. Originally, the DSG concentrated on research and discussion, seeking to build a liberal bloc of support on committee actions and in floor votes. Ultimately, they won the tacit approval of the leadership and began to see some benefits from their cooperative effort.

The DSG now has an executive committee and a task force organization that concentrates on substantive questions such as civil and human rights, consumer affairs, and international affairs. It has a small professional staff, which conducts research and furnishes members with brief fact sheets on issues of importance, and it has its own whip system, which operates much like the official whip system in the party organization of the House. In recent years the DSG has attempted to provide campaign funds for Democratic liberals running in districts targeted as marginal, and its membership has grown to between 200 and 250. One 1974 study concluded that

> for the most part DSG cohesion has increased relative to that of other groups, and . . . the positions taken on issues by DSG members usually are easily distinguishable from those of nonmembers. More important, however, the evidence is unmistakable that the Democratic Study Group members are, on most issues, quite united and that they constitute a formidable bloc, . . . and there is some evidence that, even on roll-call voting, turnout of DSG members has increased by DSG efforts.[4]

Another study has shown that the Democratic Study Group did about as well providing cues to the Democratic members in making voting decisions as did the party leaders and the party majority. It also gave slightly negative cues to Republicans.[5] All in all, the Democratic Study Group has become an influential force within the House, one that took a leading role in the major reforms of the 1970s—reforms that opened avenues of power to a larger and more diverse group of members of Congress than ever before.

Two Republican groups have been formed in recent years and are in some respects the counterparts of the DSG. The first of these was the Wednesday Group, formed in 1963–64 by fourteen liberal Republicans. Membership is by invitation and, with the recent addition of some moderates, usually runs from twenty to thirty–five members. The Wednesday Group holds weekly meetings (naturally on a Wednesday) to exchange ideas and explore issues. A small staff produces research papers, and the members occasionally form task forces to study certain issues in greater depth. Unlike the DSG, the Wednesday Group does not seek to mobilize voting strength and has no formal organization of whips. It differs from the DSG in one other important respect: whereas the Democratic Study Group represents a majority of the Democratic members of the House and cooperates with the leadership, the Wednesday Group represents a small minority of the Republican members and often disagrees with the party leadership.[6] A more recent, larger, and possibly more important programmatic group is the Republican Study Committee, formed in 1973 to promote conservative positions within the party councils. The brainchild of "New Right" leader Paul Weyrich, the RSC was by 1980 over twice as large as the Wednesday Group and had considerably more influence in House party affairs. It too publishes policy fact sheets to make known its views.

The Democratic Study Group, the Wednesday Group, and the Republican Study Committee are the three principal unofficial alliances in the House. In recent years, however, other such groups have been created in order to push for a particular type of legislation or to gain a greater voice in deliberations. The best-known of these is the Black Caucus, formed by nine black congressional representatives in 1969. Since then, the number of blacks elected to Congress has increased to twenty-one, including the nonvoting delegate from the District of Columbia. The Black Caucus has concerned itself with the legislative interests of the black population. It has organized conferences on the impact of budget cuts on programs that serve black constituents and on educational problems. It has sometimes been quite vocal, and the publicity that the group receives belies its small size. On occasion, it joins forces with other groups, such as the small Women's Caucus, with which it shares some members.

As the 98th Congress opened in 1983, a record twenty-one women took their seats. Many of them, as in the past, will be members of the Women's Caucus, which, for several years, has monitored women's legislation and sought to improve the number and role of women in government. Only about half the women members of Congress have joined the caucus, and it has not proved very effective. In 1981 the group voted to admit forty-six congressmen to its ranks because of a change in rules adopted in 1981 by the House Committee on Administration.

The rapid escalation in the number of such caucuses in recent years forced the committee to take action to gain some degree of control over them. In 1980 about eight special caucuses raised more than $1.8 million from private sources.[7] The new rule requires a caucus to move off government property if it receives contributions from outside interests or lobbyists. The Women's Caucus, for one, was forced to increase its revenue by a dues structure to make up for the money it normally received in subscriptions to its newsletter (an outside source). Other groups, such as the Black Caucus, the Sun Belt Caucus, the New England Congressional Caucus, and the Shipyard Caucus, were also affected by the rule. These groups were originally formed to provide legislative support services to House members interested in particular issues or regions, but critics contend that they have come to serve only as inside-Congress special interest groups and that some kind of control had to be exercised over them.

Finally, each class of freshmen representatives, both Democratic and Republican, has followed the practice of setting up organizations, some of which have persisted beyond the first two years of the members' terms. These groups have seldom had an impact on the House. In 1975, however, seventy-five freshmen Democrats organized early and began to involve themselves actively in the affairs of the House. The class of '74 invited committee heads to appear before them, and the poor impression made by some of these individuals contributed to their defeat for reelection as chairpersons in the Democratic Caucus.

Groups such as those discussed in this section serve as supplementary avenues through which congressional representatives can affect policy. Some are of only minor importance, but others, such as the Democratic Study Group, have carved for themselves a role of considerable influence.

Some state party delegations in the House of Representatives meet regularly as an informal method of imparting information, assessing views, and seeking agreement on matters that might affect the welfare of their home states. Sometimes delegations strive to vote together in order to improve their bargaining position with regard to matters of relevance to their state. Other delegations, however, meet regularly, even though the individual members may disagree to an extent that makes joint actions unlikely. The large Texas delegation, for instance, has been meeting weekly for many years in spite of the fact that the members of the group disagree on many policy positions. The delegation as a whole simply believes that it is beneficial to the state for them to meet in order to enhance chances for getting federal projects or federal appointments for Texas. Some state delegations work closely together, others do not. Indeed, some are unable to agree on enough matters to make themselves effective as delegations. The New York delegation in the House has been generally ineffective as a unit for years because of rapid turnover and the great disparity of views among its members.

## The Party and the Congressional Committee System

One of the major responsibilities of Congress is to pass legislation. Virtually all legislation is political in one way or another. All of it must be filtered through the standing committee system, and that process is so infused with party politics that partisan considerations cannot be overlooked when any bill of any importance is discussed. In 1982 there were fifteen standing committees and five select or special committees in the Senate and twenty-three standing and three select or special committees in the House. Most of them are further broken down into subcommittees to deal with particular subjects within the parent committee's jurisdiction. The standing committees continue from one session to the next unless the congressional majority actually votes to change the committee structure. The select or special committees are ad hoc groups set up to deal with "temporary" problems that arise. Some special committees have existed for so long that they have gained a degree of permanence.

Ninety years ago Woodrow Wilson described the committees of Congress as the "little legislatures" in which the real work of the Congress is accomplished. Since that time, they have, if anything, become even more important because of the greater complexity of the issues that come before them for consideration. Technocracy has made the actions of committees on pending legislation almost tantamount to passage by the entire body, since both houses are inclined to accept the recommendations of the appropriate standing committee.

A review of the roster of committees in either house provides an overview of the kinds of problems faced by the Congress (see "Senate and House Standing Committees," below). In the Senate these range from important groups that oversee functions of fundamental importance, such as the Appropriations, Budget, and Foreign Relations committees, to committees that serve the needs of some particular segment of society, such as the Agriculture, Nutrition and Forestry, Energy and Natural Resources, and Veterans' Affairs committees. In the House the structure of committees is often parallel to that of the Senate, although some, such as the Ways and Means Committee responsible for the constitutional authority of the House to raise revenue, are unique to that body.

The committee system contributes both to congressional order and, because of its division of responsibilities, to its fragmentation. In the House, for instance, energy legislation has become ensnarled in the multijurisdictional committee and subcommittee structure. Four major standing committees and five subcommittees have jurisdiction over some aspect of all energy bills. The failure of the House to concentrate jurisdiction is responsible for considerable inefficiency and frustration. House members, however, argue that their multicommittee approach provides greater access to the public. The Senate in 1977 established a new Standing Committee on Energy and Natural Resources and removed jurisdiction over energy matters from other committees, including the Public Works, Armed Services, and Atomic Energy committees. This consolidation of energy concerns in the hands of one committee in the Senate is more efficient and works against fragmentation and delay.

Each standing and select committee is composed of a majority of members from the party holding the majority of seats in that house, as well as a minority representation in most cases equivalent to the proportion of seats held by the minority party. Thus, the Senate Agricultural, Nutrition, and Forestry Committee, which had ten Republicans and eight Democrats in the 98th Congress of 1983, was further broken down into seven subcommittees: Agricultural Credit and Rural Electrification; Agricultural Production, Marketing, and Stabilization of Prices; Agricultural Research and General Legislation; Foreign Agricultural Policy; Forestry, Water Resources, and Environment; Rural Development, Oversight, and Investigations; and Soil and Water Conservation. Each of these subcommittees is composed of members of the full committee,

## Senate and House Standing Committees, 98th Congress, 1983–1985

| *Senate* | *House* |
|---|---|
| Agriculture, Nutrition, and Forestry | Agriculture |
| Appropriations | Appropriations |
| Armed Services | Armed Services |
| Banking, Housing, and Urban Affairs | Banking, Finance, and Urban Affairs |
| Budget | Budget |
| Commerce, Science, and Transportation | District of Columbia |
| Energy and Natural Resources | Education and Labor |
| Environment and Public Works | Energy and Commerce |
| Finance | Foreign Affairs |
| Foreign Relations | Government Operations |
| Governmental Affairs | House Administration |
| Judiciary | Interior and Insular Affairs |
| Labor and Human Resources | Interstate and Foreign Commerce |
| Rules and Administration | Judiciary |
| Veterans' Affairs | Merchant Marine and Fisheries |
|  | Post Office and Civil Service |
| *Select Committees* | Public Works and Transportation |
| Select Ethics | Rules |
| Select Indian Affairs | Science and Technology |
| Select Intelligence | Small Business |
| Select Small Business | Standards of Official Conduct |
| Special Aging | Veterans' Affairs |
|  | Ways and Means |
|  |  |
|  | *Select Committees* |
|  | Select Aging |
|  | Select Intelligence |
|  | Select Narcotics Abuse and Control |

*Source: Congressional Quarterly Weekly Report* (January 15, 1983): 139–146.

and in 1983–1984 each had a majority of Republicans and a minority of Democrats. The same pattern prevails throughout the legislative standing committee system. In the 98th Congress all of the Senate standing committees had a small majority of Republican members, and in the House all but one of them had a slightly larger margin of Democratic members, reflecting the larger margin of Democrats in the overall House membership. The very fact that each committee is carefully given a majority of members from the controlling party indicates the influence of party in that body. The only two committees that do not have a larger majority than minority membership are the Senate Select Committee on Ethics and the House Standing Committee on Standards of Conduct, both of which have equal membership from both parties.

## Choosing Committee Members

Congressional committee members are chosen differently today than in the old days of seniority dominance. Beginning in 1969, the Democratic Study Group took the lead in a seven-year fight to reform the rules, including those under which House committee chairpersons and members were selected. Until that time, the Democratic members of the House Ways and Means Committee had served ex officio as the Democratic Committee on Committees and had made committee assignments each year according to traditional seniority rules. The first step toward reform was taken in 1969 when, over the objections of the Speaker, it was voted to hold regular meetings of the Democratic Caucus, with members having the right to place items on the agenda.

In 1971 the caucus asserted the right to permit any ten members to demand a debate and vote on the nominations made by the Committee on Committees (then chaired by Congressman Wilbur Mills, chairman of the Ways and Means Committee). At the same time the caucus adopted a far-reaching change permitting no one to chair more than one legislative subcommittee, although by a "grandfather" clause it allowed those who headed more than one at that time to retain their positions. In 1973 the caucus voted to subject any chairperson to a secret ballot vote at the request of 20 percent of the caucus, although the new procedure did not deprive any chairperson of office that year. The same year the caucus adopted new rules governing subcommittees and guaranteeing members some voice in the composition and operations of the committee substructure. With the addition of seventy-five new Democrats in 1975, the caucus used its secret vote to depose three committee heads, and another, Wilbur Mills, resigned from his committee post rather than face an unfavorable vote.

Other substantive changes in the House shifted the Democratic Committee on Committees from the Ways and Means Committee to the caucus's own Steering and Policy Committee; required that all committees create at least four subcommittees; gave the Speaker sole power to nominate Democratic members of the important Rules Committee (which controls what bills get on the floor and under what conditions); opened more committee and subcommittee meetings to the public; and, gave committee members the right to bid for subcommittee membership in order of their committee seniority. Since committee members were not allowed to retain membership on more than two subcommittees, the bidding procedure had the effect of making several choice assignments available to junior members. The cumulative effect of these reforms clearly enhanced the power of subcommittee heads and caucus and party leaders. Committee heads had lost power and in the process became more deferential to relatively young, even freshmen, members to whom they had paid scant attention in earlier days.[8]

The recent strengthening of the subcommittee system is important because it has shifted power from the standing committees. The growth in the number of subcommittees to nearly three hundred has provided new avenues for advancement and public attention for relatively young House members. Individual members have been able to develop specialties and to gain prestige in a way the old seniority system did not permit. The changes have caused the political system in the House to become vastly more decentralized. Power relationships have been altered, and committee heads have considerably less influence than they once did. They can neither dominate nor manipulate the work of their committee or their subcommittees as was customary before 1971. Indeed, it is ironic that the majority party caucus was recently strengthened, thus enhancing centralized authority, while the actions that undercut the traditional committee system have decentralized power among the many subcommittees.

House Republicans have a special committee on committees comprised of one member from every state that has a Republican member. Actual committee assignments are made, however, by an executive committee, which always has representatives from those states with the largest Republican delegations (e.g., California, Illinois, Michigan, Ohio, and Pennsylvania). Voting is based on the number of Republican members from a state, so that those states with the most members dominate the selection process. Even though the states with the greatest number of Republican members are industrial and urban in nature, the members of the Committee on Committees tend to be from rural Republican areas. In recent years there has been little disposition on the part of Republicans in the House to tamper with the system.

Senate procedures for appointing committee members are less formal. Both parties have a committee on committees, but their structure and functions differ in many respects. In the Democratic party the committee on committees is called the Steering Committee; for years it was a tool of the Senate Democratic establishment. Its sole function was to choose committee members, and its decisions could not be appealed. Both Majority Leader Lyndon B. Johnson and his successor, Mike Mansfield, began a process of bringing younger and more liberal members into important committee seats.

As the old southern Senate leaders began to die or to retire, changes in the makeup of the Steering Committee were reflected in the standing committees. More and more northern Democratic liberals became committee heads, and by 1978 eight of the fifteen standing committees in the Senate were chaired by members from northern, western, or border states, as opposed to only two from those areas in 1961. Since the early 1950s an unwritten rule has held that all Democrats should be appointed to one key committee assignment before any Democrat is appointed to more than one. Once appointed to the committees, however, the members remain on by automatic reappointment.

Committee assignments took on added importance in 1980 when the Republicans won control of the Senate for the first time since 1954. The Senate Republicans make original assignments through a committee on committees that makes its choices based on seniority. In 1965 the Republicans adopted a rule that no Republican could hold seats on more than one of the four most desired committees—Appropriations, Armed Services, Finance, and Foreign Relations—until every senator of that party had had a chance to refuse such a seat. In 1982, although the Senate Republicans were a generally conservative group, committee chairs were almost equally divided between conservatives and moderates.

To place too much emphasis on the party composition of the standing committees and subcommittees can be somewhat misleading. Committees seldom vote strictly along party lines, and some committees operate almost in a nonpartisan fashion. Others are unabashedly partisan. Senate committees are more likely to downplay partisan differences when they can. The level of partisanship is determined by such factors as the personality of the chairperson, the number of ambitious committee members using the assignment as a forum, and the subject matter with which the committee deals. Much depends on the chairperson's attitude and on whether or not he or she desires to be aggressively partisan or to seek accommodation with the minority.

Heads of committees in both the House and Senate are less powerful than they once were. Especially in the House, the Democratic reforms of the past few years have made committee heads more responsive to the members and have reduced the power that they had formerly exercised by custom and tradition. Even so, committee heads are very influential in determining the final outcome of policy questions, either because of their own personal standing with the members of their committee or because they have learned how to use the resources of staff, agenda, and procedure. Sometimes committee heads are able to wield power because other members hope someday to chair a committee, and, consequently, they do not challenge the head's authority lest this permanently diminish the strength of the position.

Nevertheless, a chairperson can go too far and bring about results not to his or her liking. Probably the most famous recent example of this was the experience of the late Rep. Adam Clayton Powell of New York, chairman of the House Education and Labor Committee, one of the most partisan of all House committees. In 1966 the Powell committee reported an important antipoverty bill, but three months later Powell still had not scheduled it for floor action, even suggesting that it might not come up until after the November elections. The majority of the committee, especially the Democratic members, revolted against what they considered to be irresponsible behavior on the part of the chairman—a pattern of behavior that was not unusual for Powell. Committee members had long been critical of Powell for a high rate of absenteeism, arbitrary hiring and firing of staff, misuse of committee funds, and refusal to report favorable committee actions for floor consideration. The antipoverty bill was the final indignity for many of the committee's members, and the committee voted twenty-seven to one, with three abstentions, to strip the chairman of much of his power to dominate the committee.[9] Such actions have repercussions that extend to other committee heads who may be engaged in similar practices.

In 1982 a highly visible Democrat from Texas, Congressman Phil Gramm, was removed from his seat on the important Budget Committee because the Democrats in the House felt that he should be punished for his close two-year collaboration with the White House in adoption of the Reagan budget. Gramm had worked closely with the White House in the 97th Congress, even supplying presidential aides with reports on the budget strategy of his fellow Democrats. In early January 1983 Gramm was removed by a vote of twenty-six to four in the Steering and Policy Committee and promptly announced his resignation from Congress and his decision to run for reelection to his seat as a Republican in a special election. In the February special election he was reelected. Even though Gramm was not a committee chairperson, his ouster from the important Budget Committee was illustrative of the new committee assignment system and of the way in which the leadership can punish members who stray too far from desirable partisan behavior.

The House Rules Committee is one of the most powerful and influential committees in either house of Congress. Its influence comes from its role as "traffic cop" for legislation. The Rules Committee has the power to determine just how a bill goes to the floor—or, indeed, whether it goes to the floor at all. This power places the committee in a crucial position in the legislative process in the House. Partly because of its large size the House needs to operate under tighter and more restrictive rules than the Senate. The Rules Committee sets the time limits for debate, decides whether or not to permit amendments to bills, and defines types of amendments. The committee also sends bills to conference committees composed of members of both houses; these joint bodies reconcile the differences between companion bills that have passed their respective bodies.

Until 1910 the Rules Committee was a personal tool of the Speaker, who appointed its members and served as its chairman. From 1910 to World War II the committee still remained almost an adjunct to the Speaker, although he no longer appointed the members or served on the committee. From the late 1930s until 1960 the committee was controlled by a coalition of southern Democrats and conservative Republicans, who used it as a vehicle to kill liberal Democratic legislation and to stymie other policy initiatives with which the members disagreed. In 1961 the House increased the size of the committee temporarily so that the Democratic leadership could appoint some new members; this provided a chance for control of the committee to shift to the liberals. In 1963 the enlarged committee was made permanent, and it was clear that the ploy had worked, as the stifling of liberal legislation virtually ceased. By late 1970 the Rules Committee, dominated by liberal Democrats, had become supportive of the leadership and was working to further leadership goals. Recently, the majority leadership enhanced its influence through a Democratic rules change authorizing the Speaker to nominate all of the Democratic members of the committee.

## The Conference Committee

Earlier we mentioned the institution of the Conference Committee. When the Senate and the House pass two differing versions of the same bill, it is necessary to "send it to conference" to reconcile the differences before the final act is sent to the president for signature. Used since 1789, the Conference Committee plays an important and crucial role in the legislative process because its reports are not amendable and are ordinarily accepted by both houses as presented. Composed of the senior members of the relevant standing committees in each house, a conference becomes necessary when the committee that originally reported the bill refuses to accept the changes made in the bill by the other house. If the differences are minor, they can often be worked out without a conference, but any degree of complexity or controversy will usually force the bill to conference.

Normally, the individual delegations representing the two houses will be expected to seek agreement with their respective versions, but it is assumed that compromise will be necessary in order for a report to result. Sometimes delegates are given free reign, and on other occasions they may be instructed by the parent chamber concerning the limits of compromise that will be tolerated. Once agreed upon, however, the conference report is usually accepted by both houses, sometimes by voice vote. If no agreement is possible, the bill may die in conference. Evidence suggests that since World War II the Senate has dominated conference committees in terms of gaining acceptance of more of its provisions than the House. David J. Vogler, in studying a selected group of conferences for the period 1945 to 1966, found that the Senate won the largest number of decisions on a wide variety of issues.[10]

# Influences on Congressional Voting

To what extent do political parties in Congress affect the voting behavior of legislators? This question has been debated since representative democracy was invented.

## Concepts of Representation

There are generally three different concepts of representation:

1. *Trustee.* The first, and best-known, is the classic *trustee* model advocated by Edmund Burke in his famous "Speech to the Electors of Bristol" in 1774. Burke, a political philosopher and member of Parliament for thirty years, conceded that the representative ought to maintain close contact with his constituents, but he maintained

that he should never sacrifice his "unbiased opinion, his mature judgment, his enlightened conscience . . . to any man." The legislator, Burke believed, should not blindly follow "authoritative instructions" or "mandates" from constituents. In the Burkean view, the representative was a trustee who, once elected, should make decisions based on his own will and judgment, not the collective wishes of his constituents.[11]

2. *Delegate.* A second model of representation is that of the *delegate.* The delegate, according to those who argue in behalf of this theory, should follow the popular will. T. V. Smith, political philosopher and elected legislator, maintained that "it is indeed the primary business of Congress to discern and follow the popular will when there is a popular will, and to do nothing when there isn't, save to talk around and about until there is a popular will."[12] In other words, the representative should only act in behalf of his constituents' wishes—and should not use his own judgment in making decisions. Legislators, in Smith's view, are sent to the seat of government to represent the wishes of the majority, not to vote according to their own consciences.

3. *Politico.* The third style of representation is that of the *politico,* "who votes on different bases depending on the issues being confronted."[13] The politico attempts to balance the wishes of his constituents, his own conscience, and his personal knowledge, casting some votes because of district wishes and others because it is the right thing to do. Politicos incorporate a good measure of pragmatic flexibility into their personal decision making.

## How Legislators Decide to Vote

Discussing how decisions on voting are made in terms of trustees, delegates, and politicos is a convenient way to consider the various elements that are incorporated into the legislator's individual voting decision. Obviously, the legislator does not sit down and say, "Well, on this particular bill I am going to vote as a trustee." As the floor vote (or the committee vote, for that matter) nears, the individual representative or senator may be subjected to pressure from voters in his or her district, lobbyists, the White House, the congressional leadership of his or her party, and fellow members. On a controversial matter the legislator should weigh its merits, study the issue, seek expert advice, and discuss the political implications with the party leadership or the White House.

Most of the time, however, this kind of careful preparation and consideration does not occur. The volume of legislation is too great for much time to be spent on any particular piece of legislation. The members sometimes will be told by their legislative aides or some other staff persons how to vote. On occasion, the bill will be of such importance to their district or to some interest group to which they are beholden that it is virtually impossible for them to vote against these wishes even if they disagree personally with that position. Furthermore, legislators will usually have considerable difficulty determining how their constituents feel; even if constituents have any interest in the matter, clear-cut expressions of constituent opinion are relatively rare. True, legislators may receive some letters and telephone calls pro or con, but they have no way of knowing whether they are representative of general constituent thought or mere isolated opinions from concerned citizens. It is difficult for congressional representatives or state legislators to tell whether an outpouring of sentiment on an issue represents a ground swell of public opinion or the views of local pressure groups.

**Actors and decision making.**    Many scholars have studied the way in which House members or state legislators make up their minds. John Kingdon, in his study *Congressional Voting Decisions,* surveyed a representative sample of over two hundred House members and coded their responses to spontaneous comments as to the actors who were influential in their decision making. Kingdon presumed that, if the congressional representative mentioned the actor spontaneously, it could be assumed that the actor was of sufficient importance to be added to the decision-making equation. He classified the responses into four categories: (1) the actor was of no importance in the decision; (2) the actor was of minor importance—that is, the House member noted the position and checked it, but the actor was of no greater significance; (3) the actor was of major importance, and the actor's views were weighed carefully and had an impact on the congress member's thinking, regardless of whether or not his or her vote matched the actor's advice; and (4) the actor determined the decision to the exclusion of other influences. Kingdon also coded responses according to their "overall importance in the congressman's decision, regardless of the time it is mentioned in the interview." The pattern of the two responses was roughly the same and was summarized by Kingdon as follows:

> Party leadership and staffs turn out to be the least important of the potential influences on the decision, and reading is not much more important than they. Fellow congressmen and constituency are the most important actors, followed again by interest groups and administration, in that order. Single actors very rarely determine the congressman's vote to the exclusion of other influences, and the only actor which approaches being of major importance half the time is fellow congressmen, followed by constituency.[14]

Kingdon concluded that, "by any measure, fellow congressmen turn out to be highly important influences on votes. . . . They are readily available" and "they are also known quantities. . . ." He found that the major criteria for selecting whom to consult among one's fellows were the informant's agreement with one's point of view and the informant's expertise, that is, his or her membership on the committee that considered the bill.[15]

Another scholar, Roger Davidson, observed that over half the House members he interviewed "tended to disagree" or did "disagree" with this statement: "If a bill is important for his party's record, a member should vote with his party even if it costs him some support in his district." Clearly, both of these studies found party influence to be of relatively less importance than other considerations in the decision-making process of individual House members.[16]

**Cue givers.**    A number of studies have attempted to assess the impact of party on congressional voting. The results of these studies often appear to be dependent on the kinds of questions posed and the particular milieu in which they were asked. The evidence has not been clear as to the impact of various forces on legislative decision making. One study covering the period from 1957 to 1964 attempted to assess the relative impact on House members' voting decisions of state party delegations, the president, party leaders, party majority, House majority, committee heads, ranking committee members, and the Democratic Study Group. Each of these was identified by Matthews and Stimson as a cue giver, that is, as a source of cues to which members respond in reaching decisions that come to roll-call votes.[17] As shown in table 9-1, the most important single cue giver in both parties is the member's state party delegation. In addition,

> two additional collective cues—the party majority and the House majority—are also potent, especially among the Democrats (who were in the majority all eight years). The President as a *direct* cue-giver is seemingly less significant, although Kennedy and Johnson did considerably better among Democrats than Eisenhower did among Republicans as a direct source of cues.[18]

As noted in table 9-1, the Matthews-Stimson findings show a possible variation in the figures, ranging from 0.50 (perfect agreement between the average Democratic or Republican House member and a cue giver) to −0.50 (perfect disagreement). The table reports two periods: 1957–1960, when a Republican was president, and 1961–1964, when a Democrat was president. Party leaders were important cue givers, especially for the Democrats under a Democratic president. The party majority was consistently important for members of both parties. Clearly, cue giving and cue taking show patterns of regularity and predictability. Once the individual members have received the various cues from inside and outside the Congress, they filter them through the litmus paper of their consciences and, applying their political acumen, reach a decision.

On most important votes, the average House members do not find unusual disagreement among their friends, fellow members, staff, constituents, or party leaders. The more controversial a bill is, the greater the chance that there will be disparity within the cue-giving group, but, on most routine matters, members encounter few problems in deciding how to vote.

## Party Cohesion

A variety of studies of roll-call voting in Congress and in some of the competitive two-party state legislatures have shown that on most roll calls the voting is determined more often by party lines than by any other factor. Many of these studies have used highly complex statistical tests to determine the levels of party-line voting in the House and Senate. However, some of the better-known results have come from the application of relatively simple measurement devices. One of these is the use of the "90 percent versus 90 percent" standard, which compares roll-call votes in which 90 percent of the Democrats have voted one way and 90 percent of the Republicans another.

TABLE 9–1   Cue sources for members of Congress, 1957–1964

|  | *Average cue scores* | | | |
|  | *Democrats* | | *Republicans* | |
| *Cue source* | *1957–1960* | *1961–1964* | *1957–1960* | *1961–1964* |
|---|---|---|---|---|
| State party delegation | 0.42 | 0.43 | 0.37 | 0.38 |
| President | 0.04 | 0.32 | 0.13 | −0.16 |
| Party leaders | 0.27 | 0.34 | 0.26 | 0.28 |
| Party majority | 0.34 | 0.37 | 0.35 | 0.37 |
| House majority | 0.31 | 0.39 | 0.20 | 0.23 |
| Committee chairmen | 0.19 | 0.31 | −0.05 | −0.09 |
| Ranking members | −0.05 | −0.01 | 0.08 | 0.19 |
| Democratic Study Group | 0.29 | 0.35 | −0.09 | −0.09 |

*Source:* Cited in Randall B. Ripley, *Congress: Process and Policy*, 2nd ed. (New York: W. W. Norton & Co., 1978), p. 136, as adapted from *Political Decision Making*, ed. S. Sidney Ulmer. © 1970 by Litton Educational Publishing, Inc. Reprinted by permission of Van Nostrand Reinhold Company.

This standard is thought to be too high for American legislative bodies, with their relaxed party discipline. In a classic study covering the years 1921 to 1948, Julius Turner found that only 17 percent of the roll calls in the House of Representatives met the 90 percent standard. Edward Schneier updated Turner's work from 1950 to 1967 and discovered that party-line voting declined to between 2 and 8 percent in the House during those years, depending on the session.[19]

If one relaxes the standard of measurement to a fifty-fifty ratio, the proportion of party votes rises sharply. *Congressional Quarterly* has measured the "party unity score" of each member of the House and Senate by calculating the percentage of times the member votes with his or her party on roll calls on which the two parties are opposed. The member's score, therefore, is the percentage of party unity votes on which a member votes "yea" or "nay" in agreement with a majority of his or her party. Failure to vote, under this method, lowers the member's score. As shown in table 9-2, party unity scores vacillated considerably between 1973 and 1982.

Since 1970 the two houses of Congress have had Democratic majorities voting against Republican majorities 27 to 48 percent of the time, the percentage being lower in the second session of each Congress than in the first. There is no acknowledged reason for this, although it might reflect the greater pull of constituency over party as the election season approaches. Even so, it should be remembered that these data reflect only those roll calls that met the fifty-fifty standard; many other votes were not included.

The issues involved in the differing party votes have remained rather consistent over the years. One study found that party conflict was consistent on bills that involved agriculture, labor, business, the tariff, and social welfare legislation. With regard to agriculture, Democrats have usually argued that the federal government should take greater responsibility for the development of price-support programs, food stamps, and other proposals that they believe would aid the farmer. Republicans, on the other hand, have opposed development of extensive federal programs for agriculture and have been apt to support freedom from government controls. Democrats have been more interested in programs to support organized labor and lower-income groups, not only in the realm of labor-management legislation but also in support of govern-

TABLE 9–2    Congressional party unity votes, 1970–1982

| Year | Senate | House | Both houses |
|------|--------|-------|-------------|
| 1970 | 35% | 27% | 32% |
| 1971 | 42 | 38 | 40 |
| 1972 | 36 | 27 | 33 |
| 1973 | 40 | 42 | 41 |
| 1974 | 44 | 29 | 37 |
| 1975 | 48 | 48 | 48 |
| 1976 | 37 | 36 | 37 |
| 1977 | 42 | 42 | 42 |
| 1978 | 45 | 33 | 38 |
| 1979 | 47 | 47 | 47 |
| 1980 | 46 | 38 | 41 |
| 1981 | 48 | 37 | 43 |
| 1982 | 43 | 36 | 40 |

*Source: Congressional Quarterly Almanac, 1971–1981*
(Washington, D.C.: Congressional Quarterly, Inc.);
1982 figures from *Congressional Quarterly Weekly Report* (January 15, 1983): 107.

ment health and social welfare programs, such as medical care, aid to education, and antipoverty efforts. Republicans have been more consistent in their support of business interests and have more readily opposed increased government involvement in social welfare programs. Finally, Democrats have a long-standing record of support for low tariffs, whereas Republicans have favored higher ones.[20]

Party unity in congressional voting is a dynamic measure that changes from year to year with the political tides. The election in 1980 of Ronald Reagan and the first Republican majority in the Senate since 1954 had a decided impact on party unity scores (see table 9-2). During the first session of the 97th Congress, after President Reagan was inaugurated, Senate Republicans achieved a striking gain in solidarity as they sought to follow their president's leadership. For this and other reasons, Senate Democrats also raised their party unity scores. In the Democratic-controlled House of Representatives, however, party unity actually declined slightly from 1980, reflecting greater contentiousness in that body over the Reagan program. As in the past, though, unity scores in both houses declined in the second session of that Congress, in 1982. All of these changes over the years have not been simple responses to presidential pressure. Rather, it is reasonably safe to say that they have emerged from the characteristics of the congressional districts and states that elected the congressmen and congresswomen. They may also reflect the short-term efforts of interest-group representatives to sway votes in one direction or the other. Certainly, ideological and programmatic distinctions in voting are probably built into the differences in party unity scores between the two parties and the two houses.

In the area of foreign policy the evidence of party cohesion is less than clear. At times the differences between the parties have been notable, and at other times there has been little to distinguish them. Between 1933 and 1948, a period encompassing the Great Depression and World War II, Republican and Democratic members of Congress differed substantially, according to Robert Dahl. Democrats tended to strongly support military appropriations, selective service, international organizations, and foreign aid, whereas Republicans, in the years before the war, were opposed to those efforts. This was an era of deep-seated isolationism centered in the midwestern heartland of Republicanism. The Neutrality acts were a product of the period. The division in public opinion gave rise to the stereotypes of Isolationist Republicans and Internationalist Democrats, and before American entry into World War II these terms had considerable validity.[21]

Eisenhower, elected in 1952, was perceived by many to be a peacemaker and an internationalist. This Republican president was able to overcome some of the party division on these issues, although his principal opponents were members of Congress from the isolationist wing of his own party.

The party division over foreign policy in the 1960s and 1970s has been less clear and must be approached with some caution. The Vietnam War, with its increasingly strident support from presidents of both parties, saw congressional opinion gradually coalesce until many members of both houses supported an end to the war at almost any cost. Some foreign policy decisions during the Vietnam era continued to produce differences in voting support between the parties, but such instances were clearly less frequent than in earlier eras.

It is interesting to note, however, that on several occasions in 1978 President Carter won substantial foreign-policy victories in Congress on the basis of substantial support from the Republican minority. On the Panama Canal treaties the president won approval by a Senate vote of sixty-eight to thirty-two, with sixteen Republicans supporting the treaties. On the sale of F-15 fighter planes to Saudi Arabia, a vote on a resolution to reject the sale was forty-four to fifty-four, with the Republicans furnishing twenty-six of the president's votes. Finally, on the issue of lifting the arms embargo on Turkey, the administration won fifty-seven to forty-two, with the help of twenty-seven Republicans. A majority of Senate Republicans backed the president on the plane sale and the arms embargo to Turkey, and in each case those votes were vital to his victory. On both votes a majority of Republican senators supported the president, and a majority of his own Democratic senators opposed him. Although the two parties again differed on two of the three issues, the difference was not what one might expect from a Democratic president and an overwhelmingly Democratic Senate.[22]

In 1981 President Reagan almost suffered a similar loss of support from his own party's senators over a resolution to disapprove the sale of five Airborne Warning and Control System (AWACS) radar planes and other arms to Saudi Arabia. Under a 1976 law, each house of Congress was given the power to veto major arms sales by a majority vote. Fifty senators originally cosponsored the resolution of disapproval, and the House had already passed a resolution denying the sale by a vote of 301 to 111. Thus rejection of the resolution in the Senate was crucial to the Reagan foreign policy. The president and his staff were forced to exert considerable pressure to convince seven Republican sponsors of the resolution to vote against it, thus providing the winning margin in the 48-to-52 vote. Clearly, on foreign-policy issues, party cohesion is less likely than on other issues to be a factor in the decisions of members of Congress.

Late in the Roosevelt administration, southern Democrats, more conservative than their northern colleagues, became increasingly disillusioned with the New Deal policies, which they believed favored organized labor and the urban Northeast. As the years went by, a southern Democratic-Republican coalition formed that came to have an unusually dramatic impact on congressional decision making for many years. V. O. Key, Jr., found that in 1937 the conservative coalition, which he defined as a majority of the southern Democrats and the Republicans opposing a majority of non-southern Democrats, prevailed on almost 10 percent of the roll calls that session. By 1945 the percentage had grown to 16.[23]

*Congressional Quarterly,* using the same measurement, has plotted coalition appearances and coalition victories since 1961. The overall number of coalition appearances has not substantially changed during that period, although variations ranged from 14 percent in 1962 to 30 percent in 1971.[24] Using Key's definition of the coalition—any vote in the House or Senate on which a majority of voting southern Democrats and a majority of voting Republicans opposed a stand taken by a majority of northern Democrats—the number of coalition victories has actually gone up during the period, reaching a high point in 1981. As shown in table 9-3, the conservative coalition was victorious 55 percent of the time in 1961; in 1977 the figure had grown to 68 percent with the dawn of the Carter administration but had declined sharply to 52 percent in 1978. The decline could be attributed to the coalition's failure to defeat the Panama Canal treaties and other matters that split the usual votes that make up the bipartisan conservative group. In 1981, the first year of the Reagan administration, the coalition showed a strength unequaled in twenty-five years of measuring the alliance, outpolling the northern Democrats on 92 percent of the recorded votes in which they faced off in both houses. This represented a 20 percent increase over the coalition's success in 1980. The renewed strength came from the election of considerable numbers

**TABLE 9–3**    Conservative coalition victories, 1961–1982

| Year | Total | Senate | House |
|------|-------|--------|-------|
| 1961 | 55%   | 48%    | 74%   |
| 1962 | 62    | 71     | 44    |
| 1963 | 50    | 44     | 67    |
| 1964 | 51    | 47     | 67    |
| 1965 | 33    | 39     | 25    |
| 1966 | 45    | 51     | 32    |
| 1967 | 63    | 54     | 73    |
| 1968 | 73    | 80     | 63    |
| 1969 | 68    | 67     | 71    |
| 1970 | 66    | 64     | 70    |
| 1971 | 83    | 86     | 79    |
| 1972 | 69    | 63     | 79    |
| 1973 | 61    | 54     | 67    |
| 1974 | 59    | 54     | 67    |
| 1975 | 50    | 48     | 52    |
| 1976 | 58    | 58     | 59    |
| 1977 | 68    | 74     | 60    |
| 1978 | 52    | 46     | 57    |
| 1979 | 70    | 65     | 73    |
| 1980 | 72    | 75     | 67    |
| 1981 | 92    | 95     | 88    |
| 1982 | 85    | 90     | 78    |

*Source: Congressional Quarterly Almanac,* 1981
(Washington, D.C.: Congressional Quarterly, Inc., 1982),
p. 36-C; 1982 figure from *Congressional Quarterly
Weekly Report* (January 15, 1983): 102.

of Republicans in both houses, in spite of the fact that fewer southern Democrats were elected. According to *Congressional Quarterly,* there were 86 Republicans and southern Democrats in the Senate at the beginning of the 97th Congress, as opposed to 60 at the start of the 96th. The comparative figures for the House of Representatives were 270 and 243.[25]

An important factor in the renewed strength of the 1981 coalition was the Reagan program, which generated a considerable number of votes on economic and budget matters. The 1982 decline, by the same token, represented the reduced strength the president was able to muster for his program in the face of a major recession and declining public support.

Any measurement of this type always involves extenuating circumstances that can lead to differing interpretations. For instance, *Congressional Quarterly* noted that the 1977 results were skewed by including 128 recorded votes taken by the Senate during the course of a filibuster against decontrol of natural gas prices. The conservative coalition appeared on 69 of those votes and won all but one. Vote followed vote with little debate in between as repeated roll calls were used as a parliamentary device.[26] If those votes are eliminated from consideration, the coalition success rate drops to 59 percent, about the same as it was in 1976 and only a little higher than in 1961.

As evidenced by the renewal of the coalition in 1981 and 1982, however, it is clear that trends in congressional voting can be measured reasonably well by devices such as party unity scores and conservative coalition scores. They do not tell us everything we might want to know about congressional voting behavior, but they do assist us in understanding some of the less obvious factors at work in Congress.

## Party Influence in the State Legislatures

In the fifty state legislatures, as in Congress, political party influence is important at both the organizational and the decision-making levels. Every state except Nebraska elects legislators on a political party ballot, and every state except Nebraska has two legislative houses. With fifty legislatures, there are innumerable possibilities for partisan control. After the 1982 elections, for instance, the Democrats controlled both houses in thirty-four states; the Republicans controlled both houses in twelve states; control was split between the parties in three states; and one (Nebraska) was elected on a nonpartisan ballot.[27] The variety of patterns of control and the fact that they shift almost every year or two make it quite difficult to generalize about party influence in state legislatures.

Over the past thirty years there has been a steady trend toward annual sessions as opposed to biennial sessions (every two years). The increasing complexities of state government, the need for more up-to-date information on dynamic economic and tax matters, and the greater degree of professionalization within the legislatures have exerted pressure for more frequent meetings. In most states the legislatures are allowed to discuss and act on any matter within state jurisdiction, but in several states every other session is devoted chiefly to the adoption of a state budget.

In general, legislatures are organized much like Congress, with party leaders, standing committees, caucuses, informal groups, and professional staffs, all of which affect policy results. All but a few states have established some form of legislative council to provide continuous study of policy problems and to assist with legislative planning. These councils are usually composed of legislators and often meet between the sessions to carry on the regular work of the legislative body. In those states that do not have a legislative council, there sometimes exist interim committees that meet periodically while the legislature is not in session, hold hearings on pending legislation, supervise administration, and engage in long-range policy planning. Regardless of the system used to cover the interim periods between legislative sessions, the majority party normally maintains control over the selection of those who take part.

### Legislative Leadership

Normally, lower houses are presided over by a speaker of the house who is elected by the house and is the leader of the majority party. The speaker has broad and extensive powers, which, in most states, establish him or her as the second-ranking state officer next to the governor. Usually, speakers' powers are comparable to those of the Speaker of the House in the U.S. House of Representatives. They preside over the sessions; have the power to recognize members; control floor debate; refer measures to committee; and, often, appoint committee members. Their power to control the makeup of committees as well as their legislative agenda gives them considerable control over the everyday workings of the body, as well as of the policy product that emerges from its deliberations. In many states the speaker is a member of the key rules committee, which controls the flow of legislation, and is crucial to the determination of which bills receive consideration in the important and hectic closing days of the session.

Clearly, while serving both as presiding officer of the house and leader of the majority party, the speaker is usually a very powerful and influential person in state politics.

Here, for example, is how one member of the Michigan legislature described Speaker William Ryan:

> Nothing happens without the Speaker's approval. He works through the various committee chairmen to carry out his mandates. He gets his own way about all the time. He wears down the Governor. Well, the Governor has got a few other things to do, and he spends so much time at it. But Ryan—he's got unlimited time, seven days a week. It makes no difference to him. He'd just wear the opposition down. . . . What he wants, he gets. . . . He's at least number two man in the state, if not number one man, when it comes to determining what's going to happen.[28]

The states differ as to the number of terms a speaker may serve. In some states the established pattern, and one that is never violated, is for the speaker to serve one two-year term. In a larger number of states that may be a rule of thumb, but it is not unusual for a particularly effective or powerful speaker to be elected to succeeding terms. In two states the legislative leadership is chosen by the governor in one or both houses. Usually, however, legislators jealously protect their prerogatives to select their leaders without excessive interference.

In thirty states an elected lieutenant-governor presides over the senate as a part of his or her constitutional duties.[29] He or she is not a member of the senate, does not participate in debates, and votes only in cases of a tie. As presiding officer, the lieutenant-governor usually has no power over committee appointments and has less control over the interpretation and application of rules than does his or her counterpart in the house. Whenever there is no lieutenant-governor, or one is not designated as presiding officer, the senate normally elects a president who operates in much the same fashion as does the speaker. Where the lieutenant-governor does preside, the majority floor leader will serve as the political leader of the senate. He or she not only participates on the floor but does all of the things that an elected president of the senate or a speaker of the house does.

The minority party in each house is led by a minority leader, who is normally elected by the party caucus. If minority leaders are on good terms with the speaker or the president (and especially if they lead large minorities), their influence can be great. They will often be asked to suggest names of minority members to serve on committees and in some states can appoint the minority members. They have considerable influence over which members of the party are allowed to advance and to gain power. In most states they are considered to be an important member of the state party leadership and are often consulted on party matters.

Party caucuses are an important part of the organizational structure of many state legislative houses. Their role in the operations of the house is varied but can be important to the legislative party membership and to its leadership. Party leaders can use the caucus as a means to disseminate information and to elect party officers, or they can use it to make important policy decisions. In about one-third of the states caucuses make policy decisions, and in some cases they are of such importance that deliberation on the floor becomes redundant. In about one-fourth of the states binding votes are taken in caucus requiring party members to vote as a unit once the matter gets to the floor. Some of the caucuses meet rarely, sometimes only to elect officers, whereas others may meet daily during the legislative session.[30]

## State Legislative Committees

On the whole, committees in the state legislatures are not so important as they are in Congress. Limited staff resources, infrequent sessions, lack of time and resources for bill drafting, and other factors make it more difficult for committees to operate efficiently. Furthermore, even in those legislatures where committees are important, their work is more likely to be rejected on the floor than is the work of their counterparts in Congress. Obviously, just as in deliberative bodies everywhere, the kinds of bills that emerge from the committees depend in large part on which members sit on which committee. The assignment process usually allows the appointing authority, whether it be the speaker, the senate president, or a committee on committees, to "stack" a committee so that its policy output is predetermined. Ideology often plays a role, since a liberal leadership may see to it that liberal legislators are placed on key committees, both substantive and procedural. It is also quite common in state legislatures for interest groups and their representatives to have an important voice in the selection of members for committees that are of particular importance to them. For example, the insurance industry may be quite active in pressuring the appointing authority to select legislators who are favorably disposed toward the industry and its problems. As has been noted by many who have studied state legislatures, the standing committees represent fertile soil for interest-group cultivation.

We saw earlier that seniority still plays an important part in committee assignments and the selection of committee heads at the congressional level. Seniority is not so important in most states, although it is often one factor in the selection and appointment process. Many states, either by law or by custom, change the membership of committees at the beginning of each session. Those who have not supported the successful candidate for key leadership positions can be punished by the unforgiving leaders. By the same token, those who have had the foresight to align themselves with the winning side are often rewarded for their good judgment. In the House of Representatives of Iowa, for example, "a primary consideration in the chairman selection process . . . is whether or not an individual legislator supported the speaker at the majority party organizational caucus."[31]

Committee heads in the state legislature are normally not so influential and powerful as those in Congress. They may be viewed by the membership as influential because of their positions, but they often do not have the actual power and authority to determine the outcome of legislative battles.

## Party Voting

We have noted that party politics in the state legislative process is as varied as the states themselves. Comparisons are not easy because of the states' differing political configurations. These configurations may be the result of the partisan divisions within the state, that is, the number of Republican and Democratic voters and the way in which they cast their ballots for members of the legislatures. They may also result from long-standing urban–rural divisions, regional differences, or ideological splits. The structure of state government, indeed, the internal structure of the legislative houses themselves, may be a determination in considering the impact of party on decision making. The result, however, is that comparative analysis is difficult.

Many political scientists have studied state legislative voting behavior. Generally, these studies have been conducted within the confines of a particular state and are bound by the constraints of a given period of time. A review of these findings by William Keefe and Morris Ogul suggests a number of generalizations:

1. *In most states the political parties in the legislatures are quite flexible, changing positions as the perceptions of electoral choices manifest themselves.*

2. *In some of the northern state legislatures, however, more party voting takes place than in Congress or in most other states.* These tend to be highly urbanized states (Massachusetts, Connecticut, New York, and Pennsylvania) with competitive two-party systems. Party voting tends to be less frequent in predominantly rural states.

3. *Party unity fluctuates according to the issue being discussed.* On some matters there is considerable unity, on others there is none. Here again, unity appears to depend on the strength of the party system in the state. Some studies have shown that the greater the size of the majority in the legislative body, the greater the degree of unity on roll-call votes.

4. *Party voting is not consistent in legislatures.* In most states the great majority of legislative activity is conducted without much controversy and with a high degree of consensus cutting across party lines. Only occasionally is there a conflict that could accurately be described as a party battle. One recent study found some evidence that legislators' support for party positions fluctuates according to the election calendar. This evidence suggests that party loyalty may be less important in a reelection year than at other times.[32]

5. *A governor who uses his powers to push for a legislative program is likely to be successful—particularly a governor who has strong electoral support.* Gubernatorial initiative is an important key in influencing legislators to act cohesively in behalf of a particular program.

6. *In some of the northern states distinguished by rigorous party competition in the legislative bodies, party lines are highly visible on liberal–conservative issues.* Socioeconomic class legislation often serves as a rallying point for the parties. The Republicans are generally more concerned with supporting the interests of the business community and resisting legislation backed by organized labor or designed to regulate business. They are also more likely to sponsor legislation that provides tax benefits for business and to oppose extended state services and social programs on fiscal grounds. Democratic legislators, in contrast, are more likely to represent the interests of organized labor, minorities, and low-income people, especially on legislation governing social programs designed to aid the poor or the working man and woman. They are also more likely to support extended state services in health, welfare, and other social policy areas with less regard for the fiscal impact. Thus, in the northern state legislatures, voting is likely to show partisan and ideological division more clearly.[33]

Obviously, these "rules" are general rather than specific. They do not all apply to every state, and they do not always apply to a given state at different times. However, a survey of the growing literature on state legislative behavior suggests that all are relevant to enough states to give them some general usefulness.

The effectiveness of the legislative party is determined by the kind of party system that exists in the state as well as by the internal structure of the legislature. Externally, the constituency of legislators may be of such consequence to them that it places limits on the degree of allegiance legislators are willing to give to the leadership. Internally, however, the party's influence may be undercut by an established system of strong committees or an active and involved interest-group system. Ultimately, though, state legislators must decide individually, within the internal and external political environment in which each operates, just how much deference to pay to the party. That decision, multiplied by the entire membership of the legislative body, will largely determine the effectiveness of the party in the legislative system.

## Political Parties in the Legislative Process

Both Congress and the state legislatures have been vigorously criticized for parochialism, trivialism, unrepresentativeness, inefficiency, fragmentation of power, and weak leadership. Both levels have responded to some of these criticisms, as witnessed by the reform efforts of recent years. These changes have often resulted from efforts to impose stricter majority rule and more responsible party government. Virtually all of the changes have been accompanied by vigorous debate over the advantages and disadvantages offered by reform.

Those who advocate retention of our present legislative system hold that the United States is a heterogeneous and diverse nation and must necessarily be represented in its legislative bodies by an equally heterogeneous group of elected officials. The popular diversity virtually guarantees that achieving a more effective majority will be difficult, if not impossible. Furthermore, it is argued that those advocating greater responsibility in legislative affairs have lost sight of the benefits we have gained through the existing system. In effect, they argue that the traditional outcome of legislative consideration is one of consensus and compromise between contending factions that are well represented in the legislatures and in Congress. A third argument against change is that imposition of a system of stronger majority rule might well lead to the development of a multiparty system. The rationale for that view is that a strong and uncompromising majority might force dissidents to form third parties as a way of gaining respect and attention. This, in turn, would ultimately undermine the two-party system.

Those who advocate change note that at times during the sweep of American history Congress has been able to polish its image with the people by conducting its affairs in a statesmanlike fashion. Sometimes this has even been true when the incumbent president was suffering the slings and arrows of public opinion. That has not been the case, however, in recent years. Congress has never before scored so low in public esteem, as measured by reliable public opinion polls. The Neanderthal pace of its deliberations, the usual inability of its majority party to construct an integrated national policy, the failure of its leaders to build effective coalitions, and the developing weaknesses in its internal party system have brought that body to the nadir of its public respect.

Yet these two national institutions, the presidency and the Congress, are the principal policymaking bodies in our constitutional system. It is to them that we look for national policy leadership and innovation. We expect them, working in concert, to provide solutions to our national problems. Even when the system works, when a problem is addressed and results in a "reasonable" solution, it is often the result of a long, drawn-out process that leaves considerable bitterness among the policymakers and divisions among the populace. This is a matter for concern to the citizenry because it brings to the fore some of the inherent weaknesses in the constitutional system. Responsible party advocates maintain that changes can be made in the legislative structure that will enhance public confidence, more accurately represent public desires, and build stronger parties. The advocates of change believe that legislative bodies should be more democratic in their internal structures and that legislation would consequently be more strongly allied to the common good. In essence, they argue that the nation must be viewed as a whole—that it is more than the sum of its parts. They consider that some of those parts, represented by strong interests, have gained ascendancy over the whole and have, in the process, further undermined our legislative bodies as true representatives of all the people.

These contending views have been argued for decades, and it is unlikely that the question will be resolved in the near future. Reform efforts of the recent past have been directed at achieving a more responsive system. Some have worked, and some have disappointed their advocates. In sum, they are a part of the ongoing larger struggle that has brought considerable change to American politics since World War II. The future is uncertain, but we at least now have a clearer idea of the various forces engaged in the contest.

# Notes

1. Charles O. Jones, *Party and Policy-Making: The House Republican Policy Committee* (New Brunswick, N.J.: Rutgers University Press, 1964), ch. 8.
2. Evelyn G. Schipske, "Policy Statements and Policy-Making: An Analysis of Congressional Response to the House Republican Policy Committee (1949–74)," unpublished manuscript cited in Malcolm E. Jewell and Samuel C. Patterson, *The Legislative Process in the United States,* 3rd ed. (New York: Random House, 1977), p. 168.
3. *New York Times* (April 5, 1977): 14.
4. Arthur G. Stevens, Jr., Arthur H. Miller, and Thomas E. Mann, "Mobilization of Liberal Strength in the House, 1955–1970: The Democratic Study Group," *American Political Science Review* 68, no. 2 (June 1974): 667–681.
5. Donald R. Matthews and James A. Stimson, "Decision-Making by U.S. Representatives: A Preliminary Model," in *Political Decision Making,* ed. S. Sidney Ulmer (Cincinnati, Ohio: Van Nostrand Reinhold, 1970), p. 31.
6. Randall B. Ripley, *Congress: Process and Policy,* 2nd ed. (New York: Norton, 1978), pp. 234–235.
7. *New York Times* (December 14, 1981): 18.
8. Michael J. Malbin, "House Reforms: The Emphasis Is on Productivity, Not Power," *National Journal* (December 4, 1976): 1731–1733.
9. Ripley, *Congress,* p. 171.
10. David J. Vogler, *The Third House* (Evanston, Ill.: Northwestern University Press, 1971), p. 59.
11. Edmund Burke, "Speech to the Electors of Bristol," *Writings and Speeches of Edmund Burke* (Boston: Little, Brown, 1901), pp. 93–98.
12. T. V. Smith, "Should Congress Lead or Follow Public Opinion?" *Town Meeting* 8, no. 11 (July 9, 1942): 7–17.
13. Wilder W. Crane, Jr., "All Legislators are Politicos," taken from a doctoral dissertation at the University of Wisconsin, Madison, 1959, and reprinted in Neal Riemer, ed., *The Representative* (Boston: Heath, 1967), p. 84.
14. John W. Kingdon, *Congressmen's Voting Decisions* (New York: Harper & Row, 1973), pp. 16–20.
15. Ibid., p. 101.
16. Roger H. Davidson, *The Role of the Congressman* (New York: Pegasus, 1969).
17. Cited in Ripley, *Congress,* p. 136. From Donald R. Matthews and James A. Stimson, "Decision-Making by U.S. Representatives: A Preliminary Model," in *Political Decision Making,* ed. S. Sidney Ulmer (Van Nostrand Reinhold, 1970), p. 31.
18. Ibid.
19. Julius Turner, *Party and Constituency: Pressures on Congress,* rev. ed., ed. Edward V. Schneier (Baltimore, Md.: Johns Hopkins University Press, 1970), pp. 16–17.
20. Ibid., pp. 41–106.
21. Robert Dahl, *Congress and Foreign Policy* (New York: Harcourt Brace Jovanovich, 1950), pp. 187–197.
22. "Helping hand: Republican votes in Congress are giving Carter key foreign policy wins," *Congressional Quarterly Weekly Report* (August 5, 1978): 2042.
23. V. O. Key, Jr., *Southern Politics* (New York: Vintage Books, 1949), pp. 374–375.
24. *Congressional Quarterly Almanac, 1981*

(Washington, D.C.: Congressional Quarterly, Inc., 1982), p. 36-C; 1982 figure from *Congressional Quarterly Weekly Report* (January 15, 1983): 102.

25. *Congressional Quarterly Almanac, 1981* (Washington, D.C.: Congressional Quarterly, Inc., 1982), p. 35-C.

26. *Congressional Quarterly Weekly Report* (November 6, 1982): 2807.

27. Republican National Committee, *Chairman's Report, 1979* (Washington, D.C.: Republican National Committee, 1979), inside back cover.

28. G. H. Stollman, *Michigan State Legislators and Their Work,* (Washington, D.C.: University Press of America, 1978), p. 75.

29. Council of State Governments, *The Lieutenant Governor: The Office and Its Powers,* rev. ed.

(Lexington, Ky.: Council of State Governments, 1976), p. 24.

30. Samuel C. Patterson, "Legislators and Legislatures in the American States," in *Politics in the American States: A Comparative Analysis,* 4th ed., eds. Virginia Gray, Herbert Jacob, and Kenneth Vines (Boston: Little, Brown, 1983), p. 163.

31. Charles W. Wiggins, *The Iowa Lawmaker* (Washington, D.C.: American Political Science Association, 1971), p. 37.

32. James H. Kuklinski, "Representativeness and Elections: A Policy Analysis," *American Political Science Review* 72 (March 1978): 176–177.

33. William J. Keefe and Morris S. Ogul, *The American Legislative Process: Congress and the States,* 5th ed. (Englewood Cliffs, N.J.: Prentice-Hall, 1981), pp. 300–304.

# CHAPTER
# TEN

# Interest Groups in American Politics

LOBBYISTS PROLIFERATE
—SO DO THE HEADACHES

LOBBYING COSTS PUT AT OVER $6 MILLION IN NEW YORK

AN ANGRY YOUNG CONGRESSMAN
CRITICIZES SPECIAL INTEREST GROUPS

LOBBYISTS' ROW ON K STREET IS
TUNED UP FOR ITS CHANCE AT BUDGET

USED-CAR RULE: LESSON IN LOBBYING

POLITICAL ISSUES TOP LIST
FOR N.A.A.C.P. MEETING

AT 25, A.F.L.-C.I.O. PURSUES OLD AIMS

These recent headlines tell the story.[1] As political parties have declined in influence in the past quarter century, interest groups have blossomed and proliferated and are now occupying a position of unprecedented power and influence in American politics. Some political scientists and other close observers believe that groups will replace parties as the major contact point between the people and the government once the current transformation has run its course. In a widely noted column in the *Washington Post* in late 1978, David Broder observed:

> What we are witnessing in the 1970s is the second stage in the disintegration of a stable pattern of politics based on two party competition. In the 1960s, the candidates and office-holders divorced themselves from their parties, raising their own campaign funds and reaching their voters through targeted mailing lists and television. Now these same fund-raising and direct-communication techniques have been appropriated by the single-interest organizations to bend these candidates to their will.[2]

This change, and it may be a profound one, requires that we examine interest groups and lobbying at some length. Groups occupy an important place in the political equation as we move into the 1980s. In this chapter and the next we shall explore the role of groups as well as their use of lobbying and grass-roots techniques to attempt to accomplish their policy and electoral goals.

Politics is the organized struggle for political power, and it determines the ends to which power will be used. In democracies the main instruments of this struggle are political parties and interest groups. Both of these institutions offer the citizen a legitimate means of expression in the exercise of political power and influence. As we have seen, political parties are broadly based organizations of people seeking to capture control of the government by winning offices through free elections. Winning office is the primary goal of parties. Determining what to do with the power that was gained through the electoral victory is a major secondary concern.

Interest groups, in contrast, furnish an alternative mode of political action directed toward specific, limited goals; they operate by applying organized pressure or persuasion to political officeholders, either elected or appointed. Although some consider *pressure* a pejorative term, pressure is the stock-in-trade of interest groups. Indeed, they were formerly called *pressure groups,* a term that fell into disfavor when scholars concluded that groups were just as likely to use persuasion as pressure in seeking to gain their goals. Even so, from the point of view of the officeholder, it matters little whether or not a lobbyist's persuasive efforts in behalf of the group that employs him or her include blatant pressure tactics. If the lobbyist represents an organized group from the officeholder's constituency, the implicit threat of pressure will be there, regardless of whether it is explicitly enunciated. Nevertheless, the term *pressure groups* is so value laden that it has given way to the more neutral *interest groups,* thus placing emphasis on the ends being sought rather than the means of achieving them.

## Distinctions Between Political Parties and Interest Groups

Parties adopt positions on issues that ostensibly represent the beliefs of large numbers of members who are collectively seeking to get policy proposals implemented as government programs. Groups, too, have positions on one or more issues, and group leaders are also interested in policy outcomes. Nevertheless, given the contrasting ways in which they seek to achieve their ends and the types of goals that they have, significant differences do exist between the two. One need but review the definitions of *parties* and *groups* to see some of the more important distinctions:

1. *In the American system each party includes as members people who have widely varying interests and ideological beliefs, whereas groups are composed of those who have specialized concerns and are interested in concentrating their attention on one or a few issues of public policy.* The two-party system forces most people to participate as Democrats or Republicans. That, in turn, means that in order to win elections each party must adopt policy positions that appeal to a broad range of voter interests. Party platforms present positions on issues that are general and frequently nonspecific in nature. Party candidates must appeal to a broad spectrum of the populace and, in order to do so, often try to avoid taking clear-cut positions on controversial subjects. When opinion is sharply divided, most candidates attempt to steer a middle course rather than risk alienating some significant group of potential voters. As a consequence, parties seek to encompass all important shades of political opinion and to avoid taking positions that might cause voter disaffection.

Another factor that should not be overlooked is that parties, in order to win elections, must fashion appeals that will attract voters who call themselves Independents or whose attachment to the opposition party is weak. In this way, electoral coalitions are built. The result, to the despair of responsible party advocates, is that both parties tend to generalize their positions on issues to such an extent that distinctions between them become blurred.

Groups can concentrate their time, money, and energy on issues that are singularly narrow. The National Rifle Association (NRA) is composed of members who are interested either in limiting the use of or preventing the registration of firearms or in educating people in the safe handling of guns. The NRA does not ordinarily take public stands on issues outside that narrow range. Most groups are normally happy to maintain a small base of interests, because when they seek to widen that base they risk alienating members who are in disagreement on other issues. Unlike parties, which ordinarily must mute issue differences in order to put together winning coalitions and to capture offices, groups can take clearly defined positions on those limited issues that serve as their foundation because they know that, as long as they do, their members will remain loyal to the organization.

2. *Parties attempt to put members in public office, whereas groups are usually content to work to influence elected government officials to try to implement policies or to accomplish goals.* The key words are "elected" and "influence." Groups do not normally run candidates for office; that is a function of the political party. As a consequence, party leaders promise, and sometimes carry out, policy initiatives to appeal to a broad voting public. Groups are usually content to furnish electoral assistance to the campaigns of friendly party candidates or, more likely, to treat both sides in an evenhanded manner to avoid alienating either. By following this course, they maintain their access to government, regardless of who wins office. In short, groups are content to allow (even help) party candidates to win office, but they consider it their prerogative to influence those officeholders in the way they vote or administer programs of interest to group members. The importance with which groups view their electoral role is attested to by the rapid escalation in election activities they have undertaken in recent years.

Another aspect of this distinction is that parties seek consensus and build coalitions before an election, whereas groups, through interaction with other groups, develop necessary coalitions after the election is over. It has not been unusual in recent years for Common Cause, a major governmental reform group, to join with business, labor, or professional groups in advocating positions with which they all agree. The added weight of these collective memberships and the cooperation of group lobbyists strengthen the group's position as it seeks to achieve its goal. We shall return to the discussion of such alliances later in this chapter.

3. *Political parties are treated as though they are a part of the legal machinery of government, whereas groups are considered to be private associations outside formal governmental channels.* The activities of parties are regulated by law. Federal and state statutes—sometimes even constitutional provisions—set forth legal rules concerning campaign finances, public officials' sources of income and/or conflicts of interest, election machinery, and even the structural framework of party organizations. Legislatures, in general, are increasingly willing to make the detailed functions of political parties a part of formal law. Groups, in contrast, are private associations with private memberships and no formal ties to government. Group leaders and lobbyists may be required to register with officials of the state and may even have to file financial statements about their activities, but these regulations fall under the general heading of public disclosure rather than of regulation.

4. *Parties treat the individuals who belong as citizens, whereas groups treat them as members.* This is an important distinction. The party must approach its supporters in terms of the general welfare and the overall societal good. The president, as party leader, can exhort the citizens to hold down inflationary spending in behalf of the public good. An interest group, in contrast, approaches its members in much narrower and more selfish terms. An interest group can provide services and support on issues that it knows are important to its members, who, after all, joined the organization because of a particular orientation. Group leaders, therefore, can call upon members to write, to wire, or to call legislators to act in behalf of group goals. Group leaders have a better idea of the focus of members' attention than do party leaders—ordinarily a significant advantage.

In discussing groups and parties, one must remember that both have the same people as members. An individual citizen may be an active Democrat or Republican and at the same time be a member of one or more groups. Both political systems, that of the party and that of the group, offer the individual a method of reaching the government. In a responsible party system the voter might need to make a choice between one party and the other because of their opposite stands on policy. The dissatisfied voter could register his or her displeasure on election day by voting against those who have been in power but have not carried out their promises. Congressional leaders might have power to force compliance with party commands on policy votes. The end result, though, would be that the voter would have the means to hold his or her elected party officials responsible for their actions.

As we have seen, however, the United States does not have a responsible party system. For a wide variety of reasons, the people cannot hold officeholders and party leaders responsible for their actions. Therefore, frustrated citizens and others who seek special goals turn to interest groups in order to lend their weight to group-generated pressure directed toward specific policy gains. The distinction between parties and groups is never clear-cut. Parties sometimes perform duties normally associated with group effort, and groups sometimes engage in partylike politics. In general, though, these distinctions between interest groups and political parties hold true most of the time.

## Interest Groups: How Many Are There?

To make an accurate count of the number of interest groups in America is almost impossible. There are too many of them to count, and they come and go with little fanfare. Some are of long-standing duration, represented by well-known officers, confidentially operating from strength grounded in a long and possibly distinguished history. Others are formed to pursue one goal and, once the decision is made on that single subject, disappear forever. Many are federal in nature, that is, they not only have impressive national organizations but are also to be found in some or all of the states. A half century ago, while working on a doctoral dissertation at Harvard, the distinguished political scientist Pendleton Herring was able to count over five hundred Washington-based groups.[3]

Today that number has greatly expanded. One may safely say that there exist thousands of groups organized on a permanent basis and maintaining regular headquarters facilities (see table 10-1). One recent estimate suggests that over one thousand groups are now working out of Washington and that over eight thousand operate at both the state and national levels.[4] They range in size from the American Federation of Labor–Congress of Industrial Organizations (AFL-CIO), with fourteen million members, to many groups with a few hundred members. The largest and fastest growing union is the American Federation of State, County, and Municipal Employees (AFL-CIO), with a 1982 membership of 1,200,000, up from 99,000 in 1955.[5] Since many groups do

**TABLE 10–1**   National nonprofit organizations, by goal category, 1982

| Category | Number | Percent |
|---|---|---|
| Trade, business, and commercial | 3,344 | 20.2 |
| Health and medical | 1,582 | 9.5 |
| Cultural | 1,535 | 9.2 |
| Public affairs | 1,421 | 8.6 |
| Scientific, technical, and engineering | 1,171 | 7.0 |
| Social welfare | 1,160 | 7.0 |
| Hobby and vocational | 1,086 | 6.5 |
| Educational | 1,043 | 6.3 |
| Religious | 839 | 6.0 |
| Agricultural, and commodity exchanges | 763 | 4.6 |
| Athletics and sports | 631 | 3.8 |
| Legal, governmental, public administration, and military | 612 | 3.7 |
| Fraternal, foreign interest, nationality, and ethnic | 442 | 2.6 |
| Greek-letter societies | 321 | 1.9 |
| Labor unions, associations, and federations | 243 | 1.4 |
| Veteran, hereditary, and patriotic | 216 | 1.3 |
| Chambers of commerce | 110 | .6 |
| TOTAL | 16,519 | 100.0 |

*Source:* Denise S. Akey, ed., *Encyclopedia of Associations, 1983,* 17th ed., vols. 1 and 2 (Detroit: Gale Research Co., 1982). Reprinted by permission of the publisher; copyright © 1959, 1961, 1964, 1968, 1970, 1972, 1973, 1975, 1976, 1977, 1978, 1979, 1980, 1981, 1982 by Gale Research Company.

not make public the number of their members, however, it is difficult to get a very clear picture of group membership.

Table 10-1 clearly shows the dominance of business, trade, and commercial groups in the United States. All of the groups shown are national in scope; if local voluntary organizations were added, the numbers represented in the list would be greatly expanded. Furthermore, not all of the groups included in this list meet the definition of an interest group presented in this chapter. Some are merely private organizations that do not engage in politics or make demands on government. Nevertheless, the extent of group activity and the breadth of interests represented by groups is clearly shown in this table.

One way in which groups may be classified is as "economic" or as "public interest." *Economic* groups are organized according to the economic (often occupational) interests of their members. They promote the economic well-being of the producer group that they represent, and they may be openly selfish in behalf of their dues-paying members. That is their job, their reason for being.

There are two reasons for the dominance of economically based groups in the United States. *First,* extensive changes occurred in industry during the technological revolution, causing major changes in the components that make up industry. Assembly-line manufacture demanded assembly-line workers; mass production had begun. The workers, dissatisfied with their pay and their job conditions, formed employee unions and adopted the strike as a weapon. The success of these tactics in forcing industrial employers to raise the hourly wage, improve the fringe benefits, and create more favorable working conditions prompted business and industry to organize in order to fight the unions and to strengthen their bargaining position vis-à-vis the government. These changes resulted in a massive development of hundreds of labor and business groups with goals that are principally economic.

A *second* reason for the economic development of interest groups has arisen from the growth of big government. Government has become involved in the everyday life of the people because of need and public demand. The need has often stemmed from natural fluctuations in the economy, such as recession, depression, unemployment, and inflation. Government has been called upon to manipulate the economy in order to overcome whatever dislocation is prevalent. How the government carries out these economic policies has a major impact on some segments of the public. Consequently, all groups are interested in getting the most favorable action possible in order to benefit their own members. At the same time they may work to prevent the adoption of policies that may be detrimental to them. The impact of government policy on various segments of the population stimulates groups to involve themselves in such a way as to achieve the most favorable outcome for the group. Thus, if government is considering a new public housing program, both the construction industry and the building trades unions will become involved, sometimes on the same side. Mortgage lenders and the real estate industry will have a stake in the outcome. Architects and designers will want to compete for government contracts. One government program can stimulate dozens of interest groups into action to get what they can or to protect what they have.

*Public interest* groups are usually not easily identified with economic problems or the economic sector. They are organized around issues that they perceive to be important to the public good. These may range from a general concern about civil liberties (the American Civil Liberties Union), government reform (the League of Women Voters), or environmental protection (the Sierra Club). They are usually formed to achieve a specific end. The League of Women Voters, for instance, is an outgrowth of the National American Women's Suffrage Association, which led the fight for adoption of the Nineteenth Amendment. These groups do not have a selfish motive in the sense that their members will economically benefit from their activities. In their view, their success will benefit society as a whole. They believe that people in general will benefit from their activities and that they are protecting the public interest of the many against the private interests of a few.

The distinction between economic and public interest groups should not be over-drawn. On many occasions groups of both types were aligned against a coalition of other groups of both types. Economic interests and public interests need not be mutually exclusive. They sometimes move in the same direction. The civil rights coalition of the 1960s included the AFL-CIO, the American Jewish Congress, the American Civil Liberties Union, the National Baptist Convention, the National Association for the Advancement of Colored People (NAACP), and various other interest groups, both economic and public. On occasion a single group might see itself as falling into both categories. The NAACP, for instance, might simultaneously push for programs to improve the living standards of black people by reducing unemployment, expanding public health care, or offering better educational opportunities, while at the same time working to enhance the civil rights of black voters. In such circumstances, the NAACP seeks both strengthened civil rights and pocketbook gains for its members and can thus be categorized as both an economic and a public interest group by its own members.

## Organizational Structure

Organizationally, interest groups can be viewed from three different perspectives. The *first* of these is based on structure, that is, on whether the group is set up on a federal or a unitary basis. A *federal* organization is, in a sense, a group made up of groups. The national organization is composed of semiautonomous state organizations, and powers and functions are divided between two levels. One of the best known of the federal groups is the American Federation of Labor–Congress of Industrial Organizations (AFL-CIO). It is a national organization composed of national, state, and local unions to which individual members belong. Membership may be tied directly to the national or the subnational level. Whatever organizational implications can be drawn from the study of federated groups involve the question of cohesion versus freedom of action—that is, the degree to which the national headquarters group is able to give direction to and draw support from local member groups, while at the same time allowing the locals enough freedom to permit them to deal with the local problems and feel that they have some autonomy to do so. Farmers who belong to the American Farm Bureau Federation (AFBF) are members of their state farm bureaus (e.g., the Iowa Farm Bureau Federation), and the state groups, in turn, are members of the AFBF. It is necessary for both levels to work to maintain a proper balance between the powers and responsibilities that both may exercise.

The *unitary* organization is one in which individuals or groups belong directly to the parent national organization. The majority of trade associations fit this category.

The National Association of Manufacturers (NAM) (before its merger with the United States Chamber of Commerce in 1976) was a unitary organization composed of individual corporate firms. The Grocery Manufacturers of America (GMA), which speaks for such corporate giants as Procter and Gamble, Heinz, Quaker Oats, and General Mills, along with 150 other grocery concerns, is another example.[6] Unitary groups have a simpler chain of command and clearer lines of authority and responsibility than do federal groups. This permits the leadership to present a more coherent and cohesive program with greater confidence that member companies will be supportive.

Federations, in contrast, tend to have less cohesion because of recurring disagreements between the constituent groups and the parent group over the degree of autonomy permitted. The member groups in the states and regions often predated formation of the national group, and they are reluctant to relinquish any sovereignty over their own actions. But in order to be effective at the national government level, the national headquarters group may find that maximum advantage accrues to those who can speak for all the constituent units. If this problem cannot be resolved, the federation may not be able to maintain its cohesion and may, in fact, break up. Sometimes the degree to which the national leadership can maintain cohesion depends on how many sanctions or penalties they have the power to impose on recalcitrant state or local member groups. If the national group possesses appropriate sanctions, local affiliates may find that it is wise to cooperate in joint effort.

The *second* perspective through which interest groups can be viewed is from the standpoint of structural type. The National Association of Wholesalers is organized *horizontally* so that the group umbrella shelters a large number of diverse firms that produce many different products. The organization of the group is based on the function of wholesaling rather than on the type of product being manufactured or sold. A trade association, on the other hand, may be organized *vertically*. Firms engaged in manufacturing, wholesaling, and retailing the same product may all be members. The functions of the member firms may differ, but the product in which they deal is the same.

Finally, a *third* way of looking at the organization of groups is to determine whether they are multipurpose or single-purpose. A multipurpose group seeks to unite people who share a common background, whether it be occupational, religious, ethnic, or social. Labor unions ordinarily have an interest in a wide range of policy alternatives, such as labor–management relations, the economy, medical care, social security, and even foreign policy. Organized labor is so large and so diverse that it includes member unions with highly specialized interests; thus the national federation must take many issues into account.

In 1982 the Equal Rights Amendment failed to attract the necessary number of states to become a part of the constitution. The principal group coordinating the drive for ratification during the last few years was ERAmerica, a single-purpose coalition of groups such as the League of Women Voters, the Business and Professional Womens' Clubs, and the National Organization for Women. Most of the groups in the coalition were multipurpose, but in uniting behind the amendment through ERAmerica they became a single-purpose group. Another example of a single-purpose group is the National Abortion Rights Action League (NARAL), a "pro-choice" organization supporting abortion rights and opposing restrictive abortion legislation. NARAL had a membership of approximately 100,000 by the beginning of the 1980s. Both of these groups represented single-purpose coalitions devoted to a primary target.

Organization is important only as it affects the procedures established to coordinate the activities of the group and to bring about its specific objectives. Some groups have found that they can accomplish their objectives better as a unitary group than as a federal one. The composition of the group often determines whether it is organized in a horizontal or vertical manner, and the group's goals usually account for the breadth of issue interest. Even so, group behavior can often be traced to the manner in which the group is organized. The power of the group's leaders can sometimes be ascribed to the method of organization. For the student of groups, organizational structure offers a relatively easy way in which to gain understanding of group functions.

## Organizational Dimensions

Bicycle manufacturers want a higher tariff. Farmers want higher prices for commodities. Consumers want lower prices for food and other necessities. Airlines want fewer government regulations. States and municipalities want more federal money. Teachers want more money and more job security. Senior citizens want more Social Security and Medicare benefits. And virtually every time one of them gets something they want, some other group is negatively affected. Society has become highly complicated and now consists of an interwoven complex of specialties and specialists. Fifty years ago the farmer and his immediate family produced a steak for dinner. Today that steak is a product of the cowboy, the banker, the chemist, the oil refiner, the steelmaker, the veterinarian, the pilot, the fertilizer manufacturer, the truck driver or railroad engineer, the stockyards worker, the auctioneer, the meat packer, the butcher, and the retailer.[7] And almost every one of the people who are involved in the production of that steak is represented by an interest group. Whether the group is successful in accomplishing its purpose depends in large part on three distinct qualities associated with the type of organization used by the group: leadership, internal cohesion, and access.

---

Americans fear the country has been trending toward a psychology of self-interest so all-embracing that no room is left for commitment to national and community interest. They sense that we risk losing something precious to the meaning of the American experience. They fear that, in the pursuit of their organizational goals, the politicians and the businessmen, and the unions and the professions, have lost sight of any larger obligation to the public and are indifferent or worse to anything that does not benefit them immediately and directly. They fear that the very meaning of the public good is disappearing in a sea of self-seeking.

Bill Moyers, *Pacific Stars and Stripes* (January 18, 1980): 10.

---

### Leading a Group: The Iron Law of Oligarchy

Some group leaders are so closely associated with their organizations and have been for so long that the leader becomes almost indistinguishable from the group. George Meany was the president of the American Federation of Labor–Congress of Industrial Organizations from the merger of the independent AFL and CIO in 1955 until his retirement in 1979 at the age of eighty-five. Prior to assuming the leadership of the combined group, he was only the third president in the ninety-year history of the old AFL. An entire generation of Americans had reached maturity during his quarter century as leader. Six U.S. presidents had served during the period of Meany's presidency. He and the AFL-CIO were viewed by many as being synonymous.

John Gardner, former secretary of health, education, and welfare, founded the public interest lobby Common Cause in 1970 and served as its chairman until 1978, when he retired to the position of founding chairman. While he was active in the organization, Gardner was feared and respected by public officials throughout the national government and in many state capitals. Since its founding, the organization has focused its attention on governmental reform and institutional change. Both Meany and Gardner, representing two very different kinds of organizations, were as well known to the public and to public officials as were their groups. They represented one highly personal type of organizational leadership.

But most group leaders are not so well known outside their group. They are elected for one- or two-year terms and often defer to the established ongoing staff hierarchy, which may have dominated the administration of the group for many years. The American Medical Association (AMA) elects a new president every year. Although most of those who are elected are widely known within the ranks of the AMA, they do not have wide public recognition. The president of the group is expected to make public appearances, testify before congressional committees, and involve himself or herself in the internal politics of the AMA. The top staff person in group headquarters is often the driving force behind organizational policy and tactical decision making.

The U.S. Conference of Mayors, an organization of six hundred cities with populations of thirty thousand or more, is led by an elected president who serves a two-year term. But the chances are that John Gunther, the organization's executive director since 1958, is better known to the politicians of Washington than the organization's president. Both the American Medical Association and the Conference of Mayors are illustrative of groups run by established bureaucracies and appointed leaders. In these and other cases the current president may be better known to the public, but real power rests with professionals who serve with little public recognition. Obviously, leadership positions differ. They may be acquired and legitimized through some formal process, or they may have developed informally. The rules of some groups place authority in the hands of a few: a board of directors, an executive committee, or a house of delegates. Sometimes one of these governing bodies not only exercises power but generates it as well. Others, however, may be required to seek power from an annual convention or convocation of delegates or members. The one thing that all of them have in common is that only a few members have authority and are empowered to exercise it. Virtually all groups are run by a minority for the majority—a form of oligarchy.

Writers of all political persuasions, using every conceivable type of observation and research, have for many years agreed that most groups are ruled by a minority. Lord James Bryce, in a book published in 1921, put it this way:

> In all assemblies and groups and organized bodies of men, from a nation down to the committee of a club, direction and decisions rest in the hands of a small percentage, less and less in proportion to the larger and larger size of the body, till in a great population it becomes an infinitesimally small proportion of the whole number. This is and always has been true of all forms of government, though in different degrees.[8]

TABLE 10–2   Selected national groups with founding date, membership, and staff

| Type of group | Group | Founded | Membership | Staff |
|---|---|---|---|---|
| **Business** | National Association of Manufacturers | 1895 | 12,000 corporations | 220 |
| | Chamber of Commerce of the United States | 1912 | 4,000 associations 200,000 businesses | 1,400 |
| | National Federation of Independent Businesses | 1943 | 500,000 | 122 plus 598 field staff |
| | National Bed, Bath, and Linen Association | 1968 | 400 | 4 |
| **Labor** | American Federation of Labor–Congress of Industrial Organizations | 1955 | 13,600,000 105 locals | 600 |
| | American Federation of Teachers | 1916 | 580,000 2,100 locals | — |
| | Screen Actors Guild | 1933 | 50,000 | — |
| | United Farm Workers of America | 1962 | 100,000 | — |
| | United Steel Workers of America | 1936 | 1,400,000 | 830 |
| | National Football League Players Association | 1956 | 1,400 | 30 |
| **Farm** | National Farmers Union | 1902 | 300,000 | 40 |
| | National Grange | 1867 | 475,000 | 26 |
| | American Farm Bureau Federation | 1919 | 3,297,224 families | 102 |
| | American Fish Farmers Federation | 1965 | 438 | 5 |

Only a few years earlier a Swiss sociologist, Robert Michels, in a study of European Socialist parties before World War I, found that these parties, although proclaiming themselves as founded on pure democratic principles, were almost uniformly controlled by a small minority of leaders. His observation may be applied with equal force to groups. Labeling his conclusion "the Iron Law of Oligarchy," Michels wrote that

> the appearance of oligarchical phenomena in the very bosom of the revolutionary parties is a conclusive proof of the existence of immanent oligarchical tendencies in every kind of human organization which strives for the attainment of definite ends.[9]

Michels argued that the oligarchies that lead organizations will progressively separate themselves from the masses that make up the membership. As the elite leaders

TABLE 10-2 *(continued)*

| Type of group | Group | Founded | Membership | Staff |
|---|---|---|---|---|
| **Professional** | American Medical Association | 1847 | 282,000 | 894 |
| | National Education Association | 1857 | 1,600,800 | 600 |
| | American Bar Association | 1878 | 280,000 | 538 |
| **Particular Interest** | National Association for the Advancement of Colored People | 1909 | 500,000 | 132 |
| | American Civil Liberties Union | 1920 | 250,000 | 330 |
| | Americans for Democratic Action | 1947 | 65,000 | 20 |
| | Phi Beta Kappa | 1776 | 360,000 | — |
| **Public Interest** | Common Cause | 1970 | 225,000 | 73 |
| | League of Women Voters | 1920 | 125,000 | 55 |
| | Sierra Club | 1892 | 225,000 | 162 |
| | Wilderness Society | 1935 | 50,000 | 35 |
| | National Wildlife Federation | 1936 | 4,600,000 | 400 |
| **Government** | National Association of Counties | 1935 | 2,100 counties | 120 |
| | U.S. Conference of Mayors | 1932 | 600 cities of over 30,000 population | 65 |

*Source:* Denise S. Akey, ed., *The Encyclopedia of Associations, 1983,* 17th ed., vols. 1 and 2 (Detroit: Gale Research Co., 1982).

become more and more separated, they will become more conservative in their tactics and policies as they seek to secure their position as leaders.[10]

Forty years later, in 1955, eminent political scientist David B. Truman applied Michels's theory to the study of interest groups. Oligarchy, a system of governing in which an elite group holds power, is a useful concept to use in describing interest-group leadership. As Truman noted, leaders need a type of organizational environment that provides them with the flexibility and freedom to make decisions quickly and decisively as the politics of the moment demands. Organizational demands require that officers spend more time on the affairs of the group than members do. And, once in office, there is a tendency to self-perpetuation in the office. Leadership is time-consuming, and only a few activists are able to afford the time necessary to keep the group operating effectively. Furthermore, the longer an existing group of leaders holds power, the better equipped it is to maintain its grip on that power. Factors such as these operate to sustain the group's active minority leadership cadre.[11]

The other side of this equation, however, is just as important. The minority leadership will be left alone to rule and will be protected from challenge only so long as the rank-and-file membership is passive or apathetic. Fortunately for group leaders, even though one may find a tier of moderate activists at the middle levels of the organization, most members of most groups do not take an active part in the group's governance or decision making. Many members join because they were required or expected to join. Some were pressured by friends or colleagues to become members. Others may have once been enthusiastic over group participation but have found that their interest waned as time passed. In short, most groups are composed of an active leadership minority who, for various reasons and through various strategems, maintains control over a mass membership that collectively does not really care. As Truman noted, many people prefer to be led.

## Maintaining a Cohesive Group

People naturally fall into groups. Some groups are generic or natural—for example, men and women. Other groups are categorical; they are classified according to occupation, education, religion, or belief. Any one of these categories may serve as the base on which a group is constructed. One need but sample the number and variety of organized groups in the United States to get some appreciation for the potential of group action.

Table 10-2 shows the diversity and variety of a select number of American groups. In 1980 there were over 50,000 labor unions—including 174 that were organized nationally—with a combined membership of 21,784,000. The largest independent union, the Teamsters, had 1,890,000 members. There were 331,065 church congregations in the nation representing over 250 denominations. The number of individual farms had dwindled to 2,419,000, but an organized group existed for virtually every commodity in every state and region. In addition, there were 12,500,000 proprietorships and partnerships, 14,726 nonprofit associations, 2,200,000 teachers in 15,174 school districts, and hundreds of other kinds of groups.[12] A single public school district may be served by people belonging to teachers' unions, teachers' professional associations, principals' associations, coaches' associations, superintendents' associations, and school board associations, and furthermore, may have separate organizational structures at the local, district, regional, state, and national levels. The potential variety of groups is almost unlimited. The heterogeneous nature of American society leads to one of the principal problems faced by group leaders: overlapping membership, which has a profound effect on the ability of the group to remain cohesive.

The complexity of modern life has the effect of dispersing individual interests. One person may have many interests expressed through membership in a number of different groups. Thus a duespaying member of the Steelworkers' Union might also be an active member of the Catholic Church, a Democrat, a member of a bowling league, a Boy Scout leader, and a member of the National Rifle Association. Any one of these groups may claim his primary allegiance at any particular time, which means that the other groups cannot always claim his total support. Typically, this latter result may arise from a person's inability to maintain a consistent interest in a wide variety of disparate groups, or it may arise from the differing intensities with which a person views the particular issues promoted by the groups. Obviously, overlapping memberships represent a problem for group leadership.

Maintaining cohesion within a group is crucial if the group's leadership is to make the most effective use of the membership in staking its claims in the realm of public policy. A harmonious group can far more effectively make itself heard and attain its

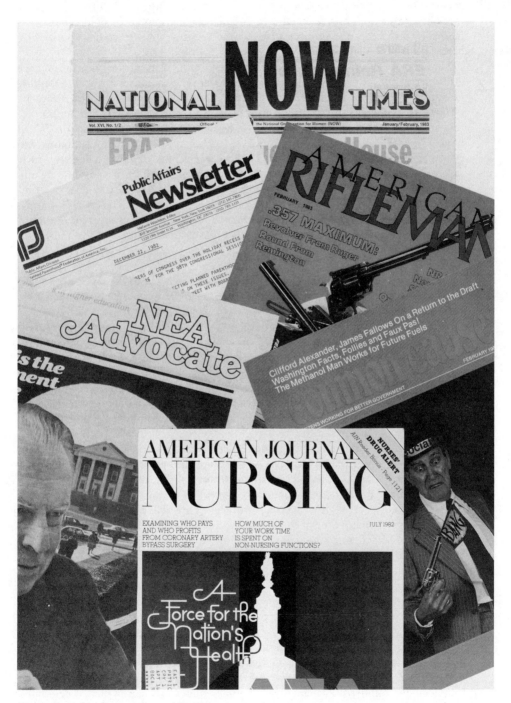

A sampling of interest groups publications.

political goals than can one ripped by dissension and disharmony. This is true for two reasons. *First,* the policymakers who are the targets of the group leaders' efforts are more likely to be responsive to a united and dedicated group. If the political officer is fearful or respectful of a group because of the membership's dedication to its goals, he or she is more likely to respond to group entreaties.

*Second,* a cohesive membership frees the leaders to concentrate on achieving the group's goals. If the leaders must keep one eye over their shoulders to watch dissenting factions jockeying for power within the group, they will be unable to concentrate the full weight of the group's influence on attaining its goals. It is, therefore, important for the group leader to work to project an image of unanimity and cohesion. When Lane Kirkland, president of the AFL-CIO, testifies before a Senate committee and claims to speak for the "working man" or for the "millions of labor unionists," he is seeking to leave the impression that labor is united in behalf of its goals and behind his leadership. When C. William Verity, Jr., chairman of the U.S. Chamber of Commerce, promised in 1980 that "Chamber members will mobilize again in 1982—at the local, state, and national levels—to support or oppose representatives according to their commitment to the enterprise system," he was intending to convey the impression to members of Congress and senators that the chamber would be unified in its election efforts.[13]

The problem of overlapping membership is highly relevant to the success or failure of group leaders' efforts to maintain a cohesive group. A woman active in a Catholic lay organization may also be an active participant (or even a leader) in a women's group, such as the National Organization for Women (NOW). She may not encounter conflict on most of the matters that become a part of each group's program, but, once NOW begins to push for liberalized abortion, the dilemma becomes obvious. If she cannot overcome her Catholic beliefs on that particular issue, NOW will lose her support to that overlapping membership. On the other hand, should she conclude that liberalized abortion is important to society, the church group may temporarily lose her support. Group leaders must work to maintain the loyalty of group members in order to mobilize group support on key group issues.

How can this be done? As any group leader will testify, it is not possible to retain enthusiastic support from all members on all issues. Virtually every position the group leaders take will cause the defection of some members. The leadership cadre must try to reduce the potential for such conflict to as great an extent as possible. As noted by David Truman twenty-eight years ago, two devices are available to the leadership to seek and retain a cohesive membership: internal propaganda techniques and sanctions.[14]

The *first, internal propaganda,* is not as nefarious as it may sound. All organizations use such techniques, and most of them can be classified under the general rubric of communications. The active minority, holding the leadership positions as it does, controls communications with the majority membership. Newspapers (the *AFL-CIO News*), magazines (the *American Rifleman*), or newsletters (*Advance/Association for the Advancement of Psychology*) are published by most groups and carry the leadership's message to the members (see "A Sampling of Interest Group Publications," page 306). Some groups send "alerts" to the members asking for immediate personal contacts with legislators or administrators. Others have long used the referendum as a means of emphasizing unity and sanctioning previously arrived-at policy positions. The U.S. Chamber of Commerce has employed the referendum for many years to determine the beliefs of local members and to demonstrate strong membership support by local and state units for national chamber policy. Many labor, public interest, conservation, environmental, and consumer organizations use the referendum as a communications device and as a way to gauge the cohesion that exists within the group. Common Cause has polled its members from its inception, and the League of Women Voters has long sought local consensus before an issue is ever adopted as a policy position.

The *second* means used by group leaders to maintain a cohesive membership is the *application of official sanctions*. Although usually imposed by the national leadership against local leaders or members, these penalties normally represent a last resort. They are applied when other leadership techniques have failed. Sanctions may take the form of a public or private slap on the wrist or, ultimately, the expulsion of the member group from the parent organization. Probably the best-known example of an applied sanction was the AFL-CIO's expulsion of the International Brotherhood of Teamsters in 1957 for corrupt practices by some of its leaders. The action not only denied the AFL-CIO its largest member union, the Teamsters, but cost it 1.5 million members. Expulsion is the ultimate sanction and, obviously, is to be avoided except in cases of recalcitrant disobedience. It always signifies a failure to maintain a cohesive organization.

The group may also take action to undercut the appeal of dissidents within the membership. The American Medical Association is implementing a tougher approach toward government, hospitals, and private insurance companies because it wishes to counter the developing American Federation of Physicians and Dentists, a group with over ten thousand members formed a few years ago to exert greater collective pressure to protect the economic and professional interests of medical practitioners. Increased activities of this kind are also aimed at alerting hospital interns and residents that the AMA is actively pursuing their interests.[15]

Instability is a common characteristic of many groups. Members come and go. Officers may be rotated regularly so that no one is ever firmly in control. Breakdowns in communications occur. Dissidents arise to disrupt the normal flow of group business. In every case the result is a lack of cohesion, and all groups take steps to try to avoid this kind of fragmentation. It is important to the group's success in achieving its goals that cohesion be maintained so that the group can make the most of any access to government officials it may have.

## Forming Alliances

On occasion a group may find that its particular interest runs parallel to that of one or more other groups. If that is the case, the group leaders may initiate discussions about forming an alliance to last until the resolution of the issue in question. Alliances serve several functions that are favorable to group success. They can multiply the number of people involved, thereby bringing more constituent pressure to bear on an issue. They also can help to distribute the work load by pooling their efforts. And they can cut expenses by combining group resources. These are all ends that are ordinarily worth seeking. Almost all issues have the potential for bringing certain groups together, and some of these alliances have been supremely successful.

One of the best-known alliances, the Leadership Conference on Civil Rights, was responsible for the passage of most of the civil rights legislation in the 1960s. This alliance comprised 139 civil rights, civic, social welfare, religious, and labor groups, who pooled their resources to bring maximum pressure to bear on Congress. First formed in 1949, the conference grew from an original 30 organizations and took an increasingly active part in the civil rights political battles of the 1960s. The coalition was effective in stopping the nomination of G. Harrold Carswell to the Supreme Court as well as in organizing lobbying efforts in behalf of voting rights legislation.[16]

Some alliances are of a more permanent nature. Groups operating within the same sphere of interest and on the same side of certain issues may decide to join permanently in a federation, while maintaining their individual identities. For example, the Consumer Federation of America (CFA) combined 140 member groups as a way to improve coordination and increase power. Consumer Union, the National Consumers Leagues, the Communication Workers of America, and various state consumer groups formed the CFA in 1967 long after consumer protection issues became an important part of the congressional agenda. Each of the members of the alliance was already established in the consumer movement, but it was decided that their efforts might be more fruitful if the groups were joined.[17]

On occasion circumstances force normally competing groups to unite to reach a mutually desirable end. The Coalition for Employment Through Exports was formed to fight Reagan administration proposals to cut back the lending authority of the Export-Import Bank. The organizational session was attended by 140 representatives of labor unions, business and industry, and several state governments. The bank was started in 1934 to encourage the export of American goods and services by offering loans to foreign importers at below-market interest rates. The threat to the lending authority of the bank brought Boeing, General Electric, Westinghouse, Caterpillar Tractor, the United Automobile Workers, the Communications Workers of America, the International Brotherhood of Electrical Workers, and the states of Florida, Wisconsin, and Washington to the coalition to seek to reverse the decision. Obviously, a group composed of 40 major and medium-size companies, 14 labor unions, and 3 states is a force of considerable importance in political decision making.[18] It also represents an excellent example of interest-group coalition politics in modern America.

Such coalitions have presented new problems to some groups not accustomed to working with others or to accommodating their views to those of other like-minded groups. In March 1982 the Committee on Political Education (COPE) of the AFL-CIO published a statement designed to gain some control over such affiliations. Particularly concerned over union marriages with nonunion groups for the purpose of endorsing political candidates, the new directive permits consultation with other nonlabor groups but forbids joint endorsements.[19]

Alliances are an effective way to gain short-term (and sometimes long-term) advantages, but they also have disadvantages that cause some groups to avoid them. Groups with good reputations cultivated over a number of years may find themselves in alliance with groups of unsavory repute, with consequent harmful effects. Nonpartisan groups may risk their standing with one or both of the parties if they align themselves too frequently with openly partisan groups. Finally, competition sometimes demands a degree of secrecy about internal group operations, and coalition with others may reveal more to competing groups about the financing, leadership, or cohesion of the group than the latter may consider desirable.

Alliances and coalitions are useful on occasion when it is possible to develop ad hoc cooperative efforts to achieve some particular end. Just as group membership may be more valuable than individual citizen involvement, a group alliance may be more valuable than independent group action.

*"Senator, according to this report, you've been marked for defeat by the A.D.A., the National Rifle Association, the A.F.L.-C.I.O., the N.A.M., the Sierra Club, Planned Parenthood, the World Student Christian Federation, the Clamshell Alliance . . ."*
(Drawing by Dana Fradon; © 1980 The New Yorker Magazine, Inc.)

## Group Involvement in Election Campaigns

When a strong and responsible party system exists, as in the United Kingdom, groups direct their efforts toward influencing the party organization and the political leadership. In fact, in the United Kingdom organized labor (an interest group in the United States) is a formal part of the party system. As we have noted earlier, the Conservative and Labour parties select their nominees for each constituency in the House of Commons, draft the platform on which they will stand for election, and control the policies of the government after the election, either as leaders or as opposition. A group wanting to have an impact on public policy must approach the party leadership to get its concerns included in the party platform or discussed in campaign debate. Party responsibility makes it less necessary for the group itself to influence the voters directly.

In the United States, with its decentralized and less responsible parties, candidates are more likely to launch themselves into politics, strike out on their own on policy matters, pay less attention to party leaders, and ignore the party platform. Once elected, the Congress or a state legislature is more apt to be a conglomerate of individuals elected independently, who practice "every man for himself" politics. Although party is the best predictor of legislative voting behavior, U.S. legislators do operate with much more freedom than their colleagues in countries with more tightly run party systems.

This greater freedom constitutes a key difference between the United States and other countries. It influences the way in which group leaders assert themselves within the political process, forcing them to place more emphasis on influencing the electorate than on prevailing with the party leadership. Not that they do not do both, but they do place greater emphasis on getting electoral support for those candidates or parties who are most closely attuned to group priorities. This is done in five ways.

## Coordinating Activities with Party

*First,* groups attempt to coordinate their activities with those of the party with which they are more closely aligned. A long-standing relationship exists between the national Democratic party and the political leadership of the Committee on Political Education (COPE) of the AFL-CIO. The leaders of COPE are often appointed to important party groups. They are brought into party councils to plan campaign strategies or to take part in internal party affairs. For instance, the original chairman of the Democratic Commission on Delegate Selection, appointed in late 1972, was Leonard Woodcock, president of the United Auto Workers Union. Woodcock later resigned, but labor's interests on the commission were protected by other members, such as Joseph A. Beirne, president of the Communications Workers of America; Edward Donahue, vice-president of the Graphic Arts International Union; William Du Chessi, general secretary-treasurer of the Textile Workers; Victor Gotbaum, executive director of the American Federation of State, County, and Municipal Employees; and Michael Johnson, executive vice-president of the Pennsylvania State AFL-CIO.[20]

Thus six of the fifty-one members of this particular party reform commission, one of a series of such groups formed during the 1960s and 1970s, were major officers in labor unions. This, of course, gave these labor representatives direct access to the affairs of the Democratic party. The advantage of this relationship to organized labor is obvious. Since this commission was revising the delegate selection rules for the 1976 national convention, it was important to the party to bring labor into the inner councils to reestablish the relationship that existed before the 1972 election (in which the AFL-CIO leadership took little formal part). Equally important was that labor should have a chance to help shape the rules for the next convention in order to guarantee itself a satisfactory role in choosing the next Democratic presidential candidate.

Since 1981 labor has enjoyed increased power within the Democratic party through expanded membership on the Democratic National Committee (DNC). Thirty union officials sit on the 362-member body, including 15 of the 25 at-large seats appointed by the national chairman. Four members of the 35-member executive committee are from labor organizations. A labor advisory council was organized in early 1982, including representatives of the 26 largest unions, and has taken an active part in party fund raising, campaign strategy, and targeting of elections. The unions gave the DNC $1 million in 1981, one-seventh of the DNC's total budget. Furthermore, the AFL-CIO executive committee decided to endorse a 1984 presidential candidate before the primaries. The plan calls for about 500 union leaders to meet in October 1983 and, if two-thirds of them agree, to back a candidate with endorsements, funds, and manpower well before the nominating process gets under way.[21]

## Using Membership as a Political Instrument

*Second,* groups must also demonstrate the effectiveness of their membership as a political instrument. Even though most groups remain nonpartisan in order to maintain access to whichever party wins an election, it is important to most groups to seek recognition for the potential strength they can deploy in an election campaign. Even if the group does not endorse candidates or work actively in an election, the leadership will often seek to impress on the parties and candidates the significance of their numbers. Although groups are seldom able to deliver the votes of members in sufficiently clear-cut fashion to claim a decisive role in the outcome, many groups may still claim to have been the deciding factor in a close election. After the 1976 presidential election, blacks, labor, and the South all took credit for playing a decisive role in the election of Jimmy Carter. As Gerald Pomper has noted:

> The results could easily have turned into an electoral landslide for either candidate. A shift of a single percentage point would have added 87 electoral votes to Carter's total, while a two-point change would have given him 440 of the total of 539 electoral voters. In the opposite direction, a change of but one vote in a hundred would have brought the incumbent President to victory by adding 43 electoral voters to his total. A two-point change would have yielded 353 electoral votes and a strong mandate.[22]

Carter won five of every six votes cast by black Americans and three of every five votes cast by union members. His victories in Ohio, New York, Pennsylvania, and Wisconsin could be properly attributed to the campaign waged by organized labor.[23] In any close election, group leaders who took an active part can lay claim to a role in the outcome. And, because of this fact, party leaders and candidates are glad to work with groups rather than to risk losing their support. Recognizing this, groups—labor and business included—make much of the vast numbers of voters that they "control."

In an election that is not close, however, it is more difficult to assess the impact of groups. At the presidential level, 1980 was a case in point. Ronald Reagan cut through the old Democratic coalition that would normally support a Democratic candidate. The general unpopularity of both of the major party candidates and the presence of a significant Independent candidate somewhat undercut the normal influence of group endorsements. Reagan's gains came almost entirely from the Democrats, while Carter lost among Independents. Although organized groups do not always reflect the same membership as generic population groups, the shifts that took place among different voter blocs suggest that interest-group support may have been less decisive in 1980.

## Helping to Shape Party Platforms

A *third* means that groups have of ensuring a role in electoral politics, whether partisan or nonpartisan, is to seek to shape party platforms so that they reflect the policy positions of the group. During the regional hearing of the Republican Platform Committee in 1976, a Washington meeting was addressed by representatives of the American Federation of Teachers, the National Abortion Rights Action League, B'nai B'rith Women, the National Association of Independent Colleges and Universities, the National Associated Businessmen, the National Forest Products Association, the Council for a Livable World, the Committee for Free China, and seventy-six other organizations. Later, at the Republican convention in Kansas City, various subcommittees of the Platform Committee heard from the Advisory Commission on Intergovernmental

## A Sampling of Interest Group Publications Distributed to Members on a Regular Basis

*Common Cause,* published in Washington by the organization of the same name, is a monthly magazine that is mailed to members. Each issue is almost totally political, reflecting the "citizens' action" goals of the group. The February 1982 issue contained articles on the Reagan budget, Federal Trade Commission regulations, and congressional campaign finance; a cover piece on the National Rifle Association; notes on various political figures; a debate on the peace-time draft; and many shorter pieces, as well as cartoons, pictures, and an envelope for remittance of money for group activities. The last page is devoted to a monthly "alert" on pending legislation, instructions for members on how to call congressional representatives and senators, and a delineation of the positions *Common Cause* has taken on particular upcoming issues.

*Advance/Association for the Advancement of Psychology,* published monthly by AAP in Washington, D.C. The March 1978 issue contains articles on pending legislation of interest to psychologists and a four-page section entitled "PLAN (Psychologists for Legislative Action Now)" analyzing the House and Senate races in that year that were of interest to members. Excerpt:

> Of the 34 U.S. Senate seats up for re-election in 1978, 17 are presently held by Democrats and 17 by Republicans. . . . It is already known that three of psychology's good friends (Senators who have cosponsored S. 123 to make psychologists autonomous providers under Medicare, as well as other issues of concern to psychology), Haskell (D) of Colorado, Hathaway (D) of Maine, and Anderson (D) of Minnesota, will have tough re-election fights. In addition, there is speculation that two very good friends of the Republican side, Senators Brooke (Mass.) and Case (N.J.), will have very tough primary challenges from conservatives. Putting these facts together, it would seem that PLAN support and psychologists' activity will be essential to a number of candidates for the U.S. Senate in 1978.

*The Public Affairs Newsletter,* published weekly by the Planned Parenthood Federation of America in New York and Washington. The December 22, 1982, issue carried a front-page notice urging local affiliate public affairs officers to begin "visits with new and returning members of Congress over the holiday recess and before Congress returns on January 26 for the 98th congressional session." It instructed that "new members would be briefed on issues affecting Planned Parenthood and provided assistance in developing and refining positions on these issues. This is a good time to invite them to tour clinic facilities to meet with board members and affiliate staff." The issue also contained brief reports on legislative victories in the waning weeks of the last session, Reagan administration proposed cuts in Medicaid and Medicare benefits, and state actions in Washington, Pennsylvania, and Missouri. An editorial from the *New York Times* was reproduced in its entirety.

The *NEA Advocate,* a monthly newspaper published by the National Education Association in Washington, D.C., devoted much of the February 1983 issue to plans for congressional lobbying. A signed editorial by the chairperson of the NEA Standing Committee on Higher Education said:

> We now have a new Congress—the 98th Congress. It is new in the traditional sense that there is a different Congress every two years, but it is new in another way. This is the first Congress in history where a majority of the members of the House of Representatives were endorsed by NEA-PAC, the NEA political action committee that raises funds from the voluntary contri-

butions of members, then endorses and makes contributions to federal candidates who have proved themselves to be pro-teacher and pro-education.

The issue also contains a full-page article on Congress and higher education and a half-page one on the higher education agenda set for the 98th Congress, with a point by point analysis of NEA proposals. The "Advocate Forum" contains a full-page article written by the west coast CTA (Classroom Teachers Association)/NEA president describing her election efforts in behalf of congressional and California legislative candidates.

The *American Journal of Nursing*, published monthly by the American Nurses' Association (ANA) in New York. The July 1982 issue includes numerous articles on professional nursing and medicine and approximately twenty-five pages of "News," including discussions of pending legislation that would affect the nursing profession. One segment reports on awards to two senators and three congressional representatives from various nursing organizations for their support of ANA legislation in the last Congress. There is also a profile of a New York nurse who combines her career with a position as a district leader in the Democratic party. There are no calls for specific action on the part of members, but the publication occasionally publishes the names, addresses, and phone numbers of key legislators with the clear implication that contacts should be made.

The *American Rifleman*, published monthly by the National Rifle Association in Washington, D.C. The February 1983 issue contains articles on guns, gunmakers, gunsmiths, trick shooters, new bullets, light rifles, and wartime weapons. In addition, the "NRA Official Journal," a six-page section in the middle of the magazine, includes editorial comment about the success of NRA lobbyists in getting an ammunition recordkeeping provision removed from federal law as well as tax relief for custom gunsmiths. Included is a report on the successes of the Institute of Legislative Action of the NRA in getting gun control measures defeated in various state legislatures and state referendums. Another brief article details the dismissal of fifteen counts in a twenty-two-count suit brought against the NRA by the Federal Election Commission for allegedly illegally advancing money to its political action committee, the Political Victory Fund, during the 1978 and 1980 election campaigns. The article notes that the charges were described by "knowledgeable sources as 'politically motivated.'"

Relations, the National Association of Counties, the National Black Republican Council, Citizens for Highway Safety, the National Association of Social Workers, the American Legion, the Polish American Congress, the National League of Families of American Prisoners and Missing in Southeast Asia, the Association of American Physicians and Surgeons, the Retired Officers Association, the National Education Association, National STOP ERA, and ERAmerica. In all, the subcommittees heard from representatives of 164 groups covering almost every possible area of concern.[24] Each group, in presenting testimony, is seeking to influence the language of the platform to reflect the policy goals of the group members. However, although all are given a courteous hearing, few have a direct impact on platform planks.

Even those groups that do not assume partisan roles are given an opportunity to be heard, and the leadership of each can inform the membership that its collective voice was heard by the highest councils of the Republican or Democratic party. If the group's views are incorporated into the platform statements, the leadership can claim a direct role, whether or not the inclusion was coincidental.

Many of these groups back the testimony of their leaders with elaborate policy booklets and brochures. The AFL-CIO presented the platform committees of both parties with a sixty-two page booklet outlining seventy topics of concern to organized labor. Common Cause not only furnished literature but also organized a letter-writing campaign from members directed to committee members. The Democratic Platform Committee accepted all of the Common Cause proposals, whereas the Republicans only included four of them in their 1976 platform.[25]

The most interesting debate over Republican platform pledges in 1980 was the conflict over two issues of importance to womens' groups—ratification of the Equal Rights Amendment and abortion rights. Michael Malbin has noted that outside groups helped to structure the framework of debates over the two issues. The main organizations active on abortion were the Pro-Life Impact Committee, on one side, and the National Women's Political Caucus, on the other. The pro-life, antiabortion group was a decentralized coalition of local pro-life organizations coordinated by people living in or near the convention city. The ERA group would have followed the same path, but their support among the delegates was slight, and they believed it to be important to be led by officials of the Women's Caucus. In both cases, though, anti-ERA and antiabortion delegates dominated the platform committee. About 80 percent of the Republican delegates who expressed a preference for a subcommittee assignment asked for the human resources subcommittee dealing with these two issues. The ensuing fight involved many groups on both sides led by the two organizations. Eventually, the ERA plank that was adopted backed away from the party's forty-year-old supportive position, and an antiabortion plank was incorporated.[26] Obviously, while this conflict was going on, the other five subcommittees of the Platform Committee were hearing from dozens of representatives of other interest groups.

## Rating Incumbent Officeholders

A *fourth* way in which groups attempt to influence election outcomes is through annual ratings of incumbent officeholders according to their voting record, as measured against the group's policy goals. The Americans for Constitutional Action (ACA), a conservative political group dedicated to electing additional conservative House members and senators, uses a sophisticated "consistency index" to demonstrate the number of times a member of Congress has voted "for safeguarding the God-given rights of the individual and promoting sound economic growth by strengthening constitutional government, against 'group morality,' a socialized economy, and centralization of governmental power."[27]

The group, formed in 1968 at the request of a number of conservative senators, periodically reports its ratings of members of both houses of Congress as to whether they were "high scorers" (supported ACA positions) or "low scorers." A 1982 ACA report, for instance, showed scores of 95 and 94 percent, respectively, for Republican senators Helms and East of North Carolina and a score of 95 percent for Independent Harry Byrd of Virginia. A zero score was given to Senator Dodd (D-Conn.). The same system is used by the ACA to rate House members.[28]

The liberal counterpart of Americans for Constitutional Action is the Americans for Democratic Action (ADA), founded in 1947 by a group that included Eleanor Roosevelt and Sen. Hubert H. Humphrey. The ADA uses a scoring system that measures the percentage of the time that each representative or senator voted in accordance with or was paired for an ADA position. In 1982 the ADA compilation was based on twenty selected issues that came to a vote in both houses. Two senators received perfect scores of 100 percent—Kennedy (D-Mass.) and Levin (D-Mich.)—and Bumpers (D-Ark.) was given a score of 95 percent. Eight Republicans received zero scores: Denton (Ala.), Goldwater (Ariz.), Symms (Idaho), East and Helms (N.C.), Thurmond (S.C.), and Garn and Hatch (Utah). Two senators, Helms and East, received zero scores from the liberal ADA and the highest scores from the conservative ACA. This fact illustrates the importance of selecting issues that reflect the views of group members. Each organization decides which key votes it will measure, and the lists vary widely.

In 1982 *Congressional Quarterly* reported on the ratings of eight principal groups: the Americans for Democratic Action, the Americans for Constitutional Action, the American Federation of Labor–Congress of Industrial Organizations, the U.S. Chamber of Commerce, the League of Conservation Voters, Public Citizen Congress Watch, the National Federation of Independent Businesses, and the National Taxpayers Union.[29] Many groups use the same votes in their measurements, some analyzing as few as four and others providing scores on as many as forty. There are now so many group ratings that almost any member of Congress can find one to make him or her look good. The selection of issues on which ratings are based reflects the particular group's internal organization and policy views. They are not always issues of great importance to the general public but are thought to reflect the members' commitment to the group's position.

The ratings of members of Congress are designed to perform three different functions: (1) to embarrass or scare the officeholder into developing a record that conforms more closely to the group's views; (2) to let the group's members know how various individual members have voted on matters of interest to the group; and (3) to provide guidance to affiliates and members for campaign finance purposes. It is not certain that ratings succeed in either regard. If an incumbent is confronted with a low score on some group's scale when his or her score should have been high, it is usually not difficult to find another group's ratings that provide the balance to make the record look better. Furthermore, although there is no reliable evidence on the matter, it is doubtful that many members of Congress consciously seek to improve their scores, since they would almost invariably be lowering other scores on the opposite side of the question.

The proliferation of ratings is itself somewhat self-defeating. So many groups now provide ratings on so many issues that people are likely to pay little attention to them. It would take a dedicated union man to decipher the record of his congressional representative from the complex charts published by the AFL-CIO. Furthermore, many groups have changed their scoring system so often that an individual member would have difficulty ascertaining the meaning of the ratings that do appear. By 1982 the U.S. Chamber of Commerce had altered its scoring system three times in three years. Depending on the particular votes selected in a given year, a member's score can show great variation from one year to the next.

In addition, publication of the ratings of individual representatives or senators in a mass-market national publication may have a greater impact than publication in group newsletters or magazines. As shown in table 10-3, the *U.S. News & World Report*'s publication of the ratings of ten groups for all senators seeking reelection in 1982 may have had an immeasurable effect on voting behavior—especially in view of the fact that the publication does not publish the actual votes included in the various ratings but provides only an overall score.

**TABLE 10–3    Example of mass-market publication's report on group ratings: *U.S. News and World Report***

How lobbies rate senators seeking re-election. Percentage of votes agreeing with the position of each group:

| | AFL-CIO | Chamber of Commerce of U.S.A. | Americans for Democratic Action | American Conservative Union | Congress Watch (Ralph Nader) | Committee for the Survival of a Free Congress | Consumer Federation of America | National Council of Senior Citizens | National Federation of Independent Business | League of Conservation Voters | National Taxpayers Union |
|---|---|---|---|---|---|---|---|---|---|---|---|
| Bentsen (D-Tex.) | 39 | 71 | 25 | 53 | 23 | 58 | 36 | 80 | 100 | 19 | 47 |
| Burdick (D-N.D.) | 74 | 44 | 75 | 13 | 28 | 43 | 50 | 100 | 75 | 50 | 37 |
| Byrd (D-W.Va.) | 89 | 39 | 70 | 14 | 45 | 43 | 64 | 100 | 75 | 75 | 36 |
| Cannon (D-Nev.) | 69 | 45 | 30 | 29 | 25 | 51 | 29 | 90 | 67 | 37 | 41 |
| Chafee (R-R.I.) | 47 | 61 | 45 | 33 | 50 | 62 | 50 | 50 | 75 | 75 | 55 |
| Chiles (D-Fla.) | 41 | 44 | 45 | 21 | 38 | 49 | 36 | 70 | 88 | 50 | 36 |
| Danforth (R-Mo.) | 17 | 89 | 25 | 73 | 38 | 73 | 36 | 10 | 75 | 31 | 53 |
| DeConcini (D-Ariz.) | 50 | 53 | 45 | 57 | 52 | 51 | 43 | 67 | 83 | 31 | 50 |
| Durenberger (R-Minn.) | 26 | 72 | 40 | 47 | 40 | 68 | 57 | 40 | 75 | 63 | 53 |
| Hatch (R-Utah) | 11 | 100 | 0 | 93 | 23 | 85 | 21 | 30 | 100 | 31 | 66 |
| Heinz (R-Pa.) | 61 | 71 | 35 | 36 | 43 | 62 | 36 | 50 | 75 | 50 | 45 |
| Jackson (D-Wash.) | 89 | 33 | 60 | 7 | 40 | 41 | 71 | 100 | 75 | 50 | 26 |
| Kennedy (D-Mass.) | 94 | 6 | 100 | 0 | 83 | 26 | 93 | 100 | 14 | 97 | 23 |
| Lugar (R-Ind.) | 0 | 94 | 5 | 100 | 40 | 83 | 29 | 0 | 100 | 31 | 66 |
| Matsunaga (D-Hawaii) | 83 | 44 | 80 | 0 | 35 | 31 | 57 | 100 | 75 | 66 | 30 |
| Melcher (D-Mont.) | 68 | 53 | 55 | 38 | 25 | 49 | 43 | 100 | 75 | 52 | 40 |
| Metzenbaum (D-Ohio) | 94 | 7 | 85 | 0 | 65 | 28 | 71 | 100 | 20 | 88 | 30 |
| Mitchell (D-Me.) | 95 | 35 | 90 | 7 | 63 | 36 | 57 | 100 | 75 | 72 | 40 |
| Moynihan (D-N.Y.) | 94 | 33 | 75 | 13 | 60 | 31 | 64 | 100 | 50 | 92 | 30 |
| Proxmire (D-Wis.) | 32 | 61 | 55 | 53 | 60 | 59 | 50 | 30 | 88 | 56 | 83 |
| Riegle (D-Mich.) | 89 | 22 | 90 | 14 | 58 | 23 | 79 | 100 | 50 | 86 | 32 |
| Roth (R-Del.) | 32 | 78 | 20 | 67 | 45 | 71 | 36 | 40 | 100 | 44 | 70 |
| Sarbanes (D-Md.) | 95 | 11 | 95 | 0 | 70 | 28 | 64 | 100 | 29 | 88 | 26 |
| Sasser (D-Tenn.) | 59 | 67 | 45 | 31 | 25 | 48 | 43 | 90 | 88 | 12 | 40 |
| Schmitt (R-N.M.) | 11 | 100 | 10 | 67 | 23 | 82 | 14 | 0 | 100 | 5 | 63 |
| Stafford (R-Vt.) | 24 | 75 | 35 | 47 | 23 | 71 | 36 | 40 | 71 | 47 | 53 |
| Stennis (D-Miss.) | 28 | 93 | 15 | 47 | 23 | 65 | 14 | 40 | 100 | 19 | 53 |
| Wallop (R-Wyo.) | 5 | 100 | 10 | 71 | 23 | 85 | 14 | 0 | 100 | 25 | 63 |
| Weicker (R-Conn.) | 64 | 60 | 55 | 23 | 40 | 54 | 43 | 78 | 50 | 48 | 43 |
| Zorinsky (D-Nebr.) | 26 | 78 | 20 | 71 | 30 | 62 | 29 | 78 | 100 | 12 | 62 |

*Source:* "The Unhappy Lobbyists on Capitol Hill," *U.S. News & World Report* (May 24, 1982): 54. Copyright, 1982, U.S. News & World Report, Inc.

In an effort to overcome the built-in bias in group ratings, political scientists and journalists have undertaken to develop rating systems that may more accurately measure congressional performance. For instance, since 1959 *Congressional Quarterly* has used its measure of the conservative coalition of Republicans and southern Democrats as one method of bringing more meaningful ratings to the fore (see chapter 9). Since 1983 *CQ* has also measured the allegiance of members of Congress to the president's program. The *National Journal* and the *Baron Report* introduced a more complex scoring system in 1982 that rates lawmakers on separate liberal–conservative scales for their votes on economic matters, defense and foreign-policy questions, and social issues. These publications hoped that the new system would help to illustrate the separate strands of each member's ideological or philosophical views. Some members who received identical scores on a rating from a particular group emerged as dramatically different personalities when their votes on different kinds of issues were charted separately.[30] It is clear that rating systems for incumbent members of Congress will continue to be used by interest groups, but it is also clear that such systems have a long way to go before they accurately reflect a member's overall record.

## Making Campaign Contributions

The *fifth* way in which groups take part in electoral politics is through campaign contributions to candidates. It must be emphasized again that many groups work hard to preserve their nonpartisanship and never overtly take part in political campaigns lest they jeopardize their access to any candidate or party emerging victorious. Others, however, make equal contributions to the candidates of both parties, and many openly endorse candidates or parties. In chapter 6 we noted that business and labor have long histories of raising and contributing funds for political purposes. Either these funds are furnished to selected candidates who, if elected or reelected, might be sympathetic to the goals of the group, or they go directly to political parties to assist with meeting the general expenses of the campaign.

Both in Congress and in the state legislatures money tends to flow to those who hold the most important committee or leadership positions. A committee vote can be crucial to the success of a group, and lobbyists and organization officers keep careful track of voting records in order to identify their friends as well as their enemies. At election time, direct campaign contributions will be made or tickets to fund-raising events will be purchased to assist those friends. Organized labor has long provided campaign assistance costing millions of dollars to candidates individually and to the Democratic party as a whole. Theodore White, in describing labor's role in the 1968 Democratic campaign, noted that contributions cannot be measured in terms of dollars alone:

> The dimension of the AFL-CIO effort . . . can be caught only in its final summary figures: the ultimate registration, by labor's efforts, of 4.6 million voters; the printing and distribution of 55 million pamphlets and leaflets out of Washington, 60 million more from local unions; telephone banks in 638 localities, using 8,055 telephones, manned by 24,611 union men and women and their families; some 72,225 house-to-house canvassers; and, on Election Day, 94,457 volunteers serving as car-poolers, materials-distributors, babysitters, poll-watchers, telephoners.[31]

As we saw in chapter 6, the 1974 Federal Election Campaign Act significantly increased the role of groups, particularly business and labor, by limiting individual contributions to $1,000 per candidate but extending that limit to $5,000 if the contribution was made through a political action committee (PAC). By the end of the 1980 presidential campaign PACs, largely representing interest groups, had contributed $130.3 million to campaigns. The Federal Election Commission reported in 1981 that at least $50.7 million had been contributed to congressional races and $1.8 million to presidential campaigns. Most of the money went to Democratic candidates and to incumbents of both parties. Corporate groups contributed nearly $19.3 million to federal candidates, favoring for the first time Republicans over Democrats $12.1 million to $7.1 million. Labor gave more than $13.7 million, about $12.8 million to Democrats and less than $1 million to Republicans.[32] As noted in chapter 6, during the first eighteen months of the 1981–1982 election cycle, these PACs gave $38 million to congressional candidates. The largest amounts were contributed by realtors, doctors, unions, and various specialized groups (see table 6-8). Almost 3,500 PACs, mostly representing groups, took an active part in the 1982 off-year elections.

An increasing number of groups are also contributing services and counsel to campaigns. In 1982 the Committee on Political Education (COPE) of the AFL-CIO provided assistance to candidates on campaign planning and public opinion polling and held training sessions for managers and candidates. The training schools were organized for candidates in different regions of the country almost entirely for congressional candidates of the Democratic party. The midwestern school was held in Chicago for two days in July and was attended by thirty candidates or campaign aides.[33]

The U.S. Chamber of Commerce, a long-time practitioner of grass-roots politics, began in 1982 to beam custom-made television programs to business subscribers around the nation. The broadcasts, including legislative and political news of interest to business, sometimes featured call-in shows with leading government officials and were designed to enhance the political sophistication of men and women in business. The chamber invested $6 million in equipment, including a satellite dish for its Washington headquarters.[34]

Business and labor are not alone in these efforts to influence elections. Most of the large professional groups, agricultural groups, and public interest organizations are developing new techniques for involving their members in campaigns and, with the advent of political action committees, have become increasingly active in the political arena. Some of them are old and well established and are simply adding a new dimension to their political sophistication. Others are new and have just organized for political purposes.

Prior to the 1980 campaign, a new phenomenon emerged as an actor in the interplay of groups and politics. The so-called New Right groups gained a great deal of media attention in their support of conservative causes and candidates. Although sharing many views on issues and a number of strategies, the New Right groups fell into two distinct categories of activity: political and evangelical. The best-known of the political groups in 1980 and 1982 was the National Conservative Political Action Committee (NCPAC). NCPAC reportedly spent $4.5 million in 1980, nearly one-fourth of which went to campaigns against six liberal Democratic senators: George McGovern (S.D.), Frank Church (Idaho), Birch Bayh (Ind.), John Culver (Iowa), Gaylord Nelson (Wis.), and Gary Hart (Colo.). Of the six, all but Hart were defeated, and NCPAC claimed credit, although considerable evidence indicates that a number of other factors were of greater importance in each of those races.

The second type of New Right group to emerge was a loose coalition of evangelical groups representing a number of conservative religious organizations, often involved

An example of advertising directed toward a specific group.

in television evangelism. The best-known of these was the Moral Majority, headed by Rev. Jerry Falwell, the "star" of television's "Old Time Gospel Hour." The Moral Majority was not successful in its efforts to raise large amounts of money through its own PAC and eventually abandoned the effort. However, it and the other evangelical groups—the Christian Voice, the Religious Roundtable, the National Christian Action Coalition, and others—claimed to have had an important impact in 1980 by emphasizing moral and family issues through sermons, through the distribution of thousands of leaflets, by word of mouth, and in mass rallies. These groups concentrated on such issues as support of prayer in the schools and opposition to abortion, the Equal Rights Amendment, and homosexual rights. They participated in several House races, in which they claimed some success in defeating incumbents, and in two Senate races in Oklahoma and Alabama, where conservative Republicans won with their support.[35] However, the efforts of these groups in 1982, both the politically oriented and the evangelical, were not widely perceived to have been effective, partly because senators and representatives targeted by these groups had apparently learned how to deal with this kind of campaign tactic and were able to counteract it during their campaigns.

Such contributions by groups to officeholders and candidates are not always designed to elicit positive action. Lester Milbrath, in his study of Washington lobbying, found a number of House members who reported that they might not take the initiative in behalf of a friendly group but would go out of their way to avoid opposing it.[36]

But groups have limited effectiveness in electoral politics. Many, particularly smaller ones, do not have the financial resources or personnel to become very actively engaged in political campaigns. Furthermore, as we have observed, some groups are unable to translate their membership rolls into voting blocs. In short, even those groups that take an active part in electoral politics do so selectively. They desire to help their friends in the political arena, but they cannot afford to suffer too many electoral defeats. Group leaders must bend every effort to be selective in choosing the candidates they will ask their members to support.

In each of these five ways, groups make themselves felt in electoral politics. They are not always effective. They do not always behave in a polished and professional manner. But they do have an interest in who gets nominated and elected because the results affect their access to power and may determine in the long run whether they can achieve their political goals.

## Interest Groups: Influencing Political Action

By now it should be clear that political parties and interest groups are dependent on each other. They share power and influence in American politics. Parties, as part of the formal framework through which officials are elected to run the government, have opportunities to put their policies into effect through their elected representatives, who control the policymaking machinery of government. Groups, however, must use whatever means they can devise to make their influence felt. As we have seen in this chapter, such means sometimes take the form of electoral action. Not all groups are organized in such ways as to make them effective in politics. Nelson Polsby and Aaron Wildavsky, both political scientists, have noted that the groups that are the most influential in elections in our society are groups that have the following characteristics:

1. They have a mass base composed of many members.

2. They are geographically concentrated, not thinly dispersed over the countryside.

3. They represent a major resource investment for their members; that is, the entire livelihoods of those who belong to the group are tied up in the group. Polsby and Wildavsky illustrated this point by noting that the producers of a commodity are inevitably tied to the success of the commodity, whereas consumers of the item view it as just one among many that they may use.

4. They involve those characteristics that provide people with their status, such as race or ethnic background.

5. An effective interest group is composed of people who are able to spare the time and money to take part in politics.[37]

Obviously, many groups possessing some or all of these characteristics can make themselves felt politically by taking part in the election process. As we noted earlier, though, such participation is not a sufficient guarantee that their goals will eventually be achieved. They must use other means to seek what they want. These means generally fall into two categories: lobbying and grass-roots politics, the subjects of the next chapter.

# Notes

1. In order of appearance, these headlines appeared in the following issues of the *New York Times:* July 25, 1982, p. E-5; November 9, 1980, p. 27; January 11, 1981, p. 22; February 26, 1981, p. 10; May 12, 1982, p. 13; June 27, 1982, p. 15; and December 5, 1980, p. B-9.

2. David Broder, *Washington Post* (September 13, 1978): A-27.

3. Pendleton Herring, *Group Representation Before Congress* (New York: Russell and Russell, 1967), p. 19. (Originally published 1929.)

4. Jerry I. Reitman and Judith Bettelhein, eds., *The Directory of Registered Federal and State Lobbyists* (New York: Academic Press, 1973).

5. The 1955 membership figure from the *New York Times* (May 7, 1978): 6-E; the 1982 membership figure from Denise S. Akey, ed., *The Encyclopedia of Associations, 1983*, 17th ed., vol. 1, (Detroit: Gale Research, 1982), p. 1412.

6. Andrea F. Schoenfeld, "Sophisticated GMA Lobby Represents Grocery Item Industry in Era of Consumerism," in *Pressure Groups* (Washington, D.C.: National Journal, 1971), pp. 3–14.

7. Based on illustration used by Ivan Hinderaker in *Party Politics* (New York: Holt, 1956), pp. 51–52.

8. James Bryce, *Modern Democracies,* vol. 2 (New York: Macmillan, 1921), p. 542.

9. Robert Michels, *Political Parties: A Sociological Study of the Oligarchical Tendencies of Modern Democracy,* trans. Eden and Cedar Paul (London: Jarrold and Sons, 1915), p. 14.

10. Ibid.

11. David B. Truman, *The Governmental Process* (New York: Knopf, 1955), pp. 139–155.

12. U.S. Department of Commerce, Bureau of the Census, *Statistical Abstract of the United States, 1981* (Washington, D.C.: Government Printing Office, 1981).

13. U.S. Chamber of Commerce, *1981 Annual Report: Let's Rebuild America* (Washington, D.C.: U.S. Chamber of Commerce, 1981), p. 2.

14. Truman, *Governmental Process,* ch. 6.

15. John K. Iglehart, "No More Doctor Nice Guy," in *Interest Groups, 1977–78* (Washington, D.C.: National Journal Reprints, 1977), p. 8.

16. Carol S. Greenwald, *Group Power: Lobbying and Public Policy* (New York: Praeger, 1977), pp. 75, 207, 264, and 285.

17. Mark V. Nadel, *The Politics of Consumer Protection* (Indianapolis, Ind.: Bobbs-Merrill, 1971), pp. 158–159.

18. "A Superlobby in Action," *New York Times* (June 5, 1982): 29.

19. "Memo from COPE," Committee on Political Education, AFL-CIO, Washington, D.C., March 8, 1982.

20. *Congressional Quarterly Weekly Report* (December 2, 1972): 3096.

21. *Congressional Quarterly Weekly Report* (September 4, 1982): 2192–2193.

22. Gerald Pomper et al., *The Election of 1976* (New York: McKay, 1977), p. 60.

23. Ibid., pp. 61–62.

24. Witness lists for regional hearings, subcommittee hearings, and full committee hearings, Republican Committee on Resolutions (Plat-

form), Republican National Convention, 1976. These lists were furnished by Dr. John F. Bibby, assistant staff director, Resolutions Committee.

25. Greenwald, *Group Power,* p. 122.

26. Michael J. Malbin, "The Conventions, Platforms, and Issue Activists," in *The American Elections of 1980,* ed. Austin Ranney (Washington, D.C.: American Enterprise Institute, 1981), pp. 100–110.

27. Ibid., pp. 126–127.

28. *Congressional Quarterly Weekly Report* (July 3, 1982): 1607–1619.

29. Ibid.

30. Ibid., p. 1609.

31. Theodore H. White, *The Making of the President, 1968* (New York: Atheneum, 1969), p. 365.

32. "Interest Groups Spent $130.3 Million in '80 Elections," *New York Times* (March 29, 1981): 31.

33. "Labor Now Also Counsels Candidates," *New York Times* (July 21, 1982): 17.

34. *Congressional Quarterly Weekly Report* (November 14, 1981): 2235.

35. *Congressional Quarterly Weekly Report* (November 15, 1980): 3372–3373.

36. Lester W. Milbrath, *The Washington Lobbyists* (Chicago: Rand McNally, 1963), p. 284.

37. Nelson W. Polsby and Aaron Wildavsky, *Presidential Elections: Strategies of American Electoral Politics,* 4th ed. (New York: Scribner's, 1976), pp. 13–14.

# Lobbying and Grass-Roots Politics

Lobbyists approach their jobs with more intelligence, hard work, and persuasive argument than ever before. While fewer than 2,000 lobbyists are registered with Congress under a largely ignored 1946 law, their actual number has soared from about 8,000 to 15,000 over the past five years. Their mass arrival has transformed Washington's downtown K Street into a virtual hall of lobbies. New office buildings springing up west of the White House along Pennsylvania Avenue fill up with lobbyists as soon as the painters walk out. It is estimated that lobbyists now spend $1 billion a year to influence Washington opinion, plus another $1 billion to orchestrate public opinion across the nation.

Excerpted from "The Swarming Lobbyists," *Time* (August 7, 1978).

*In the Age of Expansion, the railroad lobbyists were so active and so effective that Senator J. S. Morrill, a man of rare wit, once rose towards the end of a session and, calling attention to the presence in the outer lobby of the president of the Pennsylvania Railroad, moved the appointment of a committee to wait upon him and learn if there was any further legislation he desired before adjournment.*

Karl Schriftgiesser, *The Lobbyists* (Boston: Little, Brown, 1951), p. 19.

*I want to say to you that, as one legislator for almost three decades now, ... I use the services of lobbyists in my activities more than lobbyists come and see me. One of my favorite lobbyists is the Montana Power Co. I do not think that anyone would say I am subservient to the Montana Power Co., but when I want some information I go [to] the Montana Power Co.'s lobbyist who is here in Washington and ask him if he could find it out for me. With all justice, they have never given me false information.*

Former senator Lee Metcalf, a liberal Democrat from Montana, in a hearing before the Senate Committee on Government Operations, 94th Congress, 1st Session, Government Printing Office, Washington, D.C., 1976, p. 231.

Lobbying is widespread in Washington, the state capitals, the county courthouses, and the city halls. Thousands of people make their livings serving as contact points between the people, their organized groups, and their elected officeholders. In a democracy decision making on public policy matters represents the end result of the process of translating public desires into official reality. Because the population is so great and so heterogeneous and because there are no clear-cut channels through which the public can speak to the policymakers, the role of communicator, translator, and propounder has been coopted by political parties and interest groups. As we have noted before, parties have not proved to be very effective as the intermediator between the public and the government. Groups, however, are sometimes more adaptable to that role and have assumed an increasingly important place in that respect. Nevertheless, if the groups are to serve effectively as go-betweens for the people (as group members) and the government officials (as decision makers), the leadership must have the means to communicate group desires to those who have the power to make decisions to carry them out. Groups must work to maintain access to policymakers. They must also maintain working channels of communication with their members. Political effectiveness may well hinge on the degree to which these channels of communication are kept open.

## Getting the Message Across

Groups use two techniques to get their message across. One is through the direct contact of a lobbyist, employed by the group, talking with a legislator, an administrator, or another lobbyist. In some situations, however, direct lobbying is not enough or is inappropriate, and the group must resort to the use of grass-roots pressures generated by the leadership from within the membership. A cohesive group with strong leadership and dedicated members can use both techniques to accomplish its goals.

Congress has defined lobbying as any attempt "to influence, directly or indirectly, the passage or defeat of any legislation by the Congress of the United States."[1] That narrow definition has not proved to be very useful, because Congress itself limited the scope of the lobby regulation provisions to exclude executive agencies. Furthermore, in 1954 the Supreme Court, in *United States* v. *Harriss,* eliminated indirect lobbying (including grass-roots efforts) because "the Act is so broad that one who writes a letter or makes a speech or publishes an article or distributes literature . . . has no fair notice when he is close to the prohibited line."[2] These two limitations had a chilling effect on efforts to regulate the practices used by lobbyists, but attempts to define more clearly the parameters of the term have always run afoul of constitutional problems engendered by efforts to avoid conflicts with the First and Fifth amendments.

According to H. L. Mencken, the term first appeared as *lobby-agent* in the New York state legislature in the early 1800s. It was later shortened to *lobbyist* and had gained widespread use by the early 1830s. It was used to describe those men who frequented the lobbies of government buildings in order to take advantage of opportunities to speak to legislators in their efforts to gain consideration for their employers' special needs.[3] The term is often used interchangeably with *pressure group,* but it should be noted that, in a technical sense, lobbying is but a tool through which pressure groups try to accomplish their goals.

## Lobbying and Lobbyists

Have you ever heard of Karen A. Doherty, James J. Baker, Harvey Alter, John Terzano, William Gilmartin, or Leslie Loble? Probably not—but official Washington may be well aware of their identities. They are registered lobbyists who represent their respective groups in official dealings with Congress and the executive branch of government. Doherty represents the Sierra Club; Baker works for the National Rifle Association; Alter is employed by the U.S. Chamber of Commerce; Terzano lobbies for the Vietnam Veterans of America; Gilmartin represents Planned Parenthood of America; and Loble is a lobbyist for the Communications Workers of America.[4] The range of organizational interests that these lobbyists stand for suggests the wide diversity of interest groups in the United States. Some lobbyists are self-employed; others are members of law firms with interest-group clients; still others are staff members of the groups they represent.

Many lobbyists are lawyers employed full-time to represent groups in appearances before governmental agencies. Lobbying, in a sense, constitutes their law practice. They are selling expertise, not only on matters of law but also in access to lawmakers. Others are former members of Congress who, having retired voluntarily or involuntarily, open an office in Washington and offer their services to those who might need the assistance of one who knows the inner workings of Congress, to say nothing of its members and leaders. The former Congress member-lawyer may operate from a law office but engage primarily in lobbying. The former member of Congress who is not a lawyer may style himself or herself a public relations expert. Some who lobby do so part-time, practicing case law most of the time but contracting to carry a bill for some group for a regular legal fee. The job can be a relaxed ramble through government or a harried and hectic eighteen-hour daily grind of meetings and telephone calls. The latter, of course, is most likely to occur when a bill of interest is reaching the stages of final passage or approaching a key vote.

Professional lobbyists have a number of factors in their favor when dealing with Congress and the federal bureaucracy (or the state legislatures and state bureaucracies). *First,* the structure of the government is itself an advantage. Lobbyists need points of contact. They prefer to have more than one target so that, should they fail to persuade one contact, they can fall back on another. The federal nature of our government offers an advantage to lobbyists, for, if they fail in their efforts to get a law changed through congressional action, they can switch signals and seek redress through the state legislatures. If they cannot prevent a bill from getting through Congress, they can change direction and try to persuade the president to veto the bill. If lobbyists fail to influence the president, they can shift their attention to the bureaucracy and its administrators who are charged with developing the rules under which the general legislation will be implemented.

Furthermore, many laws passed in Washington must be implemented in the state and local governments. If the law requires that rules be adopted governing the administration of a new or expanded program, the rule-making authority may extend from federal agencies down through comparable state and local units. Each level, therefore, offers a target for lobbyists to get a little more of what they want. The very complexity of the governmental machinery, with its multiple layers and many chambers, provides many channels for the lobbyists' efforts.

A *second* advantage enjoyed by lobbyists is that the United States Constitution is on their side. One of the principal reasons few legislative bodies have been willing or able to enact legislation to control the actions of groups and lobbyists is that they enjoy an honorable place among those protected by the First Amendment. The right to petition provides a means through which groups of people can combine to attempt to influence policymakers. It has proved very difficult to chart a constitutional path that provides some controls of lobbying excesses but at the same time does not infringe on the group members' or lobbyists' First Amendment rights. Reform efforts to provide reasonably clear rules of lobbying behavior have often run onto the shoals of constitutional protection.

A *third* advantage of lobbyists, although more evident at the state legislative level than at the congressional level, is that they are widely used as an important source of information. Many state legislators still have not provided themselves with the resources necessary to conduct business. They have no staff, no research assistance, no legislative library, no bill-drafting service, and in some states no assigned office space. These legislators literally operate out of their hats. Yet the unavailability of these services, particularly research information and bill drafting, does not diminish the need for them. In those states lobbyists sometimes represent the only generally available source of information, biased though it may be. Even U.S. congressional representatives and senators will testify to the importance of lobbyists and groups as sources of information—as illustrated by the comments of the late former senator Lee Metcalf of Montana quoted at the opening of this chapter. Over the years many studies of congressional and state legislative voting behavior have found that groups and lobbyists represent an important source of information on which the legislator acts. A recent study of state legislatures in Massachusetts, New Hampshire, and Pennsylvania, conducted by political scientist David Ray, found that in all three states members cited groups as an important source of information so long as their material was used with care.[5]

Many initial contacts are made by the legislator with the lobbyist. The lobbyist for a particular interest, especially a complex one, may be the best source of information available, and members of Congress and state legislators are often quick to ask for help. In fact, several studies of state legislative processes have concluded that much of the information furnished by lobbyists to legislators is remarkably straightforward and reliable. Most professional group representatives are aware that their reputation for integrity and honesty is their most important possession. Once a legislator is embarrassed by disseminating erroneous information furnished by a lobbyist, he or she is unlikely to maintain open access for that particular person. A Florida speaker of the

"It's awful the way they're trying to influence
Congress. Why don't they serve cocktails and
make campaign contributions like we do?"
(From The Herblock Gallery, Simon & Schuster, 1968)

house recalls a time "when I was a freshman. A lobbyist lied to me and I was embarrassed in front of a committee. I've never forgiven him, and I could never trust him after that."[6] Nevertheless, because most state legislators do rely on lobbyists for important information, this provides lobbyists with a degree of leverage they would not ordinarily have.

It should be noted, however, that the lobbyist–legislator relationship is not always tilted toward the lobbyist. For decades most of the literature, influenced as it was by the muckrakers, has portrayed lobbyists and "pressure" groups as hidden manipulators who work behind the scenes to control the behavior of helpless and harried legislators. This ancient theory demands a certain suspension of reason if one is to believe it. Many groups and the lobbyists who represent them do not have unlimited supplies of money to spend on influence. Many lobbyists are not only not very effective but are not even possessed of the kinds of experiences or resources necessary to carry out their mission. Groups are sometimes torn with dissension and are unable to show a united front. Lobbyists sometimes are simply inept. The theory does not often square with the facts. The relationship between lobbyists and legislators is more complex than that. This theory was the principal thrust behind the effort of political scientists to change the descriptive adjective describing such groups from *pressure* to *interest*.

## Lobbyists: Who They Are and How They Operate

Many people have a predominantly negative view of lobbyists. This attitude has developed over the years in reaction to news accounts of lobbyists who have violated the norms of professional or legal behavior. It is evident that lobbying pushed to the furthest limits can breach the law and become outright bribery. Some former lobbyists are in jail because they were unable to draw the line between responsible advocacy and illegal payoffs. Needless to say, several members of Congress and legislators, too, have been convicted of accepting payoffs from lobbyists. Even so, hundreds of professional lobbyists do their jobs every day, year in and year out, and never even approach the area of unethical or illegal behavior.

One reason might be that those who lobby for a living do not differ significantly from persons engaged in other professions. Lester W. Milbrath found in a study based on 101 interviews with lobbyists and 38 with congressional targets of lobbying that the profile of group representatives does not differ significantly from that of other professional groups, either in socioeconomic characteristics or in personality traits. Lobbyists are better educated and have higher incomes than the general populace. They tend to be middle-aged, white, male, and Protestant. And they have the same respect for ethical behavior and moral codes as do the members of other professional groups.[7] Thus one may conjecture that the negative view that many persons have of lobbyists may be associated with their role in the political process and may well be an extension of the public distrust of politicians.

When carried to extremes, of course, the lobbyist's role can be objectionable. Aside from the fact that his or her behavior might alienate a legislator, thus defeating the group's purpose, there are certain unofficial rules of the game that should be followed when possible. Milbrath, after extensive interviews with lobbyists and legislators, suggests a series of "dos" and "don'ts" that lobbyists should follow in pursuing their profession. Some of them appear to be commonsense suggestions, but even they are violated from time to time. The list might be summarized as follows:

1. *Be pleasant and nonoffensive.* Congressional respondents told Milbrath that they preferred to deal with people who are sincere, enthusiastic, energetic, patient, and present a good appearance. They do not respond favorably to lobbyists (or anyone else, for that matter) who are antagonistic, arrogant, or disagreeable. Milbrath concludes that pleasantness is possibly the most important factor in maintaining access to decision makers.

2. *Convince the official that it is important for him or her to listen.* Lobbyists must demonstrate to the official that they have something important to say. Since legislators are almost always interested in constituent interests, it is helpful to be able to show them how support for the lobbyist's position can help them in their districts. If no reasonable constituent interest is at stake, the lobbyists must show the member of Congress or administrator that their group's stand is in the public interest.

3. *Be well prepared and well informed.* The most important aspect of a successful presentation by a lobbyist to a member of Congress is to be well prepared, knowledgeable, and well informed. Lobbyists must demonstrate their capabilities and their knowledge in order to avoid being considered incompetent. The stock-in-trade of the lobbyist is information, and it is essential that it be well founded and accurate.

4. *Be personally convinced.* Lobbyists, unlike attorneys, must believe in their case. Milbrath found that the lobbyist who does not appear to be personally convinced of his or her own cause is less effective. Many successful lobbyists present both sides of the case to the legislator. This suggests fairmindedness and honesty, but the committed lobbyist can demonstrate during a presentation that his or hers is the stronger case. If a lobbyist is unable to embrace the group's position on some issue, the leadership of the group may want to sideline him or her temporarily and send in someone more committed to their position on the matter at hand.

5. *Be succinct, well organized, and direct.* Since time is important to legislators and administrators, the lobbyist who can present his or her case in a concise and direct manner will score points with the legislator. Milbrath quotes one member of Congress: "The man who presents his problem or proposal, and lets the congressman get on with his other work, comes to be liked and respected."

6. *Use the soft sell.* Some lobbyists push their case too hard. They give the impression that they and their group are unwilling to compromise in an environment in which compromise is the accepted currency. Knowledgeable and experienced lobbyists try to plead but not to demand. Contrary to the concept of "pressure" politics, the successful lobbyist seldom attempts to pressure or threaten. The soft sell is more likely to be effective and better received.

7. *Leave a short written summary of the case.* Legislators appreciate receiving statements of the case in writing. Some lobbyists even send a written statement before visiting a House member so that the latter can review the case and discuss it intelligently. Furthermore, there is always a chance that the written statement might be incorporated into a speech by the member of Congress or be used in his or her election campaign. In any event, it is good to have a written statement of the group's position in the files of a House member for future use.[8]

This list represents a distillation of lobbying experiences. Presumably, lobbyists who follow these rules of the game will be more effective than those who violate them. Even when lobbyists adhere to the rules, they may not be successful in convincing legislators to support their group's position. But, even if that is the case, an appropriate approach will serve to maintain open access for the future.

Lobbyists have other ways of presenting their points of view besides direct contacts with decision makers. They often testify before congressional committees and sub-

---

## The Darker Side of Lobbying

During the 1975 efforts to reform lobby regulation legislation Senators Edward Kennedy (D–Mass.) and Robert Stafford (R–Vt.) presented a joint statement to the Senate Committee on Government Operations. The following are excerpts from their testimony:

> But there is a darker side of lobbying, a side that is responsible for the sinister connotation that lobbying often has. In large part, the connotation derives from the secrecy of lobbying and the widespread suspicion, even when totally unjustified, that secrecy breeds undue influence and corruption. It is but a short step from there to the cynical and undeserved view that government itself is the puppet of wealthy citizens and powerful interest groups with special access to Congress and the Executive Branch. Too often, the suspicions seem to be well founded. Too often the needs of the people are overridden by interest groups clamoring for favored treatment.

> Fortunes are won and lost on the basis of a single arcane sentence in a lengthy complex bill or a Treasury regulation. Page after page of the Internal Revenue Code is dotted with the fingerprints of lobbyists—special tax provisions written into the law for the benefit of a single company or individual. It is difficult enough under the present lobbying law to identify the beneficiaries of such favored tax treatment. It is virtually impossible to trace the way by which they suddenly surface in a committee bill or conference report.

*Source: "Lobby Reform Legislation," Hearings, the Committee on Government Operations, United States Senate* (Washington, D.C.: U.S. Government Printing Office, 1976), p. 24.

committees, and, even if some members are absent, they have made their case for the record so that committee members can refer to it at a later time. Other lobbyists have such a close relationship with some members of Congress that the former merely furnish accurate materials to the latter, who then may make the case to their fellow committee members. Some lobbyists build a close working relationship with key members interested in their position so that there is almost a constant exchange of information and discussion of tactics. Many officials want to establish themselves with certain lobbyists in order to gain the campaign support of the group. Others find that, because the views of a particular organization correspond closely to those of some important constituent group, a marriage between the pertinent member of Congress and the lobbyist or group is desirable. A rural midwestern member of Congress will not find it difficult to adopt the Farm Bureau's position on some agricultural issue. Several studies have shown that the relationship between legislators and lobbyists is quite complex; it is not a simple association. Many of the chips in this poker game belong to the legislators. Donald Matthews pointed out in his classic study of the U.S. Senate that legislators influence the behavior of lobbyists in at least four different ways.

*First,* the lobbyist must have the senator's cooperation in order to keep his or her access to the legislative process open. The senator can effectively block the lobbyist by noncooperation. *Second,* Matthews notes that the senator's friendship is important to the lobbyist. It makes the lobbyist indebted to the senator and, consequently, more inclined to understand the latter's political problems. Sometimes it builds a relationship that, as we have seen earlier, almost makes allies of the lobbyist and the senator. A *third* technique available to senators is to build up credit by passing on information or giving the group represented by the lobbyist favorable publicity by referring to it in a speech or inserting material favorable to the group in the *Congressional Record.* This permits the lobbyist to tell his or her employer that he or she was responsible for this reference and subtly binds him or her to the senator. *Finally,* if all else fails, the senator can always threaten an attack on the lobbyist or his or her group. This can be done through a press release or by threatening a congressional investigation. In either event, groups would ordinarily rather avoid such a reaction. In any case, clearly a good deal of reciprocity exists in the relations between legislators and lobbyists.[9] Recognizing that fact helps to explain why *interest* is a better adjective to describe the relationship than *pressure.*

Lobbyists engage in a wide variety of activities that fall within any definition of influence. These activities may be directed to officeholders or their staff members. They may be focused on the legislative, executive, or judicial branches as well as on administrative agencies. They may involve presenting testimony before a congressional committee or subcommittee or before an administrative tribunal. Lobbyists and other group representatives often take part in political campaigns as a way of trying to ensure their access once an election is over. Their role in campaigns may be business-like, or it may be carried out as an entertainment function through parties, receptions, or the working lunch. Lobbyists lobby other lobbyists, and interest groups seek support and alliance with other groups.

Government agencies themselves engage in widespread lobbying activities. Every cabinet office has an undersecretary or an assistant secretary for congressional relations—in other words, a lobbyist. During the Carter administration there were 675 lobbyists representing 32 federal agencies spending between $12 million and $15 million a year trying to sell administration programs to Congress and the people.[10] The White House legislative liaison team under President Reagan, working out of the executive branch, has a staff of fourteen people. These public officials have as their primary duty selling the agency's or the administration's program to Congress. It is commonplace, for example, for an industry engaged in defense manufacture to work closely with the Department of Defense in presenting arguments to congressional committees in behalf of new weapons systems. In short, lobbying cannot be narrowly defined, for it is broader than the strict definition contained in federal law. Lobbying is in fact a system of communications directed by organized private citizens at government decision makers who possess the power to act on their problems. The fact that the lobbyist–legislator–administrator relationship is so obviously one of direct contact goes far to explain why many people are more likely to rely on interest groups to get what they want than on the less direct, more distant activities of political parties.

---

While thinking about lobbying and pressure group politics we usually think about the American Legion or the AFL-CIO. But there are others who are busy working in Washington to get what they can for the group or organization they represent. As of 1978 eight separate taxpayer-supported offices were maintained in Washington to lobby for New York State and City agencies. Governor Carey had an office; Mayor Koch had an office; both houses of the General Assembly maintained offices; along with those operated by the city's Board of Education, the New York State Department of Education, The State University of New York, and Nassau County. All of them were staffed by lobbyists—38 in all. All told, three-quarters of a million dollars a year are being spent in the spirit of getting more Federal support for New Yorkers.

Based on a story by Edward C. Burks in the *New York Times* (April 26, 1978): 37.

---

The legislative process in the United States is complex and provides many points of access for lobbyists to present the point of view of the groups they represent. Bills, once introduced, must overcome many obstacles and pitfalls along the legislative pathways. They must survive the committee system, the subcommittee system, the Rules Committee in the House, and, ultimately, the perils of floor action. If the two houses of Congress pass a bill in differing forms, the two forms must be compromised in a conference committee made up of members from both houses. If compromise is accomplished, the bill must then receive the approval of the members of both houses. Should a bill survive this process—and only a small percentage of them do—it must then be signed by the president. Should he choose to exercise his veto power, all of the work will be for naught. And whatever the final outcome, some lobbyists and groups will be happy and others will be distressed. The process is a difficult one; should the bill fail to negotiate any step in the road toward passage, it will not become law. Thus it is much easier to defeat a bill than to get one approved, a fact that works to the advantage of organized group activities.

Obviously, the more controversial a bill, the more groups are going to either advocate or oppose it. Groups participate at almost every step of the process. Traditionally, groups have been more interested in maintaining the status quo than in trying to get new legislation passed. The recent rise of public interest and citizen's groups, however, has placed new emphasis on positive legislation, often actually initiated by the groups themselves.

Regardless of the type of bill being considered, its life is tenuous. Almost everyone agrees, however, that the principal point of danger is at the committee level. Consequently, most lobbyists concentrate their attention on committees and subcommittees. In one study, lobbyists were interviewed concerning their techniques, and one stated that

> once a bill clears committee the battle is usually four-fifths done, because they have a habit over there of backing up their committee actions in both houses. The main battle is to get proper appropriate legislation out of committee. . . . Once that happens, you don't have any problem. Once in ten times there'll be a floor fight. At that point you have to work with the entire Congress.[11]

Another lobbyist noted:

> We concentrate in both areas, but I would think that in the committee stage the concentration is on dealing with the legislative concept when it is still jelling. The concentration when you get on the floor is with the reality of what the committee is reporting out. So that you really are dealing with two different concepts of concentration and development. Sometimes, as far as success goes, there's greater success at the committee level. Other times it's at the floor stage.[12]

It is generally not necessary for lobbyists to maintain a close working relationship with each and every committee and subcommittee. Legislative power in Congress is divided along substantive policy lines represented by different committees and subcommittees. Therefore, it is usually the case that group representatives can concentrate their efforts on one or two committees that have jurisdiction over their area of legislative interest. Thus, as shown in table 11-1, agricultural interest groups, organized by commodities, are able to work with individual subcommittees of the House Agriculture Committee. Only when it comes to general appropriations or rules do they

**TABLE 11–1    Agricultural interest groups and related House subcommittees, 98th Congress**

| *House agriculture subcommittee* | *Commodity* | *Interest group* |
| --- | --- | --- |
| Cotton, Rice, and Sugar Subcommittee | Cotton, Rice, and Sugar | National Cotton Council of America |
| | | National Rice Growers Association |
| | | American Sugarbeet Growers Association |
| Livestock, Dairy, and Poultry Subcommittee | Livestock, Dairy products, Poultry products | National Wool Growers Association |
| | | Associated Milk Producers, Inc. |
| | | National Broiler Council |
| | | Pork Producers Council |
| Tobacco and Peanuts Subcommittee | Tobacco and Peanuts | Tobacco Institute |
| | | Cigar Association of America, Inc. |
| | | National Peanut Council |
| Wheat, Soybeans, and Feed Grains Subcommittee | Wheat, Soybeans, Grains | National Association of Wheat Growers |
| | | Soybean Council of America |
| | | National Corn Grower's Association |
| | | Grain Sorghum Producers Association |

need to broaden the scope of their activities. Almost every congressional committee, along with its subcommittee structure, is organized in this way, thus providing a narrower target for interest-group activities.

## Lobbyists' Relationships with Legislators

In their study of four state legislatures (California, New Jersey, Ohio, and Tennessee) Wahlke, Eulau, Ferguson, and Buchanan found that state legislators could be categorized by their orientation toward groups as follows:

*Facilitators:* those having a friendly attitude toward group activity and relatively much knowledge about it.

*Neutrals:* those having no strong attitude of favor or disfavor toward group activity (regardless of their knowledge about it) or those having very little knowledge about it (regardless of their friendliness or hostility toward it).

*Resisters:* those having a hostile attitude toward group activity and relatively much knowledge about it.

Using the most favorable opinion expressed by the respondent during the interview, the researchers found that 63 percent of those classified as facilitators believed that groups are indispensable, and another 23 percent viewed group activity as good. Only 14 percent of the facilitators had less favorable opinions of group activities. Although 40 percent of the resisters had less favorable opinions of groups, 14 percent considered them to be indispensable, and 46 percent believed their activities were generally good. Another interesting finding was that the more educated legislators tended to have more favorable reactions to group behavior and were more likely to be typed as facilitators.[13] This and other studies have shown that legislators tend to view lobbying and interest groups favorably.

Even so, a surprisingly large number of legislators are not very aware of the activities of lobbyists. These members may be so specialized themselves that only a few lobbyists representing their particular interest ever approach them. Some legislators may simply be considered hostile to group pressures and are thus not contacted by many lobbyists. Furthermore, a lobbyist representing an interest with a strong base in the legislator's district may simply be viewed as a constituent representing constituent interests rather than as a lobbyist representing a pressure group. It might also be noted that, in the years since the Wahlke study was completed, the greater activity and visibility of groups may have substantially increased the number of lawmakers familiar with their activities.

Lobbying in behalf of interest-group programs is an accepted part of the legislative and the administrative process. Many members of state legislatures and of Congress believe it to be a vital and indispensable service that, for the most part, serves good purposes. One congressman expressed his favorable attitude toward lobbying in this way:

A lot of people seem to think that lobbying is a bad thing. I think that is one misconception which still needs to be corrected as far as the general public is concerned. Lobbying is an essential part of representative government, and it needs to be encouraged and appreciated. [Lobbyists] are frequently a source of information. If they come to your offices and explain a program or factors contributing to the need for legislation, you get a better understanding of the problems and the answers to them. If you have your independence, and I think we all do, they can teach you what an issue is all about, and you can make your own decision. There can be bad lobbying techniques, of course, but basically lobbying is a good thing.[14]

So, although there are some dissenters, lobbying is generally believed to have positive attributes. Lobbyists provide information and research services that are usually welcomed by government policymakers. These services are probably not so important now as they once were because of the growth of staff and research and service facilities. Even so, lobbyists can often contribute a different dimension to debates because the information they are able to present is directly attuned to group and constituent needs. It may well be that the impact of lobbying in Congress has reduced the need for that branch of government to rely so heavily on executive agency inputs. That, in turn, may well have helped to redress the long-standing imbalance between the two branches. Furthermore, it is quite possible for government researchers and bill drafters to miss important aspects of some problem because they are not directly affected by it. Groups and their lobbyists can help to fill that void.

Harry Eckstein has suggested that lobbyists perform one other service: they help to define public opinion for decision makers with a degree of specificity that political parties, opinion polls, and research staffs are often unable to achieve. In other words, parties can take positions within a broad framework, whereas groups are able to provide detail and to define the specialized parameters within which a concerned public opinion can make itself felt.[15] Indeed, the lobbyist may be able to convey a sense of the intensity and depth of public opinion in discussions with legislators and administrators.

## Lobbyists' Relationships with Administrators

When we think of lobbying, most of us automatically think of legislators. But interest-group activity is not limited to legislators or to legislative bodies. With the burgeoning of the federal and state government administrations, especially since the 1930s, more and more decision-making authority is centered in executive agencies and the independent regulatory commissions. General legislation passed by Congress must be implemented by the executive branch; thus administrative structures peopled with government workers become necessary. The decisions made by administrators throughout the bureaucracy are fully as important as those made by Congress. The representatives and senators may pass a general law providing for an agency to administer some new program, but the administrators in that agency will be laying down the rules and regulations under which it is to be administered on a day-to-day basis. To interest groups, administrators represent targets that are as important as those in Congress.

Lobbyists must, therefore, maintain contacts with and access to the executive branch of government and the independent regulatory agencies. These may range from the president through the cabinet officers, assistant secretaries, and on down the hierarchy to the department heads. Administrators may be located in Washington, or they may be in regional offices scattered over the nation. Because of the structure of the federal bureaucracy, many agencies are organized for specific clientele groups. Thus the Agriculture Department was created to serve farmers; Labor to serve the working man; and Commerce to serve business. The independent regulatory commissions include the Federal Communications Commission, the Federal Trade Commission, the Interstate Commerce Commission, the Civil Aeronautics Board, and the Securities and Exchange Commission. Each body has rule-making and rate-setting powers within its jurisdiction. Their authority encompasses broadcasting, railroads, trucking, shipping, airlines, the stock market, and a wide variety of other elements of the nation's economic structure. Each commission represents a point of contact for interest groups. A lobbyist's success in reaching the policymakers in the commissions may well be more important than contacts with legislators in some circumstances. In truth, though, neither can be ignored. Interest groups and lobbyists must necessarily master the workings of bureaucracy in order to affect the policy machinery.

Postwar growth in state and local governments has generated large bureaucracies in the state capitals and major cities throughout the country. The problems that beset the state and local governments are no less complex than those that afflict the nation. Groups within the states, whether independent units or members of national federations, have broadened the scope of their activities in recent years and now occupy an important place in the context of state government decision making. The same, of course, is true of counties, cities, and even special districts across the nation. These groups, and their lobbyists, use the same techniques, for the same purposes, and with the same results as their counterparts in Washington.

Lewis Dexter has noted that the state and municipal governments themselves have assumed the role of interest groups in dealing with federal government agencies.[16] In recent years cities faced with bankruptcy have beaten a path to Washington as officials sought federal aid to help them bail out of dire financial straits. As noted in a boxed quotation earlier in this chapter, in 1978 the state and city of New York maintained eight separate lobbying operations in the nation's capital. Direct lobbying and organized grass-roots efforts are a part of the arsenals that belong to interest groups, regardless of location or level of government. They are techniques that extend even to governments lobbying other governments.

## Grass-Roots Politics

People join political interest groups as a means of gaining an additional voice in government. Group leaders are expected to serve as the vehicle through which that collective voice is heard. They can either present the membership's views and desires through the lobbyist as intermediary, or they can call upon the members from time to time to send messages of their own to decision makers. The latter technique is called grass-roots politics. The grass-roots approach to politics is grounded in the knowledge that group members are voters and constituents. From the group leader's point of view, it makes sense to use member-constituents as a means to apply pressure to members of Congress or other political decision makers. This is done either over an extended period of time in order to build general public goodwill, or it may be a concentrated all-out effort to focus public demands on a specific issue of the day (see "The Chamber of Commerce of the United States," page 330).

An example of the former method is the series of television commercials sponsored by the International Ladies Garment Workers' Union and designed to encourage people to buy union-label clothing. The advertisements featured a disparate group of people, men and women, black and white, old and young, singing and marching to a snappy tune urging support for the products made by the union's members. The other type of campaign is directed at a particular bill and is concentrated ordinarily into a constricted period of time. Examples abound. The National Rifle Association is always ready to send out a call to its members to contact members of Congress or legislators if passage of a gun control bill appears imminent. In 1965 the NRA triggered twelve

## The Chamber of Commerce of the United States

The Chamber of Commerce of the United States is the largest and most prestigious business group operating in the nation. It is composed of 2,500 local affiliates, 1,300 professional and trade associations, and 68,000 corporations.[a] It was established in 1912 as a defense against two threats to business that emerged in the years before World War I. The first was the rapid growth of organized labor. The second was the "hostile" actions of the federal government, such as the passage of the Sherman and Clayton acts, the vigor with which President Theodore Roosevelt prosecuted antitrust actions, and the growing response to disadvantaged groups' demands for stronger business regulation.[b]

Because of the heterogeneity of business interests and the enormous size of the business community the chamber has concentrated on protecting business interests faced with fundamental challenges on important economic and labor–management issues. Member corporations or trade associations are free to pursue more specialized interests independently.

The Chamber of Commerce operates out of a marble and limestone building one block from the White House. In recent years it has vastly increased its political resources and escalated its level of political action. In the second session of the 95th Congress (1978) the chamber took an active part on sixty-one different legislative issues, including the proposed consumer protection agency, labor law reform, and the administration's energy policy. It won 63 percent of the legislative battles in which it took part—an impressive performance on Capitol Hill, especially with a Democratic congress.[a]

The Chamber uses both principal techniques of interest-group politics:

1. It maintains a stable of experienced lobbyists who engage in direct lobbying of senators, representatives, administration officials, and regulatory commissioners.

2. It emphasizes grass-roots pressures, operating through a sophisticated network of regional, state, and local branches. Six regional offices, employing fifty operatives, study the members of Congress and senators from within their respective areas in order to ascertain possible individual electoral pressure points. They pinpoint key resource people who have personal influence with the respective members—campaign contributors, college classmates, law partners. Four of its lobbyists watch the progress of bills of interest and send alerts to twelve hundred local Congressional Action committees when action is imminent. Through the chamber's various publications the alert quickly reaches 7 million people, who are called upon to send letters, telegrams, and petitions and to make telephone calls or visits.[a]

Grass-roots techniques have recently been used to such effect that business, as represented by the chamber, has scored a number of unexpected upsets in various legislative battles. In 1968 the legislative director of the Chamber of Commerce began holding breakfast meetings for Washington-based business representatives two times each month. Issues were presented and discussed, and the chamber's position outlined. By 1978 over three hundred people were attending the breakfasts and presumably spreading the word throughout their own organizations as to the chamber's position on important issues.[c]

Another grass-roots technique begun by the chamber is sponsorship of the Citizen's Choice, a lobby group that unabashedly emulates the success of Common Cause. Citizen's Choice now has seventy thousand members paying annual dues.[d] It publishes a monthly bulletin, maintains a "hot line" toll-free telephone message, and sends "action alerts" to its members. The result is a network of members who can generate intelligent personalized letters to House members and senators on reasonably short notice. It is an acknowledged effort to hold members of Congress accountable for what they do.[c]

The chamber also maintains the National Chamber Alliance for Politics, a political action committee supported by voluntary contributions. The alliance does not provide direct contributions to the candidates or campaign committees but does provide services and materials to complement the activities of selected campaigns. Experts are employed to furnish appropriate assistance to chamber-favored candidates.[d]

The Chamber of Commerce of the United States is but one of many large and well-financed interest groups engaged in these kinds of legislative activities. Labor organizations have an even longer history of sophisticated lobbying and grass-roots efforts; and farm groups, professional associations, and citizen reform interests have all been successful in such efforts.

*Source:* The information contained in this sketch was derived from four sources: [a]"Lobbyists: Swarming Over Washington," *Time* (August 7, 1978): 14–22; [b]L. Harmon Zeigler and G. Wayne Peak, *Interest Groups in American Society* (Englewood Cliffs, N.J.: Prentice-Hall, 1972), pp. 229–231; [c]Charles Mohr, "Grass-Roots Lobby Aides Business," *New York Times* (April 17, 1978): 1 and 8; [d]Chamber of Commerce of the United States, *A Glimpse of the U.S. Chamber, 1981–82* (Washington, D.C: Chamber of Commerce of the United States, 1982).

thousand letters from its members to Congress within a one-month period. In 1977–1978 a coalition of conservative groups through direct mail and newspaper and television advertisements brought an avalanche of mail into the Senate in opposition to the treaties that ultimately turned the Panama Canal over to the Republic of Panama.

At times these organized letter-writing tactics can be quite dramatic. In August 1979 more than a million members of the United Auto Workers Union laid down their tools and shut down assembly lines for six minutes while they each signed four postcards urging passage of an energy bill. One card was addressed to the worker's congressman, one to each of his or her two senators, and one to President Carter. The cards were not mailed to Washington but were personally delivered by the union's lobbyists, thereby providing an additional opportunity to make known the organization's views.[17] Common Cause uses a telephone network to activate its members for a grass-roots campaign. Word can be disseminated from the Washington headquarters by an "action-gram" to coordinators in selected congressional districts across the country. The coordinators then contact other Common Cause members who each contact others in an ever-broadening base. In reasonably short order the group can trigger a remarkable outpouring of telegrams, letters, and phone calls to Congress.[18]

The member of Congress who receives a letter from his or her home district is sometimes not sure whether the correspondent has written as a result of a group effort or has acted individually, out of conviction. The letter may appear to be simply another missive from a constituent letting his or her representative know how he or she feels. If several dozen letters on the same side of the same issue all arrive at about the same time, most members of Congress will see through the organized letter-writing campaign. That does not mean that the effort will not be taken seriously, but many members of Congress and of the state legislatures acknowledge that they pay less attention to such a systematic drive than to spontaneous, individual letters.

When combined with lobbying, grass-roots politics can produce a truly awesome display of political power. The proposal of President Kennedy to extend the Social Security system to cover health care for the aged (the King-Anderson bill in 1961) resulted in a coalition of dozens of different groups taking stands on both sides of the issue. Those favoring the measure included the National Council of Senior Citizens Clubs, the Americans for Democratic Action, and key segments of the AFL-CIO. Those opposed to the bill were the American Medical Association, the American Dental Association, the National Association of Manufacturers, the Chamber of Commerce of the United States, and a variety of insurance companies. The King-Anderson bill died in 1961, but in 1965 a similar proposal, although contested by the same coalition of opposing groups, was passed and became law.

The success of grass-roots efforts often depends on the effectiveness of public relations. At one time public relations was not of much consequence to organized groups, but the emergence of mass-media communications and professional advertising and public relations firms changed all that. Many organized groups, especially those that are well financed, have found it advisable to undertake both long-range and short-range public relations campaigns. The underlying goal of such efforts is to try to make the public look on group goals and the general welfare as synonymous. Success sometimes depends on the public goodwill that is accorded to the group.

Finally, many groups have discovered that their effectiveness can be greatly enhanced by enlisting other groups in their cause. Alliances of this type can greatly magnify the impact of grass-roots politics by multiplying the number of members who become involved and by permitting the pooling and sharing of resources. Coalitions are formed because it seems to be the best way groups can maximize their strength to accomplish a legislative goal. A recent example of such a coalition was that formed in 1979–1980 to roll back a 1972 enactment that expanded a federal program compensating injured longshoremen and workers in "related" industries. The shipping and insurance industries both considered the 1972 extension damaging to their economic interests and had unsuccessfully tried to get it amended. In 1979, fresh from a joint campaign to kill a proposed federalization of state workman's compensation laws, lobbyists for the shipping and insurance industries decided to form a coalition to roll back the expanded longshoreman's compensation law. The Longshore Action Committee was initially composed of the Alliance of American Insurers, the U.S. Chamber of Commerce, the National Association of Manufacturers, the Associated General Contractors, and the American Farm Bureau Federation (AFBF). The participation of the farm group was brought about by convincing AFBF that fish farmers and waterfront grain elevator operators were affected by the law. The AFBF effort also helped broaden the target of the coalition from the waterfront to inland farm areas. By 1982 the coalition had enlisted seventy-four members. Early efforts to achieve the coalition's ends proved unsuccessful, but the leadership of the coalition vowed to take as long as necessary to change the law.[19] Coalitions such as this broaden the base of participants and also expand the number of targets in the decision-making milieu against which grass-roots pressures can be directed.

Both direct lobbying and indirect grass-roots pressures are effective means of translating group wishes and needs into reality. On some occasions one technique may be more effective than the other; on other occasions both techniques can be used to accomplish the group's ends. Although the group may not always be effective, the elected or appointed politicians on the receiving end of its blandishments are made aware of its existence.

Some groups, in fact, are placing more emphasis on indirect or grass-roots lobbying than on the face-to-face kind. Of 470 major trade associations and corporations engaged in lobbying activities in one recent study, over half reported that they engaged in substantial grass-roots lobbying and that they had not done so two or three years before. Most of those who organize indirect lobbying campaigns agree that arranging a meeting between a member of Congress and a prominent local businessperson-constituent is the most effective method, but that organized telephone campaigns and letters rank next. Ad hoc alliances of companies and associations have increasingly formed five- or six-member teams to call as a group on pivotal lawmakers. Company executives have been brought more and more into the effort, as have stockholders and employees. As grass-roots activities have increased, so have the budgets, staffs, and various groups assigned to such indirect lobbying.[20] Many times this expansion of activities has forced the groups to seek new funds with which to promote their goals. And even such fund raising can have a grass-roots lobbying component.

Richard Viguerie, the Virginia conservative mass-mail impresario, has noted that, contrary to his primary image as a fund raiser, his chief role is that of grass-roots lobbyist. Viguerie has said that about 90 percent of the 60 to 70 million pieces of mail he sends each year for conservative groups urge the recipient to do something other than contribute money. Virtually every letter also asks the individual who receives it to write his or her congressional representative, sign a petition, or boycott a product. Sometimes the money requested is merely a means of paying for the mailing.[21]

## Legal Controls on Lobbying

Few could remember such a strange coalition: beginning in 1974 and continuing into the latter part of the decade the AFL-CIO, the U.S. Chamber of Commerce, various of Ralph Nader's reform groups, the American Civil Liberties Union, and a variety of other organizations banded together in opposition to a Common Cause–backed bill to rewrite and strengthen the 1946 Federal Regulation of Lobbying Act. Common Cause, in fact, stood alone among all the public interest groups in support of the measure. Few public issues could weld together such a diverse collection of interest groups, but a bill to tighten legal controls over the activities of groups and their lobbyists proved to be the catalyst that brought about that unusual union.

Efforts to control lobbying by law began at the turn of the century. The first bill designed to control lobbying was passed by Congress in 1907. Other bills, such as the Public Utility Holding Company Act of 1935 and the Merchant Marine Act of 1936, contained language that affected lobbying. The Foreign Agents Registration Act of 1938 required those who represented foreign governments to register with the Department of Justice. Finally, in 1946 Congress passed the Federal Regulation of Lobbying Act as Title III of the Legislative Reorganization Act of 1946.

### The Federal Regulation of Lobbying Act of 1946

The 1946 act did not restrict the activities of lobbyists. It merely required any person hired by someone else for the principal purpose of lobbying Congress to register with the clerk of the House and the secretary of the Senate. In addition to registering, the lobbyist must file quarterly reports making his or her activities known to Congress and the public. This act has long been noted as an example of unclear, vague, ineffective, and imprecise lawmaking. The act was upheld by the Supreme Court in *United States* v. *Harris* (347 U.S. 612) in 1954, but the decision greatly reduced the effect of the law's provisions by interpreting the language narrowly. First, the Court said that the law applied only to groups and individuals that collected money for the "principal purpose" of influencing legislation through "direct" contacts with "members of Congress." That one section of the decision provided loopholes and areas of vagueness guaranteed to permit, if not to encourage, noncompliance. The decision, for instance, allowed groups or individuals to spend money from their own funds to finance activities designed to influence legislation without registering. Only those who solicited or collected money specifically for lobbying purposes were covered, according to the Court.

By including the term *principal purpose* in the definition, the Court permitted groups to decide for themselves whether they were "principally" involved in lobbying. As a result, the U.S. Chamber of Commerce and the National Association of Manufacturers, two of the largest business groups in the country, both argued that they were principally "educational" groups and thus were not covered by the law. In other words, when lobbyists for these two groups contacted members of Congress, they were "educating" the legislators rather than "lobbying" them.

A third loophole was opened by the Court's determination that "lobbying" must be through *direct* contact with members. That exempted those groups that use grassroots approaches to decision makers, or at least that portion of their effort that was of a grass-roots nature.

The language of the law did not define the meaning of what constituted a contact with a member of Congress. Testimony before a congressional committee was specifically exempted, and a later court case held that those who assisted in preparing the testimony were also exempted. Even those who appeared to be covered sometimes argued that their contacts with members of Congress were informational or educational—not lobbying.

Furthermore, the law applied only to lobbying Congress. It did not cover lobbying executive agencies or the federal bureaucracy, in spite of the fact that much legislation originates from executive offices, and most is interpreted and enforced by administrative rules handed down by executive/administrative agencies.

The law did not specify clearly how reports were to be made or what they were to contain. Consequently, the lobbyists were permitted to decide for themselves what portion of their expenditures, if any, should be reported. Some groups, with budgets in the hundreds of thousands of dollars, reported small incidental expenditures, arguing that the unreported portions were not used for lobbying but for public information.

Finally, as if to reinforce all the other weaknesses in the law, Congress did not designate any officer or agency to investigate the accuracy or the truthfulness of the reports filed by the lobbyists. The clerk of the House and the secretary of the Senate were named to receive the reports but were not empowered to investigate their accuracy or to compel anyone to comply. Although the Justice Department might prosecute violators, it was not given power to investigate the accuracy of reports, thus emasculating its prosecutorial powers. Since 1946 the Justice Department has prosecuted only four violations of the lobbying law.

In spite of all these loopholes and weaknesses, many groups and lobbyists did register within the spirit of the law. Many, however, did not, and most could find a loophole that they believed excused them. The record of registrations and of reported expenditures, therefore, is incomplete and often distorted.

## The Search for a New Lobby Law

At the beginning of this section it was noted that Common Cause, the public service reform group, has been trying since 1975 to force Congress to rewrite the lobby registration laws. The legislative process finally began to come to a head in 1978 when the House Judiciary Committee approved a broad new bill called the Public Disclosure of Lobbying Act of 1978; this act was supported by a coalition of business, environmental, labor, civil liberties, and public interest groups. A few months later, however, amendments adopted by the full House greatly expanded the scope of the bill and, in the process, destroyed the coalition supporting it. Business (particularly the U.S. Chamber of Commerce) and the American Civil Liberties Union opposed the amended bill; labor, Common Cause, Ralph Nader's Congress Watch, and the White House supported it. The bill would have required annual registration and quarterly reporting of major paid lobbying organizations that had oral or written communications on legislative matters with members of Congress or top-level executive officials, and it would have repealed the 1946 Federal Regulation of Lobbying Act. This 1978 effort failed to pass, as did a reform move by the Carter administration in 1980. These measures were merely the latest in a long series of unsuccessful efforts by Congress to reform the lobby registration laws and to close some of the loopholes in the 1946 act.[22]

To the extent that there has been progress in recent years in rewriting lobby regulation legislation, the credit must go to Common Cause. Continued pressure from the 255,000-member, heavily financed organization has focused attention on efforts to tighten the law and has kept the matter in the forefront at times when it would otherwise have dropped from view.

Nevertheless, efforts continue to be made to write new and stricter laws governing the behavior of lobbyists and the practices of interest groups. These efforts have not been successful at the national level, and with few exceptions they have been even less successful in the states.

## Lobbying and Interest Groups in the States

For many years state government was the subject of broadsides describing it as a weak link in the chain of democratic government. One persistent focus of these attacks has always been the activities of political interest groups in the state capitals. One congressional committee staff member told Lester Milbrath:

> Lobbying at the state level is cruder, more basic, and more obvious. The system is better at the federal level; the rules are good, and we do things according to the rules. . . . At the state level you oftentimes can't get a copy of a bill and you can't get committee hearings. Lobbying at the state level is faster and more freewheeling and less visible; that is why it is more open to corruption.[23]

Another reason why state legislators are sometimes more accessible to lobbyists is that they are away from home during the session (sixty to ninety days annually or biennially, in most states) and are often paid minimal salaries with small expense allowances. A member lives in a hotel room or an apartment and is often quite agreeable to having lunch or dinner with a lobbyist. Not only does the lobbyist's largesse help with the expenses, but it can be rationalized as a legitimate effort to determine what some group wants from the legislative process. Furthermore, state efforts to control lobbying practices have trailed behind those at the federal level. All state legislatures now require registration by legislative agents and legislative counsel employed for compensation. Most of the states also require that financial reports be filed with appropriate state officials—usually the secretary of state, an ethics commission, or the legislative clerks.[24]

State registration and filing requirements are inadequate, to be sure, but those that do exist reveal the great variety in the number of groups and lobbyists operating at that level. As shown in table 11-2, the numbers registered range from 1,394 in Florida to 13 in Mississippi. The median number of groups is about 200. Some of the variation can be attributed to registration requirements, but it also reflects differences in urbanization, economic diversity, and political complexity.

## Distribution of Interest-Group Strength

Malcolm Jewell and Samuel Patterson have collected data showing that business groups and associations are more extensively represented than other types of groups in both Congress and the state legislatures. Although data for the states is fragmentary, Jewell and Patterson were able to collect comparable figures for nineteen states during the 1964–1969 period. They found that at the national level the number of registered business groups is less than the aggregate number of lobbyists who represent business.

**TABLE 11–2   Registration of lobbyists by state (ranked by number registered)**

| State | Number of groups and lobbyists registered |
|---|---|
| Top ten | |
| Florida | 1,394 |
| Minnesota | 1,254 |
| Texas | 1,052 |
| California | 552 |
| Wisconsin | 437 |
| Iowa | 428 |
| Washington | 365 |
| Illinois | 355 |
| Pennsylvania | 338 |
| Ohio | 328 |
| | |
| Bottom ten | |
| Oklahoma | 103 |
| New Hampshire | 98 |
| Rhode Island | 94 |
| South Dakota | 94 |
| Alaska | 72 |
| Delaware | 63 |
| South Carolina | 63 |
| Vermont | 63 |
| Wyoming | 17 |
| Mississippi | 13 |

*Source: Directory of Registered Federal and State Lobbyists* (Chicago: Marquis Who's Who, 1973), pp. 1–525. Hawaii, Idaho, Louisiana, Nevada, Utah, and West Virginia do not require registration.

A study of a random sample of lobbyists who registered with the clerk of the House during the first two quarters of 1956 showed that 61 percent represented business groups, 16 percent were labor lobbyists, and 5 percent were employed by farm groups. The remainder were scattered among a variety of other types of groups. An analysis of lobbyists in Illinois, Kentucky, and Oklahoma over a period of several years revealed that lobbyists in those states were distributed in about the same proportion as the groups they represented (see table 11-3).[25]

Sarah McCally Morehouse has recently published a list of states categorized according to the strength of the interest group system in general, with a list of those groups considered to be the most influential in each state (see table 11-4). She found that there are twenty-two states in which groups might be characterized as "strong," eighteen states in which they are "moderately strong," and ten in which they are "weak." Generally, Morehouse found that the states with strong pressure groups do not have modern, integrated cultures. She notes, "In most of them, a single major economic enterprise dominates the economy: farming in Alabama and Iowa; oil in Alaska, Louisiana, Oklahoma, and Texas; coal in Kentucky and West Virginia; copper in Montana; power in New Hampshire and Oregon."[26] These states do not have balanced economies because wealth, professionalism, and urban/suburban life are lacking. Income is unequally distributed, and the elements of a postindustrial type of economic activity are missing. Conversely, according to Morehouse, states that exhibit weak groups are more likely to be middle-class, with a high degree of education, literacy, and media circulation. Furthermore, in these states personal income is more likely to be equally distributed. In short, states that are sparsely populated or rural are likely to have a system that is dominated by a single large company, corporation, or interest group that wields a disproportionate amount of power in the state's political system. Groups appear to have somewhat less impact on officials where a large number of them are representing diversified interests.[27]

Using Morehouse's analysis of state pressure groups by level of strength, political scientist Harmon Zeigler categorized the states according to strength and type of groups. Table 11-5 shows that business groups are unparalleled in influence, regardless of whether the states are strong, moderately strong, or weak. Labor groups, in contrast, increase in influence (as measured by the frequency with which they are mentioned) as the overall strength of the group system declines through the three levels. The same is true to a lesser extent of farm groups and education groups. Zeigler points out that the decline in business groups is matched by a growth in strength of its traditional adversary, labor, as one moves from strong group states to weak group states. It should also be noted that the range of lobbying in state legislatures is narrow, limited largely to the types of groups shown in table 11-5.[28]

Most scholars have maintained that political parties and interest groups are, to a large extent, mutually exclusive. That is, in states with strong parties, groups will have a more difficult time gaining a foothold and maintaining their strength and influence. In states with weak parties, on the other hand, the political vacuum will be filled by organized groups offering citizens an alternative way to reach their government leaders. Although this view of the relationship of groups and parties is somewhat simplistic, evidence exists to support it. With a few exceptions, an analysis by Morehouse lends support to the strong party–weak group theory. In table 11-6 Morehouse demonstrates the relationship between pressure-group strength and party strength. Party strength is measured by the strength of the governor's electoral coalition within his party. More-

**TABLE 11–3    Types of organizations, with their percentage of the total number of registered lobbyists**

| Legislature | Year | Business | Labor | Farm | Professional | Governmental, citizens | Other | Total | Number |
|---|---|---|---|---|---|---|---|---|---|
| U.S. Congress | 1969 | 53% | 11% | 6% | 6% | 22% | 2% | 100% | 269 |
| California | 1964 | 52 | 11 | 2 | 5 | 17 | 14 | 101 | 432 |
| Connecticut | 1964 | 71 | 5 | 1 | 6 | 10 | 7 | 100 | 175 |
| Florida | 1964 | 47 | 20 | 2 | 6 | 12 | 13 | 100 | 439 |
| Illinois | 1963 | 48 | 11 | 3 | 15 | 16 | 7 | 100 | 280 |
| Indiana | 1964 | 50 | 10 | 2 | 7 | 16 | 15 | 100 | 136 |
| Iowa | 1964 | 47 | 9 | 3 | 5 | 24 | 12 | 100 | 204 |
| Kansas | 1964 | 49 | 10 | 3 | 5 | 19 | 14 | 100 | 41 |
| Kentucky | 1964 | 58 | 19 | 2 | 12 | 9 | 0 | 100 | 57 |
| Maine | 1964 | 56 | 9 | 3 | 5 | 18 | 9 | 100 | 165 |
| Michigan | 1964 | 55 | 8 | 3 | 12 | 19 | 3 | 99 | 322 |
| Montana | 1964 | 54 | 14 | 4 | 4 | 15 | 8 | 99 | 180 |
| Nebraska | 1964 | 49 | 5 | 5 | 9 | 18 | 14 | 100 | 150 |
| New York | 1964 | 74 | 8 | 1 | 8 | 6 | 4 | 101 | 174 |
| Ohio | 1964 | 60 | 15 | 1 | 12 | 8 | 4 | 100 | 173 |
| Oklahoma | 1961 | 42 | 16 | 14 | 7 | 14 | 7 | 100 | 56 |
| Pennsylvania | 1964 | 63 | 10 | 1 | 12 | 11 | 2 | 99 | 243 |
| Rhode Island | 1964 | 55 | 17 | 2 | 8 | 7 | 12 | 101 | 60 |
| South Dakota | 1964 | 63 | 5 | 5 | 9 | 13 | 4 | 99 | 92 |
| Virginia | 1964 | 81 | 8 | 4 | 2 | 1 | 4 | 100 | 107 |

*Sources: Congressional Quarterly Weekly Report* (July 31, 1970): 1970; Samuel Patterson, "The Role of the Lobbyist," and Harmon Zeigler, "Interest Groups in the States," in *Politics in the American States: A Comparative Analysis,* 1st ed., ed. Herbert Jacob and Kenneth Vines (Boston: Little, Brown & Co., 1965), pp. 81 and 110. Data for Illinois and Kentucky come from unpublished studies by Ronald D. Hedlund and Malcolm E. Jewell.

**TABLE 11–4   Listing of the significant pressure groups by state**

*States in Which Pressure Groups are Strong (22)*

| | |
|---|---|
| Alabama | Farm Bureau Federation, utilities, highway interests, Associated Industries of Alabama |
| Alaska | Oil, salmon, mining, contracting, labor unions, Chamber of Commerce |
| Arkansas | Transport, agriculture, utilities, natural resources (oil, timber, bauxite), insurance, local government (County Judges Association, Arkansas Municipal League), labor, Chamber of Commerce, Arkansas Free Enterprise Association |
| Florida | Associated Industries, utilities (Florida Power Corp., Florida Power and Light), Farm Bureau, bankers, liquor interests, chain stores, race tracks, Phosphate Council |
| Georgia | Atlanta business group, Citizens and Southern Bank, Coca-Cola, Fuqua Industries, Delta Airlines, Trust Company of Georgia, Woodruff Foundation, education lobby, Georgia Municipal Association |
| Hawaii | Big Five Companies: C. Brewer and Co., Ltd. (sugar, molasses, insurance, ranching); Thro. H. Davies and Co. (sugar, merchandising, foreign investment); Amfac, Inc. (sugar and merchandising); Castle and Coke, Inc. (sugar, pineapple, bananas, seafoods, coffee, macadamia nuts, discount stores, steamship agent in Hawaii, land development, and property management); Alexander and Baldwin, Inc. (docks and warehouses, sugar, pineapples, merchandising); Dillingham Corporation (construction) |
| Iowa | Farm Bureau Federation, Truckers |
| Kentucky | Coal companies, Jockey Club, liquor interests, tobacco interests, Kentucky Education Association, rural electric cooperatives |
| Louisiana | Oil companies (Exxon, Chevron, Texaco, Gulf, Shell, Mobile, Mid-Continental Oil and Gas Association); gas pipeline interests, Louisiana Chemical Association, forest industry, rice industry, Louisiana Manufacturers Association, Farm Bureau, AFL-CIO |
| Mississippi | Mississippi Economic Council, Farm Bureau, manufacturers association, medical association, public school teachers, associations of local officials (county supervisors, mayors, sheriffs, etc.), segregationist groups (Citizens' Council, John Birch Society, Association for Preservation of the White Race, Women for Constitutional Government) |
| Montana | Anaconda Copper Company, Montana Power Company, State Chamber of Commerce, Northern Pacific Railroad, Great Northern Railroad |
| Nebraska | Farm Bureau, Omaha National Bank, Northern Natural Gas Company, Union Pacific Railroad, Northwest Bell Telephone, education lobby |
| New Hampshire | Public utilities, paper manufacturing, lumber, race-track lobby |
| New Mexico | Oil and gas, school teachers, liquor dealers, banks, truckers, cattlemen, business groups |
| North Carolina | Textile, tobacco, furniture, utilities, banks, teachers |
| Oklahoma | Phillips Petroleum, Kerr-McGee, other oil companies (Texaco, Mobile, Humble, Atlantic-Sinclair, Sun-Sunray, DX Division, Hess Oil), transportation companies, power companies, local public officials |
| Oregon | Utilities (Pacific Power and Light, Portland General Electric), lumber companies, public school teachers (Oregon Education Association), railroads and truckers, organized labor (AFL-CIO, Teamsters, Longshoremen), Farm Bureau, Agricultural Association, insurance lobby |
| South Carolina | Planters, textiles (DuPont, Stevens, Deering-Milliken, Fiberglass, Textron, Chemstrand, Lowenstein, Burlington, Bowaters), Electric and Gas Company, banks |
| Tennessee | Manufacturers association, County Services Association, Farm Bureau, Municipal League, Education Association, liquor lobby |
| Texas | Chemical Council, Mid-Continent Oil and Gas Association, Independent Producers and Royalty Owners, State Teachers' Association, Manufacturers' Association, medical association, Motor Transport Association, insurance organizations |
| Washington | Boeing Aircraft, Teamsters, government employees, school teachers, AFL-CIO, highway interests (oil, asphalt, contractors, car builders), timber, banking, commercial fishing, pinballs, public and private power, gravel, wine and beer, Grange |

**TABLE 11-4** *(Continued)*

| | |
|---|---|
| West Virginia | Union Carbide, Bethlehem Steel, Occidental Petroleum, Georgia Pacific, Baltimore and Ohio Railroad, Norfolk and Western Railway Company, Chesapeake and Ohio Railway Company, United Mine Workers |

*States in Which Pressure Groups are Moderately Strong (18)*

| | |
|---|---|
| Arizona | Copper companies (Phelps Dodge), oil companies, farm groups, Arizona Power Company, "school lobby," liquor lobby |
| California | Pacific Gas and Electric, Standard Oil of California, Bank of America, California Teachers Association, Lockheed Aircraft, Transamerica, Kern County Land Company, Bankers Association of America, California Real Estate Association, California Growers Association, University of California, AFL-CIO |
| Delaware | DuPont Chemical Company, insurance lobby |
| Idaho | Idaho Power Company, Idaho Farm Bureau, stockmen, mining and forest industries, railroads, county courthouses, Mormon Church, Idaho Education Association, AFL-CIO |
| Illinois | Illinois Manufacturers Association, Illinois Chamber of Commerce, coal operators, insurance companies (State Farm and Allstate), Illinois Education Association, Illinois Medical Society, AFL-CIO unions (Steelworkers), retail merchants, race tracks, Farm Bureau, *Chicago Tribune* |
| Indiana | AFL-CIO, Farm Bureau, Indiana State Teachers' Association, Chamber of Commerce |
| Kansas | Banks, power companies, pipeline companies, railroads, Farm Bureau |
| Maine | Big three: electric power, timber, textile and shoe manufacturing; Farm Bureau; Grange; liquor and beer lobby; horse-racing lobby; conservation groups |
| Maryland | Bankers, industrialists, AFL-CIO, liquor lobby |
| Missouri | Missouri Farmers Association, AFL-CIO, Missouri Bus and Truck Association, Teamsters, Missouri State Teachers Association, brewers |
| Nevada | Gambling, utilities, banks, mining, livestock, insurance, railroads |
| Ohio | Insurance, banking, utilities, savings and loan associations, Chamber of Commerce |
| Pennsylvania | Steel companies (U.S. Steel, Republic, Jones and Laughlin, Bethlehem); oil firms (Standard, Gulf, Sun, Atlantic); public utilities; service industries; Pennsylvania State Teachers Association; Welfare Rights Organization; AFL-CIO |
| South Dakota | Farmers Union, rural co-ops and rural electrification interests, Farm Bureau, Chamber of Commerce, banks, South Dakota Wheat Growers Association, South Dakota Stockgrowers Association, Northern States Power, Homestake Mine, liquor lobby |
| Utah | Utah Mining Association, Utah Manufacturers Association, Utah Industrial Council, Utah Farm Bureau Federation, Salt Lake City Chamber of Commerce, Utah Education Association, AFL-CIO, Farmers Union |
| Vermont | Farm Bureau, Associated Industries of Vermont |
| Virginia | Virginia Electric Power, Virginia Manufacturers Association, Chamber of Commerce, railroads |
| Wyoming | Wyoming Stock Growers Association, Rocky Mountain Oil and Gas Association, Farm Bureau Federation, Wyoming Education Association, Wyoming Association of Municipalities, Union Pacific Railroad, Truckers |

*States in Which Pressure Groups are Weak (10)*

| | |
|---|---|
| Colorado | Colorado Cattlemen's Association, Denver financial interests, oilmen, Chamber of Commerce, billboard interests, Colorado Education Association, Colorado Municipal League, AFL-CIO, Colorado Farmers Union, League of Women Voters |
| Connecticut | Connecticut Manufacturers Association, Insurance Lobby, Farm Bureau Federation, Grange, AFL-CIO |
| Massachusetts | Labor, Roman Catholic Church, public utility interests, Real Estate Lobby, Associated Industries of Massachusetts, Chamber of Commerce, Insurance Companies, Massachusetts Federation of Taxpayer's Associations, race-track interests, state employees, liquor interests |
| Michigan | General Motors, Ford, Chrysler, American Motors, United Automobile Workers, AFL-CIO |

**TABLE 11–4** *(Continued)*

| | |
|---|---|
| Minnesota | Railroads Association, 3M, Dayton Hudson Corporation, Northern States Power Company, Honeywell, Northwestern Bell Telephone, banking, beer, iron mining, liquor, Minnesota Education Association, Teamsters, Minnesota Association of Commerce and Industry, AFL-CIO, Farm Bureau, Farm Union, League of Women Voters |
| New Jersey | Johnson and Johnson, Warner-Lambert Pharmaceuticals, Prudential Insurance, Campbell's Soup, Becton Dickinson, First National State Bank in Newark, New Jersey Manufacturers Association, Hess Oil, Garden State Race Track, New Jersey Farm Bureau, New Jersey Education Association, Chamber of Commerce, AFL-CIO |
| New York | Education lobby (Board of Regents, N.Y. State Teachers' Association, N.Y. Federation of Teachers), Associated Industries of New York, Empire State Chamber of Commerce, Bankers Association, AFL-CIO, Teamsters, state medical association, Roman Catholic Church, New York City Lobby |
| North Dakota | Education lobby (North Dakota Education Association, PTA, School Boards, Department of Public Instruction), Farmers Unions, Farm Bureau, North Dakota Stockmen's Association, Association of Rural Cooperatives |
| Rhode Island | AFL-CIO, Associated Industries of Rhode Island, insurance companies, public utilities, banks, race-track associations |
| Wisconsin | AFL-CIO, United Auto Workers, business interests, Farmers' Union, liquor lobby, local public officials |

*Source:* Adapted from *State Politics, Parties and Policy* by Sarah McCally Morehouse. Copyright © 1981, CBS College Publishing. Reprinted by permission of Holt, Rinehart and Winston, CBS College Publishing. Her footnote describing sources is as follows:

[This table] is based on judicious consideration of the available evidence. It is offered with some hesitation because tabular presentation tends to "harden" the data. There are undoubtedly sins of omission and commission in this table, and the author will appreciate any correspondence on the subject. The following sources were helpful: the highly perceptive, although journalistic, volumes of Neal R. Pierce, still in the process of publication and to date: *The Megastates of America* (1972), *The Pacific States of America* (1972), *The Mountain States of America* (1972), *The Great Plains States of America* (1973), *The Deep South States of America* (1974), *The Border South States of America* (1975), all published by W. W. Norton and Company, New York; John H. Fenton's two books: *Midwest Politics* (New York: Holt, Rinehart and Winston, 1966) and *Politics in the Border States* (New Orleans: The Hauser Press, 1957); Duane Lockard, *New England State Politics* (Princeton: Princeton University Press, 1959); William C. Havard, *The Changing Politics of the South* (Baton Rouge: Louisiana State University Press, 1972); Wahlke et al., *The Legislative System;* Frank H. Jonas, *Politics in the American West* (Salt Lake City: University of Utah Press, 1969); V. O. Key, *Southern Politics in State and Nation* (New York: Knopf, 1949); and last, in an effort to find out about Delaware, Lewis A. Dexter, "Where The Elephant Fears to Dance Among the Chickens," *Human Organization* (Spring 1960–61), pp. 188–94.

house averaged the governor's vote percentage in primary elections between 1956 and 1978 and defined those with an average vote of 80 to 100 percent as "strong," between 64 and 79 percent as "moderately strong," and those between 35 and 63 percent as "weak." She classified interest groups according to estimates derived from a careful reading of the state politics literature. The results of this study, as reflected in table 11-6, tend to support the theory that strong state party organizations ordinarily go hand in hand with weak interest groups.[29]

However, other factors enter into the relationship between interest group and party. As noted earlier, the level of interest-group activity often reflects the economic strength and composition of a given state. In other places, the degree to which groups have developed is related to the interest the parties have shown in issues—weak party interest breeds strong group activity. In some states groups literally control much of what transpires under the name of the party. The best conclusion to be drawn from

**TABLE 11–5    Types of groups regarded as powerful**

| Type of group | Type of interest-group system | | |
| | Strong | Moderate | Weak |
| --- | --- | --- | --- |
| Business | 125 (75%) | 76 (71%) | 46 (58%) |
| Labor | 9 ( 5%) | 7 ( 7%) | 12 (15%) |
| Farm | 12 ( 7%) | 14 (13%) | 11 (14%) |
| Education | 11 ( 7%) | 8 ( 7%) | 10 (14%) |
| Government | 9 ( 5%) | 2 ( 2%) | — |
| Total | 166 | 107 | 79 |

*Source:* From L. Harmon Zeigler, "Interest Groups in the States," in Virginia Gray, Herbert Jacob, and Kenneth N. Vines, *Politics in the American States: A Comparative Analysis,* 4th ed., p. 103. Copyright © 1983 by L. Harmon Zeigler. Reprinted by permission of the publisher, Little, Brown, and Company. Data from *State Politics, Parties and Policy* (New York: Holt, Rinehart and Winston, 1981). As in table 11-4, states are categorized according to strength of interest groups as shown by Morehouse, who reached her conclusions from reading available state literature.

the studies that have been made is that the strength of interest groups in the states is related both to the condition of the political parties and to the diversification of the economy.

Some states are dominated by a single interest group of such consuming power that it is difficult to differentiate between the pressure and the pressured. Delaware history, for example, cannot be discussed without recognizing the role played by the E. I. DuPont Company. In many ways DuPont extends its power to Delaware state government. In 1970 nearly one-third of the state legislative committees were chaired by DuPont connections, according to a Ralph Nader study group.[30]

In Montana the Anaconda Company has long been almost synonymous with state government. Well known for the excellence of its lobbying activities, the company employs attorneys who study and analyze every bill introduced in the legislature to determine its impact on the company. Anaconda people are among the leaders of the power structure in both the state and local governments. The company's strength rests on its resources—wealth, citizens, law, business, and publishing. Until 1959, in fact, Anaconda published eight daily newspapers in the state, including all the dailies published in four of the five largest cities. Company papers, before they were sold in 1959, had about 55 percent of the total daily newspaper circulation in the state and about 60 percent of the Sunday circulation.[31] Few political decisions are made in the state without the company's intercession.

West Virginia is another example of a state that has long been run by a single industry. Through the great influence of the coal operators and other business interests in the state legislature, the tax system has been kept so regressive that, until it is changed, government services will continue to be inadequate. One former state senator pointed out to an interviewer that the entire coal industry paid less in taxes to the state of West Virginia than the state collected in cigarette taxes.[32]

Although the situation has changed somewhat in recent years with the imposition of corporate and severance taxes, the revenue generated by those taxes has equalled no more than a fraction of the revenue generated by the regressive sales tax. West Virginia exemplifies a state government so dominated by a single industry that there is little competition for power. Group influence is not static, however, and the kind of dominance that has existed in Montana and West Virginia will possibly change as

**TABLE 11–6    Pressure-group strength by party strength**

| Pressure-group Strength[b] | Party Strength[a] | | |
|---|---|---|---|
| | Strong | Moderate | Weak |
| **Weak** (10) | Connecticut New York Minnesota North Dakota Rhode Island Wisconsin Massachusetts Michigan Colorado | New Jersey | |
| **Moderate** (18) | Delaware South Dakota Arizona Vermont Virginia | Missouri Maine Nevada Utah California Idaho Maryland Kansas Wyoming Pennsylvania Ohio Indiana Illinois | |
| **Strong** (22) | Iowa | South Carolina Hawaii Washington Montana Nebraska West Virginia New Hampshire | Oregon Arkansas New Mexico Alaska Kentucky North Carolina Georgia Florida Texas Oklahoma Alabama Louisiana Mississippi Tennessee |

[a]Party strength is measured by averaging the governors' vote percentages in the gubernatorial primaries of 1956–1978. In a state with strong parties, the average primary vote received by governors-to-be was 80 to 100 percent. In states with moderately strong parties, the average primary vote received was 64 to 79 percent. In weak-party states, the governors-to-be received 35 to 63 percent of the primary vote.

[b]Pressure-group strengths are estimates derived from reading the most recent state literature. This classification agrees with an earlier one by Belle Zeller in 34 out of 45 states. Political conditions in 6 out of the 11 states in which we differ (Minnesota, Wisconsin, Michigan, Arizona, Maine, and California) have changed drastically in the 25 years since her study. See Belle Zeller, ed., *American State Legislatures* (New York: Crowell, 1954), pp. 190–191.

the economy becomes more diversified, single industries lose their grip, or new forces, such as labor unions, gain power and influence.

Examples abound of organized groups with majority membership in state legislative bodies—lawyers and veterans are a case in point. In the western and midwestern states farmers and ranchers have long held the majority in their legislatures. During the early and middle 1960s, for instance, about one-half of the members of the Wyoming state legislature were members of the Wyoming Stock Growers Association. The stock growers represented only about 1 percent of the state's population, but they were a major economic interest.[33]

Other, more homogeneous states, have many groups and interests, with a composition more closely resembling that of the United States as a whole. As we have noted, many scholars agree that, among the more homogeneous states with a number of important groups, there is less likelihood that any one will predominate. Among other factors, the overlapping of memberships tends to dilute the power of any one group.

## Techniques of Lobbying in the States

Senate President Patrick C. Whitaker of Tampa droned on from the rostrum referring bills to committee. It was 1931 and the rural-dominated "pork-chop" [Florida] senators chatted amicably with lobbyists milling in the chamber.

Railroad lobbyist LeRoy (Shorty) Allen was settled comfortably in Whitaker's chair.

But, when Whitaker hesitated in assigning a utility bill, Allen leaped to his feet shouting, "Railroads and Public Utilities," a committee loaded with senators sympathetic to his interests.

Whitaker, with a deadpan expression, acknowledged his close friend: "On the motion from the senator from Hillsborough, the bill is referred to the Committee on Railroads and Public Utilites."[34]

Times have changed—not only in Florida but in most of the other states as well. Lobbyists have been banned from the floor in both the senate and house in Florida, and they must register with the clerk of the house and the secretary of state. By 1982 over 2,600 had done so, although that number was inflated by many who were registered in behalf of a single issue or were present in the capital for only a couple of days. Most legislators in most states profess to believe that "traditional" lobbyist techniques, such as parties or bribery, are seldom effective, although entertainment remains one of the staples in the lobbyist's arsenal. As one Florida lawmaker noted, "We've come a long way from the days of booze, blondes, and bucks."[35] Lobbying can still be crude, but changes in the legislatures in recent years have had a considerable effect in modifying the lobbying system in many states.

Increased salaries, additional personal and committee staff resources, greater research capabilities, and the advent in some states of local district legislative offices have all combined to change the focus of lobbying efforts. State legislatures have always been fertile ground for group activities. The restricted length of legislative sessions, the isolated locations of many state capitals, the failure to pay adequate salaries and expenses—all made the lobbyist's job easier. Lawmaking efforts were concentrated in short annual or biennial sessions of thirty, sixty, or ninety days. Legislators were often away at the capital without their wives and families. Bill-drafting needs and research inputs were in demand and could be furnished by the representatives of interest groups. Furthermore, few states required that any lobbyists register or file expense records. Few newspapers offered in-depth coverage of state legislative sessions. The result was that legislators and lobbyists were thrown together for restricted periods of time, largely outside of public view, and with little to inhibit their behavior or their activities. These conditions still persist in some states, but at least marginal improvements have occurred in many, and in some the changes have been vast.

The worth of the lobbyists is now measured more often by the services they perform in providing information that may be hard to obtain from other sources. Not only do they provide members with tangible evidence of the policy beliefs of some group of constituents, but they often back up their interests with campaign contributions. They can also serve as conduits for information as legislators use them to send messages to members of the other house, other members of their own house, members of the press corps, or constituent groups.

In 1974 Harmon Zeigler and Michael Baer published an important study of lobbying in four states: Massachusetts, North Carolina, Oregon, and Utah. Recognizing the importance of interaction between lobbyists and legislators, the two political scientists found that the most effective forms of influence in the four legislatures were the personal presentation of arguments, the results of research, and testimony before legislative hearings. The least effective techniques, according to both groups of participants, were entertainment, campaign contributions, and bribery.[36]

As noted earlier, the stock-in-trade of professional lobbyists is friendship, information, and service. Although they are sometimes irritants, and at times some of them cross the line between the acceptable and the unethical, most legislators and staff members in those state legislatures that have been studied give them relatively high marks. And, as controversial as lobbyists may be, the student of politics should not forget that their right to practice their trade within the bounds of ethics and law is protected in the Constitution's guarantees of the right to petition and the right to free speech.

The very fact that lobbyists are important "unofficial" tools of democracy is the central obstacle to devising means to control their activities. Congress has been unable to reach a consensus on regulatory legislation since 1946. As Norman Ornstein and Shirley Elder have pointed out, the principal problem has been the failure to reach agreement on several basic questions:

> Who should be required to register?
> Should indirect lobbying be covered in the same manner [as direct lobbying]?
> Should lobbying of the executive branch be included?
> How comprehensive and complex should reporting requirements be?
> Should contributors to lobbying organizations be made public?
> How should enforcement be handled?
> How much regulation is constitutional—that is, when does lobby legislation run the risk of being invalidated or made meaningless by the Supreme Court?[37]

Each of these questions goes to the very heart of lobbying and grass-roots campaigns. Each represents a challenge to democratic principles. Until these questions are answered in such a way as to meet constitutional standards (to say nothing of standards of fair play), Congress or the state legislatures are unlikely to be able to agree on new regulatory legislation.

## Group Pressures in a Democracy

In discussing democracy we necessarily speak regularly of the individual. Individual citizens, in a sense, are the ultimate unit of value in a free society. But, even in a democracy, and particularly a vast heterogeneous democracy, individuals have a difficult time translating their desires and their thoughts into political action that is felt in the political arena. Effective expression of these thoughts and actions requires joint action—either through the political party or through an interest group. Individual needs and desires are achieved principally through cooperative group association. This does not necessarily devalue the citizen, since it may make his or her voice more easily heard. Collections of citizens' voices are heard through membership in a political interest group with internal cohesion and external access. Through group action, pressures can be applied to government entities to produce official policy that more or less reflects the desires of the group and its individual members. Interest-group activities, therefore, are but one more extension of democracy. They serve as another avenue of approach to government policymakers.

It would be a mistake to attribute too much power and influence to lobbyists and interest groups. Obviously, as we have seen, groups are sometimes the key factor in determining some particular policy outcome. Undoubtedly, on occasion the National Rifle Association, the National Association of Manufacturers, the AFL-CIO, or the League of Women Voters has "persuaded" legislators or administrators to act in a particular manner. But at the same time we must emphasize that many groups fail. On almost every issue around which any controversy swirls, some groups are on the winning side and others on the losing side. Group action is not universally successful. As Lester Milbrath noted in his study of 101 Washington lobbyists, "The weight of evidence . . . suggests that there is relatively little influence or power in lobbying per se. . . ."[38] Bauer, Pool, and Dexter, in a case study of business influence on American trade policy, found that, despite the reputation of interest groups and lobbyists, they were all hampered by lack of money, lack of time, lack of personnel, and lack of information. They were most effective when they were able to interact and stimulate other people to cooperate in the performance of their group functions.[39]

Perhaps the ordinary citizen would be wise to keep his or her political options open. Groups are not omnipotent. The activist citizen might want to maintain his or her party connections because, in the long run, electoral behavior may be more important than group pressure.

## Notes

1. *Federal Regulation of Lobbying Act of 1946* (PL. 76–60), sec. 307.
2. *United States* v. *Harriss,* 347 U.S. 612 (1954).
3. *Legislators and Lobbyists,* 2nd ed. (Washington, D.C.: Congressional Quarterly Service, 1968), p. 4.
4. *Congressional Quarterly Almanac, 1981* (Washington, D.C: Congressional Quarterly, 1982), pp. 3D–58D.
5. David Ray, "The Sources of Voting Cues in Three State Legislatures," *Journal of Politics* 44, no. 4 (November 1982): 1074–1087.
6. Martha Musgrove and Mary Ann Lindley, "Lobbyists Still Have the Clout in Tallahassee," *Palm Beach Post-Times* (April 2, 1978): D-5.
7. Lester W. Milbrath, *The Washington Lobbyists* (Chicago: Rand McNally, 1963), pp. 89–114.
8. Ibid.
9. Donald R. Matthews, *U.S. Senators and Their World* (Chapel Hill: University of North Carolina Press, 1960), pp. 180–190.
10. *New York Times* (April 16, 1978): 8.
11. John M. Bacheller, "Lobbyists and the Legisla-

tive Process: The Impact of Environmental Constraints," *American Political Science Review* 71, no. 1 (March 1977): 257.
12. Ibid.
13. John C. Wahlke, Heinz Eulau, William Buchanan, and LeRoy Ferguson, *The Legislative System* (New York: Wiley, 1962), pp. 324–325.
14. Charles L. Clapp, *The Congressman: His Work As He Sees It* (Washington, D.C.: Brookings Institution, 1963), pp. 162–163.
15. Harry Eckstein, *Pressure Group Politics: The Case of the British Medical Association* (London: Allen & Unwin, 1960), p. 162.
16. Lewis A. Dexter, *How Organizations Are Represented in Washington* (Indianapolis, Ind.: Bobbs-Merrill, 1969).
17. Ronald J. Hrebenar and Ruth K. Scott, *Interest Group Politics in America* (Englewood Cliffs, N.J.: Prentice-Hall, 1982), p. 86.
18. Ibid., p. 86–87.
19. *Congressional Quarterly Weekly Report* (January 23, 1982): 122.
20. *New York Times* (April 16, 1978): 8.

21. *Congressional Quarterly Weekly Report* (September 12, 1981): 1740.
22. *Congressional Quarterly Weekly Report* (April 22, 1978): 955–956.
23. Milbrath, *Washington Lobbyists,* pp. 302–303.
24. William J. Keefe and Morris S. Ogul, *The American Legislative Process,* 5th ed. (Englewood Cliffs, N.J.: Prentice-Hall, 1981), p. 348.
25. Malcolm E. Jewell and Samuel C. Patterson, *The Legislative Process in the United States,* 3rd ed. (New York: Random House, 1977), pp. 181–183.
26. Sarah McCally Morehouse, *State Politics, Parties and Policy* (New York: Holt, Rinehart and Winston, 1981), pp. 107–116.
27. Ibid., pp. 112–113.
28. L. Harmon Zeigler, "Interest Groups in the States," in *Politics in the American States: A Comparative Analysis,* 4th ed., eds. Virginia Gray, Herbert Jacob, and Kenneth Vines (Boston: Little, Brown, 1983), pp. 99–104.
29. Morehouse, *State Politics,* pp. 116–118.
30. James Phelan and Robert Poxen, *The Company State* (New York: Grossman, 1973), p. 304.
31. Thomas Payne, "Montana: Politics Under the Copper Dome," in *Politics in the American West,* ed. Frank H. Jonas (Salt Lake City: University of Utah Press, 1969), pp. 210–211 and 220–221.
32. Neal Pierce, *The Border South States* (New York: Norton, 1975), p. 154.
33. T. A. Larson, *History of Wyoming* (Lincoln: University of Nebraska Press, 1965), p. 578.
34. Musgrove and Lindley, "Lobbyists in Tallahassee," p. 1.
35. Ibid., p. D-5.
36. Harmon Zeigler and Michael A. Baer, *Lobbying: Interaction and Influence in American State Legislatures* (Belmont, Calif.: Wadsworth, 1969), pp. 172–173.
37. Norman J. Ornstein and Shirley Elder, *Interest Groups, Lobbying and Policy Making* (Washington, D.C: Congressional Quarterly, 1978), p. 110.
38. Milbrath, *Washington Lobbyists,* p. 354.
39. Raymond A. Bauer, Ithiel de Sola Pool, and Lewis Anthony Dexter, *American Business and Public Policy: The Politics of Foreign Trade* (New York: Atherton Press, 1963), pp. 341–349 and 357.

## CHAPTER TWELVE

# Political Parties in Transition

*Unlike the opposing armies of Clausewitzian warfare, the American political parties are a noisy and colorful rabble. They have plenty of (although often not enough) people and money and candidates but operate without any discernible strategy. They wander aimlessly from election to election, periodically experiencing disaster at the polls, periodically inheriting a government that they treat like an accidentally acquired kingdom. If the purpose of politics were not so important, the ragamuffin parade and the whole directionless game would strike the outside visitor as hilarious. Many Americans have in fact already rendered that verdict.*

*Much more is at stake today, however, than the future of the political parties. Their incapacity has a depressing effect on the process of politics itself and restricts all those who take politics seriously enough to engage in it. Admittedly there is nothing sacred about political party institutions or even the framework of the venerable two-party system. Parties are merely instruments for realizing political ends, like pieces on a chessboard to be used or bypassed as they suit specific purposes. But they are also one of the few means free men have developed historically to establish common purposes and direction.*

John S. Saloma III and Frederick H. Sontag, *Parties: The Real Opportunity for Effective Citizen Politics* (New York: Knopf, 1972), p. 372.

*The weakness of our party system has made it very difficult to build and maintain support for the long-term enterprises we need to pursue at home and abroad. The task of supporting international economic development, of constructing a stable world peace, of building a strong domestic economy and equitably distributing its products and wealth, of reforming our governmental structures and finding adequate resources for our urgent national needs, cannot be accomplished by a single Congress or a single President. We have paid a high price for the instability and weakness of our governing coalitions. Ambitious programs have been launched but funds to finance them withheld. Commitments made by a President have been undercut by Congress. Funds voted by Congress have been vetoed or impounded by a President. No party has been able to move ahead on its own agenda for very long, and the result has been sixteen years of government by fits and starts, with a mounting backlog of unkept promises and unmet needs.*

David Broder, *The Party's Over: The Failure of Politics in America* (New York: Harper & Row, 1972), pp. 244–245.

A merican political parties began as loose aggregations of people who shared beliefs and who wished to join together to seek control of government offices and policy-making. Traditionally, parties were private organizations operating outside the purview of constitutions and laws. Parties and elections were the lifeline of modern popular democracy. Parties served as the instrument through which popular will could be channeled into the selection of public officers to run the government. In an earlier era voter participation was higher among those eligible. Public support for electoral institutions was acknowledged and accepted. The principles of democracy—majority rule, popular sovereignty, and voter equality—demanded partisan institutions such as parties, in spite of the fact that the Founding Fathers almost totally ignored them. The need for parties to serve democracy was evident early in our history, and their "natural" growth arose from that necessity.

## The Decline in Party Fortunes

The first half of this century was not a good period for party development. Political scandals involving big-city machines, bosses, bribery, and fraud spurred the demand that party organizations and their leaders be brought to heel and made to abide by the law. Those who sought reform were motivated by the desire to enhance democracy and to protect the institutions of government. Unfortunately, fifty years of reformists' success has undermined the parties and caused their power and influence to wane and their effectiveness to erode.

The decline can be easily seen if we recall the position held by the parties throughout American history until approximately the time of World War II. At that time political parties possessed either legal or practical monopolies of three vital factors: legitimacy, resources, and recruitment.[1] The legitimacy of parties was apparent in the voter loyalties of their members. Most citizens retained their party identification throughout their lives. People were proud to call themselves Republicans or Democrats. Even when voter loyalties were severely strained, such as at times of critical realignment, the changes could be explained more by generational movement than by personal conversion. A review of aggregate electoral statistics for the period shows that voters cast their votes for the same party year in and year out. Almost no ticket splitting occurred, and voters retained their stamina long enough to complete the ballot so that almost no drop-off took place. Even as late as the mid-1950s survey data showed that 90 percent of the American voters sided openly and consistently with one or the other parties. Independent voters were relatively rare. Furthermore, turnout was considerably higher.

The percentage of eligible voters who voted in presidential elections has steadily declined, from 62.8 percent in 1960 to 55.5 percent in 1972 and 53.9 percent in 1980. In off-year elections for Congress the decline has been from 45.4 percent in 1962 to 36.1 percent in 1974 and back up to 41.0 percent in 1982. An election study conducted by the U.S. Bureau of the Census and based on extensive national voter surveys found that 27 percent of those who were eligible did not vote. The reasons given by nonvoters ranged from apathy to skepticism toward government and governmental institutions.[2] The growth in ticket splitting and the rapid and unprecedented increase in registered and self-proclaimed Independents both constitute further evidence of mass dissatisfaction with government and politics. The legitimacy of political parties was not seriously questioned before the middle of this century, but virtually all of our evidence today suggests that many Americans do question the legitimacy of the parties as instruments of democracy.

One of the foundation blocks of the political parties before their decline was their near monopoly over the resources of politics. Campaign resources were controlled by the parties. Precinct lists, on which canvassing and get-out-the-vote drives were based, were maintained by local party officials. Campaign finance was, to a large extent, in the hands of party officials who raised the money and distributed it to the candidates. Party leaders were responsible for determining which candidates would represent the party in the election. They controlled the nominating procedures and decided whose name would be placed on the ballot. The availability of government jobs constituted the currency of politics, and party officials usually decided which patronage award would go to whom. These resources were keys to party success. Their removal, even if attributed to good motives, undermined the muscle and sinew of the party organizations.

Finally, the avenues of political recruitment were dominated by the parties. Many studies have shown that for most governmental offices in the United States distinct ladders of political advancement were available, and access to the rungs of the ladder was controlled by the party organizations. The result was that most of those men and women elected to high office—the presidency, the U.S. Senate, the House of Representatives, and governorships—had previous political experience and had climbed the ladder of positions in lower levels of government.

## The Move to Reform

Our emphasis in this book has been on change. There has been a continuing decline in confidence in social institutions in the United States—Congress, the presidency, bureaucracy, and the political parties. The public's lowered esteem of parties is reflected in the decrease in party identification, the progressive slide in voter turnout, the increase in ticket splitting, and the failure of the party institutions to offset the transfer of political functions from the party organizations to those in the private sector. Evidence is accumulating that the traditional office-seeking functions of parties have been, to some extent, coopted by public relations firms (campaigns), government (financing), and candidate organizations (consultants). Furthermore, internal reform efforts, though possibly strengthening party democracy, have weakened the capacity of parties to maintain their traditional functions. Although some of the reform efforts were intended to improve the parties, they have sometimes had the opposite effect. The general thrust of the McGovern-Fraser reforms of 1971 was to remove party people from positions of power and control. The recent development of the New Right groups has, on the whole, been based on the premise that conservative success is dependent on bypassing the party organizations and building independent strength.

The more recent Hunt commission, however, began the process of restoring practicing politicians and officeholders to their traditional place in the delegations at the nominating convention. Furthermore, after some initial success in helping to elect President Reagan in 1980, the New Right groups did not do well in the 1982 elections and by 1983 were publicly complaining about the failures of the Reagan Administration to carry out its "conservative mandate." They showed even less disposition to work within the Republican party. These recent events may have indicated a return to politics as usual, or they may have merely been a brief aberration from a long-range political trend.

## The Move to Nationalization

Until recently the national parties were viewed as amorphous and ephemeral bodies whose purpose was to provide continuity between elections and to maintain a framework for the nomination of presidential candidates. The state party organizations were considered the real core of the party institution; they controlled their own funding, elected representatives to the national party bodies, and adopted their own rules. This was the opinion of the late influential political scientist V. O. Key, Jr., and this position formed the thinking of a generation of political scientists. In other words, the existence of a decentralized party system in the United States has seldom ever been questioned.

In recent years, however, a number of scholars have begun to speculate that the term *decentralization* may no longer explain the relationships that exist between the national and the state and local parties. Austin Ranney believes that nationalization has taken place because of the post-1968 reforms in both parties, which have had the effect of increasing the power of the national committees over the rules governing the presidential nominating process in the states. This change has come about, Ranney thinks, because the centralization of power in national party hands under the new rules has not only persisted but is being enforced both by the national party organizations and by the courts. In 1975, in *Cousins* v. *Wigoda,* the U.S. Supreme Court declared that national party rules are in most circumstances superior to state laws, thus reenforcing the right of the national parties to impose standards on state parties.[3]

Charles Longley points out that the nationalization of the Democratic party has occurred because of changes in the party rules, adoption of the party charter, required changes (reinforced by the courts) in state laws, improved fund-raising capabilities at the national level, and modest changes in the demographic makeup of the Democratic National Committee. These changes have brought more diversity among the membership while maintaining a level of substantial experience in politics. On the whole, Longley's definition of nationalization stresses the subordination of state and local parties to the national party.[4]

Cornelius P. Cotter and John F. Bibby have emphasized that the elements defining nationalization have included a narrowing of the range of differences in structures and processes of the state parties, greater interdependence between the state and national party organizations, and an increasing uniformity of norms for state party participation in national party processes. They believe that nationalization is a process both within the national party organizations and between the national party committees and the state parties. Not only have the national committees assumed more control over national nominations, but they are increasingly participating in congressional, senatorial, state legislative, and even state constitutional and local elective officer campaigns. They are bidding to become essential service agencies to state and local parties. Nationalization has taken place both horizontally and vertically.[5]

Clearly, many political scientists believe decentralization of power is being replaced by nationalization of power in our party structure. As of 1983 this is but a trend, but it is a well-developed trend that many believe to be irreversible. Many elements of our party structure still fit the old concept of decentralization, but more and more elements demonstrate the plausibility of nationalized parties in the future.

This countervailing trend toward stronger national party organizations has paralleled the general decline in party strength. Both parties have been bolstered at the national level, although the change has been more apparent among Democrats. As noted in chapter 3, the results of the various Democratic reform efforts, carried out largely through rules changes, have almost invariably led to an increase in dominance of the state parties by the national committee. Evidence abounds. As early as 1956, the Democratic National Convention required state delegations to pledge loyalty to the national ticket. Segregated delegations were banned after 1964. In 1968 the "regular" Mississippi delegation was denied seats at the national convention in Chicago, and a substitute delegation composed of "loyal" Democrats was seated.

We have discussed in detail the reforms of the McGovern-Fraser and Mikulski commissions, which not only radically changed the structure of the national convention but also enhanced its power in a variety of ways. New delegate selection rules were adopted and imposed on the state parties. State laws and party rules had to be changed in many areas to accommodate the new requirements. Proportional representation was mandated in the selection of delegates, and designated groups (racial minorities, women, and youth) were ensured increased membership. Various irregular practices, such as delegate fees and pre–election-year meetings, were abolished, and the national committee was given enforcement powers to see that the bans were carried out.

One of the most far-reaching changes occurred in 1974 when the Democrats adopted the first national party charter in American history. This document created new units of party government, such as the judicial council, the finance council, and the education and training council. The result of these changes was to establish at the national level a governing structure composed of legislative, executive, and judicial branches, with the national party at the center of control. The state party organizations, in effect, relinquished some of the traditional sovereignty they had possessed in the past. Although the recommendations of the Sanford, Winograd, and Hunt commissions were not so sweeping, their adoption continued the trend toward stronger national control.

On the Republican side, the same trend toward nationalization of party organizations can be perceived, although to a lesser extent. There, too, new delegate selection rules and guidelines for convention operations have tended to enhance the power of the Republican National Committee. By 1983 the practice by the national committee of intervening in local and state contests, both primary and general elections, has shifted attention toward the national party level. Furthermore, the Republican National Committee has far outdone the Democrats in providing campaign assistance to state and local candidates. This practice cannot help but escalate the movement toward stronger national party units. By 1983 the Democratic National Committee was striving to emulate these Republican efforts.

It should be noted that some of the structural changes in both parties have improved communications between the national and state parties and have, in reality, made state party officers more active participants in national party affairs. First the Republicans, and later the Democrats, included state party chairpersons as members of their national committee. This move has not only brought about a greater degree of cooperation between the two levels but has provided a vehicle for enhanced state party participation in important national party decision making.

Ironically, this move toward enhanced national party power and responsibility is taking place at the same time that the organizational capabilities of the state parties are also growing. Recent studies of state party organizations have found considerable evidence of revival, plus a new vitality.[6] This change has not come about as a result of public demand, nor has it resulted from national party efforts, except as they were peripheral to those outlined above. It has, in fact, been an "inside" job. A new and different breed of state party leader, bolstered by a simultaneous growth of new political techniques, has sought to challenge tradition and to initiate changes with a view toward strengthening the system. The changes and revival have not been uniform across the nation. A few state party organizations remain buried in the past, and others, because of a pervasive system of one-party politics, have had little cause to seek to grow. But the growth cycle is there, and in some states widespread change has occurred.

For a number of reasons state parties have embarked upon this strengthening process. First, the number of states in which rival parties contest with each other in a competitive two-party or modified two-party system has increased. Noncompetitive one-party systems in the South, the Northeast, and the Midwest have all experienced rapidly developing opposition parties. The increased competition and the prospect of actually winning elections have joined to revitalize the two-party system as a whole as well as party organizations in particular states.

Second, the rapid increase in the U.S. population coincided with the swift postwar development of modern campaign techniques—the new politics. The art of public opinion polling, organized fund raising, direct-mail contact, automatic data processing, and the increased demands of media campaigning all brought demands for organizational continuity and long-range planning. These demands, in turn, stimulated calls for permanent party headquarters with paid state chairpersons and/or executive directors to provide continuity.

Finally, the development of the state chairpersons' associations at the national level has stimulated action at the state level. The regular meetings of these state leaders have furnished a continuing mechanism for the exchange of ideas and the development of strategy. The state officials have responded by working to strengthen their own parties in order to remain competitive with their neighbors in the party system itself. Innovation has bred further innovation. On the whole, the result has been somewhat stronger state party organizations. The obvious increase in power of the national party organizations, however, has been at the relative expense of the state units. The commodity of this exchange was influence and sovereignty. At the same time, the state parties have enhanced themselves organizationally and now do more of the things that strong party advocates have always urged them to do. The national parties are developing as more coherent institutions and have greater power to control state party activities. But simultaneously the state parties have seen relative growth in their organizational capabilities.

## The Emergence of Interest Groups

The final two chapters in this book dealt with the role of interest groups. They were included because they represent another important factor in the ongoing transformation of the American parties. Parties have held a special place in America as a vehicle for transforming citizen choices into public policy outcomes. They have been a major bridge between the voter and the government. Nevertheless, the parties' loss of power and influence in the past half century has weakened them and has brought about a surge in interest groups, both in numbers and in strength.

The private groups have become much more active in politics, and much more influential. New campaign finance laws have provided new impetus to group political activities. The necessity for expensive media campaigns via television and radio has created an expanding need for funds to pay for them. Interest groups have proved a ready source of such funds, both at the state and national levels, thereby giving those groups a legitimate claim on the attention of those who get elected. David Broder, the highly regarded political columnist for the *Washington Post,* has suggested that the rapid and extensive growth of single-interest constituencies, each represented by its own group, has created a whole new element in the decline of party fortunes. He notes:

> Right-to-life advocates are well-mobilized, but so are their opponents, the abortion-rights supporters. The gun-owners and sportsmen are organized, and so are the gun-registration advocates. There are farmers who demand 100 percent of parity, and there are other farmers bitterly opposed to construction of power lines across their land. There are environmental activists trying to ban motor boats from the entire Boundary Waters Canoe Area, and resort owners and putt-putt operators just as determined to let them in.[7]

Broder notes that the candidates have little protection against the demands of these groups. No matter what position the candidate takes on a controversial issue, some group will be pleased and another infuriated. Furthermore, he observes, the party organizations themselves have been infiltrated and increasingly dominated by single-interest constituencies.[8]

In a series of articles in the *New York Times,* John Herbers reports that hundreds of new special-interest groups have been established with headquarters in Washington. Most of them have set up political action committees to raise and spend money in behalf of candidates, and they are all applying pressure on the government for a multitude of causes, both private and public.[9] The candidates and the parties have little protection against such incursions by interest groups, but one result has been a lessening of commitment to broad policy programs applicable to all of the people. Another has been to place candidates running under party labels out of the reach of party influence and under much greater control by special-interest groups. The candidates may be left with little room to maneuver; they may indeed find themselves in a position where one issue of little relevance to most members of the constituency may dominate the campaign.

It is too early to predict the ultimate impact of single-interest groups on the political parties or on American political outcomes. At the present time, though, many political scientists and party leaders would agree with David Broder's assessment that "eventually the American voters may rediscover the truth that, without strong political parties, Congress and the President will be unable to come to grips responsibly with serious national problems."[10] Until then the decline in voter participation, the relative weakening of party organization influence, and the new growth of competing interest groups are all factors in the party transformation that is currently under way.

## Transformation and Change in the American Party System

Politicians, journalists, and political scientists generally agree that a major transformation is taking place within the party system, but they do not agree on the form it is assuming or on the ultimate result. Some hold that the political parties are undergoing change that will eventually lead to a major ideological realignment. Some leading conservatives take this view; they are convinced that the political instability of the immediate past is a signal for a major realignment of party identifiers. Others contend that the parties as we know them are in a continuing (and possibly irreversible) process of disintegration. They note the rise in ticket splitting and the increase in the numbers of those who profess to be Independents. These people do not believe that parties will be realigned ideologically, but they also do not believe that they can ever return to the earlier days of more clear-cut partisanship between Democrats and Republicans. Finally, still other observers suggest that, although the parties and the political system are presently caught in rough weather, the situation will gradually return to normal; that is, the parties will not only survive but also have some of their powers restored and their influence revived. Let us turn now to a brief consideration of the prevailing theories of realignment, disintegration, and revival.

### Realignment

Political historians generally agree that five significant party realignments have occurred in the course of American history and that they roughly correspond to the list of party systems reviewed in chapter 2. Each was triggered by a critical election, and each had far-reaching consequences for the American party system. The *first* was the election of Thomas Jefferson in 1800 (the experimental system), an election that doomed the Federalist party's dominance of American politics. The *second* was the election of Andrew Jackson in 1828 (the democratizing system), which ushered in a period of "people's" democracy and lasted until the Civil War. The *third* was the election of Abraham Lincoln in 1860 (the Civil War system), which inaugurated the Republican party and precipitated the Civil War. The *fourth* was the election of William McKinley in 1896 (the industrial system), which helped to define the industrialization of America and spelled an end to late–nineteenth-century populism. And the *last* was the election of Franklin D. Roosevelt in 1932 (the New Deal system), which not only began the period of liberalism that we call the New Deal but also inaugurated coalition politics

"Henry, I want you to know Forbes Lockhart
—he's also a crossover Republican."
(Reprinted by permission: Tribune Company
Syndicate, Inc. © 1976.)

on a grand scale.[11] Now, in the fourth quarter of the twentieth century, some such change may well be taking place again. No one is sure what the future holds for the political party system of the United States, but one of the prevailing theories is that we are in the midst of yet another realignment.

A realignment of politics connotes a durable change in patterns of political behavior. When masses of voters move from one party to another, as happened in 1932 and 1936, and they retain their new affiliation for a period of years, one can see the political norms altering and a durable change taking place. Obviously, in every election, some voters switch parties to vote for the opposition's candidate, either because they do not like their own party's nominee or because some predominant issue or national condition triggers their action. Ordinarily, though, these voters will switch back to their regular pattern of party support in subsequent elections, and the temporary nature of their defection is more appropriately called deviation rather than realignment.

Those who hold the view that we are currently undergoing realignment believe that most of the conditions that have historically brought about such shifts are present. The usual time span of about one generation between critical elections has passed. Since World War II politics has become somewhat confused and aimless, a condition that has preceded other realignments. Millions of voters have withdrawn from political participation or have dropped their party affiliation, and substantial cynicism is expressed about government and politics in general. Almost all of these conditions have prevailed before other realignments.

Walter Dean Burnham observes that other changes are also taking place as a result of recent developments. First, an increasing majority of the active electorate has moved above the poverty line, thus undercutting the traditional voter–party links of patronage and welfare. The result has been a tendency toward depoliticization. Second, many current political issues are so complex and technical that the partisan cues that parties formerly translated for the public have become less relevant. Many people no longer feel that there is a Republican or a Democratic way to solve complex public problems. Finally, the emergence of the United States as a major world power has subordinated the role of the political party in the overall political environment. Foreign and military policy decisions are treated in a bipartisan context, and the old distinction between foreign and domestic policy has broken down, thereby weakening party influence on both kinds of issues. These factors, along with the prevalence of the traditional conditions that precede realignments, suggest that we may be in yet another period of realignment.[12] Even if we are, however, no one can predict with certainty that a realignment will actually occur.

Some conservative spokespersons have long believed not only that a realignment is taking place but that a new, truly conservative party will emerge from it. They see such a party stemming from a new coalition composed of social and economic conservatives, middle-class taxpayers revolting against high taxes, and those who feel strongly about social issues such as school prayer, abortion, and gun control. They believe that the opposition party might well be made up of liberals, the poor and their "benefactors" (the upper-class bureaucrats), minorities, and others who benefit from social programs. Some conservative observers, as well as some academic specialists, agree that such a realignment may take place, but they disagree about how and when it will come about and about which groups of voters will be in each of the newly realigned parties.[13]

Others, however, argue that such a realignment is unlikely. They point out that few issues seriously divide the parties in today's America. Party positions, as well as campaign rhetoric, tend to move toward each other until they converge, becoming indistinguishable to the voting public. In the view of these critics, nothing suggests at the present time that any one issue might emerge as the catalyst to bring together the new ideological alignment. Even the conservative leaders who believe there will be a realignment are in some disarray over the best way to approach certain shared values and the best tactics for getting them adopted. Without a united group seeking to disassociate itself from politics as usual and coalesce into a rudimentary or embryonic new party, a new realignment is unlikely to take place—and no evidence in the 1980s points to such a shift.

Furthermore, most of the talk and most of the writing about realignment speaks solely of the national party organizations and presidential elections. But there has been little discernible movement in state and local politics toward the kind of ideological division needed for party realignment. Finally, one of the notable characteristics of the historic realignments is that history attached each to the name of a leader: Jefferson, Jackson, Lincoln, McKinley, and Franklin D. Roosevelt. Many conservatives hailed Ronald Reagan as such a leader, but by midpoint in his term they were urging him not to run again because, in their view, he had betrayed the conservative cause by approaching national issues and Washington politics too pragmatically. Reagan, many of them felt, had been too willing to compromise sacred conservative principles. Thus a realignment leader does not appear to be on the political horizon today. Undoubtedly, some of the factors in today's politics have, in the past, forecast party realignment. But such factors have been present for some years now, and the predicted sorting-out has yet to take definable shape.

## Disintegration

An alternative to the realignment thesis is one that foresees party "dealignment" or disintegration. Those who believe that the parties, as we know them, may be dying out as a force in American politics base their view on some of the same factors that have influenced the realignment advocates. They note that turnout is steadily declining, independent voting and ticket splitting are on the rise, cynicism about politics and politicians is increasing, and party organizations are no longer commanding the following that they once did.

Many read in these events a disintegration of the old coalition politics of the past. The leading academic proponent of the disintegration thesis is political scientist Walter Dean Burnham. Burnham thinks that these changes in electoral politics "may have already moved beyond the possibility of critical realignment because of the dissolution of party-related identification and voting choice at the mass base." Most of the decomposition theory is grounded in the decline in voter partisan identification and the rise in the number of Independents and in split-ticket voting. Burnham speculates that American political life without parties, party voting, and party identification would allow even greater discretion for political decision makers and that interest groups would have more influence on public policy.[14] Others contend that parties might be replaced by a multicandidate and multiparty system of campaigns. They cite the recent results of some elections to support their view. An Independent was elected governor of Maine in the mid-1970s; third-party candidates for governor and senator received significant numbers of votes in recent elections; two candidates unaffiliated with the existing parties (Wallace and Anderson) received significant numbers of votes for president in recent years; and prominent political leaders have switched parties (John Connally, John Lindsay, and Strom Thurmond).

Those who disagree with the disintegration thesis maintain that declining turnout, party identification, and party voting, although apparent, may not be so serious as to bring about dissolution of the parties. They note that turnout in presidential elections has been even lower in the past, that party identification is still the best single predictor of voting behavior, and that the decline in party voting may represent little more than the idiosyncrasies of particular elections. None of these trends necessarily predicts party disintegration. Instead, the same evidence might suggest realignment or even a continuation of the current voter alignments represented by the Republicans and Democrats.[15]

## Party Revival

A third group contends that the evidence at hand does not support either the theory of party realignment or the theory of party disintegration. Despite the growth in ticket splitting and the decline in party identification and turnout, these scholars argue that the present parties will continue to coopt each other's issues. They also feel that parties will make better use of the new campaign technology but that party leaders rather than private consulting firms will control these new methods. Some believe that a perceptible organizational growth is taking place at the state party level and that it will continue, thus providing the parties with a new stronger underpinning of structure. They suggest that organizational strength is essential to the development of more effective parties and that it is already under way. They argue that the parties are old and have survived identity crises before; they point out that in the light of history the present trends in voting behavior may simply appear to have been aberrant. Furthermore, they contend, those who foresee realignment or disintegration are denying that change can take place within the existing party structures. They concede that there may be some ideological shifting of voters between parties but suggest that the organizations themselves may well be revitalized and assume their more traditional role in American politics.

James L. Sundquist of the Brookings Institution suggests that four "cross-cutting" issues have emerged since World War II that should have contributed to party realignment. The *first*, in the early postwar years, was communism, which failed to contribute to shifting voter allegiance because both parties were on the same side. The *second* issue was the Vietnam War, but it too did not lead to realignment because neither major party responded to the rising sentiment against the war in the late 1960s. The war was, in effect, a bipartisan tragedy. The *third* cross-cutting issue to emerge during the period was a cluster of related social problems, including crime, "law and order," drugs, student unrest, poor people's marches, and pornography. The Republican party tried to exploit these issues as early as 1964, but when a deliberate attempt was made in 1970 to achieve what Vice-President Spiro Agnew called "positive polarization," it failed. Essentially, Sundquist suggests, this cluster of issues failed to bring about party realignment for the same reason that the issue of communism failed: both parties were on the same side.

Finally, in Sundquist's view, the *fourth* issue that might have resulted in realignment was race. It alone is still a possible realigning issue, for it has the potential for polarization. Yet George Wallace's various presidential campaigns, Richard Nixon's direct appeals to white majority values, and overwhelmingly significant problems such as the Supreme Court–mandated school busing to achieve desegregation all failed to bring about a partisan realignment. Liberal and moderate forces in the Republican party were able to exert sufficient influence to keep the party from overt and widespread exploitation of racial antipathy, and Republican successes and the decline of the old Democratic dominance in the South have undercut the issue's potential. Sundquist thus concludes that race—the single viable issue that might lead to realignment—does not appear to be heading in that direction.[16]

Sundquist also believes that the long-term trends of growing Independent strength, declining party identification, loss by the party organizations of control over campaigning, and other factors of decreasing party strength are probably irreversible. He states that the old-fashioned, closed political system is not going to be reestablished, nor are the old-style political bosses going to be restored to power, media campaigning outlawed, or voter independence reversed. Nevertheless, he thinks it easy to overestimate how much change has taken place, and he believes it possible to overcome the problems besetting the parties while still retaining them as viable institutions. He notes:

> party systems weakened by the passage of time can be reinforced if powerful new issues arise that run along, rather than across, the existing line of party cleavage. As during a realignment period, parties become relevant again and new and durable party attachments are formed, but this time they are formed on the rationale of the existing party system.[17]

Another group of scholars has emerged in recent years to argue that the available evidence does not necessarily support the thesis of party decline. Cornelius P. Cotter, John F. Bibby, James L. Gibson, and Robert J. Huckshorn contend that the question of party decline cannot be assessed without considering the strength of the organizational components of the parties. Their study of the party system in the states has demonstrated considerable evidence of increased strength in the party organizations. They summarize a part of their study as follows:

> The state parties are a durable and persistent force. Inter-party competition within the states is substantial, and party organizations have become more sophisticated and more capable of providing a wide range of services to their clientele. As federal and state regulation has increased, the protective mantle of the law has been spread over the parties so that the parties have become quasi-public agencies performing essential public functions. Clearly, there is little in the data . . . to support the notion that parties are withering or facing disintegration. Rather, American state parties continue to command voter loyalty as organizations capable of engaging in important activities and as important forces in shaping the decisions of policy makers. American parties do not meet the requirements of the responsible party government model. However, they remain the principle agencies for making nominations, contesting elections, recruiting leaders, and providing a link between citizens and their government.[18]

Even the most pessimistic observers of the decline of parties view that troubling trend with dismay and the results with trepidation. Walter Dean Burnham has put the concern of strong party advocates well:

> Political parties, with all their well-known human and structural shortcomings, are the only devices thus far invented by the wit of Western man that can, with some effectiveness, generate countervailing collective power on behalf of the many individually powerless against the relatively few who are individually or organizationally powerful. Their disappearance as active intermediaries, if not as preliminary screening devices, would only entail the unchallenged ascendancy of the already powerful unless new structures of collective power were somehow developed to replace them, and unless conditions in America's social structure and political culture came to be such that they could be effectively used.[19]

Thus, to summarize, Walter Dean Burnham believes that party decomposition is well along and probably irreversible. James Sundquist considers that, although in the long run the prospect may be for further gradual decomposition, one may equally well take the view that in the short run the progress toward that end will be checked and reversed. Even those who believe that the parties are doomed do not welcome their passing. They recognize that parties play a useful role in mediating conflicts—conflicts that are inevitable in a pluralistic society. It would probably be a mistake to predict the demise of political parties. The parties originally grew because of a need for some form of continuing organization to channel public views to government officials and to provide a means through which ordinary voters could collectively make themselves felt in the selection of public officials. Those needs still remain today. The emphasis may have shifted to other types of organizations, such as pressure groups, but the parties remain the only vehicles recognized in law as organizations for the electorate. Even if the present parties should die at some future date, or the people should realign themselves into different coalitions, it is probable that some form of party will prevail.

## Notes

1. Gerald M. Pomper, "The Decline of Party Politics," in *The Impact of the Electoral Process,* Sage Electoral Studies Yearbook, vol. 3, eds. Louis Maisel and Joseph Cooper (Beverly Hills, Calif.: Sage, 1977), pp. 13–38.

2. Bureau of the Census, U.S. Department of Commerce, *Voting and Registration in the Election of November 1972,* Current Population Reports, series P. 20, no. 253 (Washington, D.C.: Government Printing Office, 1973).

3. Austin Ranney, "The Political Parties: Reform and Decline," in *The New American Political System,* ed. Anthony King (Washington, D.C.: American Enterprise Institute, 1978), p. 224–230.

4. Charles H. Longley, "Party Reform and Party Nationalization: The Case of the Democrats," a paper presented at the annual meeting of the Midwest Political Science Association, Chicago, April 29–May 1, 1976; and Longley, "Party Reform and Party Organization: The Compliance Review Commission of the Democratic Party," a paper presented at the annual meeting of the Northeastern Political Science Association, Mt. Pocono, Pa., November 10–12, 1977. For a published version of parts of this work, see "Party Reform and Party Nationalization: The Case of the Democrats," in *The Party Symbol: Readings on Political Parties,* ed. William Crotty, (San Francisco: Freeman, 1980), pp. 359–378.

5. Cornelius P. Cotter and John F. Bibby, "Institutional Development of Parties and the Thesis of Party Decline," *Political Science Quarterly 95,* no. 1 (Spring, 1980): 1–27; also see their "The Impact of Reform on the National Party Organizations: The Long-Term Determinants of Party Reform," a paper presented at the annual meeting of the American Political Science Association, Washington, D.C., August 30–September 2, 1979. Also see Robert J. Huckshorn and John F. Bibby, "State Parties in an Era of Political Change," in *The Future of American Political Parties,* ed. Joel L. Fleishman (Englewood Cliffs, N.J.: Prentice-Hall, 1982), pp. 70–100; and Robert J. Huckshorn, James L. Gibson, Cornelius P. Cotter, and John F. Bibby, "On the Resistance of State Party Organizations to Dealignment: National Parties as Agents of State Party Development," a paper delivered at the Shambaugh Conference on Political Science at Iowa, University of Iowa, Iowa City, December 9–10, 1982, pp. 1–52.

6. Robert J. Huckshorn, *Party Leadership in the States* (Amherst: The University of Massachusetts Press, 1976). Also see James L. Gibson, Cornelius P. Cotter, John F. Bibby, and Robert J. Huckshorn, "Assessing Party Organizational Strength," *American Journal of Political Science* (May 1983): 193–222.

7. David Broder, "The Frustrations of Single-Interest Politics," *Washington Post* (September 13, 1978): A-27.

8. Ibid.

9. John Herbers, "Special Interests Gaining Power as Voter Disillusionment Grows," *New York Times* (November 14, 1978): B-1 and B-14.

10. Broder, "Single-Interest Politics," p. A-27.

11. The descriptive adjectives in parentheses are those of Walter Dean Burnham, "Party Systems and the Political Process," in *The American Party Systems,* eds. William Nisbet Chambers and Walter Dean Burnham (New York: Oxford University Press, 1975), pp. 289–304.

12. Ibid., pp. 305–307.

13. See Walter Dean Burnham, *Critical Elections and the Mainsprings of American Politics* (New York: Norton, 1970); Kevin Phillips, *The Emerging Republican Majority* (New Rochelle, N.Y.: Arlington House, 1969); and Kevin Phillips, *Mediacracy* (Garden City, N.Y.: Doubleday, 1975).

14. Burnham, *Critical Elections,* p. 173.

15. For a good review of the realignment–disintegration debate, see "Are Parties Becoming Irrelevant?" in *Controversies in American Voting Behavior,* eds. Richard G. Niemi and Herbert Weisberg (San Francisco: Freeman, 1976), pp. 413–421.

16. James L. Sundquist, *Dynamics of the Party System: Alignment and Realignment of Political Parties in the United States* (Washington, D.C.: Brookings Institution, 1973), pp. 355–373.

17. James L. Sundquist, "Whither the American Political System?" in *Parties and Elections in an Anti-Party Age,* ed. Jeff Fishel, (Bloomington: Indiana University Press, 1978), p. 350.

18. John F. Bibby, Cornelius P. Cotter, James L. Gibson, and Robert J. Huckshorn, "Parties in State Politics," in *Politics in the American States: A Comparative Analysis,* 4th ed., eds. Virginia Gray, Herbert Jacob, and Kenneth Vines (Boston: Little, Brown, 1983), pp. 94–95.

19. Walter Dean Burnham, "The End of American Political Parties," *Trans-Action* (December 1969): 20.

# APPENDIX

Sample Ballots

*"MISSOURI*

# OFFICIAL BALLOT

GENERAL ELECTION, TUESDAY, NOVEMBER 4, 1980

STATE OF MISSOURI

| DEMOCRATIC PARTY | REPUBLICAN PARTY | SWP<br>SOCIALIST WORKERS PARTY | LIBERTARIAN PARTY | INDEPENDENT |
|---|---|---|---|---|
| ○ | ○ | ○ | ○ | |
| For President and Vice-President —<br>JIMMY CARTER<br>WALTER F. MONDALE | For President and Vice-President —<br>RONALD REAGAN<br>GEORGE BUSH | For President and Vice-President —<br>CLIFTON DeBERRY<br>MATILDA ZIMMERMAN | For President and Vice-President —<br>ED CLARK<br>DAVID KOCH | For President and Vice-President —<br>JOHN B. ANDERSON<br>PATRICK J. LUCEY |
| For United States Senator —<br>THOMAS F. EAGLETON | For United States Senator —<br>GENE McNARY | For United States Senator —<br>MARTHA PETTIT | For United States Senator — | For United States Senator — |
| For Governor —<br>JOSEPH P. TEASDALE | For Governor —<br>CHRISTOPHER (Kit) BOND | For Governor —<br>HELEN SAVIO | For Governor — | For Governor — |
| For Lieutenant-Governor —<br>KENNETH J. ROTHMAN | For Lieutenant-Governor —<br>ROY BLUNT | For Lieutenant-Governor — | For Lieutenant-Governor — | For Lieutenant-Governor — |
| For Secretary of State —<br>JAMES C. (Jim) KIRKPATRICK | For Secretary of State —<br>WALTER L. PFEFFER, II | For Secretary of State — | For Secretary of State — | For Secretary of State — |
| For State Treasurer —<br>MEL CARNAHAN | For State Treasurer —<br>GERALD E. (Gerry) WINSHIP | For State Treasurer — | For State Treasurer — | For State Treasurer — |
| For Attorney General —<br>ROBERT BAINE | For Attorney General —<br>JOHN ASHCROFT | For Attorney General — | For Attorney General — | For Attorney General — |
| For United States Representative — | For United States Representative — | For United States Representative — | For United States Representative — | For United States Representative — |
| For State Senator —<br>District — | For State Senator —<br>District — | For State Senator —<br>District — | For State Senator —<br>District — | For State Senator —<br>District — |
| For State Representative —<br>District — | For State Representative —<br>District — | For State Representative —<br>District — | For State Representative —<br>District — | For State Representative —<br>District — |
| For Judge Circuit Court —<br>Circuit No. ____ Division ____ | For Judge Circuit Court —<br>Circuit No. ____ Division ____ | For Judge Circuit Court —<br>Circuit No. ____ Division ____ | For Judge Circuit Court —<br>Circuit No. ____ Division ____ | For Judge Circuit Court —<br>Circuit No. ____ Division ____ |
| For Associate Judge County Court —<br>District — | For Associate Judge County Court —<br>District — | For Associate Judge County Court —<br>District — | For Associate Judge County Court —<br>District — | For Associate Judge County Court —<br>District — |
| For Associate Judge County Court —<br>District — | For Associate Judge County Court —<br>District — | For Associate Judge County Court —<br>District — | For Associate Judge County Court —<br>District — | For Associate Judge County Court —<br>District — |
| For Prosecuting Attorney — | For Prosecuting Attorney — | For Prosecuting Attorney — | For Prosecuting Attorney — | For Prosecuting Attorney — |
| For Sheriff — | For Sheriff — | For Sheriff — | For Sheriff — | For Sheriff — |
| For Assessor — | For Assessor — | For Assessor — | For Assessor — | For Assessor — |
| For Treasurer — | For Treasurer — | For Treasurer — | For Treasurer — | For Treasurer — |
| For Public Administrator — | For Public Administrator — | For Public Administrator — | For Public Administrator — | For Public Administrator — |
| For Coroner — | For Coroner — | For Coroner — | For Coroner — | For Coroner — |
| For County Surveyor — | For County Surveyor — | For County Surveyor — | For County Surveyor — | For County Surveyor — |

## INSTRUCTIONS TO VOTERS

On receipt of his ballot the voter shall forthwith, and without leaving the enclosed space, retire alone to one of the voting booths provided, and prepare his ballot for voting in the following manner.

**STRAIGHT TICKET**

If the voter desires to vote a straight party ticket, he may place a cross (X) mark in the circle directly below the party name at the head of the column, or he may place cross (X) marks in the squares directly to the left of the names of candidates on one party ticket.

**SPLIT TICKET**

If the voter desires to vote a split party ticket, he may place a cross (X) mark in the circle directly below one party name at the head of the column and cross (X) marks in the squares directly to the left of the names of candidates on other party tickets, or he may place cross (X) marks in the squares directly to the left of the names of candidates on different party tickets.

**WRITE-INS**

If the voter desires to vote for a person whose name does not appear on the ballot, he may cross out a name which appears on the ballot for the office and write the name of the person for whom he wishes to vote above or below the crossed-out name and place a cross (X) mark in the square directly to the left of the crossed-out name. If a write in line appears on the ballot, he may write the name of the person for whom he wishes to vote on the line and place a cross (X) mark in the square directly to the left of the name.

**SPOILED BALLOT**

If the voter accidentally spoils his ballot or ballot card or makes an error, he may return it to an election judge and receive another. The election judge shall mark "SPOILED" across the ballot or ballot card and place it in an envelope marked "SPOILED BALLOTS." After another ballot has been prepared in the manner provided in section 115.431, the ballot shall be given to the voter for voting.

(Section 115.439 RSMo 1978)

364

---
CARD B
---

**SIDE 1**

TOP

B

# OFFICIAL JUDICIAL BALLOT

### FIRST JUDICIAL DISTRICT

**GENERAL ELECTION NOVEMBER 4, 1980**
**STATE OF ALASKA**

THIS STUB TO BE REMOVED BY ELECTION BOARD

---

Submitting to the voters whether the judges named below should be retained. Each judge is seeking to succeed himself as required by law and is not in competition with any other judge on this ballot.

### OFFICIAL JUDICIAL BALLOT
**FIRST JUDICIAL DISTRICT**
VOTE "YES" or "NO"

**SUPREME COURT**

| Shall WARREN W. MATTHEWS be retained as justice of the supreme court for ten years? | YES | + |
| --- | --- | --- |
| | NO | + |

**SUPERIOR COURT**

| Shall ALLEN T. COMPTON be retained as a judge of the superior court for six years? | YES | + |
| --- | --- | --- |
| | NO | + |

**SUPERIOR COURT**

| Shall DUANE CRASKE be retained as a judge of the superior court for six years? | YES | + |
| --- | --- | --- |
| | NO | + |

**DISTRICT COURT**

| Shall GERALD O. WILLIAMS be retained as a judge of the district court for four years? | YES | + |
| --- | --- | --- |
| | NO | + |

## TURN CARD OVER
## AND CONTINUE VOTING

01201  **VOTE BOTH SIDES**  B

---

**SIDE 2**

# I HAVE VOTED

# HAVE YOU?

### STATE OF ALASKA
**General Election November 4, 1980**

#### BALLOT PROPOSITION NO. 1
**Constitutional Amendment**
**Legislative Annulment of Regulations**

This proposal would permit the legislature to annul, by adopting a resolution, regulations adopted by state agencies. Annulment of regulations by resolution was authorized by the First State Legislature in 1959; however, in 1980 the Alaska Supreme Court held that the constitution permits the legislature to annul a regulation only by passing a bill, which requires three readings of the bill and a roll call vote which is recorded. The procedures for adopting resolutions are governed by legislative rules and require only the approval of the resolution by voice vote of a majority of both houses. A bill passed by the legislature annulling a regulation could be vetoed by the governor or repealed by referendum. A resolution annulling a regulation could not.

| A vote "FOR" adopts the amendment. | FOR | + |
| --- | --- | --- |
| A vote "AGAINST" rejects the amendment. | AGAINST | + |

#### BALLOT PROPOSITION NO. 2
**Constitutional Amendment**
**Disqualification of Legislators**

This is a proposal to eliminate the prohibition which exists during his term of office and for one year thereafter against a legislator's taking a state office or position of profit, during his term of office and for one year thereafter, the salary or emoluments of which were increased while he was a member. It retains the prohibition against taking an office which was created while he was a member.

| A vote "FOR" adopts the amendment. | FOR | + |
| --- | --- | --- |
| A vote "AGAINST" rejects the amendment. | AGAINST | + |

#### BALLOT PROPOSITION NO. 3
**Constitutional Amendment**
**Interim and Special Legislative Committees**

This proposal would amend the state constitution to permit the legislature to adopt procedures for establishing interim and special committees by legislative rule, which, unlike a bill, may be adopted without three readings or a roll call vote and is not subject to veto by the governor or repeal by referendum. This proposal would also allow interim and special committees to meet during legislative sessions and would allow the legislature to vest such a committee with the power to share with the governor the authority to approve or disapprove budget revisions, including authorizations for receiving and spending federal or other non-state funds.

| A vote "FOR" adopts the amendment. | FOR | + |
| --- | --- | --- |
| A vote "AGAINST" rejects the amendment. | AGAINST | + |

01202  **VOTE BOTH SIDES**  B

# ─CARD C─

**SIDE 1** | **SIDE 2**

TOP

**C**

## OFFICIAL GENERAL ELECTION BALLOT

GENERAL ELECTION NOVEMBER 4, 1980
STATE OF ALASKA

THIS STUB TO BE REMOVED BY ELECTION BOARD

---

### STATE OF ALASKA
General Election November 4, 1980

#### BALLOT PROPOSITION NO. 4
**Constitutional Amendment
Appointment and Confirmation
of Members of Boards and Commissions**

This proposal would expand the legislature's power over the appointment and confirmation of members of state boards and commissions by giving it the power to provide for the appointments to be made other than by the governor and the power to require confirmation of members of all boards or commissions in addition to those which are at the head of principal departments or regulatory or quasi-judicial agencies.

| A vote "FOR" adopts the amendment. | FOR | + |
| A vote "AGAINST" rejects the amendment. | AGAINST | + |

#### BALLOT PROPOSITION NO. 5
**Initiative No. 79-02
Alaska General Stock
Ownership Corporation (AGSOC.)**

This measure establishes a general stock ownership corporation (AGSOC) in Alaska. It will be a private corporation owned by Alaskans. Shares will be distributed without charge to Alaska residents who wish to become stockholders. The corporation will not be subject to income tax and this is expected to enhance its financial success. Shareholders will be subject to taxes on their share of the corporation's taxable income, whether or not it is distributed to them, and may not deduct corporate losses, if any. The corporation will borrow money for investment and repay loans from income.

| A vote "FOR" approves the initiative. | FOR | + |
| A vote "AGAINST" rejects the initiative. | AGAINST | + |

### TURN CARD OVER AND CONTINUE VOTING

01301    **VOTE BOTH SIDES**    **C**

---

## OFFICIAL BONDING PROPOSITION BALLOT

GENERAL ELECTION NOVEMBER 4, 1980
STATE OF ALASKA

### STATE OF ALASKA
General Election November 4, 1980

**OFFICIAL BONDING
PROPOSITION BALLOT**

#### BONDING PROPOSITION A
(Ch. 91, SLA 1980)
**State General Obligation Fisheries Facilities
Construction Bonds $7,718,800**

Shall the State of Alaska issue its general obligation bonds in the principal amount of not more than $7,718,800 for the purpose of paying the cost of capital improvements for fisheries facilities?

| BONDS - YES | + |
| BONDS - NO | + |

#### BONDING PROPOSITION B
(Ch. 97, SLA 1980)
**State General Obligation Water Supply and Sewer
Systems, Solid Waste Facilities, and Village Safe
Water Construction Bonds $33,000,000**

Shall the State of Alaska issue its general obligation bonds in the principal amount of not more than $33,000,000 for the purpose of paying the cost of capital improvements for water and sewer systems, solid waste facilities, and village safe water facilities?

| BONDS - YES | + |
| BONDS - NO | + |

#### BONDING PROPOSITION C
(Ch. 98, SLA 1980)
**State General Obligation Facilities Upgrade
Construction Bonds $18,787,500**

Shall the State of Alaska issue its general obligation bonds in the principal amount of not more than $18,787,500 for the purpose of paying the cost of energy conservation, code upgrade, and architectural barrier removal for state facilities?

| BONDS - YES | + |
| BONDS - NO | + |

#### BONDING PROPOSITION D
(Ch. 99, SLA 1980)
**State General Obligation Correctional Facilities
Construction Bonds $28,350,000**

Shall the State of Alaska issue its general obligation bonds in the principal amount of not more than $28,350,000 for the purpose of paying the cost of capital improvements for correctional facilities?

| BONDS - YES | + |
| BONDS - NO | + |

01302    **VOTE BOTH SIDES**    **C**

# SAMPLE BALLOT

## VOTE IN ALL COLUMNS

### CONSTITUTIONAL AMENDMENTS, REFERENDUMS AND INITIATIVES

#### CONSTITUTIONAL AMENDMENT NO. 10

AN AMENDMENT TO THE CONSTITUTION PROPOSED BY THE LEGISLATURE

Attorney General's Explanatory Statement

**The legislature submitted this proposal for a vote. It would amend the Montana Constitution regarding the investment of public funds.** Currently public funds may not be invested in private corporate capital stock and school fund investments must bear a fixed rate of interest. This proposal would eliminate those restrictions.

AN ACT TO SUBMIT TO THE QUALIFIED ELECTORS OF MONTANA AN AMENDMENT TO ARTICLE VIII, SECTION 13, OF THE MONTANA CONSTITUTION REMOVING THE RESTRICTION ON INVESTMENT OF PUBLIC FUNDS IN CORPORATE CAPITAL STOCK AND THE REQUIREMENT THAT SCHOOL FUND INVESTMENTS BEAR A FIXED INTEREST RATE.

**FISCAL NOTE**
REMOVING THESE RESTRICTIONS WILL ALLOW THE LEGISLATURE TO BROADEN THE RANGE OF INVESTMENTS IN WHICH PUBLIC FUNDS MAY BE INVESTED. THE FISCAL IMPACT ON STATE FUNDS IS NOT KNOWN.

☐ **FOR** removing the restriction on investment of public funds in corporate capital stock and the requirement that school fund investments bear a fixed rate of interest.

☐ **AGAINST** removing the restriction on investment of public funds in corporate capital stock and the requirement that school fund investments bear a fixed rate of interest.

#### CONSTITUTIONAL AMENDMENT NO. 11

AN AMENDMENT TO THE CONSTITUTION PROPOSED BY THE LEGISLATURE

Attorney General's Explanatory Statement

**The legislature submitted this proposal for a vote. It would amend the Montana Constitution to require the legislature to meet yearly.** In odd-numbered years the legislature would meet for not more than 60 days and would consider legislation on all subjects except appropriations. In even-numbered years the legislature would meet for not more than 45 days and would be limited to considering revenue and appropriations matters. Legislation on excluded subjects could be considered if two-thirds of the members of either house voted to introduce such a bill. Currently the legislature meets every other year for not more than 90 days.

AN ACT TO SUBMIT TO THE QUALIFIED ELECTORS OF MONTANA AN AMENDMENT TO ARTICLE V, SECTION 6, OF THE MONTANA CONSTITUTION TO PROVIDE THAT THE LEGISLATURE SHALL MEET IN ANNUAL SESSIONS FOR 60 LEGISLATIVE DAYS IN ODD-NUMBERED YEARS AND 45 LEGISLATIVE DAYS IN EVEN-NUMBERED YEARS AND TO PROVIDE LIMITATIONS ON THE BUSINESS THAT MAY BE CONDUCTED IN EACH RESPECTIVE SESSION; AND TO PROVIDE AN EFFECTIVE DATE.

**FISCAL NOTE**
THE COST OF LEGISLATORS' SALARIES, EXPENSES AND STAFF FOR THE PRESENT 90 DAY LEGISLATIVE SESSION IS APPROXIMATELY $3.2 MILLION. THESE COSTS WOULD INCREASE ABOUT $500,000 IF THE LEGISLATURE WERE TO MEET IN YEARLY SESSIONS TOTALING 105 DAYS DURING THE SAME TWO YEAR PERIOD.

☐ **FOR** annual legislative sessions.

☐ **AGAINST** annual legislative sessions.

VOTE IN NEXT COLUMN

### CONSTITUTIONAL AMENDMENTS, REFERENDUMS AND INITIATIVES
(Continued)

#### CONSTITUTIONAL AMENDMENT NO. 12

AN AMENDMENT TO THE CONSTITUTION PROPOSED BY THE LEGISLATURE

Attorney General's Explanatory Statement

**The legislature submitted this proposal for a vote. It would amend the Montana Constitution regarding the legislature's ability to override the governor's veto.** Currently the legislature must come back into session if it wishes to reconsider a bill vetoed by the governor after the session has ended. This proposal would allow the secretary of state to poll the legislature by mail. The proposal also specifies that two-thirds of the members of each house of the legislature must vote to override any veto for a bill to become a law.

AN ACT TO SUBMIT TO THE QUALIFIED ELECTORS OF MONTANA AN AMENDMENT TO ARTICLE VI, SECTION 10, OF THE MONTANA CONSTITUTION TO PROVIDE THAT THE SECRETARY OF STATE SHALL CONDUCT A POLL OF ALL LEGISLATORS WHEN THE LEGISLATURE IS NOT IN SESSION AND THE GOVERNOR VETOES A BILL.

☐ **FOR** allowing the legislature to override a post-session veto through a poll of its members by the secretary of state.

☐ **AGAINST** allowing the legislature to override a post-session veto through a poll of its members by the secretary of state.

#### LEGISLATIVE REFERENDUM NO. 89

AN ACT REFERRED BY THE LEGISLATURE

Attorney General's Explanatory Statement

**The legislature submitted this proposal for a vote. It would amend the initiative passed by the voters in 1980 concerning the disposal of certain radioactive materials.** This proposal would allow the disposal of some uranium and thorium mill tailings. The state would regulate the disposal of tailings, monitor the maintenance of disposal sites, and may charge fees for radiation control services. The state would also have authority to condemn radioactive waste disposal sites.

AN ACT TO REMOVE THE PROHIBITION OF DISPOSAL OF CERTAIN RADIOACTIVE MATERIALS IN THE STATE OF MONTANA ENACTED BY INITIATIVE 84 AND PROVIDING FOR A REGULATORY SYSTEM; PROVIDING FOR THE CONTROL AND CONDEMNATION OF LAND USED FOR DISPOSAL OF MILL TAILINGS FROM URANIUM AND THORIUM ORE PROCESSING; AND REVISING THE LAWS CONCERNING RADIATION CONTROL; AMENDING SECTIONS 75-3-102, 75-3-103, 75-3-104, 75-3-201, 75-3-202, 75-3-302, 75-3-303, 75-30-102, MCA, AND SECTION 1 OF INITIATIVE 84; PROVIDING AN EFFECTIVE DATE; AND PROVIDING FOR A REFERENDUM.

**FISCAL NOTE**
THE COST OF ADMINISTERING THE RADIOACTIVE MATERIALS PROGRAM WILL BE $41,600 IN FISCAL YEAR 1984 AND $58,872 IN FISCAL YEAR 1985. THE COST OF OPERATION OF THE PROJECT AFTER FISCAL YEAR 1985 WILL BE FUNDED FROM LICENSE FEES.

☐ **FOR** allowing disposal in Montana of uranium mill tailings as an exception to the ban on disposal of radioactive waste and providing a regulatory system.

☐ **AGAINST** allowing disposal in Montana of uranium mill tailings as an exception to the ban on disposal of radioactive waste and providing a regulatory system.

#### INITIATIVE NO. 91

A LAW PROPOSED BY INITIATIVE PETITION

THIS INITIATIVE WOULD DECLARE THAT THE PEOPLE OF MONTANA ARE OPPOSED TO THE PLACEMENT OF MX MISSILES IN THIS STATE. IT ALSO EXPRESSES OPPOSITION TO FURTHER TESTING, DEVELOPMENT OR DEPLOYMENT OF NUCLEAR WEAPONS BY ANY NATION. PASSAGE OF THIS INITIATIVE IS AN EXPRESSION OF THE OPINION OF THE VOTERS IN MONTANA AND WOULD HAVE NO LEGAL EFFECT.

☐ **FOR** the initiative — I oppose the placement of MX missiles in Montana and the further testing, development or deployment of nuclear weapons by any nation.

☐ **AGAINST** the initiative — I do not oppose the placement of MX missiles in Montana and the further testing, development or deployment of nuclear weapons by any nation.

VOTE IN NEXT COLUMN

### CONSTITUTIONAL AMENDMENTS, REFERENDUMS AND INITIATIVES
(Continued)

#### INITIATIVE NO. 92

A LAW PROPOSED BY INITIATIVE PETITION

THIS INITIATIVE WOULD EXPAND AUTHORIZED GAMBLING IN MONTANA, AND CREATE A STATE GAMING COMMISSION. IT WOULD ALLOW BLACKJACK; PUNCHBOARDS; AND ELECTRONIC OR MECHANICAL GAMBLING DEVICES THAT SIMULATE CARD GAMES. BINGO OR KENO BINGO AND KENO PAYOFFS COULD BE MADE IN CASH. THE STATE GAMING COMMISSION WOULD LICENSE AND REGULATE ALL AUTHORIZED GAMBLING IN MONTANA INCLUDING THE MANUFACTURE, SALE AND APPROVAL OF GAMBLING DEVICES. THE COMMISSION WOULD SET PRIZE LIMITS FOR ALL GAMES. LOCAL GOVERNMENTS COULD ASSESS FEES OR TAXES ON GAMBLING ESTABLISHMENTS, TABLES AND DEVICES. OPERATION OF A GAMBLING ESTABLISHMENT WITHOUT A LICENSE WOULD BE A FELONY.

**FISCAL NOTE**
THE INITIATIVE PROVIDES THAT REVENUE GENERATED BY FEES ON GAMBLING ESTABLISHMENTS. DISTRIBUTORS AND MANUFACTURES WOULD FUND THE OPERATION OF A STATE GAMING COMMISSION, WHICH WOULD COST APPROXIMATELY $600,000 EACH YEAR. LOCAL GOVERNMENTS COULD ALSO ASSESS SPECIFIED FEES AND TAXES ON GAMBLING ESTABLISHMENTS. IT IS NOT POSSIBLE TO ESTIMATE THOSE REVENUES.

☐ **FOR** — expansion of authorized gambling to include blackjack, punchboards and certain electronic or mechanical gambling devices, and creation of a State Gaming Commission.

☐ **AGAINST** — expansion of authorized gambling to include blackjack, punchboards and certain electronic or mechanical gambling devices, and creation of a State Gaming Commission.

#### INITIATIVE NO. 94

A LAW PROPOSED BY INITIATIVE PETITION

THIS INITIATIVE WOULD ABOLISH THE QUOTA SYSTEM FOR SOME BEER AND WINE LICENSES. BUSINESSES WITH SUFFICIENT KITCHEN AND DINING ROOM EQUIPMENT TO SELL MEALS TO THE PUBLIC COULD APPLY FOR A LICENSE TO SELL BEER AND WINE. THE AVAILABILITY OF THOSE LICENSES WOULD NOT BE BASED ON POPULATION. ESTABLISHMENTS HOLDING LICENSES UNDER THE PRESENT QUOTA SYSTEM WOULD BE ENTITLED TO A TRANSFERABLE CREDIT ON THEIR STATE TAXES FOR ANY LOSS IN THE FAIR MARKET VALUE OF THAT LICENSE.

**FISCAL NOTE**
THE TRANSFERABLE TAX CREDIT GRANTED TO CURRENT LICENSE HOLDERS WOULD REDUCE STATE TAX COLLECTIONS BY APPROXIMATELY $2 - 5 MILLION OVER A FIVE YEAR PERIOD. THE STATE WOULD RECEIVE A REVENUE INCREASE FROM THE FEES FOR NEW BEER AND WINE LICENSES. THE FEES ARE GENERALLY $400 PER LICENSE.

☐ **FOR** abolishing the quota system on beer and wine licenses for restaurants and prepared food businesses.

☐ **AGAINST** abolishing the quota system on beer and wine licenses for restaurants and prepared food businesses.

#### INITIATIVE NO. 95

A LAW PROPOSED BY INITIATIVE PETITION

UNDER THIS INITIATIVE THE STATE WOULD TAKE ONE-FOURTH (25%) OF ALL FUTURE DEPOSITS TO THE PERMANENT COAL TAX TRUST AND INVEST IT IN MONTANA'S ECONOMY. THE STATE WOULD MAKE NO DIRECT LOANS, BUT WOULD EMPHASIZE INVESTMENTS IN NEW OR EXPANDING ENTERPRISES.
THE INITIATIVE WOULD ALSO CREATE AN ECONOMIC DEVELOPMENT FUND, USING A PORTION OF THE INTEREST FROM THE COAL TAX TRUST. AFTER DETERMINING HOW MUCH INTEREST TO ALLOCATE TO THE ECONOMIC DEVELOPMENT FUND THE LEGISLATURE MAY SPEND MONEY FROM THE FUND TO SUPPORT ECONOMIC DEVELOPMENT IN THE STATE.

**FISCAL NOTE**
THE AMOUNT INVESTED IN MONTANA ECONOMIC DEVELOPMENT FROM THE COAL TAX TRUST WOULD INCREASE EACH YEAR TO AN ESTIMATED TOTAL OF $134.6 MILLION BY 1989. PROJECTIONS HAVE NOT BEEN MADE BEYOND 1989. SUCH INVESTMENT COULD REDUCE THE AMOUNT OF INTEREST EARNED ON THE TRUST.

☐ **FOR** investing part of the coal severance tax permanent trust fund in the Montana economy and creating a Montana economic development fund.

☐ **AGAINST** investing part of the coal severance tax permanent trust fund in the Montana economy and creating a Montana economic development fund.

# BIBLIOGRAPHY

Abramson, Paul, Aldrich, John H., and Rohde, David W. *Change and Continuity in the 1980 Elections.* Washington, D.C.: Congressional Quarterly Press, 1982.

Adamany, David. *Campaign Financing in America.* North Scituate, Mass.: Duxbury Press, 1972.

Adamany, David, and Agree, George E. *Political Money: A Strategy for Campaign Financing in America.* Baltimore, Md.: Johns Hopkins University Press, 1975.

Agranoff, Robert. *The Management of Election Campaigns.* Boston: Holbrook Press, 1976.

———. *The New Style in Election Campaigns.* Boston: Holbrook Press, 1972.

Akey, Denise S., ed. *Encyclopedia of Associations, 1983.* 17th ed. Vols. 1 and 2. Detroit: Gale Research, 1982.

Alexander, Herbert A., ed. *Campaign Money: Reform and Reality in the States.* New York: Free Press, 1976.

———. *Financing Politics: Money Elections and Political Reform.* Washington, D.C.: Congressional Quarterly Press, 1976.

———. *Financing the 1960 Election.* Princeton, N.J.: Citizens' Research Foundation, 1962.

———. *Financing the 1964 Election.* Princeton, N.J.: Citizens' Research Foundation, 1966.

———. *Financing the 1968 Election.* Boston: Heath, 1971.

———. *Financing the 1972 Election.* Boston: Heath, 1976.

———. *Money in Politics.* Washington, D.C.: Public Affairs Press, 1972.

———. *Political Financing.* Minneapolis, Minn.: Burgess, 1972.

Almond, Gabriel A., and Verba, Sidney. *The Civic Culture.* Boston: Little, Brown, 1965.

American Political Science Association. *Toward a More Responsible Two-Party System.* New York: Holt, Rinehart and Winston, 1950.

Anderson, William, and Weidner, Edward W. *American Government.* 4th ed. New York: Holt, Rinehart and Winston, 1953.

Apter, David E., ed. *Ideology and Discontent.* New York: Free Press, 1964.

Bain, Henry M., and Hecock, Donald S. *Ballot Position and Voter's Choice.* Detroit: Wayne State University Press, 1957.

Banfield, Edward C., and Wilson, James Q. *City Politics.* New York: Vintage Books, 1963.

Barber, James David, ed. *Choosing the President.* Englewood Cliffs, N.J.: Prentice-Hall, 1974.

Bauer, Raymond A., Pool, Ithiel De Sola, and Dexter, Lewis Anthony. *American Business and Public Policy: The Politics of Foreign Trade.* New York: Atherton Press, 1963.

Baus, Herbert M., and Ross, William B. *Politics Battle Plan.* New York: Macmillan, 1968.

Berelson, Bernard, Lazarsfeld, Paul F., and McPhee, William N. *Voting.* Chicago: University of Chicago Press, 1954.

Beyle, Thad, and Williams, J. Oliver. *The American Governor in Behavioral Perspective.* New York: Harper & Row, 1972.

Bibby, John F., and Davidson, Roger. *On Capitol Hill: Studies in the Legislative Process.* 2nd ed. Hinsdale, Ill.: Dryden Press, 1972.

Binkley, Wilfred E. *American Political Parties: Their Natural History.* 4th ed. New York: Knopf, 1963.

Bone, Hugh A. *American Politics and the Party System.* 3rd ed. New York: McGraw-Hill, 1965.

Bowers, Claude C. *Jefferson and Hamilton.* Boston: Houghton Mifflin, 1925.

Broder, David S. *The Party's Over: The Failure of Politics in America.* New York: Harper & Row, 1971.

Bryce, James. *The American Commonwealth.* Putnam's, 1959.

———. *Modern Democracies.* New York: Macmillan, 1921.

Burke, Edmund. *Works of Edmund Burke.* Boston: Little, Brown, 1971.

Burnham, Walter Dean. *Critical Elections and the Mainsprings of American Politics.* New York: Norton, 1970.

Burns, James MacGregor. *The Deadlock of Democracy.* Englewood Cliffs, N.J.: Prentice-Hall, 1963.

Califano, Joseph A., Jr. *A Presidential Nation.* New York: Norton, 1975.

Campbell, Angus, Converse, Philip E., Miller, Warren E., and Stokes, Donald E. *The American Voter.* New York: Wiley, 1960.

Chambers, William N. *Political Parties in a New Nation: The American Experience 1776–1809.* New York: Oxford University Press, 1963.

Chambers, William N., and Burnham, Walter D. *The*

*American Party Systems.* 2nd ed. New York: Oxford University Press, 1967.

Chartrand, Robert L. *Computers and Political Campaigning.* Spartan Books, 1972.

Clapp, Charles L. *The Congressman: His Work As He Sees It.* Washington, D.C.: Brookings Institution, 1973.

Congressional Quarterly. *Dollar Politics.* 3rd ed. Washington, D.C.: Congressional Quarterly, 1982.

Corwin, Edward S. *The President: Office and Powers, 1787–1948.* 3rd ed. New York: New York University Press, 1948.

Cosman, Bernard C., and Huckshorn, Robert J., eds. *Republican Politics: The 1964 Campaign and Its Aftermath.* New York: Praeger, 1968.

Cotter, Cornelius P., and Hennessy, Bernard C. *Politics Without Power: The National Party Committees.* New York: Atherton Press, 1964.

Cronin, Thomas E. *The State of the Presidency.* Boston: Little, Brown, 1975.

Cronin, Thomas E., and Greenberg, Sanford D., eds. *The Presidential Advisory System.* New York: Harper & Row, 1969.

Crotty, William J., and Jacobson, Gary C. *American Political Parties in Decline.* Boston: Little, Brown, 1980.

———. *Political Reform and the American Experiment.* New York: Crowell, 1977.

———. *The Party Symbol: Readings on Political Parties.* San Francisco: Freeman, 1980.

Cunningham, Noble E., Jr. *The Jeffersonian Republicans.* Chapel Hill: University of North Carolina Press, 1957.

Dahl, Robert. *Congress and Foreign Policy.* New York: Harcourt Brace Jovanovich, 1950.

———. *Pluralist Democracy in the United States.* Chicago: Rand McNally, 1967.

David, Paul T., Goldman, Ralph M., and Bain, Richard C. *The Politics of National Party Conventions.* Washington, D.C.: Brookings Institution, 1960.

Davidson, Roger H. *The Role of the Congressman.* New York: Pegasus, 1969.

Davis, James W. *Presidential Primaries: Road to the White House.* New York: Crowell, 1967.

Dawson, Richard E., and Prewitt, Kenneth. *Political Socialization.* Boston: Little, Brown, 1969.

De Vries, Walter, and Tarrance, Lance, Jr. *The Ticket-Splitter.* Grand Rapids, Michigan: Eerdmans, 1972.

Dexter, Lewis A. *How Organizations Are Represented in Washington.* Indianapolis, Ind.: Bobbs-Merrill, 1969.

Domhoff, G. William. *Who Rules America?* Englewood Cliffs, N.J.: Prentice-Hall, 1967.

Downs, Anthony. *An Economic Theory of Democracy.* New York: Harper & Row, 1957.

Duverger, Maurice. *Political Parties.* New York: Wiley, 1954.

Dunn, Delmar D. *Financing Presidential Campaigns.* Washington, D.C.: Brookings Institution, 1972.

Easton, David. *A Framework for Political Analysis.* Englewood Cliffs, N.J.: Prentice-Hall, 1965.

Eckstein, Harry. *Pressure Group Politics: The Case of the British Medical Association.* London: Allen & Unwin, 1960.

Epstein, Leon D. *Political Parties in Western Democracies.* New York: Praeger, 1967.

Fishel, Jeff. *Parties and Elections in an Anti-Party Age.* Bloomington: Indiana University Press, 1978.

———. *Party and Opposition: Congressional Challengers in American Politics.* New York: McKay, 1973.

Fleishman, Joel L., ed. *The Future of American Political Parties.* New York: Prentice-Hall, 1982. (An American Assembly book.)

Froman, Lewis A., Jr. *The Congressional Process: Strategies, Rules and Procedures.* Boston: Little, Brown, 1967.

Graubard, Stephen R., and Holton, Gerald, eds. *Excellence and Leadership in Democracy.* New York: Columbia University Press, 1962.

Gray, Virginia, Jacob, Herbert, and Vines, Kenneth, eds. *Politics in the American States: A Comparative Analysis.* 4th ed. Boston: Little, Brown, 1983.

Greenberg, Edward S. *Political Socialization.* New York: Atherton Press, 1970.

Greenstein, Fred I. *Children and Politics.* New Haven, Conn.: Yale University Press, 1965.

Greenwald, Carol S. *Group Power: Lobbying and Public Policy.* New York: Praeger, 1977.

Gross, Bertram. *The Legislative Struggle.* New York: McGraw-Hill, 1953.

Heard, Alexander. *The Costs of Democracy.* Chapel Hill: University of North Carolina Press, 1960.

Herring, Pendleton. *Group Representation Before Congress.* Baltimore, Md.: Johns Hopkins University Press, 1929.

Hershey, Marjorie Random. *The Making of Campaign Strategy.* Boston: Heath, 1974.

Hess, Stephen. *The Presidential Campaign: The Leadership Selection Process After Watergate.* Washington, D.C.: Brookings Institution, 1974.

Hinderaker, Ivan. *Party Politics.* New York: Holt, Rinehart and Winston, 1956.

Horn, Stephen. *Unused Power: The Work of the Senate Committee on Appropriations.* Washington, D.C.: Brookings Institution, 1970.

Hrebenar, Ronald J., and Scott, Ruth K. *Interest Group Politics in America.* Englewood Cliffs, N.J.: Prentice-Hall, 1982.

Huckshorn, Robert J. *Party Leadership in the States.* Amherst: University of Massachusetts Press, 1976.

Huckshorn, Robert J., and Spencer, Robert C. *The Politics of Defeat.* Amherst: University of Massachusetts Press, 1971.

Institute of Politics, John F. Kennedy School of Government, Harvard University. *Financing Presidential Campaigns.* Cambridge, Mass.: Institute of Politics, 1982.

Jacob, Herbert, and Vines, Kenneth, eds. *Politics in the American States: A Comparative Analysis.* 3rd ed. Boston: Little, Brown, 1976.

Jennings, M. Kent, and Zeigler, L. Harmon, eds. *The*

*Electoral Process.* Englewood Cliffs, N.J.: Prentice-Hall, 1966.

Jewell, Malcolm E., and Olson, David M. *American State Political Parties and Elections.* Rev. ed. Homewood, Ill.: Dorsey Press, 1982.

Jonas, Frank, ed. *Politics in the American West.* Salt Lake City: University of Utah Press, 1969.

Jones, Charles O. *An Introduction to the Study of Public Policy.* North Scituate, Mass.: Duxbury Press, 1977.

————. *Party and Policy-Making: The House Republican Policy Committee.* New Brunswick, N.J.: Rutgers University Press, 1964.

Keech, William R., and Matthews, Donald R. *The Party's Choice.* Washington, D.C.: Brookings Institution, 1976.

Keefe, William J., and Ogul, Morris. *The American Legislative Process: Congress and the States.* 5th ed. Englewood Cliffs, N.J.: Prentice-Hall, 1981.

Kelley, Stanley. *Political Campaigning.* Washington, D.C.: Brookings Institution, 1960.

————. *Professional Public Relations and Political Power.* Baltimore, Md.: Johns Hopkins University Press, 1956.

Kent, Frank R. *The Great Game of Politics.* Rev. ed. Garden City, N.J.: Doubleday, 1930.

Kessel, John. *Presidential Campaign Politics.* Homewood, Ill.: Dorsey Press, 1980.

Key, V. O., Jr. *Politics, Parties and Pressure Groups.* 5th ed. New York: Crowell, 1964.

————. *Public Opinion and American Democracy.* New York: Knopf, 1961.

————. *Southern Politics in State and Nation.* New York: Vintage Books, 1949.

————. *The Responsible Electorate.* Cambridge, Mass.: Harvard University Press, 1966.

King, Anthony, ed. *The New American Political System.* Washington, D.C.: American Enterprise Institute, 1978.

Kingdon, John W. *Candidates for Office: Beliefs and Strategies.* New York: Random House, 1968.

————. *Congressmen's Voting Decisions.* New York: Harper & Row, 1973. (2nd ed., 1981.)

Kirkpatrick, Jeane Jordan. *Dismantling the Parties: Reflections on Party Reform and Party Decomposition.* Washington, D.C.: American Enterprise Institute, 1971.

Knoke, David. *Change and Continuity in American Politics: The Social Bases of Political Parties.* Baltimore, Md.: Johns Hopkins University Press, 1976.

Ladd, Everett Carll, Jr. *Where Have All the Voters Gone?* New York: Norton, 1978.

Ladd, Everett Carll, Jr., and Hadley, Charles D. *Transformations of the American Party System: Political Coalitions from the New Deal to the 1970s.* New York: Norton, 1975.

Lane, Robert E. *Political Ideology.* New York: Free Press, 1962.

————. *Political Life.* New York: Free Press, 1959.

Larson, T. A. *History of Wyoming.* Lincoln: University of Nebraska Press, 1965.

Lasswell, Harold D. *Politics: Who Gets What, When, How.* New York: McGraw-Hill, 1936.

Lazarsfeld, Paul F., Berelson, Bernard, and Gaudet, Hazel. *The Peoples Choice: How the Voter Makes Up His Mind in a Presidential Campaign.* 3rd ed. New York: Columbia University Press, 1968.

Lee, Eugene C. *The Politics of Nonpartisanship.* Berkeley: University of California Press, 1960.

Leuthold, David A. *Electioneering in a Democracy.* New York: Wiley, 1968.

Lipset, Seymour Martin. *Political Man.* New York: Doubleday, 1960.

Litt, Edgar. *Ethnic Politics in America.* Glenview, Ill.: Scott, Foresman, 1970.

McConnell, Grant. *The Modern Presidency.* 2nd ed. New York: St. Martin's Press, 1976.

McCormick, Richard P. *The Second American Party System: Party Formation in the Jacksonian Era.* Chapel Hill: University of North Carolina Press, 1966.

MacIver, Robert M. *The Web of Government.* New York: Crowell-Collier and Macmillan, 1957.

MacNeil, Robert. *The People Machine: The Influence of Television on American Politics.* New York: Harper & Row, 1968.

Maisel, Louis, and Sacks, Paul M. *The Future of Political Parties.* Beverly Hills, Calif.: Sage, 1975.

Maisel, Louis, and Cooper, Joseph. *The Impact of the Electoral Process.* Beverly Hills, Calif.: Sage, 1977.

Mann, Thomas E. *Unsafe at Any Margin: Interpreting Congressional Elections.* Washington, D.C.: American Enterprise Institute, 1978.

March, James G. *Handbook of Organizations.* Chicago: Rand McNally, 1965.

Matthews, Donald R. *U.S. Senators and Their World.* Chapel Hill: University of North Carolina Press, 1960.

Mencken, H. L. *Making a President.* New York: Knopf, 1932.

Michels, Robert. *Political Parties.* New York: Free Press, 1949.

Milbrath, Lester W. *The Washington Lobbyists.* Chicago: Rand McNally, 1963.

Miller, Clem. *Member of the House.* New York: Scribner's, 1962.

Miller, Warren E., and Levitin, Teresa E. *Leadership and Change: The New Politics and the American Electorate.* Cambridge, Mass.: Winthrop, 1976.

Mills, C. Wright. *The Power Elite.* New York: Oxford University Press, 1957.

Morehouse, Sarah McCally. *State Politics, Parties and Policy.* New York: Holt, Rinehart and Winston, 1981.

Mullen, William F. *Presidential Power and Politics.* New York: St. Martin's Press, 1976.

Nadel, Mark V. *The Politics of Consumer Protection.* Indianapolis, Ind.: Bobbs-Merrill, 1971.

Napolitan, Joseph. *The Election Game and How to Win It.* New York: Doubleday, 1972.

Neumann, Sigmund, ed. *Modern Political Parties: Approaches to Comparative Politics.* Chicago: University of Chicago Press, 1956.

Nichols, David. *Financing Elections: The Politics of the American Ruling Class.* New York: New Viewpoints, 1974.

Nie, Norman H., Verba, Sidney, and Petrocik, John R. *The Changing American Voter.* Cambridge, Mass.: Harvard University Press, 1976.

Niemi, Richard G., and Weisberg, Herbert F. *Controversies in American Voting Behavior.* San Francisco: Freeman, 1976.

Nimmo, Dan. *The Political Persuaders.* Englewood Cliffs, N.J.: Prentice-Hall, 1970.

Ornstein, Norman J., and Elder, Shirley. *Interest Groups, Lobbying and Policy Making.* Washington, D.C.: Congressional Quarterly Press, 1978.

Ostrogorski, M. *Democracy and the Organization of Political Parties.* Vol. 2. New York: Macmillan, 1902.

Parris, Judith H. *The Convention Problem: Issues in Reform of Presidential Nominating Procedures.* Washington, D.C.: Brookings Institution, 1972.

Patterson, Thomas E., and McClure, Robert D. *The Unseeing Eye.* New York: Putnam's, 1976.

Perry, James M. *The New Politics: The Expanding Technology of Political Manipulation.* New York: Potter, 1968.

Phelan, James, and Poxen, Robert. *The Company State.* New York: Grossman, 1973.

Phillips, Kevin. *The Emerging Republican Majority.* New Rochelle, N.Y.: Arlington House, 1969.

———. *Mediacracy.* Garden City, N.J.: Doubleday, 1975.

Pierce, Neal. *The Border South States.* New York: Norton, 1975.

———. *The Mega States of America.* New York: Norton, 1972.

———. *The People's President.* New York: Simon & Schuster, 1968.

Plano, Jack C., and Greenberg, Milton. *The American Political Dictionary.* 4th ed. Hinsdale, Ill.: Dryden Press, 1976.

Polsby, Nelson W., and Wildavsky, Aaron B. *Presidential Elections.* 4th ed. New York: Scribner's, 1976.

Pomper, Gerald M. *Elections in America.* New York: Dodd, Mead, 1971.

———. *Nominating the President: The Politics of Convention Choice.* Evanston, Ill.: Northwestern University Press, 1963.

———. *Voters' Choice: Varieties of American Electoral Behavior.* New York: Dodd, Mead, 1975.

———. ed. *The Election of 1976.* New York: McKay, 1977.

———. ed. *The Election of 1980: Reports and Interpretations.* Chatham, N.J.: Chatham House, 1980.

Ranney, Austin. *Curing the Mischiefs of Faction: Party Reform in America.* Berkeley: University of California Press, 1975.

———. *The Governing of Men.* 3rd ed. New York: Holt, Rinehart and Winston, 1971.

———, ed. *The American Elections of 1980.* Washington, D.C.: American Enterprise Institute, 1981.

Ranney, Austin, and Kendall, Willmoore. *Democracy and the American Party System.* New York: Harcourt Brace Jovanovich, 1956.

Reitman, Jerry I., and Bettelhein, Judith, eds. *The Directory of Registered Federal and State Lobbyists.* New York: Academic Press, 1973.

Riemer, Neal, ed. *The Representative.* Boston: Heath, 1967.

Ripley, Randall B., and Franklin, Grace A. *Congress, the Bureaucracy and Public Policy.* Rev. ed. Homewood, Ill.: Dorsey Press, 1980.

Ripley, Randall B. *Congress: Process and Policy.* 2nd ed. New York: Norton, 1975.

Rossiter, Clinton. *Parties and Politics in America.* Ithaca, N.Y.: Cornell University Press, 1960.

———. *The American Presidency.* New York: Harcourt Brace Jovanovich, 1956.

Royko, Mike. *Boss: Richard J. Daley of Chicago.* New York: Dutton, 1971.

Sabato, Larry J. *The Rise of Political Consultants.* New York: Basic Books, 1982.

Salisbury, Robert H., ed. *Interest Group Politics in America.* New York: Harper & Row, 1970.

Saloma, John S., III, and Sontag, Frederick H. *Parties: The Real Opportunity for Effective Citizen Politics.* New York: Knopf, 1972.

Sandoz, Ellis, and Crabb, Cecil V., Jr., eds. *The Tide of Discontent: The 1980 Elections and Their Meaning.* Washington, D.C.: Congressional Quarterly Press, 1981.

Sayre, Wallace S., and Parris, Judith H. *Voting for President: The Electoral College and the American Party System.* Washington, D.C.: Brookings Institution, 1970.

Scammon, Richard, and Wattenberg, Ben J. *The Real Majority.* New York: Coward-McCann, 1970.

Schattschneider, E. E. *The Semi-Sovereign People.* New York: Holt, Rinehart and Winston, 1960.

Shannon, Jasper. *Money and Politics.* New York: Random House, 1959.

Sheldon, George H. *The American Judicial Process.* New York: Harper & Row, 1974.

Sorauf, Frank J. *Party Politics in America.* 3rd ed. Boston: Little, Brown, 1976. (4th ed., 1980.)

Stewart, John G. *One Last Chance: The Democratic Party, 1974–76.* New York: Praeger, 1974.

Stollman, G. H. *Michigan State Legislators and Their Work.* Washington, D.C.: University Press of America, 1978.

Sundquist, James L. *Dynamics of the Party System: Alignment and Realignment of Political Parties in the United States.* Washington, D.C.: Brookings Institution, 1973.

Thomson, Charles A. H. *Television and Presidential*

*Politics*. Washington, D.C.: Brookings Institution, 1956.

Tolchin, Martin, and Tolchin, Susan. *To the Victor . . . Political Patronage from the Clubhouse to the White House*. New York: Vintage Books, 1971.

Truman, David B. *The Governmental Process*. New York: Knopf, 1951.

Tugwell, Richard G., and Cronin, Thomas E. *The Presidency Reappraised*. New York: Praeger, 1974.

Turner, Julius. *Party and Constituency: Pressures on Congress*. Baltimore, Md.: Johns Hopkins University Press, 1970.

Ulmer, Sidney, ed. *Political Decision Making*. Cincinnati, Ohio: Van Nostrand Reinhold, 1970.

Vogler, David J. *The Third House*. Evanston, Ill.: Northwestern University Press, 1971.

Wahlke, John C., Eulau, Heinz, Buchanan, William, and Ferguson, Leroy C. *The Legislative System*. New York: Wiley, 1962.

White, Theodore H. *America In Search of Itself*. New York: Harper & Row, 1982.

———. *The Making of the President, 1960*. New York: Atheneum, 1961.

———. *The Making of the President, 1964*. New York: Atheneum, 1965.

———. *The Making of the President, 1968*. New York: Atheneum, 1969.

———. *The Making of the President, 1972*. New York: Atheneum, 1973.

White, William S. *Home Place*. Boston: Houghton Mifflin, 1965.

Wildavsky, Aaron, ed. *Perspectives on the Presidency*. Boston: Little, Brown, 1975.

Zeigler, Harmon, and Baer, Michael A. *Lobbying: Interaction and Influence in American State Legislatures*. Belmont, Calif.: Wadsworth, 1969.

Zeigler, Harmon, and Peak, Wayne. *Interest Groups in American Society*. Englewood Cliffs, N.J.: Prentice-Hall, 1972.

# INDEX

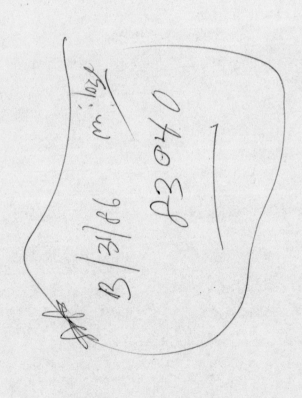

B/31/96 m. lozz

8303 0